D0982540

Texts and Monographs in Computer Science

Editors

David Gries
Fred B. Schneider

Advisory Board
F.L. Bauer
S.D. Brookes
C.E. Leiserson
M. Sipser

Texts and Monographs in Computer Science

(continued after index)

Logic for Applications

Anil Nerode
Richard A. Shore

With 66 Illustrations

Springer-Verlag

New York Berlin Heidelberg London Paris
Tokyo Hong Kong Barcelona Budapest

Anil Nerode
Department of Mathematics
Cornell University
White Hall
Ithaca, NY 14853-7901
USA

Richard A. Shore
Department of Mathematics
Cornell University
White Hall
Ithaca, NY 14853-7901
USA

Series Editors:
David Gries
Department of Computer Science
Cornell University
Upson Hall
Ithaca, NY 14853-7501
USA

Fred B. Schneider
Department of Computer Science
Cornell University
Upson Hall
Ithaca, NY 14853-7501
USA

4-25-95- 1825355

Library of Congress Cataloging-in-Publication Data
Nerode, Anil
    Logic for applications / Anil Nerode, Richard A. Shore.
        p.   cm. — (Texts and monographs in computer science)
    Includes bibliographical references and indexes.
    ISBN 0-387-94129-0. — ISBN 3-540-94129-0
    1. Logic programming.   2. Logic, Symbolic and mathematical.
    I. Shore, Richard A., 1946-   . II. Title. III. Series.
    QA76.63.N45   1993
    005.1—dc20   93-27846

Printed on acid-free paper.

Production managed by Hal Henglein; manufacturing supervised by Genieve Shaw.
Photocomposed copy produced from the authors' AMSTeX files.
Printed and bound by Hamilton Printing Co., Castleton, NY.
Printed in the United States of America.

9 8 7 6 5 4 3 2 1

ISBN 0-387-94129-0 Springer-Verlag New York Berlin Heidelberg
ISBN 3-540-94129-0 Springer-Verlag Berlin Heidelberg New York

Preface

In writing this book, our goal was to produce a text suitable for a first course in mathematical logic more attuned than the traditional textbooks to the recent dramatic growth in the applications of logic to computer science. Thus our choice of topics has been heavily influenced by such applications. Of course, we cover the basic traditional topics — syntax, semantics, soundness, completeness and compactness — as well as a few more advanced results such as the theorems of Skolem–Löwenheim and Herbrand. Much of our book, however, deals with other less traditional topics. Resolution theorem proving plays a major role in our treatment of logic, especially in its application to Logic Programming and PROLOG. We deal extensively with the mathematical foundations of all three of these subjects. In addition, we include two chapters on nonclassical logics — modal and intuitionistic — that are becoming increasingly important in computer science. We develop the basic material on the syntax and semantics (via Kripke frames) for each of these logics. In both cases, our approach to formal proofs, soundness and completeness uses modifications of the same tableau method introduced for classical logic. We indicate how it can easily be adapted to various other special types of modal logics. A number of more advanced topics (including nonmonotonic logic) are also briefly introduced both in the nonclassical logic chapters and in the material on Logic Programming and PROLOG.

The intended audience for this text consists of upper level undergraduate and beginning graduate students of mathematics or computer science. We assume a basic background in abstract reasoning as would be provided by any beginning course in algebra or theoretical computer science, as well as the usual familiarity with informal mathematical notation and argument as would be used in any such course.

If taught as a course for advanced undergraduates, essentially all the material in Chapters I–III, together with a reasonable amount of programming in PROLOG, can be covered in one semester with three hours of lectures a week. When teaching it in this way, we have had (and recommend) an additional weekly section devoted to homework problems and programming instruction. Alternatively, the material on resolution theorem proving and Logic Programming can be replaced by the chapters on modal and intuitionistic logic to get a rather different course. For two quarters, one can simply add on one of the nonclassical logics to the first suggested semester course. We have deliberately made these two chapters entirely independent of one another so as to afford a choice. There is, however, much similarity in the developments and, if both are covered, the corresponding sections of the second chapter can be covered more quickly. At the graduate level, essentially the whole book can be covered in a semester.

The text develops propositional logic in its entirety before proceeding to predicate logic. However, depending on the background of the class and the predilections of the instructor, it is possible to combine the treatments. Indeed, for a graduate course or with students with some previous exposure to propositional logic and truth tables, this may well be better. To follow such a path, begin with I.1–2 and then move on to II.1–4. If planning to introduce PROLOG and develop the foundations of Logic Programming, II.5 can be used to explain the syntax and semantics of PROLOG. To start the students on actual programming, an informal introduction to PROLOG implementation and programming can be continued in the recitation section (parts of I.10 are relevant here). Of course, the theoretical underpinnings must wait for the formal development of resolution and unification. With or without the Logic Programming, it is now possible (based on the tableau approach) to prove the soundness and completeness theorems for predicate logic in II.6–7 and to continue through the proof of Herbrand's theorem in II.10. A Hilbert–style proof system is presented without proving any results in I.7 and II.8.

The resolution–style proof system on which PROLOG is based is more intimately tied to its development in the propositional case, as the basic theorems are proven by using Herbrand's theorem to reduce predicate logic results to corresponding ones of propositional logic. Thus it is necessary, if covering this material, to do the propositional case first. The sections needed for the treatment of PROLOG are I.8, I.10 and II.11–13. The refinements of resolution considered in I.9 are strictly optional. While linear resolution (II.14) is highly relevant to PROLOG, the completeness theorem is one of the most difficult in the text. We have therefore provided in III.1 an alternate approach to the corresponding results for Horn logic and PROLOG that requires only the basic definitions of linear resolution (I.14.1–3).

A diagram of the logical dependencies between sections of the text is given on the facing page. Unless indicated otherwise by an arrow, the order of dependency runs right to left. Dotted lines (as from the propositional to predicate sections for classical logic) indicate relevance but not strict logical dependence. We should note that the very first section, I.1, simply collects definitions and facts about orderings and trees that are needed at various points in the text. This material can be covered at the beginning or inserted as needed. In particular, König's Lemma, I.1.4, is not needed until the treatment of complete systematic tableaux in I.4. At various other points in the text, certain paragraphs or even whole sections that are not needed for the later material are marked as optional by an asterisk (*). They are also printed in smaller type and with wider margins to set them off from the main line of development. In addition, there are three important possible exceptions to the order indicated above; these are of particular relevance for those courses not including very much about PROLOG.

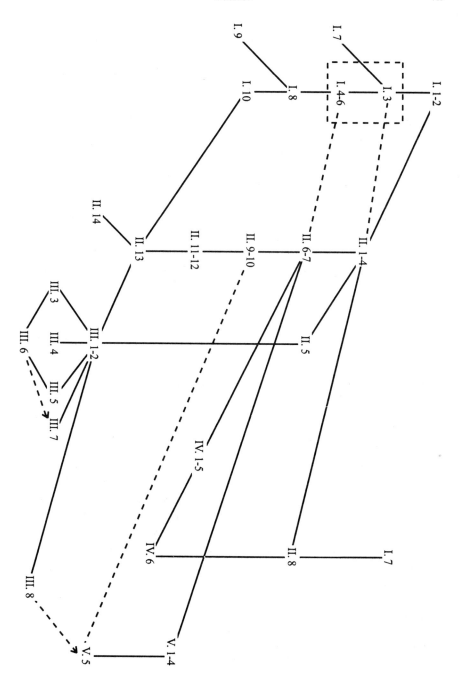

The first exception also needs a warning. Our basic approach to logic does not include a specialized equality predicate. Although no longer the common approach in texts on mathematical logic, this is the right way to develop the subject to do resolution theorem proving, Logic Programming and PROLOG. We have thus relegated to III.5 the analysis of equality, either as a special predicate with the privileged semantics of true equality and the corresponding logical axiom schemes, or as an ordinary one with the appropriate equality axioms added on to each system under consideration. It is, however, quite possible to cover the relevant material in III.5 up to III.5.3 and the proofs of the soundness and completeness theorems for equality interpretations described there immediately after II.7.

The second exception concerns the proof of Church's theorem on the undecidability of validity for predicate logic. In III.8 we present a proof designed to apply even to the fragment of predicate logic represented in PROLOG. In Exercise 3 of III.5, however, we indicate how the presentation can easily be modified to make no mention of PROLOG notation or procedures and so give a proof of Church's Theorem which is accessible after II.7.

Finally, the introduction to nonmonotonic logic given in III.7 up to III.7.6 can also be read independently of the material on Logic Programming and PROLOG. The rest of III.7 consists of an analysis of the stable models of Logic Programming with negation in terms of nonmonotonic logic. Other, more self–contained, applications to graphs and partial orders are given in Exercises 8–9 of III.7.

We should point out that there is a considerable overlap in the basic material for the development of modal and intuitionistic logic in Chapters IV and V. Indeed, a single unified development is possible albeit at some expense to the ease of intelligibility. We have instead written these chapters so that either may be read independently of the other. For the readers who wish to delve into both topics, we supply a comparative guide to basic notions of classical, modal and intuitionistic logic in V.6. We try there to point out the similarities and differences between these logics.

We have included a variety of problems at the end of almost every section of the text, including a fair number of programming problems in PROLOG which can be assigned either for theoretical analysis or actual implementation. In particular, there are series of problems based on a database consisting of the genealogical lists in the first few chapters of *Chronicles*. It is reproduced in Appendix B. We have included these problems to serve as paradigms for use with a similar database or to be appropriately modified to fit other situations. This is not, however, a text on PROLOG programming. When teaching this material, we always supplement it with one of the standard texts on PROLOG programming listed in the suggestions for further reading at the end of Chapter III. We used ARITY PROLOG and the printouts of program runs are from that implementation, but nothing in the text is actually tied to a particular version of the language; we use only standard syntax and discuss typical implementations.

When we (infrequently) cite results from the current literature, we attribute them as usual. However, as this is a basic textbook, we have made no attempt to attribute the standard results of the subject to their discoverers, other than when at times we name theorems according to common usage. We have, however, supplied a brief history of logic in an appendix that should give the student a feel for the development of the subject. In addition, suggestions for further reading that might be useful for either students or teachers using this text are given at the end of each chapter. Finally, a fairly extensive bibliography of related material, arranged by subject, is given at the end of the book.

Portions of this book appeared in various formats over many years. Very early versions of the material on classical logic appeared in lecture notes by Nerode which were distributed for courses at Cornell years ago. This material was also independently reworked by George Metakides and appeared as lecture notes in English with Nerode and in Greek as his lectures at the University of Patras. Nerode [1990, 4.2] and [1991, 4.4] contain preliminary versions of our treatment of intuitionistic and modal logic based on the tableau method which were presented in lectures at Montecatini Terme and Marktoberdorf in 1988 and 1989, respectively. Our approach to resolution was also influenced by courses on program verification given by Richard Platek at Cornell. More current versions of the material have been read and used over the past five years by a number of teachers in both mathematics and computer science departments and we have benefited considerably from their comments and suggestions. We should mention Uri Abraham (Mathematics, Ben Gurion University, Israel), John Crossley (Mathematics and Computer Science, Monash University, Australia), George Metakides (University of Patras, Greece and Information Technologies Research, EEC), Dexter Kozen (Computer Science, Cornell) and Jacob Plotkin (Mathematics, Michigan State University). Warren Goldfarb (Philosophy, Harvard) helped us avoid a number of pitfalls in the historical appendix. Particularly extensive (and highly beneficial) comments were received from Wiktor Marek (Computer Science, University of Kentucky), George Odifreddi (Computer Science, University of Turin, Italy) and Robert Soare (Mathematics and Computer Science, University of Chicago) who used several versions of the text in their courses. We also owe a debt to our graduate students who have served as assistants for our logic courses over the past few years and have made many corrections and suggestions: Jennifer Davoren, Steven Kautz, James Lipton, Sherry Marcus and Duminda Wijesekera.

We gratefully acknowledge the financial support over the past few years of the NSF under grants DMS–8601048 and DMS–8902797, the ARO under grants DAAG29–85–C–0018 and DAAL03–91–C–0027 through the Mathematical Sciences Institute at Cornell University, and IBM for an equipment grant through Project Ezra at Cornell University. We would also like to thank Arletta Havlik and Graeme Bailey for their help with the TEXing of the text, and Geraldine Brady, Jennifer Davoren and George Odifreddi for their help in proofreading.

Finally, in appreciation of their continuing support, we dedicate this book to our wives, Sally and Naomi.

Cornell University   Anil Nerode
Ithaca, NY   Richard A. Shore
December, 1992

Contents

Introduction

In 1920 logic was mostly a philosopher's garden. There were also a few mathematicians there, cultivating the logical roots of the mathematical tree. Today, Recursion Theory, Set Theory, Model Theory and Proof Theory, logic's major subdisciplines, have become full–fledged branches of mathematics. Since the 1970s, the winds of change have been blowing new seeds into the logic garden from computer science, AI, and linguistics. These winds have also uncovered a new topography with many prominences and depths, fertile soil for new logical subjects. These days, if you survey international meetings in computer science and linguistics, you will find that the language of mathematical logic is a lingua franca, that methods of mathematical logic are ubiquitous and that understanding new logics and finding feasible algorithms for implementing their inference procedures plays a central role in many disciplines. The emerging areas with an important logic component include imperative, declarative and functional programming; verification of programs; interactive, concurrent, distributed, fault tolerant and real time computing; knowledge–based systems; deductive databases; and VLSI design. Various types of logic are now also playing key roles in the modeling of reasoning in special fields from law to medicine.

These applications have widened the horizons of logical research to encompass problems and ideas that were not even considered when logic was motivated only by questions from mathematics and philosophy. Applied logic is now as much a reality as is applied mathematics, with a similarly broad, overlapping but somewhat different area of application. This situation has arisen because of the needs for automated inference in critical, real time, and large database information processing applications throughout business, government, science, and technology. Mathematical logic, coupled with some of its applications, should be as easily available to college and university students as is applied mathematics. It may well be as important to the future of many previously qualitative disciplines as ordinary applied mathematics has been to the traditionally quantitative ones.

This book is a rigorous elementary introduction to classical predicate logic emphasizing that deduction is a form of computation. We cover the standard topics of soundness, completeness and compactness: our proof methods produce only valid results, all valid sentences are provable and, if a fact is a logical consequence of an infinite set of axioms, it is actually a consequence of finitely many of them. The need for soundness seems obvious but, as we shall see in our discussion of PROLOG, even this requirement of simple correctness is often sacrificed on the altar of efficiency in actual implementations. Completeness, on the other hand, is a remarkable result connecting proofs and validity. We can prescribe an effective proof procedure that precisely captures the semantics of first order logic. A valid sentence, i.e., one true for every interpretation of the relations used to state it, always has a proof in a particular formal system and there is an algorithm to find such a proof. Compactness also has surprising applications that deduce results about infinite structures from results about finite ones. To cite just one example, it implies that every planar map is colorable with four colors as every finite planar map is so colorable. We also prove that validity is undecidable: no single algorithm can decide if any given sentence is valid. Thus although we can, using a particular algorithm, search for a proof of a given sentence φ and be assured of finding one if φ is valid, we cannot know in general whether we are searching in vain.

Our treatment begins in Chapter I with the syntax and semantics of classical propositional logic, that is the logic of compound sentences formed with connectives such as "and", "or", "if" and "not" but without consideration of the quantifiers "for all" and "there exists". We present a traditional approach to syntax in terms of strings of symbols as well as one based on tree structures. As trees have become basic objects in many computer science areas, the latter approach may well be more accessible (or at least familiar) to many students. Either approach can be adopted. We then introduce the semantic tableau proof method developed by Beth (*Foundations of Mathematics* [1959, 3.2]) and Smullyan (*First order Logic* [1968, 3.2]) for propositional logic. We have found over the years that the tableaux method is the easiest for students to learn, use and remember. This method seeks to find a proof of a sentence φ by discovering that a systematic search for a counterexample to φ fails in a finite amount of time. The procedure brings out the unadorned reasons for completeness by directly analyzing the subformulas of the formula φ for which a proof is being attempted. It presents the systematic search as a tree–constructing algorithm. The goal of the algorithm is to produce a finite tree beginning with "φ is false" with a contradiction on every branch. Such a tree shows that every analysis of "φ is false" leads to a contradiction. We call this a tableau proof of φ. Employing a systematic search for tableau proofs, we prove the soundness, completeness and compactness theorems.

We then develop the resolution method of theorem proving introduced by J. A. Robinson [1965, 5.7]. This method has played a crucial role in the development of automated reasoning and theorem proving. After again establishing soundness and completeness, we specialize this method to Horn clauses to develop the mathematical foundations of Logic Programming and PROLOG (still at the propositional level). Logic Programming is a general abstract approach to programming as logical deduction in a restricted setting. PROLOG is a type of programming language designed to implement this idea that computations are deductions.

In Chapter II we introduce the rest of predicate logic (functions and relations; variables and quantifiers) with explanations of its syntax and semantics. We present a tableau style proof system for predicate logic and prove its soundness and completeness. Our approach naturally leads to Herbrand's theorem which, in a certain sense, reduces predicate logic to propositional logic. Then, following Robinson, we add to resolution the pattern–matching algorithm, called unification, which is originally due to Herbrand. This produces Robinson's system of deduction for predicate logic; it was the first complete redesign of logical inference for the purpose of mechanization of inference on digital computers. It is really better carried out by machines than by hand. Robinson's work made automation of reasoning on digital computers a major area of research. Many of his ideas and much of his terminology have persisted to the present day.

Chapter III is devoted to the specialization of resolution to Horn clauses, a special class of predicate logic formulas that are the domain of Logic Programming and PROLOG. The predicate version of Logic Programming has applications to expert systems, intelligent databases and AI among many others. Logic Programming has a very active research community and has become a separate discipline. In addition to restricting its attention to a limited class of formulas, Logic Programming and PROLOG make various changes in proof procedures to attain computational efficiency. We cover the mathematical foundations of Horn clause logic and then of PROLOG: syntax, semantics, soundness and completeness. We also touch on proofs of termination for PROLOG programs. As an example of current trends, we give an introductory account of the so–called "general logic programs". We present views of implementation and semantics for negation in this setting in terms of both negation as failure and stable models. This area is still in considerable flux. It is one example of the larger evolving subject of nonmonotonic reasoning. Unlike the classical situation, in nonmonotonic logic the addition of new premises may force the withdrawal of conclusions deduced from the previous ones. We include a brief introduction to this area in III.7. We are not programmers, however, and do not attempt to really cover PROLOG programming beyond what is needed to illustrate the underlying logical and mathematical ideas. (References to basic books on PROLOG programming are included in the bibliography.) We do, however, deal with theoretical computability by PROLOG programs as our route to undecidability.

Standard proofs of undecidability for a theory come down to showing how to represent each effectively computable function by a logical formula so that computing the values of the function amounts to deducing instances of that formula. The noncomputability of specific functions such as the halting problem (deciding if a given program halts on a given input) are then translated into the impossibility of deciding the provability of given formulas. In this way, we prove the undecidability of PROLOG and of Horn clause logic (and so *a fortiori* of all of predicate logic) by showing that Horn clause programs and even standard implementations of PROLOG compute all effectively computable functions. As a definition of an algorithm for an effective computation, we use the model of computation given by programs on register machines. Thus we simulate each register machine program for computing a recursive function by a PROLOG program computing a coded version of that same function. As it is known that all other models of computation can be simulated by register machines, this suffices to get the desired results on computability and undecidability.

For the final chapters, we turn to some nonclassical logics that are becoming increasingly important in understanding and modeling computation and in verifying programs. "Nonclassical" has a technical meaning: the truth of a composite sentence may not depend solely on the truth of its parts and, indeed, even the truth of simple statements may depend on context, time, beliefs, etc. Although this attitude is not the traditional one in mathematics, it reflects many real life situations as well as many important problems in computer science. The truth of an implication often has temporal components. Usually sentences are evaluated within some context. If our knowledge or beliefs change, so may our evaluation of the truth of some sentence. The analysis of programs depends on the states of knowledge of the computer over time, on what may happen and on what must happen. We touch briefly on one form of such logic (nonmonotonic logic in which later information may invalidate earlier conclusions) in Chapter III. The last two chapters are devoted to a systematic study of two such logics: modal and intuitionistic.

Intuitionism incorporates a constructive view of mathematics into the underlying logic. We can claim that we have a proof of A or B only if we have a proof of one of them. We can claim to have a proof of "there exists an x with property P" only if we can actually exhibit an object c and a proof that c has property P. Modal logic attempts to capture notions of necessity and possibility to serve as a basis for the analyses of systems with temporal, dynamic or belief–based components. We describe the semantics of both of these logics in terms of Kripke frames. These are sets of classical models together with a partial ordering or some other relation on the models; it is this relation that embodies the nonclassical aspects of Kripke semantics. We then formulate tableau systems that generalize the classical ones and faithfully reflect the semantics expressed by Kripke frames. Once again, soundness and completeness play a central role in our exposition. The two logics are presented independently but a comparative guide is supplied in V.6.

For good or ill, the philosophical tenets of intuitionism play no role here, nor do the philosophers' analyses of time and necessity. Rather, we explain Kripke frames as a way of modeling the notion of a consequence of partial information and modal operators as simply expressing relations among sets of models. This explanation fits the prospective use of intuitionistic logic, as Scott has suggested, as a language for Scott domains and information systems, or for Horn clause logic, which is a subtler use of both classical and intuitionistic logic. It also fits the applications of modal logic to program analysis and verification, as initiated by Hoare with dynamic logic and continued by many in the field.

Finally, we believe that knowing the historical context in which mathematical logic and its applications have developed is important for a full understanding and appreciation of the subject. Thus we supply in an appendix a brief historical view of the origins and development of logic from the Greeks to the middle of the twentieth century. Parts of this survey may be fully appreciated only after reading the text (especially the first two chapters) but it can be profitably consulted before, after or while reading the book. It is intended only as a tourist brochure, a guide to the terrain. To supplement this guide, we have included a fairly extensive bibliography of historical references and sources for additional information on many topics in logic, including several not covered in the text. When possible, we have confined our suggestions to historical material, handbooks, surveys and basic texts at a level suitable for a reader who has finished this book. Some newer subjects, however, also require references to the current literature. This bibliography is arranged as several (partially annotated) bibliographies on individual subjects. References are made accordingly. Thus, for example, Thomas [1939, 1.1] refers to the item *Selections Illustrating the History of Greek Mathematics with an English Translation* by Ivor Thomas published in 1939 which is listed in Bibliography 1.1, Sourcebooks for the History of Mathematics. We have also included at the end of each chapter suggestions for further reading that are keyed to these bibliographies.

I Propositional Logic

1. Orders and Trees

Before starting on the basic material of this book, we introduce a general representation scheme which is one of the most important types of structures in logic and computer science: Trees. We expect that most readers will be familiar with this type of structure at least informally. A tree is something that looks like the following:

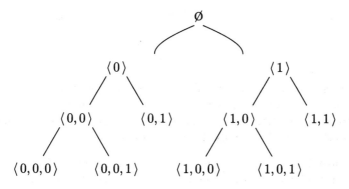

FIGURE 1

It has nodes (in this example, binary sequences) arranged in a partial order (extension as sequences means lower down in the picture of the tree). There is typically a single node (the empty set, $\emptyset$) at the top (above all the others) which is called the root of the tree. (We will draw our trees growing downwards to conform to common practice but the ordering on the tree will be arranged to mirror the situation given by extension of sequences. Thus the root will be the smallest (first) element in the ordering and the nodes will get larger as we travel down the tree.) A node on a tree may have one or more incomparable immediate successors. If it has more than one, we say the tree branches at that node. If each node has at most n immediate successors, the tree is n–ary or n–branching. (The one in the picture is a 2–ary, or as we usually say, a *binary* tree.) A terminal node, that is one with no successors, is called a leaf. Other terminology such as a path on a tree or the levels of a tree should have intuitively clear meanings. For those who wish to be formal, we give precise definitions. This material can be omitted for now and referred to as needed later. In particular König's lemma (Theorem 1.4) is not needed until §4.

Definition 1.1:

(i) A *partial order* is a set S with a binary relation called "less than", and written $<$, on S which is *transitive* and *irreflexive*:

$$x < y \text{ and } y < z \Rightarrow x < z \text{ and}$$
$$x \text{ is not less than } x \text{ for any } x.$$

(ii) The partial order $<$ is a *linear order* (or simply an *order*) if it also satisfies the *trichotomy law*:

$$x < y \text{ or } x = y \text{ or } y < x.$$

(iii) A linear order is *well ordered* if it has no infinite descending chain, i.e., there is no set of elements $x_0, x_1, \ldots$ of S such that

$$\ldots < x_2 < x_1 < x_0.$$

(iv) We use the usual notational conventions for orderings:

$$x \leq y \iff x < y \text{ or } x = y.$$
$$x > y \iff y < x.$$

Note that antisymmetry for partial orderings, $x < y \Rightarrow$ it is not the case that $y < x$, follows immediately from Definition 1.1 (i). (We follow standard mathematical practice in using "$\Rightarrow$" and "$\iff$" as abbreviations for "implies" and "if and only if", respectively.)

Definition 1.2: A *tree* is a set T (whose elements are called *nodes*) partially ordered by $<_T$, with a unique least element called the *root*, in which the predecessors of every node are well ordered by $<_T$.

A *path* on a tree T is a maximal linearly ordered subset of T.

Definition 1.3:

(i) The *levels* of T are defined by induction. The 0th level of T consists precisely of the root of T. The $k + 1^{\text{st}}$ level of T consists of the immediate successors of the nodes on the kth level of T.

(ii) The *depth* of a tree T is the maximum n such that there is a node of level n in T. If there are nodes of level n for every natural number n we say the depth of T is infinite or ω.

(iii) If each node has at most n immediate successors, the tree is *n–ary* or *n–branching*. If each node has finitely many immediate successors, we say that the tree is *finitely branching*. A node with no successors is called a *leaf* or a *terminal node*.

We will only consider trees of depth at most ω, i.e., every node on every tree we ever consider will be on level n of the tree for some natural number n (and as such will have precisely n many predecessors in the tree order).

The crucial fact about finitely branching trees is König's lemma:

Theorem 1.4 (König's Lemma): *If a finitely branching tree T is infinite, it has an infinite path.*

Proof: Suppose T is infinite. We define the sequence of elements x_0, x_1, ..., constituting a path P on T by induction (or recursion). The first element x_0 of P is, of course, the root of T. It has infinitely many successors in T by the assumption that T is infinite. Suppose that we have defined the first n elements of P to be $x_0, x_1, \ldots, x_{n-1}$ on levels $0, 1, \ldots, n-1$ of T respectively so that each x_i has infinitely many successors in T. By hypothesis, x_{n-1} has only finitely many immediate successors. As it has infinitely many successors all together, (at least) one of its immediate successors, say y, also has infinitely many successors. We now set $x_n = y$. x_n is on level n of T and has infinitely many successors in T and so we may continue our definition of P. $\square$

König's lemma is a version of the compactness theorem in propositional logic and in topology. See §6 (and especially Theorem 6.13 and Exercise 6.11) for the former and Exercises 10 and 11 for its relations to the latter.

Frequently it is just the shape of the tree that is important and not the nodes themselves. To facilitate talking about the arrangement of different materials into the same shape and to allow the same component to be used at different places in this assemblage, we will talk about labeled trees. We attach labels to the nodes of the tree. Again the picture should be clear.

Definition 1.5: A *labeled tree* T is a tree T with a function (the labeling function) which associates some object with every node. This object is called the *label* of the node.

In fact, after the first exposure or two to labeled trees we will at times simply drop the word. We will draw our trees already labeled and will let the concerned reader adjust the formalities.

Another way of putting more structure on a tree is by adding a linear ordering on the entire tree. Consider the case of the standard binary tree of finite sequences of 0's and 1's: The underlying set is the set $S = \{0,1\}^*$ of such sequences. We think of a binary sequence σ of length n as a map from $\{0, 1, \ldots, n-1\}$ into $\{0, 1\}$. We use " $\frown$ " to denote *concatenation*. Thus, for example, $\langle 0, 1 \rangle \frown 0$ is $\langle 0, 1, 0 \rangle$ while $\langle 0, 1, 0 \rangle \frown \langle 0, 1 \rangle$ is $\langle 0, 1, 0, 0, 1 \rangle$. (Note that we frequently abuse notation by identifying 0 with $\langle 0 \rangle$ and 1 with $\langle 1 \rangle$ in such situations.) The tree ordering $<_S$ is given by extension as functions $\sigma < \tau \Leftrightarrow \sigma \subset \tau$. The additional linear order usually associated with this tree is the *lexicographic ordering on sequences*: For two sequences σ and τ we say that $\sigma <_L \tau$ if $\sigma \subset \tau$ or if $\sigma(n)$, the nth entry in σ, is less than $\tau(n)$ where n is the first entry at which the sequences differ (otherwise, as one can easily see, $\tau <_L \sigma$ or $\sigma = \tau$). The same procedure can be applied to any tree to produce a linear order of all the nodes. We begin by defining a linear order on each level of the tree. This order is usually called $<_L$ and described as a *left to right ordering* for the obvious pictorial reason.

(This corresponds to ordering the binary strings of each fixed length by $\sigma <_L \tau$ if, at the first place σ and τ differ, σ is 0 and τ is 1. We then say that σ is *to the left of* τ.) The left–right orderings of each level are then extended to a linear ordering (also designated $<_L$) of all the nodes of the tree: Given two nodes x and y, we say that $x <_L y$ if $x <_T y$. If x and y are incomparable in the tree ordering, we find the largest predecessors x' and y' of x and y respectively which are on the same level of T. We then order x and y in the same way that x' and y' were ordered by $<_L$ on their own level: $x <_L y$ iff $x' <_L y'$. Any such total ordering of the nodes of a tree is also referred to as the *lexicographic ordering of the nodes*.

Exercises

1. Give an example of a finitely branching tree which is not n–branching for any n.

2. Give an example of an infinite tree of depth 3.

3. Prove that the notion of the level of a node in a tree is well defined, i.e., every node in a tree T is on exactly one level.

4. Prove that every node of a tree other than the root has exactly one immediate predecessor.

5. Let T be a tree. We say that two nodes x and y of T are *adjacent* if one is an immediate predecessor of the other, i.e., $x <_T y$ or $y <_T x$ and there is no node strictly between them. Prove that there is no sequence of nodes $x_1, \dots, x_n$ $(n > 3)$ such that each x_i is adjacent to x_{i+1}, $x_1 = x_n$ but there are no other duplications on the list. (In graph theoretic terms (see Exercise 6.8) this says that if we define the edges of a graph to be the adjacent nodes of a tree, then the graph is acyclic.) Hint: Use Exercise 3.

6. Prove that a linear order $<$ on S is well ordered iff every subset of S has a least element.

7. Prove that the lexicographic ordering $<_L$ of pairs from the natural numbers $\mathbb{N}$ is well ordered.

8. a) Prove that the lexicographic ordering $<_L$ of n–tuples of natural numbers is well ordered for each n.

   b) Prove that the lexicographic ordering of the set of all n–tuples (with $n < m$ for any $m \in \mathbb{N}$) is well ordered.

9. Consider the set of all finite sequences of natural numbers. Define an ordering $<$ as follows: $\sigma < \tau$ iff either σ is shorter than τ or, if not, $\sigma <_L \tau$. Prove that $<$ is a well ordering.

The next two exercises are for those readers familiar with the topological notions of product topologies and compactness.

10. Show that König's lemma for binary trees is equivalent to the compactness of the topological space $C = \{0,1\}^\omega$ where $\{0,1\}$ is given the discrete topology and C the product topology.

11. Show that König's lemma for all finitely branching trees is equivalent to the compactness of all spaces $\prod X_i$ for every sequence of finite sets X_i, $i \in \mathbb{N}$, where each X_i has the discrete topology.

2. Propositions, Connectives and Truth Tables

Propositions are just statements and propositional logic describes and studies the ways in which statements are combined to form other statements. This is what is called the syntactic part of logic, the one which deals with statements as just strings of symbols. We will also be concerned with ascribing meaning to the symbols in various ways. This part of language is called semantics and a major theme in the development of logic is the relationship between these two aspects of language. The analysis of the internal structure of statements is left to a later time and a subject called predicate logic. For now we will consider some of the ways in which one builds statements from other statements in English. The construction procedures we consider will be the ones basic to mathematical texts. We call the operations that combine propositions to form new ones *connectives*.

The connectives one finds most frequently in a mathematical text are "or", "and", "not", "implies" and "if and only if". The meaning given to them by the working mathematician does not precisely reflect their meaning in everyday discourse; it has been changed slightly so as to become entirely unambiguous. They should be thought of simply as part of the jargon of mathematics.

We introduce formal symbols for these connectives as follows:

$\vee$	for	"or"	*(disjunction)*
$\wedge$	for	"and"	*(conjunction)*
$\neg$	for	"not"	*(negation)*
$\rightarrow$	for	"implies"	*(conditional)*
$\leftrightarrow$	for	"if and only if"	*(biconditional)*.

Before making the meaning of these connectives precise, we describe how they are used to form statements of propositional logic. The description of the syntax of any language begins with its alphabet. The *language of propositional logic* consists of the following symbols:

(i) *Connectives*: $\vee$, $\wedge$, $\neg$, $\rightarrow$, $\leftrightarrow$

(ii) *Parentheses*:) , (

(iii) *Propositional Letters*: A, A_1, A_2, ... , B, B_1, B_2, ... , ...

Once the symbols of our language are specified, we can describe the statements of the language of propositions. The definition that follows selects out certain strings of symbols from the language and calls them propositions. It is an *inductive* definition which describes the "shortest" statements first and then describes how to build longer statements from shorter ones in accordance with certain definite rules.

Definition 2.1: (Propositions)

(i) Propositional letters are propositions.

(ii) If α and β are propositions, then $(\alpha \wedge \beta)$, $(\alpha \vee \beta)$, $(\neg \alpha)$, $(\alpha \to \beta)$ and $(\alpha \leftrightarrow \beta)$ are propositions.

(iii) A string of symbols is a proposition if and only if it can be obtained by starting with propositional letters (i) and repeatedly applying (ii).

For example, $(A \vee B)$, C, $((A \wedge B) \to C)$, $(\neg(A \wedge B) \to C)$ are all propositions while $A \wedge \neg$, $(A \vee B$, $(\wedge \to A)$ are not. We will return to these examples in 2.3 below. The importance of clause (iii) in the above definition is that it provides us with the basis for applying induction directly to propositions. We will also return to this subject after first introducing another approach to describing propositions.

Labeled (binary) trees provide us with an important way of representing propositions. It is not hard to see that each proposition φ can be represented as a finite labeled binary tree T. The leaves of T are labeled with propositional letters. If any nonterminal node of T is labeled with a proposition α, its immediate successors are labeled with propositions (one or two) which can be combined using one of the connectives to form α. The left to right ordering on the immediate successors of α is given by the syntactic position of the component propositions. This procedure can be carried out so that the original proposition φ is the label of the root of the tree T. One could take such labeled trees to define propositions and ignore the inductive definition given above. We instead offer a precise translation between these notions:

Definition 2.2: A *formation tree* is a finite tree T of binary sequences (with root $\emptyset$ and a left to right ordering given by the ordinary lexicographic ordering of sequences) whose nodes are all labeled with propositions. The labeling satisfies the following conditions:

(i) The leaves are labeled with propositional letters.

(ii) If a node σ is labeled with a proposition of the form $(\alpha \wedge \beta)$, $(\alpha \vee \beta)$, $(\alpha \to \beta)$ or $(\alpha \leftrightarrow \beta)$, its immediate successors, $\sigma{^\smallfrown}0$ and $\sigma{^\smallfrown}1$, are labeled with α and β (in that order).

(iii) If a node σ is labeled with a proposition of the form $(\neg \alpha)$, its unique immediate successor, $\sigma{^\smallfrown}0$, is labeled with α.

The formation tree T is *associated* with the proposition with which its root is labeled.

Example 2.3: We can depict the formation trees associated with the correctly formed propositions listed above by inserting the appropriate labels for nodes on the proper trees:

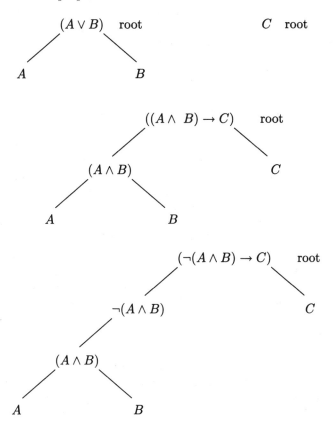

FIGURE 2

Note that in these examples we talked of *the* formation tree associated with a given proposition. Behind this usage stands a theorem that there is, in fact, a unique formation tree associated with each proposition. The method of proof for such a theorem is induction. The definition of propositions is an inductive one: the propositional letters are the base case and the formation rules given by the various connectives constitute the inductive step. Clause (iii) of the definition says that all propositions are included in this process. Corresponding to this type of definition we have both other definitions and proofs by induction. Indeed, induction is the primary method for dealing with most of the notions we will consider. Thus, for example, to define a formation tree associated with each proposition it suffices to define one for each propositional letter and to specify how to define one for a proposition constructed from others via each of the connectives in terms of the ones defined for its constituent propositions. The corresponding method of proof by induction establishes that some property P (such as there being at most one formation tree associated with each proposition) holds for every proposition by first showing that it holds for each propositional letter (the base case) and then showing that, if it holds for propositions α and β, then it holds for each of the propositions constructed from α and β via the five basic connectives. This method is really nothing more than the usual procedure of induction on natural numbers. A translation into that terminology is supplied in Exercise 15.

Theorem 2.4: *Each proposition has a unique formation tree associated with it.*

Proof: We first show by induction that each proposition α has a formation tree associated with it. The base case is that α is a propositional letter, say A. In this case the tree consisting precisely of $\emptyset$ (its root and only node) labeled with A is the desired tree. For the induction step consider the proposition $\alpha \rightarrow \beta$. By induction there are formation trees T_α and T_β associated with α and β respectively. The desired formation tree $T_{(\alpha \rightarrow \beta)}$ for $(\alpha \rightarrow \beta)$ has as its root $\emptyset$ labeled with $(\alpha \rightarrow \beta)$. Below this root we attach copies of T_α (on the left) and T_β (on the right). This can be described formally as letting the other nodes of $T_{(\alpha \rightarrow \beta)}$ be all sequences $0^\frown\sigma$ for every σ on T_α and $1^\frown\tau$ for every τ on T_β. The labels are the same as they were in the original trees. As both T_α and T_β were formation trees, it is clear that $T_{(\alpha \rightarrow \beta)}$ is one as well. (The labeling of nodes is inherited from the original trees except for that of the root by $(\alpha \rightarrow \beta)$. This labeling of the root is acceptable as the root's immediate successors are, by definition, labeled with α and β respectively.) The cases for the other binary connectives are handled in exactly the same way. For $(\neg\alpha)$ we simply add on the nodes $0^\frown\sigma$ for σ in T_α (with the same label as σ) to the root $\emptyset$ which we label with $(\neg\alpha)$. Note that if the formation trees for α and β have depth n and m respectively, the tree for any of the propositions built by applying one of the basic connectives has depth $\max\{n, m\} + 1$.

We next claim that there is at most one formation tree associated with each proposition. For the propositional letters, this claim is clear. As the root of the tree $\emptyset$ must be labeled by the propositional letter if the tree is associated with it, the definition requires that the root be a leaf, i.e., it is the entire tree. Consider now the inductive case for $\alpha \rightarrow \beta$. If T is a formation tree associated with $(\alpha \rightarrow \beta)$ then its root $\emptyset$ must be labeled with $(\alpha \rightarrow \beta)$ by definition. Again, by the definition of a formation tree, $\emptyset$ must have two immediate successors 0 and 1 which must be labeled with α and β respectively. Every node on T below $i = 0$ or 1 must be of the form $0^\frown\sigma$ or $1^\frown\sigma$ respectively for some binary sequence σ. For $i = 0, 1$ let $T_i = \{\sigma \mid i^\frown\sigma \in T\}$ have the standard ordering and be labeled as in T. It is clear that T_0 is a formation tree for α and T_1 for β. They are unique by induction and so T has been uniquely determined as required. The other connectives are handled similarly. $\square$

This theorem corresponds to what is often called the *unique readability* of propositions: There is only one way to parse a proposition into its component parts all the way down to the propositional letters. Along these lines, we will, in informal usage, abuse our notation by omitting parentheses whenever no confusion can arise. Thus, for example, we will write $\neg\alpha$ for $(\neg\alpha)$ and $\alpha \to \beta$ for $(\alpha \to \beta)$. Formally, unique readability gives us another way to define functions on the propositions and prove facts about them: induction on formation trees. Typically, we induct on the depth of the formation tree associated with a proposition. The advantage of using trees is that, if one defines a function on formation trees, one automatically has one on the associated propositions. If instead, one defined an operation directly on propositions by induction, one would not know that there is only one way of analyzing a given proposition inductively so as to guarantee that the operation is well defined. This is precisely unique readability. We will see some examples of such procedures in the next section. For now, we just note that the theorem allows us to define the depth of a proposition. We can also use it to pick out the propositional letters that are "relevant" to a given proposition:

Definition 2.5:

(i) The *depth* of a proposition is the depth of the associated formation tree.

(ii) The *support* of a proposition is the set of propositional letters that occur as labels of the leaves of the associated formation tree. (That this notion corresponds to the ones which occur syntactically in the proposition is proven by another induction argument. See Exercise 16.)

*Closure operations and inductive definitions:

Another approach to the type of inductive definition given may clarify the role of (iii) in guaranteeing that only those expressions generated by (i) and (ii) are propositions. We begin with the (algebraic) notion of closure. A set S is *closed* under a single (for example n–ary) operation $f(s_1, ..., s_n)$ iff for every $s_1, ..., s_n \in S$, $f(s_1, ... , s_n) \in S$. The *closure* of a set S under (all) the operations in a set T is the smallest set C such that

1) $S \subseteq C$ and

2) if $f \in T$ is n–ary and $s_1, ... , s_n \in C$ then $f(s_1, ... , s_n) \in C$.

To see that there is a smallest such set consider the set

$$C = \cap\{D \mid S \subseteq D \ \& \ D \text{ is closed under the operations of } T\}.$$

Of course $S \subseteq C$. Now show that C is closed under the operations of T. It is then clear that C is the smallest such set as it is contained in every set $D \supseteq S$ which is closed under the operations of T. We could now define the set of propositions as the closure of the set of propositional letters (i) under the operations $\wedge, \vee, \neg, \to$ and $\leftrightarrow$ as listed in (ii).

Turning now to semantics, we take the view that the meaning of a propositional letter is simply its truth value, that is, its truth or falsity. (Remember that we are postponing the analysis of the internal structure of propositions to the next chapter.) Each proposition will then have a unique *truth value* (T, for true or F, for false). The truth value of a compound proposition is determined from the truth values of its parts in accordance with the following *truth tables*:

Definition 2.6: (*Truth tables*):

α	β	$(\alpha \vee \beta)$
T	T	T
T	F	T
F	T	T
F	F	F

α	β	$(\alpha \wedge \beta)$
T	T	T
T	F	F
F	T	F
F	F	F

α	β	$(\alpha \to \beta)$
T	T	T
T	F	F
F	T	T
F	F	T

α	β	$(\alpha \leftrightarrow \beta)$
T	T	T
T	F	F
F	T	F
F	F	T

α	$\neg\alpha$
T	F
F	T

FIGURE 3

As pointed out earlier, the meaning of these connectives as specified by these truth tables is not exactly the same as in ordinary English. For $\vee$, the meaning is that of the inclusive or: $\alpha \vee \beta$ is true if either or both of α and β are true. The meaning of $\to$ is further removed from that in colloquial usage. In mathematics, $(\alpha \to \beta)$ is asserted to be false only when α is true and β is false. It is asserted to be true in all other cases.

The formal assignment of truth values to propositions based on those of the propositional letters will be given in the next section. Intuitively, it should be clear from the inductive definition of propositions how, given any proposition whatsoever, we can construct a truth table for it by considering it as being built up step by step starting from propositional letters. For example Figure 4 is the truth table for $((A \wedge B) \to C)$.

The eight combinations of truth values for A, B, C ($2^3 = 8$) can be thought of as all possible states of the world as far as any proposition in which only the propositional letters A, B, C appear is concerned. The column for $(A \wedge B)$ is auxiliary and could be eliminated. The result would be the *abbreviated truth table* for $((A \wedge B) \to C)$. If the convention implicit in

A	B	C	$(A \wedge B)$	$((A \wedge B) \to C)$
T	T	T	T	T
T	T	F	T	F
T	F	T	F	T
T	F	F	F	T
F	T	T	F	T
F	T	F	F	T
F	F	T	F	T
F	F	F	F	T

FIGURE 4

the above table for systematically listing the (eight) possible combinations of truth values for the propositional letters A, B and C is observed, then it is clear that to any proposition there corresponds a unique abbreviated truth table.

A priori, we might have begun with some other list of basic connectives. In general, an *n–ary connective* is any function σ which assigns a proposition $\sigma(A_1, \dots, A_n)$ to every n–tuple of propositions $A_1, \dots, A_n$. So $\neg$ is 1–ary (*unary*), while $\wedge$ and $\vee$ are 2–ary (or *binary*). An n–ary connective is *truth functional* if the truth value for $\sigma(A_1, \dots, A_n)$ is uniquely determined by the truth values for $A_1, \dots, A_n$. Our five connectives are truth functional since their meaning was defined by truth tables. On the other hand a connective like "because" is not. For let A symbolize "I had prune juice for breakfast" and B "there was an earthquake at noon". Even in the event that both A and B have truth values T it is at least debatable whether (B because A) should have truth value T. The debate might be more or less heated in other cases depending on the content of A and B. An n–ary connective which is truth functional can be completely described by means of a truth table. Here each b_i, $1 \le i \le 2^n$ is either T or F:

A_1	A_2	$\cdots$	A_n	$\sigma(A_1, \dots, A_k)$
T	T	$\cdots$	T	b_1
T	T	$\cdots$	F	b_2
.	.	$\cdots$	.	.
.	.	$\cdots$	.	.
F	F	$\cdots$	F	.

FIGURE 5

Conversely, two distinct abbreviated truth tables (with the conventional listing of truth values for $A_1, \ldots, A_n$) correspond to distinct truth functional connectives. By counting we see that there are 2^{2^n} distinct n–ary truth functional connectives. (So there are $12 = 16 - 4$ binary connectives which we are not using.)

Definition 2.7: A set S of truth functional connectives is *adequate* if, given any truth functional connective σ, we can find a proposition built up from the connectives in S with the same abbreviated truth table as σ.

Theorem 2.8 (Adequacy): $\{\neg, \wedge, \vee\}$ *is adequate.*

Proof: Let $A_1, \ldots, A_k$ be distinct propositional letters and let a_{ij} denote the entry (T or F) corresponding to the ith row and j^{th} column of the truth table for $\sigma(A_1, \ldots, A_k)$. Suppose that at least one T appears in the last column.

A_1	$\cdots$	A_j	$\cdots$	A_k	$\cdots$	$\sigma(A_1, \ldots, A_k)$
						b_1
						b_2
						.
						.
		a_{ij}				b_i

FIGURE 6

For any proposition α, let α^T be α and α^F be $(\neg \alpha)$. For the ith row denote the *conjunction* $(A_1^{a_{i1}} \wedge \ldots \wedge A_k^{a_{ik}})$ by a_i. Let $i_1, \ldots, i_m$ be the rows with a T in the last column. The desired proposition is the *disjunction* $(a_{i_1} \vee \ldots \vee a_{i_m})$. The proof that this proposition has the given truth table is left as Exercises 14. (Note that we abused our notation by leaving out a lot of parentheses in the interest of readability. The convention is that of *right associativity*, that is, $A \wedge B \wedge C$ is an abbreviation for $(A \wedge (B \wedge C))$.) We also indicate a disjunction over a set of propositions with the usual set–theoretic terminology. Thus the disjunction just constructed would be written as $\bigvee\{a_i : b_i = T\}$. $\square$

Example 2.9: The procedure given in the above proof can be illustrated by constructing a proposition built using only $\wedge$, $\vee$ and $\neg$ which has the truth table given in Figure 7.

	A	B	C	?
1	T	T	T	T
2	T	T	F	F
3	T	F	T	F
4	T	F	F	F
5	F	T	T	T
6	F	T	F	F
7	F	F	T	F
8	F	F	F	T

FIGURE 7

We begin by looking only at rows with a T in the last column. For each such row we find a proposition which is true for that row and false for every other row. The proposition we want is the disjunction of the propositions we obtain for all relevant rows (rows 1, 5, 8 in this case). For any particular row, the proposition true for only that row is obtained by taking the conjunction of the letters having a T in that row and the negations of letters having an F on that row. In this case row 1 gives $(A \wedge B \wedge C)$ (we abuse notation again!); row 5 gives $((\neg A) \wedge B \wedge C)$; and row 8 gives $((\neg A) \wedge (\neg B) \wedge (\neg C))$. Thus the proposition $(A \wedge B \wedge C) \vee ((\neg A) \wedge B \wedge C) \vee ((\neg A) \wedge (\neg B) \wedge (\neg C))$ has the given truth table.

Clearly, given any proposition α we can construct its truth table and then follow the above procedure to find another proposition which has the same truth table and is a disjunction of conjunctions of propositional letters and their negations. A proposition of this form which has the same (abbreviated) truth table as α is called a *disjunctive normal form* (DNF) of α. There is also a *conjunctive normal form* (CNF) equivalent of α which is presented in Exercise 3.3. Another method of finding DNF and CNF equivalents of α is presented at the end of the exercises for §4.

Remark 2.10: The above procedure does not tell us what to do in case the last column consists entirely of F's. See Exercise 13.

Corollary 2.11: $\{\neg, \vee\}$ *is adequate.*

Proof: We can easily check that $(A_1 \wedge A_2)$ has the same truth table as $\neg((\neg(A_1)) \vee (\neg(A_2)))$. Thus given any proposition α we can find a DNF of α and then eliminate any use of $\wedge$ by this substitution. The resulting proposition will still have the same truth table. $\square$

The sets $\{\neg, \wedge\}$ and $\{\neg, \rightarrow\}$ are also shown to be adequate in the exercises. If a set is not adequate, how do you prove that? (See Exercises 10.)

Remark 2.12: By the adequacy theorems (Theorem 2.8 and Corollary 2.11) we could, in theory, get by with just the connectives $\neg$, $\vee$ and $\wedge$ or even just $\neg$ and $\vee$. The induction clause in the definition of propositions and many related definitions and proofs (such as those involving tableaux in sections 4, 5 and 6) could then be considerably shortened. We will, however, leave the list of connectives as it is but will generally explicitly deal with only a couple of cases in any particular proof and leave the rest as exercises.

Exercises

1. Which of the following expressions are official (that is, unabbreviated) propositions of propositional logic based on the propositional letters A, B, C, D, ...?

   a) $\big((\neg(A \vee B)) \wedge C\big)$

   b) $(A \wedge B) \vee C$

   c) $A \rightarrow (B \wedge C)$

   d) $\big((A \leftrightarrow B) \rightarrow (\neg A)\big)$

   e) $\big((\neg A) \rightarrow B \vee C\big)$

   f) $\big(((C \vee B) \wedge A) \leftrightarrow D\big)$

   g) $\big((\vee A) \wedge (\neg B)\big)$

   h) $\big(A \wedge (B \wedge C))\big)$

2. Prove your answers to 1(a), (b) and (f) by either giving the step by step procedure producing the proposition in accordance with the inductive definition of propositions (you can simply draw a correctly labeled formation tree) or proving, by induction on statements, that there is some property enjoyed by all propositions but not by this expression.

3. Prove that the number of right and left parentheses are equal in every proposition.

4. Prove that the depth of a proposition is less than or equal to the number of left parentheses appearing in the proposition. (Use the official definition of proposition.)

5. Find DNF equivalents for the following propositions:

   a) $(A \rightarrow B) \rightarrow C$

   b) $(A \leftrightarrow B) \vee (\neg C)$

6. Prove that $\{\neg, \wedge\}$ is an adequate set of connectives. (Hint: Express $\vee$ in terms of $\neg$ and $\wedge$.)

7. Prove that $\{\neg, \rightarrow\}$ is an adequate set of connectives.

8. Prove that the binary connective $(\alpha \mid \beta)$ ("not both ... and") called the *Sheffer stroke* whose truth table is given by

α	β	$\alpha \mid \beta$
T	T	F
T	F	T
F	T	T
F	F	T

FIGURE 8

is adequate. (Hint: Express $\neg$ and $\wedge$ in terms of $\mid$.)

9. Show that joint denial (neither α nor β), written as $\alpha \downarrow \beta$, is also adequate.

10. Prove that $\{\wedge, \vee\}$ is not adequate.
    Hint: Show by induction that $\neg\alpha$ is not equivalent to any statement built up from α using only $\wedge$ and $\vee$

11. Prove that $\{\vee, \rightarrow\}$ is not an adequate set of connectives.

12. Prove that $\{\vee, \rightarrow, \leftrightarrow\}$ is not an adequate set of connectives.

13. Explain how to handle the case of a column of all F's in the proof of Theorem 2.8.

14. Prove that the expressions constructed in the proof of Theorem 2.8 (including the case considered in exercise 13) have the desired truth tables.

15. We say that all propositional letters are built at stage 0. If propositions α and β have been built by level n, we say that $(\neg\alpha)$, $(\alpha \vee \beta)$, $(\alpha \wedge \beta)$, $(\alpha \rightarrow \beta)$ and $(\alpha \leftrightarrow \beta)$ have been built by level $n + 1$. Clause (iii) of Definition 2.1 says that every proposition φ is built by some level n. Explain how we can rephrase proof by induction on the definition of propositions in terms of ordinary induction on the natural numbers $\mathbb{N}$.

    (Hint: Proving that all propositions have property P by induction on propositions corresponds to proving that all propositions built by level n have property P by induction on n.)

16. We say that each propositional letter A *occurs* in itself and no propositional letters other than A occur in A. The propositional letters that *occur* in $(\neg\alpha)$ are precisely the ones that occur in α. The ones that occur in $(\alpha \vee \beta)$, $(\alpha \wedge \beta)$, $(\alpha \rightarrow \beta)$ and $(\alpha \leftrightarrow \beta)$ are precisely those that occur in either α or β (or both). This notion clearly captures the idea of a syntactic occurrence of a propositional letter A in a proposition α.

    Prove that the support of a proposition α is precisely the set of propositional letters that occur in α.

3. Truth Assignments and Valuations

Our view of propositional logic is that the meaning or content of a proposition is just its truth value. Thus, the whole notion of semantics for propositional logic consists of assigning truth values to propositions. We begin with the propositional letters.

Definition 3.1: A *truth assignment* $\mathcal{A}$ is a function which assigns to each propositional letter A a unique truth value $\mathcal{A}(A) \in \{T, F\}$.

The truth values of all propositions should now be determined by the assignment to the propositional letters. The determinations are made in accordance with the truth tables for the connectives given in the last section.

Definition 3.2: A *truth valuation* $\mathcal{V}$ is a function which assigns to each proposition α a unique truth value $\mathcal{V}(\alpha)$ so that its value on a compound proposition (that is, one with a connective) is determined in accordance with the appropriate truth tables. Thus, for example, $\mathcal{V}((\neg\alpha)) = T$ iff $\mathcal{V}(\alpha) = F$ and $\mathcal{V}((\alpha \vee \beta)) = T$ iff $\mathcal{V}(\alpha) = T$ or $\mathcal{V}(\beta) = T$. We say that $\mathcal{V}$ *makes* α *true* if $\mathcal{V}(\alpha) = T$.

The basic result here is that a truth assignment to the propositional letters uniquely determines the entire truth valuation on all propositions. We analyze the situation in terms of an induction on the depth of the propositions, that is, the depth of the (unique) formation tree associated with the proposition.

Theorem 3.3: *Given a truth assignment* $\mathcal{A}$ *there is a unique truth valuation* $\mathcal{V}$ *such that* $\mathcal{V}(\alpha) = \mathcal{A}(\alpha)$ *for every propositional letter* α.

Proof: Given a truth assignment $\mathcal{A}$, define (by induction on the depth of the associated formation tree) a valuation $\mathcal{V}$ on all propositions by first setting $\mathcal{V}(\alpha) = \mathcal{A}(\alpha)$ for all propositional letters α. This takes care of all formation trees (propositions) of depth 0. Assuming that $\mathcal{V}$ has been defined on all propositions with depth at most n, the inductive steps are simply given by the truth tables associated with each connective. For example, suppose $T_{(\alpha \rightarrow \beta)}$ is the formation tree (of depth $n+1$) for $(\alpha \rightarrow \beta)$. (It is built from T_α and T_β (with the maximum of their depths being exactly n) as in Theorem 2.4.) $\mathcal{V}((\alpha \rightarrow \beta))$ is then defined to be F iff $\mathcal{V}(\alpha) = T$ and $\mathcal{V}(\beta) = F$. The valuation is defined on α and β by induction since they have depth at most n.

Clearly $\mathcal{V}$ has been defined so as to be a valuation and it does extend $\mathcal{A}$. It remains to show that any two valuations $\mathcal{V}_1$, $\mathcal{V}_2$ both extending $\mathcal{A}$ must coincide. We prove this by induction on the depth of propositions:

(i) $\mathcal{V}_1(\alpha) = \mathcal{V}_2(\alpha)$ for all propositional letters α (depth 0) since $\mathcal{V}_1$, $\mathcal{V}_2$ both extend $\mathcal{A}$.

(ii) Suppose $\mathcal{V}_1(\alpha) = \mathcal{V}_2(\alpha)$ for all propositions α of depth at most n and that α and β have depth at most n. Thus $\mathcal{V}_1(\alpha) = \mathcal{V}_2(\alpha)$ and $\mathcal{V}_1(\beta) = \mathcal{V}_2(\beta)$ by induction. $\mathcal{V}_1((\alpha \wedge \beta))$ and $\mathcal{V}_2((\alpha \wedge \beta))$ are then both given by the truth table for $\wedge$ and so are equal. The same argument works for all the other connectives and so $\mathcal{V}_1$ and $\mathcal{V}_2$ agree on every proposition. $\square$

Note that, by induction again on the depth of α, the definition of $\mathcal{V}(\alpha)$ in this construction only depends on the values of $\mathcal{A}$ on the support of α (the propositional letters occurring in α). Thus the proof of the theorem actually proves:

Corollary 3.4: *If $\mathcal{V}_1$ and $\mathcal{V}_2$ are two valuations which agree on the support of α, the finite set of propositional letters used in the construction of the proposition α, then $\mathcal{V}_1(\alpha) = \mathcal{V}_2(\alpha)$.* $\square$

Definition 3.5: A proposition σ of propositional logic is said to be *valid* if for any valuation $\mathcal{V}$, $\mathcal{V}(\sigma) = T$. Such a proposition is also called a *tautology*.

Definition 3.6: Two propositions α and β such that, for every valuation $\mathcal{V}$, $\mathcal{V}(\alpha) = \mathcal{V}(\beta)$ are called *logically equivalent*. We denote this by $\alpha \equiv \beta$.

Example 3.7:

(i) $(A \vee (\neg A))$, $\big(((A \rightarrow B) \rightarrow A) \rightarrow A\big)$ (Law of the excluded middle, Peirce's law) are tautologies. See Exercise 1.

(ii) For any proposition α and any DNF β of α, $\alpha \equiv \beta$.

(iii) We could rephrase the adequacy theorem (2.8) to say that, given any proposition α, we can find a β which uses only $\neg$, $\vee$, $\wedge$ and such that $\alpha \equiv \beta$.

Although Corollary 3.4 allows us to check whether a given proposition is a tautology or not using Definition 2.5, it also tells us that we can answer the same question by finding out whether the last column of the corresponding truth table has all T's or not. We choose not to develop these proofs by truth tables further because they do not generalize to proofs for predicate logic which we will study shortly. We close this section with some definitions and notations which will be important later and generalize nicely to the corresponding concepts in the logic of predicates.

Definition 3.8: Let Σ be a (possibly infinite) set of propositions. We say that σ *is a consequence of* Σ (and write $\Sigma \vDash \sigma$) if, for any valuation $\mathcal{V}$,

$$\mathcal{V}(\tau) = T \text{ for all } \tau \in \Sigma \quad \Rightarrow \quad \mathcal{V}(\sigma) = T.$$

Note that, if Σ is empty, $\Sigma \vDash \sigma$ (or just $\vDash \sigma$) iff σ is valid. We will also write this as $\vDash \sigma$. This definition gives a semantic notion of consequence. We will see several syntactic notions in the coming sections that correspond to different proof procedures. A major result will be the equivalence of the syntactic and semantic notions of consequence which will be embodied in the soundness and completeness theorems (§5).

Definition 3.9: We say that a valuation $\mathcal{V}$ is a *model* of Σ if $\mathcal{V}(\sigma) = T$ for every $\sigma \in \Sigma$. We denote by $\mathcal{M}(\Sigma)$ the set of all models of Σ.

Notation: Rather than writing "implies" and "if and only if" in our definitions, theorems, etc., we often use $\Rightarrow$ and $\Leftrightarrow$ instead. These are not symbols of the language of propositional logic but of the language (or metalanguage) in which we discuss propositional logic.

Proposition 3.10: *Let Σ, Σ_1, Σ_2 be sets of propositions. Let $Cn(\Sigma)$ denote the set of consequences of Σ and Taut the set of all tautologies.*

  (i) $\Sigma_1 \subseteq \Sigma_2 \Rightarrow Cn(\Sigma_1) \subseteq Cn(\Sigma_2)$.

  (ii) $\Sigma \subseteq Cn(\Sigma)$.

  (iii) *Taut* $\subseteq Cn(\Sigma)$ *for all* Σ.

  (iv) $Cn(\Sigma) = Cn(Cn(\Sigma))$.

  (v) $\Sigma_1 \subseteq \Sigma_2 \Rightarrow \mathcal{M}(\Sigma_2) \subseteq \mathcal{M}(\Sigma_1)$.

  (vi) $Cn(\Sigma) = \{\sigma \mid \mathcal{V}(\sigma) = T \text{ for all } \mathcal{V} \in \mathcal{M}(\Sigma)\}$.

  (vii) $\sigma \in Cn(\{\sigma_1, \ldots \sigma_n\}) \Leftrightarrow \sigma_1 \to (\sigma_2 \ldots \to (\sigma_n \to \sigma) \ldots) \in$ *Taut.*

We leave the proof of this proposition as Exercise 4.

The last assertion of Proposition 3.10 tells us that testing whether σ is a consequence of a finite set Σ of propositions (sometimes called "premises") with, say, n members can be done in at most 2^n steps by checking whether the proposition on the right–hand side of (vii) is a tautology. But what do we do if Σ is infinite? We had better learn how to *prove* that σ is a consequence. The first method we will consider is that of tableaux.

Exercises

1. Prove that the propositions in Example 3.7 (i) are tautologies by checking directly, using Corollary 3.4, that they are true under all valuations.

2. Prove De Morgan's laws for any propositions $\alpha_1, \ldots, \alpha_n$, i.e.,

    a) $\neg(\alpha_1 \lor \alpha_2 \lor \ldots \lor \alpha_n) \equiv \neg\alpha_1 \land \neg\alpha_2 \land \ldots \land \neg\alpha_n$

    b) $\neg(\alpha_1 \land \alpha_2 \land \ldots \land \alpha_n) \equiv \neg\alpha_1 \lor \neg\alpha_2 \lor \ldots \lor \neg\alpha_n$.

    Hint: Do not write out the truth tables. Argue directly from the truth conditions for disjunctions and conjunctions.

3. A proposition is a *literal* if it is a propositional letter or its negation. A proposition α is in *conjunctive normal form* (CNF) if there are literals $\alpha_{1,1}, \ldots, \alpha_{1,n_1}, \alpha_{2,1}, \ldots, \alpha_{2,n_2}, \ldots, \alpha_{k,1}, \ldots, \alpha_{2,n_k}$ such that α is

    $$(\alpha_{1,1} \lor \alpha_{1,2} \lor \ldots \lor \alpha_{1,n_1}) \land (\alpha_{2,1} \lor \alpha_{2,2} \lor \ldots \lor \alpha_{2,n_2}) \land \ldots \land (\alpha_{k,1} \lor \ldots \lor \alpha_{k,n_k}).$$

    Prove that every proposition is equivalent to one in CNF (i.e., one that has the same truth table). (Hint: Consider a DNF (of $\neg\alpha$) and use Exercise 2.)

4. Find a CNF for each of the following propositions:

    a) $(A \wedge B \wedge C) \rightarrow D$

    b) $(A \wedge B) \rightarrow (C \vee D)$.

5. Supply the (short) proofs from the appropriate definitions for (i)–(vii) of Proposition 3.10.

4. Tableau Proofs in Propositional Calculus

We will describe a system for building proofs of propositions. The proofs will be labeled binary trees called tableaux. The labels on the trees will be *signed propositions*, that is a proposition preceded by either a T or an F (which we can think of as indicating an assumed truth value for the proposition). We call the labels of the nodes the *entries of the tableau*. Formally we will define (or describe how to build) tableaux for propositions inductively by first specifying certain (labeled binary) trees as tableaux (the so–called atomic tableaux) and then giving a development rule defining tableaux for compound propositions from tableaux for simple propositions.

The plan of the procedure is to start with some entry, i.e., some signed proposition such as $F(\neg(A \wedge (B \vee C)))$, and analyze it into its components. We will say that an entry is correct if our assumption about the truth value of the given proposition is correct. For our current example, $F(\neg(A \wedge (B \vee C)))$, this would mean that $\neg(A \wedge (B \vee C))$ is false. The guiding principle for the analysis is that, if an entry is correct, then (at least) one of the sets of entries into which we analyze it contains only correct entries. In our sample case, we would analyze $F(\neg(A \wedge (B \vee C)))$ first into $T(A \wedge (B \vee C))$. $\big($If $\neg(A \wedge (B \vee C))$ is false, then $(A \wedge (B \vee C))$ is true.$\big)$ We would then analyze $T(A \wedge (B \vee C))$ into TA and $T(B \vee C)$. $\big($If $(A \wedge (B \vee C))$ is true then so are both A and $(B \vee C)$.$\big)$ Next we would analyze $T(B \vee C)$ into either TB or TC. $\big($If $(B \vee C)$ is true then so is one of B or C.$\big)$

The intent of the procedure, as a way of producing proofs of propositions, is to start with some signed proposition, such as $F\alpha$, as the root of our tree and to analyze it into its components in such a way as to see that any analysis leads to a contradiction. We will then conclude that we have refuted the original assumption that α is false and so have a proof of α. Suppose, for example, that we start with $F(\neg(A \wedge \neg A))$ and proceed as in the above analysis (replacing $(B \vee C)$ by $\neg A$). We reach TA and $T\neg A$ and then analyze $T\neg A$ into FA. We now have entries saying both that A is true and that it is false. This is the desired contradiction and we would conclude that we have a proof of the valid proposition $\neg(A \wedge \neg A)$.

The base case of our inductive definition of tableaux starts with the following (labeled binary) trees as the *atomic tableaux* for any propositions α and β and propositional letter A (Figure 9).

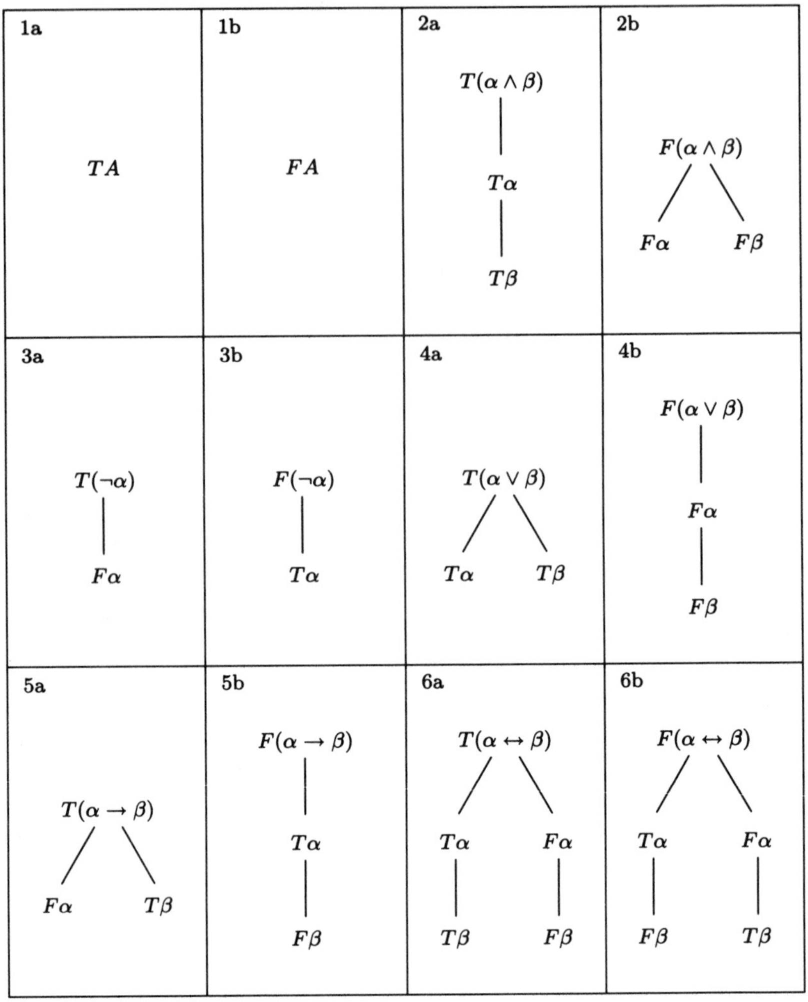

1a	1b	2a	2b
TA	FA	$T(\alpha \wedge \beta)$ $\mid$ $T\alpha$ $\mid$ $T\beta$	$F(\alpha \wedge \beta)$ $\diagup \quad \diagdown$ $F\alpha \qquad F\beta$

3a	3b	4a	4b
$T(\neg\alpha)$ $\mid$ $F\alpha$	$F(\neg\alpha)$ $\mid$ $T\alpha$	$T(\alpha \vee \beta)$ $\diagup \quad \diagdown$ $T\alpha \qquad T\beta$	$F(\alpha \vee \beta)$ $\mid$ $F\alpha$ $\mid$ $F\beta$

5a	5b	6a	6b
$T(\alpha \to \beta)$ $\diagup \quad \diagdown$ $F\alpha \qquad T\beta$	$F(\alpha \to \beta)$ $\mid$ $T\alpha$ $\mid$ $F\beta$	$T(\alpha \leftrightarrow \beta)$ $\diagup \quad \diagdown$ $T\alpha \qquad F\alpha$ $\mid \qquad \mid$ $T\beta \qquad F\beta$	$F(\alpha \leftrightarrow \beta)$ $\diagup \quad \diagdown$ $T\alpha \qquad F\alpha$ $\mid \qquad \mid$ $F\beta \qquad T\beta$

FIGURE 9

Definition 4.1 (Tableaux): A *finite tableau* is a binary tree, labeled with signed propositions called entries, which satisfies the following inductive definition:

(i) All atomic tableaux are finite tableaux.

(ii) If τ is a finite tableau, P a path on τ, E an entry of τ occurring on P and τ' is obtained from τ by adjoining the unique atomic tableau with root entry E to τ at the end of the path P then τ' is also a finite tableau.

If $\tau_0, \tau_1, ..., \tau_n, ...$ is a (finite or infinite) sequence of finite tableaux such that, for each $n \geq 0$, τ_{n+1} is constructed from τ_n by an application of (ii), then $\tau = \cup \tau_n$ is a *tableau*.

This definition describes all possible tableaux. We could get by with finite tableaux in propositional logic (see the appendix to this section) but would necessarily be driven to infinite ones in predicate logic. As they simplify some proofs even in our current situation we have introduced them here.

Each tableau is a way of analyzing a proposition. The intent is that, if it is all right to assume that all the signs on entries on a path down to some entry E in a tableau are correct, then one of the paths of the tableau that continue on through E to the next level of the tree is also correct. To see that this intention is realized, it suffices to consider the atomic tableaux. Consider for example (5a). If $\alpha \to \beta$ is true then so is one of the branches through it: α is false or β is true. Similarly for (4a), if $\alpha \vee \beta$ is true then so is one of α or β. The other atomic tableaux can be analyzed in the same way. This intuition will be developed formally in the next section as the soundness theorem for tableaux. The other major theorem about tableaux is the completeness theorem. It is connected with the idea that we can show that if α is valid, then all possible analyses of a given signed proposition $F\alpha$ lead to contradictions. This will constitute a proof α. In order to do this, we will have to develop a systematic method for generating a tableau with a given root which includes all possible procedures. First, however, some examples of tableaux.

Example 4.2: We wish to begin a tableau with the signed proposition $F\big(\big((\alpha \to \beta) \vee (\gamma \vee \delta)\big) \wedge (\alpha \vee \beta)\big)$. There is only one atomic tableau which has this entry as its root — the appropriate instance of the atomic tableau of type (2b):

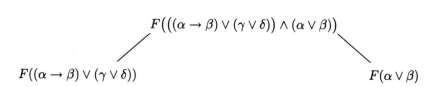

$$F\big(\big((\alpha \to \beta) \vee (\gamma \vee \delta)\big) \wedge (\alpha \vee \beta)\big)$$

$$F\big((\alpha \to \beta) \vee (\gamma \vee \delta)\big) \qquad\qquad F(\alpha \vee \beta)$$

FIGURE 10

Now this tableau has two entries other than its root either of which could be chosen to use in the induction clause to build a bigger tableau. (We could legally use the root entry again but that would not be very interesting.) The two possibilities are given in Figures 11 A and B below.

We could also do each of these steps in turn to get the tableau given in Figure 11 C.

In this last tableau we could (again ignoring duplications) choose either $F(\alpha \to \beta)$ or $F(\gamma \vee \delta)$ as the entry to d evelop. $F(\gamma \vee \delta)$ is the end of the only path in the tableau which contains either of these entries. Thus, in either case the appropriate atomic tableau would be appended to that path. Choosing $F(\alpha \to \beta)$ would give the tableau of Figure 12.

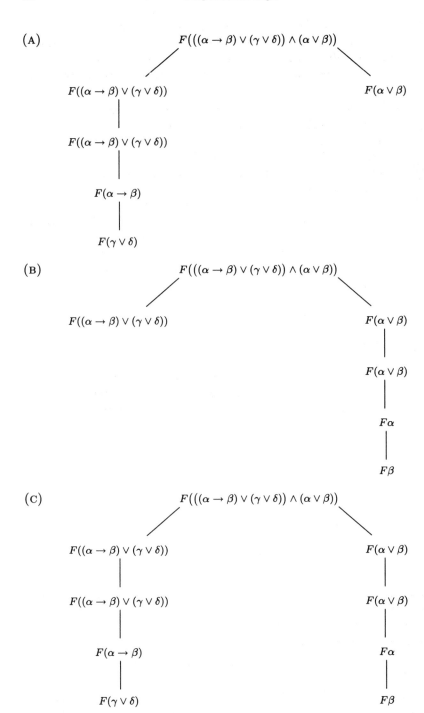

FIGURES 11 A, B, C

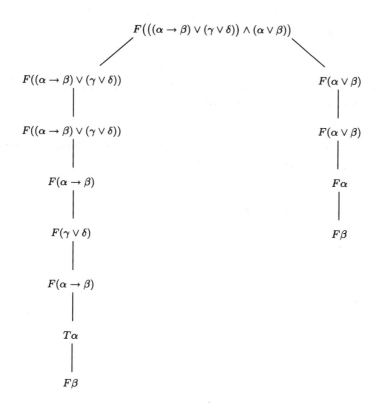

As the reader must have noticed, each time we select an entry it gets repeated at the end of the chosen path as part of the atomic tableau that we affix to the end of the path. As a notational convenience we will often omit this second occurrence when we draw tableaux although it remains part of the formal definition. (They will actually be needed when we consider the predicate calculus and so we included them in our formal definition.)

We now wish to describe those tableaux that will constitute proofs and a systematic procedure for generating them from given signed propositions. We need a number of auxiliary notions:

Definition 4.3: Let τ be a tableau, P a path on τ and E an entry occurring on P.

(i) E has been *reduced* on P if all the entries on one path through the atomic tableau with root E occur on P. (For example, TA and FA are reduced for every propositional letter A. $T\neg\alpha$ and $F\neg\alpha$ are reduced (on P) if $F\alpha$ and $T\alpha$ respectively appear on P. $T(\alpha \vee \beta)$ is reduced if either $T\alpha$ or $T\beta$ appears on P. $F(\alpha \vee \beta)$ is reduced if both $F\alpha$ and $F\beta$ appear on P.)

(ii) *P* is *contradictory* if, for some proposition α, $T\alpha$ and $F\alpha$ are both entries on *P*. *P* is *finished* if it is contradictory or every entry on *P* is reduced on *P*.

(iii) τ is *finished* if every path through τ is finished.

(iv) τ is *contradictory* if every path through τ is contradictory. (It is, of course, then finished as well.)

Example 4.4: Here is a finished tableau with three paths. The leftmost path is contradictory; the other two are not.

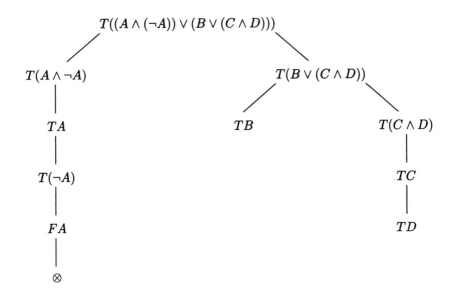

FIGURE 13

We can now define tableau proofs of α as ones that show that the assumption that α is false always leads to a contradiction:

Definition 4.5: A *tableau proof* of a proposition α is a contradictory tableau with root entry $F\alpha$. A proposition is *tableau provable*, written $\vdash \alpha$, if it has a tableau proof.

A *tableau refutation* for a proposition α is a contradictory tableau starting with $T\alpha$. A proposition is *tableau refutable* if it has a tableau refutation.

The following example is a tableau proof of an instance of Peirce's law. Remember that we don't actually recopy the entries that we are reducing. We put $\otimes$ at the end of a path to denote that it is contradictory.

Example 4.6: Peirce's Law.

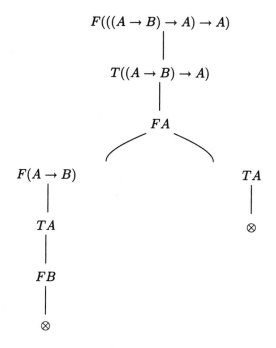

FIGURE 14

In much of what follows, for every definition or theorem dealing with a tableau proof or a logical truth (or both), there is a dual definition or theorem dealing with a tableau refutation and a logical falsehood respectively. It is left to the reader to provide these dual propositions.

The next step in producing proofs is to see that there is a finished tableau starting with any given signed proposition as root entry. We will describe a simple systematic procedure for producing such a tableau. A development that uses only finite tableaux is provided in the appendix to this section.

Definition 4.7 (Complete Systematic Tableaux): Let R be a signed proposition. We define the *complete systematic tableau* (CST) with root entry R by induction. We begin the construction by letting τ_0 be the unique atomic tableau with R at its root. Assume that τ_m has been defined. Let n be the smallest level of τ_m containing an entry which is unreduced on some noncontradictory path in τ_m and let E be the leftmost such entry of level n. We now let τ_{m+1} be the tableau gotten by adjoining the unique atomic tableau with root E to the end of every noncontradictory path of τ_m on which E is unreduced. The union of the sequence τ_m is our desired complete systematic tableau.

Theorem 4.8: *Every* CST *is finished.*

Proof: Consider any entry E which occurs at some level n of the CST τ and lies on a noncontradictory path P in τ. There are at most finitely many entries on τ at or above level n. Thus, all the entries at level n or above on τ must be in place by some point of the construction. That is, there is an m_0 such that for every $m \geq m_0$, τ_m through level n is the same as τ through level n. Now, for $m \geq m_0$, the restriction of P to τ_m is a path in τ_m containing E. At each step $m \geq m_0$ in the construction of the CST we reduce the entry on the lexicographically least node labeled with an unreduced entry which is on some noncontradictory path in the tableau τ_m. If E is not already reduced on P by stage m_0, we can proceed for at most finitely many steps in this construction before E would become the lexicographically least unreduced entry. At this point in the construction we would reduce E. $\square$

In allowing infinite tableaux, we seem to be in conflict with the intuition that proofs should be finite objects. However, by König's lemma, we can restrict our attention to finite contradictory tableaux.

Theorem 4.9: *If* $\tau = \cup \tau_n$ *is a contradictory tableau then for some* m, τ_m *is a finite contradictory tableau. Thus, in particular, if a* CST *is a proof, it is a finite tableau.*

Proof: τ is a finitely branching tree. Consider the subset of all nodes of τ with no contradiction above them. If this set is infinite, it has an infinite path by König's lemma. As this contradicts the assumption that every path in τ is contradictory, there are only finitely many such nodes. They must all appear by some level n of τ. Thus every node at level $n + 1$ of τ has a contradiction above it. Once again, as τ through level $n + 1$ is finite, there is an m such that τ_m is the same as τ through level $n + 1$. Now every path P in τ_m is either a path in τ (ending with a leaf of level $\leq n$) or a path containing a node of level $n + 1$. In the first case, P is contradictory by our assumption that τ is contradictory. In the second, P is contradictory by our choice of n and m. Thus τ_m is the desired contradictory tableau.

Note that if $\tau = \cup \tau_n$ is as in the definition of a CST and m is least such that τ_m is contradictory, then we cannot extend τ_m in the construction of τ. In this case $\tau = \tau_m$. $\square$

In the next section, we will consider the import of this argument for the semantic as well as syntactic versions of the compactness theorem.

*Appendix: Finite tableaux suffice.

We wish to show that we can develop the results of this section without recourse to infinite tableaux. We first prove that there is a finite finished tableau with any given root. We then consider systematic procedures to generate such tableaux.

Theorem 4.10: *There is a finished finite tableau τ for each possible root entry $T\alpha$ or $F\alpha$.*

Proof: We proceed by induction on the depth of the given proposition α. If its depth is 0, i.e., α is a propositional letter, then the tableau consisting of just the signed propositional letter is finished. The point here is that signed propositional letters are themselves atomic tableaux. For the inductive case consider first case (2b): $F(\alpha \wedge \beta)$. By induction there are finished tableaux τ_α and τ_β with root entries $F\alpha$ and $F\beta$ respectively. We form the desired tableau with root $F(\alpha \wedge \beta)$ by beginning with the corresponding atomic tableau (2b) and then appending copies of τ_α and τ_β below the entries $F\alpha$ and $F\beta$ respectively. It is immediate from the definition of a finished tableau that this gives the desired result. The arguments for cases (3a), (3b), (4a) and (5a) are similar.

Next consider case (2a): $T(\alpha \wedge \beta)$. As before, we have finished tableaux τ_α and τ_β. We again begin our desired tableau τ with the appropriate atomic tableau (2a). To the end of this tableau we add a copy of τ_α to get a tableau τ' in which the only possible unreduced occurrence of an entry is that of $T\beta$ in the original atomic tableau. We now add a copy of τ_β to the end of every noncontradictory path in τ' to get our desired τ.

The cases (4b) and (5b) are similar. (6a) and (6b) are handled by applying this same procedure below each of the two distinct paths introduced by the atomic tableau to the two adjoined signed propositions which are put on these paths. $\square$

The above proof actually gives a recursive procedure to construct a finished finite tableau with given root. The procedure is, however, somewhat complicated and hard to carry out. We now define a simpler systematic way of generating tableaux that will always produce a finished finite tableau with any given root entry. The idea is to always reduce the unreduced entry of greatest depth. We will see in the next section that this procedure will always produce a tableau proof of $F\alpha$.

Definition 4.11 (*Systematic Tableaux): We define *systematic tableaux* by induction:

(i) Every atomic tableau is a *systematic tableau.

(ii) If τ is a *systematic tableau and E is an entry of τ of maximal depth such that there is a noncontradictory path P of τ on which E is unreduced, then if τ' is the tableau gotten by adjoining the unique atomic tableau with root E to the end of every noncontradictory path P' of τ on which E is unreduced, then τ' is a *systematic tableau.

Our claim is that if we start with any *systematic tableau (and so in particular any atomic tableau) and repeatedly apply instances of the inductive step described in Definition 4.11(ii), then we eventually reach a finished tableau. Of course, once we have a finished tableau there is, by definition, no way of continuing this process. We can thus specify a sequence of steps that will eventually build a finished tableau with any given root entry.

Let τ_0 be the atomic tableau having the given entry as its root. Then, by induction, we form from τ_n the *systematic tableau, τ_{n+1}, gotten by applying the formation rule to say the (lexicographically) least E of maximal depth (as a proposition) which occurs unreduced on some noncontradictory path in τ_n.

The proof that this procedure eventually produces a finished tableau is a somewhat more complicated induction than the ones we have seen so far. We do not, however, actually need this result for later work. The simple existence of a finished tableau with any specified root entry (Theorem 4.10) suffices for the theorems of the next sections. Moreover, this procedure is not the most efficient way to produce such a finished tableau. We give examples and hints as to how one actually builds finished tableaux in the exercises.

The advantage of the *systematic tableaux approach is that the proof of termination, although somewhat complicated, is quite clean. It proceeds by induction on the pair consisting of the maximal depth of an entry in τ as described above and the number of unreduced occurrences of entries with this maximal depth. These pairs are ordered lexicographically and so progress is made in the induction when either the maximal depth of such an entry in this tableau is reduced or, failing that, when the number of unreduced occurrences of entries with the given maximal depth is reduced. (Exercise 1.7 says that the lexicographic ordering $<_L$ (used at the end of the proof of Theorem 4.12) of pairs of natural numbers is well founded, i.e., it has no infinite descending chains. Thus we may do a proof by induction on this ordering in the usual format: If, from the assumption that some property holds for every pair less than $\langle x, y \rangle$ in this ordering, we can prove that it holds for $\langle x, y \rangle$ as well, then we may conclude that it holds for every pair.)

Theorem 4.12: *There is no infinite sequence $\langle \tau_n \rangle$ of *systematic tableaux such that for each n, τ_{n+1} is gotten from τ_n by an application of the inductive clause (ii) of Definition 4.11.*

Proof: We proceed by induction on the lexicographic order of the pair $h(\tau_0) = \langle i, j \rangle$ where i is the maximal depth of any entry of τ_0 occurring unreduced on some noncontradictory path in τ_0 and j is the number of unreduced occurrences (on any noncontradictory path of τ_0) of entries of depth i. Now if $i = 0$, the only relevant entries are signed propositional letters. As all such are atomic tableaux, any occurrence of one is necessarily reduced. In this case then, there are no unreduced occurrences of entries ($j = 0$) and τ_0 itself is finished. (Remember that in this case there can be no τ_1 produced by applying clause (ii) to τ_0.) Thus, by induction, it suffices to prove that the application of clause (ii) of the definition of *systematic tableaux decreases h as we can then apply the induction hypothesis to the sequence beginning with τ_1. Consider a situation as described in Definition 4.11 (ii). Note that all occurrences of E in τ on noncontradictory paths in τ' are reduced: Each occurrence of E in τ on a noncontradictory path P in τ has been reduced by the addition of the atomic tableau with root E to end P. The only new occurrences of E in τ' are in these added atomic tableaux; these occurrences are already reduced by definition. Now, all the occurrences of entries other than E in τ' that are not ones of τ are nonroot entries in the atomic tableau with root E. These all have depth less than that of E. Thus τ' has fewer occurrences of unreduced entries of depth that of E than τ and no new entries of greater depth. In other words, $h(\tau') <_L h(\tau)$ as required. $\square$

The advantage of the original procedure for generating a CST is that it is not necessary to check every entry in the tableau to find the one E for which we must act. One simply checks the occurrences of entries level by level in lexicographic order until one is found which is unreduced. The *systematic procedure requires checking every entry to see that we have an unreduced one of maximal depth. The original procedure also always terminates with a finite finished tableau. Unfortunately the proof of termination for the CST procedure seems considerably more complicated than for the *systematic one. One can, however, use it in any particular example and simply notice that one has a finished tableau when it is produced.

Exercises

Give tableau proofs of each of the propositions listed in (1) – (7) below.

1. Idempotence and Commutativity of $\wedge$, $\vee$
   a) $(\alpha \vee \alpha) \leftrightarrow \alpha$
   b) $(\alpha \wedge \alpha) \leftrightarrow \alpha$
   c) $(\alpha \wedge \beta) \leftrightarrow (\beta \wedge \alpha)$
   d) $(\alpha \vee \beta) \leftrightarrow (\beta \vee \alpha)$

2. Associativity and Distributivity of $\wedge$, $\vee$
   a) $((\alpha \wedge \beta) \wedge \gamma) \leftrightarrow (\alpha \wedge (\beta \wedge \gamma))$
   b) $((\alpha \vee \beta) \vee \gamma) \leftrightarrow (\alpha \vee (\beta \vee \gamma))$
   c) $(\alpha \vee (\beta \wedge \gamma)) \leftrightarrow ((\alpha \vee \beta) \wedge (\alpha \vee \gamma))$
   d) $(\alpha \wedge (\beta \vee \gamma)) \leftrightarrow ((\alpha \wedge \beta) \vee (\alpha \wedge \gamma))$

3. Pure Implication Laws
   a) $\alpha \rightarrow \alpha$
   b) $\alpha \rightarrow (\beta \rightarrow \alpha)$
   c) $(\alpha \rightarrow \beta) \rightarrow ((\beta \rightarrow \gamma) \rightarrow (\alpha \rightarrow \gamma))$
   d) $(\alpha \rightarrow (\beta \rightarrow \gamma)) \rightarrow ((\alpha \rightarrow \beta) \rightarrow (\alpha \rightarrow \gamma))$

4. Introduction and Elimination of $\wedge$
   a) $((\alpha \rightarrow (\beta \rightarrow \gamma)) \rightarrow ((\alpha \wedge \beta) \rightarrow \gamma)$
   b) $((\alpha \wedge \beta) \rightarrow \gamma) \rightarrow ((\alpha \rightarrow (\beta \rightarrow \gamma))$

5. De Morgan's Laws
   a) $\neg(\alpha \vee \beta) \leftrightarrow (\neg\alpha \wedge \neg\beta)$
   b) $\neg(\alpha \wedge \beta) \leftrightarrow (\neg\alpha \vee \neg\beta)$

6. Contrapositive
   $(\alpha \rightarrow \beta) \leftrightarrow (\neg\beta \rightarrow \neg\alpha)$

7. Double Negation

$\alpha \leftrightarrow \neg\neg\alpha$

8. Contradiction

$\neg(\alpha \wedge \neg\alpha)$

9. a) $(\neg\alpha \vee \beta) \to (\alpha \to \beta)$
   b) $(\alpha \to \beta) \to (\neg\alpha \vee \beta)$

Conjunctive and disjunctive normal forms

Recall from Exercise 3.3 that a conjunctive normal form (CNF) for a proposition α is a conjunct of disjuncts of literals (propositional letters or their negations) which is equivalent to α. Similarly, a disjunctive normal form (DNF) for α is a disjunct of conjuncts of literals which is equivalent to α. For any proposition α, we can find equivalent conjunctive and disjunctive normal forms by the following procedure:

(i) Eliminate all uses of $\leftrightarrow$ in the formation (tree) of α by replacing any step going from β and γ to $\beta \leftrightarrow \gamma$ by one going to $(\beta \to \gamma) \wedge (\gamma \to \beta)$. This produces a proposition α_1 equivalent to α in which $\leftrightarrow$ does not occur.

(ii) Eliminate all uses of $\to$ in the formation of α_1 by replacing any step going to $\beta \to \gamma$ by one going to $\neg\beta \vee \gamma$. This produces an α_2 equivalent to α in which the only connectives are $\neg$, $\vee$ and $\wedge$.

(iii) Get a third equivalent proposition α_3 in which, in addition, $\neg$ appears only immediately before propositional letters by replacing in α_2 all occurrences of $\neg\neg\beta$ by β, of $\neg(\beta\vee\gamma)$ by $\neg\beta\wedge\neg\gamma$ and of $\neg(\beta\wedge\gamma)$ by $\neg\beta\vee\neg\gamma$.

(iv) Now use the associativity and distributivity laws above to get equivalents of α_3 which are either conjuncts of disjuncts of literals (CNF) or disjuncts of conjuncts of literals (DNF).

We provide an example of this procedure by finding both normal forms for the proposition $\alpha = (A \to B) \leftrightarrow \neg C$:

$(A \to B) \leftrightarrow \neg C$ (i)

$((A \to B) \to \neg C) \wedge (\neg C \to (A \to B))$ (ii)

$(\neg(\neg A \vee B) \vee \neg C) \wedge (\neg\neg C \vee (\neg A \vee B))$ (iii)

$((\neg\neg A \wedge \neg B) \vee \neg C) \wedge (\neg\neg C \vee (\neg A \vee B))$ (iii)

$((A \wedge \neg B) \vee \neg C) \wedge (C \vee (\neg A \vee B))$ (iii).

We can now apply step (iv) to get a CNF for α:

$(A \vee \neg C) \wedge (\neg B \vee \neg C) \wedge (C \vee \neg A \vee B)$

We can also use distributivity to produce a DNF for α:

$(((A \wedge \neg B) \vee \neg C) \wedge C) \vee (((A \wedge \neg B) \vee \neg C) \wedge (\neg A \vee B))$

$(A\wedge\neg B\wedge C)\vee(\neg C\wedge C)\vee(A\wedge\neg B\wedge\neg A)\vee(\neg C\wedge\neg A)\vee(A\wedge\neg B\wedge B)\vee(\neg C\wedge B).$

This last line is a DNF for α. It can, however be simplified by using some of the other rules proved above and simple truth table considerations. In particular, contradictions such as $C \wedge \neg C$ can be eliminated from disjuncts and tautologies such as $C \vee \neg C$ can be eliminated from conjuncts. Applying these procedures simplifies the DNF derived for α to the following:

$$(A \wedge \neg B \wedge C) \vee (\neg C \wedge \neg A) \vee (\neg C \wedge B).$$

10. Use the procedure described above to find CNF and DNF equivalents for the following propositions:

   a) $(A \rightarrow B) \leftrightarrow (A \rightarrow C)$

   b) $(A \leftrightarrow B) \rightarrow (C \vee D)$.

11. Use the laws provided in the above exercises to prove that each step of the above procedure produces a proposition equivalent to the original proposition α.

5. Soundness and Completeness of Tableau Proofs

We are going to prove the equivalence of the semantic notion of validity ($\vDash$) and the syntactic notion of provability ($\vdash$). Thus we will show that all tableau provable propositions are valid (soundness of the proof method) and that all valid propositions are tableau provable (completeness of the method).

Theorem 5.1 (Soundness): *If α is tableau provable, then α is valid, i.e.,* $\vdash \alpha \Rightarrow \vDash \alpha$.

Proof: We prove the contrapositive. Suppose α is not valid. By definition there is a valuation $\mathcal{V}$ assigning F to α. We say that the valuation $\mathcal{V}$ *agrees with* a signed proposition E in two situations: if E is $T\alpha$ and $\mathcal{V}(\alpha) = T$ or if E is $F\alpha$ and $\mathcal{V}(\alpha) = F$. We will show (Lemma 5.2) that if any valuation $\mathcal{V}$ agrees with the root node of a tableau, then there is a path P in the tableau such that $\mathcal{V}$ agrees with every entry on P. As no valuation can agree with any path on a contradictory tableau there can be no tableau proof of α. □

Lemma 5.2: *If $\mathcal{V}$ is a valuation which agrees with the root entry of a given tableau τ (given as in Definition 4.1 as $\cup \tau_n$), then τ has a path P every entry of which agrees with $\mathcal{V}$.*

Proof: We prove by induction that there is a sequence $\langle P_n \rangle$ such that, for every n, P_n is contained in P_{n+1} and P_n is a path through τ_n such that $\mathcal{V}$ agrees with every entry on P_n. The desired path P through τ will then simply be the union of the P_n. The base case of the induction is easily seen to be true by the assumption that $\mathcal{V}$ agrees with the root of τ. As an example, consider (6a) with root entry $T(\alpha \leftrightarrow \beta)$. If $\mathcal{V}(\alpha \leftrightarrow \beta) = T$, then either $\mathcal{V}(\alpha) = T$ and $\mathcal{V}(\alpha) = T$ or $\mathcal{V}(\alpha) = F$ and $\mathcal{V}(\alpha) = F$ by the truth table definition for $\leftrightarrow$. We leave the verifications for the other atomic tableaux as Exercise 1.

For the induction step, suppose that we have constructed a path P_n in τ_n every entry of which agrees with $\mathcal{V}$. If τ_{n+1} is gotten from τ_n without extending P_n, then we let $P_{n+1} = P_n$. If P_n is extended in τ_{n+1}, then it is extended by adding on to its end an atomic tableau with root E for some entry E appearing on P_n. As we know by induction that $\mathcal{V}$ agrees with E, the same analysis as used in the base case shows that $\mathcal{V}$ agrees with one of the extensions of P_n to a path P_{n+1} in τ_{n+1}. $\square$

Theorem 5.3 (Completeness): *If α is valid, then α is tableau provable, i.e., $\vDash \alpha \Rightarrow \vdash \alpha$. In fact, any finished tableau with root entry $F\alpha$ is a proof of α and so, in particular, the complete systematic tableaux with root $F\alpha$ is such a proof.*

The crucial idea in the proof of the completeness theorem is embodied in Lemma 5.4: We can always define a valuation which agrees with all entries on any noncontradictory path of any finished tableau.

Lemma 5.4: *Let P be a noncontradictory path of a finished tableau τ. Define a truth assignment $\mathcal{A}$ on all propositional letters A as follows:*

$\mathcal{A}(A) = T$ *if TA is an entry on P.*

$\mathcal{A}(A) = F$ *otherwise.*

If $\mathcal{V}$ is the unique valuation (Theorem 3.3) extending the truth assignment $\mathcal{A}$, then $\mathcal{V}$ agrees with all entries of P.

Proof: We proceed by induction on the depth of propositions on P.

(i) If α is a propositional letter and $T\alpha$ occurs on P, then $\mathcal{V}(\alpha) = T$ by definition and we are done. If $F\alpha$ occurs on P, then, as P is noncontradictory, $T\alpha$ does not and $\mathcal{V}(\alpha) = F$.

(ii) Suppose $T(\alpha \wedge \beta)$ occurs on the noncontradictory path P. Since τ is a finished tableau, both $T(\alpha)$ and $T(\beta)$ occur on P. By the induction hypothesis $\mathcal{V}(\alpha) = T = \mathcal{V}(\beta)$ and so $\mathcal{V}(\alpha \wedge \beta) = T$ as required.

(iii) Suppose $F(\alpha \wedge \beta)$ occurs on the noncontradictory path P. Again by the definition of a finished tableau, either $F\alpha$ or $F\beta$ must occur on P. Whichever it is, the induction hypothesis tells us that it agrees with $\mathcal{V}$ and so either $\mathcal{V}(\alpha) = F$ or $\mathcal{V}(\beta) = F$. In either case $\mathcal{V}(\alpha \wedge \beta) = F$ as required.

The remaining connectives are treated like one of these two cases depending on whether or not the corresponding atomic tableau branches. The details are left as Exercise 2. $\square$

Proof (of Theorem 5.3): Suppose that α is valid and so $\mathcal{V}(\alpha) = T$ for every valuation $\mathcal{V}$. Consider any finished tableau τ with root $F\alpha$. (The CST with root $F\alpha$ is one by Theorem 4.8.) If τ had a noncontradictory path P there would be, by Lemma 5.5, a valuation $\mathcal{V}$ which agrees with all its entries and so in particular with $F\alpha$. This would give us a valuation with $\mathcal{V}(\alpha) = F$ contradicting the validity of α. Thus every path on τ is contradictory and τ is a tableau proof of α. $\square$

It is clear from the proof of the completeness theorem (in fact from Lemma 5.4) that if you try to construct a tableau proof for α (i.e., one starting with $F\alpha$) and you do your best by constructing a finished tableau with root $F\alpha$ but fail to produce a proof of α (i.e., the finished tableau has at least one noncontradictory path) then the valuation defined by this noncontradictory path as in Lemma 5.4 gives us a counterexample to the assertion that α is valid. As we can always produce a finished tableau with any given root, we must, for every proposition, be able to get either a tableau proof or a counterexample to its validity!

It is this dichotomy (albeit expressed at the level of more complicated fragments of predicate logic) that forms the basis for constructive solutions to many problems. It is also the underlying rationale of PROLOG and of the implementation of other constructive theorem provers as programming languages. One starts with an assumption such as "there is no x such that $\mathcal{P}(x)$" and one either proves it true or finds a counterexample, that is, one actually produces an x such that $\mathcal{P}(x)$. We will consider these matters in II.5 and, in more detail, in Chapter III.

Exercises

1. Verify the remaining cases of atomic tableaux in Lemma 5.2.

2. Verify the cases for the remaining connectives in Lemma 5.4.

Reformulate and prove the analogs of the results of this section for tableau refutations and satisfiability:

3. If α is tableau refutable, i.e., there is a contradictory tableau with root $T\alpha$, then α is *unsatisfiable*, i.e., there is no valuation $\mathcal{V}$ such that $\mathcal{V}(\alpha) = T$.

4. If α is unsatisfiable then there is a tableau refutation of α.

6. Deductions from Premises and Compactness

Recall the treatment at the end of §3 of the consequences of a set Σ of propositions (which we called premises). A proposition σ is a consequence of Σ ($\Sigma \vDash \sigma$) if every valuation which is a model of Σ is also one of σ, i.e., every valuation which makes all the elements of Σ true also makes σ true. (See Definitions 3.2 and 3.8.) This notion of consequence and the associated one of a proof from given premises (which we are about to define) reflect common usage in mathematical arguments. A theorem is typically stated as an implication of the form $\alpha \to \beta$. The proof of the theorem, however, is generally presented in a format which begins by assuming that the hypotheses (α) are true and then argues that the conclusion (β) must be true. Viewed syntactically in terms of proofs, we might describe this procedure as "assuming" α and then "deducing" β. The semantic notion of consequence captures the first view of such an argument. We now want to capture the syntactic or proof theoretic version by defining what it means to prove a proposition from a set of premises. Once we have developed the appropriate notions, a formal version of the informal mathematical method of argument described above is (easily) provided by the deduction theorem (Exercise 6). We now turn to the abstract formulation of the notions needed to express this result.

We begin our analysis with the definition of tableaux with premises from a set of sentences. It differs from the basic definition only in that we are allowed to add on entries of the form $T\alpha$ for premises α. This variation reflects the intuition that working from a set of premises means that we are assuming them to be true.

Definition 6.1 (Tableaux from Premises): Let Σ be a (possibly infinite) set of propositions. We define the *finite tableaux with premises from Σ* (or just *from Σ* for short) by induction:

 (i) Every atomic tableau is a finite tableau from Σ.

 (ii) If τ is a finite tableau from Σ and $\alpha \in \Sigma$, then the tableau formed by putting $T\alpha$ at the end of every noncontradictory path not containing it is also a finite tableau from Σ.

 (iii) If τ is a finite tableau from Σ, P a path in τ, E an entry of τ occurring on P and τ' is obtained from τ by adjoining the unique atomic tableau with root entry E to the end of the path P, then τ' is also a finite tableau from Σ.

If $\tau_0, \tau_1, \dots, \tau_n, \dots$ is a (finite or infinite) sequence of finite tableaux from Σ such that, for each $n \geq 0$, τ_{n+1} is constructed from τ_n by an application of (ii) or (iii), then $\tau = \cup \tau_n$ is a *tableau from Σ*.

We can now define tableau proofs as before.

Definition 6.2: A *tableau proof of a proposition α from Σ* (or *with premises from Σ*) is a tableau from Σ with root entry $F\alpha$ which is contradictory, that is, one in which every path is contradictory. If there is such a proof we say that α *is provable from Σ* and write it as $\Sigma \vdash \alpha$.

Example 6.3: Figure 15 gives a tableau proof of A from the set of premises $\{\neg B, (A \lor B)\}$.

We can now mimic the development of the last section to prove the soundness and completeness theorems for deductions from premises. The only changes are in the definition of a finished tableau and the CST. A *finished tableau from Σ* is a tableau from Σ with $T\alpha$ on every noncontradictory path for every $\alpha \in \Sigma$. The idea here is again that we are incorporating the truth of the premises into the analysis.

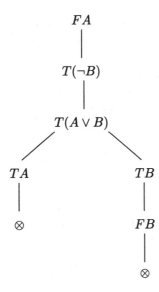

$$FA$$

$$T(\neg B)$$

$$T(A \lor B)$$

FIGURE 15

Similarly we must take steps in the construction of the CST *from* Σ to guarantee the appearance of these premises. We list the elements of Σ as α_m, $m \in \mathbb{N}$, and revise the definition of the CST by simply adding on one step to the definition of τ_{m+1}. If our new construction has produced τ_m we let τ'_{m+1} be the next tableau that would be defined by the standard CST procedure. (If that procedure would now terminate, we also terminate the current construction.) We now add on $T\alpha_m$ to the end of every noncontradictory path in τ'_{m+1} which does not already contain $T\alpha$ to form our new τ_{m+1}.

Theorem 6.4: *Every* CST *from a set of premises is finished.*

Proof: Exercise 1. $\square$

The proofs of the soundness and completeness theorems can now be carried out as before with the caveat that we must always see to it that the propositions in Σ are true in the relevant valuations. We state the appropriate lemmas and theorems and leave most of their proofs in this setting as exercises.

Lemma 6.5: *If a valuation $\mathcal{V}$ makes every $\alpha \in \Sigma$ true and agrees with the root of a tableau τ from Σ, then there is a path in τ every entry of which agrees with $\mathcal{V}$.*

Proof: Exercise 2. $\square$

Theorem 6.6 (Soundness of deductions from premises): *If there is a tableau proof of α from a set of premises Σ, then α is a consequence of Σ, i.e., $\Sigma \vdash \alpha \Rightarrow \Sigma \vDash \alpha$.*

Proof: If not, there is a valuation which makes β true for every $\beta \in \Sigma$ but makes α false. Continue now as in the proof of Theorem 5.1. □

Lemma 6.7: *Let P be a noncontradictory path in a finished tableau τ from Σ. Define a valuation $\mathcal{V}$ as in Lemma 5.4. $\mathcal{V}$ then agrees with all entries on P and so in particular makes every proposition $\beta \in \Sigma$ true (as $T\beta$ must appear on P for every $\beta \in \Sigma$ by definition of a finished tableau from Σ).*

Proof: Exercise 3. □

Theorem 6.8 (Completeness of deductions from premises): *If α is a consequence of a set Σ of premises, then there is a tableau deduction of α from Σ, i.e., $\Sigma \vDash \alpha \Rightarrow \Sigma \vdash \alpha$.*

Proof: If $\Sigma \vDash \alpha$, every valuation $\mathcal{V}$ which makes every proposition in Σ true also makes α true. Consider the CST from Σ with root $F\alpha$. It is finished by Theorem 6.4. Now apply Lemma 6.7. □

Again we consider the problem of finiteness of proofs. The argument for Theorem 4.9 using König's lemma works just as before for tableaux from premises Σ even if Σ is infinite:

Theorem 6.9: *If $\tau = \cup\tau_n$ is a contradictory tableau from Σ, then, for some m, τ_m is a finite contradictory tableau from Σ. In particular, if a CST from Σ is a proof it is finite.*

Proof: Exercise 4. □

Thus we know that if α is provable from Σ then there is a finite tableau proof of it. This can be viewed as a syntactic version of the compactness theorem. Using the completeness and soundness theorems it can be converted into a semantic one:

Theorem 6.10 (Compactness): *α is a consequence of Σ iff α is a consequence of some finite subset of Σ.*

Proof: Exercise 5. □

We have left the indirect proof, via completeness and soundness, of the semantic version of the compactness theorem as an exercise. However, a direct proof of this result is also available. The compactness theorem is genuinely deeper than the others we have proven and deserves two proofs. An advantage of the direct approach is that the completeness theorem can be proved from the compactness theorem and without recourse to infinite tableaux. The direct approach also shows that compactness is simply a consequence of König's lemma.

Definition 6.11: A set Σ of propositions is called *satisfiable* if it has a model, i.e., there is a valuation $\mathcal{V}$ such that $\mathcal{V}(\alpha) = T$ for every $\alpha \in \Sigma$. We also say that such a valuation *satisfies* Σ.

Example 6.12:

(i) $\{A_1, A_2, (A_1 \wedge A_2), A_3, (A_1 \wedge A_3), A_4, (A_1 \wedge A_4), \dots\}$ is a satisfiable infinite set of propositions.

(ii) $\{A_1, A_2, (A_1 \rightarrow A_3), (\neg A_3)\}$ is a finite set of propositions which is not satisfiable nor is any set containing it.

Theorem 6.13 (Compactness): *Let* $\Sigma = \{\alpha_i \mid i \in \omega\}$ *be an infinite set of propositions.* Σ *is satisfiable if and only if every finite subset* Γ *of* Σ *is satisfiable.*

Proof: Note that the "only if" direction of the theorem is trivially true; the other direction is not (not *trivially* that is). The problem is that finding different valuations which satisfy longer and longer initial segments does not necessarily mean that there is a single valuation satisfying the whole sequence. Building such a valuation is essentially an application of König's lemma.

Let $\langle C_i \mid i \in \omega \rangle$ be a list of all the propositional letters. We define a tree T whose nodes are binary sequences ordered by extension. We use $lth(\sigma)$ to denote the length of a sequence σ and set $T = \{\sigma \mid$ there is a valuation $\mathcal{V}$ such that, for $i \leq lth(\sigma)$, $\mathcal{V}(\alpha_i) = T$ and $\mathcal{V}(C_i) = T$ iff $\sigma(i) = 1\}$. What this definition says is that we put σ on the tree unless interpreting it as an assignment of truth values to the propositional letters C_i ($i \leq lth(\sigma)$) already forces one of the α_i to be false for $i \leq lth(\sigma)$.

Claim: There is an infinite path in T if and only if Σ is satisfiable.

Proof of Claim: If $\mathcal{V}$ satisfies Σ then, by definition, the set of all σ such that $\sigma(i) = 1$ iff $\mathcal{V}(C_i) = T$ is a path on T. On the other hand, suppose that $\langle \sigma_j \mid j \in \mathbb{N} \rangle$ is an infinite path on T. Let $\mathcal{V}$ be the unique valuation extending the assignment determined by the σ_j, i.e., the one for which C_i is true iff $\sigma_j(i) = 1$ for some j (or equivalently, as the σ_i are linearly ordered by extension, iff $\sigma_j(i) = 1$ for every i such that $i \leq lth(\sigma_j)$). If $\mathcal{V} \nvDash \Sigma$, then there is some $\alpha_j \in \Sigma$ such that $\mathcal{V}(\alpha_j) = F$. Now by Corollary 3.4 this last fact depends on the truth values assigned by $\mathcal{V}$ to only finitely many propositional letters. Let us suppose it depends only on those C_i with $i \leq n$. It is then clear from the definition of T that no σ with length $\geq n$ can be on T at all. As there are only finitely many binary sequences σ with length $\leq n$, we have contradicted the assumption that the sequence $\langle \sigma_j \rangle$ is an infinite path on T and so $\mathcal{V} \vDash \Sigma$ as claimed.

The next claim is that there is, for every n, a σ of length n in T. By assumption every finite subset of Σ is satisfiable. Thus, for each n, there is a valuation $\mathcal{V}_n$ which makes α_i true for each $i \leq n$. The string σ given by $\sigma(i) = 1$ iff $\mathcal{V}_n(C_i) = T$ for $i \leq n$ is then on T by definition.

König's lemma (Theorem 1.4) now tells us that there is an infinite path in T and so Σ is satisfiable as required. $\square$

The connection between this version of the compactness theorem for propositional logic and the compactness theorem of topology is considered in Exercises 9 and 10. Other applications of the compactness theorem can be found in Exercises 7 and 8.

*Finite tableaux suffice.

We wish to outline the development of the soundness and completeness theorems from premises based on the semantic proof of the compactness theorem without recourse to infinite tableaux. Now, if the given set of premises Σ is finite there is no trouble in proving the soundness and completeness results of §5 for proofs from Σ. One can follow the path outlined in the appendix to that section but still consider only finite tableau. One simply requires that a finished tableau have $T\alpha$ on every noncontradictory path for every $\alpha \in \Sigma$. The proofs (including that of Theorem 4.10 that there is always a finished finite tableau from Σ with any given root entry) can be carried over without difficulty.

The situation for infinite sets of premises seems more complicated. Proofs, even from infinite sets of premises, must now be finite objects. Including this restriction as part of the definition of a proof from premises can cause no difficulties in the proof of soundness since the hypothesis of the theorem starts us with such a proof. Thus the soundness theorem for finite proofs is simply a special case of Theorem 6.5.

The problem with considering only finite proofs comes in the proof of the completeness theorem. There we begin with a finished tableau τ with root $F\alpha$. If τ is contradictory, it is a proof of α. If not, we use a noncontradictory path in τ to define a valuation that agrees with Σ but makes α false. The existence of such a valuation contradicts the assumption that α is a consequence of Σ.

Now if Σ is infinite and τ being finished means that $T\alpha$ appears on every noncontradictory path on τ, then it seems as if we have to consider infinite tableaux. We can avoid this by appealing to the compactness theorem (6.13). It essentially reduces the infinite case to the finite one. Thus we can use the compactness theorem to reduce the completeness theorem for finite proofs from infinite sets of premises to the one for finite sets of premises.

Theorem 6.14 (Completeness of deductions from premises): *If α is a logical consequence of a set of premises Σ, then there is a tableau proof of α from Σ, i.e., $\Sigma \vDash \alpha \Rightarrow \Sigma \vdash \alpha$.*

Proof: As $\Sigma \vDash \alpha$, $\Sigma \cup \{\neg\alpha\}$ is not satisfiable by definition. By the compactness theorem (6.13), there is a finite $\Gamma \subset \Sigma$ such that $\Gamma \cup \{\neg\alpha\}$ is not satisfiable. Again, by definition, this means that $\Gamma \vDash \alpha$. The completeness theorem for finite sets of premises outlined above (see also Exercise 12) now tells us that there is a proof of α from Γ. As $\Gamma \subset \Sigma$, this proof is also one from Σ. $\square$

Exercises

1. Prove Theorem 6.4.

2. Prove Lemma 6.5.

3. Follow the proof of Lemma 5.4 to prove Lemma 6.7.

4. Follow the proof of Theorem 4.9 to prove Theorem 6.9.

5. Deduce Theorem 6.10 from the results preceding it.

6. **Deduction Theorem**: Let Σ be a finite set of propositions and $\bigwedge \Sigma$ the conjunction of its members. Prove that for any proposition α the following are equivalent:

    (i) $\Sigma \vDash \alpha$.

    (ii) $\vDash \bigwedge \Sigma \rightarrow \alpha$.

    (iii) $\Sigma \vdash \alpha$.

    (iv) $\vdash \bigwedge \Sigma \rightarrow \alpha$.

Applications of Compactness

For problems 7 and 8, use the compactness theorem for propositional logic or König's lemma. The key point in each case is to faithfully translate the given problem into an appropriate set of propositions (or an appropriate tree). One then applies compactness or König's lemma. Finally, one must translate the result of this application back into the terms of the problem. These problems are treated in predicate logic in Exercises II.7.5.

7. A partial order has *width at most* n if every set of pairwise incomparable elements has size at most n. A chain in a partial order $<$ is simply a subset of the order which is linearly ordered by $<$. Prove that an infinite partial order of width at most 3 can be divided into three chains (not necessarily disjoint) if every finite order of width at most 3 can be so divided.

   Hint (using compactness): Let the elements of the order be $\{p_n \mid n \in \mathbb{N}\}$. Consider propositions $Rp_i p_j$, Ap_i, Bp_i and Cp_i for $i, j \in \mathbb{N}$. Think of $Rp_i p_j$ as saying that $p_i < p_j$. Think of Ap_i as saying that p_i is in chain A and similarly for Bp_i and Cp_i. Now write down the *sets* of propositions expressing the desired conclusions: Each of A, B and C is a chain; every element is in A, B or C; the order has width 3.

   Note: Dilworth's theorem states that any partial order of width at most n can be divided into n chains. Thus Dilworth's theorem for infinite orders follows from the theorem for finite orders by compactness. As the finite case is proved by induction on the size of the given order this is a nontrivial application of compactness.

8. A *graph* G is a set of elements $\{a_0, a_1, \dots \}$ called nodes and a set of pairs of nodes $\{a_i, a_j\}$ called edges. We say that G is n-*colorable* if we can label its nodes with n colors $C_1, \dots, C_n$ so that no two nodes in a single edge of G have the same color. Suppose every finite

subgraph of G (a finite subset of the nodes and the edges between them) is 4–colorable. Prove that G is 4–colorable.

Hint (Using König's lemma): Define a tree of 4–ary sequences ordered by extension. Put a sequence σ of length $n + 1$ on the tree if and only if it defines a 4–coloring of the nodes $a_0, a_1, \ldots, a_n$ by coloring a_j with color $C_{\sigma(j)}$.

Note: The four color theorem says that every planar graph is 4–colorable. By this exercise, it suffices to prove the theorem for finite graphs as a graph is planar if and only if all its finite subgraphs are planar.

Connections with topological compactness and König's Lemma

The compactness theorem for propositional logic can be connected to the topology on the set $\mathcal{T}$ of all possible truth valuations which is determined by letting the open sets be generated by those of the form $\{\mathcal{V} : (\exists \alpha \in \Sigma)\ (\mathcal{V} \nvDash \alpha)\}$ for any set Σ of propositions.

9. Prove that the space $\mathcal{T}$ with this topology is compact.

10. Deduce the nontrivial direction of the semantic version of the compactness theorem (6.13). Hint: Prove the contrapositive from the open cover property.

11. Prove König's lemma from Theorem 6.13.

See also Exercises 1.10 and 1.11 for other connections between König's lemma and topological compactness.

Finite Sets of Premises and Tableau Proofs

12. Give a direct proof of the completeness theorem for deductions from finite sets of premises that could be used in the proof of Theorem 6.14.

7*. An Axiomatic Approach

Propositional calculus (as well as other mathematical systems) are often formulated as a collection of *axioms* and *rules of inference*. The axioms of propositional logic are certain valid propositions. A rule of inference, R, in general, "infers" a proposition α from certain n–tuples $\alpha_1, \ldots, \alpha_n$ of propositions in a way that is expected to preserve validity. Thus, for R to be an acceptable rule of inference, it must be true that, if one can use R to infer α from the valid propositions $\alpha_1, \ldots, \alpha_n$, then α must be valid as well.

We now give a brief description of one such classical formulation based on the adequate set of connectives $\{\neg, \rightarrow\}$. (For simplicity we view the other connectives as defined from $\neg$ and $\rightarrow$. This considerably reduces the number of axioms needed.)

7.1 Axioms: The axioms of our system are all propositions of the following forms:

（i） $(\alpha \to (\beta \to \alpha))$

（ii） $((\alpha \to (\beta \to \gamma)) \to ((\alpha \to \beta) \to (\alpha \to \gamma)))$

（iii） $(\neg\beta \to \neg\alpha) \to ((\neg\beta \to \alpha) \to \beta)$

where α, β and γ can be any propositions.

The forms in this list are often called *axiom schemes*. The axioms are all instances of these schemes as α, β and γ vary over all propositions. It is easy to check that these axioms are all valid. Their choice will, in some sense, be justified a bit later. Our system has only one rule of inference called *modus ponens*.

7.2 The Rule of Inference (Modus Ponens):

From α and $\alpha \to \beta$, we can infer β. This rule is written as follows:

$$\alpha$$

$$\frac{\alpha \to \beta}{\beta} \quad .$$

Systems based on axioms and rules in the style of the one presented above are generally called Hilbert–style proof systems. We therefore denote provability in this system by $\vdash_H$.

Definition 7.3: Let Σ be a set of propositions.

（i） A *proof from* Σ is a finite sequence $\alpha_1, \alpha_2, \ldots \alpha_n$ such that for each $i \le n$ either:

  （1） α_i is a member of Σ;

  （2） α_i is an axiom;

  or

  （3） α_i can be inferred from some of the previous α_j by an application of a rule of inference.

（ii） α is *provable from* Σ, $\Sigma \vdash_H \alpha$, if there is a proof $\alpha_1, \ldots, \alpha_n$ from Σ where $\alpha_n = \alpha$.

（iii） A *proof of* α is simply a proof from the empty set $\emptyset$; α is *provable* if it is provable from $\emptyset$.

Example 7.4: Here is a proof of $((\neg\beta \to \alpha) \to \beta)$ from $\Sigma = \{\neg\alpha\}$:

$\neg\alpha$	from Σ
$(\neg\alpha \to (\neg\beta \to \neg\alpha))$	axiom (i)
$(\neg\beta \to \neg\alpha)$	modus ponens
$((\neg\beta \to \neg\alpha) \to ((\neg\beta \to \alpha) \to \beta))$	axiom (iv)
$((\neg\beta \to \alpha) \to \beta)$	modus ponens.

We should note here, as we did for tableau deductions, that, although the set of premises Σ may be infinite, if α is provable from Σ then α is provable from a finite subset of Σ. Proofs are always finite!

The standard theorems are again soundness, completeness and compactness. Soundness is fairly easy to prove. One has only to check that the axioms are all valid and the rule of inference (modus ponens) preserves truth, i.e., if the premises are true for some valuation then so is the conclusion. The syntactic version of the compactness theorem is immediate in this setting as all proofs are finite. The semantic version (as stated in Theorem 6.13) remains nontrivial. Of course, the semantic proof given there also remains applicable. The theorem can also be derived from the completeness theorem for this rule–based system (which must therefore be nontrivial).

We omit the proofs of soundness and completeness for this particular system (they can be found in Mendelson [1979, 3.2] but in the next section we will consider another rule–based system and will supply the proofs of such results. For now, we simply state the theorems for the system presented here.

Theorem 7.5 (Soundness and Completeness from Premises): α *is provable from a set of propositions* Σ *if and only if* α *is a consequence of* Σ, *i.e.,* $\Sigma \vdash_H \alpha \Leftrightarrow \Sigma \vDash \alpha$.

Corollary 7.6 (Soundness and Completeness): *A proposition* α *is provable if and only if it is valid, i.e.,* $\vdash_H \alpha \Leftrightarrow \vDash \alpha$.

Remarks 7.7:

(i) *On modus ponens*: If α has a tableau proof and $\alpha \to \beta$ has a tableau proof, then α and $\alpha \to \beta$ are both valid by the soundness theorem. As modus ponens preserves validity, β is also valid. Thus by the completeness theorem for tableau proofs, β has a tableau proof. There is actually an algorithm for getting a tableau proof for β from such proofs for α and $\alpha \to \beta$. This is known as the Gentzen Hauptsatz (principle theorem) and is too long to prove here. Modus ponens is also called the cut rule and this theorem is therefore referred to as a cut elimination theorem.

(ii) *On theorems*: A *theorem* is any proposition which is provable. So any proposition which occurs as an element in a proof is a theorem. We usually think of the *conclusion* as being the last element of a proof but, any initial segment of a proof is also a proof.

(iii) *Choice of axioms*: The corollary says that the axioms are complete in the sense that we can prove any valid proposition from them by repeated applications of modus ponens. On the other hand, since the axioms are valid and modus ponens preserves validity, every theorem (i.e., every proposition provable in this system) has a tableau proof. Thus tableau proofs are sufficient and so are the axioms and rules of inference listed above. One could have more axioms (or fewer) or more (or other) rules of inference or both. Sometimes it is a matter of taste, other times a matter of expediency (e.g., what makes various proofs easier). The key point is that whatever the proof system, there is really only one set of theorems, the valid propositions.

(iv) *Efficiency*: Proving theorems efficiently from such a system of axioms and rules may be somewhat tricky since you often have to guess which axiom to use rather than having a systematic procedure as is the case for the tableaux. The source of this problem is having a plethora of axioms from which to choose. The Hilbert–style proof system presented here has many axioms and few rules. Other systems which reverse the emphasis are Gentzen systems and natural deduction systems. These are much more relevant to automatic theorem proving and, in their intuitionistic or constructivist forms, to producing systems which have the property of always being able to produce a proof or counterexample for any given proposition (as discussed at the end of §5).

8. Resolution

The proof method underlying PROLOG and most automatic theorem provers is a particularly simple and efficient system of axioms and rules called *resolution*. Like the system presented in §7, resolution has only one rule. It reduces the large amount of the guesswork involved in producing a proof by essentially eliminating all axioms. (Actually it incorporates them automatically via various formatting rules but as far as the work of producing the proof is concerned, this almost amounts to their elimination.) The resolution method, like our version of the tableau method, is a refutation procedure. That is, it tries to show that the given formula is unsatisfiable. It begins by assuming that the formula of interest is in conjunctive normal form (see Exercises 3.3 and 4.8). In typical computer science treatments this form is called *clausal form* and the associated terminology is as follows:

Definition 8.1:

 (i) A *literal* ℓ is a propositional letter p or its negation $\neg p$. If ℓ is p or $\neg p$, we write $\bar{\ell}$ for $\neg p$ or p respectively. The propositional letters are also called *positive literals* and their negations *negative literals*.

 (ii) A *clause* C is a finite set of literals (which you should think of as the disjunction of its elements). As we think of C as being true iff one of its elements is true, the *empty clause* $\square$ is always false — it has no true element.

 (iii) A *formula* S is a (not necessarily finite) set of clauses (which you should think of as the conjunction of its elements). As we think of a formula S as being true if every one of its elements is true, the *empty formula* $\emptyset$ is always true — it has no false element.

 (iv) An *assignment* $\mathcal{A}$ is a consistent set of literals, i.e., one not containing both p and $\neg p$ for any propositional letter p. (This, of course, is just the (partial) truth assignment in which those $p \in \mathcal{A}$ are assigned T and those q with $\bar{q} \in \mathcal{A}$ are assigned F.) A *complete assignment* is one containing p or $\neg p$ for every propositional letter p. It corresponds to what we called a truth assignment in Definition 3.1.

 (v) $\mathcal{A}$ *satisfies* S, $\mathcal{A} \vDash S$, iff $\forall C \in S (C \cap \mathcal{A} \neq \emptyset)$, i.e., the valuation induced by $\mathcal{A}$ makes every clause in S true.

 (vi) A formula S is *(un)satisfiable* if there is an (no) assignment $\mathcal{A}$ which satisfies it.

Examples 8.2:

(i) $p, q, r, \neg p, \bar{q}(= \neg q), \bar{r}$ and $\neg\bar{q}(= q)$ are literals.

(ii) $\{p, r\}, \{\neg q\},$ and $\{q, \neg r\}$ are clauses.

(iii) $S = \{\{p,r\}, \{q, \neg r\}, \{\neg q\}, \{\neg p, t\}, \{s, \neg t\}\}$ is a formula which, in our original notation system, would be written as $\big((p \vee r) \wedge (q \vee \neg r) \wedge (\neg q) \wedge (\neg p \vee t) \wedge (s \vee \neg t)\big)$.

(iv) If $\mathcal{A}$ is given by $\{p, q, r, s, t\}$, i.e., the (partial) assignment such that $\mathcal{A}(p) = T = \mathcal{A}(q) = \mathcal{A}(r) = \mathcal{A}(s) = \mathcal{A}(t)$, then $\mathcal{A}$ is an assignment not satisfying the formula S in (iii). S is, however, satisfiable.

*PROLOG Notation:

Another way of thinking of clausal or conjunctive normal form is in terms of implications. Suppose we have a clause C whose *positive literals* (the propositional letters contained in C) are $A_1, \ldots, A_m$ and whose *negative literals* (the propositional letters p such that $\bar{p}$ (i.e., $(\neg p)$) is an element of C) are $B_1, \ldots, B_n$. The clause C is then equivalent to $A_1 \vee A_2 \vee \ldots \vee A_m \vee \neg B_1 \vee \ldots \vee \neg B_n$. This in turn is equivalent to $B_1 \wedge B_2 \ldots \wedge B_n \to A_1 \vee \ldots \vee A_m$. If there is at most one positive literal (i.e., at most one A_i) in C then C is called a *Horn clause* (or a *program clause* if it has exactly one positive literal). If the Horn clause contains some negative literals it is a *rule*, otherwise a *fact*. A *goal clause* is one with no positive literals. It is the logic and proof theory of these clauses (which we analyze in section 10) that is the heart of PROLOG. (PROLOG is, however, not limited to propositional letters. It also allows for variables in its literals. We will elaborate on this when we deal with predicate logic in chapter II.)

The standard notations in PROLOG reverses the order used in $\to$ and instead use either $\leftarrow$ or $:-$ which are read "if". Occurrences of the $\wedge$ symbol are replaced by commas. Thus $A_1 :- B_1, B_2, \ldots, B_n$ or $A_1 \leftarrow B_1, \ldots, B_n$ is read (and means) A_1 if $(B_1$ and B_2 and $\ldots$ and $B_n)$. In terms of generating deductions or writing programs one thinks of the assertion of a clause C such as $A_1 :- B_1, \ldots, B_n$, as specifying conditions under which A_1 is true. We are usually interested in establishing some result. Thus A_1 is called the *goal* of the clause C (or at times the *head* of C) and $B_1, \ldots, B_n$ the subgoals (or *body* and with this terminology the symbol " $:-$ " is called the *neck*) of C. The idea is that C tells us that to establish A we should first establish each of $B_1, \ldots, B_n$. Along with the goal — subgoal terminology come the terms succeed and fail. One says a goal A succeeds if it is true, or more precisely from the programming point of view, if we have a proof of A. Otherwise we say the goal fails. Be warned, however, that this terminology of success and failure is (at least for now) somewhat imprecise.

It is worth noting what these views imply for the meaning of the degenerate cases of the notation $:-$, i.e., when $n = 0$ or $m = 0$. If $m = 0$ then $:- B_1, \ldots, B_n$ (or $\leftarrow B_1, \ldots, B_n$), called a *goal clause*, is equivalent to $\neg B_1 \vee \ldots \vee \neg B_n$, i.e., it asserts that one of the B_i fail (is false). If $n = 0$ then $A_1 :-$ (or $A_1 \to$), called a *unit clause*, is equivalent to simply A_1, thus this notation simply says that A_1 succeeds (is true).

The *resolution rule* is much like a version of modus ponens called cut. Modus ponens (see §7) says that from α and $\alpha \to \beta$ one can infer β. In this format, the cut rule says that from $\alpha \vee \gamma$ and $\neg\alpha \vee \beta$ infer $\gamma \vee \beta$. Thus cut is somewhat more general than modus ponens in that it allows one to carry along the extra proposition γ. Resolution is a restricted version of cut in which α must be a literal while β and γ must be clauses.

Definition 8.3 (*Resolution*)**:** In our current terminology, we say that, from clauses C_1 and C_2 of the form $\{\ell\} \sqcup C_1'$ and $\{\bar{\ell}\} \sqcup C_2'$, infer $C = C_1' \cup C_2'$ which is called a *resolvent* of C_1 and C_2. (Here ℓ is any literal and $\sqcup$ means that we are taking a union of disjoint sets.) We may also call C_1 and C_2 the *parent* and C their *child* and say that we *resolved on* (the literal) ℓ.

(Note that, compared to the classical form of the cut rule, the resolution rule also eliminates redundancies, i.e., letters common to C_1 and C_2. This takes the place of certain axioms in a classical proof system such as the Hilbert–style one of §7.)

Resolution is, of course, a sound rule, that is, it preserves satisfiability by any given truth assignment. If some assignment satisfies both C_1 and C_2, whatever it does for p it must satisfy one of C_1' or C_2'. (This argument is formalized in Lemma 8.12.) It can thus be used as the basis of a sound proof procedure.

Definition 8.4: A (*resolution*) *deduction* or *proof of C from a given formula S* is a finite sequence $C_1, C_2, \ldots, C_n = C$ of clauses such that each C_i is either a member of S or a resolvent of clauses C_j, C_k for j, $k < i$. If there is such a deduction, we say that *C is* (*resolution*) *provable from S* and write $S \vdash_{\mathcal{R}} C$. A deduction of $\square$ from S is called a (*resolution*) *refutation of S*. If there is such a deduction we say that *S is* (*resolution*) *refutable* and write $S \vdash_{\mathcal{R}} \square$.

Warning: A resolution refutation of S gives a proof of $\square$ from S. As $\square$ is always false, we should think of this as showing that S can never be true, i.e., S is unsatisfiable. This will be the content of the soundness theorem (Theorem 8.11).

Examples 8.5:

(i) From $\{p, r\}$ and $\{\neg q, \neg r\}$ conclude $\{p, \neg q\}$ by resolution (on r).

(ii) From $\{p, q, \neg r, s\}$ and $\{\neg p, q, r, t\}$ we could conclude either $\{q, \neg r, s, r, t\}$ or $\{p, q, s, \neg p, t\}$ by resolution (on p or r) respectively. Of course, both of these clauses are valid and are equivalent to the empty formula.

A more useful picture of a resolution proof is as a tree of deductions rather than just the sequence described above.

Definition 8.6: A *resolution tree proof of C from S* is a labeled binary tree T with the following properties:

(i) The root of T is labeled C.

(ii) The leaves of T are labeled with elements of S.

(iii) If any nonleaf node σ is labeled with C_2 and its immediate successors σ_0, σ_1 are labeled with C_0, C_1 respectively, then C_2 is a resolvent of C_0 and C_1.

Example 8.7: Here is a resolution tree refutation of the formula $S = \{\{p,r\}, \{q,\neg r\}, \{\neg q\}, \{\neg p,t\}, \{\neg s\}, \{s,\neg t\}\}$, i.e., a resolution tree proof of $\square$ from S:

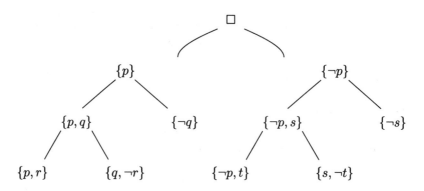

FIGURE 16

Lemma 8.8: *C has a resolution tree proof from S if and only if there is a resolution deduction of C from S.*

Proof: ($\Rightarrow$) List all the labels of the nodes σ of the tree proof of C from S in any order that reverses the $<$ ordering of the tree (so leaves are listed first and the root last). This sequence can be seen to be a resolution deduction of C from S by simply checking the definitions.

($\Leftarrow$) We proceed by induction on the length of the resolution deduction of C from S. Suppose we can get tree proofs for any deduction of length $< n$ and $C_1, \ldots, C_n$ is one of length n from S. If $C_n \in S$ there is nothing to prove. If not, then C_n is the resolvent of C_i and C_j for some i and j less than n. By induction, we have tree proofs T_i and T_j of C_i and C_j. Let T_n be the tree whose root is labeled C and to whose immediate successors we attach T_i and T_j. Again, by definition, this is the desired tree proof. $\square$

Yet another picture of resolution deduction corresponds to the inductive definition of the set of theorems or clauses provable from S.

Definition 8.9: $\mathcal{R}(S)$ is the *closure of S under resolution*, i.e., the set determined by the following inductive definition:

1) If $C \in S$, $C \in \mathcal{R}(S)$.

2) If $C_1, C_2 \in \mathcal{R}(S)$ and C is a resolvent of C_1 and C_2 then $C \in \mathcal{R}(S)$.

Proposition 8.10: *For any clause C and formula S, there is a resolution deduction of C from S iff $C \in \mathcal{R}(S)$. In particular, there is a resolution refutation of S iff $\square \in \mathcal{R}(S)$.*

Proof: Exercise 1. $\square$

The first observation to be made is that no matter how the resolution method is described, it gives a sound proof procedure.

Theorem 8.11 (Soundness of Resolution): *If there is a resolution refutation of S then S is unsatisfiable.*

We first prove a lemma which is needed for the inductive step in the proof of the theorem.

Lemma 8.12: *If the formula (i.e., set of clauses) $S = \{C_1, C_2\}$ is satisfiable and C is a resolvent of C_1 and C_2, then C is satisfiable. Indeed, any assignment $\mathcal{A}$ satisfying S satisfies C.*

Proof: As C is a resolvent of C_1 and C_2, there are ℓ, C_1' and C_2' such that $C_1 = \{\ell\} \sqcup C_1'$, $C_2 = \{\bar{\ell}\} \sqcup C_2'$ and $C = C_1' \cup C_2'$. As $\mathcal{A}$ satisfies $\{C_1, C_2\}$, it satisfies (that is it contains an element of) each of C_1 and C_2. As $\mathcal{A}$ is an assignment, it cannot be the case that both $\ell \in \mathcal{A}$ and $\bar{\ell} \in \mathcal{A}$. Say $\bar{\ell} \in \mathcal{A}$. As $\mathcal{A} \vDash C_2$ and $\bar{\ell} \notin \mathcal{A}$, $\mathcal{A} \vDash C_2'$ and so $\mathcal{A} \vDash C$. The proof for $\ell \notin \mathcal{A}$ just replaces C_2 by C_1. $\square$

Proof of Theorem 8.11: If $C_1, \ldots, C_n$ is a resolution deduction from S then the lemma shows by induction (on n) that any assignment satisfying S satisfies every C_i. If the deduction is in fact a refutation of S then $C_n = \square$. As no assignment can satisfy $\square$, S is unsatisfiable. $\square$

Remark 8.13: The soundness theorem and its proof could just as well have been phrased directly in terms of Definitions 8.6 or 8.9. We leave these formulations as exercises 2 and 3.

Our next major goal is to prove that the resolution method is complete, i.e., if S is unsatisfiable then there is a resolution refutation of S. We will then want to consider ways of implementing a search for a refutation of S. We will first consider using the resolution method as originally presented. We then introduce more and more restrictive versions of resolution which are designed to make the search more efficient without rendering the method either unsound or incomplete. Following this line of development, we will first present a simple direct proof of the completeness of the general form of resolution given in Definition 8.3. This proof will, however, rely on the (semantic form of the) compactness theorem. We will then introduce and analyze a somewhat abstract description of unsatisfiability. It will supply us with a proof of the completeness theorem for resolution deduction which does not rely on the compactness theorem and a new proof of the compactness theorem. That proof of completeness will be the paradigm for the completeness proofs of the restricted version of resolution presented in §9.

We begin our first path to completeness with a lemma that will allow us to eliminate literals in clauses which are resolution deducible from an unsatisfiable formula S. Repeated applications of the lemma will show that $\Box$, the clause with no literals, is deducible from S.

Lemma 8.14: *For any formula T and any literal ℓ, let $T(\ell) = \{C \in \mathcal{R}(T) \mid \ell, \bar{\ell} \notin C\}$. If T is unsatisfiable, then so is $T(\ell)$.*

Proof: Assume T is unsatisfiable and suppose, for the sake of a contradiction, that $\mathcal{A}$ is any assignment which satisfies $T(\ell)$ and is defined on all the literals (of T) other than ℓ. Let $\mathcal{A}_1 = \mathcal{A} \cup \{\ell\}$ and $\mathcal{A}_2 = \mathcal{A} \cup \{\bar{\ell}\}$. As T is unsatisfiable, there are clauses C_1 and C_2 in T such that $\mathcal{A}_1 \nvDash C_1$ and $\mathcal{A}_2 \nvDash C_2$. Now as $\ell \in \mathcal{A}_1$ and $\mathcal{A}_1 \nvDash C_1$, $\ell \notin C_1$. If $\bar{\ell}$ is also not in C_1 then $C_1 \in T(\ell)$ by definition. As this would contradict our assumption that $\mathcal{A} \vDash T(\ell)$, $\bar{\ell} \in C_1$. Similarly, $\ell \in C_2$. Thus we may resolve C_1 and C_2 on ℓ to get a clause D not containing ℓ and hence in $T(\ell)$. (As a resolvent of two clauses in T, D is certainly in $\mathcal{R}(T)$). Then, by our choice of $\mathcal{A}$, $\mathcal{A} \vDash D$. If $\mathcal{A}$ satisfies the resolvent D, however, it must satisfy one of the parents C_1 or C_2. Thus we have the desired contradiction. $\Box$

Theorem 8.15 (Completeness of Resolution): *If S is unsatisfiable then there is a resolution refutation of S.*

Proof: By the compactness theorem (Theorem 6.13), there is a finite subset S' of S which is unsatisfiable. As any refutation deduction from S' is one from S, we may assume that S is finite, i.e., it contains only finitely many clauses. If there are only finitely many clauses in S and each clause is finite, there are only finitely many literals, say $\ell_1, \ell_2, \ldots, \ell_n$ which are in any clause in S. For the rest of the proof we will consider only clauses and formulas based on these n literals.

We wish to consider the set of clauses $C \in \mathcal{R}(S)$ and prove that it contains $\Box$. We proceed by eliminating each literal in turn by applying Lemma 8.14. We begin with $S_n = S(\ell_n) = \{C \in \mathcal{R}(S) \mid \ell_n, \bar{\ell}_n \notin C\}$. By definition, it is a collection of resolution consequences of S none of which contain ℓ_n or $\bar{\ell}_n$. By Lemma 8.14 it is unsatisfiable. Next we let $S_{n-1} = S_n(\ell_{n-1})$. It is an unsatisfiable collection of resolution consequences of S_n (and hence of S) none of which contain $\ell_{n-1}, \bar{\ell}_{n-1}, \ell_n$ or $\bar{\ell}_n$. Continuing in this way we define $S_{n-2}, \ldots, S_0$. By repeated applications of the definitions and Lemma 8.14, we see that S_0 is an unsatisfiable set of resolution consequences of S containing no literals at all. As the only formulas with no literals are $\emptyset$ and $\{\Box\}$ and $\emptyset$ is satisfiable, $\Box \in S_0$. Thus $\Box$ is a resolution consequence of S as required. $\Box$

We now turn to a more abstract formulation of the notions and lemmas inherent in the proof of the completeness of resolution deduction. They will be needed to deal with the refinements of resolution in §9 and §10.

Definition 8.16: If S is a formula and ℓ a literal, we let

$$S^\ell = \{C - \{\bar{\ell}\} \mid C \in S \ \wedge \ \ell \notin C\}.$$

So S^ℓ consists of those clauses C of S containing neither ℓ nor $\bar{\ell}$, plus those clauses (not containing ℓ) such that $C \cup \{\bar{\ell}\} \in S$. Note that if the singleton clause $\{\bar{\ell}\}$ is in S then $\square$ is in S^ℓ.

Admittedly, this definition seems somewhat obscure at first reading. It is based on the idea that we can analyze (the satisfiability of) S by cases. S^ℓ corresponds to the result of the analysis under the assumption that ℓ is true. $S^{\bar{\ell}}$ gives the result when ℓ is assumed false. Consider, for example, the formula S under the assumption that ℓ is true. The first point here is that, if ℓ is true, then any clauses containing ℓ is satisfied since a clause is equivalent to the disjunction of its literals. As the formula S is equivalent to the conjunction of its clauses, any clause known to be true can be eliminated from S without changing its satisfiability. Thus, assuming ℓ to be true, we may omit any clause containing ℓ from S as far as satisfiability is concerned. This is precisely the point of the part of the definition of S^ℓ which restricts the clauses under consideration to those C such that $\ell \notin C$. The next point of the analysis is that, still assuming ℓ to be true, $\bar{\ell}$ can be omitted from any clause C containing it without changing the satisfiability of C. (Again C is equivalent to the disjunction of its members. If one of them is known to be false it cannot affect the satisfiability of the disjunction.) Of course, if the satisfiability of C is not affected, neither is that of the formula S containing it. This is then the point of that part of the definition of S^ℓ which says replace C by the smaller clause $C - \{\bar{\ell}\}$.

If ℓ is false, then $\bar{\ell}$ is true and the same analysis applies to $S^{\bar{\ell}}$. As one of ℓ and $\bar{\ell}$ must be true, we can argue (as we do in Lemma 8.17) that S is satisfiable if and only one of S^ℓ and $S^{\bar{\ell}}$ is satisfiable. Thus, we can reduce the satisfiability problem for S to two similar problems for formulas S^ℓ and $S^{\bar{\ell}}$ with one less propositional letter. We can then continue this procedure by considering each of the two new formulas S^ℓ and $S^{\bar{\ell}}$. In this way, we could produce a binary tree of formulas in which we would successively eliminate one literal at each level of the tree. Every path through this tree corresponds to an assignment. The branch through S^ℓ is the one that makes ℓ true. The one through $\bar{\ell}$ is the one that makes ℓ false. If every path through the tree ends with a formula containing the empty clause $\square$, we can conclude that the original formula S was unsatisfiable. On the other hand, if not all paths lead to $\square$, then, if we successively eliminate all the literals appearing in S, either there is an infinite path along which we have eliminated every literal or at least one path ends with the empty formula $\emptyset$. In either case S is satisfiable. Indeed, the appropriate path (infinite or leading to $\emptyset$) directly supplies an assignment satisfying S.

Seen in this way, the plan of the analysis is similar to that of tableau proofs beginning with $F\alpha$ for some proposition α. There too, we attempted to analyze all ways of making α false, i.e., of verifying $F\alpha$. If they all lead to contradictions ($\otimes$) we conclude that $F\alpha$ is unsatisfiable and α is valid. Here, if all paths lead to a formula containing the unsatisfiable clause $\square$, we conclude that the formula S is unsatisfiable. On the other hand, if the tableau analysis was finished and produced a noncontradictory path, we could use that path (Lemma 5.4) to define a valuation satisfying α. In the analysis here, when we eliminate all the literals (corresponding to finishing the tableau) and are left with an infinite path or one ending with the empty formula $\emptyset$, this path itself directly supplies the assignment satisfying S.

We illustrate the construction of S^ℓ from S and the general form of this analysis by considering two examples.

Example 8.17: Let $S = \{\{p\}, \{\neg q\}, \{\neg p, \neg q\}\}$. The analysis in which we eliminate first p and then q can be represented by the following tree:

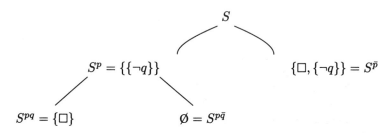

FIGURE 17

Assuming p is true, we eliminate the clause $\{p\}$ from S and the literal $\neg p$ from the clause $\{\neg p, \neg q\}$ to get S^p on the left side of the first level of the tree. Assuming that p is false, the right side ($S^{\bar p}$) reduces to $\{\square, \{\neg q\}\}$ since S asserts that p is true by having $\{p\}$ as one of its clauses. At the next level, we consider q. On the left, when q is assumed true, we again get $\square$ as S^p asserts that $\neg q$ is true. On the right, where we assume that q is false, we eliminate all clauses containing $\neg q$ to get the empty formula. Thus, we have a path ending in $\emptyset$. It supplies the assignment satisfying S: Make p true and q false.

Example 8.18: Consider the formula proven unsatisfiable in Example 8.7, $S = \{\{p, r\}, \{q, \neg r\}, \{\neg q\}, \{\neg p, t\}, \{\neg s\}, \{s, \neg t\}\}$. We begin the analysis by eliminating p. When we assume p to be true, we eliminate the clauses containing p (as they are true) and omit $\neg p$ from the others (since being false $\neg p$ cannot help to satisfy them) to get $S^p = \{\{q, \neg r\}, \{\neg q\},$ $\{t\}, \{\neg s\}, \{s, \neg t\}\}$. On the other hand, when we assume that p is false we eliminate clauses containing $\neg p$ and remove p from the others to get $S^{\bar p} = \{\{r\}, \{q, \neg r\}, \{\neg q\}, \{\neg s\}, \{s, \neg t\}\}$. Here is part of the full tree analysis:

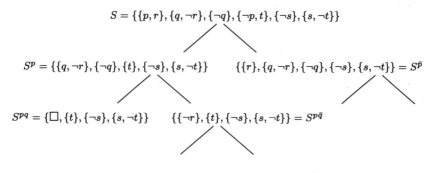

$$S = \{\{p,r\},\{q,\neg r\},\{\neg q\},\{\neg p,t\},\{\neg s\},\{s,\neg t\}\}$$

$$S^p = \{\{q,\neg r\},\{\neg q\},\{t\},\{\neg s\},\{s,\neg t\}\} \qquad \{\{r\},\{q,\neg r\},\{\neg q\},\{\neg s\},\{s,\neg t\}\} = S^{\bar{p}}$$

$$S^{pq} = \{\Box,\{t\},\{\neg s\},\{s,\neg t\}\} \qquad \{\{\neg r\},\{t\},\{\neg s\},\{s,\neg t\}\} = S^{p\bar{q}}$$

FIGURE 18

The path of the analysis through S^{pq} terminates at this point since it contains $\Box$ and so is unsatisfiable. The other paths displayed, however, continue. If continued, every path would eventually terminate with an unsatisfiable formula containing $\Box$ as a clause. This is the analog of the proof that $S \vdash_{\mathcal{R}} \Box$. We leave the completion of this analysis as Exercise 4.

We now formulate and prove the results that say that the analysis discussed above correctly captures the notion of satisfiability.

Lemma 8.19: S is satisfiable if and only if either S^ℓ or $S^{\bar{\ell}}$ is satisfiable. (Warning: In the "if" direction the assignments are not necessarily the same.)

Proof: ($\Rightarrow$) Suppose that $\mathcal{A} \vDash S$. If $\mathcal{A}$ were a complete assignment we could conclude that it must make one of ℓ, $\bar{\ell}$ true, say ℓ. We could then show that $\mathcal{A} \vDash S^\ell$. If we do not wish to make this assumption on $\mathcal{A}$, we instead start with the fact that, by definition, one of ℓ or $\bar{\ell}$ does not belong to $\mathcal{A}$. For the sake of definiteness assume that $\bar{\ell} \notin \mathcal{A}$. We now also claim that $\mathcal{A} \vDash S^\ell$. We must show that $\mathcal{A}$ satisfies every clause in S^ℓ. Consider any $C \in S^\ell$. By the definition of S^ℓ, either $C \cup \{\bar{\ell}\} \in S$ or $C \in S$ (depending on whether or not $\bar{\ell}$ is in the clause of S which "puts" C into S^ℓ). Thus, by hypothesis, $\mathcal{A} \vDash C$ or $\mathcal{A} \vDash C \cup \{\bar{\ell}\}$. As an assignment satisfies a clause only if it contains one of its literals, there is a literal k such that either $k \in C \cap \mathcal{A}$ or $k \in (C \cup \{\bar{\ell}\}) \cap \mathcal{A}$. As $\bar{\ell} \notin \mathcal{A}$ by our assumption, in either case we must have $k \in C \cap \mathcal{A}$, i.e., $\mathcal{A} \vDash C$ as required. The case that $\ell \notin \mathcal{A}$ is handled similarly.

($\Leftarrow$) Suppose for definiteness that $\mathcal{A} \vDash S^\ell$. Now neither ℓ nor $\bar{\ell}$ appear in any clause of S^ℓ and so we may adjust $\mathcal{A}$ on ℓ as we choose without disturbing the satisfiability of S^ℓ. More precisely, if we let $\mathcal{A}' = (\mathcal{A} - \{\bar{\ell}\}) \cup \{\ell\}$ then $\mathcal{A}' \vDash S^\ell$ as well. We claim that $\mathcal{A}' \vDash S$. Consider any $C \in S$. If $\ell \in C$ then $\mathcal{A}' \vDash C$ as $\ell \in \mathcal{A}'$. If $\ell \notin C$ then $C - \{\bar{\ell}\} \in S^\ell$ by definition of S^ℓ. As $\mathcal{A} \vDash S^\ell$ there is some literal $k \in (C - \{\bar{\ell}\}) \cap \mathcal{A}$. Now $\mathcal{A}$ and $\mathcal{A}'$ differ at most at ℓ and $\bar{\ell}$. As $k \neq \ell$ or $\bar{\ell}$, we see that $k \in \mathcal{A}' \cap C$ as required. $\Box$

Corollary 8.20: S *is unsatisfiable iff both S^ℓ and $S^{\bar{\ell}}$ are.* $\square$

This corollary, together with the unsatisfiability of $\square$, actually characterizes the property of unsatisfiability.

Theorem 8.21: *If* UNSAT $= \{S \mid S$ *is an unsatisfiable formula*$\}$ *then* UNSAT *is the collection $\mathcal{U}$ of formulas defined inductively by the following clauses:*

    (i) $\square \in S \;\Rightarrow\; S \in \mathcal{U}$

and

    (ii) $S^\ell \in \mathcal{U} \;\wedge\; S^{\bar{\ell}} \in \mathcal{U} \;\Rightarrow\; S \in \mathcal{U}.$

Proof: As $\square$ is unsatisfiable UNSAT satisfies (1). By Corollary 8.20 it also satisfies (ii). Thus $\mathcal{U} \subseteq$ UNSAT. We must show that UNSAT $\subseteq \mathcal{U}$. We prove the contrapositive by showing that if $S \notin \mathcal{U}$ then S is satisfiable. Let $\{p_i\}$ list the propositional letters such that p_i or $\bar{p}_i$ occurs in a clause of S. Define by induction the sequence $\{\ell_i\}$ such that $\ell_i = p_i$ or $\bar{p}_i$ and $S^{\ell_1,\ldots,\ell_i} \notin \mathcal{U}$. (Property (ii) guarantees that we can always find such an ℓ_i.) Now let $\mathcal{A} = \{\ell_i \mid i \in \mathbb{N}\}$. We claim that $\mathcal{A}$ satisfies S. Suppose $C \in S$. We must show that $C \cap \mathcal{A} \neq \emptyset$. As C is finite, there is an n such that for all propositional letters p_i occurring in C, $i < n$. If $C \cap \mathcal{A} = \emptyset$ then $\forall i < n \; (\ell_i \notin C)$ and so a clause corresponding to C is passed on to each $S^{\ell_1,\ldots,\ell_i}$ for $i < n$. At each such transfer, say to $S^{\ell_1,\ldots,\ell_i}$, we remove $\bar{\ell}_i$ from the clause. As all literals in C are among the $\bar{\ell}_i$, the clause deriving from C becomes $\square$ in $S^{\ell_1,\ldots,\ell_n}$. By our choice of the ℓ_i, $S^{\ell_1,\ldots,\ell_n} \notin \mathcal{U}$. On the other hand, any S containing $\square$ is in $\mathcal{U}$ by clause (i) and we have our desired contradiction. $\square$

This result is the analog of Lemma 5.4. The choice of the sequence ℓ_i corresponds to the definition of the assignment in Lemma 5.4 from the signed propositional letters appearing on the noncontradictory path on the finished tableau. As there, we are building an assignment that satisfies every entry on the path being constructed. Since we eventually reach the unsatisfiable clause $\square$ in this construction, we have the desired contradiction. As for tableau proofs, this characterization of unsatisfiability is really the heart of the completeness proof of the resolution method.

Theorem 8.22 (Completeness of the resolution method): *If S is unsatisfiable then there is a resolution refutation of S (equivalently, $\square \in \mathcal{R}(S)$).*

Proof: We proceed by induction according to the characterization of UNSAT provided by Theorem 8.21. Of course, if $\square \in S$, then $\square \in \mathcal{R}(S)$. For the inductive step, suppose that, for some ℓ and S, $\square \in \mathcal{R}(S^\ell)$ and $\square \in \mathcal{R}(S^{\bar{\ell}})$. We must show that $\square \in \mathcal{R}(S)$. By assumption, we have tree proofs T_0 and T_1 of $\square$ from S^ℓ and $S^{\bar{\ell}}$. Consider T_0. If every leaf in T_0 is labeled with a clause in S, then T_0 is already a proof of $\square$ from S. If not, we define a tree T_0' by changing every label C on T_0 which is above a leaf labeled with a clause not in S to $C \cup \{\bar{\ell}\}$. We claim that T_0' is a tree proof of $\{\bar{\ell}\}$ from S. Clearly, by the definition of S^ℓ, every leaf of T_0' is in S. We must now check that every nonleaf node of T_0' is labeled with a resolvent C' of its immediate successors C_0' and C_1'. Suppose they correspond to clauses C, C_0 and C_1 respectively on T_0. As T_0 is a resolution tree proof, C is a resolvent of C_0 and C_1. Note first that no resolution in T_0 is on ℓ or $\bar{\ell}$ as neither appear in any label on T_0 (by the definition of S^ℓ). Next, consider the possible forms of clauses C_0', C_1' and C' on T_0'. If, for example, both C_0 and C_1 (and hence certainly C) are above leaves labeled with clauses not in S, then $C' = C \cup \{\bar{\ell}\}$ is the resolvent of $C_0' = C_0 \cup \{\bar{\ell}\}$ and $C_1' = C_1 \cup \{\bar{\ell}\}$, as is required for T_0' to be a resolution tree proof. The other cases to consider either keep all three clauses the same in T_0' as they were in T_0 or change C and precisely one of C_0 and C_1 by adding on $\{\bar{\ell}\}$. In all these cases C' is still clearly the resolvent of C_0' and C_1' and we again verify that T_0' is a tree proof. Similarly, if we replace every label C on a node of T_1 above a leaf labeled with a clause not in S by $C \cup \{\ell\}$ we get T_1', a tree proof of $\{\ell\}$ from S (or in the case that all leaves were in S, one of $\square$). We can now define a tree proof T of $\square$ from S by simply attaching T_0' and T_1' to the immediate successors of the root node of T which we label with $\square$. As $\square$ is a resolvent of $\{\ell\}$ and $\{\bar{\ell}\}$ the resulting tree T is a proof of $\square$ from S. $\square$

*Compactness revisited

Of course there is no need to reprove the compactness theorem as it can be phrased solely in semantic terms. Nonetheless we offer another proof based on the characterization of UNSAT given by Theorem 8.21. It is the construction of the infinite sequence ℓ_i of literals in the proof of this theorem which corresponds to the path through the tree of assignments (given by König's lemma) in our original proof of compactness in Theorem 6.13.

Theorem 8.23 (Compactness): *If S is unsatisfiable, so is some finite subset of S.*

Proof: Let $\mathcal{T} = \{S \mid \exists S_1 \subseteq S \,[S_1 \text{ is finite} \wedge S_1 \text{ is unsatisfiable}]\}$. If we can show that $\mathcal{T}$ satisfies (i) and (ii) of Theorem 8.21 then we are done for it will then contain all unsatisfiable formulas.

(i) If $\square \in S$ then $S_1 = \{\square\} \subseteq S$ shows that $S \in \mathcal{T}$ as required.

(ii) Suppose S^ℓ, $S^{\bar{\ell}} \in \mathcal{T}$. We must show that $S \in \mathcal{T}$. By definition of $\mathcal{T}$, S^ℓ and $S^{\bar{\ell}}$, there are finite unsatisfiable formulas S_1, $S_2 \subseteq S$ such that $S_1^\ell \subseteq S^\ell$ and $S_2^{\bar{\ell}} \subseteq S^{\bar{\ell}}$. Let $S_3 = S_1 \cup S_2$. S_3 is a finite subset of S. It suffices to show that it is unsatisfiable. If not, then there would be an assignment $\mathcal{A}$ satisfying S_3. Now $\mathcal{A}$ must omit either ℓ or $\bar{\ell}$. Thus $\mathcal{A}$ would satisfy either $S_3^{\bar{\ell}}$ or S_3^ℓ respectively. As it would then satisfy $S_2^{\bar{\ell}}$ or S_1^ℓ (as $S_3 \supset S_2, S_1$), we have the desired contradiction. $\square$

Exercises

1. Prove Proposition 8.10 by induction. (Hint: For one direction proceed by induction on the number of lines in the proof. For the other direction proceed by induction on the definition of $\mathcal{R}(S)$.)

2. Rephrase the proof of Theorem 8.11 (soundness) in terms of resolution tree proofs and an induction on their definition.

3. Do the same for the version of resolution deductions defined in terms of $\square \in \mathcal{R}(S)$.

4. Continue the analysis in Example 8.18 until every path terminates with a formula equivalent to the unsatisfiable clause $\square$.

5. Rewrite the following in both conjunctive normal and clausal form.
   a) $((A \vee B) \rightarrow (C \vee D))$
   b) $\neg(A \wedge B \wedge \neg C)$
   c) $\neg((A \wedge B) \vee (B \vee C) \vee (A \wedge C))$.

6. Which of the following clause sets are satisfiable? Give assignments satisfying them if they are. If they are not, explain why not.
   a) $\{\{A, B\}, \{\neg A, \neg B\}, \{\neg A, B\}\}$
   b) $\{\{\neg A\}, \{A, \neg B\}, \{B\}\}$
   c) $\{\{A\}, \square\}$
   d) $\{\square\}$

7. Find all resolvents for the following pairs:
   a) $\{A, B\}, \{\neg A, \neg B\}$
   b) $\{A, \neg B\}, \{B, C, D\}$

8. Find $\mathcal{R}(S)$ for the following sets S:
   a) $\{\{A, \neg B\}, \{A, B\}, \{\neg A\}\}$
   b) $\{\{A\}, \{B\}, \{A, B\}\}$

9. Find a deduction of the empty clause from
   $$\{\{A, \neg B, C\}, \{B, C\}, \{\neg A, C\}, \{B, \neg C\}, \{\neg B\}\}$$

10. Use resolution to show that each of the following is not satisfiable by any assignment.
    a) $(A \leftrightarrow (B \rightarrow C)) \wedge ((A \leftrightarrow B) \wedge (A \leftrightarrow \neg C))$
    b) $\neg(((A \rightarrow B) \rightarrow \neg B) \rightarrow \neg B)$

11. Let α be the proposition $\neg(p \vee q) \rightarrow (\neg p \wedge \neg q)$.
    a) Give a tableau proof of α.
    b) Convert $\neg \alpha$ into CNF and clausal form. (Show the steps of the conversion.)
    c) Give a resolution proof of α.

12. Do the same for the proposition $\beta = (\neg r \vee (p \wedge q)) \rightarrow ((r \rightarrow p) \wedge (r \rightarrow q))$.

13. Prove that if $S \vdash_{\mathcal{R}} C$, then $S \vDash C$.

14. Prove that if $S \cup \{\neg C\} \in$ UNSAT, then $S \vdash_{\mathcal{R}} C$.

15. Let $\mathcal{T}$ be defined inductively by the following clauses:

   (i) $\{\Box\} \in \mathcal{T}$

   (ii) S^{ℓ}, $S^{\bar{\ell}} \in \mathcal{T} \Rightarrow S \in \mathcal{T}$

   Prove that for every finite $S \in$ UNSAT, $S \in \mathcal{T}$ but that not every $S \in$ UNSAT is in $\mathcal{T}$. (Thus the characterization of UNSAT in Theorem 8.21 cannot be changed by replacing the base step assumption that all formulas containing $\Box$ are included by the plausible alternative that just the formula consisting of $\Box$ alone be included.)

9. Refining Resolution

Resolution is already a considerable improvement, for example, on the classical system of rules and axioms in §7. Resolution is intuitively more efficient because one is never tempted to ask which (of the infinitely many) axioms (of §7) should we put down next in our proof. There is only one rule for resolution. Thus, when we try to search systematically for a resolution refutation of a given (say finite) S, we need only arrange to check the application of this one rule to elements of S and previously deduced clauses. Even so, the search space can quickly become quite large. In fact, it is known that, for a certain class of theorems, the standard resolution method takes exponential time. A major concern is then developing ways to limit the search space (preferably without giving up soundness or completeness although in actual applications both are often sacrificed; more on this point later). In all honesty, we should point out that restricting the search space for proofs means that we will miss some proofs. Thus, although we search through a smaller space, the proofs we find may well be longer than those found by a wider search. Nonetheless, pruning the search tree does seem to be more efficient. (Of course we are using efficiency in a heuristic sense. SAT $= \{S \mid S$ is satisfiable$\}$ is NP complete and no system can avoid this theoretical limitation. Nonetheless, in practice smaller search spaces tend to correspond to faster run times.) We will consider just a few of the many possible strategies for directing the search for a resolution refutation.

We can consider directing the search from two viewpoints. The first is to terminate the search along paths that are unpromising. The second is to direct it by specifying the order in which we should try to go down alternative paths. Perhaps the most obvious branches to prune are those with tautologies on them: If C is a tautology then it can't be of any use in showing that S is unsatisfiable. As it is easy to check if a clause C is a tautology (just in case it contains both p and $\bar{p}$ for some propositional letter p) this is an inexpensive and useful pruning. (The cost of checking for tautologies has been absorbed by the requirement that we consider only clausal forms. Putting an arbitrary proposition into CNF can be expensive.)

Definition 9.1: *T–resolutions* are resolutions in which neither of the parent clauses is a tautology. $\mathcal{R}^T(S)$ is the closure of S under T–resolutions.

Lemma 9.2: *Any restriction of a sound method, i.e., one which allows fewer deductions than the sound method, is itself sound. In particular, as resolution is sound, so is $\mathcal{R}^T$, i.e., if $\square \in \mathcal{R}^T(S)$, S is unsatisfiable.*

Proof: As any deduction in the restricted system is one in the original system and by soundness there is no deduction of $\square$ in the original one, there is none in the restricted system. $\square$

It is also not hard to see that $\mathcal{R}^T$ is complete.

Theorem 9.3 (Completeness of T–resolution): *If S is unsatisfiable then $\square \in \mathcal{R}^T(S)$.*

Proof: The proof of the completeness of resolution given in Theorem 8.22 remains correct for $\mathcal{R}^T$. The only remark needed is that if T_0 and T_1 have no tautologies on them then neither do the trees T_0' and T_1' gotten by adding $\bar{\ell}$ and ℓ respectively to the appropriate clauses. The point here is that no clause on T_0 (T_1) contains ℓ ($\bar{\ell}$) by assumption as T_0 (T_1) is a proof from S^ℓ ($S^{\bar{\ell}}$). $\square$

Tautologies are true in every assignment and so can surely be ignored. We can considerably strengthen this semantic approach to refining resolution by fixing one assignment $\mathcal{A}$ and requiring that in every resolution one of the clauses be false in $\mathcal{A}$. (Again, if both are true in $\mathcal{A}$, so is the resolvent and we cannot hope to get unsolvability without resorting to clauses which fail in $\mathcal{A}$. Of course, this is far from a proof that we can simply ignore all such resolutions.)

Definition 9.4: Let $\mathcal{A}$ be an assignment. An *$\mathcal{A}$–resolution* is a resolution in which at least one of the parents is false in $\mathcal{A}$. $\mathcal{R}^{\mathcal{A}}$ is the closure of S under $\mathcal{A}$–resolutions. This procedure is often called *semantic resolution*.

Theorem 9.5 (Completeness of $\mathcal{A}$–resolution): *For any $\mathcal{A}$ and S, if $S \in$ UNSAT then $\square \in \mathcal{R}^{\mathcal{A}}(S)$.*

Proof: Fix an assignment $\mathcal{A}$ and let $T^{\mathcal{A}} = \{S \mid \square \in \mathcal{R}^{\mathcal{A}}(S)\}$. We must show that UNSAT $\subseteq T^{\mathcal{A}}$. By the characterization of UNSAT of Theorem 8.21 it suffices to prove that

  (i) $\square \in S \Rightarrow S \in T^{\mathcal{A}}$ and

  (ii) For any S and ℓ, if $S^\ell \in T^{\mathcal{A}}$ and $S^{\bar{\ell}} \in T^{\mathcal{A}}$ then $S \in T^{\mathcal{A}}$.

(i) is immediate. For (ii) consider the $\mathcal{A}$–resolution proofs T_0 and T_1 of $\square$ from S^ℓ and $S^{\bar{\ell}}$ respectively. We can form T_0' (T_1') as before by adding $\bar{\ell}$ (ℓ) to the appropriate clauses of T_0 (T_1). The resulting trees are of course resolution proofs of $\{\bar{\ell}\}$ and $\{\ell\}$ respectively (or perhaps of $\square$). They may not, however, be $\mathcal{A}$–resolutions since one of $\bar{\ell}$, ℓ may be true in $\mathcal{A}$. On the other hand, as at most one of $\ell, \bar{\ell}$ is true in $\mathcal{A}$, at least one of T_0' and T_1' is an $\mathcal{A}$–resolution proof. For definiteness say that $\ell \notin \mathcal{A}$ and so T_1' is an $\mathcal{A}$–resolution proof of $\{\ell\}$ or $\square$ from S. In the latter case we are done. In the former, we can combine this proof of $\{\ell\}$ with T_0 to get the desired $\mathcal{A}$–resolution proof of $\square$ as follows: To each leaf C of T_0 which is not in S attach as children $C \cup \{\bar{\ell}\}$ and $\{\ell\}$. As $\ell \notin \mathcal{A}$, this is an $\mathcal{A}$–resolution. Since $C \notin S$, $C \cup \{\bar{\ell}\}$ is in S. Thus, except for the fact that $\{\ell\}$ may not be in S, we have the desired $\mathcal{A}$–resolution proof of $\square$ from S. We finish the construction of the required proof by attaching a copy of the tree T_1' below each leaf labeled with $\{\ell\}$. The resulting tree is now easily seen to represent an $\mathcal{A}$–resolution deduction of $\square$ from S. Other than the resolutions of $\{\ell\}$ and nodes of the form $C \cup \{\bar{\ell}\}$ that we have just considered, all the resolutions appearing in this new proof appear in one of the $\mathcal{A}$–resolution deduction trees T_0 or T_1'. Thus every resolution appearing on the tree is an $\mathcal{A}$–resolution. $\square$

As an example of a syntactic procedure which, to some extent at least, determines which resolutions we should try first we consider *ordered resolution*.

Definition 9.6: Assume that we have indexed all the propositional letters. We define $\mathcal{R}^<(S)$, for ordered resolution, as usual except that we only allow resolutions of $C_1 \sqcup \{p\}$ and $C_2 \sqcup \{\bar{p}\}$ when p has higher index than any propositional letter in C_1 or C_2.

Again if we try to mimic the proof of completeness given in Theorem 8.22 by simply restoring p and $\bar{p}$ to the ordered proofs T_0, T_1 of $\square$ from S^p and $S^{\bar{p}}$, we may no longer have ordered resolutions. All we need to do, however, is reexamine our characterization of UNSAT to see that ordering can be imposed.

Theorem 9.7: UNSAT *is equal to the class of formulas $\mathcal{U}^<$ defined inductively by the following clauses:*

(i) $\square \in S \Rightarrow S \in \mathcal{U}^<$ *and*

(ii$^<$) *If no propositional letter with index strictly smaller than that of p occurs in S, $S^p \in \mathcal{U}^<$ and $S^{\bar{p}} \in \mathcal{U}^<$ then $S \in \mathcal{U}^<$.*

Proof: As the inductive clause (ii$^<$) is weaker than (ii) of 8.21, $\mathcal{U}^<$ is surely contained in $\mathcal{U} =$ UNSAT. On the other hand, the original proof of the characterization of UNSAT (Theorem 8.21) shows that any $S \notin \mathcal{U}^<$ is satisfiable and so UNSAT is also contained in $\mathcal{U}^<$. The only point is to list the $\{p_i\}$ occurring in S in ascending order of their indices. $\square$

The proof of completeness of resolution in Theorem 8.22 with $\mathcal{R}$ replaced by $\mathcal{R}^<$ and (ii) by (ii$^<$) now proves the completeness of ordered resolution.

Theorem 9.8 (Completeness of ordered resolution): *If S is unsatisfiable, then there is an ordered resolution refutation of S, i.e., $\square \in \mathcal{R}^<(S)$.* $\square$

Ordered resolution eliminates some of the duplications resulting from different permutations of the literals on which we resolve producing the same resolvent. It therefore reduces the number of times we derive any particular clause. There are many other versions of refutation each of which eliminates some aspect of the search space. A couple of them will be discussed in the exercises while the most powerful — linear resolution — will be considered in the next section in the setting of propositional logic and in the next chapter in the setting of full predicate logic.

Exercises

1. Let S be a finite set of clauses. Arbitrarily give each **occurrence** of a literal in the clauses of S a distinct index. A *lock resolution* is a resolution in which the literal resolved on has in each parent the lowest index of any literal in that parent. The literals in the child inherit their indices from its parents with the proviso that, if a literal appears in both parents, then in the child it has the smaller of the two possible indices. (We use superscripts to indicate the indexing.)

   Example: $C_1 = \{p^1, q^2, r^3\}, \; C_2 = \{\neg p^4, q^5\},$
   $C_3 = \{\neg q^6\}; \; S = \{C_1, C_2, C_3\}.$

   Here we can lock resolve C_1 and C_2 to get $\{q^2, r^3\} = C_4$. C_4 can then be lock resolved against C_3 to get $\{r^3\}$. We cannot, however, lock resolve C_2 and C_3 as we would have to resolve on q and the occurrence of q in C_2 does not have the lowest index of any literal in C_2. (It has index 5 while $\neg p$ has index 4.)

   Prove that lock resolution is complete, i.e., if S is unsatisfiable then there is a lock resolution deduction of $\square$ from S. (Hint: Proceed by induction on the *excess literal parameter* = the total number of occurrences of literals in S minus the number of clauses in S.)

2. Show that lock resolution cannot be combined with the omission of tautologies to get a complete resolution system.

3. Suppose S is a set of clauses, $U \subseteq S$ and $S - U$ is satisfiable. A resolution has *support* U if not both parents are in $S - U$. Give a complete definition of a resolution of clauses with support U and the associated set $\mathcal{R}^U(S)$. Prove that $S \in$ UNSAT $\Leftrightarrow \square \in \mathcal{R}^U(S)$.

4. We say informally that an *F–resolution* is one in which one of the clauses is a goal clause (i.e., it contains only negative literals). Give a complete formal definition of F–resolution (that is without referring to the basic definition of resolution) and of $S \vdash_F \square$ (there is an F–resolution proof of $\square$ from S). Prove that $S \in$ UNSAT iff $S \vdash_F \square$.

10. Linear Resolution, Horn Clauses and PROLOG

We wish to consider another refinement of resolution: linear resolution. We will defer the full analysis of this method to the chapter on predicate logic. Here we will simply describe it and analyze its specialization to Horn clauses. In this form it becomes the basic theorem prover underlying PROLOG. The plan here is to try to proceed via a linear sequence of resolutions rather than a branching tree of them. We carry out a sequence of resolutions each of which (after the first) must have as one of its parents the child of the one previously carried out.

Definition 10.1:

(i) A *linear (resolution) deduction or proof* of C from S is a sequence of pairs $\langle C_0, B_0 \rangle, \ldots, \langle C_n, B_n \rangle$ such that $C = C_{n+1}$ and

  (1) C_0 and each B_i are elements of S or some C_j with $j < i$,

  (2) each C_{i+1}, $i \leq n$, is a resolvent of C_i and B_i.

(ii) As usual we say that C is *linearly deducible (or provable) from S*, $S \vdash_{\mathcal{L}} C$, if there is a linear deduction of C from S. There is a *linear refutation* of S if $S \vdash_{\mathcal{L}} \square$. $\mathcal{L}(S)$ is the set of all clauses linearly deducible from S.

The usual convention is to write linear resolutions with the starting point at the top and the conclusion at the bottom (as opposed to the picture of tree resolutions which put the node, labeled by the conclusion, at the top). Thus we picture a linear resolution as follows:

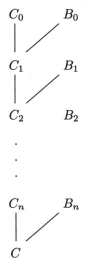

FIGURE 19

Example 10.2: Let $S = \{A_1, A_2, A_3, A_4\}$, $A_1 = \{p, q\}$, $A_2 = \{p, \neg q\}$, $A_3 = \{\neg p, q\}$, $A_4 = \{\neg p, \neg q\}$. Figure 20 gives a linear refutation of S:

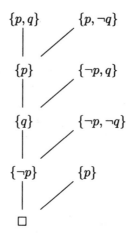

FIGURE 20

Definition 10.3: In the context of linear resolution, the elements of the set S from which we are making our deductions are frequently called *input clauses*. The C_i are called *center clauses* and the B_i *side clauses*. C_0 is called the *starting clause* of the deduction.

If we extend the parent–child terminology by defining the *ancestors* of a clause C in a resolution proof of C from S to be the clauses above it in the tree proof, we can rephrase the definition of linear deduction by saying that each C_i is resolved against an input clause or one of its own ancestors to produce C_{i+1}.

Linear resolution is clearly a refinement of resolution; that is, every linear resolution proof is an ordinary resolution proof. As resolution is sound (Theorem 8.11), so then is linear resolution. In Chapter II, Section 14 we will prove that linear resolution is complete. For now, we wish to consider only the case of Horn clauses and PROLOG programs.

Definition 10.4:

(i) A *Horn clause* is a clause which contains at most one positive literal.

(ii) A *program clause* is one which contains exactly one positive literal. (In PROLOG notation it looks like $A :\!\!- B_1, B_2, \ldots, B_n$.)

(iii) If a program clause contains some negative literals it is called a *rule* ($n > 0$ in the notation of (ii)).

(iv) A *fact* (*or unit clause*) is one which consists of exactly one positive literal (Notation: $A.$ or $A:\!\!- .$).

(v) A *goal clause* is one which contains no positive literals. (Thus in PROLOG it is entered as a question with the symbol ?– .)

(vi) A PROLOG *program* is a set of clauses containing only program clauses (rules or facts).

Notice that Horn clauses are either program or goal clauses while program clauses are either rules or facts. An important point is that an inconsistency can arise only from the combination of a goal clause and a fact. The contradiction may be mediated by rules but rules (and facts) alone cannot produce a contradiction.

Lemma 10.5: *If a set of Horn clauses S is unsatisfiable, then S must contain at least one fact and one goal clause.*

Proof: The assignment which makes every propositional letter true satisfies every program clause. The assignment which makes every propositional letter false satisfies every goal clause and every rule. Thus, any unsatisfiable set of Horn clauses must contain both a fact and a goal clause. $\square$

The general view of a PROLOG program is that we are given a collection of facts and rules and wish to deduce consequences from them. Typically, we may want to know if the conjunction of some facts $q_1, q_2, \ldots, q_n$ follows from our program P. We enter this as a question ?– $q_1, q_2, \ldots, q_n$ at the PROLOG prompt and receive an answer telling us if the q_i are consequences of the program. The general idea implemented by PROLOG is to add on a goal clause $G = \{\neg q_1, \neg q_2, \ldots, \neg q_n\}$ to the given program and ask if the resulting set $P \cup \{G\}$ of Horn clauses is unsatisfiable. The simple but crucial point here is that the conjunction of facts $q_1, q_2, \ldots, q_n$ is a consequence of our assumptions P just in case $P \cup \{G\}$ is unsatisfiable. We isolate this basic semantic transformation as a lemma. It is implicitly employed every time we ask a question in PROLOG.

Lemma 10.6: *If P is a PROLOG program and $G = \{\neg q_1, \neg q_2, \ldots, \neg q_n\}$ a goal clause, then all of the q_i are consequences of P if and only if $P \cup \{G\}$ is unsatisfiable.*

Proof: The proof simply consists of tracing through the definitions. First note that $P \cup \{G\}$ is unsatisfiable if and only if any assignment satisfying P makes G false. Next note that the goal clause G is false iff none of the $\neg q_i$ are true, i.e., G is false iff all the q_i are true. Thus, our desired conjunction of facts is a consequence of our assumptions P just in case $P \cup \{G\}$ is unsatisfiable. $\square$

Our goal now is to translate this semantic condition into a proof theoretic one that we can verify by resolution methods. In fact, we show that linear resolution suffices to decide unsatisfiability for sets of Horn clauses.

Theorem 10.7 (Completeness of linear resolution for Horn clauses): *If S is an unsatisfiable set of Horn clauses, then there is a linear resolution deduction of $\square$ from S, i.e., $\square \in \mathcal{L}(S)$.*

Proof: By the compactness theorem (Theorem 6.13 or 8.23) we may assume that S is finite. We proceed by induction on the number of literals in S. By Lemma 10.5 we know that there is at least one positive literal p occurring as a fact $\{p\}$ in S. Consider the formula S^p as described in Definition 8.16. Each clause in S^p is a subset of one in S and so is Horn by definition. We claim that S^p is unsatisfiable. The point here is that, if $\mathcal{A} \models S^p$, then $\mathcal{A} \cup \{p\} \models S$ contradicting the unsatisfiability of S. As S^p contains fewer literals than S (we omit any clause containing p and remove $\bar{p}$ from every other clause), we may apply the induction hypothesis to S^p to get a linear resolution deduction of $\square$ from S^p. As in the inductive step of the proof of the completeness theorem for the general resolution method given for Theorem 8.22, either this is already a linear proof of $\square$ from S or we can convert it into one of $\{\bar{p}\}$ from S by adding $\bar{p}$ to every clause below one not in S. We can now extend this proof one step by adding on $\{p\} \in S$ as a new side clause and resolving against the last center clause $\{\bar{p}\}$ to get $\square$ as required. $\square$

The advantage of linear resolution is obvious. We are now looking for a linear sequence to demonstrate unsatisfiability rather than a whole tree. The tree structure of the searching in PROLOG is generated by the different possibilities for side clauses. Each path in the tree of possible deductions by PROLOG represents a linear resolution. In the actual setting of a PROLOG program and a given goal clause (question to the interpreter) we can be more precise in specifying the order of clauses in the linear resolutions for which we are searching. By Lemma 10.4, we know that the goal clause must be used in the deduction. In fact, we can require our deduction of $\square$ to start with the goal clause and thereafter to use only clauses from the PROLOG program as side clauses. As these clauses are called input clauses, this restriction of resolution is called *linear input resolution*.

Definition 10.8: Let P be a set of program clauses and G a goal clause. A *linear input* (LI) *resolution refutation of* $S = P \cup \{G\}$ is a linear resolution refutation of S which starts with G and in which all the side clauses are from P (input clauses).

The method of LI–resolution is not complete in general as may be seen from the following example.

Example 10.9: Recall the clauses of Example 10.2: $S = \{A_1, A_2, A_3, A_4\}$, $A_1 = \{p, q\}$, $A_2 = \{p, \neg q\}$, $A_3 = \{\neg p, q\}$, $A_4 = \{\neg p, \neg q\}$. The only goal clause here is A_4 which we set equal to G. The remaining clauses are, however, not all program clauses. If we set $P = \{A_1, A_2, A_3\}$ and try to produce a linear input resolution refutation of $S = P \cup \{G\}$ beginning with G we are always thwarted. Figure 21 gives one attempt.

The problem here is that, no matter how we start the resolution, when we get to a center clause which contains exactly one literal, any resolution with a clause from P produces another such clause as resolvent. Thus we can never deduce $\square$.

Linear input resolution does, however, suffice for the cases of interest in PROLOG programming.

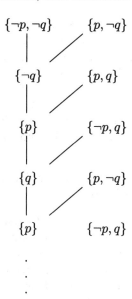

FIGURE 21

Theorem 10.10: *Let P be a set of program clauses and G be a goal clause. If $S = P \cup \{G\} \in$ UNSAT, there is a linear input resolution refutation of S.*

Proof: Note first that we can resolve a goal clause only against a program clause (as opposed to another goal clause) as we must have some literal p in one of the clauses being resolved and $\bar{p}$ in the other while goal clauses contain only negative literals. Moreover, the child of any such resolution must again be a goal clause as the single positive literal in the program clause must be the one resolved on and it is removed from the child leaving only the negative literals of the program clause and the remaining ones of the goal clause. Thus, if we have any linear proof of $\square$ from S starting with G then all the children of the resolutions in the proof must be goal clauses and all the side clauses must be program clauses as desired. It therefore suffices to prove that there is a linear proof of $\square$ from S starting with G. We again proceed by induction on the number of literals in our unsatisfiable set of clauses, but we prove a stronger assertion than that of Theorem 10.7.

Lemma 10.11: *If T is a set of Horn clauses, G a goal clause such that $T \cup \{G\} \in$ UNSAT but $T \in$ SAT, then there is a linear resolution deduction of $\square$ from $T \cup \{G\}$ starting with G.*

Proof: As before, we may assume that T is finite by the compactness theorem. We proceed by induction on the number of literals in T. As in the proof of Theorem 10.7, we know that T contains a fact $\{p\}$ for some positive literal p and that $T' = (T \cup \{G\})^p = T^p \cup \{G\}^p$ is an unsatisfiable set of Horn clauses. (As G is a goal clause, it contains no positive literals and so $\{G\}^p$ is just $\{G - \{\bar{p}\}\}$.) As T was satisfiable and contained $\{p\}$, T^p is satisfiable by the same assignment that satisfied T (by the proof of the "only if" direction of Lemma 8.19). Thus we may apply the induction hypothesis to T' to get a linear proof of $\square$ from T' starting with $G - \{\bar{p}\}$. If this proof is not already the desired one of $\square$ from T starting with G, we may, as in the proofs of Theorem 8.22 or 10.7, convert it into a proof of $\{\bar{p}\}$ from T starting with G. We can again extend this proof one step by adding on $\{p\} \in T$ as a new side clause at the end to do one more resolution to get $\square$ as desired. $\square$

As any set of program clauses is satisfiable by Lemma 10.5, this lemma suffices to prove Theorem 10.10. $\square$

We now know the general format of the resolution proofs for PROLOG : linear input resolution. There are two points left to consider before we have the precise mechanism used by the PROLOG implementation. The most important one is that PROLOG is not restricted to propositional logic; it uses predicates and variables as well. This is the topic of the next chapter. The other point is more technical; it concerns ordering considerations which come in two varieties. The first deals with the actual representation of clauses in the implementation of resolution and the choice of literal on which to resolve. The second deals with the ordering of the search for linear proofs: searching and backtracking.

We begin with the representation of clauses. Our abstract presentation of resolution deals with clauses viewed as sets of literals. As sets, the clauses are intrinsically unordered. A machine, however, typically stores clauses as sequences of literals. Moreover, it manipulates them as sequences and not as sets. Thus, set theoretic operations such as union must be replaced by some sort of merging procedure on sequences. In particular, when $G = \{\neg A_0, \neg A_1, \dots, \neg A_n\}$ and $H = \{B, \neg B_0, \dots, \neg B_m\}$ (viewed as ordered clauses) are resolved, say on $A_i = \neg B$, the interpreter simply replaces A_i by $\neg B_0, \dots, \neg B_m$. The resolvent is then (as an ordered clause) $\{\neg A_0, \neg A_1, \dots, \neg A_{i-1}, \neg B_0, \dots, \neg B_m, \neg A_{i+1}, \dots, \neg A_n\}$. In addition to the ordering itself, one should note that, as a result of this view of clauses, duplications may arise if, for example, one of the B_j is the same as some A_k ($k \neq i$). The implementation of PROLOG does not check for such duplication, it merely carries along all copies of literals in the appropriate location in the ordered clause. (Ordered clauses are sometimes referred to as *definite clauses*, hence the notation in the next definition using LD for linear–definite.) This ordering of clauses does not cause any serious changes. We embody it in the following definition and lemma.

We continue to use T to denote a set of Horn clauses, P a set of program clauses and G a goal clause.

Definition 10.12: If $P \cup \{G\}$ is given as a set of ordered clauses, then an LD–*resolution refutation* of $P \cup \{G\}$ is a sequence $\langle G_0, C_0 \rangle, \dots, \langle G_n, C_n \rangle$ of ordered clauses G_i, C_i such that $G_0 = G$, $G_{n+1} = \square$, and

(i) Each G_i, $i \leq n$, is an ordered goal clause $\{\neg A_{i,0}, \dots, \neg A_{i,n(i)}\}$ of length $n(i) + 1$.

(ii) Each $C_i = \{B_i, \neg B_{i,0}, \dots, \neg B_{i,m(i)}\}$ is an ordered program clause of length $m(i) + 2$ from P. (We include the possibility that $C_i = \{B_i\}$, i.e., $m(i) = -1$.)

(iii) For each $i < n$, there is a resolution of G_i and C_i as ordered clauses with resolvent the ordered clause G_{i+1} (of length $n(i) + m(i) + 1$) given by $\{\neg A_{i,0}, \dots, \neg A_{i,k-1}, \neg B_{i,0}, \dots, \neg B_{i,m(i)}, \neg A_{i,k+1}, \dots, \neg A_{i,n(i)}\}$. (In this resolution we resolve on $B_i = A_{i,k}$.)

Lemma 10.13: *If $P \cup \{G\} \in$ UNSAT, then there is an LD–resolution refutation of $P \cup \{G\}$ starting with G.*

Proof: This is left as Exercise 1. Proceed by induction on the length of the LI–resolution refutation of $P \cup \{G\}$. (Note that we can only resolve a program clause and a goal clause at each step of the resolution. Each center clause must be a goal clause and each side one a program clause.) $\square$

Our next task is to describe how we choose the literal of G_i to be resolved on in an LD–resolution proof. The selection rule used in virtually all implementations of PROLOG is to always resolve on the first literal in the ordered goal clause G (in our notation this is just the leftmost literal in G_i). The literals in the resolvent of C_i and G_i are then ordered as indicated in Definition 10.12. We call such linear input resolutions with ordered clauses SLD–*resolutions*. (The S stands for selection.) More generally, we can consider any selection rule R, i.e., any function choosing a literal from each ordered goal clause.

Definition 10.14: An SLD–*resolution refutation* of $P \cup \{G\}$ via (the selection rule) R is an LD–resolution proof $\langle G_0, C_0 \rangle, \dots, \langle G_n, C_n \rangle$ with $G_0 = G$ and $G_{n+1} = \square$ in which $R(G_i)$ is the literal resolved on at the $(i+1)$ step of the proof. (If no R is mentioned we assume that the standard one of choosing the leftmost literal is intended.)

Theorem 10.15 (Completeness of SLD–refutation for PROLOG): *If $P \cup \{G\} \in$ UNSAT and R is any selection rule, then there is an SLD–resolution refutation of $P \cup \{G\}$ via R.*

Proof: By Lemma 10.13, there is an LD–resolution refutation of $P \cup \{G\}$ starting with G. We prove by induction on the length n of such proofs (for any P and G) that there is an SLD one via R. For $n = 1$ there is nothing to prove as $G = G_0$ is a unit clause and so every R makes the same choice from G_0. Let $\langle G_0, C_0 \rangle, \dots, \langle G_n, C_n \rangle$, with the notation for these clauses as in Definition 10.12, be an LD–resolution refutation of length n of $\{G_0\} \cup P$. Suppose that the selection rule R chooses the clause $\neg A_{0,k}$ from G_0. As $G_{n+1} = \square$ there must be a $j < n$ at which we resolve on $\neg A_{0,k}$. If $j = 0$

we are done by induction. Suppose then that $j \geq 1$. Consider the result C of resolving G_0 and $C_j = \{B_j, \neg B_{j,0}, \dots, \neg B_{j,m(j)}\}$ on $B_j = A_{0,k}$:

$$C = \{\neg A_{0,0}, \dots, \neg A_{0,k-1}, \neg B_{j,0}, \dots, \neg B_{j,m(j)}, \neg A_{0,k+1}, \dots, \neg A_{0,n(0)}\}.$$

We claim that there is an LD–resolution refutation of length $n-1$ from $P \cup \{C\}$ which begins with C. One simply resolves in turn with $C_0, \dots, C_{j-1}$ on the same literals as in the original proof that started with G. The only change is that we carry along the sequence of clauses $\neg B_{j,0}, \dots, \neg B_{j,m(j)}$ in place of $\neg A_{0,k}$ in the center clauses of the resolution. After resolving with each side clause $C_0, \dots, C_{j-1}$, we have precisely the same result G_{j+1} as we had in the original resolution after resolving with C_j. We can then continue the resolution deduction exactly as in the original resolution with $C_{j+1}, \dots, C_n$. This procedure produces an LD–resolution refutation of length $n-1$ beginning with C. By induction, it can be replaced by an SLD–resolution refutation via R. Adding this SLD–resolution via R onto the single step resolution of G_0 with C_j described above produces the desired SLD–resolution refutation from $P \cup \{G\}$ via R starting with $G = G_0$. $\square$

We now know what the PROLOG interpreter does when a question is entered as in "?- $A_1, \dots, A_n$.". It searches for an SLD–resolution proof of $\square$ from the current program P and the goal clause $G = \{\neg A_1, \dots, \neg A_n\}$ starting with G. The remaining uncertainty in our description of its action is just how it organizes this search. At each step i of the SLD–resolution, the only choice to be made is which clause in P to use to resolve on the leftmost term in our current goal clause G_i. We can thus display the space of all possible SLD–derivations as a labeled tree T. The root of T is labeled G. If any node of T is labeled G', then its immediate successors are labeled with the results of resolving on the leftmost literal of G' with the various possible choices of clauses in P. We call such trees SLD–*trees* for P and G.

Example 10.16 (SLD–Trees): As a simple example, consider the program P_0:

p :- q,r.	(1)
p :- s	(2)
q.	(3)
q :- s.	(4)
r.	(5)
s :- t.	(6)
s.	(7)

PROGRAM P_0.

Suppose we have $G = \{\neg p\}$ as our goal clause. The corresponding SLD–tree is given below in Figure 22. Along each branching we indicate the clause of P_0 resolved against. The convention is that the successors are listed in a left to right order that agrees with the order in which the clauses used appear in P_0. *Success paths* are those ending in $\Box$. A path is a *failure path* if it ends with a clause G' such that there is no clause in P with which we can resolve on the leftmost term of G'. In this example there are five possible paths. Two end in failure and three end with success.

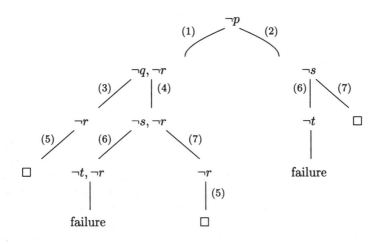

FIGURE 22

The PROLOG theorem prover searches the SLD–tree for a success path by always trying the leftmost path first. That is, it tries to resolve the current G with the first clause in P that is possible. In Figure 22 it would simply follow the path (1), (3) (5) to get the correct answer "yes". If the theorem prover hits a failure point (i.e., not $\Box$ and no resolution is possible) it backtracks, that is, it goes back up the tree until it returns to a node N which has a path leading out of it to the right of the one the theorem prover has followed upward. The prover then exits from N along the path immediately to the right of the one it just returned on (i.e., it tries the leftmost successor of N not yet attempted). This process is repeated until a success path is found.

Example 10.17 (Backtracking): If we omit clause (3) from the above program P_0 to produce P_1, we get a new SLD–tree as pictured in Figure 23.

In this case, the theorem prover first tries the path (1), (4), (6), failure. It then backtracks to $\neg s$, $\neg r$ and tries (7), (5), success, to give the answer yes.

Suppose the PROLOG interpreter has searched the tree until it has found an answer and we then enter a semicolon ";" at the prompt. The interpreter will resume backtracking to look for another resolution refutation in

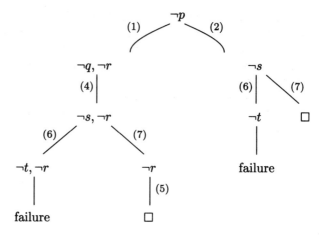

FIGURE 23

the part of the tree that it has not yet searched. A "no" answer now means that there are no more proofs. A "yes" answer indicates another one has been found. In this case, we may once more enter ";" to start the search for yet another proof. In the last example after finding the proof along the path (1), (4), (7), (5) the theorem prover answered "yes". If we asked for another proof by entering a semicolon, it would backtrack all the way up to the top node and try the path (2). It then would proceed down (6) to a failure, backtrack to $\neg s$ and follow (7) to another success and "yes" answer. One more request for a proof via entering a semicolon would finally produce a "no" answer.

If PROLOG searches through the entire SLD–tree without finding a path leading to □, it gives the answer "no" the first time we ask our question. By our general completeness theorem, we then know that in this case $P \cup \{G\}$ is satisfiable and so (by Theorem 10.6) the question asked is not a logical consequence of P.

This type of search procedure is called a *depth–first* search procedure as it tries to go as deeply as possible in the tree by running down to the end of a path before searching sideways along any other branches. In contrast, one that searches the tree in figure (1) in the order $\neg p$; $\neg q$, $\neg r$; $\neg s$; $\neg r$; $\neg s$, $\neg r$; $\neg t$; □; □; $\neg t$, $\neg r$; $\neg r$; failure; failure; □ is called a *breadth–first* search. Clearly many mixed strategies are also possible. In our case, the depth–first search was much faster than breadth–first (3 versus 6 steps). Indeed, this is a quite general phenomena. Depth–first is usually much faster than breadth–first. That, of course, is why the implementations use depth–first searches. The cost of this strategy can, however, be quite high. In a breadth–first search, it is clear that, if there is a path ending in □, we must eventually find it. In contrast, the procedure of depth–first search is not complete: There may be a path leading to □ but we may search the tree forever without finding it.

Example 10.18 (Failure of depth-first searching): Consider the following simple program:

$$q :- r. \qquad (1)$$
$$r :- q. \qquad (2)$$
$$q. \qquad (3)$$

The usual search procedure applied to the starting clause $\neg q$ will loop back and forth between $\neg q$ and $\neg r$. It will never find the contradiction supplied by (3).

This example seems easy to fix and to depend purely on the order of the clauses in the program. Unfortunately, rearranging clauses will not always produce a terminating program even when a correct proof does exist. (See program P_5 of III.2 for an example.) The full impact of these problems cannot, however, be felt until we deal with full PROLOG rather than restricting our attention to the propositional case. Indeed, it is only with the introduction of predicates and variables that one sees the true power of PROLOG. We now turn to these matters, first in the general setting of full predicate logic and then in just PROLOG.

Exercises

1. Prove Lemma 10.13.

2. Consider the following sentence in "English": If the congress refuses to enact new laws, then the strike will not be over unless it lasts more than one year and the president of the firm resigns.

    a) Represent this sentence in three ways:

        (i)   by a statement in the propositional calculus

        (ii) by one in conjunctive normal form

        (iii) as part of a PROLOG program.

    b) Suppose congress has refused to act and the strike has not yet lasted more than a month. Add these to your list (in (a), (b) and (c)) and use a tableau deduction to see if the strike is over yet. (You can try to do a deduction from the appropriate premises or an ordinary one from the appropriate conjunction but be careful how you formulate the problem.)

    c) Suppose instead that the congress refused to act, the strike is now over but the president of the firm did not resign. Use tableau deduction to see if the strike lasted more than a year.

    d) In (d) and (e) if you had a list of the relevant clauses in your PROLOG data base, what would you enter to get the answer.

3. One of the successful applications of expert systems has been analyzing the problem of which chemical syntheses are possible. We consider here an extremely simple example of such a problem.

We know we can perform the following chemical reactions:

$$(1) \quad MgO + H_2 \ \rightarrow \ Mg + H_2O$$
$$(2) \quad C + O_2 \ \rightarrow \ CO_2$$
$$(3) \quad CO_2 + H_2O \ \rightarrow \ H_2CO_3 \, .$$

a) Represent these rules and the assumptions that we have some MgO, H_2, O_2 and C by propositional logic formulas in which assertions say that we have a particular chemical and implications are understood to mean that, if we have the hypotheses, we can get the conclusion. (Thus (1) is $MgO \wedge H_2 \ \rightarrow \ Mg \wedge H_2O$.)

b) Describe the state of affairs in clausal form and as a PROLOG Program.

c) Give a resolution proof (in tree or linear form) that we can get some $H_2 CO_3$.

4. Represent the following information as a PROLOG program so that, if you are told that Jones has fallen deathly ill and Smith has gone off to his bedside, you could determine if the directors will declare a dividend.

   If Jones is ill or Smith is away, then the directors will meet and declare a dividend if Robinson comes to his senses and takes matters into his own hands. If Patterson comes, he will force Robinson back to his senses but, of course, he will come only if Jones is ill. On the other hand, if Townsend, who is inseparable from Smith, stays away, Robinson will have to take matters into his own hands.

   Give a resolution proof from your program and the added hypotheses from above that shows that the directors will declare a dividend.

5. Represent the following information as a PROLOG program:

   If congress enacts a line item veto and the president acts responsibly, there will be a decrease in both the budget and trade deficits unless there is a major lobbying campaign by both the protectionists and the advocates of high interest rates. A strong public outcry will get the congress to enact the line item veto and force the president to act responsibly. The protectionists can be kept quiet if productivity increases and the dollar is further devalued.

   (It may help to start with a formulation in propositional logic and convert it appropriately.)

   How would you add on PROLOG clauses to reflect the fact that the public is vocally outraged about the deficits, the dollar is continuing to fall on world markets and productivity is on the increase.

   How do you now ask the PROLOG program if the trade deficit will decrease?

   Give the resolution refutation that shows that it will go down.

6. Draw the SLD–tree illustrating all possible attempts at SLD–refutations using the standard selection rule (always resolve on the leftmost literal)

for the question " ?– **p.** " and following program:

(1)	**p :– s,t.**
(2)	**p :– q.**
(3)	**q.**
(4)	**q :– r.**
(5)	**r :– w.**
(6)	**r.**
(7)	**s.**
(8)	**t :– w.**

In what order will the PROLOG interpreter search this tree and what output will it give if we enter a semicolon at each yes answer?

Suggestions for Further Reading

For orderings, partial orderings and trees, consult Birkhoff [1973, 3.8], or almost any of the logic and computer science texts listed in the bibliography [5.2].

For early propositional logic, read Boole [1952, 2.3] and Post [1921, 2.3].

For various alternate formalisms for logic, read the propositional part of the following:

Tableaux: Beth [1959, 3.2], Smullyan [1976, 3.2], and Fitting [1985, 4.2].

Axioms and Rules of Inference: Hilbert and Ackermann [1950, 3.2], Mendelson [1964, 3.2] and Enderton [1976, 3.2]. For an approach at a more advanced level, see Kleene [1971, 3.2], Monk [1976, 3.2] or Shoenfield [1967, 3.2].

Resolution: Chang and Lee [1973, 5.7], J. A. Robinson [1979, 5.2], Lewis and Papadimitriou [1981, 5.2], Maier and Warren [1988, 5.4].

Natural Deduction: Prawitz [1965, 3.5], or at a more advanced level, Girard [1987, 3.5] and Girard et al. [1989, 3.5].

Sequents: Gallier [1986, 5.2], Manaster [1975, 3.2] or Girard [1987, 3.5] and Girard et al. [1989, 3.5].

For a problem–oriented text based on resolution and Horn logic, see Kowalski [1979, 5.4].

For Boolean algebra and its relations to propositional logic, see Halmos [1974, 3.8], Sikorski [1969, 3.8] or Rasiowa and Sikorski [1963, 3.8].

II Predicate Logic

1. Predicates and Quantifiers

The logic of predicates encompasses much of the reasoning in the mathematical sciences. We are already familiar with the informal idea of a property holding of an object or a relation holding between objects. Any such property or relation is an example of a *predicate*. The difference between a property and a relation is just in the arity of the predicate. Unary predicates are simply properties of objects, binary ones are relations between pairs of objects and in general n–ary predicates express relations among n–tuples of objects. A reasonable answer to the question of what are 0–ary predicates might well be that they are propositions. The point here is that they are simply statements of facts independent of any variables. Thus, for example, if we are discussing the natural numbers we may let $\varphi(x, y)$ denote the binary relation (predicate) "x is less than y". In this case $\varphi(3, y)$ denotes the property (unary predicate) of y "3 is less than y" and $\varphi(3, 4)$ denotes the (true) proposition (0–ary predicate) that 3 is less than 4.

In this discussion x and y were used as *variables* while 3 and 4 were used as *constants*. Variables act as placeholders in much the same way as pronouns act as placeholders in ordinary language. Their role is best understood with the following convention: At the beginning of any particular discourse we specify a nonempty domain of objects. All variables that show up in the ensuing discussion are thought of as ranging over this domain. Constants play the role of names for objects (individuals) in this domain. In such a setting, n–ary predicates can be viewed as simply sets of n–tuples from the domain of discourse — the ones for which the predicate holds. Thus, for example, unary predicates can be seen as the subset of the domain consisting of the elements of which the property is true. 0–ary predicates assert facts about the domain of discourse and, in the context of predicate logic, are usually called *sentences* rather than propositions.

Another important class of objects in mathematical discourse is that of *functions*. For example $f(1, 2)$ might stand for the sum of 1 and 2. Functions also have an arity which corresponds to the number of arguments the function takes as input. Ordinary addition on the natural numbers is a binary function as is multiplication. Subtraction, however, is not even a function on the natural numbers. The point here is that the difference of two natural numbers is not necessarily a natural number. We require that the outputs of any function considered always be elements of our domain of discourse. (We may change the domain of discourse, however, as the need arises or our mood dictates.) On the other hand, not every element of the domain need be a value for a function. As another example consider a ternary function $g(x, y, z)$ defined as $x \cdot y + z$. Here we see that variables can play the role of placeholders in functions as well as predicates. In analogy with our manipulations of the binary relation φ above, we can define binary and unary functions from g by replacing some of the variables by constants: $g(1, y, 1)$ is the unary function $y + 1$ and $g(x, y, 0)$ is multiplication. How then should we view $g(1, 1, 0)$? It is, of course, (the constant) 1. Thus, just as we can think of propositions as predicates of arity 0, we can think of constants as functions of arity 0. They are objects which have no dependence on any inputs; they simply denote elements of the domain of discourse. More generally, we call all the symbols generated by the function symbols, constants and variables such as $f(x, g(y, y))$, *terms*. We think of them also as ranging over our domain of discourse (or possibly just some subset of the domain — what is usually called the range of the function).

As with propositions, the truth–functional connectives can be used to build compound predicates from simpler ones. For example, if $\varphi(x, y)$ still denotes the relation "x is less than y" and $\psi(x, y)$ denotes the relation "x divides y" then $(\varphi(x, y) \wedge \psi(x, y))$ is a new binary predicate with the obvious meaning. In addition to the truth functional connectives, predicate logic uses two other predicate constructors:

> (i) the *universal quantifier* (with the intended meaning "for all")
>   denoted by "$\forall$",

and

> (ii) the *existential quantifier* (with the intended meaning "there
>   exists") denoted by "$\exists$".

Example 1.1:

(i) Let the domain of discourse consist of the natural numbers $\mathbb{N}$; let "$\varphi(x, y)$" denote "$x < y$"; $f(x, y)$ the binary function $x + y$ and a, b, c be constants naming the numbers 0, 1, and 2 respectively:

    (a) $((\exists x)\varphi(x, y))$ is a unary predicate which says of y that there is a natural number less than it. It is equivalent to "y is not zero". $((\forall x)((\exists y)\varphi(x, y)))$ is the true sentence (predicate of arity 0) saying that for any natural number x, there is a natural number y which is greater than x.

    (b) $((\forall x)\varphi(x, f(x, b)))$ is a sentence saying that $x < x + 1$ for every x, i.e., every natural number is less than its successor. $\varphi(y, f(y, y))$ is again a unary predicate saying of y that $y < y + y$. This predicate is also equivalent to y being nonzero.

(ii) Let the domain of discourse consist of all rational numbers $\mathbb{Q}$. Again $\varphi(x,y)$ denotes $x < y$, $f(x,y)$ represents addition $(x + y)$, $g(x,y)$ division $(x \div y)$ and a, b, c are constants representing 0, 1 and 2.

(a) The ternary predicate $(\varphi(x,y) \wedge \varphi(y,z))$ says that $x < y$ and $y < z$.

(b) The binary predicate $((\exists y)(\varphi(x,y) \wedge \varphi(y,z)))$ says that there is a rational number between x and z. The unary predicate $((\forall x)(\varphi(x,z) \rightarrow ((\exists y)(\varphi(x,y) \wedge \varphi(y,z)))))$ expresses a property of z which says that, for any x, if x is less than z then there is a rational number between them.

(c) $((\forall x)((\forall y)(\varphi(x,y) \rightarrow (\varphi(x,g(f(x,y),c)) \wedge \varphi(g(f(x,y),c),y)))))$ is a sentence saying that for every x and y, if $x < y$ then $x < \frac{x+y}{2} < y$.

(d) $\varphi(y, f(y,y))$ is again a unary predicate saying that $y < y + y$. Note, however, that in this domain this predicate is equivalent to y being positive.

2. The Language: Terms and Formulas

We can now give a formal definition of what constitutes an appropriate language for predicate logic and then specify the formulas of predicate logic by an inductive definition which selects certain "well formed" strings of symbols which we think of as the meaningful ones.

Definition 2.1: A *language* $\mathcal{L}$ consists of the following primitive symbols:

(i) Variables: x, y, z, v, x_0, x_1, ... , y_0, y_1, ... , ... (an infinite set)

(ii) Constants: c, d, c_0, d_0, ... (any set of them)

(iii) Connectives: $\wedge$, $\neg$, $\vee$, $\rightarrow$, $\leftrightarrow$

(iv) Quantifiers: $\forall$, $\exists$

(v) Predicate symbols: P, Q, R, P_1, P_2, ... (some set of them for each arity $n = 1, 2, \ldots$. There must be at least one predicate symbol in the language but otherwise there are no restrictions on the number of them for each arity).

(vi) Function symbols: f, g, h, f_0, f_1, ... , g_0, ... (any set of them for each arity $n = 1, 2, \ldots$. The 0-ary function symbols are simply the constants listed by convention separately in (ii). The set of constant symbols may also be empty, finite or infinite).

(vii) Parentheses:) , (.

Note that we no longer have propositional letters (which would be 0-ary predicates). They are simply unnecessary in the context of predicate logic.

A true (false) proposition can be replaced by any sentence which is always true (false) such as one of the form $\alpha \vee \neg\alpha$ $(\alpha \wedge \neg\alpha)$. (See Theorem 4.8 for an embedding of propositional logic in predicate logic.)

As a prelude to defining the formulas of a language $\mathcal{L}$, we define the terms of $\mathcal{L}$ — the symbols which, when interpreted, will represent elements of our domain of discourse. We define them inductively. (Readers who prefer to use the formation tree approach exclusively may skip the more traditional syntactic one given here in favor of the presentation of the next section. They should then take the formulations given there as definitions and omit the proofs of their equivalence to the ones given here.)

Definition 2.2: *Terms.*

   (i) Every variable is a term.

   (ii) Every constant symbol is a term.

   (iii) If f is an n–ary function symbol $(n = 1, 2, \ldots)$ and $t_1, \ldots , t_n$ are terms then $f(t_1, \ldots , t_n)$ is also a term.

Definition 2.3: Terms with no variables are called *variable–free terms* or *ground terms*.

The ground terms are the ones you should think of as naming particular elements of the domain of discourse. They are the constants and the terms built up from the constants by applications of function symbols as in (iii) above.

The base case for the definition of formulas is given by:

Definition 2.4: An *atomic formula* is an expression of the form $R(t_0, \ldots , t_{n-1})$ where R is an n–ary predicate symbol and $t_0, \ldots , t_{n-1}$ are terms.

We now give the full inductive definition of formulas.

Definition 2.5: *Formulas.*

   (i) Every atomic formula is a formula.

   (ii) If α, β are formulas, then so are $(\alpha \wedge \beta)$, $(\alpha \rightarrow \beta)$, $(\alpha \leftrightarrow \beta)$, $(\neg\alpha)$ and $(\alpha \vee \beta)$.

   (iii) If v is a variable and α is a formula, then $((\exists v)\alpha)$ and $((\forall v)\alpha)$ are also formulas.

Definition 2.6:

   (i) A *subformula* of a formula φ is a consecutive sequence of symbols from φ which is itself a formula.

   (ii) An *occurrence* of a variable v in a formula φ is *bound* if there is a subformula ψ of φ containing that occurrence of v such that ψ begins with $((\forall v)$ or $((\exists v)$. An occurrence of v in φ is *free* if it is not bound. (This includes the v in $\forall v$ or $\exists v$.)

(iii) A variable v is said to *occur free* in φ if it has at least one free occurrence there.

(iv) A *sentence* of predicate logic is a formula with no free occurrences of any variable, i.e., one in which all occurrences of all variables are bound.

(v) An *open formula* is a formula without quantifiers.

To see that the definition of sentence corresponds to the idea of a formula with a single fixed meaning and truth value, notice that all references to variables (which are the only way of moving up to predicates of arity greater than 0) occur in the context of a quantifier. That is, they occur only in the form "there exists an x such that ..." or "for all x it is true that ... ". The idea of replacing a variable by some other term to produce predicates of perhaps smaller arity (as we did in Section 1) is captured by the following definition:

Definition 2.7 *Substitution* (or *Instantiation*): If φ is a formula and v a variable we write $\varphi(v)$ to denote that fact that v occurs free in φ. If t is a term then $\varphi(t)$, or if we wish to be more explicit, $\varphi(v/t)$, is the result of substituting (or instantiating) t for all free occurrences of v in φ. We call $\varphi(t)$ an *instance* of φ. If $\varphi(t)$ contains no free variables, we call it a *ground instance* of φ.

There is one important caveat that must be heeded when doing substitutions.

Definition 2.8: If the term t contains an occurrence of some variable x (which is necessarily free in t) we say that t is *substitutable* for v in $\varphi(v)$ if all occurrences of x in t remain free in $\varphi(t)$.

Note that ground terms are always substitutable for any free variable. The problems with substituting a term t (with variables) which is not substitutable in φ will become clearer when we define the semantics of formulas. For now, we consider two examples.

Example 2.9:

(i) Consider first a unary predicate $\psi(y) = ((\exists x)\varphi(x, y))$ where our notation is as in Example 1.1(i). There is no problem substituting z or 2 or even $f(w, w)$ for y to get $((\exists x)\varphi(x, z))$, $((\exists x)\varphi(x, 2))$ and $((\exists x)\varphi(x, f(w, w)))$ respectively. These formulas simply say that z, 2 and $w + w$ are not zero as we would want and expect. However if we try to substitute $f(x, x)$ for y we get $((\exists x)\varphi(x, f(x, x)))$. This formula says nothing about x or $x + x$; it is simply the true sentence asserting that there is some x such that $x < x + x$.

(ii) Next consider a language for the integers $\mathbb{Z}$ with constants 0 and 1, a unary function symbol s for successor and a predicate $A(x, y, z)$ which is interpreted as $x + y = z$. Let φ be the sentence $\forall x \exists y A(x, y, 0)$

which is true in $\mathbb{Z}$. As a true universal sentence, φ should be true of any object. Indeed, any permissible substitution results in a formula valid in $\mathbb{Z}$. On the other hand, if we violate substitutability and substitute $s(y)$ for x we get $\forall x \exists y A(s(y), y, 0)$ which is false in $\mathbb{Z}$.

Example 2.10:

(i) $((\forall x)R(x, y))$ is a formula in which y occurs free but x does not. $((\exists y)((\forall x)R(x, y)))$ has no free variables; it is a sentence.

(ii) A variable may have both a free and a bound occurrence in a single formula as do both x and y in $(((\forall x)R(x, y)) \vee ((\exists y)R(x, y)))$.

(iii) If $\varphi(x)$ is $(((\exists y)R(x, y)) \wedge ((\forall z)\neg Q(x, z)))$ and t is $f(w, u)$ then $\varphi(t) = \varphi(x/t)$ is $(((\exists y)R(f(w, u), y)) \wedge ((\forall z)\neg Q(f(w, u), z)))$. The term $g(y, s(y))$ would, however, not be substitutable for x in $\varphi(x)$.

After the exercises for this section we will usually omit parentheses from formulas when doing so improves readability.

Exercises

For exercises 1–5 let the language be specified by the symbols listed in Definition 2.1.

1. Which of the following are terms?

   a) x e) $f(x, d)$

   b) xy f) $(\forall x)(R(c))$

   c) c g) $g(c, f(y, z))$

   d) $P(c)$ h) $g(R, d)$

2. Which of the following are formulas fully written out in accordance with Definition 2.5?

   a) $f(x, c)$ d) $\forall x(P(x))$

   b) $R(c, f(d, z))$ e) $(\neg R(z, f(w))$

   c) $(\exists y)(P(c))$ f) $((\exists x)(((\forall y)P(z)) \to R(x, y)))$

3. List all the subformulas of the formulas listed in exercise 2.

4. Which occurrences of variables are free in the formulas listed in answer to exercise 3? Which are bound?

5. Which of the following proposed substitutions are allowable by our definition of substitutable?

   a) $x/f(z, y)$ in $((\exists y)(P(y) \wedge R(x, z)))$.

   b) $x/g(f(z, y), a)$ in $(((\exists x)(P(x) \wedge R(x, y))) \to P(x)))$.

   c) $x/g(f(z, y), a)$ in $((\exists x)(P(x) \wedge R(x, y)))$.

   d) $x/g(a, b)$ in $((\exists y)(R(a, x) \wedge P(y)))$.

3. Formation Trees, Structures and Lists

As with the definition of propositions, we can make the formation rules for formulas more explicit and the definition of such terms as "occurrence" more precise by reformulating everything in terms of formation trees. This is also the preferred presentation in most texts on PROLOG programming. Our starting point is again the terms.

Definition 3.1:

(i) *Term formation trees* are ordered, finitely branching trees T labeled with terms satisfying the following condition:

    (1) The leaves of T are labeled with variables or constant symbols.

    (2) Every nonleaf node of T is labeled with a term t of the form $f(t_1, \dots, t_n)$.

    (3) A node of T which is labeled with a term of the form $f(t_1 \dots, t_n)$ has exactly n immediate successors in the tree. They are labeled in (lexicographic) order with $t_1, \dots, t_n$.

(ii) A term formation tree is *associated with* the term with which its root node is labeled.

Example 3.2: (i) The term formation trees associated with $f(c, g(x, y))$ and $h(f(d, z), g(c, a), w)$ are

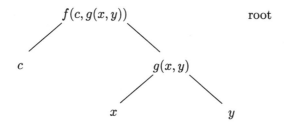

and

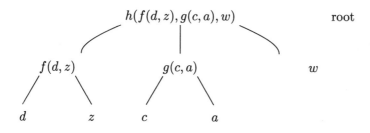

FIGURE 24

Proposition 3.3: *Every term t has a unique formation tree associated with it.*

The proof of this proposition, like those of the other results of this section, is a simple exercise in induction like that of Theorem I.2.4. We will leave them all as exercises. This one is Exercise 4.

Proposition 3.4: *The ground terms are those terms whose formation trees have no variables on their leaves.*

Proof: Exercise 5. □

The atomic formulas are handled as follows:

Definition 3.5:

(i) The *atomic formula auxiliary formation trees* are the labeled, ordered, finitely branching trees of depth one whose root node is labeled with an atomic formula. If the root node of such a tree is labeled with an n–ary relation $R(t_1, \ldots, t_n)$, then it has n immediate successors which are labeled in order with the terms $t_1, \ldots, t_n$.

(ii) The *atomic formula formation trees* are the labeled, ordered, finitely branching trees gotten from the auxiliary trees by attaching at each leaf labeled with a term t the rest of the formation tree associated with t. Such a tree is *associated with* the atomic formula with which its root is labeled.

Example 3.6: The atomic formation trees associated with the formula $R(c, f(x, y), g(a, z, w))$ is

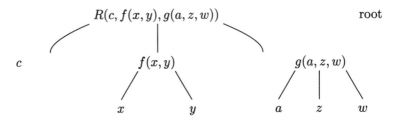

FIGURE 25

Proposition 3.7: *Every atomic formula is associated with a unique formation tree.*

Proof: Exercise 6. □

Definition 3.8:

(i) The *formula auxiliary formation trees* are the labeled, ordered, binary branching trees T such that

(1) The leaves of T are labeled with atomic formulas.

(2) If σ is a nonleaf node of T with one immediate successor $\sigma \wedge 0$ which is labeled with a formula φ, then σ is labeled with $\neg\varphi$, $\exists v\varphi$ or $\forall v\varphi$ for some variable v.

(3) If σ is a nonleaf node with two immediate successors, $\sigma \wedge 0$ and $\sigma \wedge 1$, which are labeled with formulas φ and ψ, then σ is labeled with $\varphi \wedge \psi$, $\varphi \vee \psi$, $\varphi \rightarrow \psi$ or $\varphi \leftrightarrow \psi$.

(ii) The *formula formation trees* are the ordered, labeled trees gotten from the auxiliary ones by attaching to each leaf labeled with an atomic formula the rest of its associated formation tree. Each such tree is again *associated* with the formula with which its root is labeled.

(iii) The *depth of a formula* is the depth of the associated auxiliary formation tree.

Example 3.9: The formula formation tree associated with the formula $\exists x R(c, f(x,y), g(a, z, w)) \wedge \forall y R(c, f(x,y), g(a, z, w))$ is

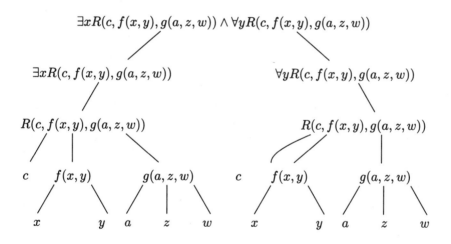

FIGURE 26

Proposition 3.10: *Every formula is associated with a unique (auxiliary) formation tree.*

Proof: Exercise 3.7. □

Formally, we continue to treat the remaining notions about formulas, subformulas and occurrences of variables as the proven equivalents of the notions defined in the last section. Those definitions could, however, actually be replaced with the ones we present here.

Proposition 3.11: *The subformulas of a formula φ are the labels of the nodes of the auxiliary formation tree associated with φ.*

Proposition 3.12:

(i) *The occurrences of a variable v in a formula φ are in one–one correspondence with the leaves of the associated formation tree which are labeled with v. (The correspondence is given by matching the typographical ordering of the occurrences of v in φ with the left–right ordering given by the tree to the leaves labeled with v.) We may also refer to the appropriate leaf labeled with v as the occurrence of v in φ.*

(ii) *An occurrence of the variable v in φ is bound if there is a formula ψ beginning with $((\forall v)$ or $((\exists v)$ which is the label of a node above the corresponding leaf of the formation tree for φ labeled with v.*

Proposition 3.13: *If φ is a formula and v a variable then $\varphi(v/t)$ is the formula associated with the formation tree gotten by replacing each leaf in the tree for $\varphi(v)$ which is labeled with a free occurrence of v with the formation tree associated with t and propagating this change through the tree.*

Proposition 3.14: *The term t is* substitutable *for v in $\varphi(v)$ if all occurrences of x in t remain free in $\varphi(t)$, i.e., any leaf in the formation tree for t which is a free occurrence of a variable x remains free in every location in which it appears in the formation tree described in Proposition 3.9.*

We leave the proofs of these propositions as Exercises 8–11.

Notice that, except for the distinction we have made in our alphabet between function symbols and predicate symbols, the formation trees for terms and atomic formulas are indistinguishable. Each has leaves labeled with constants or variables and every other node is labeled by applying one of the appropriate n–ary symbols to the labels of its immediate successors. The standard implementations of PROLOG, and so the various programming texts, in fact do not make this alphabetic distinction. Terms and atomic formulas are all lumped together and called *structures*. One can therefore have a syntactically acceptable PROLOG clause like "reading(john, reading(jack,list1))". This PROLOG clause might be rendered into English as follows: John is reading Jack's first reading list. Here "reading" is thought of both as a predicate describing who is reading what and a function giving people's items for reading. In general, however, it seems very difficult to make consistent sense out of such combined usages. The semantics we present in the next section, which is the standard one for predicate logic, makes no sense unless we maintain the distinction between function and predicate symbols. As it is the basis for the theoretical analysis of PROLOG (in terms of soundness and completeness, for example) and we know of no reason that it might ever be necessary to exploit such a confusion, we will simply assume that separate alphabets are maintained for function and predicate symbols (at least within any particular program or application).

Example 3.15: As an example of a typical PROLOG structure, we briefly consider one of its most important function symbols (or operators), the *pairing function* denoted by ".". Thus $.(a, b)$ denotes the ordered pair with first element a and second element b. This function is used to form arbitrary lists by repeated application. Practically speaking, the operator "." in PROLOG should be applied only to pairs the second element of which is already a list (the first element can be anything). To get such a procedure off the ground, PROLOG starts with a constant symbol [ ] denoting the empty list (one with no elements). Thus a list consisting of just the element b would be represented by $.(b, [\ ])$ and the ordered pair $\langle a, b \rangle$ would actually be realized as $.(a, .(b, [\ ]))$. As this notation is cumbersome, lists in PROLOG are also denoted by putting their elements in order within square brackets and separating them by commas. Thus $[a, b, c, d]$ denotes the list with elements a, b, c and d in that order. This notation is really an abbreviation for an iterated use of pairing (with the convention that we always end with the empty list). $[a, b, c, d]$ is treated as if it were $.(a, .(b, .(c, .(d, [\ ]))))$. Its formation tree is given in Figure 27 below.

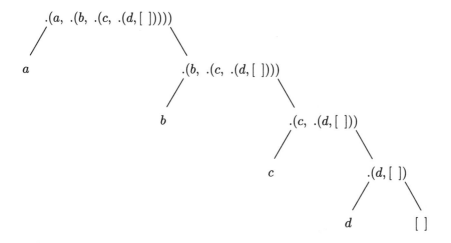

FIGURE 27

The list $[a, b, c, d]$ is also written $[a \mid [b, c, d]]$. The notation with the vertical bar, $\mid$, is another version of the function symbol . for combining lists. $[X \mid Y]$ denotes the list whose first element is X and whose succeeding elements are those of the list Y in order. The terminology that accompanies this notation is that X, the first element of the new list, is called the head of the list $[X \mid Y]$ and the list Y consisting of the remaining elements is called its tail.

The reason for avoiding terms like $[a \mid b]$ or equivalently $.(a, b)$ when b is not a list is that we usually define list handling functions by recursion. The starting point for such recursions is generally the empty list [ ]. Thus a function so defined would never be computed on an input like $.(a, b)$ when b

is not a list. We will return to this point with examples and explanations of definition by recursion in section 5 after we have defined the semantics for predicate logic and PROLOG.

Exercises

1. Draw the formation trees associated with the following terms:
   a) c
   b) $f(x, d)$
   c) $g(f(x, d), c)$
   d) $h(y, g(z, f(f(c, d), g(x, z))))$

2. Draw the formation trees associated with the following formulas:
   a) $R(c, d)$
   b) $R(f(x, y), d)$
   c) $R(c, d) \wedge R(f(x, y), d)$
   d) $\exists y \forall z (R(x, f(c, d)) \vee \neg P(h(y)))$
   e) $\forall z (R(g(x, z, z)) \rightarrow P(y)) \wedge P(z)$

3. Indicate which leaves are free occurrences of variables in the trees of exercise 2.

4. Prove Proposition 3.3.

5. Prove Proposition 3.4.

6. Prove Proposition 3.7.

7. Prove Proposition 3.10.

8. Prove Proposition 3.11.

9. Prove Proposition 3.12.

10. Prove Proposition 3.13.

11. Prove Proposition 3.14.

12. Prove that the length of every term t in a language $\mathcal{L}$ for predicate logic is greater than or equal to the depth of the associated formation tree.

13. Prove that the length of every formula φ of predicate logic is strictly greater than the depth of the associated formation tree.

4. Semantics: Meaning and Truth

A language $\mathcal{L}$ of predicate logic is specified by its predicate (or relation) symbols and function symbols. A single language will have many possible interpretations each suited to a different context or domain of discourse. Thus the language with just one binary predicate $P(x, y)$ can be viewed as talking about any of the following situations:

1) The natural numbers, $\mathbb{N}$, with $<$.

2) The rationals, $\mathbb{Q}$, with $<$.

3) The integers, $\mathbb{Z}$, with $>$.

or any of a host of other possibilities. If we add a binary function symbol $f(x, y)$, we could view f as representing, for example, $x \cdot y$, $x - y$ or $\max\{x, y\}$ in these respective domains. To begin to interpret the language, we must specify a domain of discourse and the intended meanings for the predicate and function symbols.

Definition 4.1: A *structure* $\mathcal{A}$ for a language $\mathcal{L}$ consists of a nonempty domain A, an assignment, to each n–ary predicate symbol R of $\mathcal{L}$, of an actual predicate (i.e., a relation) $R^{\mathcal{A}}$ on the n–tuples $(a_1, \ldots, a_n)$ from A, an assignment, to each constant symbol c of $\mathcal{L}$, of an element $c^{\mathcal{A}}$ of A and, to each n–ary function symbol f of $\mathcal{L}$, an n–ary function $f^{\mathcal{A}}$ from A^n to A.

In terms of the examples considered above, we can specify structures for the language with one binary predicate by letting the domain be $\mathbb{N}$, $\mathbb{Q}$, or $\mathbb{Z}$ respectively. The interpretations $P^{\mathcal{A}}$ of the binary predicate are then $<$, $<$, and $>$ respectively. When we add the binary function symbol f we must specify in each case a binary function $f^{\mathcal{A}}$ on the domain to interpret it. In each of our examples, the function would be the one specified above: multiplication, subtraction or max.

We begin the task of interpreting the formulas of $\mathcal{L}$ in the structure $\mathcal{A}$ by saying, for each ground term of the language $\mathcal{L}$, which element of the domain of discourse A it names.

Definition 4.2 (The *interpretation of ground terms*):

(i) Each constant term c *names* the element $c^{\mathcal{A}}$.

(ii) If the terms $t_1, \ldots, t_n$ of $\mathcal{L}$ *name* the elements $t_1^{\mathcal{A}}, \ldots, t_n^{\mathcal{A}}$ of A and f is an n–ary function symbol of $\mathcal{L}$ then the term $f(t_1, \ldots, t_n)$ *names* the element $f(t_1, \ldots, t_n)^{\mathcal{A}} = f^{\mathcal{A}}(t_1^{\mathcal{A}}, \ldots, t_n^{\mathcal{A}})$ of A. (Remember that $f^{\mathcal{A}}$ is an n–ary function on A and that $t_1^{\mathcal{A}}, \ldots, t_n^{\mathcal{A}}$ are elements of A so that $f^{\mathcal{A}}(t_1^{\mathcal{A}}, \ldots, t_n^{\mathcal{A}})$ is in fact an element of A.)

Continuing with our above examples, we might add constants c and d to our language and assign them to elements $c^{\mathcal{A}}$ and $d^{\mathcal{A}}$ of the structures as follows:

1) $c^{\mathcal{A}} = 0$; $d^{\mathcal{A}} = 1$.

2) $c^{\mathcal{A}} = 1/2$; $d^{\mathcal{A}} = 2/3$.

3) $c^{\mathcal{A}} = 0$; $d^{\mathcal{A}} = -2$.

Suppose f is interpreted as multiplication in each of the three structures. Then the ground terms $f(c, d)$ and $f(d, f(d, d))$ name elements of the structures as follows:

1) $(f(c,d))^{\mathcal{A}} = 0$; $(f(d,f(d,d)))^{\mathcal{A}} = 1$.
2) $(f(c,d))^{\mathcal{A}} = 1/3$; $(f(d,f(d,d)))^{\mathcal{A}} = 8/27$.
3) $(f(c,d))^{\mathcal{A}} = 0$; $(f(d,f(d,d)))^{\mathcal{A}} = -8$.

It is convenient to deal with structures $\mathcal{A}$ for languages $\mathcal{L}$ which have a ground term naming every element a of A. If we are given a structure $\mathcal{A}$ for a language $\mathcal{L}$ in which not every element of the domain is named by a ground term, we *expand* $\mathcal{L}$ by adding a new constant c_a to $\mathcal{L}$ for each $a \in A$ to get a language $\mathcal{L}^{\mathcal{A}}$ and *extend* $\mathcal{A}$ to a structure for $\mathcal{L}^{\mathcal{A}}$ by interpreting these constants in the obvious way: $c_a^{\mathcal{A}} = a$. Thus in $\mathcal{L}^{\mathcal{A}}$ every element of the domain A is named by a constant. Notice that every structure $\mathcal{A}$ for $\mathcal{L}$ becomes one for $\mathcal{L}^{\mathcal{A}}$ in this way and every structure for $\mathcal{L}^{\mathcal{A}}$ becomes one for $\mathcal{L}$ by simply ignoring the constants c_a.

We can now define when a sentence φ of a language $\mathcal{L}$ is true in a given structure for $\mathcal{L}$. We will write this as $\mathcal{A} \vDash \varphi$. The formal definition is by induction on sentences in the expected manner. The interesting case is that for the quantifiers. Here it is necessary to have ground terms which name each element of A. If there are not enough ground terms in $\mathcal{L}$, we simply use the definition in $\mathcal{L}^{\mathcal{A}}$. Thus, we assume in the following definition that every $a \in A$ is named by a ground term of $\mathcal{L}$.

Definition 4.3: The *truth* of a sentence φ of $\mathcal{L}$ in a structure $\mathcal{A}$ in which every $a \in A$ is named by a ground term of $\mathcal{L}$ is defined by induction. (If not every element of A is so named, we use the definition of $\mathcal{A} \vDash \varphi$ for $\mathcal{L}^{\mathcal{A}}$ to define $\mathcal{A} \vDash \varphi$ for sentences φ of $\mathcal{L}$.)

(i)   For an *atomic* sentence $R(t_1, \ldots, t_n)$, $\mathcal{A} \vDash R(t_1, \ldots, t_n)$ iff $R^{\mathcal{A}}(t_1^{\mathcal{A}}, \ldots, t_n^{\mathcal{A}})$, i.e., the relation $R^{\mathcal{A}}$ on A^n assigned to R holds of the elements named by the terms $t_1, \ldots, t_n$. Note that, as $R(t_1, \ldots, t_n)$ is a sentence, the t_i are all ground terms and so name particular elements of A.

(ii) $\mathcal{A} \vDash \neg\varphi \Leftrightarrow$ it is not the case that $\mathcal{A} \vDash \varphi$. [We also write this as $\mathcal{A} \nvDash \varphi$.]

(iii) $\mathcal{A} \vDash (\varphi \vee \psi) \Leftrightarrow \mathcal{A} \vDash \varphi$ or $\mathcal{A} \vDash \psi$.

(iv) $\mathcal{A} \vDash (\varphi \wedge \psi) \Leftrightarrow \mathcal{A} \vDash \varphi$ and $\mathcal{A} \vDash \psi$.

(v) $\mathcal{A} \vDash (\varphi \rightarrow \psi) \Leftrightarrow \mathcal{A} \nvDash \varphi$ or $\mathcal{A} \vDash \psi$.

(vi) $\mathcal{A} \vDash (\varphi \leftrightarrow \psi) \Leftrightarrow (\mathcal{A} \vDash \varphi$ and $\mathcal{A} \vDash \psi)$ or $(\mathcal{A} \nvDash \varphi$ and $\mathcal{A} \nvDash \psi)$.

(vii) $\mathcal{A} \vDash \exists v \varphi(v) \Leftrightarrow$ for some ground term t, $\mathcal{A} \vDash \varphi(t)$.

(viii) $\mathcal{A} \vDash \forall v \varphi(v) \Leftrightarrow$ for all ground terms t, $\mathcal{A} \vDash \varphi(t)$.

Note that truth (or *satisfaction*, as $\vDash$ is often called) for longer sentences is always defined in (ii)–(viii) in terms of truth for shorter sentences. It is for clauses (vii) and (viii) that the assumption that all elements of our structure are named by ground terms is crucial.

Definition 4.4: Fix some language $\mathcal{L}$.

(i) A sentence φ of $\mathcal{L}$ is *valid*, $\vDash \varphi$, if it is true in all structures for $\mathcal{L}$.

(ii) Given a set of sentences $\Sigma = \{\alpha_1, \ldots\}$, we say that α is *logical consequence* of Σ, $\Sigma \vDash \alpha$, if α is true in every structure in which all of the members of Σ are true.

(iii) A set of sentences $\Sigma = \{\alpha_1, \ldots\}$ is *satisfiable* if there is a structure $\mathcal{A}$ in which all the members of Σ are true. Such a structure is called a *model* of Σ. If Σ has no model it is *unsatisfiable*.

Note that we have defined truth only for sentences, that is, formulas with no free variables. The point here is that if $\varphi(v)$ has v free then the formula has no single fixed meaning in a structure $\mathcal{A}$. It rather represents an n–ary predicate on A for $n > 0$ and so we do not say that it is true or false. The notion for formulas with free variables that is analogous to truth for sentences is that of validity.

Definition 4.5: A formula φ of a language $\mathcal{L}$ with free variables $v_1, \ldots, v_n$ is *valid in a structure* $\mathcal{A}$ for $\mathcal{L}$ (also written $\mathcal{A} \vDash \varphi$) if the *universal closure* of φ, i.e., the sentence $\forall v_1 \forall v_2, \ldots \forall v_n \varphi$ gotten by putting $\forall v_i$ in front of φ for every free variable v_i in φ, is true in $\mathcal{A}$. The formula φ of $\mathcal{L}$ is *valid* if it is valid in every structure for $\mathcal{L}$.

As long as we are in a situation in which every element of the structure $\mathcal{A}$ is named by a ground term, this definition of validity in $\mathcal{A}$ is equivalent to saying that every *ground instance* of φ is true in $\mathcal{A}$, i.e., $\mathcal{A} \vDash \varphi(t_1, \ldots, t_n)$ for all ground terms $t_1, \ldots, t_n$ of $\mathcal{L}$. Also note that as sentences have no free variables, a sentence is true in a structure iff it is valid in the structure.

Warning: For a sentence φ and structure $\mathcal{A}$ either φ or $\neg\varphi$ is true in $\mathcal{A}$ (and the other false). It is not true, however, for an arbitrary formula ψ that ψ or $\neg\psi$ must be valid in $\mathcal{A}$. It may well be that some ground instances of ψ are true while others are false. Similarly, one can have a sentence such that neither it nor its negation is valid. It is true in some structures but not in others.

Definition 4.6: A set Σ of formulas with free variables is *satisfiable* if there is a structure in which all of the formulas in Σ are valid (i.e., their universal closures are true). Again such a structure is called a *model* of Σ. If Σ has no models it is *unsatisfiable*.

Example 4.7: Consider a language $\mathcal{L}$ specified by a binary relation symbol R and constants $c_0, c_1, c_2, \ldots$. Here are two possible structures for $\mathcal{L}$ corresponding to two different interpretations of the language.

(i) Let the domain A consist of the natural numbers, let $R^{\mathcal{A}}$ be the usual relation $<$, and $c_0^{\mathcal{A}} = 0$, $c_1^{\mathcal{A}} = 1, \ldots$. The sentence $(\forall x)(\exists y) R(x, y)$ says that for every natural number there is a larger one, so it is true in this structure.

(ii) Let the domain of $\mathcal{A}$ consist of the rational numbers $\mathbb{Q} = \{q_0, q_1, \dots\}$; let $R^{\mathcal{A}}$ again be $<$, and let $c_0^{\mathcal{A}} = q_0$, $c_1^{\mathcal{A}} = q_1, \dots$. The sentence $(\forall x)(\forall y)(R(x, y) \rightarrow (\exists z)(R(x, z) \wedge R(z, y))))$ is true in this structure. (It says that the rationals are dense.) It is not, however, valid as it is false in the structure of (i) for the natural numbers.

Warning: We have not included any special or reserved predicate symbol for equality in either our syntax or semantics for predicate logic. In other words, we have made no provisions in our definitions that could be used to force us to interpret some particular predicate, such as "$=$", as true equality. We have avoided this extension of our definition of a language in 2.1 and the corresponding restriction in the definition of truth in 4.3 because it does not mesh well with resolution theorem proving, logic programming and PROLOG. Some of the perhaps unexpected consequences of this choice can be seen in Exercises 2–3 of §7. A view of predicate logic with such a distinguished equality predicate (as well as an approach to equality without it) is presented in III.5. The syntax and semantics presented there can be read now. The proofs of soundness and completeness discussed there for logic with equality are simple modifications of the ones we present in §7.

Now that we have defined the semantics for predicate logic we can make precise the claim that we do not need propositions. Indeed there is a faithful embedding of propositional logic in predicate logic.

Theorem 4.8: *Let φ be an open (i.e., quantifier–free) formula of predicate logic. We may view φ as a formula φ' of propositional logic by regarding every atomic subformula of φ as a propositional letter. With this correspondence, φ is a valid formula of predicate logic if and only if φ' is valid in propositional logic.*

Proof: Exercises 9–11. □

Now that we have both the syntax and semantics for predicate logic it should be clear by analogy with our development of propositional logic what we should do next. We have to give methods of proof in predicate logic and then prove soundness and completeness theorems analogous to those we have seen for the propositional calculus. First, however, we will consider the application (or actually, the specialization) of our semantics to PROLOG.

Notation: We will often use vector notation as in $\vec{x}$, $\vec{t}$ and $\vec{c}$ to denote sequences of variables, terms and constants respectively.

Exercises

1. Let $\mathcal{L}$ contain a constant c, a binary function f and a unary predicate P. Give two structures for $\mathcal{L}$: one in which $\forall x\, P(f(x, c))$ is true and one in which it is false.

2. Show that $\forall x(p(x) \to q(f(x))) \wedge \forall x\, p(x) \wedge \exists x \neg q(x)$ is satisfiable.

3. Give an example of an unsatisfiable sentence.

4. Define a structure for the language containing constant symbols 0 and 1, a binary predicate $<$ and one binary function symbol $+$ in which $x + 1 < x$ is valid but $x + x < x$ is not. Indicate why the structure has the required properties.

5. Prove that $\mathcal{A} \vDash \neg \exists x \varphi(x) \Leftrightarrow \mathcal{A} \vDash \forall x \neg \varphi(x)$. Does it matter if φ has free variables other than x?

6. Prove that, for any sentence ψ, $\mathcal{A} \vDash (\psi \to \exists x \varphi(x)) \Leftrightarrow \mathcal{A} \vDash \exists x(\psi \to \varphi(x))$. What happens if ψ is a formula in which x is free?

7. Prove that for any sentence ψ, $\mathcal{A} \vDash (\exists x \varphi(x) \to \psi) \Leftrightarrow \mathcal{A} \vDash \forall x(\varphi(x) \to \psi)$. What happens if ψ is a formula in which x is free?

8. **Theorem on constants**: Let $\varphi(\vec{x})$ be a formula of a language $\mathcal{L}$ with a sequence $\vec{x}$ of free variables. Let $\vec{c}$ be a sequence of new constants (not in $\mathcal{L}$). Prove that $\varphi(\vec{x})$ is valid iff $\varphi(\vec{c})$ is.

9. Prove Theorem 4.8 for formulas with no free variables. (Hint: Convert between models for φ or $\neg \varphi$ to assignments making φ' or $\neg \varphi'$ true.)

10. Combine exercises 8 and 9 to prove Theorem 4.8.

5. Interpretation of PROLOG Programs

In this section we want to specialize the ideas and definitions of the last section to explain the semantics of clausal form and Horn formulas with free variables and so begin the study of the semantics of full PROLOG programs.

The syntax for clausal form and PROLOG format is the same as in the propositional case (Definition I.10.4) except that *literals* can now be any atomic formulas or their negations. Note, however, that implementations of PROLOG uniformly use (initial) capital letters for (names of) variables and lower case ones for (names of) predicates, constants and functions.

Definition 5.1 (*Clausal Notation*):

(i) *Literals* are atomic formulas or their negations. The atomic formulas are called *positive literals* and their negations, *negative literals*.

(ii) A *clause* is a finite set of literals.

(iii) A clause is a *Horn clause* if it contains at most one positive literal.

(iv) A *program clause* is a clause with exactly one positive literal. If a program clause contains some negative literals it is a *rule*, otherwise it is a *fact*.

(v) A *goal clause* is a clause with no positive literals.

(vi) A *formula* is a not necessarily finite set of clauses.

The PROLOG notation for rules and facts is as in the propositional case as well.

Definition 5.2 (PROLOG *Notation*):

(i) In PROLOG, the fact $\{p(\vec{X})\}$ consisting of the single positive literal $p(\vec{X})$ appears in PROLOG programs as follows:

$$p(\vec{X}).$$

(ii) The rule $C = \{p(\vec{X}), \neg q_1(\vec{X}, \vec{Y}), \dots, \neg q_n(\vec{X}, \vec{Y})\}$ appears in PROLOG programs as follows:

$$p(\vec{X}) :- q_1(\vec{X}, \vec{Y}), \dots, q_n(\vec{X}, \vec{Y}).$$

(iii) For a rule C as in (ii), we call $p(\vec{X})$ the *goal* or *head* of C. We call the $q_1(\vec{X}, \vec{Y}), \dots, q_n(\vec{X}, \vec{Y})$ the *subgoals* or *body* of C. When the head–body terminology is used, the symbol :– which connects the head and body of C is called the *neck*.

(iv) A (PROLOG) *program* is a formula (set of clauses) containing only program clauses (i.e., rules and facts).

The intended meaning of clauses and formulas is as in the propositional case except that we must explain how we treat the free variables. Each clause is interpreted as the universal closure of the disjunction of its elements. Thus the intended meaning of $C_1 = \{q(X,Y), r(Y)\}$ is $\forall X \forall Y[q(X,Y) \vee r(Y)]$. In this vein the intended meaning of the rule C given by $p(X) :- q_1(X,Y), \dots, q_n(X,Y)$ (in clausal notation $C = \{p(X), \neg q_1(X,Y), \dots, \neg q_n(X,Y)\}$) is $\forall X \forall Y[p(X) \vee \neg q_1(X,Y) \vee \dots \vee \neg q_n(X,Y)]$. Repeated applications of Exercises 4.8 and I.3.2 would show that this is equivalent to $\forall X[\exists Y(q_1(X,Y) \wedge \dots \wedge q_n(X,Y)) \rightarrow p(X)]$. (We will later analyze some examples to see how this equivalence is worked out.) Thus C truly embodies a rule: If, for any X, there is a Y such that $q_1(X,Y), q_2(X,Y), \dots, q_n(X,Y)$ are all true (have been verified), then $p(X)$ is also true (has been verified).

A formula S is interpreted as the conjunction of its clauses. Thus if $S = \{C_1, C_2\}$ where C_1 is as above and $C_2 = \{q(X,Y), m(Y)\}$, then S has the same meaning as $\forall X \forall Y[q(X,Y) \vee r(Y)] \wedge \forall X \forall Y[q(X,Y) \vee m(Y)]$. In particular, if the formula S is a PROLOG program then it is equivalent to a list of universal facts of the form $\forall X p(X)$ and rules like C in the previous paragraph. Implementing PROLOG consists in making deductions from such a list of facts and rules.

Note that in describing the intended meaning of a formula, each clause is universally closed before we take the conjunction. The importance of this convention will become apparent when we consider resolution for predicate calculus. Confusion can be avoided by using distinct variables in each clause. (This corresponds to what is called *standardizing the variables apart* (see §13)). We will later (§9) show that, at the expense of adding new function symbols to our language, every sentence of predicate calculus is equivalent to a formula in the sense of Definition 5.1. (This result will be the analog of CNF for the predicate calculus.) For now, after one example involving such transformations, we will simply deal with the syntax and semantics of formulas in clausal form directly. The notions of structures for, and interpretations of, formulas in clausal form are immediately specified by the above translation into predicate calculus.

*Knight's moves: an example:

Let us briefly examine the added expressive power given to us by using variables in PROLOG by considering the problem of representing information about a knight's moves on a chessboard. We can label the squares of the board by pairs of numbers from 1 to 8 in the usual way.

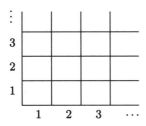

FIGURE 28

We thus might well want our language to include the constant symbols $1, 2, \ldots, 8$. One of the basic predicates of our language should be the 4–ary one, ktmove(X_1, X_2, X_3, X_4). (For the moment we want to avoid worrying about the actual representation of pairs in PROLOG via the list notation introduced in §3 and so will use a 4–ary predicate on $\{1, \ldots 8\}$ rather than a binary one on pairs of numbers.) The **intended** interpretation of "ktmove(X_1, X_2, X_3, X_4)" is that a knight is allowed to move from position $\langle X_1, X_2 \rangle$ to $\langle X_3, X_4 \rangle$. One way to represent the data involved is to simply list all the facts:

$$\text{ktmove}\,(1, 1, 2, 3).$$

$$\text{ktmove}\,(1, 1, 3, 2).$$

$$\cdots$$

The list is, however, quite long (336 facts). Moreover, the situation quickly becomes intolerable when we ask for only a little bit more. Suppose we also wish to have another predicate 2ktmove(X_1, X_2, X_3, X_4) which says that a knight can get from $\langle X_1, X_2 \rangle$ to $\langle X_3, X_4 \rangle$ in two moves. Here too we could enter a very long list of facts:

$$\text{2ktmove}\,(1, 1, 1, 1).$$

$$\text{2ktmove}\,(1, 1, 3, 5).$$

$$\cdots$$

This is really all we could hope to do were we restricted to propositional logic. That situation corresponds to simply having a pure database. Once we have variables, however, we can greatly condense the representation of the data by the introduction of rules. The one for 2ktmove is obvious: $2\text{ktmove}(X_1, X_2, X_3, X_4)$ if there are Y_1, Y_2 such that $\text{ktmove}(X_1, X_2, Y_1, Y_2)$ and ktmove (Y_1, Y_2, X_3, X_4). In predicate logic we might express this rule or definition as follows:

$$\forall X_1 \forall X_2 \forall X_3 \forall X_4 [\exists Y_1 \exists Y_2 (\text{ktmove}\,(X_1, X_2, Y_1, Y_2)$$
$$\wedge \text{ktmove}\,(Y_1, Y_2, X_3, X_4)) \to 2\text{ktmove}\,(X_1, X_2, X_3, X_4)] \quad (\#)$$

We will introduce a general method for converting all such sentences of predicate calculus to clausal equivalents (or PROLOG programs) in §9. For now we analyze this one in an ad hoc way. We begin with eliminating the implication in favor of $\neg$ and $\vee$ as in constructing a CNF in propositional logic to get the following sentence equivalent to $(\#)$:

$$\forall X_1 \forall X_2 \forall X_3 \forall X_4 [\neg(\exists Y_1 \exists Y_2)(\text{ktmove}\,(X_1, X_2, Y_1, Y_2)$$
$$\wedge \text{ktmove}\,(Y_1, Y_2, X_3, X_4)) \vee 2\text{ktmove}\,(X_1, X_2, X_3, X_4)].$$

The next steps are to apply the equivalence of $\neg \exists z \varphi$ to $\forall z \neg \varphi$ established in Exercise 4.5 and then De Morgan's laws from Exercise I.3.2 to get

$$\forall X_1 \forall X_2 \forall X_3 \forall X_4 [\forall Y_1 \forall Y_2 [\neg \text{ktmove}\,(X_1, X_2, Y_1, Y_2)]$$
$$\vee \neg \text{ktmove}\,(Y_1, Y_2, X_3, X_4)] \vee 2\text{ktmove}\,(X_1, X_2, X_3, X_4)].$$

Finally we have an equivalent of $(\#)$ which is essentially in clausal form

$$\forall X_1 \forall X_2 \forall X_3 \forall X_4 \forall Y_1 \forall Y_2 [\neg \text{ktmove}\,(X_1, X_2, Y_1, Y_2)$$
$$\vee \neg \text{ktmove}\,(Y_1, Y_2, X_3, X_4) \vee 2\text{ktmove}\,(X_1, X_2, X_3, X_4)].$$

(The semantic equivalence of these last two sentences should be clear.)

The clausal form of our rule originally stated in predicate calculus as $(\#)$ is thus simply:

$$\{\neg \text{ktmove}\,(X_1, X_2, Y_1, Y_2), \neg \text{ktmove}\,(Y_1, Y_2, X_3, X_4),$$
$$2\text{ktmove}\,(X_1, X_2, X_3, X_4)\}.$$

This is a Horn clause which we write in PROLOG notation as

$$2\text{ktmove}\,(X_1, X_2, X_3, X_4) :\!- \text{ktmove}\,(X_1, X_2, Y_1, Y_2),$$
$$\text{ktmove}\,(Y_1, Y_2, X_3, X_4).$$

Thus, we have an example of the general interpretation of a program clause of the form "$p(\vec{X}) :\!- q_1(\vec{X}, \vec{Y}), \ldots, q_n(\vec{X}, \vec{Y})$" in PROLOG. It is a rule which says that, for every choice of the variables $\vec{X}$ in the goal (*head*) $p(\vec{X})$ of the clause, p holds of $\vec{X}$ (*succeeds*) if there are $\vec{Y}$ such that all of the subgoal (*body*) clauses $q_1(\vec{X}, \vec{Y}), \ldots, q_n(\vec{X}, \vec{Y})$ hold (*succeed*). In our case, the clause says as expected that you can get from $\langle X_1, X_2 \rangle$ to $\langle X_3, X_4 \rangle$ in two knight's moves if there is a $\langle Y_1, Y_2 \rangle$ such that you can get from $\langle X_1, X_2 \rangle$ to $\langle Y_1, Y_2 \rangle$ in one move and from $\langle Y_1, Y_2 \rangle$ to $\langle X_3, X_4 \rangle$ in another.

Let us see how we might reduce the size of the program representing ktmove from 336 clauses to one of more manageable size by the introduction of other rules. One approach is to introduce symmetry type rules that would enable us to derive every knight's move from a small list of basic moves. One obvious such rule is symmetry itself:

(S1) ktmove (X_1, X_2, X_3, X_4) :– ktmove (X_3, X_4, X_1, X_2).

Remember that this rule says that (for any X_1, X_2, X_3, X_4) if a knight can move from $\langle X_3, X_4 \rangle$ to $\langle X_1, X_2 \rangle$, it can move from $\langle X_1, X_2 \rangle$ to $\langle X_3, X_4 \rangle$. Introducing this rule would allow us to cut our database in half. Other possible such rules include the following:

(S2) ktmove (X_1, X_2, X_3, X_4) :– ktmove (X_1, X_4, X_3, X_2).

(S3) ktmove (X_1, X_2, X_3, X_4) :– ktmove (X_2, X_1, X_4, X_3).

(S4) ktmove (X_1, X_2, X_3, X_4) :– ktmove (X_3, X_2, X_1, X_4).

(Check that these are in fact correct rules about a knight's behavior in chess.) We could then list just a few basic moves which, together with these program clauses, would correctly define the predicate ktmove. (It is correct in the sense that any structure satisfying all these facts and rules would give exactly the legal knight's moves as the quadruples of constants $\{1, \ldots, 8\}$ of which the predicate "ktmove" holds. The correctness of the program in terms of execution, which employs resolution–type theorem proving, will be dealt with later.)

Another tack might be to try to define "ktmove" in terms of arithmetic operations on the positions, i.e., to capture, in some sense, the rule as it is usually taught: The knight may move from $\langle X_1, X_2 \rangle$ to $\langle X_3, X_4 \rangle$ if the change in one coordinate is 1 and 2 in the other, i.e.,

(A0) ktmove (X_1, X_2, X_3, X_4) if $|X_1 - X_3| + |X_2 - X_4| = 3$.

(We must also make sure that the two positions are different. This will be taken care of by the way we define the appropriate arithmetic operations. In particular 0 will not be an allowed value for $|X_1 - X_3|$.) Now PROLOG has many arithmetic operations and predicates built in but a precise understanding of how they are used requires knowing more about how programs are implemented. So for now, we wish to avoid using the built–in predicates. We can, however, put into our program definitions of our own for as much arithmetic as we need. (Be careful not to use the names reserved for built–in predicates for the ones you define.)

To begin with, we might define the "succeeded by" predicate on the set of numbers $\{1, \ldots, 8\}$ by a database:

$$\text{suc}\,(1,2).$$

$$\text{suc}\,(2,3).$$

$$\vdots$$

$$\text{suc}\,(7,8).$$

We could then define a truncated version of addition by the following rules:

(A1)   add $(X,1,Z)$:-- suc(X,Z).

(A2)   add (X,Y,Z) :-- suc(Y_1,Y), suc(Z_1,Z), add (X,Y_1,Z_1).

We could then directly define $|X_1 - X_2| = Y$ by:

(A3)   absolute_difference (X_1, X_2, Y) :--   add (X_1, Y, X_2).

(A4)   absolute_difference (X_1, X_2, Y) :--   add (X_2, Y, X_1).

(These rules do what we want because we are only interested in truncated operations, i.e., only on what happens on $\{1, \ldots, 8\}$. They do not define the operations correctly on all the integers. We will say more about intended structures for a program later.)

So far we have been considering the meaning of clauses in a PROLOG program entered as such, e.g., by "consulting" a file containing the program as listed. We must now explain the semantics of goal clauses entered at the "?" prompt. The intended meaning of, for example, "?-- $p(X_1, X_2)$, $q(X_2, X_3)$." is "are there objects a_1, a_2, a_3 such that $p(a_1, a_2)$ and $q(a_2, a_3)$". PROLOG responds not only by answering yes or no to this question but, if the answer is yes, by giving instances that verify it, i.e., actual terms (and so names for objects) a_1, a_2 and a_3 such that $p(a_1, a_2) \wedge q(a_2, a_3)$. (As discussed in the case of propositional logic in I.10.4, entering "; " after one answer has been found asks for another. This may be repeated until there are no more, at which point PROLOG answers "no". The search for additional answers may also be terminated after any reply by simply entering a return.)

As in the propositional case, PROLOG implements the search for such witnesses a_1, a_2 and a_3 by adding the goal clause $G = \{\neg p(X_1, X_2), \neg q(X_2, X_3)\}$ to the current program P and then deciding if the result is an unsatisfiable formula. Let us list various semantic equivalents of the resulting formula to help see how this search produces an answer to our question. First, the meaning of the clause G is $\forall X_1 \forall X_2 \forall X_3 [\neg p(X_1, X_2) \vee \neg q(X_2, X_3)]$. If adding it to the program P produces an unsatisfiable formula $P \cup \{G\}$, then its negation is a logical consequence of P (check through the definitions as we did in Lemma I.10.6). Thus

$$P \vDash \neg \forall X_1 \forall X_2 \forall X_3 [\neg p(X_1, X_2) \vee \neg q(X_2, X_3)].$$

As we have seen above (and in Exercise 4.5), this is equivalent to $P \vDash \exists X_1 \exists X_2 \exists X_3 [p(X_1, X_2) \wedge q(X_2, X_3)]$. The implementation of PROLOG tries to establish this consequence relation by producing a resolution refutation of $P \cup \{G\}$. (We will define resolution refutations for predicate calculus in §13 and Chapter III.) A by–product of the proof procedure is that it actually produces witnesses, a_1, a_2, a_3 in this case, that show that $P \cup \{G\}$ is unsatisfiable by providing a proof from P that $p(a_1, a_2) \wedge q(a_2, a_3)$. From the viewpoint of resolution theorem proving, these witnesses are a mere by–product of the proof. From the programming point of view, they are the essential result. They are the output of our program; the answers to our questions.

Because of the way PROLOG represents data via logic, there is an unusual symmetry between input and output. We can put the variables anywhere in our predicate when we ask questions. Thus the simple predicate add (X, Y, Z) not only supplies $a + b$ when we enter " ?– add (a, b, Z)." it also supplies $b - a$ when we enter " ?– add (a, Z, b)." (at least if $b > a$). A single PROLOG program can thus be used to answer quite fancy questions that might be difficult to extract from a simple database. Compare asking if one can get from $\langle a, b \rangle$ to $\langle c, d \rangle$ in three knight's moves given one of the above PROLOG programs to explicitly writing such a program in some other language given only the database listing the knight's moves. The arrangement of, and orders for, searching are all done automatically. Again we will return to these points of reversibility and searching later.

Exercises

1. Verify that the symmetry rules (S1)–(S4) are legitimate. (You can do this by applying the arithmetic definition of ktmove (A0).)

2. Explain (in English) the meaning of the rules (A1)–(A2) and why they correctly represent addition on the structure $\{1, \ldots, 8\}$.

3. Explain (in English) the meaning of the rules (A3)–(A4) and why they correctly represent absolute difference on the structure $\{1, \ldots, 8\}$.

4. Suppose that suc(X, Y) were correctly defined in some way on all the natural numbers, i.e., suc(n, m) is true iff $n + 1 = m$.

   a) Do the clauses (A1)–(A2) still correctly define addition?

   b) Do the clauses (A3)–(A4) still correctly define absolute difference?

   Suppose now that suc(X, Y) defines "succeeded by" on the integers. What relations do the clauses (A1)–(A2) and (A3)–(A4) now define on the integers?

5. Suppose we switch to a language containing the constant c, a unary function symbol $s(X)$ and a ternary predicate symbol $a(X, Y, Z)$. Write a set of PROLOG clauses that will make "a" define addition in the

sense that $a(s^n(c), s^m(c), s^t(c))$ will be a consequence of the program
iff $n + m = t$. ($s^n(c)$ is shorthand for $s(\ldots(s(c))\ldots)$ where there are n
occurrences of s in the string of s's.)

6. Prove that every PROLOG program is satisfiable.

The following problems (and others later on) were designed to be used
with a database which we supplied on line. This database consists of the
genealogy given in the first few chapters of Chronicles (the last book of the
Hebrew Bible). The information there is in terms of male descent only. (Actually there are bits and pieces of information on women and their children
but so fragmentary as to make inclusion fairly useless. The information was
recorded in the database in terms of the predicate "fatherof(a, b)". Thus
the file consisted purely of (many) facts entered as follows:

> fatherof(adam, seth).
>
> fatherof(abraham, isaac).
>
> fatherof(isaac, jacob).
>
> fatherof(isaac, esau).

In problems 7 and 8 assume that this is the only type of information
available (e.g., in defining grandfather, there is no need to consider ancestry
on the mother's side as this sort of information is not available).

We provide a printout of the database as Appendix B. If the reader does
not have on–line access to this database or a similar one, the following
problems should be answered by just writing down a PROLOG program
which is semantically correct according to the interpretations of facts and
rules described in this section. Similarly descriptions of how to get the
requested information from the programs will suffice.

7. Ancestors:

   a) Write a program defining "grandfatherof".

   b) Find the grandfathers of nimrod, lud and joktan.

   c) Use this program to find a grandson of noah; to find all his grand-
      sons (use the facility which generates alternate answers by entering
      a semicolon after each answer is given until there are no more).

   d) Write a program defining "greatgrandfatherof".

   e) Find the great–grandfathers of shem and canaan.

   f) Use the program to find a great–grandson of abraham; to find ten
      of his great–grandsons.

   g) Write a program to define "ancestorof".

   h) Find three ancestors of shem.

8. Uncles:

a) Write a program defining "uncleof".

b) Find the uncles of nimrod, lud and joktan.

c) Use this program to find a nephew of shem; to find all his nephews (use the facility which generates alternate answers by entering a semicolon after each answer is given until there are no more).

d) Write a program defining "granduncleof" (recall that my grandfather's brothers are my granduncles.)

e) Find the granduncles of shelah and canaan.

f) Use the program to find a grandnephew of ham; to find eight of his grandnephews.

6. Proofs: Complete Systematic Tableaux

We will now describe a system for building proofs of sentences in predicate logic. As for propositional logic the proofs will be labeled binary trees called *tableaux*. The labels on the trees will be *signed sentences* (i.e., sentences preceded by T or F to indicate that, for the sake of the analysis, we are assuming them true or false respectively). We will again call these labels the *entries of the tableau*. Formally we will define tableaux for predicate logic inductively by first specifying certain (labeled binary) trees as tableaux (the so–called atomic tableaux) and then giving a development rule defining more complex tableaux from simpler ones. The intent of the proof procedure is to start with some signed sentence such as $F\alpha$ as the root of our tree and to analyze it into its components in such a way as to show that any analysis leads to a contradiction. We will then conclude that we have refuted the original assumption that α is false and so have a proof of α.

The analysis of the connectives will be the same as in propositional logic and the plan of the analysis will again be that if some sentence is correctly signed (T or F) then at least one of its immediate successors in the tree analysis is also correctly signed. The new problem is how to deal with quantifiers. If we consider, for example, $T\exists x\varphi(x)$, the obvious analysis of the assertion that there is an x such that $\varphi(x)$ is simply to supply such an x. Supplying such a witness means specifying a ground term t and asserting that $\varphi(t)$ is true. Thus, our first concern should be that there are as many ground terms available as we might ever need. If we therefore begin with any language $\mathcal{L}$, we immediately expand it to one $\mathcal{L}_C$ by adding on a set of constant symbols $c_0, c_1, c_2, \ldots$ not used in $\mathcal{L}$. Let A be any atomic sentence of $\mathcal{L}$ and α, β be any sentences of $\mathcal{L}_C$. The base case of our inductive definition of tableaux for the analysis of sentences of the language $\mathcal{L}$ starts with the following (labeled binary) trees as the *atomic tableaux*.

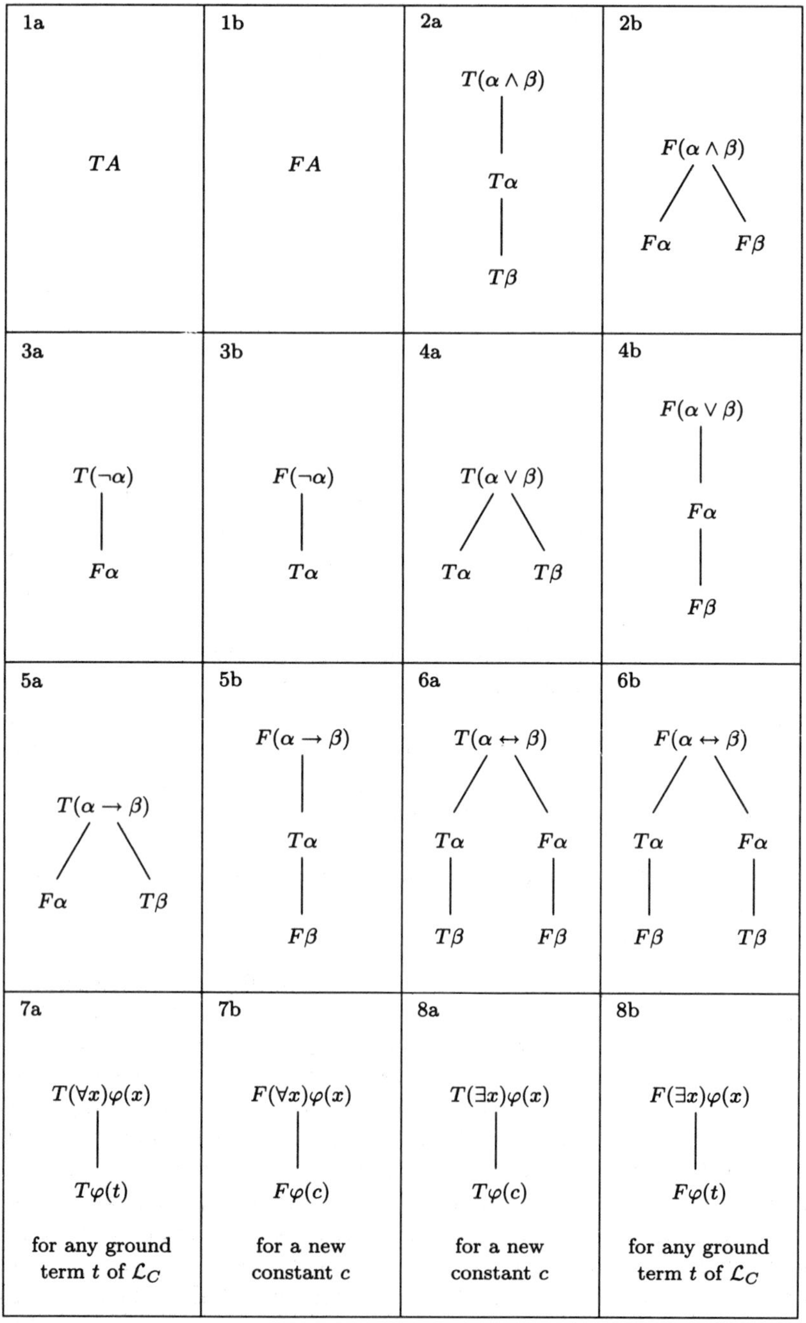

1a	1b	2a	2b
TA	FA	$T(\alpha \wedge \beta)$ $\mid$ $T\alpha$ $\mid$ $T\beta$	$F(\alpha \wedge \beta)$ $\diagup \quad \diagdown$ $F\alpha \qquad F\beta$

3a	3b	4a	4b
$T(\neg\alpha)$ $\mid$ $F\alpha$	$F(\neg\alpha)$ $\mid$ $T\alpha$	$T(\alpha \vee \beta)$ $\diagup \quad \diagdown$ $T\alpha \qquad T\beta$	$F(\alpha \vee \beta)$ $\mid$ $F\alpha$ $\mid$ $F\beta$

5a	5b	6a	6b
$T(\alpha \rightarrow \beta)$ $\diagup \quad \diagdown$ $F\alpha \qquad T\beta$	$F(\alpha \rightarrow \beta)$ $\mid$ $T\alpha$ $\mid$ $F\beta$	$T(\alpha \leftrightarrow \beta)$ $\diagup \quad \diagdown$ $T\alpha \qquad F\alpha$ $\mid \qquad \mid$ $T\beta \qquad F\beta$	$F(\alpha \leftrightarrow \beta)$ $\diagup \quad \diagdown$ $T\alpha \qquad F\alpha$ $\mid \qquad \mid$ $F\beta \qquad T\beta$

7a	7b	8a	8b
$T(\forall x)\varphi(x)$ $\mid$ $T\varphi(t)$ for any ground term t of $\mathcal{L}_C$	$F(\forall x)\varphi(x)$ $\mid$ $F\varphi(c)$ for a new constant c	$T(\exists x)\varphi(x)$ $\mid$ $T\varphi(c)$ for a new constant c	$F(\exists x)\varphi(x)$ $\mid$ $F\varphi(t)$ for any ground term t of $\mathcal{L}_C$

FIGURE 29

Intuitively the requirement that the constant introduced in cases 7b and 8a be "new" is easy to understand. The starting point of the tableau here is the assertion that an x with some property exists. There can be no danger in then asserting that c is such an x as long as we have no prior demands on c. On the other hand, if some other assertions have already been made about c, we have no right to assume that an element with these other properties can also be a witness for this new assertion. The precise syntactic meaning of "new" will be defined simultaneously with the inductive definition of *tableaux* as binary trees labeled with signed statements.

Definition 6.1: We define *tableaux* as binary trees labeled with signed sentences (of $\mathcal{L}_C$) called entries by induction:

(i) All atomic tableaux are tableaux. The requirement that c be new in cases 7b and 8a here simply means that c is one of the constants c_i added on to $\mathcal{L}$ to get $\mathcal{L}_C$ (which therefore does not appear in φ).

(ii) If τ is a finite tableau, P a path on τ, E an entry of τ occurring on P and τ' is obtained from τ by adjoining an atomic tableau with root entry E to τ at the end of the path P then τ' is also a tableau. Here the requirement that c be new in cases 7b and 8a means that it is one of the c_i which do not appear in any entries on P. [In actual practice it is simpler in terms of bookkeeping to choose one not appearing at any node of τ.]

(iii) If τ_0 is a finite tableau and $\tau_0, \tau_1, \ldots, \tau_n, \ldots$ is a sequence of tableaux such that for every $n \geq 0$, τ_{n+1} is constructed from τ_n by an application of (ii) then $\tau = \cup \tau_n$ is also a tableau.

Warning: It is crucial in the setting of predicate logic that the entry E in clause (ii) be repeated when the corresponding atomic tableau is added on to P (at least in cases 7a and 8b). The reason for this will become apparent once we analyze the action needed in these cases and the resulting definition of a finished tableau (Definition 6.7).

We would next like to define tableau proofs of sentences in predicate logic. It is important to realize, however, that in most situations one does not simply prove a sentence outright. One normally proves something based on various assumptions or axioms. The semantic aspect of this procedure was embodied in the notion of logical consequence in Definition 4.4. To capture the corresponding proof theoretic notion we need to define tableaux and proofs from premises for predicate logic analogous to the ones presented in I.6 for propositional logic. The modifications needed are like those incorporated in the definitions of I.6 for propositional logic. The key change is in the definition of a tableau from a set of sentences S. The underlying idea is that we are assuming that every sentence in S is true. Thus, in addition to the formation rules for ordinary tableaux, we may assert at any time that any sentence in S is true. We accomplish this by adding on one new formation rule for tableaux from S.

For the remainder of this section we let S be a set of sentences in the language $\mathcal{L}$. We often refer to the elements of S as *premises*.

Definition 6.1 (Continued): *Tableaux from S*. The definition for tableaux from S is the same as for ordinary tableaux except that we include an additional formation rule

(ii′) If τ is a finite tableau from S, φ a sentence from S, P a path on τ and τ' is obtained from τ by adjoining $T\varphi$ to the end of the path P then τ' is also a tableau from S.

From now on we will define our notions for tableaux from S simultaneously with the ones for ordinary tableaux. The additional clauses pertaining to tableaux from S are parenthesized, as in the following important observation.

Note: It is clear from the definition that every tableau τ (from S) is the union of a finite or infinite sequence $\tau_0, \tau_1, \ldots, \tau_n, \ldots$ of tableaux (from S) in which τ_0 is an atomic tableau and each τ_{n+1} is gotten from τ_n by an application of (ii) (or (ii′)). From now on, we will always assume that every tableau (from S) is presented as such a union.

Definition 6.2: *Tableau proofs (from S)*: Let τ be a tableau and P a path in τ.

(i) P is *contradictory* if, for some sentence α, $T\alpha$ and $F\alpha$ both appear as labels of nodes of P.

(ii) τ is *contradictory* if every path on τ is contradictory.

(iii) τ is a *proof of* α *(from S)* if τ is a finite contradictory tableau (from S) with its root node labeled $F\alpha$. If there is proof τ of α (from S), we say α is provable (from S) and write $\vdash \alpha$ $(S \vdash \alpha)$.

(iv) S is *inconsistent* if there is a proof of $\alpha \wedge \neg\alpha$ from S for some sentence α.

Note that, if there is any contradictory tableau (from S) with root node $F\alpha$, then there is one which is finite, i.e., a proof of α (from S). Just terminate each path when it becomes contradictory. As each path is now finite, the whole tree is finite by König's lemma. Thus, the added requirement that proofs be finite tableaux has no affect on the existence of proofs for any sentence. Another way of looking at this is that we could have required the path P in clause (ii) of the definition of tableaux (Definition 6.1) to be noncontradictory without affecting the existence of proofs.

Before describing the appropriate version of finished tableaux and the construction of complete systematic tableaux, it is instructive to look at some examples of proofs by tableaux in predicate logic. Note that we again abbreviate the tableaux by not repeating the entry being analyzed (or developed) unless we are dealing with either case 7a or 8b of the atomic tableaux.

Example 6.3: Suppose we want to check the validity of the formula $((\forall x)\varphi(x) \to (\exists x)\varphi(x))$. We form the following tableau:

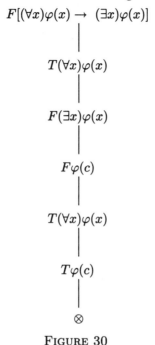

$$F[(\forall x)\varphi(x) \to (\exists x)\varphi(x)]$$

$$T(\forall x)\varphi(x)$$

$$F(\exists x)\varphi(x)$$

$$F\varphi(c)$$

$$T(\forall x)\varphi(x)$$

$$T\varphi(c)$$

$$\otimes$$

FIGURE 30

For the last entry we chose to use the same constant c as in the previous line so as to get the desired contradiction. We were able to do so because the atomic tableau for $\forall x\varphi(x)$ allows us to use *any* constant.

The next example also yields a contradictory tableau.

Example 6.4: See Figure 31.

In practice, it will generally prove more efficient to extend a tableau by first expanding the atomic tableaux which require the introduction of new terms and to then turn to those for which any ground term can be used.

Example 6.5: See Figure 32.

The atomic tableaux for $T(\forall x)\varphi(x)$ and $F(\exists x)\varphi(x)$ tell us that we can declare $\varphi(t)$ true or false, respectively, for any ground term t. On the other hand, the atomic tableau for $T(\exists x)\varphi(x)$ allows us to declare $\varphi(t)$ true only for one of the constants c_i which have not appeared so far in the tableau. The following example shows how we can get into trouble if we do not obey this proviso.

Example 6.6: Reverse the implication in Example 6.3 to get the sentence $((\exists x)\varphi(x) \to (\forall x)\varphi(x))$ which is not valid. If, however, we violate the provisions for using new constants, we can produce a "proof" of this sentence, as in Figure 33.

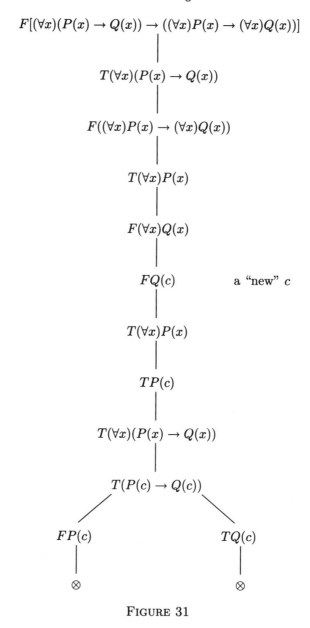

$$F[(\forall x)(P(x) \to Q(x)) \to ((\forall x)P(x) \to (\forall x)Q(x))]$$

$$T(\forall x)(P(x) \to Q(x))$$

$$F((\forall x)P(x) \to (\forall x)Q(x))$$

$$T(\forall x)P(x)$$

$$F(\forall x)Q(x)$$

$$FQ(c) \qquad \text{a "new" } c$$

$$T(\forall x)P(x)$$

$$TP(c)$$

$$T(\forall x)(P(x) \to Q(x))$$

$$T(P(c) \to Q(c))$$

$$FP(c) \qquad\qquad TQ(c)$$

$$\otimes \qquad\qquad\qquad \otimes$$

FIGURE 31

It is easy to see that tableaux in predicate logic need never terminate if no contradiction comes up. Thus, there is some question as to when we should say that an entry has been reduced and when a tableau is finished. To motivate these definitions, we first consider the role of the atomic tableaux for the quantifiers and how we use them in building tableaux. When we deal with $T(\exists x)\varphi(x)$ (or $F(\forall x)\varphi(x)$), we analyze it simply by listing $T\varphi(c)$ (or $F\varphi(c)$) for some constant c not yet appearing along the path being extended. The original sentence $(\exists x)\varphi(x)$ contains no more information

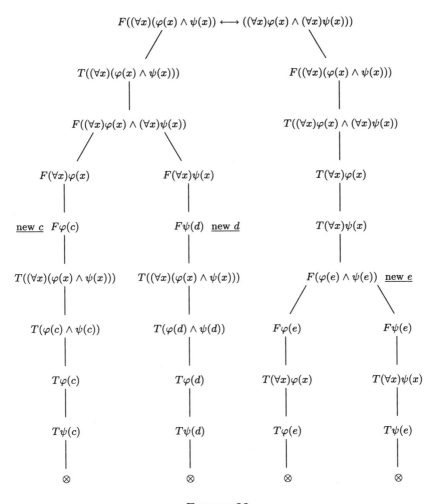

FIGURE 32

than the new one $\varphi(c)$ and so we may reasonably claim to have finished with it. On the other hand, if we are dealing with $T(\forall x)\varphi(x)$ (or $F(\exists x)\varphi(x)$) the situation is quite different. Here we may add $T\varphi(t)$ (or $F\varphi(t)$) to our tableau for any ground term t. This, however, far from exhausts the information in the original sentence. It merely gives us one instance of the universal fact asserted by $T(\forall x)\varphi(x)$. Thus, we cannot say that we have as yet finished with $T(\forall x)\varphi(x)$. With this distinction in mind we can define the notion of when an entry of a tableau has been reduced and when a tableau is finished. As in the propositional case, our goal is to describe a systematic procedure to produce a tableau proof (from S) of a given sentence φ. That this systematic procedure will always succeed if φ is valid (a logical consequence of S) will be the content of the Completeness Theorem (Theorem 7.7).

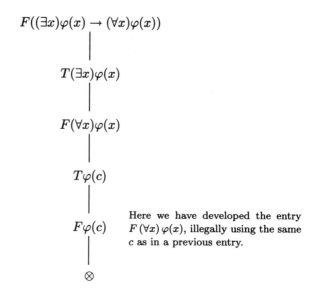

$$F((\exists x)\varphi(x) \to (\forall x)\varphi(x))$$

$$T(\exists x)\varphi(x)$$

$$F(\forall x)\varphi(x)$$

$$T\varphi(c)$$

$F\varphi(c)$ Here we have developed the entry $F\,(\forall x)\,\varphi(x)$, illegally using the same c as in a previous entry.

$\otimes$

FIGURE 33

Let $t_1, \ldots, t_n, \ldots$ be a list of all the ground terms of our language $\mathcal{L}_C$ which, we recall, includes the new constants c_i.

Definition 6.7: Let $\tau = \cup \tau_n$ be a tableau (from S), P a path in τ, E an entry on P and w the ith occurrence of E on P (i.e., the ith node on P labeled with E).

(i) w is *reduced on P* if

(1) E is neither of the form $T(\forall x)\varphi(x)$ nor $F(\exists x)\varphi(x)$ and, for some j, τ_{j+1} is gotten from τ_j by an application of rule (ii) of Definition 6.1 to E and a path on τ_j which is an initial segment of P. [In this case we say that E occurs on P as the root entry of an atomic tableau.]

     or

(2) E is of the form $T(\forall x)\varphi(x)$ or $F(\exists x)\varphi(x)$, $T\varphi(t_i)$ is an entry on P and there is an $j + 1^{\text{st}}$ occurrence of E on P.

(ii) τ is *finished* if every occurrence of every entry on τ is reduced on every noncontradictory path containing it (and $T\varphi$ appears on every noncontradictory path of τ for every φ in S). It is *unfinished* otherwise.

The idea here is that signed sentences such as $T(\forall x)\varphi(x)$ must be instantiated for each term t_i in our language before we can say that we have finished with them. We can now show that there is a finished tableau (from S) with any given entry on its root node by constructing the appropriate complete systematic tableau (from S). The plan is to devise an ordering procedure so that we can reduce each entry in turn to produce the finished tableau. We employ a variant on the lexicographic ordering on the nodes of the tableau.

Definition 6.8: Suppose T is a tree with a left–right ordering on the nodes at each of its levels. Recall (from I.1) that if T is, for example, a tree of binary sequences, the left–right ordering is given by the usual lexicographic ordering. We define the *level–lexicographic ordering* $\leq_{LL}$ on the nodes ν, μ of T as follows:

$\nu \leq_{LL} \mu \Leftrightarrow$ the level of ν in T is less than that of μ or ν and μ are on the same level of T and ν is to the left of μ.

Definition 6.9: We construct the CST, the *complete systematic tableau*, with any given signed sentence as the label of its root, by induction.

(i) We begin with τ_0 an atomic tableau with root the given signed sentence. This atomic tableau is uniquely specified by requiring that in cases 7a and 8b we use the term t_1 and that in cases 7b and 8a we use c_i for the least allowable i.

At stage n, we have, by induction, a tableau τ_n which we extend to one τ_{n+1}. As τ_n is a (finite, labeled) binary tree the level–lexicographic ordering is defined as above on its nodes. If every occurrence of every entry on T is reduced, we terminate the construction. Otherwise, let w be the level–lexicographically least node of τ_n which contains an occurrence of an entry E which is unreduced on some noncontradictory path P of τ_m. We now proceed according to one of the following two cases:

(ii) If E is not of the form $T(\forall x)\varphi(x)$ or $F(\exists x)\varphi(x)$, we adjoin the atomic tableau with apex E to the end of every noncontradictory path in τ that contains w. For E of the form $T(\exists x)\varphi(x)$ or $F(\forall x)\varphi(x)$, we use the least constant c_j not yet appearing in the tableau.

(iii) If E is of the form $T(\forall x)\varphi(x)$ or $F(\exists x)\varphi(x)$ and w is the ith occurrence of E on P we adjoin

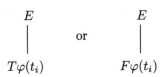

respectively, to the end of every noncontradictory path in τ containing w.

The CST from a set of premises S with a given root is defined like the ordinary CST above with one change to introduce the elements of S. At even stages $(n = 2k)$ we proceed as in (i), (ii) and (iii) above. At odd stages $(n = 2k+1)$ we adjoin $T\alpha_k$ for α_k the kth element of S to every noncontradictory path in τ_n to get τ_{n+1}. We do not terminate the construction of the CST from S unless all elements of S have been put on every noncontradictory path in this way and every occurrence of every entry is reduced on every path containing it.

Note that, in general, a CST will be an infinite tableau (even if S is finite). The crucial point is that it is always a finished tableau.

Proposition 6.10: *Every* CST *is finished.*

Proof: Consider any unreduced occurrence w of an entry E in $\tau_k \subseteq \tau$ which is on a noncontradictory path P of the given CST τ. (If there is none, τ is finished by definition.) Suppose there are n nodes of T which are level–lexicographically less than w. It is clear from the definition of the CST that we must reduce w on P by the time we form τ_{k+n+1}. Thus, every occurrence of each entry on a noncontradictory path in τ is reduced as required.

If we consider the CST from S, the same considerations apply to show that every entry is reduced on every path. (It just takes twice as many steps to get there.) The procedure of adding on the kth member of S at stage $2k+1$ guarantees that every element of S is put on every path of the CST from S. It is therefore a finished tableau from S. □

Example 6.11: Figure 34 gives an example of a finished tableau.

Exercises

In exercises 1–11, let φ and ψ be any formulas either with no free variables or with only x free as appropriate. Give tableau proofs of each of the following.

1. $(\exists x)(\varphi(x) \vee \psi(x)) \leftrightarrow (\exists x)\varphi(x) \vee (\exists x)\psi(x)$.
2. $(\forall x)(\varphi(x) \wedge \psi(x)) \leftrightarrow (\forall x)\varphi(x) \wedge (\forall x)\psi(x)$.
3. $(\varphi \vee (\forall x)\psi(x)) \rightarrow (\forall x)(\varphi \vee \psi(x))$, x not free in φ.
4. $(\varphi \wedge (\exists x)\psi(x)) \rightarrow (\exists x)(\varphi \wedge \psi(x))$, x not free in φ.
5. $(\exists x)(\varphi \rightarrow \psi(x)) \rightarrow (\varphi \rightarrow (\exists x)\psi(x))$, x not free in φ.
6. $(\exists x)(\varphi \wedge \psi(x)) \rightarrow (\varphi \wedge (\exists x)\psi(x))$, x not free in φ.
7. $\neg(\exists x)\varphi(x) \rightarrow (\forall x)\neg\varphi(x)$.
8. $(\forall x)\neg\varphi(x) \rightarrow \neg(\exists x)\varphi(x)$.
9. $(\exists x)\neg\varphi(x) \rightarrow \neg(\forall x)\varphi(x)$.
10. $(\exists x)(\varphi(x) \rightarrow \psi) \rightarrow ((\forall x)\varphi(x) \rightarrow \psi)$, x not free in ψ.
11. $((\exists x)\varphi(x) \rightarrow \psi) \rightarrow (\forall x)(\varphi(x) \rightarrow \psi)$, x not free in ψ.
12. Let φ and ψ be any formulas with free variables x, y and z; let w be any variable not appearing in φ or ψ. Give tableau proofs of the following.
    a) $\forall x \exists y \neg \forall z\, \varphi(x,y,z) \leftrightarrow \forall x \exists y \exists z \neg \varphi(x,y,z)$.
    b) $\exists x \forall y (\forall z \varphi \vee \psi) \leftrightarrow \exists x \forall y \forall w (\varphi(z/w) \vee \psi)$.
    c) $\forall x \exists y (\varphi \vee \exists z \psi) \leftrightarrow \forall x \exists y \exists w (\varphi \vee \psi(z/w))$.
    d) $\forall x \exists y (\varphi \rightarrow \forall z \psi(z)) \rightarrow \forall x \exists y \forall w (\varphi \rightarrow \psi(z/w))$.

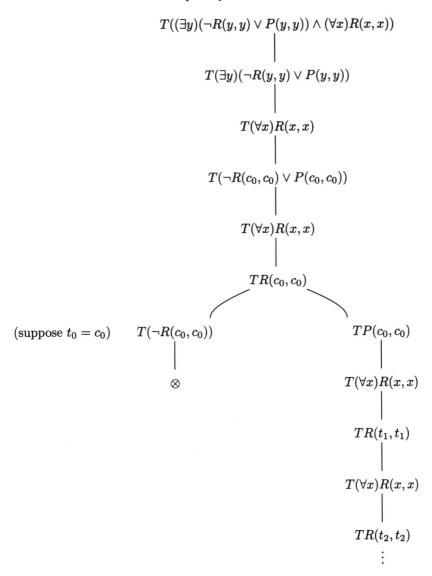

FIGURE 34

13. **Theorem on Constants:** Let $\varphi(x_1, \ldots, x_n)$ be a formula in a language $\mathcal{L}$ with all free variables displayed and let $c_1, \ldots, c_n$ be constant symbols not in $\mathcal{L}$. Show that $\forall x_1 \ldots \forall x_n \varphi(x_1, \ldots, x_n)$ is tableau provable iff $\varphi(c_1, \ldots, c_n)$ is. Argue syntactically to show that, given a proof of one of the formulas, one can construct a proof of the other. (You may assume the proof is given by the CST procedure.)

14. If the left–right orderings on each level of T is a well–ordering (i.e., every subset has a least element), then the ordering $\leq_{LL}$ is a well–ordering of the nodes of T.

7. Soundness and Completeness of Tableau Proofs

We can now exploit the complete systematic tableaux to prove the basic theorems about predicate logic and provability: Soundness, Completeness and Compactness. We begin with the soundness of proofs by tableaux in predicate logic. Throughout this section, $\mathcal{L}$ is a fixed language of predicate calculus and S is a set of sentences in $\mathcal{L}$. The case of pure tableaux, i.e., with no set S of premises, is simply the case $S = \emptyset$. This remark applies to all the results of this section and so we will deal only with the case of proofs and tableaux from S. The root nodes of our tableaux will also be taken from $\mathcal{L}$.

Lemma 7.1: *If $\tau = \cup \tau_n$ is a tableau from a set of sentences S with root $F\alpha$, then any $\mathcal{L}$-structure $\mathcal{A}$ which is a model of $S \cup \{\neg\alpha\}$ can be expanded to one agreeing with every entry on some path P through τ. (Recall that $\mathcal{A}$ agrees with $T\alpha$ ($F\alpha$) if α is true (false) in $\mathcal{A}$.)*

Proof: The only expansion of $\mathcal{A}$ that is necessary to make it a structure for all the sentences appearing in τ is to define $c_i^{\mathcal{A}}$ for the constants c_i in $\mathcal{L}_C - \mathcal{L}$ appearing on P. (Remember, these are the constants used in τ as the "new" constants in instantiations.)

We define P and $c_i^{\mathcal{A}}$ by an induction on the sequence τ_n giving the construction of τ. At each step n we will have a path P_n through τ_n and an extension $\mathcal{A}_n$ of $\mathcal{A}$ (with the same domain) which interprets all the c_i on P_n and agrees with P_n. This clearly suffices to prove the lemma. When τ_{n+1} is gotten from τ_n by extending some path other than P_n we need make no changes in P_n or $\mathcal{A}_n$. Suppose then that τ_{n+1} is gotten by adding on to the end of P_n either an atomic tableau with root E an entry on P_n or an element α_k of S. In the latter case we extend P_n in the only way possible by attaching α_k to its end. No extension of $\mathcal{A}_n$ is necessary and it agrees with α_k (and hence P_{n+1}) by hypothesis. We consider then the case of extending τ_n by adding on an atomic tableau τ' with root E. By induction we may assume that $\mathcal{A}_n$ agrees with E. We wish to extend $\mathcal{A}_n$ to $\mathcal{A}_{n+1}$ and find a path P_{n+1} extending P_n through τ_{n+1} agreeing with $\mathcal{A}_{n+1}$. (The base case of our induction is the atomic tableau τ_0 whose root $F\alpha$ agrees with $\mathcal{A}$ by hypothesis. The analysis of the base case is then exactly as in the inductive step: We wish to extend $\mathcal{A}$ to $\mathcal{A}_0$ and find a path P_0 through τ_0 agreeing with $\mathcal{A}_0$.) We consider each type of atomic tableau τ'.

(i) The situation for the propositional connectives is the same as in the proof of soundness for propositional logic (Lemma I.5.4). In particular, no extension of $\mathcal{A}_n$ is necessary. If, for example, we added on

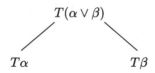

then we know by induction that $\mathcal{A}_n \vDash \alpha \vee \beta$ and so $\mathcal{A}_n \vDash \alpha$ or $\mathcal{A}_n \vDash \beta$. We choose to extend P_n accordingly. The analysis for the other propositional connectives is left as Exercise 7.

(ii) If we added on

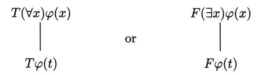

we again have no problem. $\mathcal{A}_n \vDash \forall x \varphi(x)$ (or $\mathcal{A}_n \vDash \neg\exists x \varphi(x)$) and so $\mathcal{A}_n \vDash \varphi(t)$ ($\mathcal{A}_n \vDash \neg\varphi(t)$). (Note that if $t^{\mathcal{A}}$ is not yet defined by our inductive procedure we can now define it arbitrarily and still maintain our inductive hypothesis as we know that $\mathcal{A}_n \vDash \forall x \varphi(x)$ (or $\mathcal{A}_n \vDash \neg\exists x \varphi(x)$).

(iii) Finally, if we added on

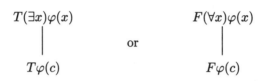

for some *new constant* symbol c (i.e., one not appearing either in S or in an entry on P_n), we must define $c^{\mathcal{A}}$. By induction, we know that $\mathcal{A}_n \vDash \exists x \varphi(x)(\mathcal{A}_n \vDash \neg\forall x \varphi(x))$ and so we may choose an element $a \in A$ ($= A_n$ by construction) such that, if we expand $\mathcal{A}_n$ to $\mathcal{A}_{n+1}$ by letting $c^{\mathcal{A}} = a$, we have $\mathcal{A}_{n+1} \vDash \varphi(c)(\mathcal{A}_{n+1} \vDash \neg\varphi(c))$ as required. $\square$

Theorem 7.2 (Soundness): *If there is a tableau proof τ of α from S, then $S \vDash \alpha$.*

Proof: If not, then there is a structure $\mathcal{A} \vDash \neg\alpha$ in which every α_k in S is true. Lemma 7.1 then tells us that there is a path P through τ and an expansion $\mathcal{A}'$ of $\mathcal{A}$ which agrees with every node on P. As P is contradictory by assumption, we have our desired contradiction. $\square$

We now turn to the completeness of the tableau method of proof for predicate logic. As in the propositional case (Theorem I.5.3 and especially Lemma I.5.4) the plan is to use a noncontradictory path in a CST to build a structure for $\mathcal{L}_C$ which agrees with every entry on P. The underlying idea here is to build the desired structure out of the only available materials — the syntactic objects, in particular, the ground terms appearing on the path. This idea and its application in the proof of the completeness theorem will be crucial ingredients in the proofs of many other important results including Herbrand's theorem (Theorem 10.4) and the Skolem–Löwenheim theorem (Theorem 7.7).

Theorem 7.3: *Suppose P is a noncontradictory path through a complete systematic tableau τ from S with root $F\alpha$. There is then a structure $\mathcal{A}$ in which α is false and every sentence in S is true.*

Proof: Let the domain of this structure be the set A of ground terms t_i on the master list of ground terms of our expanded language $\mathcal{L}_C$. We define the functions $f^{\mathcal{A}}$ associated with the n–ary function symbols f of our language in the natural way corresponding to the syntax of $\mathcal{L}_C$:

$$f^{\mathcal{A}}(t_{i_1}, t_{i_2}, \ldots, t_{i_n}) = f(t_{i_1}, \ldots, t_{i_n}).$$

Remember that the elements of our structure are the ground terms and so the t_i appearing on the left–hand side of this equation are being viewed as elements of our structure to which we apply the function $f^{\mathcal{A}}$. On the right–hand side we have another term, and so an element of our structure, which we declare to be the value of this function. If R is an n–ary predicate letter, we define $R^{\mathcal{A}}$ as dictated by the path P:

$$R^{\mathcal{A}}(t_{i_1}, \ldots, t_{i_n}) \iff TR(t_{i_1}, \ldots, t_{i_n}) \text{ is an entry on } P.$$

We now prove the theorem by establishing a slightly stronger assertion by induction.

Lemma 7.4: *Let the notation be as above.*

(i) *If $F\beta$ occurs on P, then β is false in $\mathcal{A}$.*

(ii) *If $T\beta$ occurs on P, then β is true in $\mathcal{A}$.*

Proof: First recall that, by Proposition 6.10, every occurrence of every entry on P is reduced on P. We now proceed by induction on the depth of β (more precisely, on the depth of the associated auxiliary formation tree as given in Definition 3.8).

(i) If β is an atomic sentence, then β is of the form $R(t_{i_1}, \ldots, t_{i_n})$. If $T\beta$ occurs on P then $R^{\mathcal{A}}$ has been declared true of $t_{i_1}, \ldots, t_{i_n}$. If $F\beta$ occurs on P then, as P is noncontradictory, $T\beta$ does not occur on P and $R^{\mathcal{A}}$ has been declared false of $t_{i_1}, \ldots, t_{i_n}$.

(ii) Suppose β is built using a connective, e.g., β is $(\beta_1 \vee \beta_2)$. As τ is finished, we know that if $T\beta$ occurs on P, then either $T\beta_1$ or $T\beta_2$ occurs on P. By induction hypothesis if $T\beta_1$ occurs on P then β_1 is true in $\mathcal{A}$ (and similarly for β_2). Thus, one of β_1, β_2 is true so $(\beta_1 \vee \beta_2)$ is true in $\mathcal{A}$ (by the inductive definition of truth). On the other hand, if $F(\beta_1 \vee \beta_2)$ appears on P, then we know that both $F\beta_1$ and $F\beta_2$ appear on P. Our inductive hypothesis then tells us that both β_1 and β_2 are false in $\mathcal{A}$. We then have that $(\beta_1 \vee \beta_2)$ is false in $\mathcal{A}$ as required. The cases for the other connectives are similar and are left as Exercise 8.

(iii) Suppose β is of the form $(\forall v)\varphi(v)$. If w is the ith occurrence of $T((\forall v)\varphi(v))$ on P, then $T\varphi(t_i)$ occurs on P and there is an $i+1^{\text{st}}$ occurrence of $T((\forall x)\varphi(x))$ on P. Thus, if $T((\forall v)\varphi(v))$ appears on P, then $\varphi(t)$ appears on P for every ground term t. As the depth of $\varphi(t)$ is less than that of $(\forall v)\varphi(v)$, the inductive hypothesis tells us that $\varphi(t)$ is true in $\mathcal{A}$ for every ground term t. As these terms constitute the universe of our structure $\mathcal{A}$, $(\forall v)\varphi(v)$ is true in $\mathcal{A}$ as required.

If $F(\forall v)\varphi(v)$ occurs on P then, again as τ is finished, $F\varphi(t)$ occurs on P for some t. By induction hypothesis $\varphi(t)$ is false in $\mathcal{A}$. So $(\forall v)\varphi(v)$ is false in $\mathcal{A}$.

(iv) The case for the existential quantifier $\exists v\varphi(v)$ is similar and is left as Exercise 9. $\square$

This also completes the proof of Theorem 7.3. $\square$

We now specialize our general remarks on the finiteness of proofs to complete systematic tableaux.

Proposition 7.5: *If every path of a complete systematic tableau is contradictory, then it is a finite tableau.*

Proof: By construction, we never extend a path on a CST once it is contradictory. Thus, every contradictory path on a CST is finite. The theorem then follows from König's lemma (Theorem I.1.4). $\square$

We have thus proven an effective version of the completeness theorem. For any given sentence α and any set of sentences S, we can produce either a proof that α is logical consequence of S or a model of S in which α fails.

Corollary 7.6: *For every sentence α and set of sentences S of $\mathcal{L}$, either*

(i) *the* CST *from S with root $F\alpha$ is a tableau proof of α from S*

or

(ii) *there is a noncontradictory branch through the complete systematic tableau which yields a structure in which α is false and every element of S is true.*

As the path in (ii) of Corollary 7.6 is countable (i.e., there is a one–one correspondence between its symbols (and hence its terms and formulas) and a subset of the natural numbers), so is the structure associated with it. We have thus also proven the Skolem–Löwenheim theorem. $\square$

Theorem 7.7 (Skolem–Löwenheim): *If a countable set of sentences S is satisfiable (that is, it has some model) then it has a countable model.*

Proof: Consider the CST from S that starts with a contradiction $\alpha \wedge \neg\alpha$ at its root. By the soundness theorem (Theorem 7.2) it cannot be a tableau proof of $\alpha \wedge \neg\alpha$ from S. Thus, it must have a noncontradictory path P. As there are only countably many ground terms in $\mathcal{L}_C$, the structure defined in the proof of Theorem 7.4 is the desired countable model of S. $\square$

The analogous theorem can also be proved for arbitrary cardinalities. Also note that we use countable in the sense of at most countable, that is the model may be finite. In our setting, however, one can always guarantee that the model is infinite (Exercise 3). One can guarantee that a set of sentences has only finite models only by the special treatment of equality which we consider in III.5. Ignoring the remarks on PROLOG, this treatment of equality can be read at this point.

We can reformulate Corollary 7.6, in analogy with the completeness and soundness theorems for propositional calculus, in terms of the equivalences between provability and logical consequence. The point to keep in mind is that, if α is false in some model for S, then it cannot be a logical consequence of S.

Theorem 7.8: (Completeness and Soundness):

(i) α *is tableau provable from S $\Leftrightarrow$ α is a logical consequence of S.*

(ii) *If we take α to be any contradiction such as $\beta \wedge \neg\beta$ in (i) we see that S is inconsistent if and only if S is unsatisfiable.* $\square$

The compactness theorem for predicate logic is also a consequence of these results.

Theorem 7.9 (Compactness): *Let $S = \{\alpha_1, \alpha_2, \dots\}$ be a set of sentences of predicate logic. S is satisfiable if and only if every finite subset of S is satisfiable.*

Proof: The only if direction is immediate. For the if direction consider the CST from S with root entry $F(\alpha \wedge \neg\alpha)$. If the CST is contradictory it is finite by Proposition 7.5. If it is infinite, it has a noncontradictory path and so by Corollary 7.6 there is a structure in which every α_i is true. If it is contradictory and finite then $\alpha \wedge \neg\alpha$ is a logical consequence of the finite subset of S whose elements are those appearing on this tableau. This finite subset can have no model as $\alpha \wedge \neg\alpha$ has no model. $\square$

We should point out one important difference between the completeness proofs for predicate and propositional logic. The finished tableaux for propositional logic were always finite and so for every proposition α we can effectively decide if it is valid or actually produce a counterexample. For predicate logic, if a given sentence φ is valid we eventually find a proof. On the other hand, if it is not valid, the finished tableau and the path providing a counterexample may well be infinite. Thus we may never in the course of our construction actually know that φ is not valid. This phenomena is unavoidable. Church's theorem states that there is no effective method for deciding if a given sentence in the predicate calculus is valid. We prove this result in Corollary III.8.10 as a corollary to a result on termination of PROLOG programs. A proof suitable for insertion at this point can, however, be based on the semantic approach indicated in Exercise III.8.3.

Exercises

1. Give a semantic proof of Exercise 6.13: Let $\varphi(x_1, \ldots, x_n)$ be a formula in a language $\mathcal{L}$ with all free variables displayed and let $c_1, \ldots, c_n$ be constant symbols not in $\mathcal{L}$. Show that $\forall x_1 \ldots \forall x_n \varphi(x_1, \ldots, x_n)$ is tableau provable iff $\varphi(c_1, \ldots, c_n)$ is by showing that $\varphi(x_1, \ldots, x_n)$ is valid iff $\varphi(c_1, \ldots, c_n)$ is valid. Now apply the completeness theorem.

2. Let $\mathcal{L}$ be any language which includes a binary relation symbol $\leq$ and S any set of sentences of $\mathcal{L}$ which has an infinite model and includes the axioms for linear orderings:

    (i) $(x \leq y) \vee (y \leq x)$ and

    (ii) $(x \leq y) \wedge (y \leq z) \to (x \leq z)$.

    (a) Show that there is a model $\mathcal{M}$ for S with an infinite descending chain, that is, one in which there are elements $c_0, c_1, \ldots$ such that $\ldots \leq c_{n+1} \leq c_n \leq \ldots \leq c_0$.

    (b) How can you also guarantee that $c_i \neq c_j$ for $i \neq j$?

    (This problem shows that the notion of well ordering is not definable in predicate logic.)

3. Let $\mathcal{L}$ be any language for predicate logic and S be any set of sentences in $\mathcal{L}$. Prove that S is satisfiable iff it has an infinite model.

4. Let $\mathcal{L}$ be a language for arithmetic on the natural numbers $\mathbb{N} (= \{0, 1, 2, \ldots\})$ including 0, 1, $+$, $\cdot$ and $>$. Let $Th(\mathbb{N})$ be the set of all sentences of $\mathcal{L}$ true in $\mathbb{N}$. Show that there is a nonstandard model of $Th(\mathbb{N})$, i.e., a structure $\mathcal{M}$ for $\mathcal{L}$ in which every sentence of $Th(\mathbb{N})$ is true but in which there is an element c greater than every $n \in \mathbb{N}$.

5. Reconsider the applications of compactness in the exercises for propositional logic. Use predicate logic to give considerably simpler proofs of Exercises I.6.7 and I.6.8. (Note that the planarity of a graph G is expressible in predicate logic since by a theorem of Kuratowski it is equivalent to two specific finite graphs not being subgraphs of G.)

6. **Deduction Theorem:** Let Σ be a finite set of sentences in a language $\mathcal{L}$ and $\wedge \Sigma$ the conjunction of its members. Prove that, for any sentence φ of $\mathcal{L}$, the following are equivalent:

    (i) $\Sigma \vDash \varphi$.

    (ii) $\vDash \wedge \Sigma \to \varphi$.

    (iii) $\Sigma \vdash \varphi$.

    (iv) $\vdash \wedge \Sigma \to \varphi$.

7. Complete the proof case (i) of Lemma 7.1 by describing the required extensions of P_n for the other propositional connectives.

8. Complete the proof case (ii) of Lemma 7.4 by handling the other propositional connectives.

9. Complete the proof of case (iv) of Lemma 7.4 by considering the case that β is $\exists v \varphi(v)$.

10. Let $\mathcal{L}$ be a language with no function symbols. Describe a procedure which, given any sentence ψ of the form $\forall x_1 \ldots \forall x_n \exists y_1 \ldots \exists y_m \varphi$, with φ quantifier free, decides if ψ is valid. (Hint: First use Exercise 6.13 to reduce the validity of ψ to that of $\exists y_1 \ldots \exists y_m \varphi(c_1, \ldots, c_n, y_1, \ldots, y_m)$ for new constants $c_1, \ldots, c_n$. Consider all formulas of the form $\varphi(c_1, \ldots, c_n, d_1, \ldots, d_m)$ where $d_i \in \{c_1, \ldots, c_n\}$. Apply the ideas of Theorem 4.8 and the methods of Chapter I to decide the validity of each of these sentences. If one is provable then so is φ. If none are provable, argue that $\neg \varphi$ has a model.)

11. Let R be a binary relation symbol, and let $R^{\mathcal{A}}$ be its interpretation in a structure $\mathcal{A}$. The *transitive closure* of $R^{\mathcal{A}}$ is the set of all pairs (a, b) for which there exists a finite $R^{\mathcal{A}}$–path from a to b, i.e., a sequence $a_0, a_1, \ldots, a_n$, $n \geq 1$, of elements of $\mathcal{A}$ with $a_0 = a$, $a_n = b$, and $R^{\mathcal{A}}(a_i, a_{i+1})$, $0 \leq i < n$. Show that transitive closure is not first–order definable; i.e., show that there does not exist a formula $TC(x, y)$ of predicate logic such that for all structures $\mathcal{A}$ and $a, b \in \mathcal{A}$, $\mathcal{A} \vDash TC(a, b)$ if and only if (a, b) is in the transitive closure of $R^{\mathcal{A}}$. (Hint: Define the formulas $\rho_n(x, y)$ inductively by:

$$\rho_1(x, y) \equiv R(x, y)$$
$$\rho_{n+1}(x, y) \equiv \exists z (R(x, z) \wedge \rho_n(z, y)).$$

Show that in any structure $\mathcal{A}$, the pair (a, b) is in the transitive closure of $R^{\mathcal{A}}$ iff $\mathcal{A} \vDash \rho_n(a, b)$ for some n. Suppose there were such a formula $TC(x, y)$ expressing the transitive closure of R. Consider the infinite set of sentences

$$\{TC(a, b)\} \cup \{\neg \rho_n(a, b) \mid n \geq 1\}.$$

Obtain a contradiction using the compactness of predicate logic.)

8*. An Axiomatic Approach

As for the propositional logic we give a brief sketch of a classical approach to predicate logic via axioms and rules. For the sake of brevity, we use as propositional connectives only $\neg$ and $\rightarrow$ as we did in I.7. In the same vein we view the existential quantifier $\exists$ as a defined symbol as well: We replace $\exists x \varphi(x)$ by $\neg \forall x \neg \varphi(x)$. (They are equivalent by Exercise 4.5.) We also fix some list of constants, function symbols and predicate symbols to complete our language $\mathcal{L}$. The axioms include the schemes (I.7.1) for propositional logic but now the variables α, β and γ range over all formulas of $\mathcal{L}$. In addition we include two schemes that express the meaning of the universal quantifier. Note that we are considering all formulas, not just sentences and remember that validity for a formula with free variables is the same as for its universal closure.

8.1 Axioms: Let α, β and γ be any formulas of $\mathcal{L}$. The axioms of our system are all formulas of $\mathcal{L}$ of the following forms:

(i) $(\alpha \rightarrow (\beta \rightarrow \alpha))$

(ii) $((\alpha \rightarrow (\beta \rightarrow \gamma)) \rightarrow ((\alpha \rightarrow \beta) \rightarrow (\alpha \rightarrow \gamma)))$

(iii) $((\neg\alpha) \rightarrow (\alpha \rightarrow \beta))$

(iv) $(\forall x)\alpha(x) \rightarrow \alpha(t)$ for any term t which is substitutable for x in α.

(v) $(\forall x)(\alpha \rightarrow \beta) \rightarrow (\alpha \rightarrow (\forall x)\beta)$ if α contains no free occurrences of x.

It is easy to check that all instances of these axiom schemes are valid. The restriction in (iv) is necessary as we explained when we defined substitutability (Definition 2.8). Recall that we considered in Example 2.9 (ii) the structure $\mathbb{Z}$ of the integers with constants for 0 and 1, a function s for successor and a predicate $A(x, y, z)$ which is interpreted as $x + y = z$. In particular, we considered the true sentence $\varphi = \forall x \exists y A(x, y, 0)$. As a true universal sentence, φ should be true of any object. Indeed (iv) asserts that any permissible substitution results in a formula valid in $\mathbb{Z}$. On the other hand, if we substitute $s(y)$ for x we get $\forall x \exists y A(s(y), y, 0)$ which is false in $\mathbb{Z}$. As for the restriction in (v), consider the true (in $\mathbb{Z}$) sentence $\varphi = \forall x(\forall y A(x, y, y) \rightarrow A(x, 1, 1))$. If we could ignore the restriction in (v) we could conclude from φ (via the rule of modus ponens given below) that $\forall y A(x, y, y) \rightarrow \forall x A(x, 1, 1))$. This formula is not valid in $\mathbb{Z}$ as can be seen by setting the free occurrence of x to 0. (This substitution only affects the left side of the implication by making it the true sentence $\forall y A(0, y, y)$. The right side of the implication is, however, false.)

Our system has two rules of inference. The first rule is modus ponens applied to the formulas of $\mathcal{L}$. The second captures one direction of the equivalence between the validity of a formula with free variables and that of its universal closure. (The other direction is included in axiom scheme (iv). Just take t to be x.)

8.2 The rules of inference:

(i) *Modus Ponens*: From α and $\alpha \rightarrow \beta$, we can infer β for any formulas α and β.

(ii) *Generalization*: From $\forall x \alpha$ infer α.

As in propositional logic, such axiom and rule based systems are generally called Hilbert–style proof systems. The definition of a proof from a set of formulas Σ is the same as for propositional logic except that we have more axioms and rules.

Definition 8.3: Let Σ be a set of formulas of $\mathcal{L}$.

(i) A *proof from* Σ is a finite sequence $\alpha_1, \alpha_2, \ldots \alpha_n$ of formulas of $\mathcal{L}$ such that, for each $i \leq n$, one of the following is true:

   (1) α_i is a member of Σ;

   (2) α_i is an axiom;

   (3) α_i can be inferred from some of the previous α_j by an application of a rule of inference.

(ii) α is *provable* (a *theorem*) *from* Σ if there is a proof $\alpha_1, \ldots, \alpha_n$ from Σ with $\alpha_n = \alpha$.

(iii) A *proof* of α is simply a proof from $\emptyset$. α is provable if it is *provable* from $\emptyset$.

The standard soundness, completeness and compactness theorems can be proven for the system presented here. It is taken from Elliot Mendelson's *Introduction to Mathematical Logic* [1964, 3.2] and a development of predicate logic using it can be found there. In §13, we will extend the rule based system of resolution to a fragment of predicate logic and prove the corresponding results for it.

9. Prenex Normal Form and Skolemization

We would like to show that, in a certain sense, predicate logic can almost be reduced to propositional logic. Roughly speaking, we want to eliminate the quantifiers by introducing new function symbols and terms. The basic idea is that a formula such as:

$$\varphi = \forall x_1 \ldots \forall x_n \exists y_1 \ldots \exists y_m R(x_1, \ldots, x_n, y_1, \ldots, y_m)$$

will be replaced by one

$$\psi = \forall x_1 \ldots \forall x_n R(x_1, \ldots, x_n, f_1(x_1, \ldots, x_n), f_2(x_1, \ldots, x_n),$$
$$\ldots, f_n(x_1, \ldots, x_n)).$$

Here each f_i is a new function symbol. The intended interpretation of f_i is as a function choosing, for any given $x_1, \ldots, x_n$, a y_i which makes the formula true if one exists. Such functions are called Skolem functions. It is clear that φ and ψ are equisatisfiable (i.e., φ is satisfiable iff ψ is) and so we could try to find a tableau (or other) refutation of ψ just as well as one of φ. In order to reap the full benefits from such a procedure, it is convenient to first replace φ by an equivalent formula φ' called a *prenex normal form* of φ in which all the quantifiers are at the beginning. We can then hope to eliminate successive blocks of quantifiers $\forall \vec{x} \exists \vec{y}$ by introducing appropriate Skolem functions. The ultimate goal is to get a *universal formula* ψ (i.e., one with only universal quantifiers which all occur as the initial symbols of ψ) which is *equisatisfiable* with the original φ. (We say that φ and ψ are *equisatisfiable* if both are satisfiable or if neither are.) We would then only need to consider universal formulas in any refutation proof scheme. (Of course, we have resolution in mind.)

As we know how to replace all uses of connectives by expressions involving only $\neg$ and $\lor$ (they form an adequate set of connectives by Corollary I.2.11), we assume for convenience that our given formula φ has no other connectives. We will show how to find a prenex equivalent for such a φ. We first need the basic moves to handle $\neg$ and $\lor$.

Lemma 9.1: *For any string of quantifiers* $\overrightarrow{Qx} = Q_1 x_1 Q_2 x_2 \ldots Q_n x_n$ *(each Q_i is $\forall$ or $\exists$) and any formulas φ, ψ we have the following provable* *equivalences:*

(1a) $\vdash \overrightarrow{Qx}\neg\forall y\varphi \leftrightarrow \overrightarrow{Qx}\exists y\neg\varphi.$

(1b) $\vdash \overrightarrow{Qx}\neg\exists y\varphi \leftrightarrow \overrightarrow{Qx}\forall y\neg\varphi.$

(2a) $\vdash \overrightarrow{Qx}(\forall y\varphi \vee \psi) \leftrightarrow \overrightarrow{Qx}\forall z(\varphi(y/z) \vee \psi).$

(2a′) $\vdash \overrightarrow{Qx}(\varphi \vee \forall y\psi) \leftrightarrow \overrightarrow{Qx}\forall z(\varphi \vee \psi(y/z)).$

(2b) $\vdash \overrightarrow{Qx}(\exists y\varphi \vee \psi) \leftrightarrow \overrightarrow{Qx}\exists z(\varphi(y/z) \vee \psi).$

(2b′) $\vdash \overrightarrow{Qx}(\varphi \vee \exists y\psi) \leftrightarrow \overrightarrow{Qx}\exists z(\varphi \vee \psi(y/z)).$

where z is a variable not occurring in φ or ψ or among the x_i.

Proof: Tableaux proofs of such equivalences are fairly simple and are left as exercises. (Samples of (1), (2a) and (2b′) were given in Exercise 6.12 (a), (b) and (c) respectively.) Alternatively one can argue semantically for the equivalences and then apply the completeness theorem. (Exercise 4.5 essentially gives (1a) and (1b).) A general approach to these equivalences is outlined in Exercises 1–3.

Note: In the context of resolution proofs, the practice of renaming variables as in 2a and 2b to avoid possible conflicts is often called *standardizing the variables apart.*

We can now prove that every formula φ has a prenex equivalent.

Theorem 9.2 (Prenex Normal Form): *For every formula φ there is an equivalent formula φ' with the same free variables in which all quantifiers appear at the beginning. Such an equivalent of φ is called a prenex normal form (PNF) of φ.*

Proof: By induction on the depth of φ. Remember that, by Corollary I.2.11, we may assume that the only propositional connectives occurring in φ are $\neg$ and $\vee$. If φ is atomic there is nothing to prove. If φ is $\forall y\psi$ or $\exists y\psi$ and ψ' is a PNF of ψ then $\forall y\psi'$ or $\exists y\psi'$ is one for φ. (This fact is the base case for the induction in Exercise 1.) If $\varphi = \neg\psi$ and ψ' is a PNF of ψ then repeated applications of the clauses (1a) and (1b) of the lemma will produce the desired PNF for φ. If $\varphi = \psi \vee \theta$ then repeated applications of the clauses (2a), (2a′), (2b) and (2b′) will give the result for φ. $\square$

Note: One can easily introduce prenexing rules that deal directly with the other connectives. The following equivalences may be used to put formulas in PNF without first eliminating any of the connectives except $\leftrightarrow$:

(3a) $\vdash \overrightarrow{Qx}(\forall y\varphi \wedge \psi) \leftrightarrow \overrightarrow{Qx}\forall z(\varphi(y/z) \wedge \psi).$

(3a′) $\vdash \overrightarrow{Qx}(\varphi \wedge \forall y\psi) \leftrightarrow \overrightarrow{Qx}\forall z(\varphi \wedge \psi(y/z)).$

(3b) $\vdash \overrightarrow{Qx}(\exists y\varphi \wedge \psi) \leftrightarrow \overrightarrow{Qx}\exists z(\varphi(y/z) \wedge \psi).$

(3b′) $\vdash \overrightarrow{Qx}(\varphi \wedge \exists y\psi) \leftrightarrow \overrightarrow{Qx}\exists z(\varphi \wedge \psi(y/z)).$

(4a) $\vdash \overrightarrow{Qx}(\forall y\varphi \rightarrow \psi) \leftrightarrow \overrightarrow{Qx}\exists z(\varphi(y/z) \rightarrow \psi).$

(4a′) $\vdash \overrightarrow{Qx}(\varphi \rightarrow \forall y\psi) \leftrightarrow \overrightarrow{Qx}\forall z(\varphi \rightarrow \psi(y/z)).$

(4b) $\vdash \overrightarrow{Qx}(\exists y\varphi \rightarrow \psi) \leftrightarrow \overrightarrow{Qx}\forall z(\varphi(y/z) \rightarrow \psi).$

(4b′) $\vdash \overrightarrow{Qx}(\varphi \rightarrow \exists y\psi) \leftrightarrow \overrightarrow{Qx}\exists z(\varphi \rightarrow \psi(y/z)).$

Again z is a variable not occurring on the left–hand side of the equivalences.

Example 9.3: We find PNF's for two formulas:

(i) $\forall x \exists y P(x, y) \vee \neg \exists x \forall y Q(x, y)$:

$\forall u [\exists y P(u, y) \vee \neg \exists x \forall y Q(x, y)]$

$\forall u \exists v [P(u, v) \vee \neg \exists x \forall y Q(x, y)]$

$\forall u \exists v [P(u, v) \vee \forall x \neg \forall y \; Q(x, y)]$

$\forall u \exists v [P(u, v) \vee \forall x \exists y \neg Q(x, y)]$

$\forall u \exists v \forall w [P(u, v) \vee \exists y \neg Q(w, y)]$

$\forall u \exists v \forall w \exists z [P(u, v) \vee \neg Q(w, z)]$.

(ii) $\forall x \forall y [(\exists z)(P(x, z) \wedge P(y, z)) \rightarrow \exists u Q(x, y, u)]$:

$\forall x \forall y \forall w [P(x, w) \wedge P(y, w) \rightarrow \exists u Q(x, y, u)]$

$\forall x \forall y \forall w \exists z [P(x, w) \wedge P(y, w) \rightarrow Q(x, y, z)]$.

(iii) Alternatively we could get a different PNF for (i) as follows:

$\forall u [\exists y P(u, y) \vee \neg \exists x \forall y Q(x, y)]$

$\forall u [\exists y P(u, y) \vee \forall x \neg \forall y \; Q(x, y)]$

$\forall u \forall w [\exists y P(u, y) \vee \neg \forall y Q(w, y)]$

$\forall u \forall w \exists v [P(u, v) \vee \neg \forall y Q(w, y)]$

$\forall u \forall w \exists v [P(u, v) \vee \exists y \neg Q(w, y)]$

$\forall u \forall w \exists v \exists z [P(u, v) \vee \neg Q(w, z)]$.

We can now reduce the problem of giving refutation proofs of arbitrary sentences of the predicate calculus to that for universal ones.

Theorem 9.4 (Skolemization): *For every sentence φ in a given language $\mathcal{L}$ there is a universal formula φ' in an expanded language $\mathcal{L}'$ gotten by the addition of new function symbols such that φ and φ' are equisatisfiable.*

(Note that we do not claim that the formulas are equivalent. The procedure will always produce a φ' such that $\varphi' \rightarrow \varphi$ is valid but $\varphi \rightarrow \varphi'$ need not always hold. See Exercise 9.4 for an example.)

Proof: By Theorem 9.2 we may assume that φ is in prenex normal form. Let $y_1, \dots, y_n$ be the existentially quantified variables of φ in the order in which they appear in φ from left to right and, for each $i \leq n$, let $x_1, \dots, x_{n_i}$ be all the universally quantified variables preceding y_i. We expand $\mathcal{L}$ to $\mathcal{L}'$ by adding new n_i–ary function symbols f_i for each $i \leq n$. We now form φ' by first deleting each $\exists y_i$ and then replacing each remaining occurrence of y_i by $f_i(x_1, \dots, x_{n_i})$. We claim that φ' is the desired sentence equisatisfiable with φ. To verify this claim it suffices to apply the following lemma n times:

Lemma 9.5: *For any sentence $\varphi = \forall x_1 \dots \forall x_n \exists y \psi$ of a language $\mathcal{L}$, φ and $\varphi' = \forall x_1 \dots \forall x_n \psi(y/f(x_1, \dots, x_n))$ are equisatisfiable when f is a function symbol not in $\mathcal{L}$.*

Proof: Let $\mathcal{L}'$ be the language obtained from $\mathcal{L}$ by adding the function symbol f. It is clear that if $\mathcal{A}'$ is a structure for $\mathcal{L}'$, $\mathcal{A}$ is the structure obtained from $\mathcal{A}'$ by omitting the function interpeting f and $\mathcal{A}' \vDash \varphi'$, then $\mathcal{A} \vDash \varphi$. On the other hand, if $\mathcal{A}$ is a structure for $\mathcal{L}$ and $\mathcal{A} \vDash \varphi$, we can expand $\mathcal{A}$ to a structure $\mathcal{A}'$ by defining $f^{\mathcal{A}'}$ so thatfor every $a_1, \ldots, a_n \in A = A'$, $\mathcal{A} \vDash \psi(y/f(a_1, \ldots, a_n))$. Of course, $\mathcal{A}' \vDash \varphi'$. Note that n may be 0, that is, f may be a constant symbol. $\square$

Corollary 9.6: *For any set S of sentences of a language $\mathcal{L}$ we can construct a set S' of universal sentences of a language $\mathcal{L}'$ which is an expansion of $\mathcal{L}$ gotten by adding on new function symbols such that S and S' are equisatisfiable.*

Proof: Apply the construction supplied by Theorem 9.4 to each sentence φ of S separately to introduce new function symbols f_φ for each sentence φ of S and form the corresponding universal sentence φ'. Let S' be the collection of all of these sentences φ' and $\mathcal{L}'$ the corresponding expansion of $\mathcal{L}$. As in the proof of the theorem it is clear that, if a structure $\mathcal{A}'$ for $\mathcal{L}'$ is a model of S', then it is one of S. The proof also shows how to expand any model of S to one of S' by defining each new function symbol f_φ independently of what is done for the others. $\square$

Example 9.7: Possible Skolemizations corresponding to the prenex normal forms of Example 9.3 above are as follows:

    (i) $\forall u \forall w [P(u, f_1(u)) \vee \neg Q(w, f_2(u, w))]$

    (ii) $\forall x \forall y \forall w [P(x, w) \wedge P(y, w) \rightarrow Q(x, y, f(x, y, w))]$

and

    (iii) $\forall u \forall w [P(u, f_1(u, w)) \vee \neg Q(w, f_2(u, w))]$.

Example 9.8: There are many familiar examples of Skolemization in the construction of axiom systems for standard mathematical structures such as groups or rings. In these situations, axioms of the form $\forall x \exists y \varphi(x, y)$ can be replaced by open formulas of the form $\varphi(x, f(x))$ by introducing the appropriate Skolem functions.

As a particular example let us reconsider the structure of Example 2.9 for the integers $\mathbb{Z}$ and the sentence $\forall x \exists y A(x, y, 0)$ which says that every integer has an additive inverse. The Skolemization of this sentence is $\forall x A(x, f(x), 0)$. The interpretation of f should be the unary function taking every integer x to its additive inverse $-x$. The Skolemized sentence then simply says that, for all x, $x + (-x) = 0$.

Harking back to the clausal forms for predicate calculus introduced in §5, we now see that every set of sentences has an equisatisfiable clausal form.

Corollary 9.9: *For any set S of sentences of $\mathcal{L}$, there is (in the terminology of §5) a formula, that is, a set T of clauses in a language $\mathcal{L}'$ gotten by adding new function symbols to $\mathcal{L}$ such that S and T are equisatisfiable.*

Proof: Consider the set S' of universal sentences $\forall \vec{x} \varphi'(\vec{x})$ equisatisfiable with S given by Corollary 9.6. Let T' consist of the equivalent open formulas $\varphi'(\vec{x})$ gotten by dropping the initial universal quantifiers from the elements of S'. (φ and φ' are equivalent by Exercise 4.8 or 6.13.) If we view each atomic formula of $\mathcal{L}'$ as a propositional letter and form the CNF equivalent $\psi_\varphi = \wedge \psi_{\varphi,i}$ of each formula $\varphi' \in T'$, we get a set of formulas T'' each in CNF and each equivalent to the one of $T' : \wedge \psi_{\varphi,i} = \psi_\varphi \equiv \varphi' \equiv \varphi$ for each $\varphi \in S$. (For each φ, ψ_φ is equivalent to φ' by Theorem 4.8.) The desired set T of clauses then consists precisely of the set of all conjuncts from all of the formulas φ in $T'' : T = \{\psi_{\varphi,i} \mid \varphi \in S\}$. $\square$

Exercises

1. Let φ and ψ be any formulas (with free variables) and let $\overrightarrow{Qx} = Q_1 x_1 Q_2 x_2 \ldots Q_n x_n$ be any string of quantifiers. Prove that if φ and ψ are equivalent then so are $\overrightarrow{Qx}\varphi$ and $\overrightarrow{Qx}\psi$. (Hint: proceed by induction on the length n of $\overrightarrow{Qx}$.) Thus in proving the equivalences (1a)–(4b′) we may assume that the formulas have free variables but the strings $\overrightarrow{Qx}$ of initial quantifiers are empty.

2. Use the theorem on constants (Exercise 4.8) to show that we may also assume that there are no free variables in formulas in the equivalences (1a)–(4b′).

3. Now argue for the validity of each equivalence (1a)–(4b′) either semantically or by giving a tableau proof. (Use exercises 1 and 2 to assume that the $\overrightarrow{Qx}$ are empty and that there are no free variables present.)

4. Let $\varphi(x, y)$ be an atomic formula and f a function symbol not appearing in φ. Show that the sentence $\forall x \varphi(x, f(x)) \rightarrow \forall x \exists y \varphi(x, y)$ is valid but its converse, $\forall x \exists y \varphi(x, y) \rightarrow \forall x \varphi(x, f(x))$, is not.

5. Find prenex equivalents and Skolemizations for the following sentences:
   (a) $\forall y (\exists x P(x, y) \rightarrow Q(y, z)) \wedge \exists y (\forall x R(x, y) \vee Q(x, y))$.
   (b) $\exists x R(x, y) \leftrightarrow \forall y P(x, y)$.
   (c) $\forall x \exists y Q(x, y) \vee \exists x \forall y P(x, y) \wedge \neg \exists x \exists y P(x, y)$.
   (d) $\neg(\forall x \exists y P(x, y) \rightarrow \exists x \exists y R(x, y)) \wedge \forall x \neg \exists y Q(x, y)$.

10. Herbrand's Theorem

The introduction of Skolem functions and the reduction of any set of sentences to universal ones gives us a more concrete approach to the dichotomy of unsatisfiability and model building implicit in the completeness theorem for tableau proofs. Consider any set S of universal sentences in a language $\mathcal{L}$ with various Skolem functions already included. We also assume that $\mathcal{L}$ contains at least one constant c. We claim that either S is inconsistent (i.e., unsatisfiable) or there is a model $\mathcal{A}$ of S whose elements are simply the ground terms of the language $\mathcal{L}$. As all such terms must be interpreted in any structure for $\mathcal{L}$, this is in some sense a minimal structure for $\mathcal{L}$.

Definition 10.1: The set of ground (i.e., variable–free) terms of a language $\mathcal{L}$ is called the *Herbrand universe* of $\mathcal{L}$. A structure $\mathcal{A}$ for $\mathcal{L}$ is an *Herbrand structure* if its universe A is the Herbrand universe of $\mathcal{L}$ and, for every function symbol f of $\mathcal{L}$ and elements $t_1, \dots, t_n$ of A,

$$f^{\mathcal{A}}(t_1, \dots, t_n) = f(t_1, \dots, t_n).$$

(We include here the requirement that $c^{\mathcal{A}} = c$ for each constant symbol c of $\mathcal{L}$.)

The Herbrand universe is reminiscent of the structure produced in the proof of the completeness theorem (Theorem 7.3). As we shall see, they are intimately related. Note also that no restrictions are placed on the interpretations of the predicates of $\mathcal{L}$ so there can be many Herbrand structures for a given language $\mathcal{L}$.

Definition 10.2: If S is a set of sentences of $\mathcal{L}$ then an *Herbrand model* $\mathcal{M}$ of S is an Herbrand structure for $\mathcal{L}$ which is a model of S, i.e., every sentence of S is true in $\mathcal{M}$.

Example 10.3: If our language $\mathcal{L}$ contains the constants a and c, a unary function symbol f and a binary one g and predicates P, Q, R then the Herbrand universe H for $\mathcal{L}$ is $\{a, c, f(a), f(c), g(a, c), ff(a), ff(c), f(g(a, c)), g(a, f(a)), g(a, f(c)), g(a, g(a, c)), \dots, g(f(a), f(c)), \dots, fff(a), \dots\}$.

We claim not only that there is an Herbrand model for any consistent set of universal sentences (or open formulas) S but also that, if S is inconsistent, then its unsatisfiability is demonstrable at the truth–functional level via ground instances of the formulas (that is, instances of substitutions of terms from the Herbrand structure for the universally quantified (free) variables in S).

Theorem 10.4 (Herbrand's Theorem): *Let* $S = \{\varphi_i(x_1, \dots, x_{n_i})\}$ *be a set of open formulas of a language $\mathcal{L}$. Either*

(i) *S has an Herbrand model or*

(ii) *S is unsatisfiable and, in particular, there are finitely many ground instances of elements of S whose conjunction is unsatisfiable.*

The latter case, (ii), is equivalent to

(ii′) *There are finitely many ground instances of the negations of formulas of S whose disjunction is valid. (As we may view these ground instances as built from propositional letters, the disjunction being valid is equivalent to its being a truth–functional tautology.)*

Proof: Let S' consist of all ground instances from $\mathcal{L}$ of formulas from S. Consider the CST from S' (in the language $\mathcal{L}$ alone, i.e., with no additional constant symbols added on) starting with $F(\alpha \wedge \neg\alpha)$ for any sentence α. There are two possible outcomes. First, there might be a (possibly infinite) noncontradictory path in the tableau. In this case, the proof of Theorem 7.3 supplies us with a model $\mathcal{A}$ of S' whose elements are the ground terms of $\mathcal{L}$, i.e., an Herbrand model for S'. By definition of S' and of tableau proofs from S', $\varphi(t_1, \ldots, t_n)$ is true in $\mathcal{A}$ for every $\varphi \in S$ and every $t_1, \ldots, t_n$ in the Herbrand universe. Thus the structure $\mathcal{A}$ defined on the Herbrand universe by the path is a model for S.

The other possibility is that the tableau is finite and contradictory. In this case, the tableau is, by definition, a proof of the unsatisfiability of the set of elements of S' appearing in the tableau and so we have the unsatisfiable conjunction required in (ii). Moreover, S cannot be satisfiable: A model for S is one in which $\varphi_i(x_1, \ldots, x_{n_i})$ is valid, i.e., true for every instance of the free variables $x_1, \ldots, x_{n_i}$, for every $\varphi_i \in S$. Any example of (ii), however, directly exhibits a set of such instances which cannot be simultaneously satisfied in any model.

Finally, by Theorem 4.8 we may manipulate the variable–free formulas as propositional letters. The unsatisfiability of the conjunction as required in (ii) is then equivalent by propositional rules to the disjunction of their negations being valid or a tautology. Thus, (ii) and (ii') are equivalent. $\square$

Note that if S is unsatisfiable (and so (i) fails), then (ii) directly exhibits the unsatisfiability of S. Thus we have a method for producing either an Herbrand model for S or a particular finite counterexample to the existence of any model of S.

We can now give some variations on Herbrand's theorem which will be particularly useful in our study of resolution theorem proving and PRO-LOG. We can also phrase our results positively to give a direct reduction of provability or validity in predicate logic to provability or validity in propositional logic. We begin with the special case of an existential formula.

Corollary 10.5: *If $\varphi(\vec{x})$ is a quantifier–free formula in a language $\mathcal{L}$ with at least one constant symbol, then $\exists \vec{x}\varphi(\vec{x})$ is valid if and only if there are ground terms $\vec{t_i}$ of $\mathcal{L}$ such that $\varphi(\vec{t_1}) \vee \ldots \vee \varphi(\vec{t_n})$ is a tautology.*

Proof: First, note that $\exists \vec{x}\varphi(\vec{x})$ is valid $\Leftrightarrow$ $\forall \vec{x}\neg\varphi(\vec{x})$ is unsatisfiable $\Leftrightarrow$ $\neg\varphi(\vec{x})$ is unsatisfiable. By Theorem 10.4 (ii), $\neg\varphi(\vec{x})$ is unsatisfiable iff there are finitely many ground terms $\vec{t_i}$ of $\mathcal{L}$ such that $\varphi(\vec{t_1}) \vee \ldots \vee \varphi(\vec{t_n})$ is a tautology. $\square$

Translating these results into the terminology of clauses of §5, we have what will be the key to resolution theorem proving in the predicate calculus.

Theorem 10.6: *A set S of clauses is unsatisfiable if and only if the set S' of all ground instances from the Herbrand universe of the clauses in S is unsatisfiable.*

Proof: If some set of instances of elements of S (instantiated with terms from the Herbrand universe) is unsatisfiable then S, which asserts the validity of its member clauses, is surely unsatisfiable. In the other direction, if S is unsatisfiable then, by Herbrand's theorem (ii), there is, in fact, a finite set of instances of clauses of S which is unsatisfiable. $\square$

The restriction in our version of Herbrand's theorem that S contain only universal formulas (or equivalently that we consider only sets of clauses) is necessary as can be seen from the example in Exercise 1. On the other hand, further restricting S to consists of only program clauses allows us to establish the existence of minimal and indeed least Herbrand models. (See Exercises 3.) Moreover, in the case of a deduction from a set of program clauses, which is the case of interest for PROLOG, we can eliminate the disjunction in the analog of Corollary 10.5 in favor of a single valid instance. That is, if P is a set of program clauses and $\theta(\vec{x})$ is an atomic formula, then $P \vDash \exists \vec{x} \theta(\vec{x}) \Leftrightarrow$ there are Herbrand terms $\vec{t}$ such that $P \vDash \theta(\vec{t})$ (Exercise 5).

Finally, although it is not directly relevant to resolution theorem proving, we can use Skolemization to get a generalization of Corollary 10.5 to arbitrary sentences. This result provides a propositional equivalent for validity in predicate logic.

Theorem 10.7: *Let φ be a sentence in prenex normal form in a language $\mathcal{L}$, ψ a prenex equivalent of $\neg\varphi$ and $\theta(\vec{x})$ an open Skolemization of ψ in the language $\mathcal{L}'$ as in Theorem 9.4. (Note that the free variables in ψ are precisely the existentially quantified ones of φ.) Then φ is valid if and only if there are terms $\vec{t}_1, \ldots, \vec{t}_n$, of $\mathcal{L}'$ such that $\neg\theta(\vec{t}_1) \vee \ldots \vee \neg\theta(\vec{t}_n)$ is a tautology.*

Proof: By Corollary 10.5, it suffices to prove that φ is valid if and only if $\exists \vec{x} \neg \theta(\vec{x})$ is valid. Now φ is valid iff $\neg\varphi$ is not satisfiable. On the other hand, Theorem 9.4 says that $\neg\varphi$ is satisfiable if and only if $\theta(\vec{x})$ is satisfiable. Thus, φ is valid iff $\theta(\vec{x})$ is not satisfiable. Finally, note that $\theta(\vec{x})$ (or, equivalently, $\forall \vec{x} \theta$) is not satisfiable iff $\exists \vec{x} \neg \theta(\vec{x})$ is valid. $\square$

Exercises

1. Let $\mathcal{L}$ consist of the constant c and the unary predicate R.

   (a) What is the Herbrand universe for $\mathcal{L}$?

   (b) What are the possible Herbrand structures for $\mathcal{L}$?

   (c) Let $S = \{R(c), \exists x \neg R(x)\}$. Note that S does not consist solely of universal formulas and so is not in clausal form. Show that while S is satisfiable, it has no Herbrand model.

2. Let $\mathcal{L}$ consist of the constants c and the function symbol f.

   (a) What is the Herbrand universe for $\mathcal{L}$?

   (b) Describe infinitely many possible Herbrand structures for $\mathcal{L}$.

3. Prove that every set P of program clauses has a minimal (indeed least) Herbrand model. (Hint: Prove that the intersection of all Herbrand models for P is itself an Herbrand model for P.)

4. Let M_P be the minimal Herbrand model for a set P of program clauses in a language $\mathcal{L}$. Prove that for each atomic formula φ of $\mathcal{L}$, $M_P \vDash \varphi$ iff φ is a logical consequence of P.

5. Let P be a set of program clauses and $G = \neg\theta(\vec{x})$ be a goal clause. Prove that, if $P \vDash \exists\vec{x}\theta(\vec{x})$ (or equivalently, $P \cup \{G\}$ is unsatisfiable), then there are Herbrand terms $\vec{t}$ such that $P \vDash \theta(\vec{t})$. (Hint: If $P \vDash \exists\vec{x}\theta(\vec{x})$, look at the minimal model $\mathcal{M}_P$ and apply Exercise 4.)

11. Unification

We saw in Theorem 9.4 that, for every formula φ of predicate logic, there is another one ψ which is open, in conjunctive normal form and equisatisfiable with φ. Thus if we are interested in the satisfiability of (sets of) formulas in predicate logic, it suffices to consider open formulas in clausal form. The only difference from the propositional case is that literals are now atomic formulas (possibly with free variables and the added Skolem function symbols) rather than simply propositional letters. Of course, a clause with free variables is understood to be equivalent to its universal closure. From the viewpoint of resolution theorem proving, the only difference between predicate and propositional logic in deducing $\square$ from S is the problem of how to instantiate the free variables (i.e., make substitutions) in the available clauses so that we may then apply the reduction rule.

Of course, we could, as in the tableau proof of Herbrand's theorem, simply list all ground term substitutions in the Herbrand structure and start running our resolution machine with all of them as inputs. Needless to say, this is not an efficient procedure. We need a better guide.

For example, if we have $C_1 = \{P(f(x), y), \neg Q(a, b, x)\}$ and $C_2 = \{\neg P(f(g(c)), g(d))\}$ we should be able to resolve C_1 and C_2 by directly substituting $g(c)$ for x and $g(d)$ for y to get $\{\neg Q(a, b, g(c))\}$. (Remember that C_1 is equivalent to its universal closure $\forall x\forall y(P(f(x), y) \vee \neg Q(a, b, x))$ from which we can deduce any substitution instance.) The general approach to the problem of which substitutions to make when doing resolution proofs is called *unification* (or *matching*). We describe it before giving the resolution algorithm for predicate calculus. First, we need some notation for substitutions.

Definition 11.1: A *substitution* θ is a finite set of the form $\{x_1/t_1, x_2/t_2,$ $\ldots, x_n/t_n\}$ where the x_i are distinct variables and each t_i is a term other than x_i. If the t_i are all ground terms, we call θ a *ground substitution*. If the t_i are distinct variables, we call θ a *renaming substitution*.

As we are concerned with substitutions in clauses, we must define the action of θ on a clause C. In order to define the composition (successive application) of different substitutions, it is convenient to define the action of a substitution θ on terms as well.

Definition 11.2: An *expression* is any term or literal. Given a substitution θ and an expression E (or a set of expressions S) we write $E\theta$ ($S\theta$) for the result of replacing each occurrence of x_i in E (in every element of S), by t_i for every $i \leq n$. If the resulting expression $E\theta$ (set of expressions $S\theta$) is ground, i.e., variable–free, then the substitution is called a *ground instance* of E (S).

Note: The substitution θ is written as a set of elements of the form x_i/t_i rather than as a sequence of such terms because the intended substitutions of t_i for each x_i are performed simultaneously rather than successively. Thus, in $E\{x_1/t_1, x_2/t_2\}$, any occurrences of x_2 in t_1 will be unaffected by the substitution of t_2 for x_2.

Example 11.3:

(i) Let $S = \{f(x, g(y)), P(a, x), Q(y, z, b), \neg P(y, x)\}$ and $\theta = \{x/h(a),$ $y/g(b), z/c\}$. Then $S\theta = \{f(h(a), g(g(b)), P(a, h(a)), Q(g(b), c, b),$ $\neg P(g(b), h(a))\}$. Here θ is a ground substitution and $S\theta$ is a ground instance of S.

(ii) Let S be as in (i) and let $\sigma = \{x/h(y), y/g(z), z/c\}$. Then $S\sigma = \{f(h(y), g(g(z))), P(a, h(y)), Q(g(z), c, b), \neg P(g(z), h(y))\}$.

Composition is a natural operation on substitutions, i.e., we want to define $\theta\sigma$ to be the substitution which when applied to any expression E to get $E(\theta\sigma)$ gives the same result as applying σ to $E\theta$, i.e., $(E\theta)\sigma$.

Example 11.4: Let $E = P(x, y, w, u)$, $\theta = \{x/f(y), y/g(z), w/v\}$ and $\sigma = \{x/a, y/b, z/f(y), v/w, u/c\}$. Then $E\theta = P(f(y), g(z), v, u)$ and $(E\theta)\sigma = P(f(b), g(f(y)), w, c)$. What then should $\theta\sigma$ be? Well, x is replaced first by $f(y)$. We then replace y by b. The result is $x/f(b)$. y is replaced by $g(z)$ and then z by $f(y)$ and so we get $y/g(f(y))$. w gets replaced by v which is in turn replaced by w. The result might be written w/w but this is omitted from the description as it causes no changes. The substitution x/a in σ also has no bearing on the final outcome since there are no $x's$ left after applying θ. The final substitution in σ, u/c, however, acts unimpeded as there is no substitution for u made by θ. Thus $\theta\sigma = \{x/f(b), y/g(f(y)), u/c\}$.

Guided by this example we can write out the formal definition of composition of substitutions.

Definition 11.5:

(i) If $\theta = \{x_1/t_1, \ldots, x_n/t_n\}$ and $\sigma = \{y_1/s_1, \ldots, y_m/s_m\}$ then $\theta\sigma$ is $\{x_1/t_1\sigma, \ldots, x_n/t_n\sigma, y_1/s_1, \ldots, y_m/s_m\}$ less any $x_i/t_i\sigma$ for which $x_i = t_i\sigma$ and any y_j/s_j for which $y_j \in \{x_1, \ldots, x_n\}$.

(ii) The *empty substitution* ϵ (which does nothing to any expression) is an identity for this operation, i.e., $\theta\epsilon = \epsilon\theta = \theta$ for every substitution θ.

We now check that we have defined composition correctly and that it is associative.

Proposition 11.6: *For any expression E and substitutions θ, ψ, and σ:*

(i) $(E\theta)\sigma = E(\theta\sigma)$ *and*

(ii) $(\psi\theta)\sigma = \psi(\theta\sigma)$.

Proof: Let θ and σ be as in the definition of composition and let $\psi = \{z_1/r_1, \ldots, z_k/r_k\}$. As the result of a substitution consists simply of replacing each variable in an expression by some term, it suffices to consider the case in which E is a variable, say v, in (i) and the result of applying $(\psi\theta)\sigma$ and $\psi(\theta\sigma)$ to v in (ii).

(i) We divide the argument into two cases.

Case 1: $v \notin \{x_1, \ldots, x_n\}$. In this case $v\theta = v$ and $(v\theta)\sigma = v\sigma$. If $v \notin \{y_1, \ldots, y_m\}$ then $v\sigma = v = v(\theta\sigma)$ as $v \notin \{x_1, \ldots, x_n, y_1, \ldots, y_m\}$ and so no substitution is made. If, on the other hand, $v = y_j$ for some $j \leq n$ then $y_j \notin \{x_1, \ldots, x_n\}$, $(v\theta)\sigma = v\sigma = s_j = v(\theta\sigma)$.

Case 2: $v = x_i$ for some $i \leq n$. In this case $v\theta = t_i$ and $(v\theta)\sigma = t_i\sigma$ but this is exactly $v(\theta\sigma)$ by definition.

(ii) The result follows from several applications of (i):

$$
\begin{aligned}
v((\psi\theta)\sigma) &= (v(\psi\theta))\sigma \\
&= ((v\psi)\theta)\sigma \\
&= (v\psi)(\theta\sigma) \\
&= v(\psi(\theta\sigma)) \qquad \square
\end{aligned}
$$

Thus we may omit parentheses when composing sequences of compositions. The composition operation on substitutions is, however, not commutative. (Exercise 3 asks for a counterexample.)

Our interest in substitutions, we recall, is to make certain elements of different clauses identical so that we may apply the resolution rule. The process of making substitutions that identify expressions is called *unification*.

Definition 11.7: If $S = \{E_1, \ldots, E_n\}$ is a set of expressions we say a substitution θ is a *unifier* for S if $E_1\theta = E_2\theta = \ldots = E_n\theta$, i.e., $S\theta$ is a singleton. S is said to be *unifiable* if it has a unifier.

Example 11.8: (i) Neither $\{P(x, a), P(b, c)\}$ nor $\{P(f(x), z), P(a, w)\}$ are unifiable. (Exercise 2).

(ii) $S_1 = \{P(x, c),\ P(b, c)\}$ and $S_2 = \{P(f(x), y), P(f(a), w)\}$ are, however, both unifiable. The first can be unified by $\{x/b\}$ and only by this substitution. The situation for S_2 is a bit different. $\theta = \{x/a, y/w\}$ unifies S_2 but so do $\sigma = \{x/a, y/a, w/a\}$ and $\psi = \{x/a, y/b, w/b\}$ as well as many others. Here θ has a certain advantage over the other substitutions in that it allows more scope for future substitutions. If we first applied θ to unify S_2 we could then unify the resulting set with the expression $P(f(a), c)$ by applying $\{w/c\}$. Had we used either of σ or ψ, however, we would be stuck. On the other hand, we can always go from θ to σ or ψ by applying the substitution $\{w/a\}$ or $\{w/b\}$ respectively. We capture this property of θ in the following definition.

Definition 11.9: A unifier θ for S is a *most general unifier (mgu) for S* if for every unifier σ for S there is a substitution λ such that $\theta\lambda = \sigma$.

Up to renaming variables there is only one result of applying an mgu:

Theorem 11.10: *If θ and ψ are both mgu's for S then there are renaming substitutions σ and λ (i.e., ones which consist solely of replacements of distinct variables by other distinct variables) such that $S\theta\sigma = S\psi$ and $S\theta = S\psi\lambda$.*

Proof: By the definition of an mgu there are σ and λ such that $S\theta\sigma = S\psi$ and $S\psi\lambda = S\theta$. Clearly, we may assume that σ and λ make substitutions only for variables occurring in $S\theta$ and $S\psi$ respectively. (They consist of the single terms $E\theta$ and $E\psi$, respectively, as θ and ψ both unify S.) Suppose σ makes some substitution x_i/t_i where t_i is not a variable or a constant. In this case the complexity (e.g., length) of the expression $E\theta\sigma$ in $S\theta\sigma = \{E\theta\sigma\}$ must be strictly larger than that of $E\theta$ in $S\theta$. As no substitutions of terms for variables (e.g., λ) can decrease the length of an expression we could not then have $S\psi\lambda = S\theta\sigma\lambda = S\theta$ as required. If there were in σ a substitution x_i/c, for some constant c, then no further substitution (e.g., λ) could return the resulting instances of c in an expression $E\theta\sigma$ in $S\theta\sigma$ back to instances of the variable x_i in $E\theta \in S\theta$. Thus, once again, we could not have $S\theta\sigma\lambda = S\theta$ for any λ. We now know that σ can contain only substitutions of one variable by another. If σ identified distinct variables by such a substitution, then λ could not distinguish them again. Thus σ (and similarly λ) is simply a renaming substitution. $\square$

Exercises

1. Find substitutions which will unify the following sets of expressions.
   (a) $\{P(x, f(y), z), P(g(a), f(w), u), P(v, f(b), c)\}$.
   (b) $\{Q(h(x, y), w), Q(h(g(v), a), f(v)), Q(h(g(v), a), f(b))\}$.
2. Explain why neither expression in Example 8 (i) is unifiable.

3. Show that composition of substitutions is not commutative, that is, find two substitutions σ and λ such that $\sigma\lambda \neq \lambda\sigma$.

4. We say that expressions E and F are *variants* (or E is a variant of F) if there are substitutions θ and ψ such that $E\theta = F$ and $F\psi = E$. Recall that a renaming substitution is one of the form $\{x_1/y_1, \ldots, x_n/y_n\}$ where $x_1, \ldots, x_n$ are distinct variables in E and the $y_1, \ldots, y_n$ are distinct variables not including any variables in E other than perhaps some of $x_1, \ldots, x_n$. Prove that if E and F are variants, then there is a renaming substitution σ for E such that $E\sigma = F$.

12. The Unification Algorithm

In this section we will give an effective procedure for finding an mgu for a finite set of expressions S. We start with two illustrations, $S_1 = \{f(x, g(x)), f(h(y), g(h(z)))\}$ and $S_2 = \{f(h(x), g(x)), f(g(x), h(x))\}$. We begin our search for mgu's for S_1 and S_2 by noting that in each case the terms to be unified begin with f. Of course, if they each began with different function or predicate symbols there would be no hope as unification only replaces variables. The next step must be to check the first and second place arguments of f in the terms of S_1 (S_2). If we can unify them both by a single substitution, then we can unify S_1 (S_2). For S_1, we get $T_1 = \{x, h(y)\}$ and $T_2 = \{g(x), g(h(z))\}$ respectively. In order to unify T_1 in the most general way, we should substitute $h(y)$ for x. As we must do the substitution throughout the expressions being unified, the second place arguments in T_2 become $g(h(y))$ and $g(h(z))$. These first differ at y. We can now unify them by applying $\{y/z\}$. Again this must be applied to the entire expression and we get $f(h(z), g(h(z)))$ and $f(h(z), g(h(z)))$ as required for unification. Thus the composition $\{x/h(y)\}\{y/z\} = \{x/h(z)\}$ is our desired unifier. For S_2 the process halts when we try to unify the arguments of f. Here the first difference occurs in the set of first arguments where we get $\{h(x), g(x)\}$. As these terms differ at the function symbol rather than at a variable there is no hope of unifying them and so S_2 is not unifiable.

The general procedure for unification is to move along each of the expressions in the given set to the first position of disagreement. If, in any one of the expressions, it is not a variable the set is not unifiable. If it does not contain a variable in one of the expressions, we can replace it by one of the terms in the corresponding position at another expression. As long as the variable being replaced does not occur in the term replacing it, this substitution makes some progress towards unification. We can now try to repeat the process in the hope of eventually unifying the set of expressions. We now formalize this process.

Definition 12.1: Let S be a finite nonempty set of expressions. To define the *disagreement set* of S find the first (i.e., leftmost) position at which not all elements E of S have the same symbol. The set of subexpressions of each $E \in S$ that begin at this position is the disagreement set $D(S)$ of S. (In terms of formation trees, we find the lexicographically least node of the formation trees associated with each expression such that not all the labels of these nodes begin with the same symbol. $D(S)$ is then the set of labels of these nodes.)

Note that any unifier ψ of S must necessarily unify $D(S)$.

Example 12.2: For $S_1 = \{f(x, g(x)), f(h(y), g(h(z)))\}$ and $S_2 = \{f(h(x), g(x)), f(g(x), h(x))\}$ as above, the disagreement sets are $D(S_1) = \{x, h(y)\}$ and $D(S_2) = \{h(x), g(x)\}$. For $T_1 = S_1\{x/h(y)\} = \{f(h(y), g(h(y))), f(h(y), g(h(z)))\}$ the disagreement set is $\{y, z\}$.

12.3 The Unification Algorithm for S: Let S be a set of expressions. We attempt to unify it as follows:

Step 0. Set $S_0 = S$, $\sigma_0 = \epsilon$.

Step $k + 1$. If S_k is a singleton, terminate the algorithm with the announcement that $\sigma_0\sigma_1\sigma_2 \ldots \sigma_k$ is an mgu for S. Otherwise, see if there is a variable v and a term t not containing v both of which are in $D(S_k)$. If not, terminate the algorithm with the announcement that S has no mgu. (Note that, in this case, it is at least clear that S_k is not unifiable.) If so, let v and t be the least such pair (in any fixed ordering of terms). (Indeed, we could nondeterministically choose any such t and v as will become clear from the proof that the algorithm succeeds.) Set $\sigma_{k+1} = \{v/t\}$ and $S_{k+1} = S_k\sigma_{k+1}$ and go on to step $k + 2$.

Example 12.4: Consider the set of expressions

$$S = \{P(f(y, g(z)), h(b)),\ P(f(h(w), g(a)), t),\ P(f(h(b), g(z)), y)\}.$$

Step 1. $S = S\epsilon = S_0\sigma_0$ is not a singleton. $D(S_0) = \{y, h(w), h(b)\}$. Depending on the ordering of terms, there are two possibilities for σ_1: $\{y/h(w)\}$ and $\{y/h(b)\}$. It is better to choose the second (see step 2) but suppose we are not so clever and blindly set $\sigma_1 = \{y/h(w)\}$. We then get $S_1 = S_0\sigma_1$ which is

$\{P(f(h(w), g(z)), h(b)),\ P(f(h(w), g(a)), t),\ P(f(h(b), g(z)), h(w))\}.$

Step 2. $D(S_1) = \{w, b\}$, $\sigma_2 = \{w/b\}$ (and so we get to $\{y/h(b)\}$ after all). Then S_2 is

$\{P(f(h(b), g(z)), h(b)),\ P(f(h(b), g(a)), t),\ P(f(h(b), g(z)), h(b))\}.$

Step 3. $D(S_2) = \{z, a\}$, $\sigma_3 = \{z/a\}$. Then S_3 is

$\{P(f(h(b), g(a)), h(b)),\ P(f(h(b), g(a)), t),\ P(f(h(b), g(a)), h(b))\}.$

Step 4. $D(S_3) = \{h(b), t\}$, $\sigma_4 = \{t/h(b)\}$. Then S_4 is

$\{P(f(h(b), g(a)), h(b)),\ P(f(h(b), g(a)), h(b)),\ P(f(h(b), g(a)), h(b))\}.$

Step 5. S_4 is a singleton and the mgu for S is

$\{y/h(w)\}\{w/b\}\{z/a\}\{t/h(b)\} = \{y/h(b), w/b, z/a, t/h(b)\}.$

Theorem 12.5: *For any S, the unification algorithm terminates at some step $k+1$ with a correct solution, i.e., either S is not unifiable as announced or $\psi = \sigma_0 \sigma_1 \ldots \sigma_k$ is in fact an mgu for S. Moreover, ψ has the special property that for any unifier θ of S, $\theta = \psi \theta$.*

Proof: First of all, the algorithm always terminates as each nonterminal step eliminates all occurrences of one of the finitely many variables in S. It is obvious that if the algorithm terminates with an announcement that there is no unifier, then S is not unifiable. On the other hand, if the algorithm terminates with the announcement that $\psi = \sigma_0 \ldots \sigma_n$ is an mgu for S, then it is at least clear that ψ is a unifier for S. Suppose then that θ is any unifier for S. We must show that $\theta = \psi \theta$. We prove by induction that, for every i, $\theta = \sigma_0 \ldots \sigma_i \theta$.

For $i = 0$, the claim clearly holds. Suppose we have $\theta = \sigma_0 \sigma_1 \ldots \sigma_i \theta$ and $\sigma_{i+1} = \{v/t\}$. It suffices to show that the substitutions $\sigma_{i+1}\theta$ and θ are equal. We show that their actions on each variable are the same. For $x \neq v$, $x\sigma_{i+1}\theta$ is clearly the same as $x\theta$. For v itself $v\sigma_{i+1}\theta = t\theta$. As θ unifies $S\sigma_0 \ldots \sigma_i$ and v and t belong to $D(S\sigma_0 \ldots \sigma_i)$, θ must unify v and t as well, i.e., $t\theta = v\theta$ as required. $\square$

The unification algorithm given here is simple but inefficient. As presented, it is the search for a v and t with v not occurring in t that can take excessive amounts of time. The problem is that we may have to check each pair of items in the disagreement set rather than simply taking the first variable and term that we come across. As an example, consider the problem of unifying $S = \{P(x_1, \ldots, x_n), P(f(x_0, x_0), \ldots, f(x_{n-1}, x_{n-1}))\}$:

$$D(S_0) = \{x_1, f(x_0, x_0)\}; \quad \sigma_1 = \{x_1/f(x_0, x_0)\};$$
$$S_1 = \{P(f(x_0, x_0), x_2, \ldots, x_n), P(f(x_0, x_0),$$
$$f(f(x_0, x_0), f(x_0, x_0)), f(x_2, x_2), \ldots, f(x_{n-1}, x_{n-1}))\}.$$
$$D(S_1) = \{x_2, f(f(x_0, x_0), f(x_0, x_0))\}; \quad \sigma_2 = \{x_2/f(f(x_0, x_0), f(x_0, x_0))\};$$
$$\text{etc.}$$

Note that before announcing σ_1 we had to check that x_1 was not either of the two occurrences of variables in $f(x_0, x_0)$. For σ_2 there were four occurrences to check. In general $D(S_{i+1})$ will have twice as many occurrences of variables as $D(S_i)$ and so the "occurs check" takes exponential time.

More efficient (even linear time) procedures for unification are now available (Martelli and Montanari [1982, 5.4]). Unfortunately, all current PROLOG implementations simply omit the "occurs check". They simply take the first variable x in $D(S_k)$ and substitute for it the first term t other than x in $D(S_k)$ in the expressions contributing x to $D(S_k)$. Thus, the implementations believe that $S = \{x, f(x)\}$ is unifiable. (They cannot actually carry out the substitution. They would try to replace x by $f(x)$ and then return to x which would again be replaced by $f(x)$ and so on forever.) Needless to say, this type of unification destroys the soundness of the resolution method. Some protections against such incorrect deductions can be put into programs. We will discuss one in III.2 after we have more fully described the actual deduction procedure of PROLOG. Unfortunately, almost nothing the programmer can do can fully compensate for omitting the occurs check. We will, however, prove (Corollary II.8.7) that certain programs sufficient to calculate all effective functions do in fact run correctly even without the occurs check.

Exercises

1. Apply the unification algorithm to each of the following sets to find an mgu or show that none exists.

   (a) $\{P(x, y), P(y, f(z))\}$

   (b) $\{P(a, y, f(y)), P(z, z, u)\}$

   (c) $\{P(x, g(x)), P(y, y)\}$

   (d) $\{P(x, g(x), y), P(z, u, g(a)), P(a, g(a), v)\}$

   (e) $\{P(g(x), y), P(y, y), P(y, f(u))\}$

2. Apply the unification algorithm to each of the following sets to find mgu's or show that they are not unifiable.

   (a) $\{P(h(y), a, z), P(hf(w), a, w), P(hf(a), a, u)\}$

   (b) $\{P(h(y), a, z), P(hf(w), a, w), P(hf(a), a, b)\}$

13. Resolution

We now describe how to combine unification with the resolution method for propositional logic to give a proof scheme for full predicate logic. As before, we consider formulas in clausal form. Remember, however, that literals are now atomic formulas or their negations with free variables allowed. The results of §9 and §10 show that, as long as we are willing to add function symbols to our language, every sentence has an equisatisfiable version in clausal form. Note that all the variables in a sentence S are local, that is, each clause is understood as its universal closure. S is then the conjunction of the universally quantified clauses. Thus, there are no connections between the variables of distinct clauses. To reflect this syntactically, we will generally rename variables when using two clauses together so that they have no variables in common. (This procedure is called *standardizing the variables apart.*)

As in the propositional case, clauses with at most one positive literal are called *Horn clauses*. The rest of the terminology from Definition I.10.4 (or II.5.1) describing *program clauses, rules, facts* and *goals*, is also carried over intact from the propositional case. Thus, for example, a (PROLOG) *program* is a formula which contains only program clauses, that is ones with exactly one positive literal. We continue to use PROLOG notation.

Example 13.1: Consider the following list of clauses:

mother (X,Y) :− daughter(Y,X), female (X).	(1)
mother (X,Y) :− son (Y,X), female (X).	(2)
daughter (X,Y) :− mother (Y,X), female (X).	(3)
son (X,Y) :− mother (Y,X), male (X).	(4)
father (X,Y) :− son (Y,X), male (X).	(5)
father (X,Y) :− daughter (Y,X), male (X).	(6)
daughter (X,Y) :− father (Y,X), female(X).	(7)
son (X,Y) :− father (Y,X), male (X).	(8)
male (jim).	(9)
male (tim).	(10)
female(jane).	(11)
female (pam).	(12)
father (jim, tim).	(13)
father (jim, pam).	(14)
mother (jane, tim).	(15)
mother (jane, pam).	(16)

These clauses are the PROLOG versions of

$$\{\{\text{mother}(x, y), \neg\text{daughter}(y, x), \neg\text{female}(x)\},$$
$$\{\text{mother}(x, y), \neg\text{son}(y, x), \neg\text{female}(x)\},$$

$$\vdots$$

$$\{\text{mother}(\text{jane}, \text{pam})\}\}.$$

Which are in turn the clausal forms of

$$\forall x \forall y [\text{daughter}(y, x) \wedge \text{female}(x) \rightarrow \text{mother}(x, y)] \wedge$$
$$\forall x \forall y [\text{son}(y, x) \wedge \text{female}(x) \rightarrow \text{mother}(x, y)] \wedge$$
$$\dots \wedge$$
$$\dots \wedge$$
$$\dots \wedge$$
$$\text{mother}(\text{jane}, \text{pam}).$$

Definition 13.2: Suppose that we can rename the variables of C_1 and C_2 so that they have no variables in common and are of the form $C_1' \sqcup \{P\vec{t}_1, \dots, P\vec{t}_n\}$ and $C_2' \sqcup \{\neg P\vec{s}_1, \dots, \neg P\vec{s}_m\}$ respectively. If σ is an mgu for $\{P\vec{t}_1, \dots, P\vec{t}_n, P\vec{s}_1, \dots, P\vec{s}_m\}$ then $C_1'\sigma \cup C_2'\sigma$ is a *resolvent* of C_1 and C_2. ($C_1'\sigma \cup C_2'\sigma$ is also called the *child* of the *parents* C_1 and C_2.)

Resolution proofs of C from S and resolution refutations of S in both linear and tree form are now defined as in the propositional case (Definitions I.8.4 and I.8.6) except that we use the version of the resolution rule given above and allow the premises inserted from S, or equivalently the leaves of the tree proof, to be $C\sigma$ for any renaming substitution σ and any $C \in S$. Similarly, we define $\mathcal{R}(S)$ as the closure under resolution of the set of all renamings of elements of S.

Two points should be noted in this definition of resolvent. The first is that the renaming of variables is necessary. For example, the sentence $\{\{P(x)\}, \{\neg P(f(x))\}\}$ is (unsatisfiable and) resolution refutable but the clauses cannot be unified without renaming the variables. The second point is that we cannot assume in the above definition that n or m are equal to 1 as we did in propositional logic. We must be able to eliminate several literals at once. (This aspect of the procedure is often called *factoring*.) As an example, consider $S = \{\{P(x), P(y)\}, \{\neg P(x), \neg P(y)\}\}$. It is (unsatisfiable and) resolution refutable but no resolution proof from S which eliminates only one literal at a time can produce $\square$.

Example 13.3:

(i) We can resolve

$$C_1 = \{Q(x), \neg R(y), P(x,y), P(f(z), f(z))\}$$

and

$$C_2 = \{\neg N(u), \neg R(w), \neg P(f(a), f(a)), \neg P(f(w), f(w))\}$$

to get

$$C_3 = \{Q(f(a)), \neg R(f(a)), \neg N(u), \neg R(a)\}.$$

To do this we unify $\{P(x, y), P(f(z), f(z)), P(f(a), f(a)), P(f(w), f(w))\}$ via the mgu $\{x/f(a), y/f(a), z/a, w/a\}$ and perform the appropriate substitutions and union on C_1 and C_2.

(ii) From the clauses corresponding to (3) and (16) in Example 13.1 above, we can form the resolvent $\{\text{daughter(pam, jane)}, \neg\text{female(pam)}\}$ by the substitution $\{X/\text{pam}, Y/\text{jane}\}$.

Example 13.4:

(i) From (a) and (b) below we wish to conclude (c):

   (a) $\forall x \forall y \forall z[P(x,y) \wedge P(y,z) \rightarrow P(x,z)]$ (transitivity)   and

   (b) $\forall x \forall y[P(x,y) \rightarrow P(y,x)]$ (symmetry)

   (c) $\forall x \forall y \forall z[P(x,y) \wedge P(z,y) \rightarrow P(x,z)]$.

In clausal form, we wish to derive C_3 from $S = \{C_1, C_2\}$ where

$$C_1 = \{\neg P(x,y), \neg P(y,z), P(x,z)\},$$
$$C_2 = \{\neg P(u,v), P(v,u)\},$$

and

$$C_3 = \{\neg P(x, y), \neg P(z, y), P(x, z)\}.$$

(Note that we have standardized the clauses of S apart.)

We exhibit a resolution tree proof with the substitutions used in the resolution displayed on the branches. For clarity, we also underline the literal on which we resolve.

$$C_1 = \{\neg P(x, y), \underline{\neg P(y, z)}, P(x, z)\} \qquad \{\neg P(u, v), \underline{P(v, u)}\} = C_2$$

$$\epsilon \qquad \{u/z, v/y\}$$

$$\{\neg P(x, y), \neg P(z, y), P(x, z)\} = C_3$$

FIGURE 35

(ii) We can show that son(tim, jim) follows from the clauses in example 13.1 by the following resolution proof:

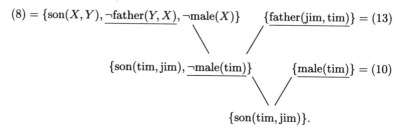

FIGURE 36

One can ask for the results gotten by resolution in the above examples from PROLOG. If one has the clauses of Example 13.1 in the database, one enters the desired result at the " ?– " prompt as "?– son(tim, jim).". One then gets the answer yes. PROLOG interprets the question as a request to prove son(tim, jim) from the database. More precisely, if positive literals $C_1, C_2, \ldots, C_n$ are entered at the "?" prompt, PROLOG tries to deduce $\square$ from the database S and the goal clause $G = \{\neg C_1, \ldots, \neg C_n\}$ which is also written :– $C_1, C_2, \ldots, C_n$. (Recall that a goal clause is one without positive literals, i.e., one of the form :– $A_1, \ldots, A_n$ where the A_i are positive. The reason for this terminology is apparent from such examples.)

If the C_i are ground, then we would expect a successful deduction of $\square$ from $S \cup \{\neg C_1, \ldots, \neg C_n\}$ to imply that all of the C_i are consequences of S. (This implication will follow from the soundness of resolution for predicate logic, Theorem 13.6 below. With some syntactic effort it can also be viewed, in the case that the C_i are ground, as a consequence of the soundness of resolution for propositional logic.) Consider, however, the meaning of entering an atomic formula with free variables such as "male(X), female(Y)" at the "?" prompt. Again PROLOG takes this as a request to prove $\square$ from S and the added goal clause $\{\neg \text{male}(X), \neg \text{female}(Y)\}$. Success here only means that from S we can conclude $\neg \forall X \forall Y [\neg male(X) \lor \neg female(Y)]$ as the clause $\{\neg male(X), \neg female(Y)\}$ means $\forall X \forall Y [\neg male(X) \lor \neg female(Y)]$. That is, we conclude $\exists X \exists Y [male(X) \land female(Y)]$. What PROLOG actually does is return a substitution, say $X = \text{jim}$, $Y = \text{jane}$ which demonstrates the truth of the conclusion $\exists X \exists Y [male(X) \land female(Y)]$ based on the information in S – i.e., $\{\neg male(\text{jim}), \neg female(\text{jane})\}$ is inconsistent with S. Of course, in applications it is almost always this correct answer substitution that we really want, not the mere assertion that $\exists X \exists Y [male(X) \land female(Y)]$.

Definition 13.5: If P is a program and $G = \{\neg A_1, \ldots, \neg A_n\}$ a goal clause, we say that the substitution θ (for the variables of G) is a *correct answer substitution* if $(A_1 \land A_2 \land \ldots \land A_n)\theta$ is a logical consequence of P (that is, of its universal closure).

Note that, by an application of Herbrand's theorem given in Exercise 10.5, if $P \cup \{G\}$ is unsatisfiable then there is a correct answer substitution which is a ground substitution. That one can always find such a substitution via resolution is essentially a statement of the completeness theorem. We will return to the issue of completeness of resolution after proving its soundness. We discuss general resolution methods in this and the next sections and leave the specific search procedures used in PROLOG to Chapter III.

Theorem 13.6 (Soundness of Resolution): *If $\square \in \mathcal{R}(S)$ then S is unsatisfiable.*

Proof: Suppose, for the sake of a contradiction, that $\mathcal{A} \vDash S$. Let the notation for a resolution be as in Definition 13.2. It suffices to show that if $\mathcal{A} \vDash C_1$, C_2 and C is a resolvent of C_1, C_2 then $\mathcal{A} \vDash C$, i.e., $\mathcal{A} \vDash C\tau$ for every ground substitution τ. (If so, we could show by induction that $\mathcal{A} \vDash C$ for every $C \in \mathcal{R}(S)$. As $\mathcal{R}(S)$ contains $\square$, we would have the desired contradiction.) The only point to notice here is that if $\mathcal{A} \vDash C_i$ then $\mathcal{A} \vDash C_i \sigma_i$ for any σ_i as the C_i are open. For every ground instantiation τ of the variables of $C = C_1'\sigma \cup C_2'\sigma$ we can argue as in the propositional case. (See Lemma I.8.12 and Theorem I.8.11.) As, for each ground instantiation τ, either $C_1'\sigma\tau$ or $C_2'\sigma\tau$ is true in $\mathcal{A}$ (depending on whether the literal resolved on is true in $\mathcal{A}$ or not and in which of the $C_i'\tau$ it appears positively), then so is their union $C\tau$. $\square$

We now want to prove the completeness of the resolution method for predicate logic by reducing it to the case of propositional logic. We begin with two lemmas. The first (Lemma 13.7) relates single resolutions in propositional and predicate logic. The second (Lemma 13.8) extends the correspondence to resolution proofs. This lemma (which is often called the lifting lemma as it "lifts" proofs in propositional logic to ones in predicate logic) will be quite useful in the analysis of restricted versions of resolution in §14 and III.1. The special case of proofs of $\square$ will be especially useful and is singled out as Corollary 13.9.

Lemma 13.7: *If C_1' and C_2' are ground instances (via the substitutions θ_1 and θ_2) of C_1 and C_2 respectively and C' is a resolvent of C_1' and C_2', then there is a resolvent C of C_1 and C_2 such that C' is a ground instance of C (via $\theta_1\theta_2$ if C_1 and C_2 have no variables in common).*

Proof: As the resolution rule allows us to rename the variables in C_1 and C_2 as part of the resolution, we may as well assume that they (and so also θ_1 and θ_2) have no variables in common. As $C_1' = C_1\theta_1$ and $C_2' = C_2\theta_2$ are resolvable, say on the ground literal $P(t_1, \dots, t_n)$, there are sets of literals

$$A_1 = \{P(\vec{s}_{1,1}), \dots, P(\vec{s}_{1,n_1})\} \subseteq C_1$$

and

$$A_2 = \{\neg P(\vec{s}_{2,1}), \dots, \neg P(\vec{s}_{2,n_2})\} \subseteq C_2$$

which become unified to $\{P(t_1, \dots, t_n)\}$ and $\{\neg P(t_1, \dots, t_n)\}$ by θ_1 and θ_2 respectively. As the sets of variables in θ_1 and θ_2 are disjoint, $\theta_1\theta_2$ unifies both sets of literals A_1 and A_2 simultaneously. Thus, by the definition of resolution for the predicate calculus (Definition 13.2), $C = ((C_1 - A_1) \cup (C_2 - A_2))\sigma$ is a resolvent of C_1 and C_2 where σ is the mgu for

$$\{\neg P(\vec{s}_{1,1}), \dots, \neg P(\vec{s}_{1,n_1})\} \cup \{\neg P(\vec{s}_{2,1}), \dots, \neg P(\vec{s}_{2,n_2})\}$$

given by the unification algorithm. The only point left to verify is that C' is an instance of C. We claim that $C' = C\theta_1\theta_2$. Note that as $\theta_1\theta_2$ unifies $\neg A_1 \cup A_2$, the special property of the mgu given by our algorithm (Theorem 12.5) guarantees that $\sigma\theta_1\theta_2 = \theta_1\theta_2$. Thus

$$
\begin{aligned}
C\theta_1\theta_2 &= ((C_1 - A_1) \cup (C_2 - A_2))\sigma\theta_1\theta_2 \\
&= ((C_1 - A_1) \cup (C_2 - A_2))\theta_1\theta_2 \\
&= (C_1\theta_1 - A_1\theta_1) \cup (C_2\theta_2 - A_2\theta_2) \quad \text{(by disjointness of variables)} \\
&= (C_1' - \{P(t_1, \dots, t_n)\}) \cup (C_2' - \{\neg P(t_1, \dots, t_n)\}) \\
&= C' \quad \text{(by definition).} \qquad \square
\end{aligned}
$$

Lemma 13.8 (Lifting Lemma): *Let S be a formula in a language $\mathcal{L}$ and let S' be the set of all ground instances of clauses in S in the Herbrand universe for $\mathcal{L}$. If T' is a resolution tree proof of C' from S', then there is a clause C of $\mathcal{L}$, a resolution tree proof T of C from S and a substitution θ such that $T\theta = T'$ (i.e., T and T' are labelings of the same tree and $C_i\theta = C_i'$ for C_i, C_i' the respective labels of each node of the common tree underlying T and T'. Thus, in particular, $C' = C\theta$.) Moreover, if the leaves of T' are labeled R_i and each R_i is an instance of an S_i in S, then we may arrange it so that the corresponding leaves of T are labeled with renamings of the appropriate S_i.*

Proof: We proceed by induction on the depth of resolution tree proofs from S'. For the base case of elements R_i of S', the lemma is immediate as each such R_i is a substitution instance of an element of S. Consider now a proof of C' from S' of depth $n + 1$. It consists of two proofs, T_1' and T_2' (of depth $\leq n$) of ground clauses C_1', C_2' from S' and a final resolution of C_1' and C_2' to get C'. Suppose that $P(t_1, \ldots, t_n) \in C_1'$, $\neg P(t_1, \ldots, t_n) \in C_2'$ and that we resolved on this literal to get

$$C' = C_1' \cup C_2' - \{P(t_1, \ldots, t_n), \neg P(t_1, \ldots, t_n)\}.$$

By induction, we have predicate clauses C_1 and C_2, proof trees T_1 and T_2 of C_1 and C_2 and substitutions θ_1 and θ_2 such that $T_i \theta_i = T_i'$. (The leaves of T_i are also labeled appropriately by induction.) At the cost perhaps of renaming variables in T_1 and T_2, we may assume that θ_1 and θ_2 have no variables in common. (As the resolution rule allows for arbitrary renamings of the parents, the T_i remain resolution proofs. As our lemma only calls for the leaves to be labeled with some renamings of the given clauses from S, this renaming does not alter the fact that we have the leaves appropriately labeled.) We now apply Lemma 13.7 to get a resolvent C of C_1 and C_2 with $C' = C\theta_1\theta_2$. We can now form a resolution tree proof T from S of C by combining T_1 and T_2. As θ_1 and θ_2 are disjoint, $T\theta_1\theta_2$ restricted to T_1 and T_2 simply gives us back $T_1\theta_1$ and $T_2\theta_2$. Of course, on the remaining node C of T we have $C\theta_1\theta_2 = C'$. Thus T is the required predicate logic resolution proof from S' of C and $\theta_1\theta_2$ is the substitution required in our lemma. $\square$

Corollary 13.9: *If T' is a resolution tree proof of $\square$ each of whose leaves L_i is labeled with a ground instance R_i of the clause S_i, then there is a relabeling T of the underlying tree of T' which gives a resolution proof of $\square$ each of whose leaves L_i is labeled with (a renaming) of S_i.*

Proof: This is simply the special case of the theorem with $C' = \square$. The only point to notice is that the only clause C which can have $\square$ as a substitution instance is $\square$ itself. $\square$

Theorem 13.10 (Completeness of Resolution): *If S is unsatisfiable then $\square \in \mathcal{R}(S)$.*

Proof: Let S' be the set of all ground instances of clauses in S in the Herbrand universe for the language $\mathcal{L}$ of S. By one of the consequences (Theorem 10.6) of Herbrand's theorem, S and S' are equisatisfiable. Thus if we assume that S is unsatisfiable then so is S'. By the completeness of resolution for propositional logic (Theorem I.8.15 or I.8.22) we then know that $\square \in \mathcal{R}_p(S')$ where we use $\mathcal{R}_p$ to represent the resolution procedure in propositional logic. (As usual we consider the atomic formulas as propositional letters in this situation.) The completeness of resolution for predicate logic (i.e., $\square \in \mathcal{R}(S)$ if S is unsatisfiable) is now immediate from Corollary 13.9. $\square$

Exercises

1. Find resolvents for the following:

   a) $\{P(x,y), P(y,z)\}, \{\neg P(u, f(u))\}$

   b) $\{P(x,x), \neg R(x, f(x))\}, \{R(x,y), Q(y,z)\}$

   c) $\{P(x,y), \neg P(x,x), Q(x, f(x), z)\}, \{\neg Q(f(x), x, z), P(x,z)\}$.

2. Translate the following sentences into predicate logic, put in clausal form and prove by resolution:

   a) Suppose all barbers shave everyone who does not shave himself. Moreover, no barber shaves anyone who shaves himself. Conclude that there are no barbers.

   b) Suppose John likes anyone who doesn't like himself. Conclude that it is not the case that John likes no one who likes himself.

3. Suppose I believe the following:

   (i) There exists a dragon.

   (ii) The dragon either sleeps in its cave or hunts in the forest.

   (iii) If the dragon is hungry, it cannot sleep.

   (iv) If the dragon is tired, it cannot hunt.

   Translate (i)–(iv) into predicate logic. Use resolution to answer the following questions:

   (a) What does the dragon do when it is hungry?

   (b) What does the dragon do when it is tired?

   (Assume that if X cannot do Y then X does not do Y.)

4. (a) Express the following in clausal form:
       Everyone admires a hero.
       A failure admires everyone.
       Anyone who is not a hero is a failure.

   (b) Use resolution to find X and Y who admire each other.

5. Give a resolution refutation of the following set of clauses. Indicate the literals being resolved on and the substitutions being made to do the resolutions:

   1) $\{P(a, x, f(y)), P(a, z, f(h(b))), \neg Q(y, z)\}$

   2) $\{\neg Q(h(b), w), H(w, a)\}$

   3) $\{\neg P(a, w, f(h(b))), H(x, a)\}$

   4) $\{P(a, u, f(h(u))), H(u, a), Q(h(b), b)\}$

   5) $\{\neg H(v, a)\}$.

6. Consider the following sentences.

1) All the stockholders who will have real estate partners will vote against the proposal but no others.

2) john and jim (and similarly mary and jane) will form real estate partnerships if some bank will give them a loan unless none of the lawyers can get them the needed zoning variance.

3) No banker will give a loan to form a real estate partnership without a lawyer's getting the needed zoning variances. With such an assurance they require only a good appraisal to agree to the loan.

4) john and jane are stockholders.

5) joyce is a lawyer who can get zoning approval for anyone with enough money.

6) john is immensely wealthy and his and jim's land has been given a good appraisal.

Translate these sentences into predicate logic, put them in clausal form and use resolution to deduce that someone will vote against the proposal. Who is it?

14. Refining Resolution: Linear Resolution

Systematic attempts at generating resolution proofs are often redundant and inefficient. As in the propositional case, we can impose various restrictions to make the procedure more efficient. The analogous procedures (to those considered in I.9) are covered in the exercises. We now wish to analyze, in the setting of full predicate logic, the refinement dealt with in I.10 for propositional Horn clauses: linear resolution. The plan here is to try to proceed via a linear sequence of resolutions rather than a branching tree. We carry out a sequence of resolutions each of which (after the first) must have one of its parents the child of the one previously carried out.

Definition 14.1: Let C be a clause and S a formula.

(i) A *linear deduction of C from S* is a sequence of pairs of clauses $\langle C_0, B_0 \rangle, \ldots, \langle C_n, B_n \rangle$ such that C_0 and each B_i are either renaming substitutions of elements of S or some C_j for $j < i$; each C_{i+1}, $i \leq n$, is a resolvent of C_i and B_i; and $C_{n+1} = C$.

(ii) C *is linear deducible from S, $S \vdash_{\mathcal{L}} C$*, if there is a linear deduction of C from S. There is a *linear resolution refutation* of S if $\square$ is linearly deducible from S. $\mathcal{L}(S)$ is the set of all clauses linearly deducible from S.

We picture a linear resolution as follows:

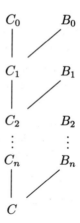

FIGURE 37

as in the following familiar example (I.10.2):

$$S = \{A_1, A_2, A_3, A_4\}, \quad A_1 = \{p(x), q(x)\}, \quad A_2 = \{p(x), \neg q(x)\},$$
$$A_3 = \{\neg p(x), q(x)\}, \quad A_4 = \{\neg p(x), \neg q(x)\}.$$

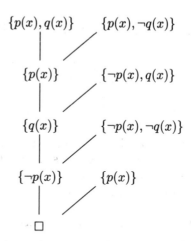

FIGURE 38

Definition 14.2: In this context, the elements of S are frequently called *input clauses*. The C_i are called *center clauses* and the B_i *side clauses*.

If we extend the parent–child terminology by defining the *ancestors* of a clause C in a resolution proof of C from S to be the clauses above it in the tree proof, we can rephrase the definition of linear deduction by saying that each C_i is resolved against an input clause or one of its own ancestors to produce C_{i+1}.

We want to prove that linear resolution is complete. (As it is a restriction of the sound method of full resolution its soundness is, as usual, automatic.) For the sake of the eventual induction argument as well as applications to the special case of proofs in PROLOG, we will actually prove a stronger result which gives us some control over the starting point of the linear proof (C_0 in the above notation).

Definition 14.3: $U \subseteq S$ is a *set of support* for S if $S - U$ is satisfiable. We say that a linear resolution proof $\langle C_i, B_i \rangle$, $i \leq n$, of C from S *has support* U if $C_0 \in U$.

The intuition here is that we will consider a formula $S \in$ UNSAT. In this case the "cause" of the unsatisfiability has been isolated in U (which "supports" the fact that $S \in$ UNSAT).

We can now state a strengthened version of the completeness theorem.

Theorem 14.4: *If $S \in$ UNSAT and U is a set of support for S, then there is a linear refutation of S with support U.*

Our first step is to reduce the proof of Theorem 14.4 to the case in which every nonempty subset of S is a set of support for S.

Definition 14.5: S is *minimally unsatisfiable* if it is unsatisfiable but every proper subset is satisfiable, i.e., $\{C\}$ is a set of support for S for every $C \in S$.

Lemma 14.6: *If $S \in$ UNSAT then there is a minimally unsatisfiable $S' \subseteq S$. Moreover, if U is a set of support for S, $U \cap S'$ is one for S'.*

Proof: By compactness, some finite subset of S is unsatisfiable. If S' is an unsatisfiable subset of S with the least possible number of clauses, S' is certainly a minimally unsatisfiable subset of S. Let U be any set of support for S. If $U \cap S' = \emptyset$, S' would be contained in the satisfiable set $S - U$ for a contradiction. Thus $S' - (S' \cap U)$ is a proper subset of S' and so, by the minimality of S', is satisfiable. $\square$

Proof (of Theorem 14.4): Our plan now is once again to reduce the proof to the case of propositional logic. (We supply a proof for this case below.) As in the case of general resolution, we apply Herbrand's theorem. If S is unsatisfiable and has support U, so is S', the set of all ground instances of elements of S, and it has support U', the set of all ground instances of elements of U. We wish to show that any linear resolution proof T' of $\square$ from S' with support U' lifts to one from S with support U. This is immediate from Corollary 13.9 to the lifting lemma. The lifting lemma preserves the shape of the resolution tree and so lifts linear proofs to linear proofs. It also lifts instances R_i of clauses S_i on the leaves of the tree to (renamings of) S_i. Thus if the clause C_0' of the proof T' is in U' and so is an instance of a clause C in U, then it lifts to a (renaming of) the same clause C. $\square$

We now turn to the proof of the strengthened completeness theorem for linear resolution in the propositional calculus. The proof here is more difficult than for semantic or ordered resolution but is connected with the set of support and lock resolution methods considered in the exercises for I.9.

Proof (of the propositional version of Theorem 14.4): By Lemma 14.6, it suffices to consider only those S which are minimally unsatisfiable. (Any linear resolution refutation of $S' \subseteq S$ with support $U \cap S'$ is one of S with support U by definition.) We proceed by induction on $E(S) =$ the *excess literal number* of S, that is, the number of occurrences of literals in all clauses of S minus the number of clauses in S. (Note that we need S to be finite to even define the excess literal number.) We in fact prove by induction that, for any $C \in S$, there is a linear refutation of S which begins with C, i.e. $C = C_0$ in the proof tree. At the bottom, if $E(S) = -1, \square \in S$ and there is nothing to prove. Suppose now that $E(S) \geq 0$.

Case 1. C is a unit clause, i.e., it contains exactly one literal ℓ. There must be a clause $C' \in S$ with $\bar{\ell} \in C'$ as otherwise any assignment satisfying $S - C$ (which is satisfiable by the minimality of S) could be extended to one satisfying S by adding on ℓ. Note that $\ell \notin C'$ for if it did, C' would be a tautology and S would not be minimally unsatisfiable contrary to our assumption. Thus $C' - \{\bar{\ell}\}$ is in S^ℓ by the definition of S^ℓ (Definition I.8.16). If $C' = \{\bar{\ell}\}$, we are done as we can simply resolve C and C' to get $\square$. Suppose then that $C' = \{\bar{\ell}, \ldots\}$ has more than one literal. As $S \in$ UNSAT, $S^\ell \in$ UNSAT by Lemma I.8.19. Each clause removed from S in forming S^ℓ has at least one literal (ℓ) (again by definition). Thus their removal cannot increase the excess literal number. On the other hand, at least C' loses one literal ($\bar{\ell}$) in its transition to S^ℓ. Thus $E(S^\ell) < E(S)$.

We next claim that S^ℓ is also minimally unsatisfiable: Suppose $D \in S^\ell$ but $S^\ell - \{D\}$ is unsatisfiable. Now, by the definition of S^ℓ, $D \in S$ or $D \cup \{\bar{\ell}\} \in S$ and in either case $\ell \notin D$. Let D' represent whichever clause belongs to S. We know, by the minimal unsatisfiability of S, that $S - \{D'\}$ is satisfiable. Let $\mathcal{A}$ be an assignment satisfying it. As $C = \{\ell\} \in S - \{D'\}$, $\mathcal{A} \vDash \ell$. Consider now any $F \in S^\ell - \{D\}$ and the associated $F' \in S - \{D'\}$. As $\mathcal{A} \vDash \ell$ and $\mathcal{A} \vDash F'$, $\mathcal{A} \vDash F$ in either case of the definition of F'. (F' is defined from F as D' was defined from D.) Thus $\mathcal{A} \vDash S^\ell - \{D\}$ contrary to our assumption.

Our induction hypothesis now gives us a linear resolution deduction of $\square$ from S^ℓ starting with $C' - \{\bar{\ell}\}$: $\langle C_0, B_1 \rangle, \ldots, \langle C_n, B_n \rangle$ with $C_0 = C' - \{\bar{\ell}\}$. Each B_i is a member of S^ℓ or is C_j for some $j < i$ and C_n, B_n resolve to $\square$. We construct a new proof $\langle D_j, A_j \rangle$ in segments with the ith one ending with $D_k = C_i$. We begin by setting $D_0 = \{\ell\} = C$ and $A_0 = C'$. Of course, they can be resolved to get $D_1 = C_0$. Now we proceed by induction. Suppose we have A_j, $j < k$ and $D_k = C_i$. If $B_i = C_j$ for some $j < i$, we let $A_k = C_j$ (which by induction is a previous D_m) and resolve to get $D_{k+1} = C_{k+1}$. Otherwise, $B_i \in S^\ell$ and we have two cases to consider. If $B_i \in S$ we set $A_k = B_i$ and resolve to get $D_{k+1} = C_{i+1}$. If $B_i \notin S$ then $B_i \cup \{\bar{\ell}\} \in S$. We set $A_k = B_i \cup \{\bar{\ell}\}$ and resolve to get $D_{k+1} = C_{i+1} \cup \{\bar{\ell}\}$. In this case, we set $A_{k+1} = \{\ell\}$ and resolve to get $D_{k+2} = C_{i+1}$ and so continue the induction. As $\{\ell\} = D_0$, we now have a linear resolution refutation of S as required.

Case 2. $C = \{\ell, \dots\}$ has more than one literal. Now consider $S^{\bar{\ell}}$. As above, it is minimally unsatisfiable and has lower excess literal number than S. We thus have, by induction, a linear resolution deduction of $\square$ from $S^{\bar{\ell}}$ starting with $C - \{\ell\}$. If we add on ℓ to every center clause and to any side clause which is in $S^{\bar{\ell}}$ but not S, we get a linear proof of $\{\ell\}$ from S starting with C. Consider now $S' = S - \{C\} \cup \{\{\ell\}\}$. It too is unsatisfiable. (Any assignment satisfying it satisfies S.) As C has more than one literal, $E(S') < E(S)$. Now as $\square \notin S'$, for any $S'' \subseteq S'$, $E(S'') \le E(S)$. If we take $S'' \subseteq S'$ to be minimally unsatisfiable we have, by induction, a linear resolution proof of $\square$ from $S'' \subseteq S \cup \{\{\ell\}\}$ beginning with $\{\ell\}$. (Note that $S' - \{\ell\} = S - \{C\}$ is satisfiable by the minimal unsatisfiability of S. Thus, any unsatisfiable subset S'' of S' must contain $\{\ell\}$.) Attaching this proof to the end of the one of $\{\ell\}$ from S gives the desired linear refutation of S starting with C. $\square$

Further refinements of general resolution are possible. Some of these (such as ordered linear resolution) are considered in the exercises. Instead of pursuing the general problem further, we turn our attention to the special case of resolution from Horn clauses — that is, the deduction mechanisms for PROLOG.

Exercises

1. Following the model in I.9 for ordered resolution in propositional logic, give a complete definition of an ordered resolution and an ordered resolution refutation for the predicate calculus in which you index the predicate symbols of the language.

2. State and prove the soundness theorem for ordered resolution for predicate logic.

3. State and prove the completeness theorem for ordered resolution for predicate logic.

4. Give the definitions and prove the soundness and completeness theorems for the predicate version of F–resolution (Exercise I.9.4).

5. Give the definitions and prove the soundness and completeness theorems for the predicate version of lock resolution (Exercise I.9.1).

Suggestions for Further Reading

To see how predicate logic got its start, read Frege [1879] in van Heijenoort [1967, 2.1].

For more on the predicate logic versions of tableaux, axioms and rules of inference, resolution, natural deduction and sequents, see the references to these topics at the end of Chapter I.

The basic development of model theory (beyond the few theorems given here) can be found in Chang and Keisler [1973, 3.4] or any of the other texts in list 3.4 of the bibliography.

To see where Herbrand universes and unification come from, read the first few pages of Herbrand [1930] in van Heijenoort [1967, 2.1] or Herbrand [1971, 2.3].

To see Herbrand's theorem used as a basis for the exposition of logic, see Chang and Lee [1972, 5.7]. Many varieties of resolution can be found there; see also Loveland [1978, 5.7] and Bibel [1982, 5.7].

The standard text on the theory of PROLOG is Lloyd [1987, 5.4] which also has an extensive bibliography. Other suggestions for reading about PROLOG can be found at the end of Chapter III.

III PROLOG

1. SLD–Resolution

In this chapter we will consider the full PROLOG language for logic programming in predicate logic. Much of the basic terminology is simply the predicate logic version of that introduced in I.10. We will, nonetheless, restate the basic definitions in a form suitable for resolution theorem proving in the predicate calculus. PROLOG employs a refinement of linear resolution but we have made the presentation independent of the (rather difficult) completeness theorem for linear resolution (Theorem II.14.4). We do, however, assume familiarity with the definitions for linear resolution in Definitions II.14.1–3. Thus our proofs will be based on the analysis of the propositional version of PROLOG discussed in I.10, together with Herbrand's theorem (II.10.4) and the reduction of predicate logic to propositional logic that it entails. At times when a knowledge of II.14 would illuminate certain ideas or simplify proofs, we mark such alternate results or proofs with an *.

Recall from II.5.1 that a PROLOG program P is a set of *program* clauses, i.e., ones with precisely one positive literal. We ask questions by entering a sequence of positive literals $A_1, \ldots, A_n$ at the " ?– " prompt. The PROLOG interpreter answers the question by converting our entry into a goal clause $G = \{\neg A_1, \ldots, \neg A_n\}$ and asking if $P \cup \{G\}$ is unsatisfiable. We will now describe the way in which PROLOG discovers if $P \cup \{G\}$ is unsatisfiable. Our starting point is the method of linear resolution introduced in I.10 for propositional logic and proved complete for predicate logic in II.14. We next restrict ourselves to an input version of linear resolution. Although this is not in general a complete version of resolution (as can be seen from the example following Definition II.14.1), it turns out to be complete in the setting of PROLOG. For the remainder of this section P is a PROLOG program and G a goal clause.

Definition 1.1: A linear resolution proof $\langle G_0, C_0 \rangle, \ldots, \langle G_n, C_n \rangle$, G_{n+1} is a *linear input*, or LI, *(resolution) refutation* of $P \cup \{G\}$ if $G_0 = G$, $G_{n+1} = \square$, each G_i is a goal clause and each C_i is a (renaming of a) clause in P.

*Theorem 1.2: *If $P \cup \{G\} \in$ UNSAT, there is a linear resolution refutation of $P \cup \{G\}$.*

*Proof: As every PROLOG program is satisfiable (Exercise II.5.6), $\{G\}$ is a set of support for $P \cup \{G\}$. By the completeness theorem for linear resolution (Theorem II.14.4) there is a linear refutation $\langle G_0, C_0 \rangle, \ldots, \langle G_n, C_n \rangle$

with $G_0 = G$. We claim that every G_i is a goal clause and, modulo renaming, every $C_i \in P$. Proceeding by induction, the only point to notice
is that we cannot resolve two goal clauses and so the next C_i must be from
P while the result of the resolution of a goal clause and a program clause
is again a goal clause or $\square$. $\square$

We now know the general format of resolution proofs for PROLOG: linear
input resolution. Before continuing to examine the additional refinements
implemented in PROLOG, we should note (and this is usually true of implementations of all resolution methods) that when $G = \{\neg A_0, \dots, \neg A_n\}$
and $C = \{B, \neg B_0, \dots, \neg B_m\}$ are resolved, say on $A_i = B$ via mgu θ, the
interpreter does not check to see if perhaps some resulting duplications
should be eliminated (e.g., $A_j\theta = A_\ell\theta$ or $A_j\theta = B_\ell\theta$ or $B_k\theta = B_\ell\theta$) . It
simply replaces $\neg A_i$ by $\neg B_0, \dots, \neg B_m$ and then applies θ to each term. It
does no further simplification. To understand the actual implementations,
we should therefore think of clauses (as the machine does) not as sets of
literals but as *ordered clauses*, i.e., sequences of literals. A resolution as
above then inserts the literals $\neg B_0, \dots, \neg B_m$ in place of $\neg A_i$ and applies θ
to each literal in the sequence to get the next (ordered) goal clause. This
ordering of clauses does not cause any serious changes. We embody it in
the following definition and lemma.

Definition 1.3:

(i) If $G = \{\neg A_0, \dots, \neg A_n\}$ and $C = \{B, \neg B_0, \dots, \neg B_m\}$ are ordered
clauses and θ is an mgu for A_i and B, then we can perform an *ordered
resolution* of G and C on the literal A_i. The *(ordered) resolvent* of
this resolution is the ordered clause $\{\neg A_0, \dots, \neg A_{i-1}, \neg B_0, \dots, \neg B_m,$
$\neg A_{i+1}, \dots, \neg A_n\}\theta$.

(ii) If $P \cup \{G\}$ is given as a set of ordered clauses, then a *linear definite*
or LD–*refutation* of $P \cup \{G\}$ is a sequence $\langle G_0, C_0 \rangle, \dots, \langle G_n, C_n \rangle$
of ordered clauses G_i, C_i in which $G = G_0$, $G_{n+1} = \square$, each G_i
is an ordered goal clause, each C_i is a renaming of an element of P
containing only variables which do not appear in G_j for $j \le i$ or C_k
for $k < i$ and each G_{i+1} $(0 \le i \le n)$ is an ordered resolvent of G_i and
C_i. If C_n is not $\square$, we call the sequence, as usual, an LD–*resolution
proof*.

Note that this method does not employ the strategy of collapsing literals.
We resolve on one literal from each clause and remove only these two literals
from the resolvent.

Lemma 1.4 (Completeness of LD–resolution): *If $P \cup \{G\}$ is an unsatisfiable set of ordered clauses, then there is an LD–refutation of $P \cup \{G\}$
beginning with G.*

Proof: Consider all (ordered) ground instances $P' \cup G'$ of the (ordered)
clauses in $P \cup \{G\}$ in the appropriate Herbrand universe. By Herbrand's
theorem (Corollary II.10.6) $P' \cup G'$ is unsatisfiable. By the compactness

theorem (II.7.9), some finite subset of $P' \cup G'$ is unsatisfiable. As all sets of program clauses are satisfiable (Exercise II.5.6), any such subset must include elements of G', i.e., instances of G. Let $P'' \cup G''$ be an unsatisfiable subset of $P' \cup G'$ of minimal size. By minimality there is a $G_0'' \in G''$ such that $P'' \cup G'' - \{G_0''\}$ is satisfiable. By Lemma I.10.11, there is then an LD–resolution refutation of $P'' \cup G''$ starting with G_0''. By Lemma 1.5 below this can be lifted to the desired LD–refutation of $P \cup G$. $\square$

Proof: Let P' and $\{G'\}$ be the sets of unordered clauses corresponding to P and $\{G\}$ respectively. The proof proceeds by a simple induction on the length of the LI–refutation of $P' \cup \{G'\}$. Note, however, that one LI–resolution may be replaced by a sequence of LD–resolutions to compensate for the collapsing of literals allowed in LI–resolution. We leave the details as Exercises 1–2. $\square$

Lemma 1.5: *The lifting lemma holds for* LD*–resolution proofs. More precisely II.13.7 holds for ordered resolutions;* II.13.8 *holds for* LD*–resolution proofs; and* II.13.9 *holds for* LD*–resolution refutations.*

Proof: The proofs are essentially the same as in II.13. The lifting of a single resolution (II.13.7) is, however, somewhat simpler in that no collapsing of literals occurs here (and so the parameters n_1 and n_2 are both equal to 1 in the proof). In the proof of the lifting lemma itself, we note that, for linear resolutions, an induction on the depth of the tree is the same as one on the length of the proof. The leaves of the tree are the starting clause and the side clauses. We leave the details of rewriting the proofs of II.13 in this setting as Exercises 3–5. $\square$

Our next task is to describe how, in an LD–resolution proof, we should choose the literal of G_i on which to resolve. The *selection rule* used in essentially all implementations of PROLOG is to always resolve on the first, i.e., the leftmost, literal in G_i. The literals in the resolvent deriving from C_i are then always inherited with their original order and put to the left of all of the clauses coming from G_i. We call this an SLD–*resolution*. (The S stands for *selection*.) More generally, we can consider any selection rule R, i.e., any function choosing a literal from each ordered goal clause.

Definition 1.6: A *selection rule* R is simply a function that chooses a literal $R(C)$ from every nonempty ordered clause C. An SLD–*refutation* of $P \cup \{G\}$ *via* R is an LD–resolution proof $\langle G_0, C_0 \rangle, \ldots, \langle G_n, C_n \rangle$ with $G_0 = G$, $G_{n+1} = \square$ in which $R(G_i)$ is the literal resolved on at step i of the proof. (If no R is mentioned we assume that the standard one of choosing the leftmost literal is intended.)

Our next goal is to prove a completeness theorem for SLD–refutations. We first give a simple proof along the lines of our previous arguments that uses a version of the lifting lemma for SLD–proofs. On the propositional level, the heart of this proof is essentially that of Theorem I.10.13, the completeness of SLD–resolution for propositional logic. The difficulty with lifting that result directly to predicate logic is that the lifting lemma does not apply directly to SLD–proofs with arbitrary selection rules. The problem is that the rule may choose a literal out of the predicate lifting of a given clause which is not the lifting of the literal chosen by the rule from the ground instance of the given clause. However, this problem does not arise for a wide class of selection rules, including the standard one of always choosing the leftmost literal. So in the case in which we are interested for implementations of PROLOG, we can directly lift the completeness theorem.

Definition 1.7: A selection rule R is *invariant* if, for every (ordered) clause C and every substitution θ, $R(C\theta) = (R(C))\theta$.

Note that the standard selection rule is obviously invariant.

Theorem 1.8 (Completeness of SLD–refutations): *If $P \cup \{G\} \in$ UNSAT, there is an SLD–resolution refutation of $P \cup \{G\}$ via R for any selection rule R.*

Proof (for invariant selection rules): We argue exactly as in the proof of Lemma 1.4 except that we apply Theorem I.10.13 in place of Lemma I.10.9. We then apply the lifting lemma for SLD–resolutions with an invariant selection rule (Exercise 6). □

We could now supply a direct but fairly complicated proof of Theorem 1.8 for arbitrary selection rules. It is somewhat simpler to instead prove a lemma asserting an independence result: given an LD–refutation starting from G, we can find an SLD one via any selection rule R. The general form of Theorem 1.8 would then follow directly from Lemma 1.4. The proof of this independence result is itself somewhat technical and we postpone it to Lemma 1.12.

We now know what the PROLOG interpreter does when a question is entered as "?– $A_1, \ldots, A_n$.". It searches for an SLD–resolution proof of □ from the current program P and the goal clause $G = \{\neg A_1, \ldots, \neg A_n\}$. Before analyzing the search method for finding such a proof, let us consider what happens at the end. If all attempts at finding a proof fail PROLOG answers "no". If a proof is found, PROLOG gives us an *answer substitution*, that is a substitution for the variables in G. In fact, if the proof found by the interpreter is $\langle G_0, C_0 \rangle, \ldots, \langle G_n, C_n \rangle$ with mgu's $\theta_0, \ldots, \theta_n$ then it gives us the answer substitution $\theta = \theta_0 \ldots \theta_n$ restricted to the variables of G. Most importantly, these are always correct answer substitutions, i.e., $(A_1 \wedge \ldots \wedge A_n)\theta$ is a logical consequence of P.

Theorem 1.9 (Soundness of implementation): *If θ is an answer substitution given by an SLD–refutation of $P \cup \{G\}$ (via R for any R) then θ is correct, i.e., $(A_1 \wedge \ldots \wedge A_n)\theta$ is a logical consequence of P.*

Proof: We proceed by induction on the length of the SLD–refutation. For the base case of a refutation of length one, $G = G_0 = \{\neg A\}$ and $C_0 = \{B\}$ are singletons with θ an mgu for $\{A\}$ and $\{B\}$. As $B \in P$, it is a logical consequence of P as is its substitution instance $B\theta$. As θ is a unifier, $B\theta = A\theta$ which is then also a logical consequence of P as required. Suppose now that $G = \{\neg A_0, \ldots, \neg A_n\}$ and $P \cup \{G\}$ has an SLD–refutation of length $n + 1$ starting with $G_0 = G$ and $C_0 = \{B, \neg B_0, \ldots, \neg B_m\}$ and a resolution on $\neg A_i$ with mgu θ_0. The resolvent $G_1 = \{\neg A_0, \ldots, \neg A_{i-1}, \neg B_0, \ldots, \neg B_m, \neg A_{i+1}, ..., \neg A_n\}\theta_0$ has an SLD–refutation from P of length n with mgu $\theta' = \theta_1 \ldots \theta_n$. Thus, by the induction hypothesis, $G_1\theta_0\theta'$ is a logical consequence of P. Let $\theta = \theta_0\theta'$. As $C_0 \in P$, $C_0\theta$ is also a logical consequence of P. Now $C_0\theta$ is equivalent to $(B_0\theta \wedge \ldots \wedge B_m\theta) \rightarrow B\theta$. So by propositional logic, $\{\neg A_0\theta, \ldots, \neg A_{i-1}\theta, \neg B\theta, \neg A_{i+1}\theta, \ldots, \neg A_n\theta\}$ is then also a consequence of P. As $\theta = \theta_0\theta'$, θ also unifies A_i and B, i.e., $A_i\theta = B\theta$. Thus $G\theta$ is a logical consequence of P as required. $\square$

The answers supplied by SLD–resolutions are, in a sense, all the correct ones there are.

Theorem 1.10 (Completeness of implementation): *Let R be a selection rule. If $P \vDash (A_1 \wedge \ldots \wedge A_n)\sigma$ then there is an SLD–refutation $T = \langle\, \langle G_i, C_i \rangle \mid i \leq n\,\rangle$ of $P \cup \{G\}$ via R with answer substitution θ and also a substitution ψ such that $G\sigma = G\theta\psi$.*

Proof (for invariant selection rules): We prove by induction on the length n of an SLD–refutation of $P \cup \{G\sigma\}$ via R that there is a refutation with answer substitution θ and a ψ such that $\sigma = \theta\psi$ on the variables of G. Choose a substitution γ instantiating all the variables of $G\sigma$ to new constants (i.e., ones not appearing in $P \cup \{G\}$). As $P \vDash (A_1 \wedge \ldots \wedge A_n)\sigma$ it is clear that $P \cup \{G\sigma\gamma\} \in$ UNSAT. Let $T = \langle\, \langle G_i, C_i \rangle \mid i < n\,\rangle$ be a ground SLD–refutation of $P \cup \{G\sigma\gamma\}$ via R. By the invariance of R, reversing the substitution γ (i.e., replacing the constants by the original variables) gives an SLD–refutation $T' = \langle\, \langle G_i', C_i' \rangle \mid i < n\,\rangle$ of $P \cup \{G\sigma\}$ via R in which the unifiers ψ_i restricted to the variables in $G\sigma$ are the identity. The ground refutation can also be lifted, by Exercise 6, to one

$$T'' = \langle\, \langle G_i'', C_i'' \rangle \mid i < n\,\rangle$$

of $P \cup \{G\}$ with mgu's $\theta_0, \ldots, \theta_n$. Suppose that R selects the literal A_i from G. We can now apply the induction hypothesis to

$$G_1' = \{\neg A_0\sigma, \ldots, \neg A_{i-1}\sigma, \neg B_{0,1}\psi_0, \ldots, \neg B_{0,m_0}\psi_0, \neg A_{i+1}\sigma, \ldots, \neg A_n\sigma\}$$

and

$$G_1'' = \{\neg A_0\theta_0, \ldots, \neg A_{i-1}\theta_0, \neg B_{0,1}\theta_0, \ldots, \neg B_{0,m_0}\theta_0, \neg A_{i+1}\theta_0, \ldots, \neg A_n\theta_0\}$$

as $G'_1 = G''_1 \sigma \psi_0 = G''_1 \psi_0 \sigma$ (remember that $G \sigma \psi_0 = G \sigma$ and, as $\sigma \psi_0$ unifies A_0 and B_0, $\theta_0 \sigma \psi_0 = \sigma \psi_0$). Thus, we have an SLD–refutation of $P \cup \{G''_1\}$ via R with mgu's $\theta'_1 \ldots \theta'_n$ and a λ' such that $\theta'_1 \ldots \theta'_n \lambda' = \sigma$ on the variables in G''_1. If x occurs in $G = G_0$, but $x\theta_0$ does not appear in G''_1, then $x\theta_0$ does not appear in $\theta'_1, \ldots, \theta'_n$. Since $\theta_0 \sigma = \sigma$ on the variables in A_0, we can extend λ' to λ by setting $\lambda(x) = \sigma(x)$ for each variable x in A_0 such that $x\theta_0$ is not in G''_1. Then $\theta_0 \theta'_1 \ldots \theta'_n \lambda = \sigma$ on all the variables of G, as required. (Keep in mind that $y\theta_0 \sigma = y\sigma$ for y occurring in G.) □

To provide proofs for Theorem 1.8 and 1.10 for arbitrary selection rules, we now prove the independence lemma, as promised. We begin with a basic procedure to change a single choice of literal in an LD–refutation.

Lemma 1.11 (Switching Lemma): *Let $G = G_0 = \{\neg A_0, \ldots, \neg A_n\}$ and let $\langle G_0, C_0 \rangle, \ldots, \langle G_k, C_k \rangle$ be an LD–refutation of $P \cup \{G_0\}$ with answer substitution $\psi = \psi_0 \ldots \psi_k$. Suppose that $A_j \psi_0 \ldots \psi_{s-1}$ is the literal resolved on at step $s > 0$. There is then an LD–refutation $\langle G_0, C'_0 \rangle, \ldots, \langle G'_k, C'_k \rangle$ of $P \cup \{G_0\}$ with answer substitution $\theta = \theta_0 \ldots \theta_k$ in which we resolve on $A_j \theta_0 \ldots \theta_{s-2} = A_j \psi_0 \ldots \psi_{s-2}$ at step $s - 1$ such that $G\theta$ is a renaming of $G\psi$.*

Proof: Let $C_i = \{B_i, \neg B_{i,0}, \ldots, \neg B_{i,m_i}\}$ for $i \leq k$. Let $G_{s-1} = \{\neg A'_0, \neg A'_1, \ldots, \neg A'_t\}$ where $A_j \psi_0 \ldots \psi_{s-2} = A'_{j'}$ and suppose we resolved on A'_r at stage $s-1$. Thus $G_s = \{\neg A'_0, \neg A'_1, \ldots, \neg A'_{r-1}, \neg B_{s-1,0}, \ldots, \neg B_{s-1,m_{s-1}}, \neg A'_{r+1}, \ldots, \neg A'_t\} \psi_{s-1}$ and G_{s+1} is ψ_s applied to the result of replacing $\neg A_j = \neg A'_{j'}$ by $\neg B_{s,0}, \ldots, \neg B_{s,m_s}$ in G_s. (Recall that by the definition of LD refutations, $\neg B_{s,0}, \ldots, \neg B_{s,m_s}$ have no variables acted on by ψ_{s-1}.) We know that $A'_{j'} \psi_{s-1} \psi_s = B_s \psi_s = B_s \psi_{s-1} \psi_s$ and so we can unify $A'_{j'}$ and B_s. Let ψ'_{s-1} be the corresponding mgu and let λ be such that $\psi_{s-1} \psi_s = \psi'_{s-1} \lambda$. We now replace step $s - 1$ of the original refutation by this resolution. We want to show that we can resolve with C_{s-1} on the literal $A'_r \psi'_{s-1}$ at step s with mgu ψ'_s. If we can also show that the result of this resolution is a renaming of G_{s+1}, we can continue the refutation, modulo renamings, to get the desired result.

We first note that, from our original refutation, $A'_r \psi_{s-1} = B_{s-1} \psi_{s-1}$. Combining this fact with the relation for λ above we can get the following sequence of equalities: $A'_r \psi'_{s-1} \lambda = A'_r \psi_{s-1} \psi_s = B_{s-1} \psi_{s-1} \psi_s = B_{s-1} \psi'_{s-1} \lambda$. Thus λ unifies $A'_r \psi'_{s-1}$ and $B_{s-1} = B_{s-1} \psi'_{s-1}$ (by convention, B_{s-1} has no variables acted on by ψ'_{s-1}). We may therefore resolve on $A'_r \psi'_{s-1}$ with mgu ψ'_s as required. We also get a λ' such that $\lambda = \psi'_s \lambda'$. Combining the equations for λ, we have $\psi_{s-1} \psi_s = \psi'_{s-1} \psi'_s \lambda'$. If we can now prove the existence of a substitution φ' such that $\psi'_{s-1} \psi'_s = \psi_{s-1} \psi_s \varphi'$, then, by Exercise II.11.4, we will have established that $\psi'_{s-1} \psi'_s$ is a renaming of $\psi_{s-1} \psi_s$ as required to complete the proof. The argument for the existence of φ' is similar to that of λ'. We know that $A'_r \psi'_{s-1} \psi'_s = B_{s-1} \psi'_{s-1} \psi'_s$ while in the original proof ψ_{s-1} is an mgu for A'_r and B_{s-1}. Thus there is a φ

such that $\psi'_{s-1}\psi'_s = \psi_{s-1}\varphi$. We next note that $A'_{j'}\psi_{s-1}\varphi = A'_{j'}\psi'_{s-1}\psi'_s = B_s\psi'_s\psi'_{s-1} = B_s\psi_{s-1}\varphi$. Thus φ unifies $A'_{j'}\psi_{s-1}$ and $B_s\psi_{s-1}$. As ψ_s in the original proof is an mgu for this unification, there is a φ' such that $\varphi = \psi_s\varphi'$. Combining this with the first equation for φ, we see that $\psi'_{s-1}\psi'_s = \psi_{s-1}\psi_s\varphi'$ as required. $\square$

Lemma 1.12 (Independence Lemma): *For any* LD*–refutation of* $P \cup \{G\}$ *of length* n *with answer substitution* θ *and any selection rule* R, *there is an* SLD*–refutation of* $P \cup \{G\}$ *via* R *of length* n *with an answer substitution* ψ *such that* $G\psi$ *is a renaming of* $G\theta$.

Proof: We proceed by induction on the length of the given LD–refutation. As usual, there is nothing to prove if it has length 1. Suppose we have an LD–refutation of G of length $k + 1$ with answer substitution φ. Let A_j be the literal selected from G by R and suppose it is resolved on at step s of the given LD–refutation. Apply Lemma 1.11 $s-1$ times to get an LD–refutation $\langle G_0, C_0 \rangle, \ldots, \langle G_k, C_k \rangle$ of $P \cup \{G\} = P \cup \{G_0\}$ with answer substitution $\varphi = \varphi_0\varphi_1 \ldots \varphi_k$ in which A_j is the literal resolved on at step 1 and such that φ is a renaming of θ via λ. Now apply the induction hypothesis to the LD–refutation $\langle G_1, C_1 \rangle, \ldots, \langle G_k, C_k \rangle$ to get one of G_1 via R with answer substitution θ' such that $\varphi_1 \ldots \varphi_k\lambda' = \theta'$ with λ' a renaming substitution. We can now prefix the resolution of $G = G_0$ with C_0 on A_j (with mgu φ_0) to this refutation to get the desired SLD–refutation of $P \cup \{G\}$ via R with answer substitution $\varphi_0\theta'$. We complete the induction argument by noting that $G_0\varphi_0\theta' = G_0\varphi_0\varphi_1 \ldots \varphi_k\lambda' = G_0\varphi\lambda' = G_0\psi\lambda\lambda'$. We have now found the required SLD–refutation and renaming substitution $\lambda\lambda'$. $\square$

Proof (of Theorems 1.8 and 1.10): It is now clear that, by applying Lemma 1.12, Theorem 1.8 follows immediately from Lemma 1.4. Similarly, Theorem 1.10 follows from Lemma 1.4 together with the special case proved above for invariant selection rules. $\square$

Exercises

1. Prove the following lemma: If G is an ordered goal clause, C an ordered program clause, G' and C' the unordered clauses corresponding to G and C respectively (i.e., the union of the elements of the sequence) and the goal clause D' is an LI–resolvent of G' and C', then there is a sequence of LD–resolutions starting with G and C and ending with an ordered goal clause D which corresponds to D'.

2. Use the results of Exercise 1 to carry out the inductive *proof of Lemma 1.4.

3. Prove Lemma II.13.7 for ordered clauses and LD–resolution.

4. Prove Lemma II.13.8 for ordered clauses and LD–resolution.

5. Prove Corollary II.13.9 for ordered clauses and LD–refutations.

6. Notice that the proofs of Exercises 3-5 work for SLD–resolutions if the selection rule is invariant.

7. Let S be a set of clauses in a language $\mathcal{L}$. The *success set* of S is the set of all ground instances $A(t_1, \dots, t_n)$ in $\mathcal{L}$ of the predicates of $\mathcal{L}$ such that there is a resolution refutation of $S \cup \{\neg A(t_1, \dots, t_n)\}$. Prove that if P is a PROLOG program then a ground atomic formula $A(t_1, \dots, t_n)$ is in the success set of P iff it is true in every Herbrand model of P.

8. Suppose a graph G is represented as a database of edges via the list of facts "edge(n, m)." for each pair of nodes, n, m for which there is an edge connecting them in the graph. (Assume that the graph is undirected and so "edge(n,m)." appears in the database iff "edge(m,n)." also appears.) Define, via a PROLOG program, the predicate "connected(X,Y)" so that connected(n,m) is a logical consequence of the program iff there is a sequence of nodes $n = n_1, n_2, \dots$; $n_k = m$ such that each successive pair of nodes n_i, n_{i+1} is joined by an edge.

2. Implementations: Searching and Backtracking

Although SLD–resolution is both sound and complete, the available implementations of PROLOG are neither. There are two sources of problems. The first, and at least theoretically relatively minor one, is in the implementation of the unification algorithm. As we have mentioned, the available PROLOG implementations omit the "occurs check" in the unification algorithm. Thus, for example, the PROLOG unifier believes that X and $f(X)$ are unifiable. In addition, the PROLOG theorem prover does not make the substitutions needed by the unifier until they are required in theSLD–resolution. These two facts combine to destroy the soundness of the system. Thus, for example, given the program:

$$\text{test :– } p(X, X).$$
$$p(X, f(X)).$$

and the question " ?– test." PROLOG will answer "yes.". What has happened here is that the theorem prover says that to verify "test", we must verify $p(X, X)$. As $p(X, f(X))$ is given, it suffices to see if $p(X, X)$ and $p(X, f(X))$ can be unified. The unifier answers that they can. As no further information is needed (to instantiate "test", for example) the theorem prover gives the answer "yes" to our question. Thus, it gives an answer which is not a logical consequence of the program — a violation of soundness.

A key point in the above implementation is that the theorem prover did not have to carry out the substitution $\{X/f(X)\}$ implicit in the unifier's answer. If it had tried, it would have fallen into the endless loop of trying to output the results of the substitution. This situation is illustrated by the program:

$$\text{test1}(X) :- p(X, X).$$
$$p(X, f(X)).$$

If we now ask "?– test1(X).", the result of the looping is displayed as PROLOG tries to give the "correct" answer substitution of $X = f(f(f(\ldots$. (Hit control–break to stop the display.) This type of failure can also occur undisplayed in the search for an SLD–resolution. Consider the program:

$$\text{test2} :- p(X, X).$$
$$p(X, f(X)) :- p(X, X).$$

In this case, the only indication that something has gone wrong is that no answer is forthcoming.

Unfortunately, these problems may well occur in natural programs as well. Of course, both of these problems could be eliminated by implementing the unification algorithm correctly. As there are now reasonably efficient (i.e., linear) unification algorithms, this is not an unreasonable expectation. For now, however, one can fairly easily eliminate the first type of problem in favor of the second. One simply writes programs in which any variable appearing in the head of a clause also appears in the body. This can be done by simply adding $X = X$ to the body for any variable X in the head not already in the body. The first program would then become

$$\text{test} :- p(X, X).$$
$$p(X, f(X)) :- X = X.$$

Now, when the theorem prover tries to resolve on $p(X, X)$ and $P(X, f(X))$ and the unifier says they are unifiable, the prover asks for the substitution so that it can put the expression resulting from $X = X$ into the goal clause in place of $p(X, X)$. As the substitution is circular, it never gets to complete the proof. Thus, this simple programming trick will restore the soundness of the PROLOG theorem prover (at the expense, of course, of taking longer to run). Completeness, however, is another matter.

The source of the incompleteness of the PROLOG implementation is the method employed to search for an SLD–refutation. Suppose we are given a program P and a goal clause G. We wish to find an SLD–resolution refutation of $P \cup \{G\}$ beginning with G. At each step i of the SLD–resolution, the only choice to make is which clause in P to use to resolve on the leftmost term in our current goal clause G_i. We can thus display the space of all possible SLD–derivations as a tree: the root node is labeled G and if a node is labeled G' then the labels of it successors are the results of all possible choices of clauses of P for the next resolution on the leftmost term of G'.

We call such trees SLD–*trees for P and G*. As a simple example, consider the program P_1:

$$p(X, X) :\!- q(X, Y), r(X, Z). \qquad (1)$$
$$p(X, X) :\!- s(X). \qquad (2)$$
$$q(b, a). \qquad (3)$$
$$q(a, a). \qquad (4)$$
$$q(X, Y) :\!- r(a, Y) \qquad (5)$$
$$r(b, Z). \qquad (6)$$
$$s(X) :\!- q(X, a). \qquad (7)$$

The SLD–tree for P_1 starting with the goal clause $G = \{\neg p(X, X)\}$ is displayed in Figure 39. Along each branching we indicate the clause of P_1 resolved against. The convention is that the successors are listed in a left to right order that agrees with the order in which the clauses used appear in P_1. *Success paths*, corresponding to yes answers, are those ending in $\square$. At the end of each such success path we put the answer substitution given by the proof (of $\square$) represented by the path. A path is a *failure path* if it ends with a clause G' such that there is no clause in P with which we can resolve on the leftmost term of G'.

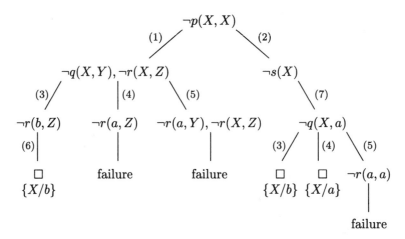

FIGURE 39

We see here that, of the six possible paths, three end in failure, two end with the correct substitution $\{X/b\}$ and one with $\{X/a\}$.

The PROLOG theorem prover searches the SLD–tree for a success path by always trying the leftmost path first. That is, it tries to resolve the current G with the first clause in P that is possible. In Figure 39 it would simply-follow the path (1), (3), (6) to get the correct answer substitution $\{X/b\}$. If the theorem prover hits a *failure point* (i.e., not $\square$ and no resolution is possible) it *backtracks*. Backtracking means retracing the path one has just followed until one finds a node with a branch to the right of the path being retraced. If there is more than one such path, take the leftmost one. The theorem prover repeats this backtracking procedure until a success path is found.

Copies of printouts for runs of the programs P_1 (and other programs listed in this section) are included at the end of the section. We also include printouts of the runs with "tracing". (Tracing is a facility supplied with most implementations of PROLOG that displays the actual steps of the search of the SLD–tree. It is an important tool for understanding the flow of control in a program and for debugging. Note that items of the form "$\_0nnn$" are just names for variables.)

If, for example, we omit clause (3) from the above program P_1 to produce P_2 , we get a new SLD–tree as pictured in Figure 40.

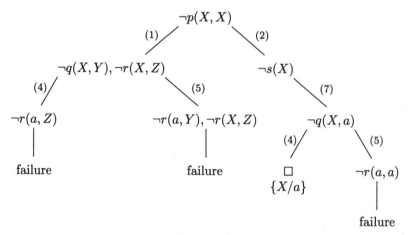

FIGURE 40

In this case, the theorem prover first tries the path (1), (4), failure. It then backtracks to $\neg q(X, Y), \neg r(X, Z)$ and tries (5), failure. It then backtracks all the way to $\neg p(X, X)$ and tries (2), (7), (4), success to give the answer substitution $X = a$.

The same backtracking procedure is implemented when we ask PROLOG for a second answer. Thus, with the original program P_1 and goal $\{\neg p(X, X)\}$, i.e., "?– $p(X, X)$." we got the reply "$X = b \rightarrow$". If we now ask for another answer by entering "$;$" the theorem prover backtracks from the success node until it hits a node with alternate paths — here $\neg q(X, Y)$, $\neg r(X, Z)$. It then tries (4), failure and (5), failure and then backtracks to $\neg p(X, X)$. It now tries (2), (7), (3) giving once again the answer $X = b$. If we enter "$;$" , once again, it backtracks from the success node to $\neg q(X, a)$ to try (4) and give the answer $X = a$. Should we once again ask for another answer, PROLOG will backtrack to $\neg q(X, a)$, try the remaining path (5), fail and report no — no more success nodes have been found and there are no more paths to try.

The situation is similar if we get a "no" answer on first entering our question. Here it means that all paths in the SLD–tree have been traversed and they are all failures. By our general completeness theorem, we then know that $P \cup \{G\}$ is satisfiable and so there is no substitution for which the question asked is a logical consequence of P_1. By the completeness theorem for the implementation we also know that when we finally get a no after a series of "; " requests, every correct answer substitution is an instance of one of the answer substitutions already displayed.

This type of search procedure is called a *depth–first search* procedure as it tries to go as deeply as possible in the tree by running down to the end of a path before searching along any other branches. In contrast, a procedure that searches the tree in Figure 40 in the order $\neg p(X, X)$; $\neg q(X, Y)$; $\neg r(X, Z)$; $\neg s(X)$; $\neg r(b, Z)$; $\neg r(a, Z)$; $\neg r(a, Y)$; $\neg r(a, Z)$; $\neg q(X, a)$; $\square$; failure; failure; $\square$; $\square$; $\neg r(a, a)$; failure, is called a *breadth–first search*. Clearly many mixed strategies are also possible. In our case, the depth–first search was much faster than breadth–first (3 versus 9 steps). Indeed, this is a quite general phenomena. Depth–first is usually much faster than breadth–first. That, of course, is why the implementations use depth–first searches. The cost, however, is quite high — we lose the completeness of the SLD–resolution method (quite independently of the procedure used to implement unification).

The general completeness theorem guarantees that, if $P \cup \{G\} \in$ UNSAT, there is a (necessarily finite) SLD–refutation proof beginning with G. If there is one of length n it is clear that in a breadth–first search we must find such a proof by the time we have searched the tree to depth n, i.e., we have traversed every possible path of length n. Unfortunately, there are no such guarantees for depth-first searching. The problem is that some paths of the tree may be infinite. Depth–first searching may then keep us on such a path forever when a short proof lies along another path. As an example, consider the program P_3 gotten by replacing (6) in P_1 by

$$r(W, Z) :\!- \ r(b, Z). \qquad (6')$$

The SLD–tree for P_3 beginning with $\neg p(X, X)$ is displayed in Figure 41.

Here we see that, even though there are SLD–refutations along the paths (2), (7), (3) and (2), (7), (4), the depth–first search employed by PROLOG will not find them. Instead, it will endlessly pursue the leftmost path (1), (3), (6') and then continue trying to use clause (6') again and again forever.

We can now see why the ordering of the clauses plays a crucial role in the actual running of a PROLOG program. If we rearranged P_3 to get P_4 by interchanging clauses (1) and (2), the theorem prover would first find the proof (2), (7), (3) and then (2), (7), (4). Only then, if asked for another answer, would it fall into the endless search part of the tree. Unfortunately,

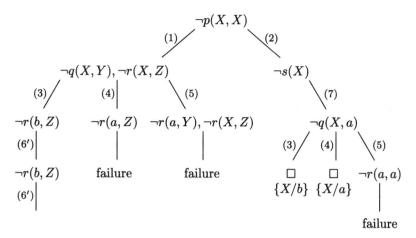

FIGURE 41

the arrangement of clauses, though an important programming consideration, is not enough to guarantee completeness. To see this, consider the program P_5 :

$$\text{equivalent}(X, Y) :- \text{equivalent}(Y, X). \tag{1}$$
$$\text{equivalent}(X, Z) :- \text{equivalent}(X, Y), \text{equivalent}(Y, Z). \tag{2}$$
$$\text{equivalent}(a, b). \tag{3}$$
$$\text{equivalent}(b, c). \tag{4}$$

and the goal $G = \neg\text{equivalent}(c, a)$. It is clear that $\text{equivalent}(c, a)$ is a logical consequence of P_5 (Exercise 1). The problem is that no matter in which order clauses (1) and (2) are listed in the program, a depth–first search will always keep trying to apply the first of them since both heads will unify with any expression of the form $\text{equivalent}(t_2, t_3)$ for any terms t_2 and t_3. Thus the theorem prover will be able to use one of (1) and (2) but not both. It is, however, easy to see that if either clause is omitted from P_5 then the result together with G is satisfiable. Thus, no depth–first search procedure can find an SLD–refutation of $P \cup \{G\}$ regardless of the ordering of the clauses in P. (Note that the depth–first implementation remains unable to find the proof here even if we use another selection rule.) Thus, depth–first search methods, although efficient, are inherently incomplete. In the next section we present a programming tool to minimize or get around these problems. In §4 we briefly consider the general problem of guaranteeing termination (for certain types) of programs in pure PROLOG with the standard selection rule and depth–first searching of SLD–trees. In §8 we show that the general termination problem for PROLOG programs is undecidable.

Exercises

1. Find an SLD–refutation of $P_5 \cup \{\neg \text{equivalent}(c, a)\}$.

2. Prove that every set P of program clauses has a *minimal* (actually least) *Herbrand model* M_P (i.e., prove that the intersection of all Herbrand models of P is also a model of P) but not every set S of universal sentences has a minimal Herbrand model.

3. Consider the program P

$$p(X, Z) :- q(X, Y), p(Y, Z). \qquad (1)$$
$$p(X, X). \qquad (2)$$
$$q(a, b). \qquad (3)$$

Draw SLD–trees for P and goal "?– $p(X, Y)$." for the standard selection rule and also for the rule which always chooses the rightmost literal from a clause.

4. a) Draw the SLD–refutation tree illustrating all possible attempts at SLD–proofs using the standard selection rule and the associated correct answer substitutions for the following program and goal:

(1) $p(X, Y) :- s(X), t(X).$
(2) $p(X, Y) :- q(X, f(X)), r(X, f(Y)).$
(3) $q(b, Y).$
(4) $q(a, Y) :- r(a, f(a)).$
(5) $r(a, f(a)).$
(6) $r(b, f(b)).$
(7) $s(a).$
(8) $s(b).$
(9) $t(a).$

Goal: ?– $p(X, Y).$

b) Explain what happens in terms of PROLOG searching and backtracking when we enter "?– $p(X, Y)$." and then repeatedly ask for more answers via ";".

5. Define PROLOG programs for the following operations on lists. (The basic notations for lists were introduced in II.3.)

a) second_element (X, Y) which is to define the predicate "X is the second element of the list Y".

b) substitute_for_second_element $(Y, L1, L2)$ which is to define the predicate "$L2$ is $L1$ with Y substituted for its second element".

c) switch (L, M) which is to define the predicate "M is L with its first and last elements exchanged".

d) Check that your programs work correctly, at least when all variables are instantiated, by running some examples: Is b the second element of $[a, [b, c], d, e]$ or of $[a, b, c]$? Is $[b, c]$ the second element of either of them? Is $[a, [b, c], d]$ the result of replacing the second element of $[a, b, c]$ with $[a, [b, c], d]$? Is $[a, [a, [b, c], d], c]$? Is $[a, c, b]$ the result of interchanging the first and last elements of $[a, b, c]$? Is $[c, b, a]$?

e) Try a couple of examples with uninstantiated variables as well: find the second element of $[a, [b, c], d, e]$ and $[a, b, c]$; replace the second element of $[a, b, c]$ with $[a, [b, c], d]$ and then replace the second element of the result with b; interchange the first and last elements of $[a, b, c]$ and then of the resulting list. Now some examples with the roles of the variables interchanged: Find a list with second element b; one which, when its second element is replaced by b, would be $[a, b, c]$; one which, when its first and last elements are interchanged, would be $[a, b, c]$.

f) What simple universal statements suggested by the above examples should be true about your programs? Try asking as a PROLOG question if substituting the second element of a list X for its own second element returns the original list. Similarly for the result of switching the first and last elements twice. Explain the output when these questions are entered.

6. Trace the execution of your programs on the examples in Exercise 5 and explain any anomalous behavior (depending on your program there may not be any).

In Exercises 7–8 we use a unary function symbol s (with the intended meaning "successor of") to define a counter beginning with the constant 0. Thus 0 corresponds to 0, $s(0)$ to 1, $s(s(0))$ to 2, and in general $s^n(0)$ ($= s \ldots s(0)$ with n repetitions of the function s) corresponds to n. Do not try to use the built-in arithmetic operations supplied with PROLOG.

7. Write a program to calculate the length of a list using this counter. Try it on a couple of inputs: $[a, b, c]$, $[a, b, c, [b, c], [d, c, e]]$. What happens when you try to find a list of length three?

8. We add on to our language two predicate symbols "add(X, Y, Z)" and "multiply(X, Y, Z)".

a) Prove that, if we interpret "0" as 0 in the natural numbers and "s" as successor, then the following PROLOG program defines addition on the natural numbers as represented by $\{0, s(0), s(s(0)), \ldots\}$ in the sense that "add$(s^n(0), s^m(0), s^r(0))$" is a consequence of the program iff $n + m = r$:

add$(X, 0, X)$.

add$(X, s(Y), s(Z)) :- $ add(X, Y, Z).

b) Write a similar PROLOG program to define multiplication in terms of addition and successor so that "multiply$(s^n(0), s^m(0), s^r(0))$ will be a consequence of the program iff $mn = r$. (Hint: $x(y + 1) = xy + x$.)

c) Prove that "multiply$(s^n(0), s^m(0), s^r(0))$ is in fact a consequence of the program iff $mn = r$.

9. Recall the procedure in II.5 for defining a knight's move on the chess board.

a) Write a program defining a queen's move. (It can move horizontally, vertically or diagonally.)

b) Write one defining when a queen cannot move from one position to another.

c) Write a program to find a way to put a queen in each column so that none of them could move to any square occupied by any of the others.

Do not use any built–in predicates (i.e., no arithmetic, no cut, no "not").

d) Find two solutions to the problem in (c).

10. Write a program for the function FLATTEN which strips off all brackets from a list except the outermost, i.e., it returns a list of atoms in the order in which they would appear on the page when the input list is written out.

11. Consider the following program:

$$tc(X, Y) :- r(X, Y).$$
$$tc(X, Y) :- r(X, Z), tc(Z, Y).$$

The goal

$$?- tc(a, b).$$

will succeed exactly when the pair (a, b) is in the transitive closure of the relation $r(,)$ as defined in Exercise 11 of II.7. How do you reconcile this with the result of that exercise? (This problem is also relevant to Exercise 1.8.)

The following problems are continuations of Exercises II.5.7–8 and follow the same conventions about the assumed genealogical database. A printout of the database and some words of warning are included in Appendix B. They also make use of the counter defined in Exercise 7. Once again, if not using the database simply write out the programs defining the required predicates and explain how one would obtain the desired information. Now, in addition to explaining why your answersare semantically correct, discuss how they would run as implemented by PROLOG.

12. a) Define nthgrandfather($X, Y, s^n(c)$) to mean that X is an ancestor of Y n generations up. (Start with $n = 1$ for X is the father of Y.)

   b) Use this program to find libni's grandfather's great–grandfather.

   c) Can you find more than one such ancestor? Should you be able to do so if all were well with the database?

   d) Use this program to find four of levi's great-great-great–grandchildren.

   e) Find three of esau's grandchildren.

13. a) Define cousin(X, Y) to give the usual meaning of first cousin.

   b) Find five cousins of tola.

   c) Define secondcousin(X, Y).

   d) Find six second cousins of libni.

   Recall the usage in English: My children and my brother's children are first cousins; my grandchildren and his grandchildren are second cousins; my children and his grandchildren are first cousins once removed; my children and his great–grandchildren are first cousins twice removed; my grandchildren and his great–grandchildren are second cousins once removed.

   e) Define cousin($X, Y, s^n(c), s^m(c)$) to mean that X is the nth cousin m times removed of Y.

   f) Find seven second cousins once removed of libni. Can you tell or guess and verify what relation they are to the people listed in (d)?

   g) Find three third cousins twice removed of libni. Can you predict from your program how they are likely to be related to libni (i.e., what routing istaken to find these instances)?

14. Various anomalies may creep into your results when implemented with an actual genealogical database. Consider how the following typical problems with such databases might affect your programs.

   a) The same data may be recorded twice. For example the fact fatherof(abraham,isaac) appears twice in the database. Will this cause any wrong answers to be reported? What effect if any will it have on running a program such as the one for ancestor or for n^{th} cousins m times removed?

   b) Different people may have the same name and not be distinguished in the database. (Try to see who is the father of enoch.) How will this affect the ancestor and cousin programs? Can you devise a method for identifying people in the database that might be used to eliminate or reduce the impact of this problem? (Hint consider using a counter.) Try the father of enoch again. Also see if you have eliminated all solutions to ancestor(X, X).

c) The same person may appear under more than one name. We know, for example, from other Biblical passages that esau is seir. How will this affect the ancestor and cousin programs? What could you do (short of editing the data file) to correct for such a situation? Can you add rules to the database that would take care of this problem without editing the database? (Examples in the database used for trying your solution out are finding the grandfather of lotan and the cousins of hori.)

Runs of Programs $P_1 - P_4$

PROGRAM P_1.

```
?- listing.
p(A,A) :-
    q(A,B),
    r(A,C).
p(A,A) :-
    s(A).
q(b,a).
q(a,a).
q(A,B) :-
    r(a,B).
r(b,A).
s(A) :-
    q(A,a).
yes
?- p(X,X).
X = b →;
X = b →;
X = a →;
no
?- trace.
yes
?- leash(full).
yes
?- spy(p/2).
yes
?- p(X,X).
   ** (0) CALL: p(_0085,_0085)? >
   (1) CALL: q(_0085,_0255)? >
   (1) EXIT: q(b,a)? >
   (2) CALL: r(b,_0261)? >
   (2) EXIT: r(b,_0261)? >
   ** (0) EXIT: p(b,b)? >
X = b →;
   ** (0) REDO: p(b,b)? >
   (2) REDO: r(b,_0262)? >
```

```
   (2) FAIL: r(b,_0261)? >
   (1) REDO: q(b,a)? >
   (1) EXIT: q(a,a)? >
   (3) CALL: r(a,_0261)? >
   (3) FAIL: r(a,_0261)? >
   (1) REDO: q(a,a)? >
   (4) CALL: r(a,_0255)? >
   (4) FAIL: r(a,_0255)? >
   (1) FAIL: q(_0085,_0255)? >
   (5) CALL: s(_0085)? >
   (6) CALL: q(_0085,a)? >
   (6) EXIT: q(b,a)? >
   (5) EXIT: s(b)? >
   ** (0) EXIT: p(b,b)? >
X = b →;
   ** (0) REDO: p(b,b)?
   (5) REDO: s(b)? >
   (6) REDO: q(b,a)? >
   (6) EXIT: q(a,a)? >
   (5) EXIT: s(a)? >
   ** (0) EXIT: p(a,a)? >
X = a →;
   ** (0) REDO: p(a,a)? >
   (5) REDO: s(a)? >
   (6) REDO: q(a,a)? >
   (7) CALL: r(a,a)? >
   (7) FAIL: r(a,a)? >
   (6) FAIL: q(_0085,a)? >
   (5) FAIL: s(_0085)? >
   ** (0) FAIL: p(_0085,_0085)? >
no
```

PROGRAM P_2.

```
?- listing.
p(A,A) :-
   q(A,B),
   r(A,C).
p(A,A) :-
   s(A).
q(a,a).
q(A,B) :-
   r(a,B).
r(b,A).
s(A) :-
   q(A,a).
yes
?- p(X,X).
X = a →;
no
?- trace.
yes
?- leash (full).
yes
?- spy(p/2).
yes
?- p(X,X).
   ** (0) CALL: p(_005D,_005D)? >
   (1) CALL: q(_005D,_022D)? >
```

```
   (1) EXIT: q(a,a)? >
   (2) CALL: r(a,_0239)? >
   (2) FAIL: r(a,_0239)? >
   (1) REDO: q(a,a)? >
   (3) CALL: r(a,_022D)? >
   (3) FAIL: r(a,_022D)? >
   (1) FAIL: q(_005D,_022D)? >
   (4) CALL: s(_005D)? >
   (5) CALL: Q(_005D,a)? >
   (5) EXIT: q(a,a)? >
   (4) EXIT: s(a)? >
   ** (0) EXIT p(a,a)? >
X = a →;
   ** (0) REDO: p(a,a)? >
   (4) REDO: s(a)? >
   (5) REDO: q(a,a)? >
   (6) CALL: r(a,a)? >
   (6) FAIL: r(a,a)? >
   (5) FAIL: q(_005D,a)? >
   (4) FAIL: s(_005D)? >
   ** (0) FAIL: p(_005D,_005D)? >
no
```

PROGRAM P_3.

```
?- listing.
p(A,A) :-
   q(A,B),
   r(A,C).
p(A,A) :-
   s(A).
q(b,a).
q(a,a).
q(A,B) :-
   r(a,B).
r(A,B) :-
   r(b,B).
s(A) :-
   q(A,a).
yes
?- p(X,X).
```

```
?- trace.
yes
?- leash(full).
yes
?- spy(p/2).
yes
?- p(X,X).
   ** (0) CALL: p(_005D,_005D)? >
   (1) CALL: q(_005D,_022D)? >
   (1) EXIT: q(b,a)? >
   (2) CALL: r(b,_0239)? >
   (3) CALL: r(b,_0239)? >
   (4) CALL: r(b,_0239)? >
   (5) CALL: r(b,_0239)? >
```

PROGRAM P_4.

```
?-  listing.
p(A,A)  :-
    s(A).
p(A,A)  :-
    q(A,B),
    r(A,C).
q(b,a).
q(a,a).
q(A,B)  :-
    r(a,B).
r(A,B)  :-
    r(b,B).
s(A)  :-
    q(A,a).

yes
?-  p(X,X).
X = b  →;

X = a  →;
?-  trace.
yes
?-  leash(full).
yes
?-  spy(p/2).
yes
```

```
?-  p(X,X).
 ** (0) CALL: p(_005D,_005D)? >
    (1) CALL: s(_005D)? >
    (2) CALL: q(_005D,a)? >
    (2) EXIT: q(b,a)? >
    (1) EXIT: s(b)? >
 ** (0) EXIT: p(b,b)? >
X = b  →;
 ** (0) REDO: p(b,b)? >
    (1) REDO: s(b)? >
    (2) REDO: q(b,a)? >
    (2) EXIT: q(a,a)? >
    (1) EXIT: s(a)? >
 ** (0) EXIT: p(a,a)? >
X = a  →;
 ** (0) REDO: p(a,a)? >
    (1) REDO: s(a)? >
    (2) REDO: q(a,a)? >
    (3) CALL: r(a,a)? >
    (4) CALL: r(b,a)? >
    (5) CALL: r(b,a)? >
```

3. Controlling the Implementation: Cut

We have seen that the success of an execution of even a semantically correct PROLOG program depends in many ways on the specifics of the implementation. So far, the only control we have had over the path of execution has been the ordering of clauses in the program. We know, for example, that the base case of a recursion should always precede the inductive case (why?). Similarly, facts about a predicate should generally precede the asserted rules. Such heuristics can, however, go only so far. At times we might wish to exercise more detailed control over implementing the searching of the SLD–tree. Sometimes this is "merely" for the sake of efficiency. At other times there just seems to be no other way of getting a program that will run at all. In this section we consider one such built–in control facility — cut.

Syntactically *cut*, written "!", appears to be simply another literal. Thus we write:

$$p :- q_1, q_2, !, q_3, q_4.$$

It does not, however, have any (declarative) semantics. Instead, it alters the implementation of the program. When the above clause is called in a search of the SLD–tree, the subgoals q_1, q_2, !, q_3 , q_4 are inserted at the beginning of our current goal clause as usual. We try to satisfy q_1 and q_2 in turn, as before. If we succeed, we skip over the cut and attempt to satisfy q_3 and q_4 . If we succeed in satisfying q_3 and q_4 all continues as if there were no cut. Should we, however, fail and so by backtracking be returned to the cut, we act as if p has failed and we are returned by "*deep backtracking*" to the node of the SLD–tree immediately above that for p, called the *parent* goal, and try the next branch to the right out of that node. (If none exists, the current search fails as usual.)

Example 3.1: Consider the following program:

$$t :\!- \ p, r. \qquad (1)$$
$$t :\!- \ s. \qquad (2)$$
$$p :\!- \ q_1, q_2, !, q_3, q_4. \qquad (3)$$
$$p :\!- \ u, v. \qquad (4)$$
$$q_1. \qquad (5)$$
$$q_2. \qquad (6)$$
$$s. \qquad (7)$$
$$u. \qquad (8)$$

For the goal $\{\neg t\}$ we get the following SLD–tree:

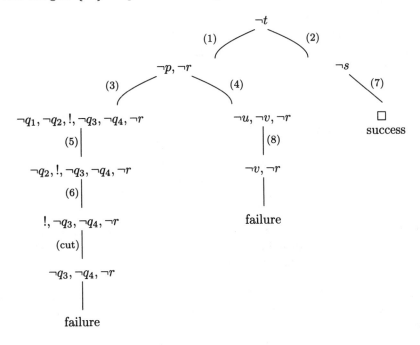

FIGURE 42

When we run the search we travel down the leftmost branch, as usual, going through the cut until we hit the failure point. (Note that ! succeeds by definition the first time through; we simply remove it when reached.) However, when we hit the failure node at the end of the leftmost path, control is passed to the node labeled $\neg s$ from which we immediately succeed. The point is that, once the goal clauses after the cut, $\neg q_3, \neg q_4, \neg r$, have failed, we return not to the parent, $(\neg p, \neg r)$, of the clause with the cut, but instead go back to *its* parent $(\neg t)$. We then try the next branch to the right (through $\neg s$) and proceed with our search.

The use of cut in this example merely saved us time in the execution of the program by pruning the SLD–tree without cutting off any success branches. Such uses of cut are, of course, innocuous (or *safe*). It is, however, difficult to write programs so that the uses of cut are always restricted to such safe situations. In general, the cut can be a source of both incompleteness and unsoundness. Clearly, if the cut prunes a success path, we may lose some correct answer substitutions. Worse yet, it could prune all the success paths. In this case we might wind up running down an infinite path — demonstrating the incompleteness of the search system much as in the analysis of depth–first searching. Finally it might prune both all success paths and all infinite paths. In this case PROLOG will answer "no" when in fact $P \cup \{G\}$ is unsatisfiable. In this way cut can introduce an actual unsoundness into programs, as a "no" answer means that $P \cup \{G\}$ is satisfiable.

Nonetheless, cut can be very useful if extreme care is taken when using it. Some implementations of PROLOG have other facilities for controlling the implementation of searching. One such is called *snip*. It acts like a restricted form of cut. For example when a clause $p :\!- q_1, q_2, [!q_3, q_4!], q_5$ is encountered, the search progresses normally through the snip (q_4), that is through the clauses between the exclamation points. Should backtracking return you to right end of the snip, however, it instead skips over the snip to return to q_2. Although this is at times a convenient tool, we will see in the exercises that a snip can always be replaced by a use of cut. In general, we simply warn the reader — be very careful, cut can have unexpected consequences. At the very least, uses of cut which subvert the declarative semantics of the program should be avoided. We will, however, briefly consider one important use of cut — defining negation — as a lead in to some other topics.

Although "not" comes as a built–in predicate in PROLOG, we can see what it really means by defining it in terms of cut. Its meaning in PROLOG is different from the usual logical meaning of negation. "not(P)" means that we have a demonstration that P fails (i.e., is not provable). Thus PROLOG answers "yes" to the goal "not(A)" if and only if it would answer "no" to the goal A. We could replace uses of "not" by uses of cut by inserting a definition of not(A) :

$$\text{not(A)} :\!- \text{A, !, fail.}$$
$$\text{not(A).}$$

We see here that if not(A) is called, PROLOG turns to the first clause defining it and calls A. If A succeeds, we pass over the cut and hit "fail". "fail" is a built–in predicate which always fails (and so could be replaced with any other clause which always fails). Thus, if A succeeds, not(A) fails. On the other hand, if A fails, we try the second clause defining not(A) and it succeeds.

In fact, the tables can often be turned. Many uses of cut can and should be replaced by uses of "not". We say "should" because "not" can have some declarative sense in PROLOG programs (even though not the classical one) while cut is much more problematic. We will explore the theoretical semantic underpinnings of PROLOG's use of "not" in §6. In order to do that, however, we will first make a start on dealing with equality in §5.

Exercises

1. In Exercise 2.4 what would be the effect of inserting a cut, !, between the two literals in the body of clause (2) on your answer to (b)?

   Recall the list notation introduced in Example II.3.15. Consider the following program APPEND for appending one list to another:

   (a1) $a([\ ], Y, Y)$.
   (a2) $a([X|Y], Z, [X|W]) :- a(Y, Z, W)$.

2. What is the advantage of modifying this program to APPEND':

   (a1) $a([\ ], Y, Y) :- !$.
   (a2) $a([X|Y], Z, [X|W]) :- a(Y, Z, W)$.

   Consider the situation when we have two given lists x and y and we wish to find out the result of appending one to the front of the other, that is consider goals of the form ?– $a([x, y, z], [u, v], Z)$. Consider also ones of the form ?– $a([x, y, z], V, W)$.

3. What problems arise in the implementation of APPEND' (in contrast to that of APPEND) when considering a goal of the form ?–$a(X, Y, [x, y, z])$. Consider what happens when you try to get more than one answer substitution for the variables.

4. This question is somewhat open–ended and refers to the database mentioned in the exercises for II.7–8 and III.11–12. Can you use cut to take advantage of the ordering of clauses in the genealogical database to alleviate any of the problems that you had earlier on with the family relation programs such as grandfather, uncle or cousin? Assume that the clauses in the database reflect births in chronological order. You might consider both rewriting your programs and writing a new program (with cut) to revise the database in some way to prevent such results as someone being his own grandfather.

4. Termination Conditions for PROLOG Programs

An important problem in the analysis of programs is that of determining when programs terminate. Of course, the problem in general is undecidable (Theorem 8.9 and Corollary 8.10), but it may be manageable for specific programs of practical interest. In this section we present a method of analysis that can be used to abstractly characterize termination of programs running with the standard selection rule of always choosing the leftmost literal. The approach presented is that of Apt and Pedreschi [1991, 5.4]. They adapted the ideas of Bezem [1989, 5.4] for characterizing termination of all LD–proofs from a given program and goal to deal with the situation where the selection rule is fixed as the standard one.

For the rest of this section P will be a PROLOG program and G a goal in a language $\mathcal{L}$. All clauses and resolutions are ordered. We let P' and G' be the set of ground instances of P and G respectively. SLD–proofs will mean ones using the standard selection rule. The basic property of the program P that we wish to characterize is given in the following definition:

Definition 4.1: P is *left–terminating for a goal* G if all SLD–proofs from $P \cup \{G\}$ starting with G are finite. P is *left–terminating* if it is left–terminating for every ground goal G.

Note that if P is left–terminating for G, then the standard implementation of P in PROLOG (using leftmost selection and depth–first search) will terminate on the goal G. Indeed, as all SLD–proofs starting with G are finite, it would terminate with any search rule. Thus, if we can prove left–termination for the goal clauses of interest, we will be guaranteed that our programs terminate under the standard implementation.

The basic strategy in nearly all proofs of termination of deductions has two parts. First, one carefully defines a well ordering of clauses or proofs. Then one shows that individual deductions (or in our case resolutions) produce decreases in this ordering. Once we have reached such a situation, it is clear that all proofs terminate as each step represents a decrease in a well ordering. The description of the well ordering we want begins with the basic notion of a level mapping.

Definition 4.2:

(i) A *level mapping* for P is a function f from the atomic sentences (positive ground literals) of $\mathcal{L}$ to $\mathbb{N}$. We denote the value of this function on a literal A by $|A|_f$, called *the level of* A *with respect to* f. If the function f is clear from the context, we will omit the subscript.

(ii) If $\mathcal{M}$ is a structure for $\mathcal{L}$ and $\vec{A} = A_1, \ldots, A_n$ a sequence of atomic sentences, we let $\mathcal{M}(\vec{A})$ be the least $i \leq n$ such that $\mathcal{M} \not\models A_i$, if there is one, and n itself otherwise. If $G = \{\neg A_1, \ldots, \neg A_n\}$, we also write $\mathcal{M}(G)$ for $\mathcal{M}(A_1, \ldots, A_n)$.

(iii) *P is acceptable with respect to a level mapping f and a model $\mathcal{M}$ of P*
   if for every $B :- \vec{A}$ in P', i.e., every ground instance of a clause in P,
   $|B| > |A_i|$ for each $i \leq \mathcal{M}(\vec{A})$. P is *acceptable* if it is acceptable with
   respect to some level mapping and model.

To grasp the idea behind this definition, consider first a level mapping
without any mention of a model. It is then clear that, if P is acceptable,
every ground resolution of a goal clause $G = \{\neg A_1, \ldots, \neg A_n\}$ with a clause
in P gives a resolvent of lower level than G. This modified notion of acceptability corresponds to the condition that all LD–proofs from P starting
with G are finite. (See Exercises 1–2.) The restriction to SLD–proofs will
be captured by the restriction to literals A_i for $i \leq \mathcal{M}(G)$ by the right
choice of the model $\mathcal{M}$. The basic idea is that, if there is no SLD–refutation
of $\{\neg A_i\}$, then no SLD–refutation starting with G can get beyond A_i. Thus
there is no need to consider later literals in an analysis of the SLD–tree
from G. On the other hand, if there is no SLD–refutation of $\{\neg A_i\}$, there
is a model $\mathcal{M}$ in which A_i is false. Thus the right choice of model will cut
off the level function precisely at the point at which one need not consider
any more literals.

To begin our analysis we define, from a given level mapping f and model
$\mathcal{M}$ of P, the required well ordering of clauses. We must consider first the
ground goal clauses and then certain nonground ones.

Definition 4.3:

(i) Let P be acceptable with respect to f and $\mathcal{M}$. We extend f to ground
   goal clauses $G_i = \{\neg A_{i,1}, \ldots, \neg A_{i,n_i}\}$ by setting $|G_i| = \langle |A_{i,j_1}|, \ldots,$
   $|A_{i,j_k}|\rangle$ where we have listed the literals $A_{i,1}, \ldots, A_{i,\mathcal{M}(G_i)}$ in decreas-
   ing (although not necessarily strictly decreasing) order of their level.
   We order these tuples by the lexicographic ordering. (Formally, to
   make this literally an extension of f we identify each $n \in \mathbb{N}$ with the
   one element sequence $\langle n \rangle$.) Note that the lexicographic ordering on
   finite sequences is a well ordering by Exercise I.1.8(b).

(ii) A goal clause G is *bounded* (with respect to f and $\mathcal{M}$) if there is a
   maximal element in $\{|G^*| : G^* \in G'\}$. (Recall that G' is the set of
   ground instances of G.) If G is bounded, we denote this maximal
   element by $|G|$. (Note that with the identification of n and $\langle n \rangle$ this
   agrees with the definition in (i) if G is ground.)

The use of the word bounded is justified by the following lemma.

Lemma 4.4: $G = \{\neg A_1, \ldots, \neg A_n\}$ *is bounded (with respect to f and $\mathcal{M}$)
if and only if there is a sequence τ such that $G^* \leq \tau$ for every $G^* \in G'$.*

Proof: The "only if" direction is immediate. Suppose then that there is
a τ as described in the Lemma. Let t be a number larger than any element
of τ. If $G^* \in G'$, then there are at most n elements in the sequence $|G^*|$.
By the choice of τ and t, each of these elements is less than t. Thus there
are only finitely many sequences of the form $|G^*|$ for $G^* \in G'$. As every
finite set has a maximum in any ordering we are done. $\square$

Our next task is to prove that any acceptable program which starts with a bounded goal must terminate. As the ordering induced on the goal clauses is a well ordering, it suffices to show that resolutions with clauses in P decreases the level of the goal clause. We begin with ground resolutions.

Lemma 4.5: *Let P be acceptable with respect to a level mapping f and a model M. If $G = \{\neg A_1, \ldots, \neg A_n\}$ is a ground goal and $H = \{\neg B_1, \ldots, \neg B_m, \neg A_2, \ldots, \neg A_n\}$ is an SLD–resolvent of G with some ground clause $C = \{B, \neg B_1, \ldots, \neg B_m\}$ in P', then $|H| < |G|$.*

Proof: We proceed by cases. First, suppose that $M(G) = 1$, i.e., $M \not\models A_1$ and so by definition $|G| = \langle |A_1| \rangle$. As we resolved G and C, $B = A_1$ and it is false in M by assumption. As $C \in P'$, it must be true in the model M of P. Thus, B_i must be false in M for some $i \leq m$ and so by definition $M(H) \leq m$. As $|B_i| < |A_1|$ for every $i \leq m$ by acceptability, $|H| < |G| = |A_1|$ by the definition of the ordering.

Next suppose that $M(G) > 1$. In this case H and G succeed in M for the first time at the same literal, i.e., $M(H) = M(G) + m - 1$. Thus the sequence $|H|$ has the same elements as $|G|$ except that $|A_1|$ is replaced by the set of elements $|B_i|$ for $1 \leq i \leq m$. As $|B_i| < |A|$ for each i, it is clear from the definition of the extension of the level mapping to clauses and the ordering on these sequences that $|H| < |G|$ as required. $\square$

We now prove our lemma for bounded goals.

Lemma 4.6: *Let P be acceptable with respect to a level mapping f and a model M. If $G = \{\neg A_1, \ldots, \neg A_n\}$ is a bounded (with respect to f and M) goal and $H = \{\neg B_1, \ldots, \neg B_m, \neg A_2, \ldots, \neg A_n\}\theta$ an SLD–resolvent of G with some $C = \{B, \neg B_1, \ldots, \neg B_m\}$ in P, then H is bounded and $|H| < |G|$.*

Proof: Consider any ground instance $H\gamma$ of H. By extending γ if necessary, we may assume that $\theta\gamma$ also grounds B. $H\gamma$ is then a resolvent of $G\theta\gamma$ and $C\theta\gamma \in P'$ and so by Lemma 4.5 $|H\gamma| < |G\theta\gamma|$. As G is bounded, $|G\theta\gamma| \leq |G|$. As $H\gamma$ was an arbitrary ground instance of H, H is bounded by Lemma 4.4. If we now choose γ so that $|H\gamma| = |H|$ we see that $|H| < |G|$ as required. $\square$

Theorem 4.7: *If P is acceptable and G is a goal clause which is bounded (with respect to any level mapping and model showing that P is acceptable) then every SLD–proof from $P \cup \{G\}$ beginning with G is finite.*

Proof: Consider any SLD–proof from $P \cup \{G\}$ starting with $G = G_0$. Each successive resolution produces a new goal clause G_n. By Lemma 4.6, the sequence $|G_n|$ is strictly decreasing. As the ordering on goal clauses is a well ordering, the sequence of resolutions must be finite. $\square$

Corollary 4.8: *Every acceptable program is left–terminating.*

Proof: The corollary follows from the theorem as every ground goal is by definition bounded. □

We now wish to characterize the left–terminating programs by proving the converse to Corollary 4.8. We also want to deal with nonground goals by proving some form of converse to Theorem 4.7. We begin with the ingredients of our level mapping.

Definition 4.9: If the SLD–tree from $P \cup \{G\}$ beginning with G is finite, $N(G)$ is the number of its nodes; otherwise, $N(G)$ is undefined.

Theorem 4.10: *If P is left–terminating, there is a level mapping f and a model $\mathcal{M}$ such that*

(i) *P is acceptable with respect to f and $\mathcal{M}$ and*

(ii) *For every goal clause G, G is bounded with respect to f and $\mathcal{M}$ if and only if every SLD–proof from $P \cup \{G\}$ beginning with G is finite.*

Proof: We define the required level mapping f and model $\mathcal{M}$ by setting $|A| = N(\{\neg A\})$ for each atomic sentence A of $\mathcal{L}$ and requiring that $\mathcal{M} \vDash A \Leftrightarrow$ there is an SLD–refutation of $P \cup \{\neg A\}$. Note that, as we are assuming that P is left–terminating, f is well defined. Also, by the completeness of SLD–resolution, each atomic sentence A is true in $\mathcal{M}$ if and only if it is a logical consequence of P. We now prove that f and $\mathcal{M}$ have the desired properties.

(i)   Consider any clause $C = A :\!- B_1, \dots, B_m$ in P'. Let $n = \mathcal{M}(B_1, \dots, B_m)$. There is an SLD–proof from $P \cup \{\neg A\}$ beginning with $\{\neg A\}$ and a resolution with C. By the definition of $\mathcal{M}$, there is an SLD–refutation of $P \cup \{\neg B_i\}$ beginning with $\neg B_i$ for each $i < n$. The SLD–search tree for each such refutation is clearly a subtree of the SLD–tree for $\{\neg A\}$. As each such search for $i < n$ succeeds, the SLD–tree for $\neg B_n$ is attached to the end of each successful search for refutations of all of the $\neg B_i$ for $i < n$. Thus the SLD–tree for $\{\neg A\}$ contains copies of the SLD–tree for $\{\neg B_i\}$ for every $i \leq n$. The definition of f then tells us that $|A| > |B_i|$ for each $i \leq n$ as required.

(ii)   Let G be a bounded goal clause. Suppose, for the sake of a contradiction, that there is a nonterminating SLD–proof $\langle G_0, C_0 \rangle, \langle G_1, C_1 \rangle, \dots$ starting with $G = G_0$. For any n, we can (starting with $\langle G_n, C_n \rangle$) find a substitution θ which grounds all the clauses of $\langle G_0, C_0 \rangle, \langle G_1, C_1 \rangle, \dots, \langle G_n, C_n \rangle$. This gives an SLD–proof beginning with the ground instance $G\theta$ of G of length n. As n was arbitrary, this contradicts the assumption that G is bounded.

Finally, suppose that every SLD–proof beginning with G terminates. Notice that the SLD–tree from any goal clause is finitely branching: Each immediate successor of a fixed node corresponds to a clause in the finite program P. Thus, by König's lemma (Theorem I.1.4) the SLD–tree for G is finite. Suppose it has n nodes. Again, as every SLD–tree has branchings of at most the number of clauses in P, there can be SLD–trees from ground instances of G with arbitrarily large numbers of nodes only if there are ones of arbitrarily large depth. Thus, if G is not bounded, there is an SLD–proof beginning with a ground instance of G of length $n + 1$. The lifting lemma for SLD–proofs (Exercise 1.6) then lifts such a proof to one of length $n + 1$ beginning with G. As this proof must be a path on the SLD–tree beginning with G we have the desired contradiction. $\square$

Corollary 4.11: *P is left–terminating if and only if it is acceptable.*

As an example we will show that the program PERM for deciding if one list is a permutation of another is left–terminating. The language of our program consists of a constant [ ] for the empty list and the binary list combining function "." of Example II.3.15. We also use the alternate notations and abbreviations introduced there such as $[a] \mid [b, c, d]$ for $[a, b, c, d]$. The ground terms of the language, i.e., its Herbrand universe H, consists of the closure of the constant [ ] under the list combining operation. The program for PERM includes a program APPEND (consisting of (a1) and (a2) below) for appending one list to another as well as two clauses (p1) and (p2) defining PERM from APPEND:

$(a1) \quad a([\,], Y, Y).$

$(a2) \quad a([X|Y], Z, [X|W]) :\!- a(Y, Z, W).$

$(p1) \quad p([\,], [\,]).$

$(p2) \quad p(X, [Y, Z]) :\!- a(W, [Y|V], X), a(W, V, U), p(U, Z).$

Now not all LD–proofs from PERM starting with a ground goal are finite (Exercise 3) but we will show that PERM is acceptable and so all SLD–proofs starting with ground goals will terminate.

Theorem 4.12: PERM *is acceptable (and so left–terminating).*

Proof: We first let $|x|$ be the length of x for any list x in the Herbrand universe, H. Thus, for example, $||[y|v]|| = |v| + 1$ for all $y, v \in H$. We define a level mapping by setting $|p(x, y)| = |x| + |y| + 1$ and $|a(x, y, z)| = \min\{|x|, |z|\}$. As our model we could take the intended interpretations for p and a on B (Exercise 6). Rather than verifying the semantic correctness of the program, however, it is easier to create an artificial model that embodies just enough to cut off the resolutions when needed. We define $\mathcal{M}$ with universe H by saying that $p(x, y)$ holds for every $x, y \in H$ and that $a(x, y, z)$ holds iff $|x| + |y| = |z|$. It is obvious from the definitions that $\mathcal{M}$ is a model of PERM. We prove that, with this choice of level mapping and model, PERM is acceptable.

We only have to check ground instances of clauses (a2) and (p2). For (a2) just note that, for any $x, y \in H$, $|y| < ||[x|y]||$ by definition. Thus for any $x, y, z, w \in H$,

$$|a(y, z, w)| = \min\{|y|, |w|\} < |a([x|y], z, [x|w])| = \min\{||[x|y]||, ||[x|w]||\}$$

as required. Now consider any ground instance of (p2):

$$p(x, [y, z]) :- a(w, [y|v], x),\ a(w, v, u),\ p(u, z).$$

It is clear that

$$|p(x, [y, z])| = |x| + |[y|z]| + 1 > |a(w, [y|v], x)| = \min\{|w|, |x|\}.$$

If $|w| + |[y|v]| \neq |x|$, then we are done by our choice of $\mathcal{M}$ and the definition of acceptability. Suppose then that $|w| + |[y|v]| = |x|$ and so $|w| \leq |x|$. Thus $|p(x, [y, z])| = |x| + |[y|z]| + 1 > |w| \geq |a(w, v, u)|$. Once again we are done unless $|w| + |v| = |u|$ as well. In this case, $|u| < |x|$ and so $|p(x, [y, z])| = |x| + |[y|z]| + 1 > |u| + |[y|z]| + 1 = |p(u, z)|$ as required to complete the proof of acceptability. $\square$

As acceptability implies left–termination, we have shown that PERM running with the standard implementation of PROLOG will terminate on any ground clause. As the logical consequences of PERM are the intended ones by Exercise 5, PERM will terminate with a correct answer on any ground goal. Thus we have a proven method for checking if one list is a permutation of another. More interestingly, we can use the characterization of termination in terms of boundedness to prove that it can do much more. For example, by starting with a goal of the form $G = \{\neg p(x, X)\}$ we would hope to be able to find all the permutations of a given list x. To see this, it suffices to prove that G is bounded. We prove much more.

Theorem 4.13: *For all terms $t, t_1, \ldots, t_n$ of $\mathcal{L}$, every goal G of the form $\{\neg p([t_1, \ldots, t_n], t)\}$ is bounded (with respect to the level mapping and model of the proof of Theorem 4.12).*

Proof: For any ground instance $G\gamma$ of G, $|G\gamma| = n + m + 1$ where $m = |t\gamma|$. As the length of $t\gamma$ is constant for any ground substitution γ, G is bounded. $\square$

Many other types of goal clauses can be proven bounded for PERM. See, for example, Exercise 7.

Exercises

Definition:

(i) P is *terminating for a goal G* if all LD–proofs from $P \cup \{G\}$ starting with G are finite. P is *terminating* if it is terminating for every ground goal G.

(ii) P is *recurrent with respect to a level mapping f* if, for every clause $A :- A_1, \ldots, A_n$ in P', $|A| > |A_i|$ for each $1 \leq i \leq n$. P is *recurrent* *if* it is recurrent with respect to some level mapping.

1. Prove that if P is recurrent it is terminating.
2. Prove that if P is terminating it is recurrent.
3. Prove that PERM is not terminating.
4. Prove that APPEND is recurrent.
5. Prove that the logical consequences of PERM of the form $p(x, y)$ for $x, y \in B$ are the intended ones.
6. Prove that one could use the intended interpretation of p and a on B as the model in the proof of Theorem 4.12.
7. Suppose $G = \{\neg A_1, \ldots, \neg A_n\}$. Prove that, if each A_i is bounded (with respect to some level mapping and model), then so is G.

5. Equality

Until now, we have ignored the whole question of mathematical equality. (Recall that in PROLOG, "$t_1 = t_2$" is used to mean that t_1 and t_2 can be unified.) The time has come to at least face the problem of "true" equality for it is indeed a problem for PROLOG. Syntactically, we introduce a special (reserved) two–place predicate written infix as $x = y$. (The use of $=$ for equality is too widespread to give it up in our exposition simply because PROLOG syntax took it for some other use. In all contexts other than PROLOG programs, we will use "$=$" for the equality relation.) We must now expand our deduction methods and semantics for predicate calculus to deal with this new special predicate.

The basic properties of equality (in a language $\mathcal{L}$) are captured by the following:

Definition 5.1: *The equality axioms for $\mathcal{L}$:*

(1) $x = x$.
(2) $x_1 = y_1 \wedge \ldots \wedge x_n = y_n \rightarrow f(x_1, \ldots, x_n) = f(y_1, \ldots, y_n)$ for each n–ary function symbol f of $\mathcal{L}$.
(3) $x_1 = y_1 \wedge \ldots \wedge x_n = y_n \rightarrow (P(x_1, \ldots, x_n) \rightarrow P(y_1, \ldots, y_n))$ for each n–ary predicate symbol P of $\mathcal{L}$ (including the binary one "$=$").

Reflexivity of "$=$" is guaranteed by (1). The other usual properties of equality (symmetry and transitivity) follow from (3) by taking P to be $=$ (Exercise 4).

We can now think of these axioms as being added to any set of sentences we are dealing with under any proof system. Thus, by a tableau refutation proof of a sentence S with "$=$" in its language, we mean one from the set of sentences S^* where S^* is S plus the universal closures of (1)–(3) for all the function and predicate symbols of S. Similarly, a resolution refutation of S is one from S^*. Unfortunately, simply adding in these clauses makes for a very inefficient procedure. We will return to this point shortly when we consider more specialized methods such as paramodulation.

The next step is to decide on the intended semantics for equality. Here there are two choices. We can treat equality as we did all other predicates and simply require that the interpretation of "=" be a two–place relation which satisfies all the equality axioms. From the proof theoretic, and so the PROLOG point of view, this is the only approach on which we have any real handle, and within the confines of a fixed language, it is all we can say about equality. On the other hand, from an abstract mathematical point of view, we would like to require that "=" always be interpreted as true equality.

We can, in fact, require this of our interpretations and still prove all the basic theorems of II.7 as before: soundness, completeness, compactness, etc.. The only problem arises in the proof of the completeness theorem. In the proof of Theorem II.7.3, our construction via the CST gives us a structure in which the interpretation of "=" satisfies all the above axioms but this does not guarantee that it is true equality. The solution is to divide out by the equivalence relation induced by "=". To be precise, let $\mathcal{A}$ be the structure determined by a noncontradictory path on the CST for a given set of sentence S. The elements of $\mathcal{A}$, we recall, are the ground terms t of a language $\mathcal{L}$. We define a relation $\equiv$ on them by: $t_1 \equiv t_2 \Leftrightarrow \mathcal{A} \vDash t_1 = t_2$. Using the equality axioms, it is easy to see that $\equiv$ is an equivalence relation (i.e., $t \equiv t$ for every t, if $t_1 \equiv t_2$ then $t_2 \equiv t_1$ and if $t_1 \equiv t_2$ and $t_2 \equiv t_3$, then $t_1 \equiv t_3$). We then define a structure $\mathcal{B}$ for $\mathcal{L}$ on the equivalence classes of $\equiv$. That is, the elements of $\mathcal{B}$ are the sets of the form $[t_1] = \{t \,|\, t \equiv t_1\}$ for each $t_1 \in \mathcal{A}$. The functions and relations are defined on $\mathcal{B}$ by choosing representatives and referring to $\mathcal{A}: \mathcal{B} \vDash P([t]_1, \dots, [t_n]) \Leftrightarrow \mathcal{A} \vDash P(t_1, \dots, t_n)$ (for P other than "=") and $f^{\mathcal{B}}([t]_1, \dots, [t_n]) = [f^{\mathcal{A}}(t_1, \dots, t_n)]$. Of course "=" is interpreted as true equality in $\mathcal{B}$. At this point, one must check that these definitions are independent of the choice of representatives (that is, the elements t_i chosen from the sets $[t_i]$). The final step is to show by induction, as we did for $\mathcal{A}$, that $\mathcal{B}$ agrees with every signed statement on the path used to construct $\mathcal{A}$. Thus $\mathcal{B}$ is the required model for S in which "=" is interpreted as true equality.

Theorem 5.2 (Completeness): *If S is any set of sentences which includes the equality axioms for the language of S, then either there is a tableau proof of $\square$ from S or there is a model for S in which $=$ is interpreted as true equality.*

As our main concern now is with the proof theoretic, i.e., resolution method, point of view we leave the details of this construction and the proof of the appropriate compactness theorem for such interpretations as exercises. From now on we use "=" simply as a reserved predicate symbol.

Definition 5.3: An *equality structure for a language* $\mathcal{L}$ with "=" is any structure for $\mathcal{L}$ which satisfies the equality axioms. Similarly, an *equality model of a set of sentences* S of $\mathcal{L}$ is an equality structure for $\mathcal{L}$ in which all sentences of S are true. An *equality resolution* (*or tableau*) *proof* from S is then one from S plus the equality axioms.

The soundness, completeness and compactness theorems for resolution (or tableaux) are then by definition true for equality interpretations and proofs. In terms of actually carrying out equality resolutions with any sort of efficiency, however, we are considerably worse off than in the original case. There are simply too many new rules. At this point we will give one revised resolution rule to handle equality that goes a long way towards alleviating the problem.

The inference scheme (paramodulation) we want will take the place of the equality axioms (2) and (3). That is, we want a rule (like resolution) which, when combined with resolution, will be complete for equality interpretations: If $\{x = x\} \in S$ and S has no equality model, then $\square$ is derivable from S using resolution and paramodulation. (The point here is that S may mention "=" but contain no equality axioms other than $x = x$.) The basic idea is that if we have a clause C_1 containing a literal $L(t, \ldots)$ in which a term t occurs and a clause C_2 (with no variables in common with C_1) containing $t = s$ then we can conclude from C_1 and C_2 not only $C_1 \cup C_2$ but also the modification of $C_1 \cup C_2$ in which we replace t by s in $L(t, \ldots)$. Of course we need not replace t by s everywhere in L. Thus, we want to consider replacement of a single occurrence of t by s in L. (Obviously, multiple replacements can then be generated by repeated uses of the rule.) We use $L[t/s]$ to represent the result of replacing some one occurrence of t by s in L.

Example 5.4: From $C_1 = \{\neg P(a),\, Q(b)\}$ and $C_2 = \{a = b, R(b)\}$ conclude $\{\neg P(b), Q(b), R(b)\}$. Note that we also drop $a = b$ from the result. As in resolution, it has been used and absorbed.

Of course as in resolution, we must consider the possibilities introduced by unifications.

Example 5.5: From $C_1 = \{\neg P(x), Q(x)\}$ and $C_2 = \{b = b, R(b)\}$ we can conclude $\{\neg P(b), Q(b), R(b)\}$. This is simply instantiation via unification.

More generally we should consider the following:

Example 5.6: From $C_1 = \{\neg P(f(g(x))), Q(x)\}$ and $C_2 = \{g(h(c)) = a, R(c)\}$ we can conclude $\{\neg P(f(a)), Q(h(c)), R(c)\}$. Here $g(x)$ is the term t being considered. We unified it with $g(h(c))$ by the substitution $\{x/h(c)\}$. After applying this substitution to C_1 to get $\{\neg P(fgh(c)), Q(h(c))\}$ we replaced the occurrence of $gh(c)$ by a as allowed by $gh(c) = a$ of C_2 and combined to get our result.

As with resolution, we may also collapse literals via unification before applying the substitution. Here it is necessary to separate these operations.

Definition 5.7: Suppose we can rename the variables of C_1 and C_2 so that they have no variables in common and C_1 is of the form $\{L(t_1), \ldots, L(t_n)\} \sqcup C_1'$ and C_2 is of the form $\{r_1 = s_1, \ldots, r_m = s_m\} \sqcup C_2'$. If σ_1 is an mgu for $\{L(t_1), \ldots, L(t_n)\}$, σ_2 one for $\{r_1 = s_1, \ldots, r_m = s_m\}$ and σ one for $\{t_1\sigma_1, r_1\sigma_2\}$ then any clause of the form

$$\{L \ \sigma_1\sigma[t_1\sigma_1\sigma/s_1\sigma_2\sigma]\} \cup C_1'\sigma_1\sigma \cup C_2'\sigma_2\sigma$$

is a *paramodulant* of C_1 and C_2.

Together with resolution, this rule is complete for equality interpretations. In fact, as with resolution, a linear version is also complete.

Theorem 5.8: *If $\{x = x\} \in S$, $C \in S$ and $S - \{C\}$ has an equality interpretation but S does not, then there is a linear proof of $\Box$ from S starting with C via resolution and paramodulation.* (As you would expect, such a linear proof is a sequence $\langle C_0, B_0 \rangle, \ldots, \langle C_n, B_n \rangle$ in which $C_0 = C$, $C_{n+1} = \Box$, each B_i is in S or is a C_j for $j < i$ and each C_{i+1} follows from C_i and B_i via one resolution or paramodulation step.)

The proof is very much like that for resolution alone and we omit it. The general problem of dealing with just equality is quite complicated. It is a well developed subject on its own, that of rewrite rules. The problems of integrating equality with PROLOG or more general theorem provers is an as yet underdeveloped topic of current research that lies beyond the scope of this book.

Exercises

1. Prove that the tableau method with equality axioms is sound for the class of interpretations in which $=$ is interpreted as true equality.

2. Give a complete proof of the completeness theorem for tableau proofs (from the equality axioms) with the true equality interpretation (Theorem 5.2).

3. Prove the compactness theorem (a set of sentences is satisfiable iff every finite subset is) for the true equality interpretation.

4. Prove that the symmetry and transitivity of "$=$" follow from (1)–(3) of Definition 5.1. (Hint: For the first let $x_1 = x$, $x_2 = x$, $y_1 = y$ and $y_2 = x$ in (3). For the second let $x_1 = x$, $x_2 = y$, $y_1 = x$ and $z_2 = z$.)

6. Negation as Failure

PROLOG, as we have described it so far, has no way to derive negative information. (The Herbrand structure for a PROLOG program P in which every ground atomic formula is true is obviously a model of P.) Nonetheless, it is often the case that we want to conclude that certain facts do not hold.

In PROLOG derivations, negation is implemented in terms of failure, i.e., the goal $\neg A$, often written "not(A)", succeeds if and only if PROLOG would return "no" to the goal A. There are a number of ways of understanding negation which are used to justify this implementation. The two earliest are the *closed world assumption* (CWA) and the *completed database* (CDB) view. The first falls outside the scope of predicate logic so we will explain it fairly briefly; we will give a more detailed treatment of the second. These two approaches also apply to a more general implementation of negation as failure which allows arbitrary clauses in the program as well as in the goal.

In the next section we will describe a more recent approach to negation, that of stable models. The characterization of such models also goes beyond predicate logic. It is closely related to nonmonotonic logic which we will also describe in §7.

The CWA arises naturally in the context of databases. If we are given a database of grades for students in the math department, we may have reason to believe that it is a correct and complete list. Thus, if the fact that Jones got an A in Math 486 does not appear, we may reasonably assume that it is false. The extension of this principle to a setting like PROLOG with rules as well as data leads to the CWA for a program P: If a ground atomic formula (positive literal) A is not a logical consequence of P then we may infer $\neg A$.

The first thing to note here is that the CWA deals with the abstract notion of logical consequence or, equivalently, provability in some complete proof systems for predicate logic. By the undecidability of provability in predicate logic (Corollary 8.10), however, we cannot hope to implement such a rule even in theory. The closest we can expect to come is to conclude $\neg A$ when we have a proof that A is not a logical consequence of P. For a PROLOG–like system such a proof might reasonably consist of a finite SLD–tree starting with the goal $\neg A$ in which every branch ends a failure. In this case, we know that there is no SLD–refutation starting with the given goal. The completeness theorem for SLD–refutations (Theorem 1.8) then tells us that A is not a logical consequence of P. Such a tree is called a *finitely failed* SLD*–tree for* $P \cup \{A\}$.

The usual implementations of PROLOG only check for a finitely failed SLD–tree via the standard selection rule. For theoretical analyses, however, we are better off considering a more general definition which has a clearer semantic content. To this end, we will have to consider refutation search procedures which do not follow the standard rule or even any selection rule that always chooses the same literal from a given goal. (See Exercise 2.)

We begin with a generalized notion of a selection rule that makes its choice of literal at any step based on the entire history of the proof up to that point rather than on just the current goal clause.

Definition 6.1:

(i) A *generalized selection rule* R is a function which, given any LD–proof $\langle G_0, C_0 \rangle, \ldots, \langle G_n, C_n \rangle$, chooses a literal from G_n.

(ii) An LD–proof $\langle G_0, C_0 \rangle, \ldots, \langle G_n, C_n \rangle$ is a *proof via a generalized selection rule* R if the literal resolved on at each step i, $0 \le i < n$ is the one chosen by R from the proof $\langle G_0, C_0 \rangle, \ldots, \langle G_i, C_i \rangle$ up to that point.

We now give the formal definition of the SLD–tree associated with a given goal, program and generalized selection rule.

Definition 6.2: Let P be PROLOG program, G a goal clause and R a generalized selection rule. The *associated* SLD*–tree (from P starting with G via R)* is a finitely branching tree T labeled with goal clauses such that each path of T is associated with an SLD proof via R. We define T by induction. The root node of T is labeled with G. If any node σ of T is labeled with a goal clause G' and the generalized selection rule R chooses the literal $\neg A$ from G' given the proof associated with the path through T leading to G', then the immediate successors of σ correspond to the clauses C_i of P which can be resolved with G' on $\neg A$. These nodes are labeled with the results of resolving G' on $\neg A$ with the corresponding clause C_i of P. (The proof associated with the path to a successor of G' is the one associated with the path to G' followed by the appropriate resolution.)

Note that, in general, the SLD–tree associated with some P, G and R may be infinite. Some paths may succeed, i.e., end with $\square$ (success) and so be (necessarily) finite refutations of G from P. Others may be failed, i.e., there is no clause of P with which the final goal can be resolved on the selected literal. Other paths, however, may never terminate.

We can now approximate the set of literals A which are not logical consequences of a program P by considering those for which the search for a refutation of A fails in a finite and hence observable way.

Definition 6.3:

(i) The SLD–tree associated with P, G and R is *finitely failed* if it is finite and every path ends because of a failure to find a clause of P with which the selected literal can be resolved. (In particular no path ends with success, i.e., $\square$.)

(ii) The SLD *finite failure set* of a PROLOG program P is the set of ground atoms A such that there is a generalized selection rule R such that the SLD–tree associated with P, $\{\neg A\}$ and R is finitely failed.

Recall the contrast between breadth–first and depth–first searches of SLD–trees in terms of completeness. In this setting, there are generalized selection rules R which guarantee that if A is in the finite failure set of P then the SLD–tree via R is finitely failed and there are others which do not have this property.

Definition 6.4: An SLD–proof (via R) is *fair* if it is either finite (and so either failed or a successful refutation) or, for every occurrence of a literal Q in the proof (say in G_i), either R selects Q at step i or there is a stage $j > i$ at which $Q\theta_i \ldots \theta_{j-1}$ is selected by R, where θ_k is the mgu used at step k of the proof. A generalized selection rule R is *fair* if every SLD–proof via R is fair.

It is not hard to design a fair generalized selection rule R. However, no ordinary selection rule can be fair. (See Exercises 1–2.) The following result says that we can restrict our attention to any fair generalized selection rule.

Theorem 6.5: *For a program P and ground atomic formula A, A is in the SLD–finite failure set of P iff the SLD–tree for A via R is failed for every fair generalized selection rule R. Thus, there is a finitely failed SLD–tree for A using any selection rule if and only if the SLD–tree for A is finitely failed for any fair generalized selection rule.*

Proof: The "if" direction is immediate from the definition of the finite failure set. Suppose, therefore, that A is in the finite failure set of P and R is any fair generalized selection rule. We wish to prove that the SLD–tree via R starting with $\{\neg A\}$ is finitely failed. We prove a stronger lemma by induction.

Lemma 6.6: *Let P be a PROLOG program and R a fair generalized selection rule. If a goal clause $G = \{\neg A_1, \ldots, \neg A_m\}$ has a finitely failed SLD–tree of depth k (via any generalized selection rule) and $\langle G_0, C_0 \rangle, \ldots, \langle G_n, C_n \rangle$ is an SLD–proof from P via R with $G_n = G$, then every path on the SLD–tree via R that has $\langle G_0, C_0 \rangle, \ldots, \langle G_n, C_n \rangle$ as an initial segment is finitely failed.*

Proof: We proceed by induction on k. Suppose $k = 1$ and A_s is the literal selected from G in the given failed SLD–tree S of depth 1. By the definition of a failed SLD–tree, no clause in P has a head that will unify with A_s. Now consider any path Q on the SLD–tree T via R starting with $\langle G_0, C_0 \rangle, \ldots, \langle G_n, C_n \rangle$. As R is fair there is a node on Q at which R chooses $A_s\theta$ for some substitution θ. By our assumption about A_s, no clause of P has a head which can be unified with $A_s\theta$. Thus the path Q terminates with a failure at this point. As Q was an arbitrary path on T with the specified initial segment, T is finitely failed below this point.

For the induction step, let A_s be the literal chosen at the first level of the given finitely failed SLD–tree S of depth $k + 1$. The first level of S then consists of all the resolvents of all resolutions on A_s with clauses in P. Each node at this level then has the form

$$H = \{\neg A_1, \ldots, \neg A_{s-1}, \neg B_1, \ldots, \neg B_k, \neg A_{s+1}, \ldots, \neg A_n\}\theta$$

where θ is the mgu associated with the appropriate resolution and clause C of P. Note that H has a finitely failed SLD–tree of depth k.

Now let Q be any path on the SLD–tree T via R starting with $\langle G_0, C_0 \rangle$, $\ldots, \langle G_n, C_n \rangle$ with $G_n = G$. Again, by the fairness of R, there is some level, say $m - 1$, of Q at which we first select a literal of the form $A_s \psi$ coming from A_s in G. Let $\langle G_0, C_0 \rangle, \ldots, \langle G_m, C_m \rangle$ be the path up to the point at which we have performed the resolution on $A_s \psi$. The last resolution on this path was with some $C \in P$ whose head unified with $A_s \psi$ and so with A_s. The proof of the switching lemma (Lemma 1.11) shows that G_m is a renaming of the clause H on the first level of S which corresponds to C_{m-1}. As starting a finitely failed SLD–tree is obviously invariant under renamings, G_m starts a finitely failed SLD–tree of depth k and we can apply the induction hypothesis to $\langle G_0, C_0 \rangle, \ldots, \langle G_m, C_m \rangle$ to conclude that Q is finitely failed. $\square$

In view of Theorem 6.5, we may assume that we have specified any fair generalized selection rule R to define our SLD–trees. It is now reasonably clear how a PROLOG type system equipped with an implementation of a fair R should attack a question asking for negative as well as positive conclusions. We start with a clause G containing both positive and negative literals. We then carry out an SLD–proof via R except that when we select a positive literal A we try to construct a finitely failed SLD–tree via R starting with A. If we succeed, we eliminate the literal A and continue. If we fail, the attempt at refutation of G fails as well. We formalize this procedure as SLDNF–refutations (SLD–refutations with negation as failure).

Definition 6.7:

(i) A *general goal clause* G is simply an arbitrary clause.

(ii) Let P be a PROLOG program. An SLDNF–*proof via R from P beginning with G* is a sequence $\langle G_i, C_i \rangle$ of general goal clauses G_i and clauses $C_i \in P$ with $G_0 = G$ and $G_{n+1} = \square$ which is generated as follows: If $R(G_i)$, the literal chosen by R, is negative, then G_{i+1} is a resolvent of G_i and C_i via mgu θ_i on literal $R(G_i)$. If $R(G_i)$ is positive, it must be a ground literal A. In this case, there must be a finitely failed SLD–tree (via R) starting with the goal $\neg A$. We then have G_{i+1} equal to G_i with A deleted, C_i plays no role and θ_i is the identity.

As usual, the composition sequence of mgu's $\theta_0 \ldots \theta_1 = \theta$ for such a proof is called its *answer substitution*.

The definition of the SLDNF–*tree* from P starting with G via R is the same as that of the corresponding SLD–tree (Definition 6.2), modulo the modification in (ii). A path on the tree is just an attempt to construct such an SLDNF–refutation. The path *succeeds* if the attempt eventually produces $\square$. Suppose at some point on such a path we encounter an SLD–tree T starting with some $\neg R(G_i)$ where $R(G_i)$ is a positive ground literal. If T has $\square$ on one of its paths, T is not finitely failed. In this case, we say that this attempt at finding an SLDNF–refutation *fails*. (Of course, even if the SLDNF–tree is not finitely failed, we may never discover this fact and the proof procedure may simply fall into an infinite search.) If $R(G_i)$ is positive but not ground, we say that the proof *flounders* at this point.

Warning: We allow the SLDNF–refutation to proceed when R chooses a positive literal only if it is ground. Such a choice is called *safe*. This restriction is essential as we are interpreting the success of $\neg q$ as the failure of q. If q has a free variable X, this is clearly unfounded. A question "?– $\neg q(X)$." asks for a c such that $\neg q(c)$ holds while "?– $q(X)$." asks for a d such that $q(d)$ holds. Clearly neither one is the negation or failure of the other. Unfortunately, most PROLOG systems do not bother to check that a positive literal is ground before applying the negation as failure procedure. This can lead to unexpected (and indeed false) results.

Before describing the relationship between negation as failure and the CWA, we introduce a more general approach in terms of "*completed data–bases*" (CDB). The idea here is that, when one specifies the conditions under which something occurs, one specifies them all. In terms of a particular program P, suppose we consider one n–ary predicate r and all the clauses of P with r in their heads:

$$r(t_{1,1}, \ldots, t_{1,n}) :- q_{1,1}, \ldots, q_{1,n_1}.$$

$$\vdots$$

$$r(t_{k,1}, \ldots, t_{k,n}) :- q_{k,1}, \ldots, q_{k,n_k}.$$

If we view this list as a complete description of when $r(X_1, \ldots, X_n)$ holds (for new variables X_i), then we can express this view by the sentence

$$r(X_1, \ldots, X_n) \leftrightarrow q_1 \vee \ldots \vee q_k.$$

where $Y_1, \ldots, Y_{p_i}$ are the variables in $q_{i,1}, \ldots, q_{i,n_i}$, $X_1, \ldots, X_n$ are new variables and q_i is $\exists Y_1, \ldots, Y_{p_i}(X_1 = t_{i,1} \wedge \ldots \wedge X_n = t_{i,n} \wedge q_{i,1} \wedge \ldots \wedge q_{i,n_i})$. The "if" ($\leftarrow$) direction in these equivalences is simply the assertions of the given program. The "only if" ($\rightarrow$) direction say that we have completely specified r by the program clauses. Comp(P), *the completion of P*, includes such an axiom for each predicate r appearing in P. If r does not occur in the head of any clause of P, we include the axiom $\forall \vec{X} \neg r(\vec{X})$ in Comp(P). In the absence of equality, Comp(P) consists of these axioms and no others.

To deal with equality, we include in Comp(P) the basic equality axioms (1)–(3) of §5 for the language of P. In addition, the database point of view dictates that distinct terms (names) represent distinct objects. We incorporate this point of view (to the extent possible in first order logic) by including the following axioms in Comp(P) as well:

(4) $f(x_1, \ldots, x_n) \neq g(y_1, \ldots, y_m)$ for each distinct pair of function symbols f and g of arities n, $m \geq 0$ respectively.

(5) $t(x) \neq x$ for each term $t(x)$ (other than x itself) in which x occurs.

(6) $f(x_1, \ldots, x_n) = f(y_1, \ldots, y_n) \rightarrow x_1 = y_1 \wedge \ldots \wedge x_n = y_n$ for each n–ary function symbol f.

This completes the construction of $\text{Comp}(P)$ from P. Every clause in P is clearly a consequence of $\text{Comp}(P)$ and so $\text{Comp}(P) \vDash P$. Moreover, if P is a PROLOG program, $\text{Comp}(P)$ is consistent. (Again, the Herbrand structure in which "=" is interpreted as true equality and every other ground atomic formula is true is a model.) We can now use $\text{Comp}(P)$ to prove soundness and completeness theorems "justifying" the negation as failure rule. We begin with a lemma relating unification and the equality axioms (1)–(6).

Lemma 6.8: *Let $S = \{s_1 = t_1, \ldots, s_n = t_n\}$.*

(i) *If S is unifiable and $\theta = \{x_1/r_1, \ldots, x_m/r_m\}$ is the mgu given by the unification algorithm (II.12.3), then* (1)–(6) $\vDash (s_1 = t_1 \wedge \ldots \wedge s_n = t_n) \to (x_1 = r_1 \wedge \ldots \wedge x_m = r_m)$.

(ii) *If S is not unifiable, then* (1)–(6) $\vDash (s_1 = t_1 \wedge \ldots \wedge s_n = t_n) \to A \wedge \neg A$ *for any sentence A.*

Proof: Consider the unification algorithm as applied to S. It produces a sequence of substitutions $\theta_0, \theta_1, \ldots, \theta_n$. Let $\{x_1/r_{k,1}, \ldots, x_m/r_{k,m}\}$ be the composition $\theta_0 \ldots \theta_k$. One proves by induction on k that (1)–(6) $\vDash (s_1 = t_1 \wedge \ldots \wedge s_n = t_n)\theta_0 \ldots \theta_k \to (x_1 = r_{k,1} \wedge \ldots \wedge x_m = r_{k,m})$ for each k up to the point at which the algorithm terminates. If it terminates with a unifier we have proved (i). If it terminates with the announcement that S is not unifiable, it is easy to see that (1)–(6) prove that no instance of $(s_1 = t_1 \wedge \ldots \wedge s_n = t_n)\theta_0 \ldots \theta_k$ can be true, as is required for (ii). We leave the details of the induction and verifications asExercise 3. $\square$

Theorem 6.9 (Soundness of SLDNF–refutation): *Let P be a PROLOG program.*

(i) *If the SLDNF–tree via R from P beginning with a general goal $G = \{L_1, \ldots, L_m\}$ is finitely failed, then $\text{Comp}(P) \vDash L_1 \vee \ldots \vee L_m$.*

(ii) *If there is a success path, i.e., an SLDNF–refutation of G from P, on the tree with answer substitution θ, then $\text{Comp}(P) \vDash (\neg L_1 \wedge \ldots \wedge \neg L_m)\theta$.*

Proof:

(i) We proceed by induction on the depth of the finitely failed SLDNF–tree starting with G. We begin with the case that the tree is finitely failed at its first level.

If $R(G)$ is a negative literal $L = \neg r(s_1, \ldots, s_n)$, then there is no clause $C \in P$ with whose head we can unify $r(s_1, \ldots, s_n)$. If there is no clause in P with r in its head then $\text{Comp}(P)$ includes the axiom $\forall \vec{X} \neg r(\vec{X})$ and so $\text{Comp}(P) \vDash \neg r(s_1, \ldots, s_n)$. Otherwise, with the notation as in the definition of $\text{Comp}(P)$, we see that $\text{Comp}(P) \vDash r(s_1, \ldots, s_n) \leftrightarrow \vee\{\exists Y_1, \ldots, Y_{p_i} (s_1 = t_{i,1} \wedge \ldots \wedge s_n = t_{i,n} \wedge q_{i,1} \wedge \ldots \wedge q_{i,n_i}) | i \leq k\}$. As $r(s_1, \ldots, s_n)$ does not unify with any $r(t_{i,1}, \ldots, t_{i,n})$, by assumption, the falsity of each of the disjuncts follows from the equality axioms by Lemma 6.8(ii). Thus $\text{Comp}(P) \vDash \neg r(s_1, \ldots, s_n)$ and so $\text{Comp}(P) \vDash G$ as required.

If $R(G)$ is a positive literal L, it must be ground (or the proof would flounder rather than fail) and the SLD–tree starting with $\neg L$ must have a path ending in $\square$. Thus, by the soundness of SLD–refutations (Theorem 1.9), $P \vDash L$ as required. (Note that as L is ground, the answer substitution given by the SLD–refutation is irrelevant.)

Now consider the inductive step. Suppose that G has a finitely failed SLDNF–tree of depth $k + 1$. If $R(G)$ is a positive ground literal L, then the SLD–tree starting with $\neg L$ is finitely failed and G_1 is $G - \{L\}$. It has a finitely failed SLDNF–tree of depth k and so by induction, $\text{Comp}(P) \vDash G_1$. As G contains G_1, $\text{Comp}(P) \vDash G$ as well.

Finally, suppose $R(G)$ is a negative literal $L = \neg r(s_1, \dots, s_n)$. (Again we adopt the notation of the definition of $\text{Comp}(P)$.) Each immediate successor H_i of G on level 1 of the given failed SLDNF–tree is the result of applying the appropriate mgu θ_i to G with L replaced by $\neg q_{i,1}, \dots, \neg q_{i,n_i}$ (for $i \leq k$). Each has a failed SLDNF–tree of depth $\leq k$ and so, by induction, $\text{Comp}(P) \vDash H_i$ for each $i \leq k$. It thus suffices to prove that $\text{Comp}(P) \vDash \wedge H_i \to \forall \vec{X} G$. To see this, it suffices in turn to prove that

$$\text{Comp}(P) \vDash \wedge \{(\neg q_{i,1} \vee \dots \vee \neg q_{i,n_i})\theta_i | i \leq k\} \to \neg r(s_1, \dots, s_n).$$

Now by the definition of $\text{Comp}(P)$, $\neg r(s_1, \dots, s_n)$ can fail to hold only if $\exists Y_1, \dots, Y_{p_i}(s_1 = t_{i,1} \wedge \dots \wedge s_n = t_{i,n} \wedge q_{i,1} \wedge \dots \wedge q_{i,n_i})$ for some $i \leq k$. By Lemma 6.8, this can happen only if there is a $\vec{Y}$ which unifies s_j and $t_{i,j}$ for each $j \leq n$ as well as witness $q_{i,1} \wedge \dots \wedge q_{i,n_i}$. As θ_i is the mgu for this unification, the assumption that $(\neg q_{i,1} \vee \dots \vee \neg q_{i,n_i})\theta_i$ implies that there are no such $\vec{Y}$ as required. $\square$

(ii) We proceed by induction on the length of the SLDNF–refutation. Suppose first that the refutation has length 1 and so G contains only one literal L. If L is positive, it is ground and there is a finitely failed SLD–tree starting with $\neg L$. By (i), $\text{Comp}(P) \vDash \neg L$ as required. If L is negative, say $\neg r(s_1, \dots, s_n)$, then there is a clause of the form $r(t_1, \dots, t_n)$ in P that can be unified with L by some θ. Thus $\neg L\theta$ is a consequence of P and hence of $\text{Comp}(P)$ as required.

Next, consider an SLDNF–refutation of G of length $k + 1$. If $R(G)$ is a positive literal L_i, then L_i is ground, θ_0 is the identity and $G_1 = \{L_1, \dots, L_{i-1}, L_{i+1}, \dots, L_m\}$ has an SLDNF–refutation of length k with mgu's $\theta_1 \dots \theta_k$. As in the base case, $\text{Comp}(P) \vDash \neg L_i$; by the induction hypothesis $\text{Comp}(P) \vDash (\neg L_1 \wedge \dots \wedge \neg L_{i-1} \wedge \neg L_{i+1} \wedge \dots \wedge \neg L_m)\theta_1 \dots \theta_k$. Thus, $\text{Comp}(P) \vDash (\neg L_1 \wedge \dots \wedge \neg L_m)\theta_0\theta_1 \dots \theta_k$ as required.

Finally, suppose $R(G)$ is a negative literal $L_i = \neg r(s_1, \dots, s_n)$, and $G_1 = \{L_1, \dots, L_{i-1}, \neg q_{j,1}, \dots, \neg q_{j,n_j}, L_{i+1}, \dots, L_m\}\theta_0$. By induction, $\text{Comp}(P) \vDash \{\neg L_1 \wedge \dots \wedge \neg L_{i-1} \wedge q_{j,1} \wedge \dots \wedge q_{j,n_j} \wedge \neg L_{i+1} \wedge \dots \wedge \neg L_m\}\theta_0 \dots \theta_{k+1}$. Now by the definition of $\text{Comp}(P)$, the fact that θ_0 unifies $r(s_1, \dots, s_n)$ and $r(t_{j,1}, \dots, t_{j,n})$ and Lemma 6.8(i), $\text{Comp}(P) \vDash (q_{j,1} \wedge \dots \wedge q_{j,n_j})\theta_0 \to r(s_1, \dots, s_n)\theta_0$. Thus we see that $\text{Comp}(P) \vDash \neg L_i\theta_0 \dots \theta_k$ as required to complete the induction step. $\square$

Theorem 6.10 (Completeness of SLDNF–refutation): *If P is a* PROLOG *program, $G = \{\neg A_1, \ldots, \neg A_k\}$ an ordinary goal clause, R a fair generalized selection rule and $Comp(P) \vDash \neg A_1 \vee \ldots \vee \neg A_k$ then there is a finitely failed* SLD–*tree from P via R beginning with G.*

Proof: The idea of the proof is much like that for the proof of completeness of the tableau method (II.7) as modified to handle equality in §5. If the SLD–tree beginning with G is not finitely failed, then it has a (possibly infinite) path Q. We use the terms and formulas appearing on Q to define a model $\mathcal{M}$ of $Comp(P)$ such that $\mathcal{M} \vDash \exists \vec{X}(A_1 \wedge \ldots \wedge A_k)$. ($\vec{X}$ lists the free variables of G.) The construction of $\mathcal{M}$ then establishes the contrapositive of the desired theorem.

Let $G_0, G_1, \ldots$ and $\theta_0, \theta_1, \ldots$ be the goals and the mgu's appearing in the SLD–proof associated with Q. As in §5, the elements of M are equivalence classes of terms of the language and the function symbols operate on them in the obvious way defined there. The crucial new idea here is to use the sequence of mgu's to define the equivalence relation on the terms. We say that two terms s and t are equivalent, $s \equiv t$, if they are eventually identified by the sequence of mgu's, i.e., there is an m such that $s\theta_0 \ldots \theta_m = t\theta_0 \ldots \theta_m$. It is easy to see that this relation is, in fact, an equivalence relation (Exercise 4). We denote the equivalence class of a term t by $[t]$ and let the universe M of our intended model be the set of these equivalence classes. It is now easy to see that the equality axioms (1)–(6) of $Comp(P)$ are satisfied in M when $=$ is interpreted as true equality on the equivalence classes (Exercises 5).

As the first step in defining the atomic formulas true in $\mathcal{M}$, we declare $r([t_1], \ldots, [t_n])$ true if there are $s_i \in [t_i]$ such that $\neg r(s_1, \ldots, s_n)$ appears as a literal in one of the goal clauses G_m. Note that this immediately makes $\mathcal{M} \vDash \exists \vec{X}(A_1 \wedge \ldots \wedge A_k)$ (as the (classes of the) terms in G provide the witnesses).

Our next, and most critical, claim is that the set S of atomic facts declared true so far satisfies the "only if" direction of the axioms for predicate letters in $Comp(P)$. Suppose $\neg r(s_1, \ldots, s_n)$ first appears as a literal in the goal clause G_m. By the fairness of R, there is a $u > m$ at which $\neg r(s_1, \ldots, s_n)\theta_m \ldots \theta_u$ is selected. Note that $\neg r(s_1, \ldots, s_n)\theta_m \ldots \theta_u = \neg r(s_1, \ldots, s_n)\theta_0 \ldots \theta_u$ by the usual convention on the choice of variables and mgu's. At that step it is replaced by the literals $(\neg q_{i,1}, \ldots, \neg q_{i,n_i})\theta_{u+1}$ $(= (\neg q_{i,1}, \ldots, \neg q_{i,n_i})\theta_0 \ldots \theta_{u+1})$ from the body of the appropriate clause of P. As θ_{u+1} is an mgu for this resolution, each $q_{i,j}\theta_{u+1}$ is in S. So by Lemma 6.8(i) we have the desired witnesses for the disjunct q_i of the instance of the axiom of $Comp(P)$ associated with $r([s_1], \ldots, [s_n])$.

We now have to extend S so as to make $\mathcal{M}$ a model of the "if" direction of the axioms, i.e. of P, without losing the "only if" direction. Let P' be the set of ground substitution instances of clauses of P by elements of M and let S' be the set of resolution consequences of $S \cup P'$. Let $\mathcal{M}$ be such that S' is the set of atomic facts true in M. We claim that $\mathcal{M}$ is the desired model of $\text{Comp}(P)$. As it is obviously a model of P, we only have to check that the "only if" direction of the axioms for each predicate r have been preserved as well. This claim is immediate by induction on the length of the resolution deduction putting any $r(t_1, \ldots, t_n)$ into S': It can be deduced only if some appropriate instances of the $q_{i,1}, \ldots, q_{i,n_i}$ in one of the clauses of P with r in its head have already been deduced. $\square$

The definition of $\text{Comp}(P)$ formalizes the intuition behind the CDB approach. Analogously, $\text{CWA}(P)$ is the set of all sentences which should be associated with P according to the CWA (closed world assumption). The basic intuition of the CWA is that, for any positive ground literal L, if $P \nvdash L$ then we should infer $\neg L$. We can thus view it as adjoining to P the following clauses:

(0) $\{\neg L\}$ for each ground positive literal L such that $P \nvdash L$.

While the CWA shares with CDB the view that the domain of discourse is correctly captured by the ground terms, the CWA takes it even farther. In addition to the equality axioms (1)–(6) described above, it asserts that the universe consists precisely of the ground terms. This assertion cannot, however, be guaranteed by a formula of predicate logic (Exercise 6). If we consider only logical consequence ($\vDash$) rather than provability, we can express this requirement by an infinitary clause, DCA, the *domain closure axiom*:

(7) $x = t_1 \vee \ldots \vee x = t_n \vee \ldots$

where $\langle t_i \rangle$ a list of all the ground terms.

We now write $\text{CWA}(P)$ to denote the extension of P by (0)–(7). Note that any model for $\text{CWA}(P)$ is an Herbrand model for P. As the adjunction of (0) guarantees that the truth of every ground literal is determined by $\text{CWA}(P)$, there can be at most one such model. Indeed for any PROLOG program P, $\text{CWA}(P)$ is always satisfiable and its only model is the minimal Herbrand model for P (Exercise 7). As this model is also one of $\text{Comp}(P)$ (Exercise 8), the soundness results (Theorem 6.9) proved for negation as failure and $\text{Comp}(P)$ hold automatically for $\text{CWA}(P)$ as well. There can, however, be no completeness theorem comparable to Theorem 6.10 for $\text{CWA}(P)$. Indeed, no effective procedure (such as searching for an SLDNF–refutation) can list all the logical consequences of $\text{CWA}(P)$ for every P (Exercise 8.6).

In addition to sometimes wanting to derive negative information, the PROLOG programmer might like to use such expressions in the program as well. This leads to the notion of general programs and general SLDNF–resolution.

Definition 6.11: A *general program clause* is one which contains at least one positive literal (but perhaps more). A *general program* is a set of general program clauses.

In any given general program clause $\{R, \bar{L}_1, \ldots, \bar{L}_n\}$ we single out one positive literal, R, as the head and consider all others as the body of the clause. We then write the clause in PROLOG notation (with $\neg$) as $R :- L_1, \ldots, L_n$. (Unfortunately, the interpretation and analysis will depend on which positive literal is chosen as the head.) In the same vein, we write general goal clauses in the form $\{\neg L_1, \ldots, \neg L_n\}$; however, as before the hope is to show that $P \vDash \exists X_1 \ldots X_m (L_1 \wedge \ldots \wedge L_n)\theta$ by deriving $\square$ (via some form of resolution) from $P \cup \{G\}$ with mgu's $\theta_0 \ldots \theta_k = \theta$.

We can now extend the definition of SLDNF–refutations to general programs by introducing a recursion at the point at which we search for a finitely failed tree. We now look for a finitely failed SLDNF–tree. The extensions of a general program P to CWA(P) and Comp(P) are defined as before. Soundness results like those of Theorems 6.8, 6.9 can be proved in this general setting as well. The completeness result of Theorem 6.10 no longer holds. Indeed, the completeness theorem cannot be extended to general goal clauses even for all PROLOG programs (Exercise 9). Weaker forms that deal only with the cases in which every branch of the SLDNF–tree ends in success or failure do hold. Under these conditions, it is possible to show that the SLDNF–tree gives, in some sense, "all" the answers that are consequences of CWA(P) or Comp(P). We refer the reader to Shepherdson [1984, 5.4] for a treatment of CWA(P) and to Chapter 3 of Lloyd [1987, 5.4] for a thorough discussion of the CDB approach and Comp(P).

The crucial caveat in the setting of general programs P is that it may turn out that CWA(P) or Comp(P) or both are unsatisfiable even though P is satisfiable (Exercises 10–12). Conditions like those of recurrence and acceptability considered in §4 can, however, be used to guarantee the consistency of Comp(P) and to produce a completeness theorem for SLDNF–refutations with respect to the semantics given by Comp(P). (Again we refer the reader to Lloyd [1987, 5.4].)

Exercises

1. Show that no selection rule that always chooses the same literal from each goal clause can be fair.

   (Hint: Consider the program P with three clauses:

   $$(1) \;\; r :- p, q. \qquad (2) \;\; p :- p. \qquad (3) \;\; q :- q. \;)$$

2. Describe a fair generalized selection rule and prove that it is fair.

   (Hint: Always choose the first literal to appear in the proof so far that has not yet been chosen.)

3. Complete the proof of Lemma 6.8.

4. Verify that the relation $\equiv$ defined in the proof of Theorem 6.10 is an equivalence relation.

5. Verify that the equality axioms (1)–(6) are satisfied in the set M defined in the proof of Theorem 6.10 when "=" is interpreted as true equality of equivalence classes.

6. Prove that no set of sentences of predicate logic can imply axiom (7) of CWA. (Hint: Use the compactness theorem.)

7. Prove that the unique model for $\text{CWA}(P)$ for a PROLOG program P is the minimal Herbrand model for P.

8. Prove that the minimal Herbrand model for a PROLOG program P is also a model of $\text{Comp}(P)$.

9. Give a counterexample to the generalization of Theorem 6.10 to general goal clauses. (Hint: Write a short program and choose a general goal such that every attempted SLDNF–refutation flounders.)

10. Give an example of a general program P such that $\text{Comp}(P)$ (and hence P) is satisfiable but $\text{CWA}(P)$ is not.

11. Give an example of a general program P such that $\text{CWA}(P)$ (and hence P) is satisfiable but $\text{Comp}(P)$ is not.

12. Give an example of a satisfiable general program P such that neither $\text{Comp}(P)$ nor CWA is satisfiable.

7. Negation and Nonmonotonic Logic

The general procedure of implementing negation as failure described in the last section is both useful and important. Nonetheless, it violates one of the most basic tenets of mathematical reasoning. In mathematical reasoning (and indeed in all the systems we consider elsewhere in this book) a conclusion drawn from a set of premises can be also be drawn from any larger set of premises. More information or axioms cannot invalidate deductions already made. This property of monotonicity of inferences is basic to standard mathematical reasoning, yet it is violated by many real life procedures as well as by the negation as failure rule.

In the absence of evidence to the contrary, we typically take consistency with the rest of our general belief system to provide grounds for a belief. The classic example concerns Tweety the bird. At some stage in the development of our knowledge we observe and learn about various birds. Based on this information we conclude that birds fly. One day we are told about Tweety the bird and naturally assume that he can fly. When we are later introduced to Tweety, we discover that he is a pet ostrich and can no more fly than we can. We reject our previous belief that all birds fly and revise our conclusions about Tweety. We now face the world with a new set of beliefs from which we continue to make deductions until new evidence once again proves our beliefs false. Such a process is typical of the growth of knowledge in almost all subjects except mathematics. Beliefs and conclusions are often based on a lack of evidence to the contrary.

A similar approach is embodied in the notion of negation as failure. If we have no evidence to the contrary (i.e., a deduction of L), we assume that L is false. This procedure clearly embodies a nonmonotonic system of reasoning. Minsky [1975, 5.5] was the first to propose such systems and beginning with McCarthy's study of circumscription [1980, 5.5] various researchers have proposed and studied a large number of nonmonotonic systems which have been suggested by various problems in computer science and AI. To list just a few: Hintikka's theory of multiple believers, Doyle's truth maintenance system, Reiter's default logic and Moore's autoepistemic logic as well as various versions of negation as failure in extensions of PROLOG by Apt, Clark and others.

We will now briefly present a new approach to an abstract view of non-monotonic systems as given in Marek, Nerode and Remmel [1990, 5.5]. It seems to capture the common content of many of the systems mentioned. The literature has dealt primarily with the propositional case and we restrict ourselves to it as well. For negation in PROLOG, this means that we will always be looking at the set of ground instances of a given program in the appropriate Herbrand universe. After describing the general system we will connect it to one interesting way of picking out a distinguished Herbrand model that captures many aspects of negation in PROLOG (although it is not precisely the same as the negation as failure rules of §6): the stable model semantics of Gelfond and Lifschitz [1988, 5.4].

We present the idea of nonmonotonic systems in the form of rules of inference like resolution or the one given for classical monotonic logic in I.7. In such a setting, a rule of inference is specified by giving a list of hypotheses and a conclusion which may be drawn from them. The standard rule of modus ponens (I.7.2) concludes β from the hypotheses α and $\alpha \to \beta$. An appropriate style for describing this rule is to write the hypotheses in a list above the line and the conclusion below:

$$\frac{\alpha, \alpha \to \beta}{\beta} \; .$$

In this notation, the axioms are simply rules without hypotheses such as in I.7.1(i):

$$\overline{(\alpha \to (\beta \to \alpha))}$$

The crucial extension of such a system to nonmonotonic logic is to add restraints to the deduction. In addition to knowing each proposition in the set of hypotheses, it may be necessary to not know (believe, have a proof of, have already established, etc.) each of some other collection of propositions in order to draw the conclusion permitted by a given rule. The notation for this situation is to list the usual kind of premises first and then, separated by a colon, follow them with the list of restraints. The restraints are the propositions which the rule requires us not to know (believe, etc.). Thus we read the rule

$$\frac{\alpha_1, \ldots, \alpha_n : \beta_1, \ldots, \beta_m}{\gamma}$$

as saying that if $\alpha_1, \ldots, \alpha_n$ are known (proven, established) and $\beta_1, \ldots, \beta_m$ are not, then we may conclude that we know (can prove or establish) γ.

Definition 7.1 (*Nonmonotonic formal systems*): Let U be a set (of propositional letters).

(i) A *nonmonotonic rule of inference* is a triple $\langle P, G, \varphi \rangle$ where $P = \{\alpha_1, \ldots, \alpha_n\}$ and $G = \{\beta_1, \ldots, \beta_m\}$ are finite lists of elements of U and $\varphi \in U$. Each such rule is written in the form

$$r = \frac{\alpha_1, \ldots, \alpha_n : \beta_1, \ldots, \beta_m}{\varphi}.$$

We call $\alpha_1, \ldots, \alpha_n$ the *premises* of the rule r and $\beta_1, \ldots, \beta_m$ its *restraints*. Note that either P or G or both may be empty.

(ii) If $P = G = \emptyset$, then the rule r is called an *axiom*.

(iii) A *nonmonotonic formal system* is a pair $\langle U, N \rangle$ where U is a non–empty set (of propositional letters) and N is a set of nonmonotonic rules.

(iv) A subset S of U is *deductively closed* in the system $\langle U, N \rangle$ if, for each rule r of N such that all the premises $\alpha_1, \ldots, \alpha_n$ of r are in S and none of its restraints $\beta_1, \ldots, \beta_m$ are in S, the conclusion φ of r is in S.

The essence of the nonmonotonicity of a formal system is that the deductively closed sets are not in general closed under arbitrary intersections. Thus there is, in general, no deductive closure of a set I of propositional letters; i.e., no least set $S \supseteq I$ which is deductively closed. The intersection of a decreasing sequence of deductively closed sets is, however, deductively closed (Exercise 1) and so there is always (at least one) minimal deductively closed subset of U (Exercise 2).

The deductively closed sets containing I can be viewed as the rational points of view possible in a given system when one assumes all the elements of I to be true. Each one expresses a set of beliefs which is closed under all the rules. There may, however, be many such points of view which are mutually contradictory. The intersection of all deductively closed sets containing I represents the information common to all such rational points of view. It is often called the set of *secured consequences* of I or the *skeptical reasoning* associated with the system and I.

Example 7.2: Let $U = \{\alpha, \beta, \gamma\}$ and let

$$r_1 = \frac{}{\alpha} \qquad\qquad r_3 = \frac{\alpha : \beta}{\gamma}$$

$$r_2 = \frac{\alpha : \beta}{\beta} \qquad\qquad r_4 = \frac{\alpha : \gamma}{\beta}$$

(i) Let $N_1 = \{r_1, r_2\}$. There is only one minimal deductively closed set for $\langle U, N_1 \rangle : S = \{\alpha, \beta\}$. S is then the set of secured consequences of $\langle U, N_1 \rangle$.

(ii) Let $N_2 = \{r_1, r_3, r_4\}$. There are two minimal deductively closed set for $\langle U, N_2 \rangle : S_1 = \{\alpha, \beta\}$ and $S_2 = \{\alpha, \gamma\}$. $S = \{\alpha\}$ is then the set of secured consequences of $\langle U, N_2 \rangle$. In this case the set of secured consequences is not deductively closed.

The analog in nonmonotonic logic of a classical deduction from premises I involves a parameter S for the set of propositions we are assuming we do not know. We use this notion of deduction to characterize the *extensions* of a nonmonotonic system which are analogous to the set of consequences of a monotonic system.

Definition 7.3: Let $\langle U, N \rangle$ be a nonmonotonic formal system and let $S, I \subseteq U$. An *S–deduction* of φ *from* I in $\langle U, N \rangle$ is a finite sequence $\varphi_1, \ldots, \varphi_k$ such that $\varphi = \varphi_k$ and, for all $i \leq k$, φ_i is either in I, an axiom of $\langle U, N \rangle$ or the conclusion of a rule $r \in N$ all of whose premises are included among $\varphi_1, \ldots, \varphi_{i-1}$ and all of whose restraints are contained in $U - S$. In this situation φ is called an *S–consequence of* I and we denote by $C_S(I)$ the set of all S–consequences of I.

Note that the role of S in the above definitions is to prevent applications of rules with any restraint in S; it does not contribute any members of U directly to $C_S(I)$. Indeed, $C_S(I)$ may not contain S and may not be deductively closed.

Example 7.4: With the notation as in Example 7.2, define a system $\langle U, N \rangle$ by setting $N = \{r_1, r_3\}$. If $S = \{\beta\}$, then $C_S(\emptyset) = \{\alpha\}$ is not deductively closed as it does not contain γ in violation of rule r_3.

Proposition 7.5: *If* $S \subseteq C_S(I)$, *then* $C_S(I)$ *is deductively closed.*

Proof: Suppose all the premises of a rule r with conclusion φ are in $C_S(I)$ and all of r's restraints are outside it. By the definition of $C_S(I)$, we can produce an S–deduction containing all the premises of r. All of the restraints in r are outside S by hypothesis. We can thus extend the S–deduction to one of φ by applying r to get $\varphi \in C_S(I)$ as desired. $\square$

Definition 7.6: $S \subseteq U$ is an *extension of* I if $C_S(I) = S$. S is an *extension* if it is an extension of the empty set $\emptyset$.

The extensions S of I are the analogs for nonmonotonic systems of the logical consequences of I. Every member of an extension is deducible from I and all the S–consequences of I are in fact in S. We give some basic properties of extensions in Exercises 3–5.

It turns out that extensions capture many procedures in mathematics and computer science. We give some mathematical examples in Exercises 8–9. Now we return to PROLOG programs with negation and their connection to extensions through the notion of stable models.

From our current point of view, it is natural to try to consider the negation as failure as a nonmonotonic system. The underlying idea of negation as failure as presented in the last section is that we may assert $\neg p$ when we do not know (cannot deduce) p. This suggests a natural translation of a general PROLOG program into a nonmonotonic formal system.

Recall from Definition 6.11 that a general program clause has the form $p :- q_1, \ldots, q_n, \neg s_1, \ldots, \neg s_m$ where p, q_i and s_j are atoms.

Remember also that we are in the propositional case. Thus, if a program of interest has variables, we consider instead all ground instances of the program clauses in the Herbrand universe. We can now easily translate a general program P containing only ground atoms into a nonmonotonic formal system in a natural way. We consider each ground atom as a propositional letter. These atoms constitute our universe U. Each program clause C of P of the form $p :- q_1, \ldots, q_n, \neg s_1, \ldots, \neg s_m$ is translated into a rule $tr(C)$:

$$\frac{q_1, \ldots, q_n : s_1, \ldots, s_m}{p}$$

The nonmonotonic system is then specified by letting its set of rules N be the collection $\{tr(C) : C \in P\}$ of translations of clauses of P.

Definition 7.7: Let P be a general program with only ground clauses. $tr(P)$, the *translation of* P, is the nonmonotonic system $\langle U, N \rangle$ where U is the set of atoms appearing in P and $N = \{tr(C) : C \in P\}$ is the set of translations of clauses of P.

It turns out that it is precisely the extensions of $tr(P)$ which are the stable models of P introduced by Gelfond and Lifschitz [1988, 5.4] to capture a strong notion of semantics for general programs with negation as failure.

Definition 7.8: If U is the set of atoms appearing in a ground general program P and $M \subseteq U$, then P_M is the program obtained from P by deleting each clause which has in its body a negative literal $\neg s$ with $s \in M$ and also deleting all negative literals in the bodies of the remaining clauses. As P_M is clearly a PROLOG program (it has no negative literals), it has a unique minimal Herbrand model by Exercise II.10.3. A *stable model* of P is an $M \subseteq U$ such that M is the unique minimal Hebrand model of P_M.

This terminology is justified by the following theorem which shows that stable models of P are in fact models of P.

Theorem 7.9: *Every stable model of P is a minimal model of P.*

Proof: Suppose M is a stable model of P. Consider a clause C of P of the form $p :- q_1, \ldots, q_n, \neg s_1, \ldots, \neg s_m$. If some $s_j \in M$, then M trivially satisfies C. If none of the s_j are in M, then $p :- q_1, \ldots, q_n$ is in P_M. As M is a model of P_M, $p \in M$ if $q_1, \ldots, q_n \in M$. Thus M satisfies C in this case as well and so M is a model of P.

To see that M is a minimal model of P, consider any $M' \subseteq M$ which is also a model of P. We need to show that $M = M'$. By the definition of a stable model, it suffices to show that M' is a model of P_M. Now any clause C' of P_M comes from some C in P as above with $s_j \notin M$ for $1 \leq j \leq m$. It is then of the form $p :- q_1, \ldots, q_n$. Suppose then that $q_1, \ldots, q_n \in M'$. We need to show that $p \in M'$. As $M' \subseteq M$, $s_j \notin M'$ for every $1 \leq j \leq m$. Thus, as M' is a model of $C \in P$, $p \in M'$ as required. $\square$

Example 7.10: Let Q be the following general program of Gelfond and Lifschitz [1988, 5.4]:

$$p(1,2).$$
$$q(x) :- p(x,y), \neg q(y).$$

Q has two minimal Herbrand models: $M_1 = \{p(1,2), q(1)\}$ and $M_2 = \{p(1,2), q(2)\}$ (Exercise 6). The usual negation as failure rule applied to this program answers "no" to the question "$?- q(2)$." but "yes" to the question "$?- q(1)$." Thus we should prefer the first model over the second.

Now consider the possible subsets of the Herbrand universe as candidates for stable models of the ground instances of this program. First, the program itself is transformed into the following ground version P:

$$p(1,2).$$
$$q(1) :- p(1,1), \neg q(1).$$
$$q(1) :- p(1,2), \neg q(2).$$
$$q(2) :- p(2,1), \neg q(1).$$
$$q(2) :- p(2,2), \neg q(2).$$

We now consider the subset $M = \{q(1)\}$ of the Herbrand universe. P_M is then

$$p(1,2).$$
$$q(1) :- p(1,2).$$
$$q(2) :- p(2,2).$$

The minimal Herbrand model of P_M is $\{p(1,2), q(1)\} \neq M$. Thus, M is not a stable model of P. Indeed, any set M not containing $p(1,2)$ is not a model of P and so by Theorem 7.9 not a stable model of P.

Next, we consider the two minimal Herbrand models M_1 and M_2 of the original program Q. We claim that M_1 is stable but not M_2. First, P_{M_1} is

$$p(1,2).$$
$$q(1) :\!- \ p(1,2).$$
$$q(2) :\!- \ p(2,2).$$

The minimal model of this program is clearly M_1 which is therefore stable. On the other hand, P_{M_2} is

$$p(1,2).$$
$$q(1) :\!- \ p(1,1).$$
$$q(2) :\!- \ p(2,1).$$

Its minimal model is $\{p(1,2)\} \neq M_2$. Thus M_2 is not stable.

In fact, M_1 is the only stable model of P (Exercise 7) and so the stable model is the "right" one from the viewpoint of negation as failure.

A direct and precise connection of stable models with nonmonotonic formal systems is provided by the Theorem 7.12. We continue with the notation introduced above and begin with a lemma.

Lemma 7.11: *If M' is a model of P_M, then $M' \supseteq C_M(\emptyset)$.*

Proof: Suppose that M' is a model of P_M. We prove by induction on the length of M–deductions that every member of $C_M(\emptyset)$ is contained in M'. Consider any M–deduction $\varphi_1, \ldots, \varphi_k, p$ (from $\emptyset$) and suppose the rule applied at the last step of this deduction to conclude p is $tr(C)$ for some clause C in P. By induction, we may assume that $\varphi_i \in M'$ for every $1 \le i \le k$ and so every premise q_i of $tr(C)$ is in M'. As this is an M–deduction, no restraint s_j of $tr(C)$ is in M. By definition then, $p :\!- \ q_1, \ldots . q_n$ is one of the clauses of P_M. As M' is a model of P_M, $p \in M'$ as required. $\square$

Theorem 7.12: *A subset M of U is a stable model of P if and only if it is an extension of $tr(P)$.*

Proof: Suppose that M is an extension of $\langle U, tr(P) \rangle$. First, we claim that M is a model of P_M. Consider any clause $p :\!- \ q_1, \ldots, q_n$ in P_M such that $q_1, \ldots, q_n \in M$. By the definition of P_M, there is a clause $C = p :\!- \ q_1, \ldots, q_n, \neg s_1, \ldots, s_m$ in P with no s_j in M. Thus there is a rule $tr(C)$ in $tr(P)$ with all its premises in M and none of its restraints in M. As extensions are deductively closed by Proposition 7.5, $q \in M$ as required. Next, we must prove that no M' strictly contained in M is a model of P_M. As $M = C_M(\emptyset)$, this is immediate from Lemma 7.11.

For the converse, suppose that M is a minimal Herbrand model of P_M. We first note that, by Lemma 7.11, $M \supseteq C_M(\emptyset)$. By the minimality assumption on M, it suffices to prove that $C_M(\emptyset)$ is a model of P_M to conclude that $M = C_M(\emptyset)$ as required. Consider, therefore, any clause $p :- q_1, \ldots, q_n$ in P_M with all the q_i in $C_M(\emptyset)$. There is then an M-deduction $\varphi_1, \ldots, \varphi_k$ containing all of the q_i. By definition of P_M, there is a clause $C = p :- q_1, \ldots, q_n, \neg s_1, \ldots, \neg s_m$ in P with none of the s_j in M and so a rule $tr(C)$ in $tr(P)$ with all its premises in $C_M(\emptyset)$. We may thus form an M-deduction with p as the consequence. So $p \in C_M(\emptyset)$ as required. $\square$

Gelfond and Lifschitz show that certain classes of programs with properties like those considered in §4 have unique stable models and propose the term stable model semantics for such programs. The special case of a unique stable model is certainly of particular interest. From the viewpoint of nonmonotonic logic, however, all the extensions of $tr(P)$ are equally good candidates for models of the system.

Exercises

1. Let $S_1 \supseteq S_2 \supseteq \ldots$ be a nested sequence of deductively closed sets for a nonmonotonic system $\langle U, N \rangle$. Prove that $\cap S_i$ is deductively closed.

2. Zorn's lemma (an equivalent of the axiom of choice) states that any nonempty family of sets closed under the intersection of downwardly nested sequences has a minimal element. Use it and Exercise 1 to prove that every nonmonotonic formal system has a minimal deductively closed subset.

3. Prove that the operation $C_S(I)$ is monotonic in I and antimonotonic in S, that is if $I \subseteq J$, then $C_S(I) \subseteq C_S(J)$ and if $S \subseteq T$, then $C_S(I) \supseteq C_T(I)$.

4. Prove that, if S is an extension of I, then S is a minimal deductively closed superset of I and for every J such that $I \subseteq J \subseteq S$ we have $C_S(J) = S$.

5. If S and T are extensions of I and $S \subseteq T$, then $S = T$.

6. Prove that the minimal Herbrand models of programs P and Q of Example 7.10 are the sets M_1 and M_2 given there.

7. Prove that M_1 is the only stable model of P in Example 7.10.

   (Hint: To begin the analysis note that any candidate must contain $p(1, 2)$ to be a model of P but will not contain any other instance of P by minimality considerations.)

Refer to Exercises I.6.7–8 for the basic terminology about graphs and partial orderings used below.

8. Let n be a natural number and G be a locally finite graph, i.e., a graph in which, for each node x there are at most finitely many nodes y such that $\{x, y\}$ is an edge of G. We define a nonmonotonic formal system $\langle U(G), N(G) \rangle$ by first setting $U(G) = \{Cxi \mid x$ is a node of G and $i \leq n\}$. We then put into $N(G)$, for each node x of G and $j \leq n$, the rule

$$\frac{: Cx1, \ldots, Cx(j-1), Cx(j+1), \ldots, Cxn}{Cxj}.$$

Finally, we put into $N(G)$, for each pair x, y of distinct nodes of G, each $i \leq n$ and each $\varphi \in U9G)$, the rule

$$\frac{Cxi, Cyi}{\varphi}$$

Prove that $S \subseteq U(G)$ is an extension for $\langle U(G), N(G) \rangle$ if and only if coloring each node x of G with color i iff $Cxi \in S$ produces an n–coloring of G.

9. Let P be a partial ordering of width n. We define a nonmonotonic system $\langle U(P), N(P) \rangle$ by first setting $U(P) = \{Cxi | x \in P$ and $i \leq n\}$. For each $x \in P$ we put into $N(P)$ the rule

$$\frac{: Cx1, \ldots, Cx(j-1), Cx(j+1), \ldots, Cxn}{Cxj}.$$

Finally, for each x and y in P which are incomparable in the partial ordering, we put into $N(P)$ the rule

$$\frac{Cxi, Cyi}{\varphi}.$$

Prove that $S \subseteq U$ is an extension of $\langle U(P), N(P) \rangle$ if and only if $\{C_1, \ldots, C_n\}$ is a set of disjoint chains covering P where $C_i = \{x | C_{x_i} \in S\}$.

8. Computability and Undecidability

One of the major tasks of the logicians of the 30's and 40's was the formalization of the basic intuitive notion of an algorithm or an effective procedure. (For convenience we consider procedures on the natural numbers.) Many seemingly different definitions were proposed by a number of researchers including Church, Gödel, Herbrand, Kleene, Markov and Post. They suggested schemes involving recursion, equational deduction systems, idealized models of computing machines and others. Perhaps the philosophically most convincing proposal was that of Turing. He gave what is undoubtedly now the best known definition in terms of a simple machine model of computation: the Turing machine.

Every function calculable by any of these models was clearly effective. As investigations progressed, it became evident that any function that was intuitively computable could be calculated in any of the systems. Indeed, over a number of years all these proposals were proven equivalent, that is, the class of functions computable in any one model is the same as that computable in any other. These functions are now called the *recursive functions*. Early results along these lines led Church to formulate what is now known as *Church's thesis*: the effectively calculable functions are precisely the recursive ones. The weight of the evidence has by now produced an almost universal acceptance of this thesis. Thus, to prove that any computation scheme is universal in the sense that it computes every effective function, it suffices to prove that it computes every function computable by any of the schemes known to define the class of recursive functions.

It is not difficult to model almost any of the standard definitions by deduction in predicate logic: for each recursive function f, we can write down axioms in a language for arithmetic which includes a term $\bar{n}$ for each natural number n and a two–place predicate symbol p_f such that $f(n) = m$ iff $p_f(\bar{n}, \bar{m})$ is a logical consequence of the axioms. (We restrict our attention to unary functions simply to avoid strings of variables. Everything we do will work just as well for functions of any specified arity m by simply replacing the single variable x_1 by a sequence of variables $x_1, x_2, \ldots , x_m$.) For the most part, these representations can be naturally expressed in the form of PROLOG programs. (See Exercises 1–2 for an example.)   Thus, any sound and complete implementation of PROLOG (e.g. with breadth–first searching) will correctly compute all recursive functions. By choosing the right model of computation (Shepherdson's register machines as described in Definition 8.1) and exercising some cleverness in the translation into PROLOG (Definition 8.4), we will prove that the standard implementation via the leftmost literal selection rule and depth-first searching of the SLD–tree also suffices to compute all recursive functions. (In fact, the "right" programs will run correctly with essentially any selection rule and search procedure.)   Thus PROLOG is a universal computing machine model (Corollaries 8.6–8.7).

Once one has an agreed upon the mathematical definition of an algorithm or the class of effectively computable functions, one can hope to prove that various procedures (or decisions) cannot be carried out (made) by any algorithm or that particular functions cannot be computed effectively. (These notions really coincide. Decision procedures such as deciding if a number n is in some given set A, or if some polynomial has an integral root or the like correspond to calculating the characteristic function C_A of A ($C_A(n) = 1$ if $n \in A$ and $C_A(n) = 0$ if $n \notin A$) or of the set of tuples of numbers which correspond to the coefficients of polynomials with integral roots.)   Indeed, beginning with the first definitions of the recursive functions and continuing to the present, many classical problems asking for algorithms have been solved negatively by showing that there is no recursive function which computes the desired result. One of the earliest and best known of these results is Turing's proof of the undecidability of the halting problem: There is no algorithm (recursive function) for deciding if a given computer program halts on a given input. Thus, once we have provided a translation of a standard model of computation into PROLOG, we will have proven the undecidability of the termination problem for PROLOG programs with the standard implementation. As the arguments apply to semantically complete implementations as well, we will also have proven Church's celebrated result on the undecidability of validity for predicate logic (Theorem 8.10).

We begin our proof of the universality of PROLOG for computation by presenting Shepherdson's register machine model for computability. It is "mechanically" simpler than Turing's model and considerably easier to implement in PROLOG. A *register machine* consists of some number of storage locations called registers. Each register contains a natural number. There are only two types of operations that these machines can perform in implementing a program. First, they can increase the content of any register by one and then proceed to the next instruction. Second, they can check if any given register contains the number 0 or not. If so they go on to the next instruction. If not they decrease the given register by one and can be told to proceed to any instruction in the program. Formally, we define register machine programs and their execution as follows:

Definition 8.1: A *register machine program* I is a finite sequence $I_1, \ldots ,$ I_t, I_{t+1} of instructions operating on a sequence of numbers $x_1, \ldots , x_r$, where each instruction I_m, for $m \leq t$, is of one of the following two forms:

(i) $x_k := x_k + 1$ (replace x_k by $x_k + 1$)

(ii) If $x_k \neq 0$, then $x_k := x_k - 1$ and go to j. (If $x_k \neq 0$, replace it by $x_k - 1$ and proceed to instruction I_j.)

It is assumed that after executing some instruction I_m, the execution procedes to I_{m+1}, the next instruction on the list, unless I_m directs otherwise. The execution of such a program proceeds in the obvious way on any input of values for $x_1, \ldots , x_r$ (the initial content of the registers) to change the values of the x_k and progress through the list of instructions.

The final instruction, I_{t+1}, is always a halt instruction. Thus, if I_{t+1} is ever reached, the execution terminates with the current values of the x_k. In general, we denote the assertion that an execution of the program I is at instruction I_m with values $n_1, \ldots , n_r$ of the variables by $I_m(n_1, \ldots , n_r)$.

Definition 8.2: A register machine program I *computes a function* $f :$ $\mathbb{N} \rightarrow \mathbb{N}$, if, when started at instruction I_1 with $x_1 = n$ and $x_k = 0$ for all $k > 1$, its execution eventually terminates (at instruction I_{t+1}) with $x_1 = n$ and $x_2 = f(n)$, i.e., we eventually have $I_{t+1}(n, f(n), n_3, \ldots , n_r)$ for some numbers $n_3, \ldots , n_r$. If f is partial function from $\mathbb{N}$ into $\mathbb{N}$, i.e., it is not defined at every $n \in \mathbb{N}$, we also require that the execution of the program beginning at $I_1(n, 0, \ldots , 0)$ terminates if and only if n is in the domain of f.

A (partial) function from $\mathbb{N}$ to $\mathbb{N}$ is *(partial) recursive* if it is computed by some register machine program.

The reader familiar with Turing machines can find proofs that the partial functions computable by a register machine program are exactly those computed by a Turing machine program or any of the other more common models in the original papers of Shepherdson and Sturgis [1963, 3.6] and Minsky [1961, 3.6] or in many basic texts on computability such as Cutland [1980, 3.6] or Tourlakis [1984, 3.6]. For our purposes, we simply take this model as the defining one for the class of partial recursive functions.

For the sake of definiteness, we give a specific definition of what it means for a PROLOG program with a particular implementation to compute a partial function f. We assume that a minimum amount of arithmetic is represented in our language. In fact, all we need is a constant for the number zero, say 0, and a unary function s representing the successor function on $\mathbb{N}$. In this setting (which we considered in Exercises 2.7–8), $s(x)$ represents $x + 1$ and the term $s^n(0)$ represents the number n.

Definition 8.3: A PROLOG program P with a (two–place) predicate p *computes the partial function f* (under some specific implementation) if, for any natural number a, asking the question "$?-\ p(s^a(0), Z)$" produces a nonterminating computation if $f(a)$ is undefined and a terminating one with the answer substitution $Z = s^b(0)$ (and no other answers) if $f(a) = b$. If no implementation is mentioned, we assume that any sound and complete one is intended (they are, of course, all equivalent). By the standard implementation, we mean the sound but incomplete one using the leftmost selection rule and depth–first search.

Perhaps the most natural way to represent a register machine in the language of predicate, or even Horn, logic is to introduce a predicate letter p_m of r variables for each instruction I_m. The intended interpretation of $p_m(n_1, \ldots, n_r)$ is that the machine is at instruction m with values $n_1, \ldots, n_r$ for the variables. We can now easily express the step by step execution of a given program by implications corresponding to its instructions.

A first attempt at such a translation might well proceed as follows:

For each instruction I_m, $1 \leq m \leq t$, include an axiom of the appropriate form:

(i) $p_m(x_1, \ldots, x_r) \rightarrow p_{m+1}(x_1, \ldots, x_{k-1}, s(x_k), x_{k+1}, \ldots, x_r)$.

(ii) $p_m(x_1, \ldots, x_{k-1}, 0, x_{k+1}, \ldots, x_r)$
$$\rightarrow p_{m+1}(x_1, \ldots, x_{k-1}, 0, x_{k+1}, \ldots, x_r)$$
$\wedge\ p_m(x_1, \ldots, x_{k-1}, s(y), x_{k+1}, \ldots x_r)$
$$\rightarrow p_j(x_1, \ldots, x_{k-1}, y, x_{k+1}, \ldots, x_r).$$

(Note that being a successor is equivalent to being nonzero.)

Let $Q(I)$ be the finite set of axioms corresponding under this translation to register program I. It is not hard to prove that, if program I computes the partial function f, then, for any n, m and $r - 2$ numbers $a, b, c \ldots$, $p_1(s^n(0), 0 \ldots 0) \rightarrow p_{t+1}(s^n(0), s^m(0), a, b, c \ldots)$ is a logical consequence of $Q(I)$ if and only if $f(n)$ is defined and equal to m. Such a translation then suffices to give the computability of all recursive functions by, and so the undecidability of, any sound and complete version of Horn clause deduction or PROLOG. (See Exercise 3.) Unfortunately, the standard implementation will not always find the terminating computation (Exercise 4).

Shepherdson's strategy (as presented in Bezem [1989, 5.4]) for converting a register machine program into a PROLOG program that will correctly compute the same function (even, as we shall see, with the standard implementation) involves two ideas. The first is to reverse the direction of the implications, thus translating the calculation into a verification. The second is to move the variable in the goal clause out of the way so as to eliminate the possibility of unnecessary and unwanted attempts at unifying it.

Definition 8.4: The PROLOG program $P(I)$ associated with a register machine program I contains the following clauses:

A clause transferring the variable in the goal clause out of the way and passing control to the first instruction:

$$p(X_1, Z) :- p_1(X_1, 0, \ldots, 0, Z).$$

(The string of zeros has length $r - 1$.)

For each instruction I_m of type (i), the single clause:

$$p_m(X_1, \ldots, X_r, Z) :- p_{m+1}(X_1, \ldots, X_{k-1}, s(X_k), X_{k+1}, \ldots, X_r, Z).$$

For each instruction of type (ii), the two clauses:

$$p_m(X_1, \ldots, X_{k-1}, 0, X_{k+1}, \ldots X_r, Z) :-$$
$$p_{m+1}(X_1, \ldots, X_{k-1}, 0, X_{k+1}, \ldots X_r, Z)$$
$$p_m(X_1, \ldots, X_{k-1}, s(Y), X_{k+1}, \ldots X_r, Z) :-$$
$$p_j(X_1, \ldots, X_{k-1}, Y, X_{k+1}, \ldots X_r, Z).$$

Finally, the clause corresponding to the terminal states of the register machine:
$$p_{t+1}(X_1, X_2, \ldots, X_r, X_2).$$

Theorem 8.5: *For every register program I, the PROLOG program $P(I)$ with any implementation computes the same partial function as I.*

Proof: Fix a natural number a and a register machine program I which computes a partial recursive function f. Consider the program $P(I)$ with the goal clause $G_0 = \{\neg p(s^a(0), Z)\}$. Notice first that every clause in the program $P(I)$ has at most one literal in its body. Thus every goal clause appearing in any SLD–proof beginning with G has at most one literal.

Thus the course of any such SLD–proof is independent of the selection rule. We also wish to show that result of the search for an SLD–refutation is both correct and independent of the search procedure. To see this we need a more detailed analysis of the execution.

When we start with the goal clause $G_0 = \{\neg p(s^a(0), Z)\}$ the first resolution must be with the first clause in $P(I)$; the result is

$$G_1 = \{\neg p_1(s^a(0), 0, \ldots, 0, Z)\}.$$

Suppose the execution of the register program I produces at its nth step the state $I_{m(n)}(m(1,n), m(2,n), \ldots, m(r,n))$ with $m(n) \leq t+1$. We claim that, as long as the machine has not halted before step n, the succeeding goal clause G_n of the SLD–proof is precisely

$$\{\neg p_{m(n)}(s^{m(1,n)}(0), s^{m(2,n)}(0), \ldots, s^{m(r,n)}(0), Z)\}$$

and that no substitutions are made for Z. The proof is by induction so suppose the claim is true for n.

If $I_{m(n)}$ is of type (i) the register machine moves to state

$$I_{m(n)+1}(m(1,n), \ldots m(k-1,n), m(k,n)+1, m(k+1,n), \ldots, m(r,n)).$$

There is only one program clause with $p_{m(n)}$ in its head (the one corresponding to $I_{m(n)}$) and so only one with which we can resolve G_n. This resolution obviously produces the desired result:

$$\{\neg p_{m(n)+1}(s^{m(1,n)}(0), s^{m(2,n)}(0), \ldots, s^{m(k,n)+1}(0), \ldots, s^{m(r,n)}(0), Z)\}.$$

If $I_{m(n)}$ is of type (ii) there are two program clauses whose heads contain $p_{m(n)}$. The argument divides into cases according to whether or not $m(k,n) = 0$. In either case there is exactly one clause whose head can be unified with G_n so the resolution is uniquely determined and G_{n+1} has the required form.

Thus, if I is nonterminating when started in state $I_1(a,0)$ (i. e. f is not defined at a), then $P(I)$ is nonterminating when started with the goal $\{\neg p(s^a(0), Z)\}$ as required. Suppose then $f(a) = b$. If I is started in state $I_1(a,0)$ then it must terminate at step $n+1$ of its execution by entering some state $I_{t+1}(a, b, c_2, \ldots, c_r)$. By the above induction argument, clause G_{n+1} of the (unique) SLD–proof is

$$\{\neg p_{t+1}(s^a(0), s^b(0), s^{c_2}(0), \ldots, s^{c_r}(0), Z)\}.$$

Once again, there is exactly one program clause with p_{t+1} in its head: the final one of the program. Resolving G_{n+1} with this fact gives $\square$ with an mgu including the substitution $Z/s^b(0)$, as desired. $\square$

Corollary 8.6: *Every (partial) recursive function f is computable by a* PROLOG *program P_f that executes correctly under any implementation of* PROLOG.

Proof: Every (partial) recursive function f is computed by some register machine program I_f. By the theorem, $P(I_f)$ is a PROLOG program that computes f under any implementation. $\square$

Of course, when referring to implementations of PROLOG, we have (tacitly) assumed we had one which correctly implements resolution (otherwise it would be meaningless). In particular, contrary to all actual implementations, one must typically assume some correct unification algorithm to be assured of the correctness of any result. It is worth pointing out that the PROLOG programs $P(I)$ constructed above from register machine programs run correctly even when the occurs check is omitted from the unification algorithm.

Corollary 8.7: *Every (partial) recursive function f is computable by a* PROLOG *program P_f that executes correctly under any implementation of* PROLOG *(even with the occurs check omitted from its unification algorithm).*

Proof: A careful look at the progression of the SLD–proof from $P(I)\cup\{G\}$ starting with $G = \{p(s^a(0), Z)\}$, as analyzed in the proof of Theorem 8.5, shows that all substitutions employed are ground. The unifications always work on a goal clause in which Z is the only nonground term and, until the last step of the proof, no substitution is made for Z. Thus all substitutions for variables in the program clauses before the last step are ground. At the last step (if there is one), we make a ground substitution for all the variables in the program clause including Z. As no ground substitution can violate the occurs condition on substitutions, the fact that we omitted the check has no significance. $\square$

We can now prove the undecidability of the halting problem for PROLOG and the general validity problem for predicate calculus.

Theorem 8.8: *The halting problem for register machine programs is undecidable, that is, there is no effective procedure for determining if a given program halts on a given input.*

Proof: We assume Church's thesis that every effectively calculable function is recursive, i.e., can be computed by a register machine program. A formal proof that there is no recursive solution for the halting problem can be obtained without Church's thesis by explicitly writing the programs for the few functions that appear in the following argument. Such programs can be found in the basic papers or many standard texts on computability. Just as we can make a list of all finite sequences of numbers, we can make an effective list of all programs for register machines. If the halting problem were decidable, there would be a recursive function $h(x)$ such that, if the xth program on this lists halts on input x with output y, then $h(x) = y + 1$ and otherwise $h(x) = 0$. We immediately deduce a contradiction by the classical diagonalization argument: As h is recursive (by Church's thesis), it is computed by some register machine program. Suppose h is computed by the nth program on our list. Consider $h(n)$. As h is defined on every number, the nth program with input n halts with some value y. By definition then, $h(n) = y + 1$ contradicting the assumption that the nth program computes h. □

Corollary 8.9: *The halting problem for* PROLOG *programs with any implementation, with or without the occurs check in the unification algorithm, is undecidable.*

Proof: The proof is immediate from the theorem and results 8.5–8.7. □

Corollary 8.10 (Church's Theorem): *The validity problem for predicate logic is undecidable, i.e., there is no effective procedure for deciding if a given sentence of the predicate calculus is valid.*

Proof: If I is a register machine program then I halts with input a if and only if the search for an SLD–refutation of $P(I) \cup \{\neg p(s^a(0), Z)\}$ terminates successfully by Theorem 8.5. By the completeness and soundness of SLD–resolution this happens if and only if $\exists Z p(s^a(0), Z)$ is a logical consequence of $P(I)$. As $P(I)$ consists of a finite set $\{C_1, \ldots, C_n\}$ of clauses, the termination is equivalent to the conjunction of the universal closure of the clauses C_i implying $\exists Z p(s^a(0), Z)$. Thus, if we could decide the validity problem for predicate calculus, we could decide the halting problem and contradict Theorems 8.8–9. □

Exercises

A very common definition of the *partial recursive functions* proceeds by closing some simple functions under composition, primitive recursion and a least number operator:

The successor function $s(x) = x + 1$ is partial recursive.

The constant function $c(x) = 0$ is partial recursive.

For each i and j the projection function $p_{i,r}(x_1, \ldots, x_r) = x_i$ is partial recursive.

If $g_1, \ldots, g_n$ and h are partial recursive, then so is $f(x_1, \ldots, x_r) = h(g_1(x_1, \ldots, x_r), \ldots, g_n(x_1, \ldots, x_r))$.

If $r > 1$ and g and h are partial recursive, then so is the function f defined "by primitive recursion" as follows:

$$f(0, x_2, \ldots, x_r) = g(x_2, \ldots, x_r)$$
$$f(x_1 + 1, x_2, \ldots, x_r) = h(x_1, f(x_1, x_2, \ldots, x_r), x_2, \ldots, x_r).$$

If $f(x_1, \ldots, x_r, y)$ is partial recursive then so is the function $g(x_1, \ldots, x_r)$ defined by setting $g(x_1, \ldots, x_r)$ equal to the least number y such that $f(x_1 \ldots, x_r, z)$ is defined for every $z \leq y$ and $f(x_1, \ldots, x_r, y) = 0$.

1. Show (by induction on the definition given above) how to write PROLOG programs that compute each partial recursive function.

2. Prove that the programs given in answer to Exercise 1 compute correctly for any sound and complete implementation of PROLOG. (Hint: By completeness of the implementation, it suffices to find one LD–refutation for each desired computation. Now follow the path of the computation. For the other direction, use soundness and the fact $\mathbb{N}$ is a natural model for the program with the intended semantics.)

3. Let $Q(I)$ be the set of clauses corresponding to register machine program I for the partial recursive function f as given before Definition 8.4.

   (i) Argue semantically to show that, for any numbers $n, m, a, b, c, \ldots$, $p_1(s^n(0), 0, \ldots, 0) \to p_{t+1}(s^n(0), s^m(0), s^a(0), s^b(0), \ldots,)$ is a logical consequence of $Q(I)$ if and only if $f(n)$ is defined and equal to m.

   (ii) Apply Theorem 8.8 to give a proof of Theorem 8.10 that does not depend on the notions of PROLOG implementation or even resolution.

   (iii) Prove that $Q(I)$ as a PROLOG program correctly computes the same partial function as register machine I for any sound and complete implementation. (Hint: Follow the hint for Exercise 2.)

4. Give an example of a register machine program I such that $Q(I)$ as a PROLOG program does not correctly compute the same partial function as does I if the standard implementation of PROLOG is used.

5. A set W of natural numbers is *recursively enumerable* if there is an effective procedure to list its members, i.e., it is empty or the range of a (total) recursive function. Use Church's Thesis to prove that a set S is recursive iff both W and its complement, $\mathbb{N} - W$, are recursively enumerable. (Hint: Argue informally that, given listings for both S and $\mathbb{N} - W$, you can calculate the characteristic function of S.)

6. Show that there is a PROLOG program P such that the logical consequences of CWA(P) as defined in §6 are not recursively enumerable. (Hint: By Church's Thesis and the results of this section, there is a program P which computes the partial recursive function f such that $f(n, x) = 0$ iff the nth register machine program halts on input x. As the only model of CWA(P) is $\mathbb{N}$, the logical consequences of CWA(P) are precisely the true facts about this function. In particular, $\neg p(s^n(0), 0)$ is a logical consequence of CWA(P) iff the nth register program does not halt on input x. Now use Exercise 5 to argue that this would contradict Theorem 8.8.)

Suggestions for Further Reading

A good survey article on logic programming is Apt [1990, 5.4]. The March 1992 issue of the *Communications of the ACM* is devoted to Logic Programming. It includes a brief history (Robinson [1992, 5.4]) as well as surveys of the impact of logic programming on databases (Grant and Minker [1992, 5.4]) and the Fifth Generation Computing Project (Furukawa [1992, 5.4]). The standard text on the theory of PROLOG is Lloyd [1987, 5.4] which also has an extensive bibliography. Another text which stresses resolution and the connection of logic programming to relational databases is Maier and Warren [1988, 5.4].

For practical programming in PROLOG, see Bratko [1986, 5.4], Sterling and Shapiro [1987, 5.4] and Dodd [1989, 5.4]. Clocksin and Mellish [1981, 5.4] used to be the standard text and is still good.

For more on termination problems in logic programming and PROLOG, see Apt and Pedreschi [1991, 5.4] and the references there.

Logic with equality is treated in all the standard texts on mathematical logic mentioned in the suggestions for further reading at the end of Chaper I. Consider in particular, Mendelson [1964, 3.2], Enderton [1976, 3.2] or Shoenfield [1967, 3.2]. A basic model theory book such as Chang and Keisler [1973, 3.4] is also a good place to look

For the treatment of negation as failure in PROLOG, see Chapters 3–4 of Lloyd [1987, 5.4] and the appropriate references including Clark [1978, 5.4] and Shepherdson [1984, 1985 and 1987, 5.4]. A good current survey and extensive bibliography can be found in Shepherdson [1992, 5.4].

For basic articles on nonmonotonic logic, see Ginsberg [1979, 5.5]. For further developments along the lines of §7, we recommend the series of papers by Marek, Remmel and Nerode [1990, 5.5]. For the different approaches and sources of nonmonotonic logics mentioned at the beginning of §7, see Apt, Blair and Walker [1987, 5.4], Clark [1978, 5.4], Doyle [1979, 5.5], Hintikka [1962, 5.5], McCarthy [1980, 5.5], Minsky [1975, 5.5], Moore [1985, 5.5] and Reiter [1980, 5.5]. A good source of current research articles which are often quite accessible are the TARK (*Theoretical Aspects of Reasoning about Knowledge*) volumes in list 5.5.

For an excellent introduction to recursive function theory (the theory of computability) from an informal viewpoint assuming Church's thesis, we recommend Rogers [1967, 3.6]. For more details on the equivalence of various definitions and actual "implementations", we suggest Davis and Weyuker [1983, 5.2] and Odifreddi [1989, 3.6]. For more specifically on register machines, see Fitting [1987, 5.2], Cutland [1980, 3.6], Tourlakis [1984, 3.2] or the original papers by Shepherdson and Sturgis [1961, 3.6] and Minsky [1961, 3.6]. An approach somewhat more oriented to computer science can be found in Machtey and Young [1978, 5.4].

The next result along the lines of the undecidability of predicate logic is Gödel's celebrated incompleteness theorem: There are sentences φ in the predicate logic language for arithmetic such that neither φ nor $\neg\varphi$ is provable from any reasonable axioms for arithmetic. For a brief introduction to incompleteness, see Crossley [1990, 3.2]. Expositions of this result can also be found in many standard textbooks such as Boolos and Jeffrey [1989, 3.2], Enderton [1972, 3.2] and Mendelson [1979, 3.2]. A treatment from a recursion–theoretic point of view is in Odifreddi [1989, 3.6]. A puzzler's approach can be found in Smullyan [1987 and 1978, 3.2]. The original paper Gödel [1931, 2.3] is still worth reading.

IV Modal Logic

1. Possibility and Necessity; Knowledge or Belief

Formal modal logics were developed to make precise the mathematical properties of differing conceptions of such notions as possibility, necessity, belief, knowledge and temporal progression which arise in philosophy and natural languages. In the last twenty–five years modal logics have emerged as useful tools for expressing essential ideas in computer science and artificial intelligence.

Formally, modal logic is an extension of classical propositional or predicate logic. The language of classical logic is enriched by adding of new "modal operators". The standard basic operators are traditionally denoted by $\square$ and $\Diamond$. Syntactically, they can be viewed as new unary connectives. (We omit a separate treatment of propositional logic and move directly to predicate logic. As we noted for classical logic in II.4.8, propositional logic can be viewed as a subset of predicate logic and so is subsumed by it. The same translation works for modal logic.)

Definition 1.1: If $\mathcal{L}$ is a language for (classical) predicate logic (as defined in II.2) we extend it to a *modal language* $\mathcal{L}_{\square,\Diamond}$ by adding (to Definition II.2.1) two new primitive symbols $\square$ and $\Diamond$. We add a new clause to the definition (II.2.5) of formulas:

(iv)   If φ is formula then so are $(\square\varphi)$ and $(\Diamond\varphi)$.

The definitions of all other related notions such as subformula, bound variable and sentence are now carried over verbatim.

When no confusion is likely to result we drop the subscripts and refer to $\mathcal{L}_{\square,\Diamond}$ as simply the (modal) language $\mathcal{L}$.

Interpretations of modal languages were originally motivated by philosophical considerations. One common reading of $\square$ and $\Diamond$ are "it is necessary that" and "it is possible that". Another is "it will always be true that" and "it will eventually be true that". One should note that the intended relation between $\square$ and $\Diamond$ is like that between $\forall$ and $\exists$. They are dual operators in the sense that the intended meaning of $\Diamond\varphi$ is usually $\neg\square\neg\varphi$. The two interpretations just mentioned have ordinary names for both operators. At times it is natural to use just one. Interpretations involving knowledge or belief, for example, are typically phrased in a language with just the operator $\square$ (which could be denoted by $\mathcal{L}_{\square}$) and $\square\varphi$ is understood as "I know φ" or "I believe that φ". It is also possible to add on additional modal operators $\Box_i$ and $\Diamond_i$ and provide various interpretations. We prefer to read $\Box$ and $\Diamond$ simply as "box" and "diamond" so as not to prejudge the intended interpretation.

The semantics for a modal language $\mathcal{L}_{\Box,\Diamond}$ is based on a generalization of the structures for classical predicate logic of II.4 known as *Kripke frames*. Intuitively, we consider a collection W of "*possible worlds*". Each world $w \in W$ constitutes a view of reality as represented by a structure $\mathcal{C}(w)$ associated with it. We adopt the notation of forcing from set theory and write $w \Vdash \varphi$ to mean φ is true in the possible world w. (We read $w \Vdash \varphi$ as "w forces φ" or "φ is true at w".) If φ is a sentence of the classical language $\mathcal{L}$, this should be understood as simply asserting that φ is true in the structure $\mathcal{C}(w)$. If $\Box$ is interpreted as necessity, this notion can be understood as truth in all possible worlds; the notion of possibility expressed by $\Diamond$ would then mean truth in some possible world.

Temporal notions, or assertions of the necessity or possibility of some fact φ given some preexisting state of affairs, are expressed by including an accessibility (or successor) relation S between the possible worlds. Thus we write $w \Vdash \Box\varphi$ to mean that φ is true in all possible successor worlds of w or all worlds accessible from w. This is a reasonable interpretation of "φ is necessarily true in world w".

Before formalizing the semantics for modal logic in §2, we give some additional motivation by considering two types of applications to computer science.

The first area of application is to theories of program behavior. Modalities are implicit in the works of Turing [1949, 5.7], Von Neumann [1963, 5.7], Floyd [1967, 5.7], Hoare [1973, 5.7], and Burstall [1972, 5.7] on program correctness. The underlying systems of modal logic were brought to the surface by many later workers. Examples of the logics recently developed for the analysis of programs include algorithmic logic, dynamic logic, process logic, and temporal logic. Here are the primitive modalities of one system, the dynamic logic of sequential programs.

Let α be a sequential (possibly nondeterministic) program, let s be a state of the machine executing α. Let φ be a predicate or property of states. We introduce modal operators $\Box_\alpha$ and $\Diamond_\alpha$ into the description of the execution of the program α with the intended interpretation of $\Box_\alpha\varphi$ being that φ is necessarily or always true after α is executed. The meaning of $\Diamond_\alpha$ is intended to be that φ is sometimes true when α is executed (i.e., there is some execution of α which makes φ true). Thus $\Box_\alpha$ is a modal necessity operator and $\Diamond_\alpha$ is a modal possibility operator.

We can make this language more useful by invoking the ideas of possible worlds as described above. Here the "possible worlds" are the states of the machine and the accessibility relation is determined by the possible execution sequences of the program α. More precisely, we interpret forcing assertions about modal formulas as follows:

$s \Vdash \Box_\alpha \varphi$ asserts that φ is true at any state s' such that there exists a legal execution sequence for α which starts in state s and eventually reaches state s'.

$s \Vdash \Diamond_\alpha \varphi$ asserts that φ is true at (at least) one state s' such that there exists a legal execution sequence for α which starts in state s and eventually reaches state s'.

Thus, the intended accessibility relation, S_α, is that s' is accessible from s, $sS_\alpha s'$, if and only if some execution of program α starting in state s ends in state s'.

We could just as well introduce separate operators $\Box_\alpha$, $\Diamond_\alpha$ for each program α. A modal Kripke semantics could then be developed with distinct accessibility relations S_α for each pair of operators $\Box_\alpha$ and $\Diamond_\alpha$. Such a language is very useful in discussing invariants of programs and, in general, proving their correctness. After all, correctness is simply the assertion that, no matter what the starting state, some situation φ is always true when the execution of α is finished: $\Box_\alpha \varphi$. (See, for example, Goldblatt [1982, 5.6], [1987, 5.6] and Harel [1979, 5.7].)

Many interesting and useful variations on this theme have been proposed. One could, for example, interpret $s \Vdash \Box_\alpha \varphi$ to mean that φ is true at every state s' which can be visited during an execution of α starting at s. In this vein, $s \Vdash \Diamond_\alpha \varphi$ would mean that φ is true at some state s' which is reached during some execution of α starting at s. We have simply changed the accessibility relation and we have what is called process logic. This interpretation is closely related to temporal logic. In temporal logic, $\Box \varphi$ means that φ is always true and $\Diamond \varphi$ means that φ will eventually (or at some time) be true. This logic can be augmented in various ways with other modal operators depending on one's view of time. In a digital sequential machine, it may be reasonable to view time as ordered as are the natural numbers. In this situation, for example, one can introduce a modal operator $\circ$ and read $t \Vdash \circ \varphi$ as φ is true at the moment which is the immediate successor of t. Various notions of fairness, for example, can be formulated in these systems (even without $\circ$): every constantly active process will eventually be scheduled (for execution or inspection etc.) — $\Box \varphi(c) \rightarrow \Diamond \psi(c)$; every process which is ever active is scheduled at least once — $\varphi(c) \rightarrow \Diamond \psi(c)$; every process active infinitely often will be scheduled infinitely often — $\Box \Diamond \varphi(c) \rightarrow \Box \Diamond \psi(c)$; etc.. Thus these logics are relevant to analyses of the general behavior and, in particular, the correctness of concurrent or perpetual programs. (Another good reference here is Manna and Waldinger [1985, 5.6].)

A quite different source of applications of modal logic in computer science is in theories of knowledge and belief for AI. Here we may understand $\Box_K \varphi$ as "some (fixed) agent or processor knows φ (i.e., that φ is true)" or $\Box_B \varphi$ as "some (fixed) agent or processor believes φ (i.e., that φ is true)". Again, we may wish to discuss not one processor but many. We can then introduce modal operators such as $\Box_{K,\alpha}\varphi$ to be understood as "processor α knows φ". Thus, for example, $\Box_{K,\alpha}\Box_{K,\beta}\varphi$ says that α knows that β knows φ; $\Box_{K,\alpha}\varphi \to \Box_{K,\beta}\psi$ says that if α knows φ then β knows ψ. (A general reference for AI logics is Turner [1984, 5.6].)

This language clearly allows one to formulate notions about communication and knowledge in distributed or concurrent systems. Another related avenue of investigation considers attempts to axiomatize belief or knowledge in humans as well as machine systems. One can then deduce what other properties of knowledge or belief follow from the axioms. On the basis of such deductions, one may either modify one's epistemological views or change the axioms about knowledge that one is willing to accept. The view of modal logic as a logic of belief or knowledge is particularly relevant to analyses of database management. In this light, it is also closely related to nonmonotonic logic as presented in III.7. (See Halpern and Moses [1985, 5.6] for a survey of logics of knowledge and beliefs and Thayse [1989, 5.6] for a thorough treatment of modal logic aimed at deductive databases and AI applications.)

In the next sections we will give a formal semantics for modal logic (§2) and a tableau style proof system (§3). In §4 we will prove soundness and completeness theorems for our proof system. Many applications of modal logic concern systems in which there are agreed (or suggested) restrictions on the interpretations corresponding to varying views of the properties of necessity, knowledge, time, etc., that one is trying to capture. We devote §5 to the relation between restrictions on the accessibility relation, adding axioms about the modal operators to the underlying logic and adjoining new tableau proof rules. The final section (§6) describes a traditional Hilbert style system for modal logic extending that presented for classical logic in II.8.

2. Frames and Forcing

For technical convenience, we make a couple of modifications to the basic notion of a (modal) language $\mathcal{L}$. First, we omit the connective $\leftrightarrow$ from our formal language and view $\varphi \leftrightarrow \psi$ as an abbreviation for $\varphi \to \psi \wedge \psi \to \varphi$. Second, we assume throughout this chapter that every language $\mathcal{L}$ has at least one constant symbol but no function symbols other than constants. (The elimination of function symbols does not result in a serious loss of expressiveness. We can systematically replace function symbols with relations. The work of a binary function symbol $f(x,y)$, for example, can be taken over by a ternary relation symbol $R_f(x,y,z)$ whose intended interpretation is that $f(x,y) = z$. A formula $\varphi(f(x,y))$ can then be systematically replaced by the formula $\exists z(R_f(x,y,z) \wedge \varphi(z))$.)

We now present the precise notion of a frame used to formalize the semantics of modal logic. As we have explained, a frame consists of a set W of "possible worlds", an accessibility (or successor) relation S between the possible worlds and an assignment of a classical structure $C(p)$ to each $p \in W$. We have chosen to require that the domains $C(p)$ of the structures $C(p)$ be monotonic in the successor relation, i.e., if q is a successor world of p, pSq, then $C(p) \subseteq C(q)$. This weak monotonicity requirement is not a serious restriction. As even the atomic predicates are not assumed to be monotonic, i.e., an element c of $C(p)$ can have some property R in $C(p)$ but not in $C(q)$. As any object can be declared to no longer be in the domain of a particular database or other predicate. One can provide frame semantics that do not incorporate this restriction but there are many difficulties involved that we wish to avoid. For example, if all objects cease to exist, i.e., some $C(q) = \emptyset$, we have entirely left the realm of classical predicate logic which is formulated only for nonempty domains.

Definition 2.1: Let $C = (W, S, \{C(p)\}_{p \in W})$ consist of a set W, a binary relation S on W and a function which assigns to each p in W a (classical) structure $C(p)$ for $\mathcal{L}$ (in the sense of Definition II.4.1). To simplify the notation we will write $C = (W, S, C(p))$ instead of the more formally precise version, $C = (W, S, \{C(p)\}_{p \in W})$. As usual, we let $C(p)$ denote the domain of the structure $C(p)$. We also let $\mathcal{L}(p)$ denote the extension of $\mathcal{L}$ gotten by adding on a name c_a for each element a of $C(p)$ in the style of the definition of truth in II.4. We write either pSq or $(p, q) \in S$ to denote the fact that the relation S holds between p and q. We also describe this state by saying that q is *accessible* from (or a *successor* of) p. We say that C is a *frame* for the language $\mathcal{L}$, or simply an $\mathcal{L}$–*frame* if, for every p and q in W, pSq implies that $C(p) \subseteq C(q)$ and the interpretations of the constants in $\mathcal{L}(p) \subseteq \mathcal{L}(q)$ are the same in $C(p)$ as in $C(q)$.

We now define the forcing relation for $\mathcal{L}$–frames. While reading the definition and working through the later examples, it may help to keep in mind the following paradigm interpretation: each $p \in W$ is a possible world; pSq means that q is a possible future of p; $p \Vdash \varphi$ means that φ is true in the world p; $\Box\varphi$ means that φ will always be true and $\Diamond\varphi$ means that φ will be true sometime in the future.

Definition 2.2 (*Forcing for frames*): Let $C = (W, S, C(p))$ be a frame for a language $\mathcal{L}$, p be in W and φ be a sentence of the language $\mathcal{L}(p)$. We give a definition of p *forces* φ, written $p \Vdash \varphi$ by induction on sentences φ.

   (i) For atomic sentences φ, $p \Vdash \varphi \Leftrightarrow \varphi$ is true in $C(p)$.

   (ii) $p \Vdash (\varphi \to \psi) \Leftrightarrow p \Vdash \varphi$ implies $p \Vdash \psi$.

   (iii) $p \Vdash \neg\varphi \Leftrightarrow p$ does not force φ (written $p \nVdash \varphi$).

   (iv) $p \Vdash (\forall x)\varphi(x) \Leftrightarrow$ for every constant c in $\mathcal{L}(p)$, $p \Vdash \varphi(c)$.

   (v) $p \Vdash (\exists x)\varphi(x) \Leftrightarrow$ there is a constant c in $\mathcal{L}(p)$ such that $p \Vdash \varphi(c)$.

   (vi) $p \Vdash (\varphi \wedge \psi) \Leftrightarrow p \Vdash \varphi$ and $p \Vdash \psi$.

   (vii) $p \Vdash (\varphi \vee \psi) \Leftrightarrow p \Vdash \varphi$ or $p \Vdash \psi$.

   (viii) $p \Vdash \Box\varphi \Leftrightarrow$ for all $q \in W$ such that pSq, $q \Vdash \varphi$.

   (ix) $p \Vdash \Diamond\varphi \Leftrightarrow$ there is a $q \in W$ such that pSq and $q \Vdash \varphi$.

If we need to make the frame explicit, we will say that p *forces* φ *in* C and write $p \Vdash_C \varphi$.

Definition 2.3: Let φ be a sentence of the language $\mathcal{L}$. We say that φ *is forced in the $\mathcal{L}$–frame C*, $\Vdash_C \varphi$, if every p in W forces φ. We say φ is *valid*, $\vDash \varphi$, if φ is forced in every $\mathcal{L}$–frame C.

Example 2.4: For any sentence φ, the sentence $\Box\varphi \rightarrow \neg\Diamond\neg\varphi$ is valid: Consider any frame $C = (W, S, C(p))$ and any $p \in W$. We must verify that $p \Vdash \Box\varphi \rightarrow \neg\Diamond\neg\varphi$ in accordance with clause (ii) of Definition 2.2. Suppose then that $p \Vdash \Box\varphi$. If $p \nVdash \neg\Diamond\neg\varphi$, then $p \Vdash \Diamond\neg\varphi$ (by (iii)). By clause (x), there is a $q \in W$ such that pSq and $q \Vdash \neg\varphi$. Our assumption that $p \Vdash \Box\varphi$ and clause (ix) then tell us that $p \Vdash \varphi$, contradicting clause (iii). Exercise 1 shows that the converse, $\neg\Diamond\neg\varphi \rightarrow \Box\varphi$, is also valid.

Example 2.5: We claim that $\Box\forall x\varphi(x) \rightarrow \forall x\Box\varphi(x)$ is valid. If not, there is a frame C and a p such that $p \Vdash \Box\forall x\varphi(x)$ but $p \nVdash \forall x\Box\varphi(x)$. If $p \nVdash \forall x\Box\varphi(x)$, there is, by clause (iv), a $c \in \mathcal{L}(p)$ such that $p \nVdash \Box\varphi(c)$. There is then, by clause (ix), a $q \in W$ such that pSq and $q \nVdash \varphi(c)$. As $p \Vdash \Box\forall x\varphi(x)$, $q \Vdash \forall x\varphi(x)$ by (ix). Finally, $q \Vdash \varphi(c)$ by (iv) for the desired contradiction. Note that the assumption that the domains $C(p)$ are monotonic, in the sense that $pSq \Rightarrow C(p) \subseteq C(q)$, plays a key role in this argument.

Example 2.6: $\Box\varphi(c) \rightarrow \varphi(c)$ is not valid: Consider any frame in which the atomic sentence $\varphi(c)$ is not true in some $C(p)$ and there is no q such that pSq. In such a frame $p \Vdash \Box\varphi(c)$ but $p \nVdash \varphi(c)$.

Example 2.7: $\forall x\varphi(x) \rightarrow \Box\forall x\varphi(x)$ is not valid: Let C be the frame in which $W = \{p, q\}$, $S = \{(p, q)\}$, $C(p) = \{c\}$, $C(q) = \{c, d\}$, $C(p) \vDash \varphi(c)$ and $C(q) \vDash \varphi(c) \wedge \neg\varphi(d)$. Now $p \Vdash \forall x\varphi(x)$ but $p \nVdash \Box\forall x\varphi(x)$ as $q \nVdash \varphi(d)$. It is crucial in this example that the domains $C(p)$ of a frame C are not assumed to all be the same. Modal logic restricted to constant domains is considered in Exercises 4.8.

Note that validity as defined here coincides with that for classical predicate logic for sentences φ with no modal operators (Exercise 10).

Some care must be taken now in the definition of "logical consequence" for modal logic. If one keeps in mind that the basic structure is the entire frame and not the individual worlds within it, one is lead to the following definition:

Definition 2.8: Let Σ be a set of sentences in a modal language $\mathcal{L}$ and φ a single sentence of $\mathcal{L}$. φ *is a logical consequence of* Σ, $\Sigma \vDash \varphi$, if φ is forced in every $\mathcal{L}$ frame C in which every $\psi \in \Sigma$ is forced.

Warning: This notion of logical consequence is not the same as requiring that, in every $\mathcal{L}$ frame C, φ is true (forced) at every world w at which every $\psi \in \Sigma$ is forced (Exercise 11). In particular, the deduction theorem (Exercise II.7.6) fails for modal logic as can be seen from Examples 2.7 and 2.9.

Example 2.9: $\forall x \varphi(x) \vDash \Box \forall x \varphi(x)$: Suppose C is a frame in which $p \Vdash \forall x \varphi(x)$ for every possible world $p \in W$. If $q \in W$, we claim that $q \Vdash \Box \forall x \varphi(x)$. If not, there would be a $p \in W$ such that qSp and $p \not\Vdash \forall x \varphi(x)$ contradicting our assumption.

Example 2.10: If φ is an atomic unary predicate, $\Box \varphi(c) \not\vDash \Diamond \varphi(c)$: Consider a frame C in which $S = \emptyset$ and in which $C(p) \not\vDash \varphi(c)$ and so $p \not\Vdash \varphi(c)$ for every p. In C, every p forces $\Box \varphi(c)$ but none forces $\varphi(c)$ and so none forces $\Diamond \varphi(c)$.

There are other notions of validity (and so of logical consequence) that result from putting further restrictions on the set W of possible worlds or (more frequently) on the accessibility relation S. For example, it is often useful to consider only reflexive and transitive accessibility relations. We will discuss several such alternatives in §5.

One should be aware that although $\Box$ and $\Diamond$ are treated syntactically like propositional connectives, their semantics involves quantification over all possible accessible worlds. $\Box \varphi$ says that, no matter what successor world one might move to, φ will be true there. $\Diamond \varphi$ says that there is some successor world to which one could move and make φ true. The construction of tableaux appropriate to such semantics will involve, of course, the introduction of new worlds and instantiations for elements of old ones.

Exercises

Prove, on the basis of the semantic definition of validity in Definition 2.3, that the following are valid modal sentences.

1. $\neg \Diamond \neg \varphi \rightarrow \Box \varphi$ (for any sentence φ).

2. $\forall x \Box \varphi(x) \rightarrow \exists x \Box \varphi(x)$ (for any formula $\varphi(x)$ with only x free).

Prove that the following are not, in general, valid modal sentences. Let φ be any modal sentence.

3. $\varphi \rightarrow \Diamond \varphi$.

4. $\varphi \rightarrow \Box \varphi$.

5. $\Diamond \varphi \rightarrow \varphi$.

Verify the following instances of logical consequence for modal sentences φ:

6. $\varphi \vDash \Box \varphi$.

7. $(\varphi \rightarrow \Box \varphi) \vDash (\Box \varphi \rightarrow \Box \Box \varphi)$.

Give frames that demonstrate the following failures of logical consequence:

8. $\Box \varphi \not\vDash \varphi$.

9. $(\Box \varphi \rightarrow \varphi) \not\vDash (\Box \varphi \rightarrow \Box \Box \varphi)$.

10. If φ is sentence with no occurrences of $\square$ or $\Diamond$, prove that validity for φ in the sense of Definition 3.1 coincides with that of II.4.4.

11. We say that φ *is a local consequence of* Σ if, for every $\mathcal{L}$ frame $\mathcal{C} = (W, S, \mathcal{C}(p))$, $\forall p \in W[(\forall \psi \in \Sigma)(p \Vdash \psi) \to p \Vdash \varphi]$.

   (i) Prove that if φ is a local consequence of Σ then it is a logical consequence of Σ.

   (ii) Prove that the converse of (i) fails, i.e., φ may be a logical consequence of Σ without being a local consequence.

3. Modal Tableaux

We will describe a proof procedure for modal logic based on a tableau style system like that used for classical logic in II.6. In classical logic, the plan guiding tableau proofs is to systematically search for a structure agreeing with the starting signed sentence. We either get such a structure or see that each possible analysis leads to a contradiction. When we begin with a signed sentence $F\varphi$, we thus either find a structure in which φ fails or decide that we have a proof of φ. For modal logic we instead begin with a *signed forcing assertion* $Tp \Vdash \varphi$ or $Fp \Vdash \varphi$ (φ is again a sentence) and try either to build a frame agreeing with the assertion or decide that any such attempt leads to a contradiction. If we begin with $Fp \Vdash \varphi$, we either find a frame in which p does not force φ or decide that we have a modal proof of φ.

The definitions of tableau and tableau proof for modal logic are formally very much like those of II.6 for classical logic. *Modal tableaux* and *tableau proofs* are labeled binary trees. The labels (again called the *entries of the tableau*) are now either *signed forcing assertions* (i.e., labels of the form $Tp \Vdash \varphi$ or $Fq \Vdash \varphi$ for φ a sentence of any given appropriate language) or accessibility assertions pSq. We read $Tp \Vdash \varphi$ as p forces φ and $Fp \Vdash \varphi$ as p does not force φ.

As we are using ordinary predicate logic within each possible world, the atomic tableaux for the propositional connectives $\vee, \wedge, \neg$ and $\to$ are as in the classical treatment in I.4 or II.6 except that their entries are now signed forcing assertions. The atomic tableaux for the quantifiers $\forall$ and $\exists$ are designed to reflect both the previous concerns in predicate logic as well as our monotonicity assumptions about the domains of possible worlds under the accessibility relation. Thus we still require that only "new" constants be used as witnesses for a true existential sentence or as counterexamples to false universal ones. Roughly speaking, a "new" constant is one for which no previous commitments have been made, e.g., one not in $\mathcal{L}$ or appearing so far in the tableau. Consider, on the other hand, a true universal sentence, $Tp \Vdash \forall x \varphi(x)$. In classical predicate logic we could substitute any constant at all for the universally quantified variable x. Here we can conclude $Tp \Vdash \varphi(c)$ only for constants c which we know to be in $C(p)$ or in $C(q)$ for some world q from which p is accessible, qSp. This idea translates into the requirement that c is in $\mathcal{L}$ or has appeared in a forcing assertion on the path so far which involves p or some q for which qSp has also appeared on the path so far. The point here is that, if qSp and c is in $C(q)$, then by monotonicity it must be in $C(p)$ as well. In the description of modal tableaux, we will refer to these constants as "any appropriate c". Of course, the formal definitions of both "new" and "appropriate" constants are given along with the definition of tableaux.

The other crucial element is the treatment of signed forcing sentences beginning with $\Box$ or $\Diamond$. In classical logic, the elements of the structure built by developing a tableau were the constant symbols appearing on some path of the tableau. We are now attempting to build an entire frame. The p's and q's appearing in the entries of some path P through our tableau will constitute the possible worlds of the frame. We must also specify some appropriate accessibility relation S along each path of the tableau. It is convenient to include this information directly on the path. Thus we allow as entries in the tableau facts of the form pSq for possible worlds p and q that appear in signed forcing assertions on the path up to the entry. Entries of this form will be put on the tableau by some of the atomic tableaux for $\Box$ and $\Diamond$. For example, from $Tp \Vdash \Diamond\varphi$ we can (semantically) conclude that $Tq \Vdash \varphi$ for some q such that pSq. Thus the atomic tableau for $Tp \Vdash \Diamond\varphi$ puts both pSq and $Tq \Vdash \varphi$ on the path for some new q (i.e., one not appearing in the tableau so far). On the other hand, the atomic tableau for $Tp \Vdash \Box\varphi$ will reflect the idea that the meaning of $p \Vdash \Box\varphi$ is that φ is true in every world q such that pSq. It will put on the path the assertion $Tq \Vdash \varphi$ for any appropriate q, i.e., any q for which we already know that pSq by virtue of the fact that pSq has itself appeared on the path so far. In this way, we are attempting to build a suitable frame along every path of the tableau.

We now formally specify the *atomic tableaux*.

Definition 3.1 (*Atomic Tableaux*): We begin by fixing a modal language $\mathcal{L}$ and an expansion to $\mathcal{L}_C$ given by adding new constant symbols c_i for $i \in \mathbf{N}$. We list in Figure 43 the atomic tableaux (for the language $\mathcal{L}$). In the tableaux in the following list, φ and ψ, if unquantified, are any sentences in the language $\mathcal{L}_C$. If quantified, they are formulas in which only x is free.

Warning: In (T$\Box$) and (F$\Diamond$) we allow for the possibility that there is no appropriate q by admitting $Tp \Vdash \Box\varphi$ and $Fp \Vdash \Diamond\varphi$ as instances of (T$\Box$) and (F$\Diamond$) respectively.

The formal definition of tableaux is now quite similar to that for classical logic in II.3.

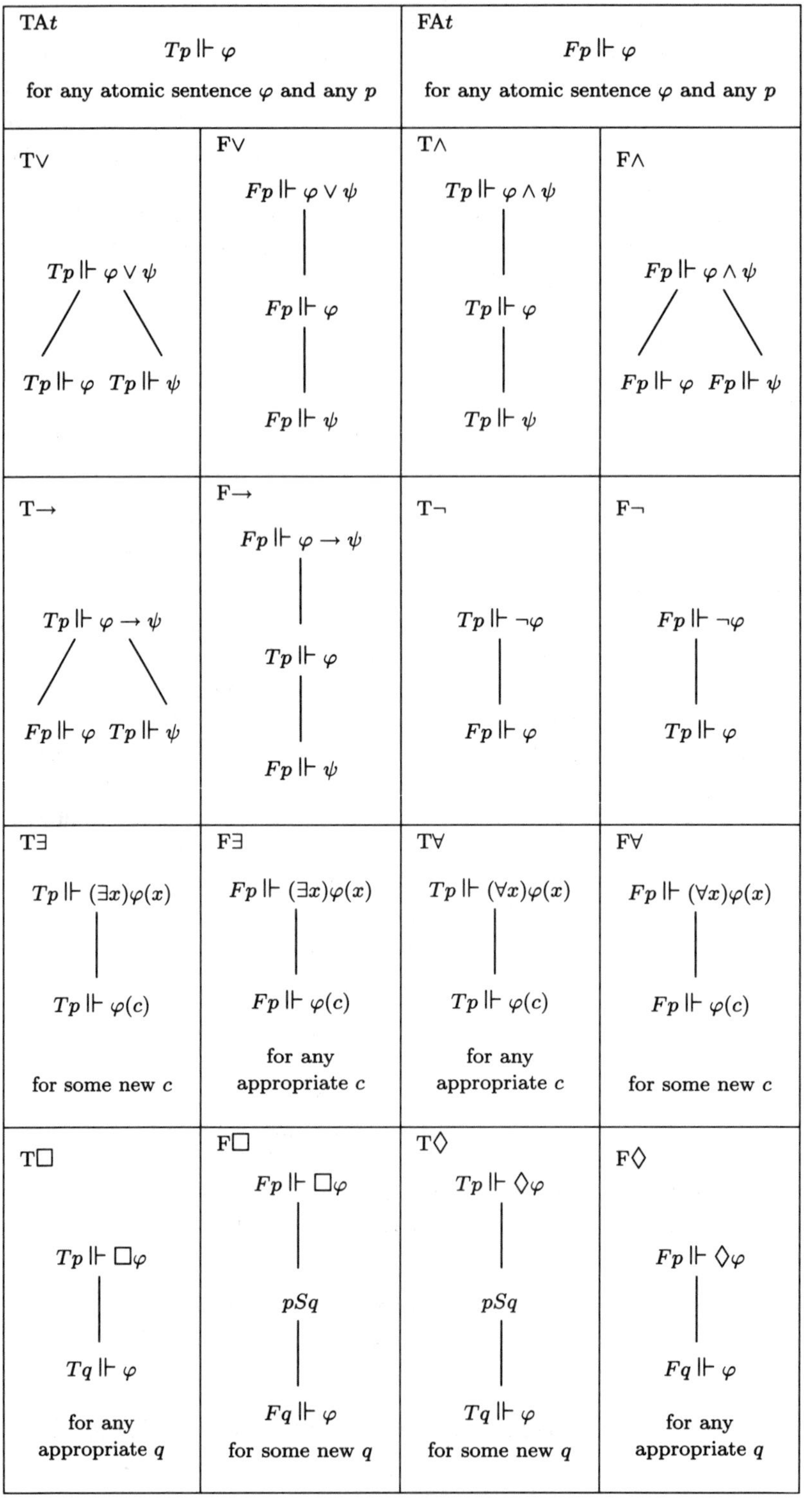

TAt		FAt	
$Tp \Vdash \varphi$ for any atomic sentence φ and any p		$Fp \Vdash \varphi$ for any atomic sentence φ and any p	

T∨	F∨	T∧	F∧
$Tp \Vdash \varphi \vee \psi$ ╱ ╲ $Tp \Vdash \varphi$　$Tp \Vdash \psi$	$Fp \Vdash \varphi \vee \psi$ | $Fp \Vdash \varphi$ | $Fp \Vdash \psi$	$Tp \Vdash \varphi \wedge \psi$ | $Tp \Vdash \varphi$ | $Tp \Vdash \psi$	$Fp \Vdash \varphi \wedge \psi$ ╱ ╲ $Fp \Vdash \varphi$　$Fp \Vdash \psi$

T→	F→	T¬	F¬
$Tp \Vdash \varphi \rightarrow \psi$ ╱ ╲ $Fp \Vdash \varphi$　$Tp \Vdash \psi$	$Fp \Vdash \varphi \rightarrow \psi$ | $Tp \Vdash \varphi$ | $Fp \Vdash \psi$	$Tp \Vdash \neg\varphi$ | $Fp \Vdash \varphi$	$Fp \Vdash \neg\varphi$ | $Tp \Vdash \varphi$

T∃	F∃	T∀	F∀
$Tp \Vdash (\exists x)\varphi(x)$ | $Tp \Vdash \varphi(c)$ for some new c	$Fp \Vdash (\exists x)\varphi(x)$ | $Fp \Vdash \varphi(c)$ for any appropriate c	$Tp \Vdash (\forall x)\varphi(x)$ | $Tp \Vdash \varphi(c)$ for any appropriate c	$Fp \Vdash (\forall x)\varphi(x)$ | $Fp \Vdash \varphi(c)$ for some new c

T□	F□	T◇	F◇
$Tp \Vdash \Box\varphi$ | $Tq \Vdash \varphi$ for any appropriate q	$Fp \Vdash \Box\varphi$ | pSq | $Fq \Vdash \varphi$ for some new q	$Tp \Vdash \Diamond\varphi$ | pSq | $Tq \Vdash \varphi$ for some new q	$Fp \Vdash \Diamond\varphi$ | $Fq \Vdash \varphi$ for any appropriate q

FIGURE 43

Definition 3.2: We continue to use our fixed modal language $\mathcal{L}$ and its extension by constants $\mathcal{L}_C$. We also fix a set $\{p_i : i \in \mathbb{N}\}$ of potential candidates for the p's and q's in our forcing assertions. A *modal tableau* (for $\mathcal{L}$) is a binary tree labeled with signed forcing assertions or accessibility assertions; both sorts of labels are called *entries* of the tableau. The class of modal tableaux (for $\mathcal{L}$) is defined inductively as follows.

(i) Each atomic tableau τ is a tableau. The requirement that c be new in cases (T∃) and (F∀) here simply means that c is one of the constants c_i added on to $\mathcal{L}$ to get $\mathcal{L}_C$ which does not appear in φ. The phrase "any appropriate c" in (F∃) and (T∀) means any constant in $\mathcal{L}$ or in φ. The requirement that q be new in (F□) and (T◊) here means that q is any of the p_i other than p. The phrase "any appropriate q" in (T□) and (F◊) in this case simply means that the tableau is just $Tp \Vdash \Box\varphi$ or $Fp \Vdash \Diamond\varphi$ as there is no appropriate q.

(ii) If τ is a finite tableau, P a path on τ, E an entry of τ occurring on P and τ' is obtained from τ by adjoining an atomic tableau with root entry E to τ at the end of the path P then τ' is also a tableau.

The requirement that c be new in cases (T∃) and (F∀) here means that it is one of the c_i (and so not in $\mathcal{L}$) which do not appear in any entry on τ. The phrase "any appropriate c" in (F∃) and (T∀) here means any c in $\mathcal{L}$ or appearing in an entry on P of the form $Tq \Vdash \psi$ or $Fq \Vdash \psi$ such that qSp also appears on P.

In (F□) and (T◊) the requirement that q be new means that we choose a p_i not appearing in τ as q. The phrase "any appropriate q" in (T□) and (F◊) means we can choose any q such that pSq is an entry on P.

(iii) If $\tau_0, \tau_1, ..., \tau_n, ...$ is a sequence of finite tableaux such that, for every $n \geq 0$, τ_{n+1} is constructed from τ_n by an application of (ii) then $\tau = \cup\tau_n$ is also a tableau.

As in the previous definitions, we insist that the entry E in clause (ii) formally be repeated when the corresponding atomic tableau is added on to P to guarantee the property corresponding to a classical tableau being finished. The atomic tableaux for which they are actually needed are (F∃), (T∀), (T□) and (F◊). We will, however, generally omit the repetition of the root entry in our examples as a notational convenience. The definition of tableau proofs now follows the familiar pattern.

Definition 3.3 (*Tableau Proofs*): Let τ be a modal tableau and P a path in τ.

(i) P is *contradictory* if, for some forcing assertion $p \Vdash \varphi$, both $Tp \Vdash \varphi$ and $Fp \Vdash \varphi$ appear as entries on P.

(ii) τ is *contradictory* if every path through τ is contradictory.

(iii) τ is a *proof of* φ if τ is a finite contradictory modal tableau with its root node labeled $Fp \Vdash \varphi$ for some p. φ is *provable*, $\vdash \varphi$, if there is a proof of φ.

Note that, as in classical logic, if there is any contradictory tableau with root node $Fp \Vdash \varphi$, then there is one which is finite, i.e., a proof of φ : Just terminate each path when it becomes contradictory. As each path is now finite, the whole tree is finite by König's lemma. Thus, the added requirement that proofs be finite (tableaux) has no affect on the existence of proofs for any sentence. Another point of view is that we could have required that the path P in clause (ii) of the definition of tableaux be noncontradictory without affecting the existence of proofs. Thus, in practice, when attempting to construct proofs we mark any contradictory path with the symbol $\otimes$ and terminate the development of the tableau along that path.

Before dealing with the soundness and completeness of the tableau method for modal logic, we look at some examples of modal tableau proofs. Remember that we are abbreviating the tableaux by generally not repeating the entry which we are expanding. We also number the levels of the tableau on the left and indicate on the right the level of the atomic tableau whose development produced the line.

Example 3.4: There is a natural correspondence between the tableaux of classical predicate logic and those of modal logic beginning with sentences without modal operators. One goes from the modal tableau to the classical one by replacing signed forcing assertions $Tp \Vdash \varphi$ and $Fp \Vdash \varphi$ by the corresponding signed sentences $T\varphi$ and $F\varphi$ respectively. (Formally one must account for the alternate notion of new constant used in II.6.1 when going in the other direction.) Note that this correspondence takes proofs to proofs. (See Exercise 1.)

Example 3.5: $\varphi \to \Box\varphi$, sometimes called the *scheme of necessitation*, is not valid. Figure 44 gives an attempt at a tableau proof.

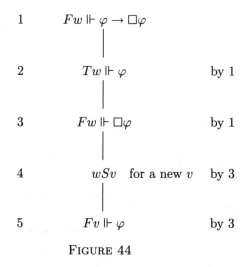

1	$Fw \Vdash \varphi \to \Box\varphi$	
2	$Tw \Vdash \varphi$	by 1
3	$Fw \Vdash \Box\varphi$	by 1
4	wSv for a new v	by 3
5	$Fv \Vdash \varphi$	by 3

FIGURE 44

This failed attempt at a proof suggests a frame counterexample $\mathcal{C}$ with $W = \{w, v\}$, $S = \{(w, v)\}$ and structures such that φ is true at w but not at v. Such a frame demonstrates that $\varphi \to \Box\varphi$ is not valid as in this frame, w does not force $\varphi \to \Box\varphi$.

Example 3.6: Similarly $\Box\varphi \to \varphi$ is not valid as can be seen from the attempted proof in Figure 45.

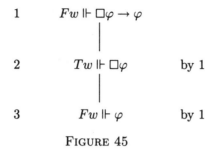

FIGURE 45

The frame counterexample suggested here consists of a one world $W = \{w\}$ with empty accessibility relation S and φ false at w. It shows that $\Box\varphi \to \varphi$ is not valid.

Various interpretations of $\Box$ might tempt one to think that $\Box\varphi \to \varphi$ should be valid. For example, probably all philosophers would agree that if φ is necessarily true it in fact is true. On the other hand, most but perhaps not all epistemologists would argue that if I know φ it must also be true. Finally, few people would claim that (for any φ) if I believe φ then φ is true. $\Box\varphi \to \varphi$ is traditionally called "T" or the "knowledge axiom". Under many interpretations of $\Box$, it should be valid. A glance at the attempted proof above shows us that, if we knew that wSw, we could quickly get the desired contradiction. Thus, there is a relation between T and the assumption that the accessibility relation is reflexive. In fact, not only is T valid in all frames with reflexive accessibility relations, but conversely any sentence valid in all such frames can be deduced from T. We will make this correspondence and others like it precise in §5.

Example 3.7: We show in Figure 46 that $\Box(\forall x)\varphi(x) \to (\forall x)\Box\varphi(x)$ is provable.

Note the use of monotonicity in the derivation of lines 6 and 8 corresponding to the semantic argument in Example 2.5.

Example 3.8: Figure 47 gives a tableau proof of

$$\Box(\varphi \to \psi) \to (\Box\varphi \to \Box\psi).$$

(This scheme plays an important role in the Hilbert–style systems of modal logic presented in §6.)

Example 3.9: Figure 48 gives an incorrect proof of $\forall x\Box\varphi(x) \to \Box\forall x\varphi(x)$.

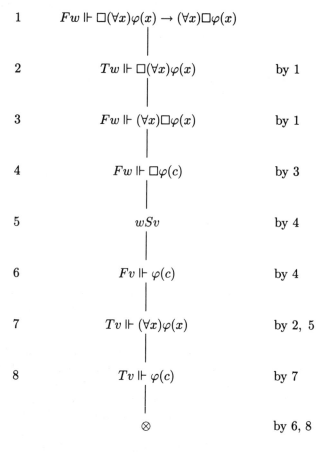

1      $Fw \Vdash \Box(\forall x)\varphi(x) \to (\forall x)\Box\varphi(x)$

2      $Tw \Vdash \Box(\forall x)\varphi(x)$ by 1

3      $Fw \Vdash (\forall x)\Box\varphi(x)$ by 1

4      $Fw \Vdash \Box\varphi(c)$ by 3

5   wSv by 4

6      $Fv \Vdash \varphi(c)$ by 4

7      $Tv \Vdash (\forall x)\varphi(x)$ by 2, 5

8      $Tv \Vdash \varphi(c)$ by 7

     $\otimes$ by 6, 8

FIGURE 46

The false step occurs at line 7. On the basis of line 6 we can use c for instantiations in forcing assertions about v or any world accessible from v but we have no basis to use it in assertions about w. As in Example 2.7, such a move would be appropriate for an analysis of constant domain frames. (See Exercises 4.8)

Example 3.10: $(\forall x)\neg\Box\varphi \to \neg\Box(\exists x)\varphi$ is not valid. (See Figure 49.)

This is not a proof. With the constant domain $C = \{c, d\}$, and two worlds w, v, with v accessible from w, no atomic sentences true at w and the sentence $\varphi(d)$ true at v, we get a frame counterexample.

As with the semantic definition of logical consequence, one must take care in defining the notion of a modal tableau proof from a set Σ of sentences (which we often call premises). We must match the intuition that we are restricting our attention to frames in which the premises are forced. To do this, we allow the insertion in the tableau of entries of the form $Tp \Vdash \varphi$ for any appropriate possible world p and any $\varphi \in \Sigma$.

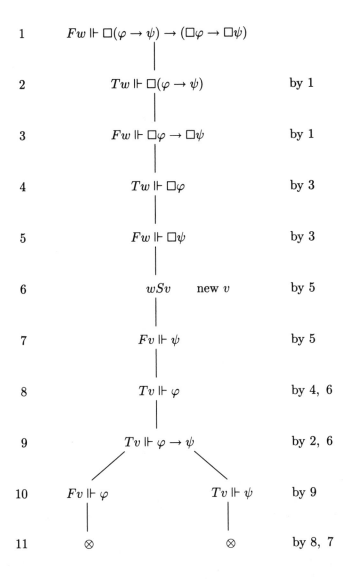

FIGURE 47

Definition 3.11: The definition of *modal tableaux from* Σ, a set of sentences of a modal language called premises, is the same as for simple modal tableaux in Definition 3.2 except that we allow one additional formation rule:

(ii′) If τ is a finite tableau from Σ, $\varphi \in \Sigma$, P a path in τ and p a possible world appearing in some signed forcing assertion on P, then appending $Tp \Vdash \varphi$ to the end of P produces a tableau τ' from Σ.

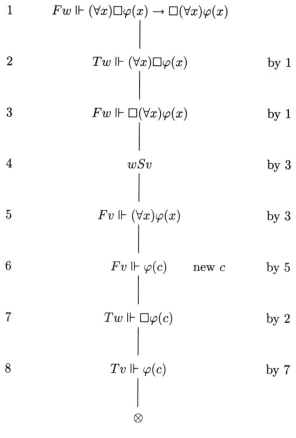

1        $Fw \Vdash (\forall x)\Box\varphi(x) \rightarrow \Box(\forall x)\varphi(x)$

2              $Tw \Vdash (\forall x)\Box\varphi(x)$ by 1

3              $Fw \Vdash \Box(\forall x)\varphi(x)$ by 1

4   wSv by 3

5              $Fv \Vdash (\forall x)\varphi(x)$ by 3

6              $Fv \Vdash \varphi(c)$ new c by 5

7              $Tw \Vdash \Box\varphi(c)$ by 2

8              $Tv \Vdash \varphi(c)$ by 7

                        $\otimes$

FIGURE 48

The notions used to define a tableau proof are now carried over from Definition 3.3 to *tableau proofs from* Σ by simply replacing "tableau" by "tableau from Σ". We write $\Sigma \vdash \varphi$ to denote that φ *is provable from* Σ, i.e., there is a proof of φ from Σ.

Example 3.12: Figure 50 gives a tableau proof of $\Box\forall x\varphi(x)$ from the premise $\forall x\varphi(x)$

Exercises

1. Make precise the correspondence described in Example 3.4 and show that it takes tableau proofs in classical predicate logic to ones in modal logic. Conversely, if τ is a modal tableau proof of a sentence φ of classical logic, describe the appropriate transformation in the other direction and show that it takes τ to a classical proof of φ.

In exercises 2–8, let φ and ψ be any formulas with either no free variables or only x free as appropriate. Give modal tableau proofs of each one.

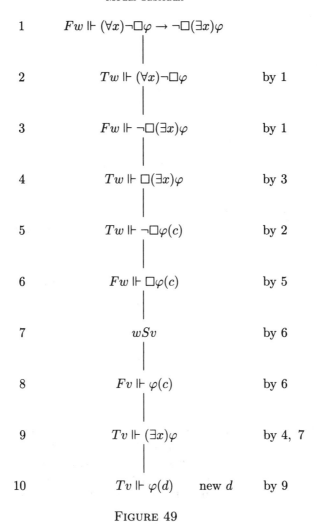

1          $Fw \Vdash (\forall x)\neg\Box\varphi \to \neg\Box(\exists x)\varphi$

2          $Tw \Vdash (\forall x)\neg\Box\varphi$ by 1

3          $Fw \Vdash \neg\Box(\exists x)\varphi$ by 1

4          $Tw \Vdash \Box(\exists x)\varphi$ by 3

5          $Tw \Vdash \neg\Box\varphi(c)$ by 2

6          $Fw \Vdash \Box\varphi(c)$ by 5

7   wSv by 6

8          $Fv \Vdash \varphi(c)$ by 6

9          $Tv \Vdash (\exists x)\varphi$ by 4, 7

10         $Tv \Vdash \varphi(d)$ new d by 9

FIGURE 49

2. $\neg\Diamond\neg\varphi \to \Box\varphi$.
3. $\forall x\Box\varphi(x) \to \exists x\Box\varphi(x)$.
4. $\Box\Box((\varphi \lor (\forall x)\psi(x)) \to (\forall x)(\varphi \lor \psi(x)))$, x not free in φ.
5. $\neg\Diamond(\neg(\varphi \land (\exists x)\psi(x)) \land (\exists x)(\varphi \land \psi(x)))$, x not free in φ.
6. $\Box(\varphi \lor \neg\psi) \to (\Diamond\psi \to \Diamond\varphi)$.
7. $\Box(\exists x)(\varphi \land \psi(x)) \to \Box(\varphi \land (\exists x)\psi(x))$, x not free in φ.
8. $\Diamond(\exists x)(\varphi(x) \to \Box\psi) \to \Diamond((\forall x)\varphi(x) \to \Box\psi)$, x not free in ψ.

Give modal tableau proofs of the following:

9. $\varphi \Vdash \Box\varphi$.
10. $(\varphi \to \Box\varphi) \Vdash \Box\varphi \to \Box\Box\varphi$.
11. $\forall x\varphi(x) \Vdash \forall x\Box\varphi(x)$.

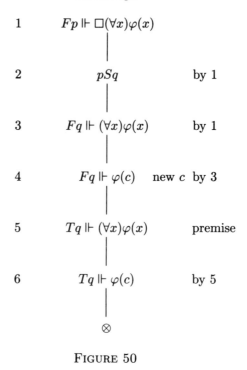

1        $Fp \Vdash \Box(\forall x)\varphi(x)$

2   pSq by 1

3        $Fq \Vdash (\forall x)\varphi(x)$ by 1

4        $Fq \Vdash \varphi(c)$ new c by 3

5        $Tq \Vdash (\forall x)\varphi(x)$ premise

6        $Tq \Vdash \varphi(c)$ by 5

$\otimes$

FIGURE 50

12. **Theorem on Constants**: Let $\varphi(x_1, ..., x_n)$ be a formula in a modal language $\mathcal{L}$ with all free variables displayed and let $c_1, ..., c_n$ be constant symbols not in $\mathcal{L}$. Show that $\forall x_1...\forall x_n \varphi(x_1, ..., x_n)$ is tableau provable iff $\varphi(c_1, ..., c_n)$ is. Argue syntactically to show that given a proof of one of the formulas one can construct a proof of the other.

4. Soundness and Completeness

Our first goal in this section is to show that in modal logic (as in classical logic) provability implies validity. As in the classical soundness theorem (II.7.2), we begin by proving that a frame which "agrees" with the root node of a tableau "agrees" with every entry along some path of the tableau. In the classical case (Definition II.7.1), we construct the path in the tableau and define a structure whose domain consists of the constants c occurring in the signed sentences along this path. In the modal case, we must define a set W of possible worlds and, for each $p \in W$, a structure based on constants occurring on the path. W will consist of the p's occurring in signed forcing assertions along the path. The accessibility relation on W will then be defined by the assertions pSq occurring on the path.

Definition 4.1: Suppose $C = (V, T, C(p))$ is a frame for a modal language $\mathcal{L}$, τ is a tableau whose root is labeled with a forcing assertion about a sentence φ of $\mathcal{L}$ and P is a path through τ. Let W be the set of p's appearing in forcing assertions on P and let S be the accessibility relation on W determined by the assertions pSq occurring on P. We say that C *agrees with* P if there are maps f and g such that

  (i) f is a map from W into V which preserves the accessibility relation, i.e., $pSq \Rightarrow f(p)Tf(q)$. (Note that f is not assumed to be one–one.)

 (ii) g sends each constant c occurring in any sentence ψ of a forcing assertion $Tp \Vdash \psi$ or $Fp \Vdash \psi$ on P to a constant in $\mathcal{L}(f(p))$. Moreover, g is the identity on constants of $\mathcal{L}$. We also extend g to be a map on formulas in the obvious way: To get $g(\psi)$ simply replace every constant c in ψ by $g(c)$.

(iii) If $Tp \Vdash \psi$ is on P, then $f(p)$ forces $g(\psi)$ in C and if $Fp \Vdash \psi$ is on P, then $f(p)$ does not force $g(\psi)$ in C.

Theorem 4.2: *Suppose $C = (V, T, C(p))$ is a frame for a language $\mathcal{L}$ and τ is a tableau whose root is labeled with a forcing assertion about a sentence φ of $\mathcal{L}$. If $q \in V$ and either*

  (i) *$Fr \Vdash \varphi$ is the root of τ and q does not force φ in C*

or

 (ii) *$Tr \Vdash \varphi$ is the root of τ and q does force φ in C,*

then there is a path P through τ which agrees with C with a witness function f (as required in Definition 4.1) that sends r to q.

The proof of this theorem proceeds by induction on the construction of the tableau τ. Before providing the details, we reformulate the result as the standard version of the soundness theorem.

Theorem 4.3 (Soundness, $\vdash \varphi \Rightarrow \vDash \varphi$): *If there is a (modal) tableau proof of a sentence φ (of modal logic), then φ is (modally) valid.*

Proof (of Soundness): A modal tableau proof of φ is a tableau τ with a root of the form $Fr \Vdash \varphi$ in which every path is contradictory. If φ is not valid, then there is a frame $C = (V, T, C(p))$ and a $q \in V$ such that q does not force φ in C. Now apply Theorem 4.2 to get a path P through τ and functions f and g with the properties listed in Definition 4.1. As τ is contradictory, there is a p and a sentence ψ such that both $Tp \Vdash \psi$ and $Fp \Vdash \psi$ occur on P. Definition 4.1(iii) then provides an immediate contradiction. $\square$

We break the inductive proof of Theorem 4.2 into its component parts. First, there are eighteen base cases corresponding to clause (i) of Definition 3.2 and the eighteen atomic tableaux.

Lemma 4.4: *For each atomic tableau τ which satisfies the hypotheses of Theorem 4.2, there are P, f and g as required in its conclusion.*

There are then sixteen induction cases corresponding to the type of atomic tableau chosen for development in clause (ii) of Definition 3.2. We in fact prove an assertion somewhat stronger than the theorem to facilitate the induction.

Lemma 4.5: *If f and g are witnesses that a path P of a tableau τ agrees with $\mathcal{C}$ and τ' is gotten from τ by an application of clause (ii) of Definition 3.2, then there are extensions P', f' and g' of P, f and g respectively such that f' and g' are witnesses that the path P' through τ' also agrees with $\mathcal{C}$.*

Theorem 4.2 is an easy consequence of these two lemmas so we present its proof before considering the proofs of the lemmas.

Proof (of Theorem 4.2): Lemma 4.4 establishes the theorem for atomic tableau. Lemma 4.5 then proves the theorem for all finite tableaux by induction. In fact, it proves it for infinite tableaux as well: Suppose $\tau = \cup \tau_n$ is an infinite tableau as defined by clause (iii) of Definition 3.2. We begin by applying the appropriate case of Lemma 4.4 to τ_0 to get suitable P_0, f_0 and g_0. We then apply Lemma 4.5 to each τ_n in turn to construct P_n, f_n and g_n. The required P, f and g for τ are then simply the unions of the P_n, f_n and g_n respectively. □

Proof (of Lemma 4.4): We begin by defining $f(p) = r$ and g to be the identity on the constants of $\mathcal{L}_C$. With this choice of f and g, the root itself agrees with $\mathcal{C}$ by the hypothesis of the theorem. This completes the argument for TAt and FAt. The argument needed for each of the other atomic tableaux is precisely the same as the one for the corresponding case of Lemma 4.5. The inductive argument applied to the rest of the atomic tableau then provides the required extensions. (Perhaps technically the degenerate cases of $(T\square)$ and $(F\lozenge)$ are exceptions but in those cases the conclusion is precisely the hypothesis.) Thus we have reduced the proof of this lemma to that of Lemma 4.5. □

Proof (of Lemma 4.5): First note that if τ' is gotten by extending τ somewhere other than at the end of P, then the witnesses for τ work for τ' as well. Thus, we may assume that we form τ' by adjoining one of the atomic tableaux at the end of P in τ. We now consider the sixteen cases given by the atomic tableaux of Definition 3.1.

The cases other than $(T\exists)$, $(F\forall)$, $(F\square)$ and $(T\lozenge)$ require no extension of f or g. In each of these cases it is obvious from the induction hypothesis and the corresponding case of the definition of forcing (Definition 2.2) (and the monotonicity assumption on the domains $C(p)$ for cases $(F\exists)$ and $(T\forall)$) that one of the extensions of P to a path through τ' satisfies the requirements of the lemma.

We present cases (T∃) and (T◊) in detail. Cases (F∀) and (F□) are similar and are left as Exercise 1. In case (T∃) the entry of P being developed is $Tp \Vdash (\exists x)\varphi(x)$. P', the required extension of P, is the only one possible. It is determined by adding $Tp \Vdash \varphi(c)$ to the end of P. By our induction hypothesis, $f(p) \Vdash_C g((\exists x)\varphi(x))$. By the definition of forcing an existential sentence (2.2(v)), there is a $c' \in \mathcal{L}(p)$ such that $f(p) \Vdash g(\varphi(c'))$. Fix such a c' and extend g to g' by setting $g'(c) = c'$. It is now obvious that P', $f' = f$ and g' satisfy the requirements of the lemma, i.e., f' and g' witness that P' agrees with C.

Finally, in case (T◊) the entry of P being developed is $Tp \Vdash \Diamond\varphi$. The required extension of P to P' is the only possible one. It is determined by adding both pSq and $Tq \Vdash \varphi$ onto the end of P. By our induction hypothesis, $f(p) \Vdash_C g(\Diamond\varphi)$. As $g(\Diamond\varphi) = \Diamond g(\varphi)$, there is, by the definition of forcing for ◊ (2.2(x)), a $q' \in V$ such that $f(p)Tq'$ and $q' \Vdash g(\varphi)$. Fix such a q' and extend f to f' by setting $f'(q) = q'$. It is now obvious that P', f' and $g' = g$ satisfy the requirements of the lemma, i.e., f' and g' witness that P' agrees with C. □

Our next goal is to prove that the tableau method of proof is complete for modal logic. We will define a procedure (like that of II.6.9) for constructing the appropriate complete systematic tableau starting with a given signed forcing assertion at its root. We will then prove that, for any non-contradictory path P through this tableau, we can build a frame C which agrees with P. Thus if our systematic procedure applied to any forcing assertion $Fp \Vdash \varphi$ fails to produce a modal tableau proof of φ, then we will have built a frame in which φ is not forced and so demonstrated that φ is not valid.

We begin by extending the notion of a reduced entry and a finished tableau (Definition II.6.7) to modal logic.

Recall that $c_1, ..., c_n, ...$ is a list of all the constants of our expanded language $\mathcal{L}_C$ and $p_1, p_2, ...$ a list of our stock of possible worlds. For convenience we assume that c_1 is in $\mathcal{L}$.

Definition 4.6: Let $\tau = \cup\tau_n$ be a tableau, P a path in τ, E an entry on P and w the ith occurrence of E on P (i.e., the ith node on P labeled with E).

(i) w is *reduced on* P if one of the following four situations hold:

    (1) E is not of the form of the root of an atomic tableau of type (F∃), (T∀), (T□) or (F◊) (of Definition 3.1) and, for some j, τ_{j+1} is gotten from τ_j by an application of rule (ii) of Definition 3.2 to E and a path on τ_j which is an initial segment of P. [In this case we say that E occurs on P as the root entry of an atomic tableau.]

    (2) E is of the form $Fp \Vdash (\exists x)\varphi(x)$ or $Tp \Vdash (\forall x)\varphi(x)$ (cases (F∃) and (T∀) respectively), there is an $i+1^{\text{st}}$ occurrence of E on P and either

c_i does not occur in any assertion on P about a possible world q such that qSp occurs on P or

$Fp \Vdash \varphi(c_i)$ or $Tp \Vdash \varphi(c_i)$ is an entry on P.

(3) E is of the form $Tp \Vdash \Box\varphi$ or $Fp \Vdash \Diamond\varphi$ (cases (T$\Box$) and (F$\Diamond$) respectively), there is an $i + 1^{\text{st}}$ occurrence of E on P and either

pSp_i is not an entry on P or

$Tp_i \Vdash \varphi$ or $Fp_i \Vdash \varphi$ is an entry on P

(4) E is of the form pSq.

(ii) τ is *finished* if every occurrence of every entry on τ is reduced on every noncontradictory path containing it. It is *unfinished* otherwise.

As in the treatment of classical tableaux, a signed forcing assertion of the form $Tp \Vdash (\forall x)\varphi(x)$ must be instantiated for each constant c_i in our language before we can say that we have finished with it. Here, in addition, if p forces $\Box\varphi$ then φ must be forced by every successor q of p. We can now show that there is a finished tableau with any given signed forcing assertion as its root by constructing the appropriate complete systematic tableau. We use the same scheme as in the classical case based on $\leq_{LL}$, the level–lexicographic ordering, introduced in Definition II.6.8.

Lemma 4.7: *Suppose w is the ith occurrence of an entry E on a path P of a tableau τ and is reduced on P in τ. If τ' is an extension of τ and P' is an extension of P to a path in τ', the only way w could fail to be reduced on P' in τ' is if*

(i) *E is of the form $Fp \Vdash \exists x\varphi(x)$ $(Tp \Vdash \forall x\varphi(x))$ and c_i does not occur in any assertion on P about a possible world q such that qSp occurs on P but c_i does occur in such an assertion on P' and $Fp \Vdash \varphi(c_i)$ $(Tp \Vdash \varphi(c_i))$ is not an entry on P'; or*

(ii) *E is of the form $Tp \Vdash \Box\varphi$ $(Fp \Vdash \Diamond p)$ and pSp_i occurs on P' but not on P and $Fp_i \Vdash \varphi$ $(Tp_i \Vdash \varphi)$ does not occur on P'.*

Proof: This claim is obvious from the definitions. □

Definition 4.8: We define the *complete systematic modal tableau* (the CSMT) *starting with a sentence φ* by induction as follows.

(i) τ_0 is the atomic tableau with root $Fp_1 \Vdash \varphi$. This atomic tableau is uniquely specified by requiring that in cases (F$\exists$) and (T$\forall$) we use the constant c_1, in cases (T$\exists$) and (F$\forall$) we use c_i for the least allowable i and in cases (F$\Box$) and (T$\Diamond$) we use the least p_i not occurring in the root. (Note that in cases (T$\Box$) and (F$\Diamond$) the tableau consists of just the root entry. It is finished and constitutes our CSMT.)

At stage n we have, by induction, a tableau τ_n. If τ_n is finished, we terminate the construction. Otherwise, we let w be the level–lexicographically least node of τ_n which contains an occurrence of an entry E which is unreduced on some noncontradictory path P of τ_n. We now extend τ_n to a tableau τ_{n+1} by applying one of the following three procedures:

(ii) If E is not of the form occurring in the root node of case (F∃), (T∀), (T□) or (F◇), we adjoin the atomic tableau with root E to the end of every noncontradictory path in τ that contains w. For E of type (T∃) or (F∀) we use the least constant c_j not yet appearing in the tableau. If E is of type (F□) or (T◇), we choose p_j for q where j is least such that p_j does not appear in the tableau.

(iii) If E is of type (F∃) or (T∀) and w is the ith occurrence of E on P, we adjoin the corresponding atomic tableau with c_j as the required c, where j is least such that c_j is appropriate and $Fp \Vdash \varphi(c_j)$ or $Tp \Vdash \varphi(c_j)$, respectively, does not appear as an entry on P. We take c to be c_1 if there is no such c_j.

(iv) If E is of type (T□) or (F◇) and w is the ith occurrence of E on P, we adjoin the corresponding atomic tableau with q_j as the required q where j is least such that q_j is appropriate and $Tq_j \Vdash \varphi$ or $Fq_j \Vdash \varphi$, respectively, does not appear as an entry on P. If $Tq_j \Vdash \varphi$ (or $Fq_j \Vdash \varphi$) already appears on P for every appropriate q_j, we simply repeat the assertion $Tq_j \Vdash \varphi$ (or $Fq_j \Vdash \varphi$), where j is least such that q_j is appropriate. (There is at least one appropriate q_j by the assumption that E is not reduced on P.)

The union τ of the sequence of tableaux τ_n is the CSMT starting with φ.

Note that in general a CSMT will be an infinite tableau (even if S is finite). The crucial point is that it is always a finished tableau.

Lemma 4.9: *If p_iSp_j appears as an entry on a CSMT then $i < j$.*

Proof: New possible worlds p_j and new instances of the accessibility relation appear on a CSMT $\tau = \cup\tau_n$ only when an entry of the form p_iSp_j is put on the tableau by an application of clause (ii) of Definition 3.8 for cases (F□) or (T◇). Thus they are put on the CSMT in numerical order and so when p_iSp_j is put on the tree, $i < j$ as required. □

Proposition 4.10: *Every CSMT is finished.*

Proof: Consider any entry E and any unreduced occurrence w of E on a noncontradictory path P of the given CSMT τ. (If there is no such w, τ is finished by definition.) Suppose that E makes a forcing assertion about some possible world p_m, w is the ith occurrence of E on P and that there are n nodes of T which are level–lexicographically less than w. Let k be large enough so that

(i) The occurrence w of E is in τ_k.

(ii) p_mSp_i is on P in τ_k if it is on P at all.

(iii) If any assertion about a possible world p_j (for which $p_j S p_m$ occurs on P) and the constant c_i appear on P, then $p_j S p_m$ and some occurrence of an assertion involving both p_j and c_i occurs on P in τ_k.

Note that by Lemma 4.9 there are only finitely many p_j which are relevant to (iii) and so we can find a k large enough to accommodate them all.

It is clear from the definition of the CSMT that we must reduce w on P by the time we form τ_{k+n+1}. Moreover, once reduced in this way, w remains reduced forever by Lemma 4.7. Thus every occurrence of each entry on a noncontradictory path in τ is reduced, as required. $\square$

We can now prove a completeness theorem by showing that the CSMT beginning with $Fp_1 \Vdash \varphi$ is either a proof or supplies us with a frame counterexample.

Theorem 4.11: *Suppose that $\tau = \cup \tau_n$ is a CSMT and P is a noncontradictory path in τ. We define a frame $\mathcal{C} = (W, S, \mathcal{C}(p))$ associated with P as follows:*

W is the set of all p_i appearing in forcing assertions on P. S is the set of all pairs (p_i, p_j) such that $p_i S p_j$ appears on P.

For each $p_i \in S$, $\mathcal{C}(p_i)$ is defined by induction on i as the set consisting of all the constants of $\mathcal{L}$ and all other constants appearing in forcing assertions $Tq \Vdash \psi$ or $Fq \Vdash \psi$ on P such that qSp. (Note that by Lemma 4.10, if $p_j S p_i$ appears on P then $j < i$. Thus $\mathcal{C}(p_i)$ is well defined by induction.)

For each $p \in W$, $\mathcal{C}(p)$ is defined by setting each atomic sentence ψ true in $\mathcal{C}(p)$ if and only if $Tp \Vdash \psi$ occurs on P. (Warning: We are using the convention that every $c \in \mathcal{C}(p)$ is named by itself in $\mathcal{L}(p)$.)

If we let f and g be the identity functions on W and on the set of constants appearing on P, respectively, then they are witnesses that $\mathcal{C}$ agrees with P.

Proof: First note that the clauses of the definition of $\mathcal{C}$ are designed to guarantee that $\mathcal{C}$ is a frame for $\mathcal{L}$ according to Definition 2.1. Just remember that every constant c in $\mathcal{L}(p)$ names itself.

We now wish to prove that (f and g witness that) P agrees with $\mathcal{C}$. We use induction on the depth of sentences φ appearing in forcing assertions on P. The key point in the induction is that, by Proposition 4.9, every occurrence of every entry is reduced on P.

(i) Atomic φ : If $Tp \Vdash \varphi$ appears on P then φ is true in $\mathcal{C}(p)$, and so forced by p. If $Fp \Vdash \varphi$ appears on P then $Tp \Vdash \varphi$ does not appear on P as P is noncontradictory. As this is the only way that p could come to force φ in $\mathcal{C}$, we can conclude that p does not force φ, as required.

The inductive cases are each handled by the corresponding clauses of Definition 4.6 and the definition of forcing (Definition 2.2) together with the induction hypothesis for the theorem. We consider some representative cases and leave the others as exercises.

(ii) The propositional connectives: Suppose φ is built using a connective, e.g., φ is $(\varphi_1 \vee \varphi_2)$. As τ is finished, we know that if $Tp \Vdash \varphi$ occurs on P, then either $Tp \Vdash \varphi_1$ or $Tp \Vdash \varphi_2$ occurs on P. By the induction hypothesis if, say, $Tp \Vdash \varphi_1$ occurs on P then p forces φ_1 and so, by the definition of forcing (Definition 2.2(vii)), p forces φ, as required. Similarly, if $Fp \Vdash \varphi$ occurs on P, then both $Fp \Vdash \varphi_1$ and $Fp \Vdash \varphi_2$ appear on P. Thus, by induction and Definition 2.2(vii), p does not force φ, as required. The other classical propositional connectives are treated similarly. (See Exercise 2.)

(iii) Quantifiers: Suppose φ is of the form $(\forall v)\psi(v)$. If w is the ith occurrence of $Tp \Vdash (\forall v)\psi(v)$ on P, then there is an $i + 1^{\text{st}}$ occurrence of $Tp \Vdash (\forall v)\psi(v)$ on P. Moreover, if $c_i \in C(p)$ then $Tp \Vdash \psi(c_i)$ occurs on P. Thus, if $Tp \Vdash (\forall v)\psi(v)$ appears on P, then $Tp \Vdash \psi(c)$ appears on P for every constant $c \in C(p)$. As the depth of $\psi(c)$ is less than that of $(\forall v)\psi(v)$, p forces $\psi(c)$ for every $c \in C(p)$. Thus p forces $\forall v \psi(v)$ by Definition 2.2(iv).

If $Fp \Vdash (\forall v)\psi(v)$ occurs on P, then again as τ is finished, $Fp \Vdash \psi(c)$ occurs on P for some c. By induction hypothesis, p does not force $\psi(c)$. Thus, by Definition 2.2(iv), p does not force $\forall v \psi(v)$ as required.

The analysis for the existential quantifier is similar and is left as Exercise 3.

(iv) The modal operators: If $Tp \Vdash \Box\varphi$ and pSq appear on P, then $Tq \Vdash \varphi$ appears on P as the tableau is finished. (Note that being finished guarantees that if there is one occurrence of $Tp \Vdash \Box\varphi$, there are infinitely many and so in particular a jth one where $q = p_j$.) Thus q forces φ by induction and p forces $\Box\varphi$ by Definition 2.2(ix).

If $Fp \Vdash \Box\varphi$ appears on P, then both pSq and $Fq \Vdash \varphi$ appear on P for some q. Thus q does not force φ by induction and q is a successor of p by definition. So by Definition 2.2(ix), p does not force $\Box\varphi$.

The cases for $\lozenge$ are similar and are left as Exercise 4. $\Box$

We can now state the standard form of the completeness theorem.

Theorem 4.12 (Completeness, $\vDash \varphi \Rightarrow \vdash \varphi$): *If a sentence φ of modal logic is valid (in the frame semantics) then it has a (modal) tableau proof.*

Proof: Suppose φ is valid. Consider the CSMT τ starting with root $Fp_1 \Vdash \varphi$. By definition, every contradictory path of τ is finite. Thus if every path of τ is contradictory, τ is finite by König's Lemma. In particular, if τ is not a tableau proof of φ, it has a noncontradictory path P. Theorem 4.9 then provides a frame $\mathcal{C}$ in which p_1 does not force φ. Thus φ is not valid and we have the desired contradiction. $\Box$

It is now routine to extend the soundness and completeness theorems to the modal notions of logical consequence and tableaux deductions from premises.

Theorem 4.13 (Soundness, $\Sigma \vdash \varphi \Rightarrow \Sigma \vDash \varphi$): *If there is a modal tableau proof of φ from a set Σ of sentences, then φ is a logical consequence of Σ.*

Proof: The proof of the basic ingredient (Theorem 4.2) of the soundness theorem (Theorem 4.3) shows that if τ is a tableau from Σ and $\mathcal{C}$ is a frame which forces every $\psi \in \Sigma$ which agrees with the root of τ, then $\mathcal{C}$ agrees with some path P of τ. The only new point is that a tableaux can be extended by adding, for any $\psi \in \Sigma$, the assertion $Tp \Vdash \psi$ to the end of any path mentioning p. The proof of Lemma 4.5 is easily modified to incorporate this difference. As $q \Vdash_{\mathcal{C}} \psi$ for every possible world q of $\mathcal{C}$ (by assumption), the inductive hypothesis of the proof of Lemma 4.5 can be immediately verified in this new case as well. The deduction of the theorem from this result is now the same as that of Theorem 4.3 from Theorem 4.2. $\square$

To prove the completeness theorem for deductions from premises, we need the obvious notion of a CSMT from set of premises.

Definition 4.14 (CSMT): We define the *complete systematic modal tableau* (CSMT) *from a set Σ of sentences* starting with a sentence φ by induction as follows. τ_0 is the atomic tableaux with root $Fp_1 \Vdash \varphi$. For the inductive step, we modify Definition 4.8 in much the same same way that the notion of a CST was modified in Definition II.6.9 to accommodate premises. Let $\Sigma = \{\psi_j \mid j \in \mathbf{N}\}$. At even stages of the construction we proceed as in (i)–(iv) of Definition 4.8 as appropriate. At odd stages $n = 2k + 1$, we adjoin $Tp_i \Vdash \psi_j$ for every $i, j < k$ to every noncontradictory path P in τ_n on which p_i occurs. We do not terminate the construction unless, for every $\psi \in \Sigma$, $Tp \Vdash \psi$ appears on every noncontradictory path P on which p is mentioned.

Theorem 4.15 (Completeness, $\Sigma \vDash \varphi \Rightarrow \Sigma \vdash \varphi$): *If φ is a logical consequence of a set Σ of sentences of modal logic, then there is a modal tableau proof of φ from Σ.*

Proof: Suppose φ is a logical consequence of Σ. The argument for Proposition 4.10 still shows that the CSMT from Σ is finished. Its definition also guarantees that, for every $\psi \in \Sigma$, $Tp \Vdash \psi$ appears on any noncontradictory path P on which p is mentioned. The argument for Theorem 4.11 now shows that if the CSMT from Σ with root node $Fp_1 \Vdash \varphi$ is not a tableau proof of φ from Σ, then there is a frame $\mathcal{C}$ in which every $\psi \in \Sigma$ is forced but in which φ is not forced. So we have the desired contradiction. $\square$

It is worth remarking that the particular construction we have given of the CSMT and the accompanying proof of completeness shows that, as far as validity (in modal logic) is concerned, we could restrict our attention to frames in which each possible world has at most finitely many predecessors. Indeed, we could even require the transitive closure of the accessibility relation to have this finite predecessor property. (See Exercises 5–7.) The innocuousness of these restrictions should be compared with the very real changes in the notion of validity that are effected by other restrictions on the accessibility relation. Various such restrictions, including reflexivity and transitivity, are considered in §5.

Exercises

1. Complete the proof of Lemma 4.5 by considering cases (F∀) and (F□).

2. Complete part (ii) of the proof of Lemma 4.11 by dealing with the connectives ¬, ∧ and → .

3. Verify the case of the existential quantifier in part (iii) of the proof of Theorem 4.11.

4. Verify the case of ◊ in part (iv) of the proof of Theorem 4.11.

5. Prove that a modal sentence φ is valid if and only if it is forced in every frame $C = (W, S, C(p))$ for which S has the *finite predecessor property*, i.e., for each $p \in W$, the set $\{q \in W \mid qSp\}$ is finite.

6. If S is a binary relation on a set W, the *transitive–reflexive closure* of S, TRC(S), is the intersection of all reflexive and transitive binary relations T on W which contain S. Prove that TRC$(S) = \cup S_n$ where $S_0 = S$, $S_1 = S \cup \{(p,p) \mid \exists q(pSq \vee qSp)\}$ and $S_{n+1} = S_n \cup \{(p,q) \mid \exists w(pS_n w \wedge wS_n q)\}$.

7. Prove that a modal sentence φ is valid if and only if it is forced in all frames $C = (W, S, C(p))$ in which, for each $p \in W$, the set $\{q \in W \mid q\text{TRC}(S)p\}$ is finite.

8. **Constant Domains**: We can modify our conception of modal logic to incorporate the restriction that the domains of all possible worlds be the same. In the Definition 2.1 of a frame we require that $C(p) = C(q)$ for every $p, q \in W$. Definitions 2.2 and 2.3 of forcing and validity remain unchanged. In Definition 3.2 of tableaux we change the notion of "any appropriate c" in (ii) to mean any c in $\mathcal{L}$ or appearing in any entry on P. With these definitions, prove the soundness and completeness theorems for constant domain modal logic.

5. Modal Axioms and Special Accessibility Relations

For many particular applications of modal logic various special types of accessibility relations seem appropriate. For example, in analyzing the behavior of a computing machine one might want to insist that the accessibility relation reflect some aspects of time as seen by the machine. In such situations it might be appropriate to require that the accessibility relation be reflexive or transitive. If one is interested in perpetual processes, one might want to require that every state have a strict successor. From another point of view, some particular intended interpretation of the modal operators might suggest axioms that one might wish to add to modal logic. Thus, for example, if $\Box$ means "it is necessarily true that" or "I know that", one might want to include an axiom scheme asserting $\Box\varphi \to \varphi$ for every sentence φ. On the other hand, if $\Box$ is intended to mean "I believe that", then we might well reject $\Box\varphi \to \varphi$ as an axiom: I can have false beliefs. In the case of modeling belief, however, we might want to incorporate an "introspection" axiom like $\Box\varphi \to \Box\Box\varphi$ (what I believe, I believe I believe) or $\neg\Box\varphi \to \Box\neg\Box\varphi$ (what I don't believe, I believe I don't believe). But if $\Box$ is intended to mean "it is necessarily true that", then the last of these axioms $(\neg\Box\varphi \to \Box\neg\Box\varphi)$ is not all compelling.

As it turns out, there are close connections between certain natural restrictions on the accessibility relation in frames and various common axioms for modal logics. Indeed, it is often possible to formulate precise equivalents in the sense that the sentences forced in all frames with a specified type of accessibility relation are precisely the logical consequences of some axiom system. In this section we will present several examples of this phenomena. In the next section we will describe traditional Hilbert style axiom and rule systems for these various modal logics in the style of I.7 and II.8.

Before considering specific examples, we introduce some general notation that will simplify our discussion.

Definition 5.1:

(i) Let $\mathcal{F}$ be a class of frames and φ a sentence of a modal language $\mathcal{L}$. We say that φ is $\mathcal{F}$–valid, $\vDash_{\mathcal{F}} \varphi$, if φ is forced in every frame $\mathcal{C} \in \mathcal{F}$.

(ii) Let F be a rule or a family of rules for developing tableaux, i.e., a rule or set of rules of the form "if τ is a tableau, P a path on τ and τ' is gotten from τ by adding some entry E (of a specified type) to the end of P then τ' is a tableau". The F–tableaux are defined by induction as in Definition 3.2 with clause (ii) extended to include the formation rules in F. An F–tableau is an F–tableau proof of a sentence φ if it is finite, has a root node of the form $Fp \Vdash \varphi$, and every path is contradictory. We say that φ is F–provable (or F–tableau provable), $\vdash_F \varphi$, if it has an F–tableau proof.

Example 5.2 (The knowledge axiom and reflexivity): We saw in Example 3.7 that the scheme $\Box\varphi \to \varphi$ is not valid. This scheme is traditionally called the *knowledge axiom* and is denoted by T. If one is modeling knowledge and is of the opinion that one cannot know φ unless φ is true, then this is a plausible axiom. One might well want to restrict one's attention to its logical consequences. We know one way to handle this restriction proof theoretically: We can consider only tableaux deductions from the set of premises consisting of all (closures of) instances of T.

Syntactically, this approach is fairly unwieldy. It to a large extent vitiates the considerable advantages of the tableaux method over a Hilbert style system. The major problem is that if we are trying to get a clever short proof (rather than using the CSMT), we have no good way of knowing which instances of the axiom to insert at any particular point. The basic tableau method, however, generally leads to proofs in fairly direct and easily predictable ways. In addition, this axiomatic approach gives us little direct insight into any semantics corresponding to T. It is far from obvious how the requirement that every instance of T be forced in every frame being considered can give us a characterization of the appropriate class of frames.

The solution to both of these problems is suggested by the attempt (in Example 3.6) to prove a typical instance of T:

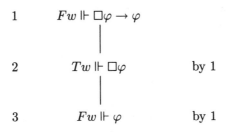

1	$Fw \Vdash \Box\varphi \to \varphi$	
2	$Tw \Vdash \Box\varphi$	by 1
3	$Fw \Vdash \varphi$	by 1

At this point, the attempted proof flounders. It is, however, obvious that if we knew that wSw, we would have a complete proof. This suggests that we incorporate reflexivity into both our semantics and tableau proof rules for T.

Definition 5.3:

(i) $\mathcal{R}$ is the class of all *reflexive frames*, i.e., all frames in which the accessibility relation is reflexive (wSw holds for every $w \in W$).

(ii) R is the *reflexive tableau development rule* which says that, given a tableau τ, we may form a new tableau τ' by adding wSw to the end of any path P in τ on which w occurs.

(iii) $\mathcal{T}$ is the set of universal closures of all instances of the scheme T:
$\Box\varphi \to \varphi$.

We claim that these notions correctly capture the import of T in the following precise sense:

Theorem 5.4: *For any sentence φ of our modal language $\mathcal{L}$, the following conditions are equivalent:*

(i) $\mathcal{T} \vDash \varphi$, φ *is a logical consequence of* $\mathcal{T}$.

(ii) $\mathcal{T} \vdash \varphi$, φ *is a tableau provable from* $\mathcal{T}$.

(iii) $\vDash_\mathcal{R} \varphi$, φ *is forced in every reflexive $\mathcal{L}$-frame.*

(iv) $\vdash_R \varphi$, φ *is provable with the reflexive tableau development rule.*

Note that this theorem not only characterizes the logical consequences of the axiom scheme T, it also includes a soundness (iv $\Rightarrow$ iii) and completeness (iii $\Rightarrow$ iv) theorem for the modal logic with a semantics in which validity means being forced in all reflexive frames and a proof system consisting of the usual construction principles plus R. The equivalence of (i) and (ii) is just the soundness and completeness theorems for deductions from sets of premises (Theorems 4.13 and 4.15). To complete the proof of equivalences we will prove the soundness and completeness results for R (iii $\Leftrightarrow$ iv) and the equivalence of (i) and (iii).

Proof (Soundness, $\vdash_R \varphi \Rightarrow \vDash_R \varphi$): Suppose τ is an R–tableau with root $Fp \Vdash \varphi$ and $\mathcal{C} = (W, S, \mathcal{C}(p))$ is a reflexive frame. If there is a $p \in W$ such that $p \not\Vdash \varphi$, then the proof of Theorem 4.2 shows that $\mathcal{C}$ agrees with some path on τ. The only new point is that when the rule R is used to put some entry wSw on τ, it is true in $\mathcal{C}$ by the reflexivity of S. Thus, if τ is an R–proof of φ ($\vdash_R \varphi$), there cannot be a reflexive frame which fails to force φ, i.e., $\vDash_R \varphi$. $\square$

Proof (Completeness, $\vDash_R \varphi \Rightarrow \vdash_R \varphi$): We begin with the obvious notion of a *complete systematic reflexive modal tableau*, R–CSMT, with root $Fp_1 \Vdash \varphi$. It is defined as was the CSMT from premises Σ in Definition 4.14 except that at odd stages $n = 2k + 1$ we adjoin $p_i Sp_i$ to every noncontradictory path P on which p_i occurs, for every $i < k$. If the R–CSMT beginning with $Fp_1 \Vdash \varphi$ is not an R–proof of φ, then there is a noncontradictory path P through it. Once again, the argument for Proposition 4.10 shows that any R–CSMT is finished. Its definition easily implies that pSp appears on every noncontradictory path P on which p occurs. Thus the proof of Theorem 4.11 defines a reflexive frame $\mathcal{C}$ from P which agrees with P. This shows that φ is not $\mathcal{R}$–valid, as required. $\square$

Proof ($\mathcal{T} \vDash \varphi \Rightarrow \vDash_R \varphi$): It is immediate from Definition 2.2(ix) of forcing $\Box \varphi$ that every instance of $\mathcal{T}$ is forced in every reflexive frame. Thus if φ is forced in every frame in which all instances of $\mathcal{T}$ are forced, φ is forced in every reflexive frame, i.e., $\mathcal{T} \vDash \varphi \Rightarrow \vDash_R \varphi$.

Alternatively, recall that the attempt at a tableau proof of a typical member $\Box \varphi \to \varphi$ of $\mathcal{T}$ presented at the beginning of this example easily becomes, as we noted, an R–proof. (Note that an arbitrary member of $\mathcal{T}$ is of the form $\forall \vec{x}(\Box \varphi \to \varphi)$. In this case the tableau proof just begins by instantiating the universally quantified variables with new constants. It then proceeds as before.) Thus $\vdash_R \theta$ for every $\theta \in \mathcal{T}$. The soundness theorem just proved for $\vdash_R$ then says that $\vDash_R \theta$ for every $\theta \in \mathcal{T}$. In particular, if $\mathcal{T} \vDash \varphi$, φ is forced in every reflexive frame, i.e., $\vDash_R \varphi$ as required. (Since this alternative proof is easier, it will be mimicked in late examples.) $\square$

Proof ($\vDash_R \varphi \Rightarrow \mathcal{T} \vDash \varphi$): Suppose, for the sake of a contradiction, that $\vDash_R \varphi$ but $\mathcal{T} \not\vDash \varphi$. Let τ be the CSMT from $\mathcal{T}$ with root $Fp_1 \Vdash \varphi$. By assumption and Theorem 4.13, τ is not a proof of φ, i.e., there is a noncontradictory path P in τ. Let $\mathcal{C} = (W, S, \mathcal{C}(p))$ be the frame defined from P as in Theorem 4.11. Let $\mathcal{C}' = (W', S', \mathcal{C}'(p))$ be the reflexive closure of $\mathcal{C}$, i.e., $W' = W$ and $\mathcal{C}'(p) = \mathcal{C}(p)$ but $S' = S \cup \{(w, w) \mid p \in W\}$ is the reflexive closure of S. We claim that the reflexive frame $\mathcal{C}'$ agrees with P. Hence $p_1 \not\Vdash_{\mathcal{C}'} \varphi$ and we have the desired contradiction. $\square$

The proof that C' agrees with P is the same as that for C in Theorem 4.11 except that new arguments are needed in the induction step to conclude, from the appearance of $Tp \Vdash \Box\psi$ or $Fp \Vdash \Diamond\psi$ on P, that $p \Vdash_{C'} \psi$ or $p \nVdash_{C'} \psi$, respectively. It clearly suffices to prove the following lemma (the case that $p = q$ is the nontrivial one and the one of immediate interest):

Lemma 5.5:

(i) *If* $Tp \Vdash \Box\psi$ *appears on* P *and* $pS'q$, *then* $Tq \Vdash \psi$ *appears on* P.

(ii) *If* $Fp \Vdash \Diamond\psi$ *appears on* P *and* $pS'q$, *then* $Fq \Vdash \psi$ *appears on* P.

Proof: First note that if $p \neq q$ then pSq appears on P and the fact that τ is finished yields our conclusion. Suppose then that $p = q$.

(i) Suppose $Tp \Vdash \Box\psi$ appears on P and ψ is of the form $\theta(c_1, ... c_n)$ where the c_i displayed are all the constants in ψ not in the original language. The element $\forall x_1 ... \forall x_n(\Box\theta(x_1, ..., x_n) \rightarrow \theta(x_1, ... x_n))$ of T appears on P as τ is a CSMT from T. As τ is finished and $Tp \Vdash \Box\theta(c_1, ... c_n)$ appears on P, so does $Tp \Vdash \Box\theta(c_1, ..., c_n) \rightarrow \theta(c_1, ... c_n)$. Thus, $Tp \Vdash \Box\psi \rightarrow \psi$ appears on P.) As τ is finished, either $Fp \Vdash \Box\psi$ or $Tp \Vdash \psi$ appear on P. The former would make P contradictory. Thus $Tp \Vdash \psi$ appears on P as required.

(ii) If $Fp \Vdash \Diamond\psi$ appears on P, then (as in (i)) $Tp \Vdash \Box\neg\psi \rightarrow \neg\psi$ appears on P. Thus either $Fp \Vdash \Box\neg\psi$ or $Tp \Vdash \neg\psi$ appears on P. In the former case, we eventually reduce $Fp \Vdash \Box\neg\psi$ on P by putting both pSw and $Fw \Vdash \neg\psi$ on P for some w. As τ is finished, the first of these, pSw, combines with $Fp \Vdash \Diamond\psi$ to guarantee that $Fw \Vdash \psi$ appears on P. Similarly, the second, $Fw \Vdash \neg\psi$, guarantees that $Tw \Vdash \psi$ appears on P. Thus in this case, P would be contradictory contrary to our assumption. In the latter case, $Fp \Vdash \psi$ appears on P as required. □

The proof of Theorem 5.4 is now complete. □

Example 5.6 (Introspection and Transitivity): The scheme PI, $\Box\varphi \rightarrow \Box\Box\varphi$, was traditionally called "4". It is now often called the *scheme of positive introspection* as it expresses the view that what I believe, I believe I believe. Once again, an attempt at proving a typical instance provides the clue to the appropriate semantics and proof rule. (See Figure 51.)

There is no contradiction. By reading off the true atomic statements from the tableaux, we get a three world frame $C = (W, S, C(p))$ with $W = \{w, v, u\}$, $S = \{(v, u), (w, v)\}$, $C(v) \vDash \varphi$ and $C(u), C(w) \nvDash \varphi$. Such a frame C is a counterexample to the validity of $\Box\varphi \rightarrow \Box\Box\varphi$ as this sentence is not forced at w in C. We can, however, produce a contradiction by adding wSu to the accessibility relation. The key here is transitivity.

Definition 5.7:

(i) TR is the class of all *transitive frames*, i.e., all frames $C = (W, S, C(p))$ in which S is transitive: $wSv \wedge vSu \Rightarrow wSu$.

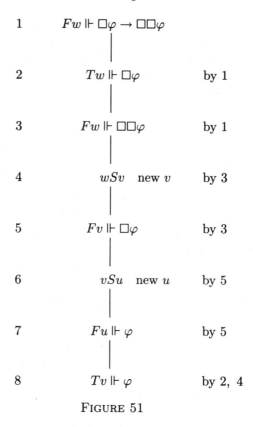

1     $Fw \Vdash \Box\varphi \to \Box\Box\varphi$

2     $Tw \Vdash \Box\varphi$ by 1

3     $Fw \Vdash \Box\Box\varphi$ by 1

4   wSv new v by 3

5     $Fv \Vdash \Box\varphi$ by 3

6   vSu new u by 5

7     $Fu \Vdash \varphi$ by 5

8     $Tv \Vdash \varphi$ by 2, 4

FIGURE 51

(ii) TR is the *transitive tableau development rule* which says that if wSv and vSu appear on a path P of a tableau τ then we can produce another tableau τ' by appending wSu to the end of P.

(iii) $\mathcal{PI}$ is the set of all universal closures of instances of the scheme PI: $\Box\varphi \to \Box\Box\varphi$.

The situation is now much the same as in Example 5.2.

Theorem 5.8: *For any sentence φ of our modal language $\mathcal{L}$, the following conditions are equivalent:*

(i) $\mathcal{PI} \vDash \varphi$, φ *is a logical consequence of $\mathcal{PI}$.*

(ii) $\mathcal{PI} \vdash \varphi$, φ *is a tableau provable from $\mathcal{PI}$.*

(iii) $\vDash_{T\mathcal{R}} \varphi$, φ *is forced in every transitive $\mathcal{L}$–frame.*

(iv) $\vdash_{TR} \varphi$, φ *is provable with the transitive tableau development rule.*

The proof of this theorem is essentially the same as for the corresponding results for reflexive frames (Theorem 5.4). We of course replace reflexive, R, $\mathcal{R}$ and $\mathcal{T}$ by transitive, TR, $T\mathcal{R}$ and $\mathcal{PI}$, respectively and make the other obvious changes. For example, the TR–CSMT at stage $n = 2k + 1$ adjoins to the end of every noncontradictory path P the entry p_iSp_j if there is some q such that p_iSq and qSp_j appear on P. The only part of the proof that is not essentially the same as that of Theorem 5.4 is the proof that $\vDash_{TR} \varphi \Rightarrow \mathcal{PI} \vDash \varphi$ and, in particular, the proof of the analog of Lemma 5.5.

Proof ($\vDash_{TR} \varphi \Rightarrow \mathcal{PI} \vDash \varphi$): Suppose, for the sake of a contradiction, that $\vDash_{TR} \varphi$ but $\mathcal{PI} \nvDash \varphi$. Let τ be the CSMT from $\mathcal{PI}$ with root $Fp_1 \Vdash \varphi$. By assumption and Theorem 4.13, τ is not a proof of φ. So there is a noncontradictory path P in τ. Let $\mathcal{C} = (W, S, \mathcal{C}(p))$ be the frame defined from P as in Theorem 4.11. Let $\mathcal{C}'(W', S', \mathcal{C}'(p))$ be the transitive closure of $\mathcal{C}$, i.e., $W' = W$ and $\mathcal{C}'(p) = \mathcal{C}(p)$ but S' is the *transitive closure* of S, i.e., $S' \equiv \cup S_n$ where $S_0 = S$ and $S_{n+1} = S_n \cup \{(p,q) \mid \exists w(pS_n \ w \wedge wS_nq)\}$. (Note that it S' is transitive by construction.) We claim that the transitive frame $\mathcal{C}'$ agrees with P. Hence $p_1 \nVdash_{\mathcal{C}'} \varphi$ and we have the desired contradiction. $\square$

The proof that $\mathcal{C}'$ agrees with P is again the same as that for $\mathcal{C}$ in Theorem 4.11 except that new arguments are needed in the induction step to conclude, from the appearance of $Tp \Vdash \Box\psi$ or $Fp \Vdash \Diamond\psi$ on P, that $q \Vdash_{\mathcal{C}'} \psi$ or $q \nVdash_{\mathcal{C}'} \psi$, respectively, for every q such that $pS'q$. Once again, it clearly suffices to prove the following lemma:

Lemma 5.9:

(i) If $Tp \Vdash \Box\psi$ appears on P and $pS'q$, then $Tq \Vdash \psi$ appears on P.

(ii) If $Fp \Vdash \Diamond\psi$ appears on P and $pS'q$, then $Fq \Vdash \psi$ appears on P.

Proof: We proceed by induction on the stage n at which (p,q) enters S'. For $n = 0$, the conclusion in both cases follows from the fact that τ is finished. Suppose that the lemma holds for $(u,v) \in S_n$ and that $(p,q) \in S_{n+1}$. Let w be such that $(p,w), (w,q) \in S_n$.

(i) If $Tp \Vdash \Box\psi$ appears on P, then (as argued in the proof of Lemma 5.5) so does $Tp \Vdash \Box\psi \to \Box\Box\psi$. As τ is finished, either $Fp \Vdash \Box\psi$ or $Tp \Vdash \Box\Box\psi$ appears on P. As P is not contradictory, it must be $Tp \Vdash \Box\Box\psi$ that appears on P. As $(p,w) \in S_n$, $Tw \Vdash \Box\psi$ appears on P by induction. As $(w,q) \in S_n$ as well, $Tq \Vdash \psi$ also appears on P, as required.

(ii) The dual case is similar and we leave it as Exercise 1. $\square$

Example 5.10 (Negative introspection and Euclidean frames): The next scheme we consider is NI, the *negative introspection scheme* (what I don't believe, I believe I don't believe): $\neg\Box\varphi \to \Box\neg\Box\varphi$. This scheme has traditionally been denoted by "E" (for Euclidean) or "5". Figure 52 gives an attempt at proving an instance of NI.

The key to completing a proof here is to be able to adjoin uSv when we have both wSv and wSu. We could then conclude $Tv \Vdash \varphi$ from line 9 contracting line 6. The story should by now be quite familiar.

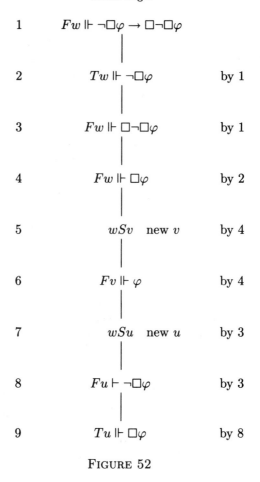

FIGURE 52

Definition 5.11:

(i) $\mathcal{E}$ is the class of all *Euclidean frames*, i.e., all frames $\mathcal{C} = (W, S, \mathcal{C}(p))$ in which S is *Euclidean*: $wSv \wedge wSu \Rightarrow uSv$.

(ii) E is the *Euclidean tableau development rule* which says that if wSv and wSu appear on a path P of a tableau τ then we can produce another tableau τ' by appending uSv to the end of P.

(iii) $\mathcal{NI}$ is the set of all universal closures of instances of the scheme NI: $\neg\Box\varphi \to \Box\neg\Box\varphi$.

Theorem 5.12: *For any sentence φ of our modal language $\mathcal{L}$, the following conditions are equivalent:*

(i) $\mathcal{NI} \vDash \varphi$, φ is a logical consequence of $\mathcal{NI}$.

(ii) $\mathcal{NI} \vdash \varphi$, φ is a tableau provable from $\mathcal{NI}$.

(iii) $\vDash_\mathcal{E} \varphi$, φ is forced in every Euclidean $\mathcal{L}$-frame.

(iv) $\vdash_E \varphi$, φ is provable with the Euclidean tableau development rule.

The proof of this theorem is essentially the same as for the corresponding results for reflexive or transitive frames (Theorems 5.4 and 5.9). The frame C' needed in the proof of $\vDash_{\mathcal{E}} \varphi \Rightarrow \mathcal{N}\mathcal{I} \vDash \varphi$ is the *Euclidean closure* of C. It is defined by setting $S' = \cup S_n$, where $S_0 = S$ and $S_{n+1} = \{(p, q) \mid \exists w((w, p), (w, q) \in S_n)\}$. The crucial point is again the analog of Lemma 5.5:

Lemma 5.13:

(i) *If $Tp \Vdash \Box\psi$ appears on P and $pS'q$, then $Tq \Vdash \psi$ appears on P.*

(ii) *If $Fp \Vdash \Diamond\psi$ appears on P and $pS'q$, then $Fq \Vdash \psi$ appears on P.*

Proof: We proceed by induction on the stage n at which (p, q) enters S'. For $n = 0$, the conclusion in both cases follows from the fact that τ is finished. Suppose that the lemma holds for $(u, v) \in S_n$ and that $(p, q) \in S_{n+1}$. Let w be such that $(w, p), (w, q) \in S_n$.

(i) If $Tp \Vdash \Box\psi$ appears on P, then (as before) $Tw \Vdash \neg\Box\psi \to \Box\neg\Box\psi$ appears on P. As τ is finished either $Fw \Vdash \neg\Box\psi$ or $Tw \Vdash \Box\neg\Box\psi$ appears on P. In the former case, $Tw \Vdash \Box\psi$ appears on P and, as required, so does $Tq \Vdash \psi$, by induction. In the latter case, $Tp \Vdash \neg\Box\psi$ would appear on P. As this would guarantee that $Fp \Vdash \Box\psi$ appears on P, it would make P contradictory contrary to our assumption. Thus $Fw \Vdash \neg\Box\psi$ and so $Tq \Vdash \psi$ appear on P as required.

(ii) The dual case is similar and is left as Exercise 2. □

Example 5.14 (Serial axioms and frames): Our next example is the scheme traditionally called "D": $\Box\varphi \to \neg\Box\neg\varphi$. It says that if I believe φ then I don't believe $\neg\varphi$. It is now often referred to as the *serial scheme*. Once again we begin with an attempt to prove an instance of D:

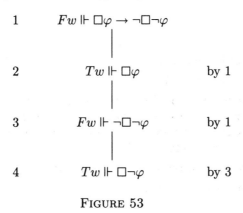

1      $Fw \Vdash \Box\varphi \to \neg\Box\neg\varphi$

2      $Tw \Vdash \Box\varphi$ by 1

3      $Fw \Vdash \neg\Box\neg\varphi$ by 1

4      $Tw \Vdash \Box\neg\varphi$ by 3

FIGURE 53

A frame with an empty accessibility relation will provide a counterexample. The existence of a v such that wSv would allow us to deduce the desired contradiction. (We could conclude $Tv \Vdash \varphi$ from $(T\Box)$ and $Fv \Vdash \varphi$ from $(T\Box$ and $F\neg)$.)

Definition 5.15:

(i) $\mathcal{SE}$ is the class of all *serial frames*, i.e., all frames $\mathcal{C} = (W, S, \mathcal{C}(p))$ in which there is, for every $p \in W$, a q such that pSq.

(ii) SE is the *serial tableau development rule* which says that if p appears on a path P of a tableau τ then we can produce another tableau τ' by appending pSq to the end of P for a new q.

(iii) $\mathcal{D}$ is the set of all universal closures of instances of the scheme D: $\Box\varphi \rightarrow \neg\Box\neg\varphi$.

Theorem 5.16: *For any sentence φ of our modal language $\mathcal{L}$, the following conditions are equivalent:*

(i) $\mathcal{D} \vDash \varphi$, φ is a logical consequence of $\mathcal{D}$.

(ii) $\mathcal{D} \vdash \varphi$, φ is a tableau provable from $\mathcal{D}$.

(iii) $\vDash_{\mathcal{SE}} \varphi$, φ is forced in every serial $\mathcal{L}$-frame.

(iv) $\vdash_{\mathrm{SE}} \varphi$, φ is provable with the serial tableau development rule.

The proof is as before. In this case the crucial point in the verification that $\vDash_{\mathcal{SE}} \varphi \Rightarrow \mathcal{D} \vDash \varphi$ is that the frame $\mathcal{C}$ defined from a path P on the CSMT τ from $\mathcal{D}$ is automatically serial. If p appears on P, then so does $Tp \Vdash \Box\psi \rightarrow \neg\Box\neg\psi$ for some ψ. As τ is finished, either $Fp \Vdash \Box\psi$ or $Tp \Vdash \neg\Box\neg\psi$ appears on P. In either case one or two more appeals to the fact that τ is finished produces an entry pSq on P for some new q as required. $\square$

Additional examples of tableau rules and their corresponding classes of frames can be found in Exercises 3–4 and 6.1–4.

Exercises

1. Prove (ii) of Lemma 5.9.

2. Prove (ii) of Lemma 5.13.

3. **Tree frames**: A frame $\mathcal{C}$ is a *tree frame* if its accessibility relation S defines a tree (in the sense of Definition I.1.1) on W by setting $p < q$ iff pSq. Extend Theorem 5.8 by proving that the following additional equivalence can be added to the list:

    (v) φ is forced in every tree frame.

    (Hint: Look at Exercises 4.5–7.)

$$wSv \qquad\qquad vSw$$

FIGURE 54

4. **Linear frames**: A frame C is a *linear frame* if its accessibility relation S defines a linear ordering on W by setting $p < q$ iff pSq. The linear tableau rule L says that if the possible worlds w and v appear on a path P of a tableau τ then we can produce another tableau τ' by appending the new tableau (Figure 54) to the end of P. Prove that a sentence φ of a modal language $\mathcal{L}$ is valid in all linear frames if and only if it is provable using the linear tableau rule.

6*. An Axiomatic Approach

We conclude this chapter with a description of a basic Hilbert–style system for modal logic and a brief catalog of some of the standard modal systems with their traditional nomenclature. In line with the view taken in II.8 where we used a language containing only the connectives $\neg$ and $\rightarrow$ and the quantifier $\forall$, we here use only the modal operator $\square$ and view $\Diamond$ as a defined symbol by replacing $\Diamond\varphi$ with $\neg\square\neg\varphi$.

The proof system for classical logic presented in II.8 can be extended to one called K for modal logic by adding on one new axiom scheme and one new rule:

6.1 Axiom scheme (vi): $\square(\alpha \rightarrow \beta) \rightarrow (\square\alpha \rightarrow \square\beta)$.

6.2 Rule (iii) *Necessitation*: From α infer $\square\alpha$.

Of course, we now include all instances in our modal language $\mathcal{L}$ of the original axiom schemes (i)–(v) as well as (vi). Similarly, the rules apply to all formulas of $\mathcal{L}$.

The definitions of proofs and proofs from a set Σ of sentences are now the same as in classical logic. It is easy to see that all instances of the axioms of K are valid. (Example 3.5 gives a tableau proof for a typical instance of (vi). The classical tableau proofs for the other axioms remain correct for instances in $\mathcal{L}$ as well. Note that by the validity of an open formula we mean the validity of its universal closure.) As the rules of K also preserve validity, all theorems of this system are valid. (Note that $\alpha \vDash \square\alpha$ is immediate even for open α once one remembers that the validity of α means that its universal closure is forced in every frame. Alternatively, one can construct a tableau proof showing that $\forall\vec{x}\alpha(\vec{x}) \Vdash \forall\vec{x}\square\alpha(\vec{x})$ as in Exercise 3.11.) A standard style completeness theorem for K then shows that it defines the same set of theorems as does our tableau system.

The schemes we have analyzed in §5 are often added to K to produce axiom systems for specialized study. Completeness theorems for each of the Hilbert–style systems listed below can be found in Chapter 9 of Hughes and Cresswell [1984, 4.4]. Thus each has the same theorems as the analogous system of §5.

T is the system consisting of K and the axiom scheme T of Example 5.2: $\square\varphi \rightarrow \varphi$. It is often regarded as the logic of knowledge. As we have seen, its theorems are precisely those sentences forced in all reflexive frames.

S4 is the system consisting of T and the scheme PI of Example 5.6: $\Box\varphi \to \Box\Box\varphi$. It is routine to combine the results of Theorems 5.4 and 5.8 to see that the theorems of S4 are precisely the sentences forced in every reflexive and transitive frame (Exercise 1.) If T is omitted we have the system K4 consisting of K and the scheme PI.

S5 is the system consisting of S4 and the scheme E of Example 5.10: $\neg\Box\varphi \to \Box\neg\Box\varphi$. Its theorems are precisely those sentences forced in every reflexive, transitive, Euclidean frame. As the reflexive, transitive Euclidean relations are precisely the equivalence relations (Exercise 2), the theorems of S5 are those sentences forced in every frame whose accessibility relation is an equivalence relation (Exercise 3). Omitting T gives us the system K5 consisting of K4 and the scheme E.

In fact, we can say somewhat more about S5. Its theorems are the sentences forced in all *complete frames*.

Definition 6.3:

(i) $\mathcal{M}$ is the class of all *complete frames*, i.e., all frames $C = (W, S, C(p))$ in which pSq for every $p, q \in W$.

(ii) M is the *complete tableau development rule* which says that if p and q appear on a path P of a tableau τ then we can produce another tableau τ' by appending pSq.

(iii) $\mathcal{S}5$ is the set of all universal closures of instances of the schemes T, PI and NI.

Theorem 6.4: *For any sentence φ of our modal language $\mathcal{L}$, the following conditions are equivalent:*

(i) $\mathcal{S}5 \vDash \varphi$, φ *is a logical consequence of* $\mathcal{S}5$.

(ii) $\mathcal{S}5 \vdash \varphi$, φ *is a tableau provable from* $\mathcal{S}5$.

(iii) $\vDash_\mathcal{M} \varphi$, φ *is forced in every complete $\mathcal{L}$–frame.*

(iv) $\vdash_M \varphi$, φ *is provable with the complete tableau development rule.*

Of course, this theorem can be proven as were the previous ones (Exercise 4). It can also be deduced (Exercise 6) from the one for frames with equivalence relations (Exercise 3) by the reduction supplied in Exercise 5.

Similar systems have been used (Moore [1984, 5.5] and [1985, 5.5]) as a basis for autoepistemic logic. If extended to have multiple modal operators $\Box_A$, one for each processor A, they are suitable for reasoning about distributed networks of agents (Halpern and Moses [1984, 5.5]).

Exercises

1. Prove that the theorems of S4, i.e., the (logical) consequences of the union of $\mathcal{T}$ and $\mathcal{TR}$, are the ones provable in a system using both the reflexive and transitive tableau rules. These are also the sentences forced in every frame which is both reflexive and transitive.

2. A binary relation S is an *equivalence relation* if it is reflexive (wSw), symmetric ($wSv \Rightarrow vSw$) and transitive ($uSv \wedge vSw \Rightarrow uSw$). Prove that a reflexive, transitive binary relation S is an equivalence relation if and only if it is Euclidean.

3. Prove that the theorems of S5, i.e., the (logical) consequences of the union of $\mathcal{T}$, $\mathcal{TR}$ and $\mathcal{NI}$ are the ones provable in a system using the reflexive, transitive and Euclidean tableau rules. These are also the sentences forced in every frame in which the accessibility relation is an equivalence relation.

4. Give a direct proof of Theorem 6.4.

5. Let $\mathcal{C} = (W, S, \mathcal{C}(p))$ be a frame in which S is an equivalence relation. For $w \in W$, let $[w] = \{p \in W \mid pSw\}$ be the equivalence class of w. If $\mathcal{C}_w$ is the restriction of $\mathcal{C}$ to $[w]$, i.e., the frame $([w], S \upharpoonright [w] \times [w], \mathcal{C}(p))$, then $w \Vdash_\mathcal{C} \varphi \Leftrightarrow w \Vdash_{\mathcal{C}_w} \varphi$ for every sentence φ.

6. Use Exercises 3 and 5 to give an alternate proof of Theorem 6.4.

Suggestions for Further Reading

Two good beginning texts on modal logic are Hughes and Cresswell [1984, 4.4] and Chellas [1980, 4.4]. The latter seems to be the common reference in the computer science literature for the basic material. A more advanced text is van Bentham [1983, 4.4] and van Bentham [1988, 4.4] is also useful. The encyclopedic treatment of tableau models in modal logic is Fitting [1983, 4.4]. In particular, this last book contains a proof of the decidability of propositional modal logic in §7 of Chapter 8. Many variations in the definition of both syntax and semantics can also be found there.

Linsky [1971, 4.4] is a good collection of important early articles on modal logic which includes Kripke's pioneering work and various pieces with a philosophical point of view. Some additional background information about applications of modal logic as well as a more comprehensive bibliography can be found in Nerode [1991, 4.1].

Galton [1987, 5.6], Goldblatt [1982, 5.6] and [1987, 5.6] and Turner [1984, 5.6] all stress the uses of various types of modal logics in computer science. Halpern and Moses [1985, 5.6] is a survey of logics of knowledge and belief. Thayse [1989, 5.6] is a thorough presentation of many types of modal logics directed towards deductive databases and AI. Thayse [1991, 5.6] supplies a wide ranging view of applications of these ideas in many areas of AI.

V Intuitionistic Logic

1. Intuitionism and Constructivism

During the past century, a major debate in the philosophy of mathematics has centered on the question of how to regard noneffective or nonconstructive proofs in mathematics. Is it legitimate to claim to have proven the existence of a number with some property without actually being able, even in principle, to produce one? Is it legitimate to claim to have proven the existence of a function without providing any way to calculate it? L. E. J. Brouwer is perhaps the best known early proponent of an extreme constructivist point of view. He rejected much of early twentieth century mathematics on the grounds that it did not provide acceptable existence proofs. He held that a proof of $p \vee q$ must consist of either a proof of p or one of q and that a proof of $\exists x P(x)$ must contain a construction of a witness c and a proof that $P(c)$ is true. At the heart of most nonconstructive proofs lies the law of the excluded middle: For every sentence A, $A \vee \neg A$ is true. Based on this law of classical logic one can prove that $\exists x P(x)$ by showing that its negation leads to a contradiction without providing any hint as to how to find an x satisfying P. Similarly, one can prove $p \vee q$ by proving $\neg(\neg p \wedge \neg q)$ without knowing which of p and q is true.

Example 1.1: We wish to prove that there are two irrational numbers a and b such that a^b is rational. Let $c = \sqrt{2}^{\sqrt{2}}$. If c is rational, then we may take $a = \sqrt{2} = b$. On the other hand, if c is not rational, then $c^{\sqrt{2}} = 2$ is rational and we may take $a = c$ and $b = \sqrt{2}$. Thus, in either case, we have two irrational numbers a and b such that a^b is rational. This proof depends on the the law of the excluded middle in that we assume that either c is rational or it is not. It gives us no clue as to which of the two pairs contain the desired numbers.

Example 1.2: Consider the proof of König's lemma (Theorem I.1.4). We defined the infinite path by induction. At each step we knew by induction that one of the finitely many immediate successors has infinitely many nodes below it. We then "picked" one such successor as the next node in our path. We had proved by induction that a disjunction is true and then simply continued the argument "by cases". As we had not in any way established which successor had infinitely many nodes below it, we have no actual construction of (no algorithm for defining) the infinite path that we proved to exist. Similar considerations apply to our proofs of completeness, compactness and other theorems.

A formal logic that attempts to capture Brouwer's philosophical position was developed by his student Heyting. This logic is called intuitionistic logic. It is an important attempt at capturing constructive reasoning. In particular, the law of the excluded middle is not valid in intuitionistic logic.

A number of paradigms have been suggested for explaining Brouwer's views. Each one can provide models or semantics for intuitionistic logic. One paradigm considers mathematical statements as assertions about our (or someone's) knowledge or possession of proofs. A sentence is true only when we know it to be so or only after we have proven it. At any moment we cannot know what new facts will be discovered or proven later. This interpretation fits well with a number of situations in computer science involving both databases and program verification. In terms of databases, one caveat is necessary. We view our knowledge as always increasing so new facts may be added but no old ones removed or contradicted. This is a plausible view of the advance of mathematical knowledge but in many other situations it is not accurate. Much of the time this model can still be used by simply attaching time stamps to facts. Thus the database records what we knew and when we knew it. The intuitionistic model is then a good one for dealing with deductions from such a database.

In terms of program verification, intuitionistic logic has played a basic role in the development of constructive proof checkers and reasoning systems. A key idea here is that, in accordance with Brouwer's ideas, the proof of an existential statement entails the construction of a witness. Similarly, the proof that for every x there is a y such that $P(x, y)$ entails the construction of an algorithm for computing a value of y from one for x. The appeal of such a logical system is obvious. On a practical level, there are now implementations of large–scale systems which (interactively) provide intuitionistic proofs of such assertions. The systems can then actually extract the algorithm computing the intended function. One then has a verified algorithm since the proof of existence is in fact a proof that the algorithm specified actually runs correctly. One such system is NUPRL developed at Cornell University by R. Constable [1986, 5.6] and others.

In this chapter, we present the basics of intuitionistic logic including a semantics developed by Kripke that reflects the "state of knowledge" interpretation of Heyting's formalism. In addition to the intuitive considerations, the claim that this choice of semantics adequately reflects constructivist reasoning is confirmed by the fact that the following *disjunction* and *existence properties* hold:

Theorem 2.20:   *If $(\varphi \vee \psi)$ is intuitionistically valid, then either φ or ψ is intuitionistically valid.*

Theorem 2.21:   *If $\exists x \varphi(x)$ is intuitionistically valid, then so is $\varphi(c)$ for some constant c.*

We then develop an intuitionistic proof theory based on a tableau method like that for classical logic and prove the appropriate soundness and completeness theorems. Of course, the completeness theorem converts the above theorems into ones about provability. We can (intuitionistically) prove $\varphi \vee \psi$ only if we can prove one of them. We can prove $\exists x \varphi(x)$ only if we can prove $\varphi(c)$ for some explicit constant c.

The presentation in this chapter is designed to be independent of Chapter IV. Thus there is some overlap of material. For those readers who have read Chapter IV, we supply a guide comparing classical, modal and intuitionistic logics in §6.

2. Frames and Forcing

Our notion of a language is the same as that for classical predicate logic in Chapter II except that we make one modification and two restrictions that simplify the technical details in the development of forcing. The modification is that we formally omit the logical connective $\leftrightarrow$ from our language. We instead view $\varphi \leftrightarrow \psi$ as an abbreviation for $(\varphi \to \psi) \wedge (\psi \to \varphi)$. Our restrictions are on the nonlogical components of our language. We assume throughout this chapter that every language $\mathcal{L}$ has at least one constant symbol but no function symbols other than constants.

We now present a semantics for intuitionistic logic which formalizes the "state of knowledge" interpretation.

Definition 2.1: Let $\mathcal{C} = (R, \leq, \{\mathcal{C}(p)\}_{p \in R})$ consist of a partially ordered set $(R, \leq)$ together with an assignment, to each p in R, of a structure $\mathcal{C}(p)$ for $\mathcal{L}$ (in the sense of Definition II.4.1). To simplify the notation, we will write $\mathcal{C} = (R, \leq, \mathcal{C}(p))$ instead of the more formally precise version, $\mathcal{C} = (R, \leq, \{\mathcal{C}(p)\}_{p \in R})$. As usual, we let $C(p)$ denote the domain of the structure $\mathcal{C}(p)$. We also let $\mathcal{L}(p)$ denote the extension of $\mathcal{L}$ gotten by adding on a name c_a for each element a of $C(p)$ in the style of the definition of truth in II.4. $A(p)$ denotes the set of atomic formulas of $\mathcal{L}(p)$ true in $\mathcal{C}(p)$. We say that $\mathcal{C}$ is a *frame for the language $\mathcal{L}$*, or simply an *$\mathcal{L}$-frame* if, for every p and q in R, $p \leq q$ implies that $C(p) \subseteq C(q)$, the interpretations of the constants in $\mathcal{L}(p) \subseteq \mathcal{L}(q)$ are the same in $\mathcal{C}(p)$ as in $\mathcal{C}(q)$ and $A(p) \subseteq A(q)$.

Often $p \leq q$ is read "q *extends* p", or "q *is a future of* p". The elements of R are called *forcing conditions, possible worlds*, or *states of knowledge*.

We now define the forcing relation for frames.

Definition 2.2 (Forcing for frames): Let $\mathcal{C} = (R, \leq, \mathcal{C}(p))$ be a frame for a language $\mathcal{L}$, p be in R and φ be a sentence of the language $\mathcal{L}(p)$. We give a definition of p *forces* φ, written $p \Vdash \varphi$ by induction on sentences φ.

(i) For atomic sentences φ, $p \Vdash \varphi \Leftrightarrow \varphi$ is in $A(p)$.

(ii) $p \Vdash (\varphi \rightarrow \psi) \Leftrightarrow$ for all $q \geq p$, $q \Vdash \varphi$ implies $q \Vdash \psi$.

(iii) $p \Vdash \neg\varphi \Leftrightarrow$ for all $q \geq p$, q does not force φ .

(iv) $p \Vdash (\forall x)\varphi(x) \Leftrightarrow$ for every $q \geq p$ and for every constant c in $\mathcal{L}(q)$, $q \Vdash \varphi(c)$.

(v) $p \Vdash (\exists x)\varphi(x) \Leftrightarrow$ there is a constant c in $\mathcal{L}(p)$ such that $p \Vdash \varphi(c)$.

(vi) $p \Vdash (\varphi \wedge \psi) \Leftrightarrow p \Vdash \varphi$ and $p \Vdash \psi$.

(vii) $p \Vdash (\varphi \vee \psi) \Leftrightarrow p \Vdash \varphi$ or $p \Vdash \psi$.

If we need to make the frame explicit, we will say that p *forces* φ *in* $\mathcal{C}$ and write $p \Vdash_{\mathcal{C}} \varphi$.

Definition 2.3: Let φ be a sentence of the language $\mathcal{L}$. We say that φ *is forced in the* $\mathcal{L}$*-frame* $\mathcal{C}$ if every p in R forces φ. We say φ *is intuitionistically valid* if it is forced in every $\mathcal{L}$-frame.

Clauses (ii), (iii) and (iv) defining $p \Vdash \varphi \rightarrow \psi$, $p \Vdash \neg\varphi$ and $p \Vdash (\forall x)\varphi(x)$ respectively each have a quantifier ranging over elements of the partial ordering, namely "for all q, if $q \geq p$, then ...". Clause (ii) says that p forces an implication $\varphi \rightarrow \psi$ only if any greater state of knowledge q which forces the antecedent φ also forces the consequent ψ. This is a sort of permanence of implication in the face of more knowledge. Clause (iii) says p forces the negation of φ when no greater state of knowledge forces φ. This says that $\neg\varphi$ is forced if φ cannot be forced by supplying more knowledge than p supplies. Clause (iv) says p forces a universally quantified sentence only if in all greater states of knowledge all instances of the sentence are forced. This is a permanence of forcing universal sentences in the face of any new knowledge beyond that supplied by p. Another aspect of the permanence of forcing that says the past does not count in forcing, only the future, is given by the following lemma. (Note that the logic of our metalanguage remains classical throughout this chapter. Thus, for example, in clause (ii) "implies" has the same meaning it had in Chapter I.)

Lemma 2.4 (Restriction Lemma): *Let* $\mathcal{C} = (R, \leq, \mathcal{C}(p))$ *be a frame, let* q *be in* R *and let* $R_q = \{r \in R \mid r \geq q\}$. *Then*

$$\mathcal{C}_q = (R_p, \leq, \mathcal{C}(p))$$

is a frame, where $\leq$ *and the function* $\mathcal{C}(p)$ *are restricted to* R_q. *Moreover, for* r *in* R_q, r *forces* φ *in* $\mathcal{C}$ *iff* r *forces* φ *in* $\mathcal{C}_q$.

Proof: By an induction on the length of formulas which we leave as Exercise 7. $\square$

Consider the classical structures $\mathcal{C}(p)$ in an $\mathcal{L}$-frame $\mathcal{C}$. As we go from p to a $q > p$, we go from the classical structure $\mathcal{C}(p)$ associated with p to a (possibly) larger one $\mathcal{C}(q)$ associated with q with more atomic sentences classically true, and therefore fewer atomic sentences classically false.

Clauses (i), (v), (vi) and (vii) for the cases of atomic sentences, "and", "or" and "there exists" respectively are exactly as in the definition of truth in $C(p)$ given in II.4.3. The other clauses have a new flavor and indeed the classical truth of φ in $C(p)$ and $p's$ forcing φ do not in general coincide. They do, however, in an important special case.

Lemma 2.5 (Degeneracy Lemma): *Let C be a frame for a language $\mathcal{L}$ and φ a sentence of $\mathcal{L}$. If p is a maximal element of the partial ordering R associated with C, then φ is classically true in $C(p)$, i.e., $C(p) \vDash \varphi$, if and only if $p \Vdash \varphi$. In particular, if there is only one state of knowledge p in R, then $C(p) \Vdash \varphi$ if and only if $p \Vdash \varphi$.*

Proof: The proof procedes by an induction on formulas. For a maximal element p of R the clauses in the definition of $p \Vdash \varphi$ coincide with those in II.4.3 for $C(p) \vDash \varphi$. In clauses (ii), (iii) and (iv) the dependence on future states of knowledge reduces simply to the classical situation at p. Consider, for example, clause (ii): $p \Vdash \varphi \to \psi \Leftrightarrow (\forall q \geq p)(q \Vdash \varphi$ implies $q \Vdash \psi)$. Since p is maximal in R, $q \geq p$ is the same as $q = p$. Thus clause (ii) reduces to $(p \Vdash \varphi \to \psi$ iff $p \Vdash \varphi$ implies $p \Vdash \psi)$ which is the analog as the corresponding clause, II.4.3(v), for classical implication. We leave the verification that all the other clauses are also equivalent as Exercise 8. □

Theorem 2.6: *Any intuitionistically valid sentence is classically valid.*

Proof: By the degeneracy lemma (Lemma 2.5), every classical model is a frame model with a one–element partially ordered set in which forcing and classical truth are equivalent. As a sentence is classically valid if true in all classical models, it is valid if forced in every frame. □

It remains to see which classically valid sentences are intuitionistically valid and which are not. We show how to verify that some classically valid sentences are not intuitionistically valid by constructing frame counterexamples. Before presenting the examples, we want to establish some notational conventions for displaying frames. All the examples below will have orderings which are suborderings of the full binary tree. We can therefore view the associated frames as labeled binary trees with the label of a node p being the structure $C(p)$, or equivalently, the pair consisting of $C(p)$ and $A(p)$. We will thus draw frames as labeled binary trees in our usual style and display the labels in the form $\langle C(p), A(p) \rangle$. The theoretical development of tableaux and the proof of their completeness will require somewhat more general trees but we leave that for the next section.

In the examples below of sentences which are not intuitionistically valid (2.7–2.11), φ and ψ will denote atomic formulas of $\mathcal{L}$ with no free variables or only x free as displayed. In each of these examples, $C(\emptyset)$, the structure associated with the bottom node $\emptyset$ of our partial ordering, will be C with all the constants of $\mathcal{L}$ interpreted as c. We begin with the archetypal classically valid sentence which is not intuitionistically valid.

Example 2.7: As expected, the sentence $\varphi \vee \neg\varphi$ is not intuitionistically valid. Let the frame $\mathcal{C}$ be

(Thus we have taken C as the domain at both nodes, $\emptyset$ and 0, of the frame.) At the bottom node, no atomic facts are true, i.e., $A(\emptyset)$ is empty. At the upper node 0, we have made the single atomic fact φ true by setting $A(0) = \{\varphi\}$).

Consider now whether or not $\emptyset \Vdash \varphi \vee \neg\varphi$. Certainly $\emptyset$ does not force φ since φ is atomic and not true in $\mathcal{C}(\emptyset)$, i.e., not in $A(\emptyset)$. On the other hand, $0 \Vdash \varphi$ since $\varphi \in A(0)$. Thus $\emptyset$ does not force $\neg\varphi$ since it has an extension 0 forcing φ. So by definition, $\emptyset$ does not force $\varphi \vee \neg\varphi$ and this sentence is not intuitionistically valid.

Example 2.8: The sentence $(\neg\varphi \rightarrow \neg\psi) \rightarrow (\psi \rightarrow \varphi)$ is not intuitionistically valid. Let the frame $\mathcal{C}$ be

$$\langle C, \{\varphi, \psi\} \rangle$$
$$|$$
$$\langle C, \{\psi\} \rangle$$

Suppose, for the sake of a contradiction, that $\emptyset \Vdash (\neg\varphi \rightarrow \neg\psi) \rightarrow (\psi \rightarrow \varphi)$. Then $\emptyset \Vdash (\neg\varphi \rightarrow \neg\psi)$ would imply $\emptyset \Vdash (\psi \rightarrow \varphi)$ by clause (ii) of the definition of forcing (Definition 2.2). Now by clause (iii) of the definition, neither $\emptyset$ nor 0 forces $\neg\varphi$ since φ is in $A(0)$ and so forced at 0. Thus we see that $\emptyset$ does in fact force $(\neg\varphi \rightarrow \neg\psi)$ by applying clause (ii) again and the fact that $\emptyset$ and 0 are the only elements $\geq \emptyset$. On the other hand, $\emptyset$ does not force $(\psi \rightarrow \varphi)$ because $\emptyset$ forces ψ but not φ and so we have our desired contradiction.

Example 2.9: The sentence $(\varphi \rightarrow \psi) \vee (\psi \rightarrow \varphi)$ is not intuitionistically valid. Let the frame $\mathcal{C}$ be

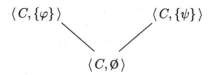

In this frame, $\emptyset$ forces neither φ nor ψ, 0 forces φ but not ψ and 1 forces ψ but not φ. Since there is a node above $\emptyset$, namely 0, which forces φ but not ψ, $\emptyset$ does not force $\varphi \rightarrow \psi$. Similarly, $\emptyset$ does not force $\psi \rightarrow \varphi$. So $\emptyset$ does not force $(\varphi \rightarrow \psi) \vee (\psi \rightarrow \varphi)$.

Example 2.10: The sentence $\neg(\forall x)\varphi(x) \to (\exists x)\neg\varphi(x)$ is not intuitionistically valid. Let b be anything other than the sole element c of C. Let the frame C be

$$\langle\, \{b, c\}, \{\varphi(c)\} \,\rangle$$
$$|$$
$$\langle\, C, \varnothing \,\rangle$$

Now by clause (iv) of Definition 2.2, neither $\varnothing$ nor 0 forces $(\forall x)\varphi(x)$ since $b \in C(0)$ but 0 does not force $\varphi(b)$. Thus $\varnothing \Vdash \neg(\forall x)\varphi(x)$. If $\varnothing \Vdash \neg(\forall x)\varphi(x) \to (\exists x)\neg\varphi(x)$, as it would were our given sentence valid, then $\varnothing$ would also force $(\exists x)\neg\varphi(x)$. By clause (v) of the definition this can happen only if there is a $c \in C$ such that $\varnothing \Vdash \neg\varphi(c)$. As c is the only element of C and $0 \Vdash \varphi(c)$, $\varnothing$ does not force $(\exists x)\neg\varphi(x)$.

Example 2.11: The sentence $(\forall x)(\varphi \vee \psi(x)) \to \varphi \vee (\forall x)\psi(x)$ is not intuitionistically valid. The required frame is

$$\langle\, \{b, c\}, \{\psi(c), \varphi\} \,\rangle$$
$$|$$
$$\langle\, C, \{\psi(c)\} \,\rangle$$

We first claim that $\varnothing \Vdash (\forall x)(\varphi \vee \psi(x))$. As $\varnothing \Vdash \psi(c)$ and $0 \Vdash \varphi$, combining the clauses for disjunction (vii) and universal quantification (iv) we see that $\varnothing \Vdash (\forall x)(\varphi \vee \psi(x))$ as claimed. Suppose now for the sake of a contradiction that $\varnothing \Vdash (\forall x)(\varphi \vee \psi(x)) \to \varphi \vee (\forall x)\psi(x)$. We would then have that $\varnothing \Vdash \varphi \vee (\forall x)\psi(x)$. However, $\varnothing$ does not force φ and, as 0 does not force $\psi(b)$, $\varnothing$ does not force $(\forall x)\psi(x)$ either. Thus $\varnothing$ does not force the disjunction $\varphi \vee (\forall x)\psi(x)$, so we have the desired contradiction.

We would now like to give some examples of intuitionistically valid sentences whose validity can be verified directly using the definition of forcing. Before presenting the examples, we will prove a few basic facts about the forcing relation that will be useful for these verifications as well as future arguments. The first is perhaps the single most useful fact about forcing. It expresses the stability of forcing as one moves up in the partial ordering.

Lemma 2.12 (Monotonicity Lemma): *For every sentence φ of $\mathcal{L}$ and every $p, q \in R$, if $p \Vdash \varphi$ and $q \geq p$, then $q \Vdash \varphi$.*

Proof: We prove the lemma by induction on the logical complexity of φ. The inductive hypothesis is not needed to verify the conclusion that $q \Vdash \varphi$ for clauses (i), (ii), (iii) and (iv). The first follows immediately from the definition of a frame and clause (i) itself which defines forcing for atomic

sentences. The other clauses define the meaning of (intuitionistic) implication, negation, and universal quantification precisely so as to make this
lemma work. We use the induction hypothesis in the verifications of clauses
(v), (vi) and (vii) which define forcing for the existential quantifier, conjunction and disjunction respectively.

(i) If φ is atomic and $p \Vdash \varphi$, then φ is in $A(p)$. By the definition
of a frame, however, $A(p) \subseteq A(q)$, and so φ is in $A(q)$. Thus, by
definition, $q \Vdash \varphi$.

(ii) Suppose $p \Vdash \varphi \rightarrow \psi$ and $q \geq p$. We show that $q \Vdash \varphi \rightarrow \psi$ by showing
that if $r \geq q$ and $r \Vdash \varphi$ then $r \Vdash \psi$. Now $r \geq p$ by transitivity and
so our assumptions that $p \Vdash \varphi \rightarrow \psi$ and $r \Vdash \varphi$ imply that $r \Vdash \psi$, as
required.

(iii) Suppose $p \Vdash \neg\varphi$ and $q \geq p$. We show that $q \Vdash \neg\varphi$ by showing that
if $r \geq q$ then r does not force φ. Again by transitivity, $r \geq p$. The
definition of $p \Vdash \neg\varphi$ then implies that r does not force φ.

(iv) Suppose $p \Vdash (\forall x)\varphi(x)$ and $q \geq p$. We show that $q \Vdash (\forall x)\varphi(x)$ by
showing that, for any $r \geq q$ and any $c \in C(r)$, $r \Vdash \varphi(c)$. Again,
$r \geq p$ by transitivity. The definition of $p \Vdash (\forall x)\varphi(x)$ then implies
that for any c in $C(r)$, $r \Vdash \varphi(c)$.

(v) Suppose $p \Vdash (\exists x)A(x)$ and $q \geq p$. Then by the definition of forcing
there is a c in $C(p)$ such that $p \Vdash \varphi(c)$. By the inductive hypothesis,
$q \geq p$ and $p \Vdash \varphi(c)$ imply that $q \Vdash \varphi(c)$. Thus $q \Vdash (\exists x)\varphi(x)$.

(vi) Suppose $p \Vdash (\varphi \wedge \psi)$ and $q \geq p$. Then by the definition of forcing
$p \Vdash \varphi$ and $p \Vdash \psi$. By the inductive hypothesis, $q \Vdash \varphi$ and $q \Vdash \psi$.
Thus $q \Vdash (\varphi \wedge \psi)$.

(vii) Suppose $p \Vdash (\varphi \vee \psi)$, and $q \geq p$. Then by the definition of forcing
either $p \Vdash \varphi$ or $p \Vdash \psi$. By the inductive hypothesis, we get that
either $q \Vdash \varphi$ or $q \Vdash \psi$. By the definition of forcing a disjunction, this
says that $q \Vdash (\varphi \vee \psi)$. □

Monotonicity says that the addition of new atomic sentences at later
states of knowledge q will not change forcing at earlier states of knowledge.
This monotone character distinguishes "truth" in an intuitionistic frame
from "truth" in "nonmonotonic logics", as discussed in III.7. In those
logics, sentences forced at state of knowledge p need not be forced at states
of knowledge $q > p$. In frames, as time evolves, we learn new "facts" but
never discover that old ones are false.

Lemma 2.13 (Double Negation Lemma): $p \Vdash \neg\neg\varphi$ *if and only if for any*
$q \geq p$ *there is an* $r \geq q$ *such that* $r \Vdash \varphi$.

Proof: $p \Vdash \neg\neg\varphi$ if and only if every $q \geq p$ fails to force $\neg\varphi$, or equivalently,
if and only if every $q \geq p$ has an $r \geq q$ forcing φ. □

Lemma 2.14 (Weak Quantifier Lemma):

(i) $p \Vdash \neg(\exists x)\neg\varphi(x)$ *if and only if for all $q \geq p$ and for all $c \in C(q)$ there is an $r \geq q$ such that $r \Vdash \varphi(c)$.*

(ii) $p \Vdash \neg(\forall x)\neg\varphi(x)$ *if and only if for all $q \geq p$, there exists an $s \geq q$ and a $c \in C(s)$ such that $s \Vdash \varphi(c)$.*

Proof:

(i) This claim follows immediately from the definition.

(ii) $q \Vdash (\forall x)\neg\varphi(x)$ if and only if for all $r \geq q$ and all $c \in C(r)$ there is no $s \geq r$ such that $s \Vdash \varphi(c)$. Thus q does not force $(\forall x)\neg\varphi(x)$ if and only if there is an $r \geq q$ and a $c \in C(r)$ such that for some $s \geq r$, $s \Vdash \varphi(c)$. So $p \Vdash \neg(\forall x)\neg\varphi(x)$ if and only if for all $q \geq p$, there is an $r \geq q$ and a $c \in C(r)$ such that for some $s \geq r$, $s \Vdash \varphi(c)$. By transitivity $s \geq q$ and c is in $C(s)$ as required in the claim. $\square$

We now produce the promised examples of intuitionistic validity. In the following examples (2.15–2.19) φ are ψ are arbitrary sentences.

Example 2.15: $\varphi \rightarrow \neg\neg\varphi$ is intuitionistically valid. To see that any p forces $\varphi \rightarrow \neg\neg\varphi$ we assume that $q \geq p$ and $q \Vdash \varphi$. We must show that $q \Vdash \neg\neg\varphi$. By the double negation lemma, it suffices to show that for every $r \geq q$ there is an $s \geq r$ such that $s \Vdash \varphi$. By the monotonicity lemma $r \Vdash \varphi$, and so r is the required s.

Example 2.16: $\neg(\varphi \wedge \neg\varphi)$ is intuitionistically valid. To show that any p forces $\neg(\varphi \wedge \neg\varphi)$ we need to show that no $q \geq p$ forces $\varphi \wedge \neg\varphi$, or equivalently no $q \geq p$ forces both φ and $\neg\varphi$. Suppose then that q forces both φ and $\neg\varphi$. Now $q \Vdash \neg\varphi$ means no $r \geq q$ forces φ. Since $q \geq q$, we have both q forces φ and q does not force φ for the desired contradiction.

Example 2.17: $(\exists x)\neg\varphi(x) \rightarrow \neg(\forall x)\varphi(x)$ is intuitionistically valid. To see that any p forces $(\exists x)\neg\varphi(x) \rightarrow \neg(\forall x)\varphi(x)$, we need to show that if $q \geq p$ and $q \Vdash (\exists x)\neg\varphi(x)$, then $q \Vdash \neg(\forall x)\varphi(x)$. Now $q \Vdash (\exists x)\neg\varphi(x)$ says there is a c in $C(q)$ such that $q \Vdash \neg\varphi(c)$. By monotonicity, any $r \geq q$ forces $\neg\varphi(c)$ as well, so no such r forces $(\forall x)\varphi(x)$, thus $q \Vdash \neg(\forall x)\varphi(x)$. This example should be compared with its contrapositive (Example 2.10) which is classically but not intuitionistically valid.

Example 2.18: $\neg(\exists x)\varphi(x) \rightarrow (\forall x)\neg\varphi(x)$ is intuitionistically valid. To see that any p forces $\neg(\exists x)\varphi(x) \rightarrow (\forall x)\neg\varphi(x)$ we have to show that for any $q \geq p$, if $q \Vdash \neg(\exists x)\varphi(x)$, then $q \Vdash (\forall x)\neg\varphi(x)$. Now $q \Vdash \neg(\exists x)\varphi(x)$ says that, for every $r \geq q$ and every c in $C(r)$, r does not force $\varphi(c)$. By transitivity $s \geq r$ implies $s \geq q$. So for every $r \geq q$ and every c in $C(r)$, no $s \geq r$ forces $\varphi(c)$. This says $q \Vdash (\forall x)\neg\varphi(x)$.

Example 2.19: If x is not free in φ, then $\varphi \vee (\forall x)\psi(x) \rightarrow (\forall x)(\varphi \vee \psi(x))$ is intuitionistically valid. To see that any p forces $\varphi \vee (\forall x)\psi(x) \rightarrow (\forall x)(\varphi \vee \psi(x))$ we must show that, for any $q \geq p$, if $q \Vdash \varphi$ or $q \Vdash (\forall x)\psi(x)$ then $q \Vdash (\forall x)(\varphi \vee \psi(x))$. There are two cases. If $q \Vdash \varphi$, then for any $r \geq q$ and any c in $C(r)$, $r \Vdash \varphi \vee \psi(c)$, so $q \Vdash (\forall x)(\varphi \vee \psi(x))$. If $q \Vdash (\forall x)\psi(x)$, then for all $r \geq q$ and all c in $C(r)$, $r \Vdash \psi(c)$, so $r \Vdash \varphi \vee \psi(c)$. This says that $q \Vdash (\forall x)(\varphi \vee \psi(x))$. This example should be compared with Example 2.11.

The frame definition of intuitionistic validity makes it remarkably simple to prove two important properties of intuitionistic logic which embody its constructivity: the disjunction and existence properties. The first says that, if a disjunction is valid, then one of its disjuncts is valid. The second says that, if an existential sentence of $\mathcal{L}$ is valid, then one of its instances via a constant from $\mathcal{L}$ is also valid. When we combine this with the completeness theorem for intuitionistic logic (Theorem 4.10), we will see that this means that if we can prove an existential sentence we can in fact prove some particular instance. Similarly, if we can prove a disjunction then we can prove one of the disjuncts.

Theorem 2.20 (Disjunction Property): *If $(\varphi_1 \vee \varphi_2)$ is intuitionistically valid then one of φ_1, φ_2 is intuitionistically valid.*

Proof: We prove the theorem by establishing its contrapositive. So suppose neither φ_1 nor φ_2 is intuitionistically valid. Thus there are, for $i = 1, 2$, frames $\mathcal{C}_i$ and elements p_i of the associated partial orderings R_i such that φ_1 is not forced by p_1 in $\mathcal{C}_1$ and φ_2 is not forced by p_2 in $\mathcal{C}_2$. By the restriction lemma (2.4), we may assume that p_i is the least element of R_i. Fix a constant c in $\mathcal{L}$. Simply by relabeling the elements of $\mathcal{C}_i(p)$ and R_i we may assume that the interpretation of c in both $\mathcal{C}_i(p_i)$ is the same, say d, and that the R_i are disjoint. Let R be the union of R_1, R_2, and $\{p_b\}$, with p_b not in either R_i. Make R into a partial order by ordering R_1 and R_2 as before and putting p_b below p_1 and p_2.

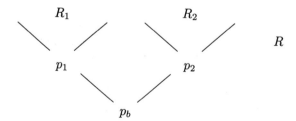

We define a frame $\mathcal{C}$ with this ordering on R by setting $\mathcal{C}(p)$ equal to $\mathcal{C}_i(p)$ for $p \in R_i$ and $C(p_b) = \{d\}$ with $A(p_b) = \emptyset$. In this frame $\mathcal{C}$, p_1 does not force φ_1 by the restriction lemma (2.4). Thus, p_b does not force φ_1 by the monotonicity lemma (2.21). Similarly, p_b does not force φ_2 as p_2 does not. Thus p_b does not force $\varphi_1 \vee \varphi_2$; hence $\varphi_1 \vee \varphi_2$ is not intuitionistically valid: contradiction. $\square$

Theorem 2.21 (Existence Property): *If $(\exists x)\varphi(x)$ is an intuitionistically valid sentence of a language $\mathcal{L}$, then for some constant c in $\mathcal{L}$, $\varphi(c)$ is also intuitionistically valid. (Remember that, by convention, $\mathcal{L}$ has at least one constant.)*

Proof: Suppose that, for each constant a in $\mathcal{L}$, $\varphi(a)$ is not intuitionistically valid. Then, for each such constant, there is an $\mathcal{L}$–frame C_a with a partially ordered set R_a containing an element p_a which does not force $\varphi(a)$. As in the previous proof, we may, without loss of generality, assume that p_a is the least element of R_a and all the R_a's are pairwise disjoint. We also assume that the interpretation of some fixed constant c of $\mathcal{L}$ is the same element d in every $C(p_a)$. We now form a new partial ordering R by taking the union of all R_a and the union of the partial orders and adding on a new bottom element p_b under all the p_a. We next define an $\mathcal{L}$–frame associated with R, as in the previous proof, by letting $C(p_b) = \{d\}$, $A(p_b) = \emptyset$ and $C(p) = C_a(p)$ for every $p \in R_a$ and every constant a of $\mathcal{L}$. We can now imitate the argument in Theorem 2.20. As we are assuming that $\exists x\varphi(x)$ is intuitionistically valid, we must have $p_b \Vdash_C \exists x\varphi(x)$. Then, by definition, $p_b \Vdash \varphi(a)$ for some constant a in $\mathcal{L}$. Applying first the monotonicity lemma and then the restriction lemma we would have p_a forcing $\varphi(a)$ first in C and then in C_a; this contradicts our initial hypothesis that p_a and C_a show that $\varphi(a)$ is not intuitionistically valid. $\square$

Exercises

Sentences (1)–(6) below are classically valid. Verify that they are intuitionistically valid by direct arguments with frames. Remember that $\varphi \leftrightarrow \psi$ is an abbreviation for $(\varphi \to \psi) \wedge (\psi \to \varphi)$.

1. $\neg\varphi \leftrightarrow \neg\neg\neg\varphi$

2. $(\varphi \wedge \neg\psi) \to \neg(\varphi \to \psi)$

3. $(\varphi \to \psi) \to (\neg\neg\varphi \to \neg\neg\psi)$

4. $(\neg\neg(\varphi \to \psi) \leftrightarrow (\neg\neg\varphi \to \neg\neg\psi)$

5. $\neg\neg(\varphi \wedge \psi) \leftrightarrow (\neg\neg\varphi \wedge \neg\neg\psi)$

6. $\neg\neg(\forall x)\varphi(x) \to (\forall x)\neg\neg\varphi(x)$

7. Supply the proof for Lemma 2.4.

8. Supply the proofs for the remaining cases of Lemma 2.5.

9. Let K be the set of constants occurring in $(\exists x)\varphi(x)$ and suppose that $(\exists x)\varphi(x)$ is intuitionistically valid. Show that, if K is nonempty, then for some c in K, $\varphi(c)$ is intuitionistically valid. (Hint: Define the restriction of a given frame C for a language $\mathcal{L}$ to one C' for a given restriction $\mathcal{L}'$ of $\mathcal{L}$. Now prove that, for any sentence φ of $\mathcal{L}'$ and any element p of the appropriate partial ordering, $p \Vdash_C \varphi$ if and only if $p \Vdash_{C'} \varphi$.)

10. In case K is empty in the previous exercise, show that $\varphi(c)$ is intuitionistically valid for any constant c. (Hint: For any constants a and c of $\mathcal{L}$ define a map Θ on formulas of $\mathcal{L}$ and on the frames for $\mathcal{L}$ which interchanges a and c. Prove that, for every C and p, $p \Vdash_C \varphi$ if and only if $p \Vdash_{\Theta(C)} \Theta(\varphi)$.)

3. Intuitionistic Tableaux

We will describe a proof procedure for intuitionistic logic based on a tableau style system like that used for classical logic in II.6. In classical logic, the idea of a tableau proof is to systematically search for a structure agreeing with the starting signed sentence. We either get such a structure or see that each possible analysis leads to a contradiction. When we begin with a signed sentence $F\varphi$, we thus either find a structure in which φ fails or decide that we have a proof of φ. For intuitionistic logic we instead begin with a *signed forcing assertion* $Tp \Vdash \varphi$ or $Fp \Vdash \varphi$ (φ is again a sentence) and try to either build a frame agreeing with the assertion or decide that any such attempt leads to a contradiction. If we begin with $Fp \Vdash \varphi$, we either find a frame in which p does not force φ or decide that we have an intuitionistic proof of φ.

There are many possible variants on the tableau method suitable for intuitionistic propositional and predicate logic due to Kripke, Hughes and Cresswell, Fitting, and others. The one we choose is designed to precisely match our definition of frame so that the systematic tableau will represent a systematic search for a frame agreeing with the starting signed forcing assertion. It is a variant of Fitting's [1983, 4.1] prefixed tableau.

The definitions of tableau and tableau proof for intuitionistic logic are formally very much like those of II.6 for classical logic. *Intuitionistic tableaux* and *tableau proofs* are labeled binary trees. The labels (again called the *entries of the tableau*) are now *signed forcing assertions*, i.e., labels of the form $Tp \Vdash \varphi$ or $Fp \Vdash \varphi$ for φ a sentence of any appropriate language. We read $Tp \Vdash \varphi$ as p forces φ and $Fp \Vdash \varphi$ as p does not force φ.

In classical logic, the elements of the structure we built by developing a tableau were the constant symbols appearing on some path of the tableau. We are now attempting to build an entire frame. The p's and q's appearing in the entries of some path P through our intuitionistic tableau will constitute the elements of the partial ordering for the frame. The ordering on them will also be specified as part of the development of the tableau. As in the classical case, we always build a tableau based on a language expanded from the one for the starting signed assertion by adding on new constants $c_0, c_1, \ldots$. The constants appearing in the sentences φ of entries on P of the form $Tq \Vdash \varphi$ or $Fq \Vdash \varphi$ for $q \leq p$ will be the elements of the required domains $C(p)$. (We use the entries with $q \leq p$ so as to ensure the monotonicity required for domains in the definition of a frame.)

With this motivation in mind, we can specify the *atomic intuitionistic tableaux*.

Definition 3.1: We begin by fixing a language $\mathcal{L}$ and an expansion $\mathcal{L}_C$ given by adding new constant symbols c_i for $i \in \mathbb{N}$. We list in Figure 55 the atomic intuitionistic tableaux (for the language $\mathcal{L}$). In the tableaux in this list, φ and ψ, if unquantified, are any sentences in the language $\mathcal{L}_C$. If quantified, they are formulas in which only x is free.

Formally, the precise meaning of "new c" and "new p" will be defined along with the definition of intuitionistic tableau. The intention for the constants is essentially as in the classical case: When we develop $T\forall x\varphi(x)$, we can put in any c for x and add on $T\varphi(c)$ but, when we develop $\exists x\varphi(x)$ by adding $T\varphi(c)$ on to the tableau, we can only use a c for which no previous commitments have been made. One warning is necessary here. When we say "any appropriate c" we mean any c in the appropriate language. In the classical case that meant any c in $\mathcal{L}_C$. Here, in developing $Tp \Vdash \forall x\varphi(x)$ as in (T$\forall$) above, it will mean any c in $\mathcal{L}$ or appearing on the path so far in a forcing assertion about a $q \leq p$. These restrictions correspond to our intention to define $C(p)$ in accordance with the requirement in the definition of frame that $C(q) \subseteq C(p)$ for $q \leq p$. Technically, similar considerations could be applied to the use of a new c as in (T$\exists$) although as a practical matter we can always choose c from among the c_i in $\mathcal{L}_C$ which have not yet appeared anywhere in the tableau. We will in fact incorporate such a choice into our formal definition.

The restrictions on the elements p introduced into the ordering should also be understood in terms of the definition of frames. In (TAt), for example, we follow the requirement in the definition of a frame that $A(p) \subseteq A(p')$ if $p \leq p'$. The reader should also keep in mind that we are determining the elements p of the partial ordering for our frame as well as defining the ordering itself as we develop the tableau. Thus, for example, when developing $Tp \Vdash \neg\varphi$ we can, in accordance with the definition of forcing a negation, add on $Fp' \Vdash \varphi$ for any $p' \geq p$ which appears on the path so far. On the other hand, if we wish to assert that p does not force $\neg\varphi$, i.e., $Fp \Vdash \neg\varphi$, then the definition of forcing tells us that there must be some $p' \geq p$ which does force φ. As with putting in a new constant, we cannot use a p' for which other commitments have already been made. Thus we can develop $Fp \Vdash \neg\varphi$ as in (F$\neg$) by adding on $Tp' \Vdash \varphi$ for a new element p' of the ordering of which we can only say that it is bigger than p. Thus, we require that p' is larger than p (and so by the requirement of transitivity bigger than any $q \leq p$) but that p' is incomparable with all other elements of the ordering introduced so far. (Again, technically, we only need to worry about the relation between p' and the q appearing on the branch so far. It is simpler to just take an entirely new p', i.e., one not yet appearing anywhere in the tableau. It will then automatically be true that $p \leq q$ only if p and q are on the same path through the tableau.)

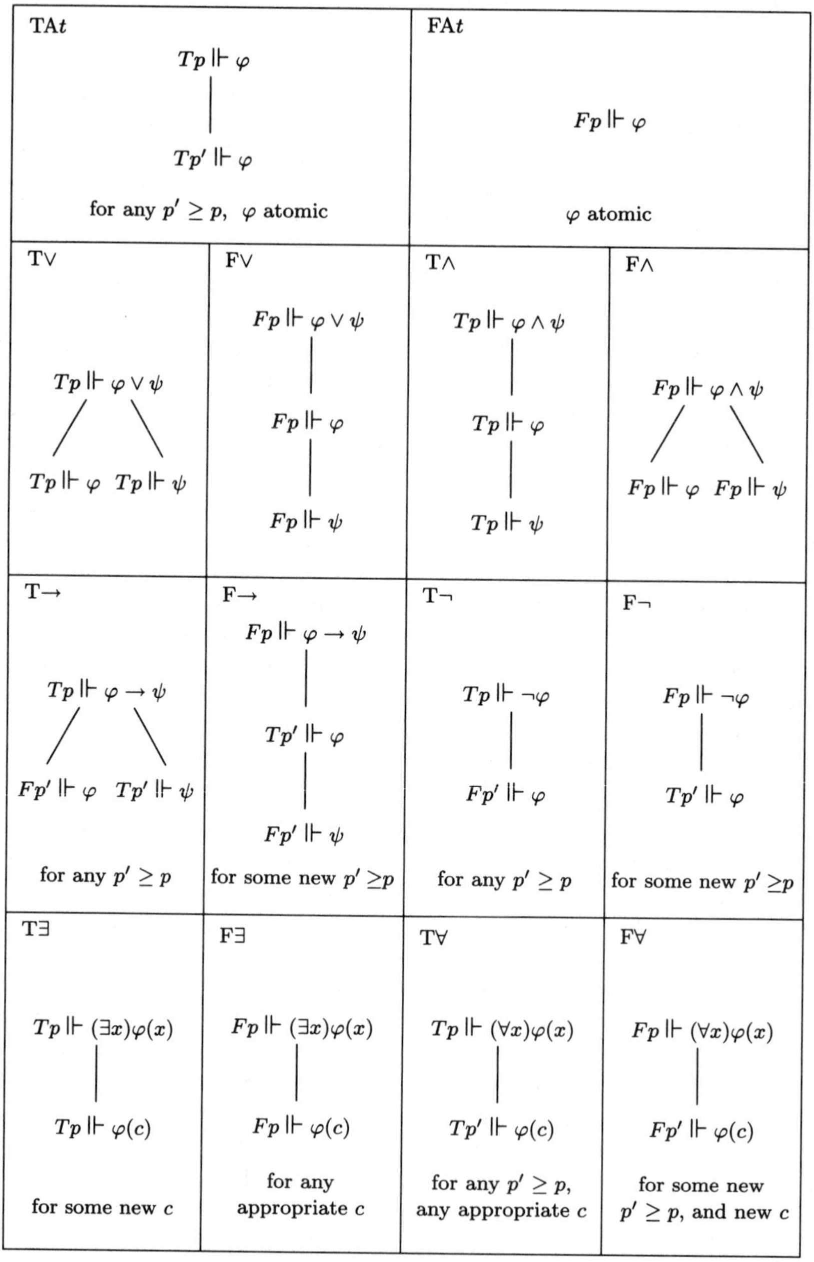

TAt	FAt
$Tp \Vdash \varphi$ | $Tp' \Vdash \varphi$ for any $p' \geq p$, φ atomic	$Fp \Vdash \varphi$ φ atomic

TV	FV	T∧	F∧
$Tp \Vdash \varphi \vee \psi$ / \ $Tp \Vdash \varphi \quad Tp \Vdash \psi$	$Fp \Vdash \varphi \vee \psi$ | $Fp \Vdash \varphi$ | $Fp \Vdash \psi$	$Tp \Vdash \varphi \wedge \psi$ | $Tp \Vdash \varphi$ | $Tp \Vdash \psi$	$Fp \Vdash \varphi \wedge \psi$ / \ $Fp \Vdash \varphi \quad Fp \Vdash \psi$

T→	F→	T¬	F¬
$Tp \Vdash \varphi \to \psi$ / \ $Fp' \Vdash \varphi \quad Tp' \Vdash \psi$ for any $p' \geq p$	$Fp \Vdash \varphi \to \psi$ | $Tp' \Vdash \varphi$ | $Fp' \Vdash \psi$ for some new $p' \geq p$	$Tp \Vdash \neg\varphi$ | $Fp' \Vdash \varphi$ for any $p' \geq p$	$Fp \Vdash \neg\varphi$ | $Tp' \Vdash \varphi$ for some new $p' \geq p$

T∃	F∃	T∀	F∀
$Tp \Vdash (\exists x)\varphi(x)$ | $Tp \Vdash \varphi(c)$ for some new c	$Fp \Vdash (\exists x)\varphi(x)$ | $Fp \Vdash \varphi(c)$ for any appropriate c	$Tp \Vdash (\forall x)\varphi(x)$ | $Tp' \Vdash \varphi(c)$ for any $p' \geq p$, any appropriate c	$Fp \Vdash (\forall x)\varphi(x)$ | $Fp' \Vdash \varphi(c)$ for some new $p' \geq p$, and new c

FIGURE 55

The formal definitions of tableaux and tableau proof for intuitionistic logic could perhaps even be left as an exercise. As it would be an exercise with many pitfalls for the unwary we give them in full detail.

Definition 3.2: We continue to use our fixed language $\mathcal{L}$ and extension by constants $\mathcal{L}_C$. We also fix a set $S = \{p_i : i \in \mathbb{N}\}$ of potential candidates for the p's and q's in our forcing assertions. An *intuitionistic tableau* (for $\mathcal{L}$) is a binary tree labeled with signed forcing assertions which are called the *entries* of the tableau. The class of all intuitionistic tableaux (for $\mathcal{L}$) is defined by induction. We simultaneously define, for each tableau τ, an ordering $\leq_\tau$ the elements of S appearing in τ.

(i) Each atomic tableau τ is a tableau. The requirement that c be new in cases (T∃) and (F∀) here simply means that c is one of the constants c_i added on to $\mathcal{L}$ to get $\mathcal{L}_C$ which does not appear in φ. The phrase "any c" in (F∃) and (T∀) means any constant in $\mathcal{L}$ or in φ. The requirement that p' be new in (F→), (F¬) and (F∀) here means that p' is any of the p_i other than p. We also declare p' to be larger than p in the associated ordering. The phrase "any $p' \geq p$" in (T→), (T¬), (T∀) and (TAt) in this case simply means that p' is p. (Of course we always declare $p \leq p$ for every p in every ordering we define.)

(ii) If τ is a finite tableau, P a path on τ, E an entry of τ occurring on P and τ' is obtained from τ by adjoining an atomic tableau with root entry E to τ at the end of the path P then τ' is also a tableau. The ordering $\leq_{\tau'}$ agrees with $\leq_\tau$ on the p_i appearing in τ. Its behavior on any new element is defined below when we explain the meaning of the restrictions on p' in the atomic tableaux for cases (F→), (F¬) and (F∀).

The requirement that c be new in cases (T∃) and (F∀) here means that it is one of the c_i (and so not in $\mathcal{L}$) which do not appear in any entry on τ. The phrase "any c" in (F∃) and (T∀) here means any c in $\mathcal{L}$ or appearing in an entry on P of the form $Tq \Vdash \psi$ or $Fq \Vdash \psi$ with $q \leq_\tau p$.

In (F→), (F¬) and (F∀) the requirement that $p' \geq p$ be new means that we choose a p_i not appearing in τ as p' and we declare that it is larger than p in $\leq_{\tau'}$. (Of course we insure transitivity by declaring that $q \leq_\tau p'$ for every $q \leq_\tau p$.) The phrase "any $p' \geq p$" in (T→), (T¬), (T∀) and (TAt) means we can choose any p' which appears in an entry on P and has already been declared greater than or equal to p in $\leq_\tau$.

(iii) If $\tau_0, \tau_1, \dots, \tau_n, \dots$ is a sequence of finite tableaux such that, for every $n \geq 0$, τ_{n+1} is constructed from τ_n by an application of (ii) then $\tau = \cup \tau_n$ is also a tableau.

As in predicate logic, we insist that the entry E in clause (ii) formally be repeated when the corresponding atomic tableau is added on to P. This is again crucial to the properties corresponding to a classical tableau being finished. In our examples below, however, we will typically omit them purely as a notational convenience.

Note that if we do not declare that either $p \leq p'$ or $p' \leq p$ in our definition of $\leq_\tau$ then p and p' are incomparable in $\leq_\tau$.

We make good on our previous remark about the relation of the ordering $\leq_\tau$ to paths through the tableau τ with the following lemma.

Lemma 3.3: *For any intuitionistic tableau τ with associated ordering $\leq_\tau$, if $p' \leq_\tau p$ then p and p' both appear on some common path through τ.*

Proof: The proof proceeds by an induction on the definition of τ and $\leq_\tau$. We leave it as Exercise 31. $\square$

Definition 3.4 (*Intuitionistic Tableau Proofs*)**:** Let τ be a intuitionistic tableau and P a path in τ.

(i) P is *contradictory* if, for some forcing assertion $p \Vdash \varphi$, both $Tp \Vdash \varphi$ and $Fp \Vdash \varphi$ appear as entries on P.

(ii) τ is *contradictory* if every path through τ is contradictory.

(iii) τ is an *intuitionistic proof of* φ if τ is a finite contradictory intuitionistic tableau with its root node labeled $Fp \Vdash \varphi$ for some $p \in R$. φ is *intuitionistically provable*, $\vdash \varphi$, if there is an intuitionistic proof of φ.

Note that, as in classical logic, if there is any contradictory tableau with root node $Fp \Vdash \varphi$, then there is one which is finite, i.e., a proof of φ : Just terminate each path when it becomes contradictory. As each path is now finite, the whole tree is finite by König's lemma. Thus, the added requirement that proofs be finite (tableaux) has no affect on the existence of proofs for any sentence. Another point of view is that we could have required the path P in clause (ii) of the definition of tableaux be noncontradictory without affecting the existence of proofs. Thus, in practice, when attempting to construct proofs we mark any contradictory path with the symbol $\otimes$ and terminate the development of the tableau along that path.

Before dealing with the soundness and completeness of the tableau method for intuitionistic logic we look at some examples of intuitionistic tableau proofs. Remember that we are abbreviating the tableaux by not repeating the entry which we are developing. We also number the levels of the tableau on the left and indicate on the right the level of the atomic tableau whose development produced the line. In all our examples, the set S from which we choose the domain of our partial order will be the set of finite binary sequences. The declarations of ordering relations are dictated by the atomic tableau added on at each step and so can also be omitted. In fact, we will always choose our p's and q's so as to define our orderings to agree with the usual ordering of inclusion on binary sequences.

Example 3.5: Let φ and ψ be any atomic sentences of $\mathcal{L}$. Figure 56 provides an intuitionistic proof of $\varphi \rightarrow (\psi \rightarrow \varphi)$.

In this proof the first three lines are an instance of (F$\rightarrow$) from the list of atomic tableaux. Lines 4 and 5 are introduced by developing line 3 in accordance with (F$\rightarrow$) again. Line 6, which, together with line 5, provides our contradiction, follows from line 2 by atomic tableau (TAt).

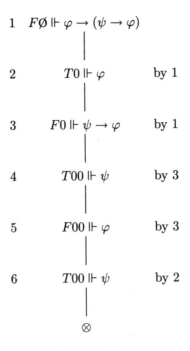

$$1 \quad F\emptyset \Vdash \varphi \to (\psi \to \varphi)$$

2	$T0 \Vdash \varphi$	by 1
3	$F0 \Vdash \psi \to \varphi$	by 1
4	$T00 \Vdash \psi$	by 3
5	$F00 \Vdash \varphi$	by 3
6	$T00 \Vdash \psi$	by 2

$\otimes$

FIGURE 56

Example 3.6: Any sentence of $\mathcal{L}$ of the following form is intuitionistically provable:

$$(\exists x)(\varphi(x) \vee \psi(x)) \to (\exists x)\varphi(x) \vee (\exists x)\psi(x)$$

In this proof (Figure 57) the first three lines are an instance of (F→). Line 4 follows by applying (T∃) to line 2. Lines 5 and 6 follow by applying (F∨) to line 3. Lines 7 and 8 are applications of (F∨) to lines 5 and 6 respectively. Line 9, which supplies the contradictions to lines 7 or 8 on its two branches, is an application of (T∨) to line 4.

Example 3.7: Consider $(\forall x)(\varphi(x) \wedge \psi(x)) \to (\forall x)\varphi(x) \wedge (\forall x)\psi(x)$.

Note here (Figure 58) that we develop both sides of the branching at line 4 and write the parallel developments side by side. Also of note is the use of (T∀) applied to line 2 to get line 6. We took advantage of the ability to chose both the constants c and d and the elements of the ordering 00 and 01.

Exercises

Let φ and ψ be any atomic formulas either with no free variables or with only x free as appropriate. For each sentence θ in (1)–(30) below, construct a tableau starting with $F\emptyset \Vdash \theta$ to show that the classically valid θ is also intuitionistically provable. (Remember that $\varphi \leftrightarrow \psi$ is an abbreviation for $(\varphi \to \psi) \wedge (\psi \to \varphi)$).

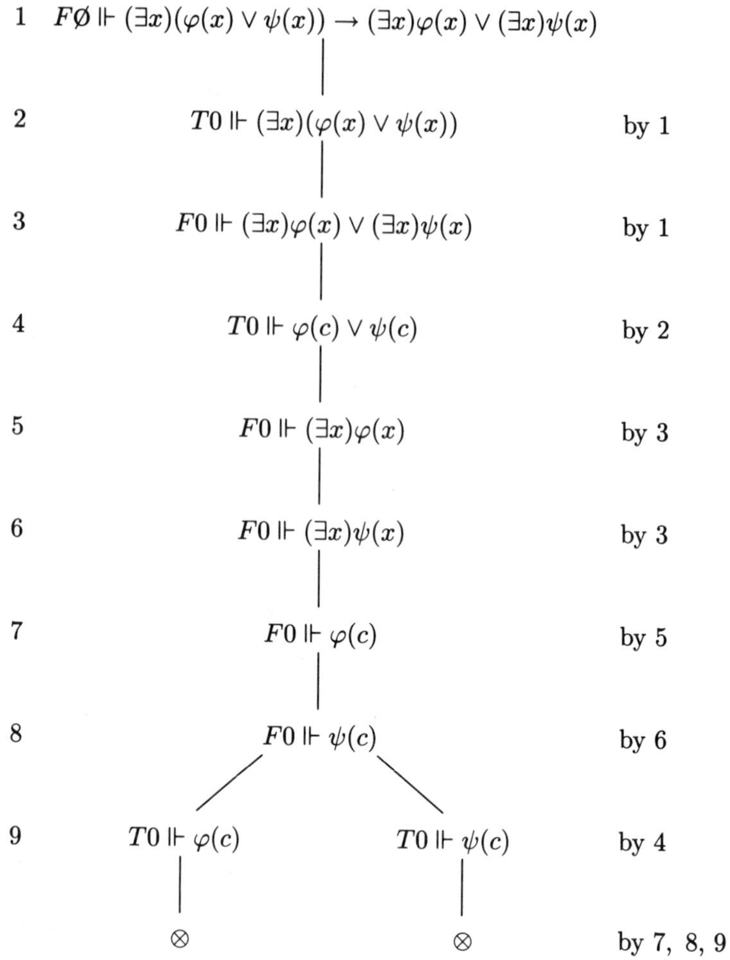

1   $F\emptyset \Vdash (\exists x)(\varphi(x) \vee \psi(x)) \rightarrow (\exists x)\varphi(x) \vee (\exists x)\psi(x)$

2            $T0 \Vdash (\exists x)(\varphi(x) \vee \psi(x))$ by 1

3            $F0 \Vdash (\exists x)\varphi(x) \vee (\exists x)\psi(x)$ by 1

4            $T0 \Vdash \varphi(c) \vee \psi(c)$ by 2

5            $F0 \Vdash (\exists x)\varphi(x)$ by 3

6            $F0 \Vdash (\exists x)\psi(x)$ by 3

7            $F0 \Vdash \varphi(c)$ by 5

8            $F0 \Vdash \psi(c)$ by 6

9        $T0 \Vdash \varphi(c)$ $T0 \Vdash \psi(c)$ by 4

            $\otimes$ $\otimes$ by 7, 8, 9

FIGURE 57

Distributive Lattice Laws

1. $(\varphi \vee \varphi) \leftrightarrow \varphi$
2. $(\varphi \wedge \varphi) \leftrightarrow \varphi$
3. $(\varphi \wedge \psi) \leftrightarrow (\psi \wedge \varphi)$
4. $(\varphi \vee \psi) \leftrightarrow (\psi \vee \varphi)$
5. $((\varphi \wedge \psi) \wedge \sigma) \leftrightarrow (\varphi \wedge (\psi \wedge \sigma))$
6. $((\varphi \vee \psi) \vee \sigma) \leftrightarrow (\varphi \vee (\psi \vee \sigma))$
7. $(\varphi \vee (\psi \wedge \sigma)) \leftrightarrow ((\varphi \vee \psi) \wedge (\varphi \vee \sigma))$
8. $(\varphi \wedge (\psi \vee \sigma)) \leftrightarrow ((\varphi \wedge \psi) \vee (\varphi \wedge \sigma))$

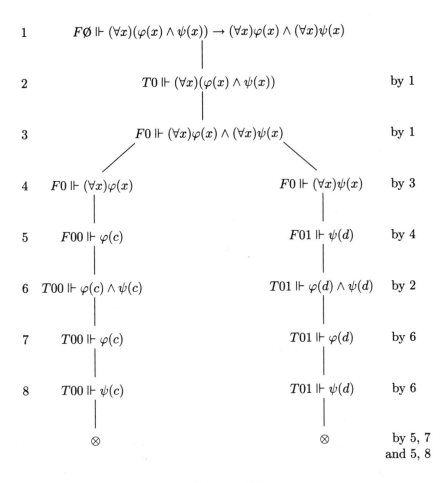

FIGURE 58

Pure Implication Laws

9. $\varphi \to \varphi$

10. $\varphi \to (\psi \to \varphi)$

11. $(\varphi \to (\psi \to \sigma)) \to ((\varphi \to \psi) \to (\varphi \to \sigma))$

Introduction and Elimination of $\wedge$

12. $((\varphi \to (\psi \to \sigma)) \to ((\varphi \wedge \psi) \to \sigma)$

13. $((\varphi \wedge \psi) \to \sigma) \to ((\varphi \to (\psi \to \sigma))$

14. $(\neg\varphi \vee \psi) \to (\varphi \to \psi)$

De Morgan's Laws

15. $\neg(\varphi \vee \psi) \leftrightarrow (\neg\varphi \wedge \neg\psi)$

16. $(\neg\varphi \vee \neg\psi) \to \neg(\varphi \wedge \psi)$

Contrapositive

   17. $(\varphi \to \psi) \to (\neg\psi \to \neg\varphi)$

Double Negation

   18. $\varphi \to \neg\neg\varphi$

Contradiction

   19. $\neg(\varphi \wedge \neg\varphi)$

Distributive Laws

   20. $(\exists x)(\varphi(x) \vee \psi(x)) \leftrightarrow (\exists x)\varphi(x) \vee (\exists x)\psi(x)$

   21. $((\forall x)(\varphi(x) \wedge \psi(x)) \leftrightarrow (\forall x)\varphi(x) \wedge (\forall x)\psi(x)$

   22. $(\varphi \vee (\forall x)\psi(x)) \to (\forall x)(\varphi \vee \psi(x))$, x not free in φ

   23. $(\varphi \wedge (\exists x)\psi(x)) \to (\exists x)(\varphi \wedge \psi(x))$, x not free in φ

   24. $(\exists x)(\varphi \to \psi(x)) \to (\varphi \to (\exists x)\psi(x))$, x not free in φ

   25. $(\exists x)(\varphi \wedge \psi(x)) \to (\varphi \wedge (\exists x)\psi(x))$, x not free in φ

De Morgan's Laws

   26. $\neg(\exists x)\varphi(x) \to (\forall x)\neg\varphi(x)$

   27. $(\forall x)\neg\varphi(x) \to \neg(\exists x)\varphi(x)$

   28. $(\exists x)\neg\varphi(x) \to \neg(\forall x)\varphi(x)$

   29. $(\exists x)(\varphi(x) \to \psi) \to ((\forall x)\varphi(x) \to \psi)$, x not free in ψ

   30. $((\exists x)\varphi(x) \to \psi) \to (\forall x)(\varphi(x) \to \psi)$, x not free in ψ

   31. Prove Lemma 3.3.

   32. (**Theorem on Constants**) Prove the intuitionistic version of Exercise II.6.13: Let $\varphi(x_1, \ldots, x_n)$ be a formula with all free variables displayed and let $c_1, \ldots, c_n$ be constants not appearing in φ. Prove that there is an intuitionistic tableau proof of $\forall x_1 \ldots \forall x_n \varphi(x_1, \ldots, x_n)$ iff there is one of $\varphi(c_1, \ldots, c_n)$.

4. Soundness and Completeness

    Our first goal in this section is to show that in intuitionistic logic (as in classical logic) provability implies validity. As in the classical soundness theorem (II.7.2), we begin by proving that a frame which "agrees" with the root node of a tableau "agrees" with every entry along some path of the tableau. In the classical case (Definition II.7.1) we constructed the path and defined a structure whose domain consists of the constants c occurring in the signed sentences along this path. Now, in addition to interpreting the constants occurring in the assertions along our path P in the appropriate structures $\mathcal{C}(p)$, we must "interpret" the partial ordering elements p occurring in the signed forcing assertions on P in the ordering R of the given frame.

Definition 4.1: Suppose $\mathcal{C} = (R, \leq_R, \mathcal{C}(p))$ is a frame for a language $\mathcal{L}$, τ is a tableau whose root is labeled with a forcing assertion about a sentence φ of $\mathcal{L}$ and P is a path through τ. Let S be the set of p's appearing in forcing assertions on P and let $\leq_S$ be the ordering on S defined in the construction of τ. We say that $\mathcal{C}$ *agrees with* P if there are maps f and g such that

(i) f is an order preserving (but not necessarily one–one) map from S into R.

(ii) g sends each constant c occurring in any sentence ψ of a forcing assertion $Tp \Vdash \psi$ or $Fp \Vdash \psi$ on P to a constant in $\mathcal{L}(f(p))$. Moreover, g is the identity on constants of $\mathcal{L}$. We also extend g to be a map on formulas in the obvious way: To get $g(\psi)$ simply replace every constant c in ψ by $g(c)$.

(iii) If $Tp \Vdash \psi$ is on P, then $f(p)$ forces $g(\psi)$ in $\mathcal{C}$ and if $Fp \Vdash \psi$ is on P, then $f(p)$ does not force $g(\psi)$ in $\mathcal{C}$.

Theorem 4.2: *Suppose $\mathcal{C} = (R, \leq_R, \mathcal{C}(p))$ is a frame for a language $\mathcal{L}$ and τ is a tableau whose root is labeled with a forcing assertion about a sentence φ of $\mathcal{L}$. If either*

(i) *$Fr \Vdash \varphi$ is at the root of τ and $q \in R$ does not force φ in $\mathcal{C}$*

or

(ii) *$Tr \Vdash \varphi$ is at the root of τ and $q \in R$ does force φ in $\mathcal{C}$,*

then there is a path P through τ which agrees with $\mathcal{C}$; moreover, there is a witness function f (as required in Definition 4.1) that sends r to q.

The proof of this theorem proceeds by induction on the construction of the tableau τ. Before providing the details we reformulate the result as the standard version of the soundness theorem.

Theorem 4.3 (Soundness): *If there is an intuitionistic tableau proof of a sentence φ, then φ is intuitionistically valid.*

Proof (of Soundness): An intuitionistic proof of φ is an intuitionistic tableau τ with a root of the form $Fr \Vdash \varphi$ in which every path is contradictory. If φ is not intuitionistically valid, then there is a frame $\mathcal{C} = (R, \leq_R, \mathcal{C}(p))$ and a $q \in R$ such that q does not force φ in $\mathcal{C}$. Now apply Theorem 4.2 to get a path P through τ and functions f and g with the properties listed in Definition 4.1. As τ is contradictory, there is a p and a sentence ψ such that both $Tp \Vdash \psi$ and $Fp \Vdash \psi$ occur on P. Definition 4.1(iii) then provides an immediate contradiction. $\square$

We break the inductive proof of Theorem 4.2 into its component parts. First, there are fourteen base cases corresponding to clause (i) of Definition 3.2 and the fourteen atomic tableaux.

Lemma 4.4: *For each atomic tableau τ which satisfies the hypotheses of Theorem 4.2, there are P, f and g as required in its conclusion.*

There are then fourteen induction cases corresponding to the type of atomic tableau chosen for development in clause (ii) of Definition 3.2. We in fact prove an assertion somewhat stronger than the theorem to facilitate the induction.

Lemma 4.5: *If f and g witness that a path P of a tableau τ agrees with C and τ' is gotten from τ by an application of clause (ii) of Definition 3.2, then there are extensions P', f' and g' of P, f and g respectively such that f' and g' witness that the path P' through τ' also agrees with C.*

Theorem 4.2 is an easy consequence of these two lemmas so we present its proof before considering the proofs of the lemmas.

Proof (of Theorem 4.2): Lemma 4.4 establishes the theorem for atomic tableaux. Lemma 4.5 then proves the theorem for all finite tableaux by induction. In fact, it proves it for infinite tableaux as well. Suppose $\tau = \cup \tau_n$ is an infinite tableau as defined by clause (iii) of Definition 3.2. We begin by applying the appropriate case of Lemma 4.4 to τ_0 to get suitable P_0, f_0 and g_0. We then apply Lemma 4.5 to each τ_n in turn to construct P_n, f_n and g_n. The required P, f and g for τ are then simply the unions of the P_n, f_n and g_n respectively. $\square$

Proof (of Lemma 4.4): We begin by defining $f(p) = r$ and g to be the identity on the constants of $\mathcal{L}$. The argument now needed for each atomic tableau is precisely the same as the one for the corresponding case of Lemma 4.5. The point here is that, with this choice of f and g, the root itself agrees with C by the hypothesis of the theorem. The inductive argument applied to the rest of the atomic tableau then provides the required extensions. Thus, we have reduced the proof of this lemma to that of Lemma 4.5. $\square$

Proof (of Lemma 4.5): First, note that, if τ' is gotten by extending τ somewhere other than at the end of P, then the witnesses for τ work for τ' as well. Thus, we may assume that we form τ' by adjoining one of the atomic tableaux at the end of P in τ. We now consider the fourteen cases given by the atomic tableaux of Definition 3.1.

Cases (T$\vee$), (F$\vee$), (T$\wedge$), (F$\wedge$), (T$\rightarrow$), (T$\neg$), (F$\exists$), (T$\forall$) and (FAt) require no extension of f or g. In each of these cases it is obvious from the induction hypothesis and the corresponding case of the definition of forcing (Definition 2.2) that one of the extensions of P to a path through τ' satisfies the requirements of the lemma. Note that (TAt) also requires the monotonicity assumption on $A(p)$.

The arguments for the remaining cases are all illustrated by that for case (F∀). Here the entry of P being developed is $Fp \Vdash (\forall x)\varphi(x)$. The required extension of P to P' is the only possible one. It is determined by adding $Fp' \Vdash \varphi(c)$ to the end of P. By our induction hypothesis, $f(p) \not\Vdash_C g((\forall x)\varphi(x))$. By the definition of forcing a universal sentence (2.2(iv)), there is a $q' \in R$ and a $c' \in \mathcal{L}(q')$ such that $q' \geq f(p)$ and q' does not force $g(\varphi(c'))$. Fix such q' and c' and extend f and g to f' and g' by setting $f'(p') = q'$ and $g'(c) = c'$. It is now obvious that P', f' and g' satisfy the requirements of the lemma, i.e., f' and g' witness that P' agrees with C.

We leave cases (F→), (F¬) and (T∃) as Exercise 1. □

Our next goal is to prove that the tableau method of proof is complete for intuitionistic logic. We will define a procedure for constructing the appropriate complete systematic tableau starting with a given signed forcing assertion as its root. We will then prove that, for any noncontradictory path P through this tableau, we can build a frame C which agrees with P. Thus if our systematic procedure applied to any forcing assertion $Fp \Vdash \varphi$ fails to produce an intuitionistic tableau proof of φ, then we will have built a frame in which φ is not forced and so demonstrated that φ is not intuitionistically valid.

Rather than trying to first give an abstract definition of when an entry is reduced and a tableau finished, we will directly define the construction procedure and prove it has the properties needed to carry out the completeness proof. (The construction procedure will define a notion of "properly developed" for occurrences of entries in the tableau that will take the place of being "reduced". The properties of a tableau that correspond to its being finished will be listed in Lemma 4.8.) The major simplification that this procedure allows is that, rather than dealing with some abstract partial ordering being constructed with the tableau, we can specify a particular partial ordering from which we will choose all our p's and q's. Any sufficiently rich partial ordering would do. We only have to be able to choose a q from the ordering which extends any given p and is incomparable with any given finite set of elements all of which are incomparable with p. We choose the set S of finite sequences of natural numbers partially ordered by extension, i.e., $p \leq q$ iff q extends p as a sequence. We will take care to declare ordering relations in our tableau so as to agree with this ordering on S. The tableau we construct will use only an initial segment of this ordering. In fact, we will arrange the construction so that, if some sequence p appears on level n of a path P of our tableau, then each initial segment of p appears on P at some level $m < n$ of the tableau.

The procedure for handling the various entries can be motivated considerating the atomic tableaux of (T∀) and (F∀). If we develop $Fp \Vdash \forall x\varphi(x)$ by putting down $Fp' \Vdash \varphi(c)$ for some new p' and c, we have exhausted the information contained in the original assertion that p does not force $\forall x\varphi(x)$. On the other hand, developing $Tp \Vdash \forall x\varphi(x)$ by putting down

$Tp' \Vdash \varphi(c)$ for some c and $p' \geq p$ leaves much to be said in terms of the full meaning of the original assertion. $Tp \Vdash \forall x \varphi(x)$ says that for every $p' \geq p$ (in the appropriate partial ordering) and every $c \in \mathcal{L}(p')$, p' forces $\varphi(c)$. Thus, we must arrange to put all of these instances of the forcing assertion on every path containing $Tp \Vdash \forall x \varphi(x)$. Note that we do not need to instantiate φ with every constant, only with those in $\mathcal{L}(p')$. Similarly, we do not have to assert that p' forces $\varphi(c)$ for every $p' \geq p$. As the frame we intend to construct will be built from the information along one non-contradictory path through our finished tableau, we need only consider the constants on the path P which we are extending.

Definition 4.6 (CSIT, *Complete Systematic Intuitionistic Tableaux*): Let φ be a sentence of a language $\mathcal{L}$. Let $d_1, d_2, \ldots, d_n, \ldots$ be a listing of the set D consisting of all the constants of our standard extension $\mathcal{L}_C$ of $\mathcal{L}$ by new constants. For convenience we assume that d_1 is in $\mathcal{L}$. Let $p_1, p_2, \ldots, p_n, \ldots$ be a listing of the set S of all finite sequences of elements of $\mathbb{N}$ which we partially order by extension and let $v_1, v_2, \ldots, v_k, \ldots$ be a listing of the set V of all pairs $\langle d_i, p_j \rangle$ consisting of an element from D and one from S. From now on, when we speak of the least element of D, S or V with some property, we mean the first one in the above lists for the appropriate sets.

We define a sequence τ_n of tableaux and what it means for an occurrence w of an entry E of τ_n to be *properly developed*. The union τ of our sequence of tableaux τ_n will be the *complete systematic intuitionistic tableau (the CSIT) starting with φ*.

τ_0 is the atomic tableau with root $F\emptyset \Vdash \varphi$. If this tableau requires a partial ordering element p' or a constant c we choose the least elements of S or D which will make it into a tableau according to clause (i) of the Definition 3.2.

Suppose we have constructed τ_n. Let m be the least level of τ_n containing an occurrence of an entry which has not been properly developed and let w be the leftmost such occurrence (say of entry E) on level m of τ_n. We form τ_{n+1} by adding an atomic tableau with root E to the end of every noncontradictory path P through τ_n which contains w. To be precise, we list the noncontradictory paths $P_1, P_2, \ldots, P_k$ of τ_n which contain w. We deal with each P_j in turn by appending an atomic tableau with root E to the end of P_j. Suppose we have reached some P_j on our list. We must now describe the atomic tableau with root E added on to the end of P_j. Cases (T$\vee$), (F$\vee$), (T$\wedge$), (F$\wedge$) and (FAt) of the list of atomic tableaux require no further information to determine the added tableau. Each of the other cases requires fixing some p' and/or some c:

(T$\rightarrow$) Let p' be the least q in S which is on P_j, extends p and is such that neither $Fq \Vdash \varphi$ nor $Tq \Vdash \varphi$ occurs on P_j. If there is no such q, let $p' = p$.

(F→) Let $k \in \mathbb{N}$ be least such that $p\char`^k$ has not occurred in the construction so far and let $p' = p\char`^k$. (Note that p' is incomparable with everything that has occurred so far except those that are initial segments of p.)

(T¬) Let p' be the least q in S which is on P_j, extends p and is such that $Fq \Vdash \varphi$ does not occur on P_j. If there is no such q, let $p' = p$.

(F¬) Proceed as in case (F→).

(T∃) Let c be the least element of D not occurring in the construction so far.

(F∃) Let c be the least element d of D which is either in $\mathcal{L}$ or else occurs in a forcing assertion $Tq \Vdash \psi$ or $Fq \Vdash \psi$ on P_j for any $q \leq p$ such that $Fp \Vdash \varphi(d)$ does not appear on P_j. If there is no such $d \in D$, let $c = d_1$.

(T∀) Let $\langle p', c \rangle$ be the least $v = \langle r, d \rangle$ in V such that r appears on P_j, d is either in $\mathcal{L}$ or else occurs in a forcing assertion $Tq \Vdash \psi$ or $Fq \Vdash \psi$ on P_j for any $q \leq p$, r extends p and $Tr \Vdash \varphi(d)$ does not appear on P_j. If there is no such pair, we let $p' = p$ and $c = d_1$.

(F∀) Let $k \in \mathbb{N}$ be least such that $p\char`^k$ has not occurred in the construction so far. We set $p' = p\char`^k$ and let c be the least element of D not occurring in the construction so far.

(TAt) Let p' be the least q in S on P_j such that $Tq \Vdash \varphi$ does not appear on P_j. If there is no such q, let $p' = p$.

In all of these cases we say that we have *properly developed* the occurrence w of entry E.

Before proceeding with the proofs of the theorems we state some basic properties of CSIT, in particular, the ones that correspond to the classical CST being finished, that allow us to prove the completeness theorem.

Lemma 4.7: *Let $\tau = \cup \tau_n$ be a CSIT as defined above and P a path through τ.*

(i) *If a sequence $p \in S$ occurs in an assertion at level n of P, then every initial segment q of p occurs on P at some level $m \leq n$ of τ.*

(ii) *τ is a tableau in accordance with Definition 3.2.*

Proof: (i)   We proceed by induction through the construction of τ. The only cases in which we actually introduce a new p on P are (F→) and (F∀). In both cases we introduce some sequence $p\char`^k$ for a p already on P.

(ii)   The only point to verify is that, in the construction of τ_{n+1}, if we add on an atomic tableau with root entry E to the end of some path P_j in τ_n, the p' and c used (if any) satisfy the conditions of Definition 3.2(ii). Otherwise, we obviously are following the prescription for building new tableaux from old ones given in that definition. A simple inspection of the cases shows that we are obeying these restrictions.   □

Lemma 4.8: *Let* $\tau = \cup \tau_n$ *be a* CSIT *as defined above and* P *a noncontradictory path through* τ.

(T$\vee$) *If* $Tp \Vdash \varphi \vee \psi$ *appears on* P, *then either* $Tp \Vdash \varphi$ *or* $Tp \Vdash \psi$ *appears on* P.

(F$\vee$) *If* $Fp \Vdash \varphi \vee \psi$ *appears on* P, *then both* $Fp \Vdash \varphi$ *and* $Fp \Vdash \psi$ *appear on* P.

(T$\wedge$) *If* $Tp \Vdash \varphi \wedge \psi$ *appears on* P, *then both* $Tp \Vdash \varphi$ *and* $Tp \Vdash \psi$ *appear on* P.

(F$\wedge$) *If* $Fp \Vdash \varphi \wedge \psi$ *appears on* P, *then either* $Fp \Vdash \varphi$ *or* $Fp \Vdash \psi$ *appears on* P.

(T$\rightarrow$) *If* $Tp \Vdash \varphi \rightarrow \psi$ *and* p' *appear on* P *with* $p' \geq p$, *then either* $Fp' \Vdash \varphi$ *or* $Tp' \Vdash \psi$ *appears on* P.

(F$\rightarrow$) *If* $Fp \Vdash \varphi \rightarrow \psi$ *appears on* P, *then for some* $p' \geq p$ *both* $Tp' \Vdash \varphi$ *and* $Fp' \Vdash \psi$ *appear on* P.

(T$\neg$) *If* $Tp \Vdash \neg\varphi$ *and* p' *appear on* P *with* $p' \geq p$, *then* $Fp' \Vdash \varphi$ *appears on* P.

(F$\neg$) *If* $Fp \Vdash \neg\varphi$ *appears on* P, *then* $Tp' \Vdash \varphi$ *appears on* P *for some* $p' \geq p$.

(T$\exists$) *If* $Tp \Vdash \exists x\varphi(x)$ *appears on* P, *then* $Tp \Vdash \varphi(c)$ *appears on* P *for some* c.

(F$\exists$) *If* $Fp \Vdash \exists x\varphi(x)$ *appears on* P *and* c *is in* $\mathcal{L}$ *or occurs in a forcing assertion* $Tq \Vdash \psi$ *or* $Fq \Vdash \psi$ *on* P *for any* $q \leq p$, *then* $Fp \Vdash \varphi(c)$ *appears on* P.

(T$\forall$) *If* $Tp \Vdash \forall x\varphi(x)$ *appears on* P, c *is in* $\mathcal{L}$ *or occurs in a forcing assertion* $Tq \Vdash \psi$ *or* $Fq \Vdash \psi$ *on* P *for any* $q \leq p$ *and* p' *appears on* P *with* $p' \geq p$, *then* $Tp' \Vdash \varphi(c)$ *appears on* P.

(F$\forall$) *If* $Fp \Vdash \forall x\varphi(x)$ *appears on* P, *then* $Fp' \Vdash \varphi(c)$ *appears on* P *for some* c *and* $p' \geq p$.

(TA*t*) *If* p *and* $Tq \Vdash \varphi$ *appear on* P *for any atomic* φ *and* $q \leq p$, *then* $Tp \Vdash \varphi$ *appears on* P.

Proof: First note that every occurrence w in τ of any entry E is properly developed at some stage of the construction. (Consider any w at level n of τ. It is clear that, by the first stage s after all w' at levels $m \leq n$ which are ever properly developed have been so developed, we would have properly developed w.)

Cases (T∨), (F∨), (T∧), (F∧), (F→), (F¬), (T∃) and (F∀) are now almost immediate. Let w be the occurrence of the appropriate signed forcing condition on P. Suppose we properly develop w at stage n of the construction. As w is on P (which is noncontradictory), one of the P_j that we deal with at stage n is an initial segment of P. We add the appropriate atomic tableau to the end of this P_j as part of our construction of τ_n. Thus P must go through one of the branches of this atomic tableau. This immediately gives the desired conclusion.

Next, note that every entry E occurring on P occurs infinitely often on P. The point here is that each occurrence w of E on P is properly developed. When we properly develop w, we add on another occurrence of E to the end of every noncontradictory path in τ_n that goes through w. Thus we make sure that there there is another occurrence of E on P. As every occurrence of each entry E on P is properly developed, the entry itself is properly developed infinitely often. It is now easy to deal with the remaining cases of the lemma. We choose a few examples.

(T→) Suppose for the sake of a contradiction that p' is the least (in our master listing of S) extension of p that occurs on P such that neither $Fp' \Vdash \varphi$ nor $Tp' \Vdash \psi$ occurs on P. Let Q be the finite set of $q \geq p$ which precede p in our master listing of S. For each $q \in Q$, either $Fq \Vdash \varphi$ or $Tq \Vdash \psi$ occurs on P by our choice of p'. Let m be a stage in the construction of τ by which, for each $q \in Q$, either $Fq \Vdash \varphi$ or $Tq \Vdash \psi$ occurs on the initial segment of P constructed so far. Consider the first stage $n \geq m$ at which we properly develop an occurrence on P of $E = Tp \Vdash \varphi \to \psi$. (As we properly develop an occurrence of E infinitely often in our construction, there must be such a stage.) The definition of the CSIT then guarantees that we add on the atomic tableau with root E using the given p' to the end of some path P_j which is an initial segment of P. As P_j is an initial segment of P, one of the branches through this atomic tableau must also be an initial segment of P as required.

(T∀) Suppose, for the sake of a contradiction, that $v = \langle p', c \rangle$ is the least pair (in our master listing of V) satisfying the hypotheses of (T∀) but not the conclusion, i.e., $Tp' \Vdash \varphi(c)$ does not occur on P. Let Q be the finite set of pairs $\langle q, d \rangle$ which precede v and satisfy the hypotheses of $T\forall$. Let m be a stage by which, for each $\langle q, d \rangle \in Q$, we already have an occurrence of $Fq \Vdash \varphi(d)$ on the initial segment of P defined so far. Consider the first stage $n \geq m$ at which we properly develop an occurrence on P of $E = Fp \Vdash \forall x \varphi(x)$. The definition of the CSIT then guarantees that we add on the atomic tableau with root E using the given p' and c to the end of some path P_j which is an initial segment of P. As P_j is an initial segment of P, the unique branch through this atomic tableau must also be an initial segment of P as required.

All the remaining cases, (T¬), (F∃) and (TAt), are proved in a similar fashion. We leave them as Exercise 3. □

Theorem 4.9: *Suppose that $\tau = \cup \tau_n$ is a* CSIT *and P is a noncontradictory path in τ. We define a frame $\mathcal{C} = (R, \leq, \mathcal{C}(p))$ associated with P as follows:*

> *R is the set of all sequences in S appearing in forcing assertions on P. The partial ordering on R is the same as that on S: extension.*
>
> *For each $p \in R$, $C(p)$ is the set consisting of the constants of $\mathcal{L}$ and all other constants appearing in forcing assertions $Tq \Vdash \psi$ or $Fq \Vdash \psi$ on P with $q \leq p$.*
>
> *For each $p \in R$, $A(p)$ is the set of all atomic sentences ψ such that $Tq \Vdash \psi$ occurs on P for some $q \leq p$. (Warning: We are using the convention that every $c \in C(p)$ is named by itself in $\mathcal{L}(p)$.)*

If we set f and g to be the identity functions on R and on the set of constants appearing on P, respectively, then they are witnesses that $\mathcal{C}$ agrees with P.

Proof: First, note that the clauses of the definition of $\mathcal{C}$ are designed to guarantee that $\mathcal{C}$ is a frame for $\mathcal{L}$ according to Definition 2.1. Just remember that every constant c in $\mathcal{L}(p)$ names itself.

We now wish to prove that P agrees with $\mathcal{C}$; we use induction on the complexity of sentences φ appearing in forcing assertions on P.

Atomic φ: If $Tp \Vdash \varphi$ appears on P then φ is in $A(p)$ and so forced by p. If $Fp \Vdash \varphi$ appears on P then we must show that $Tq \Vdash \varphi$ does not appear on P for any $q \leq p$. (This is the only way that p could come to force φ in $\mathcal{C}$.) If there were such an occurrence of $Tq \Vdash \varphi$ on P then, by Lemma 4.8 (TAt), $Tp \Vdash \varphi$ would also occur on P contradicting the assumption that P is noncontradictory.

The inductive cases are each handled by the corresponding clauses of Lemma 4.8 and of the definition of forcing (Definition 2.2) together with the induction assumption for the theorem, i.e. the requirements for $\mathcal{C}$ to agree with P are met for sentences of lower complexity.

As a sample we consider $F\forall$: $Fp \Vdash \forall x \varphi(x)$ appears on P. By Lemma 4.8 ($F\forall$), $Fp' \Vdash \varphi(c)$ appears on P for some c and $p' \geq p$. The inductive hypothesis then says that p' does not force $\varphi(c)$ in $\mathcal{C}$. The definition of forcing a universal sentence (2.2(v)) then tells us that p does not force $\forall x \varphi(x)$ in $\mathcal{C}$, as required.

The remaining cases are left as Exercise 4. $\square$

We can now state the standard form of the completeness theorem.

Theorem 4.10: *If φ is intuitionistically valid then it has an intuitionistic tableau proof.*

Proof: Consider the CSIT τ starting with an intuitionistically valid φ. If τ is not an intuitionistic tableau proof of φ, then it has by definition a non-contradictory path P. Theorem 4.9 then provides a frame $\mathcal{C}$ in which $\emptyset$ does not force φ. Thus φ can not be intuitionistically valid for a contradiction. $\square$

Exercises

1. Complete the remaining cases (F→), (F¬) and (T∃) in the proof of Lemma 4.5.
2. Prove that any CSIT is finite if and only if it is contradictory.
3. Complete the remaining cases (T¬), (F∃) and (TAt) in the proof of Lemma 4.8.
4. Complete the remaining cases in the proof of Theorem 4.9.

5. Decidability and Undecidability

The CSIT gives us a systematic method for searching for either an intuitionistic proof of a given sentence φ or a frame counterexample. As we have noted before, if a proof exists there is a finite proof and the CSIT will give such a proof by the completeness theorem. On the other hand, if φ is not intuitionistically valid, the frame counterexample constructed in the proof of the completeness theorem will usually be infinite. Indeed, there is in general no way of avoiding such a situation. Intuitionistic logic, like classical logic, is undecidable: There is no algorithm which is guaranteed to terminate in a finite time and to tell us if φ is intuitionistically valid (Theorem 5.16). Nonetheless, there are special classes of sentence whose intuitionistic validity can be decided and there are ways of improving our chances of finding both proofs and finite counterexamples in many cases.

On the side of generating proofs more quickly and efficiently, we note that the completeness theorem tells us that we can add on any sound procedure for generating tableaux without changing the class of provable sentences. That is, whatever extension we make to the schemes for generating tableau proofs, if we can still prove a soundness theorem, then the new schemes (as our current ones) generate proofs for exactly the intuitionistically valid sentences. Of course, there is a trade-off. The more rules we add on, the more possibilities there are for developing the tableau. Viewed as a search through all possible tableau proofs, adding on new procedures increases the breadth of the search space for the sake of possibly decreasing the depth of the search, i.e., the size of the proof we construct. We introduce one such rule which considerably shortens many proofs and, in addition, allows us to redress a certain imbalance in the tableau rules we have presented.

To motivate this additional rule, we first reconsider Example 3.5 which proved the intuitionistic validity of $\varphi \to (\psi \to \varphi)$ for atomic φ and ψ:

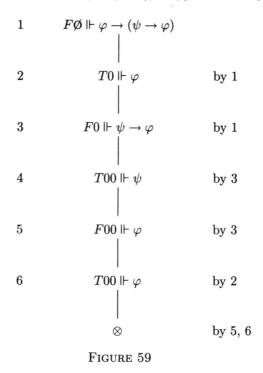

1	$F\emptyset \Vdash \varphi \to (\psi \to \varphi)$	
2	$T0 \Vdash \varphi$	by 1
3	$F0 \Vdash \psi \to \varphi$	by 1
4	$T00 \Vdash \psi$	by 3
5	$F00 \Vdash \varphi$	by 3
6	$T00 \Vdash \varphi$	by 2
	$\otimes$	by 5, 6

FIGURE 59

Our interest now is in the last step of the proof: Line 6 (which together with line 5 provides our contradiction) follows from line 2 by atomic tableau (TAt). It is at this point (and only at this point) in the proof that we used the fact that φ and ψ were atomic sentences as atomic tableau TAt applied only to atomic sentences. We chose this rule to correspond to the definition of a frame which demands monotonicity only for atomic tableau. On the other hand, the monotonicity lemma (Lemma 2.12) shows that the rule is sound for any sentence φ: If $p \Vdash \varphi$ and $p' \geq p$, then $p' \Vdash \varphi$ in any frame. Thus we may revise our tableau procedures by strengthening atomic tableau TAt to apply to all sentences φ:

$$T\varphi$$
$$Tp \Vdash \varphi$$
$$Tp' \Vdash \varphi$$
$$\text{for any } p' \geq p$$

MONOTONICITY

The proof of the soundness theorem with this strengthened atomic tableau is exactly as with the original one for atomic φ. Thus we have not changed the class of provable sentences but we have greatly expanded the applicability of our proofs. All the tableau proofs in the examples and exercises in §3 for which φ and ψ were assumed atomic are now seen to prove the validity of the specified expressions for any sentences φ and ψ. Indeed, as (TAt) was the only way of developing a tableau that was not equally applicable to all sentences, we now see that any tableau proof of a sentence built up from atomic φ, ψ, etc., actually proves all instances of the sentence gotten by replacing φ, ψ, etc., by arbitrary formulas. (Warning: There is one proviso to be observed in such replacements. As our tableau procedures apply only to sentences, we must take care not to introduce any free variables into our formulas.)

Let us now turn to using the tableau proof procedure to try to produce frame counterexamples to sentences that are not intuitionistically valid. Remember, there are are no guaranteed methods here. We can, however, convert the proof of the completeness theorem into a somewhat more general test for having produced a frame counterexample by formulating a notion of a finished tableau based on the assertions in Lemma 4.8.

Definition 5.1: If τ is a tableau and $\leq$ is the ordering defined on the p's and q's appearing in τ then τ is *finished* if every noncontradictory path P through τ has the thirteen properties listed in Lemma 4.8.

Theorem 5.2: *If τ is a finished tableau with root $Fp \Vdash \varphi$ and P is a noncontradictory path through τ, then there is a frame $\mathcal{C}$ which agrees with P (and so φ is not intuitionistically valid).*

Proof: We proceed exactly as in Theorem 4.9 except that the ordering on the p's occurring in forcing assertions on P is now defined by τ (rather than being given in advance by extension of sequences). The proof of Theorem 4.9 then makes no use of any properties of the CSIT other than those specified in Lemma 4.8. These properties of P are now guaranteed by the definition of τ being finished. $\square$

Thus if we can produce any noncontradictory finished tableau with a root of the form $Fp \Vdash \varphi$, then we know that we have built a frame counterexample to φ and so shown that it is not intuitionistically valid.

Example 5.3: Consider trying to prove the nonvalid sentence

$$\varphi \rightarrow (\varphi \rightarrow \psi).$$

We begin by developing the two implications to reach line 5 of Figure 60. Now if φ and ψ are atomic sentences, it is easy to see that this tableau is finished. As it is noncontradictory, we have shown that $\varphi \rightarrow (\varphi \rightarrow \psi)$ is not intuitionistically valid for atomic sentences φ and ψ.

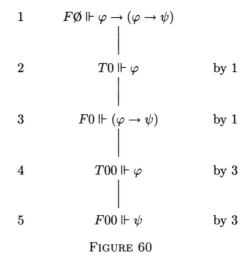

1          $F\emptyset \Vdash \varphi \rightarrow (\varphi \rightarrow \psi)$

2                 $T0 \Vdash \varphi$ by 1

3             $F0 \Vdash (\varphi \rightarrow \psi)$ by 1

4                $T00 \Vdash \varphi$ by 3

5                $F00 \Vdash \psi$ by 3

FIGURE 60

We can carry the analysis one step further by actually displaying a frame in which $\varphi \rightarrow (\varphi \rightarrow \psi)$ is not forced; such a frame can be constructed from the tableau in Figure 60 above.

$$\langle \{c\}, \{\varphi\} \rangle$$

$$\langle \{c\}, \{\varphi\} \rangle$$

$$\langle \{c\}, \emptyset \rangle$$

Of course, we could just as well eliminate the top line of the frame as it adds nothing to the second one. We also see that this frame provides us with a template to produce counterexamples to $\varphi \rightarrow (\varphi \rightarrow \psi)$ for some nonatomic φ and ψ. If we can arrange that $\emptyset$ does not force φ while 0 forces φ but not ψ, we will have the desired counterexample.

Example 5.4: Consider $\varphi \vee \neg\varphi$.

1          $F\emptyset \Vdash \varphi \vee \neg\varphi$

2             $F\emptyset \Vdash \varphi$ by 1

3             $F\emptyset \Vdash \neg\varphi$ by 1

4                $T0 \Vdash \varphi$ by 3

FIGURE 61

Again, if φ and ψ are atomic sentences, we have a finished tableau and so a proof that $\varphi \lor \neg\varphi$ is not intuitionistically valid. The frame counterexample corresponding to this finished tableau is the same one produced in Example 2.7. The difference here is that it was produced automatically.

Example 5.5: Consider the sentence $(\neg\varphi \rightarrow \neg\psi) \rightarrow (\psi \rightarrow \varphi)$.

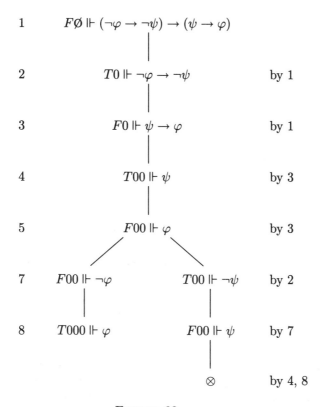

FIGURE 62

This is not a finished tableau but we can use it to produce a frame counterexample if we are sufficiently clever. The key idea is that no further development will produce any true forcing assertions $Tp \Vdash \theta$ for any new θ. Thus we must have as much information as we need to build the counterexample. In fact, letting $\varnothing$ and 0 force no atomic statements, $00 \Vdash \psi$, $000 \Vdash \psi$ and $000 \Vdash \varphi$ will give the desired frame counterexample. Now, from the viewpoint of forcing, $\varnothing$ and 0 are indistinguishable. Thus we might as well collapse them. So we end up with $\varnothing$, 0 and 00 as the partially ordered set,

$$A(\varnothing) = \varnothing, \quad A(0) = \{\psi\}, \quad A(00) = \{\varphi, \psi\}.$$

We leave the verification that this is indeed a frame counterexample as Exercise 13.

Example 5.6: Consider the sentence $(\varphi \to \psi) \vee (\psi \to \varphi)$.

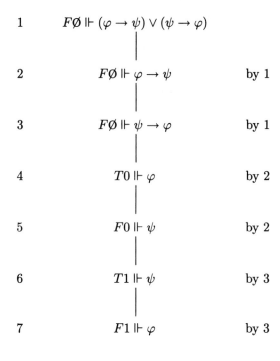

1	$F\emptyset \Vdash (\varphi \to \psi) \vee (\psi \to \varphi)$	
2	$F\emptyset \Vdash \varphi \to \psi$	by 1
3	$F\emptyset \Vdash \psi \to \varphi$	by 1
4	$T0 \Vdash \varphi$	by 2
5	$F0 \Vdash \psi$	by 2
6	$T1 \Vdash \psi$	by 3
7	$F1 \Vdash \varphi$	by 3

FIGURE 63

Observe that this is the first example in which the "new" $p' \geq p$ stipulation of rule $(F\to)$ (applied here to line 3 to obtain lines 6 and 7) forces our frame to *branch*. Node 1 in line 6 was chosen as the least node greater than $\emptyset$ incomparable with every p on the tree not $\leq \emptyset$ in accordance with rule $(F\to)$ of Definition 4.6 of a CSIT. In fact, no linear (nonbranching) frame can fail to force $(\varphi \to \psi) \vee (\psi \to \varphi)$. The above tableau, however, is finished and not contradictory, so we see that $(\varphi \to \psi) \vee (\psi \to \varphi)$ is not intuitionistically valid.

We conclude with an example of a sentence which is not intuitionistically valid and for which developing the CSIT for a few steps does not obviously supply a frame counterexample. Indeed, this is an example for which no finite frame can be a counterexample.

Example 5.7: Consider the sentence $\forall x \neg\neg\varphi(x) \to \neg\neg\forall x \varphi(x)$.

The CSIT for this sentence begins, in a somewhat abbreviated form, as in Figure 64.

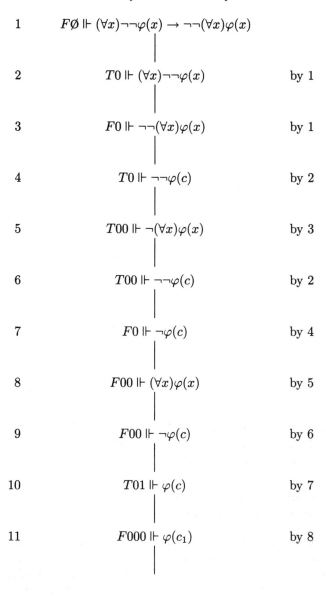

1        $F\emptyset \Vdash (\forall x)\neg\neg\varphi(x) \rightarrow \neg\neg(\forall x)\varphi(x)$

2        $T0 \Vdash (\forall x)\neg\neg\varphi(x)$ by 1

3        $F0 \Vdash \neg\neg(\forall x)\varphi(x)$ by 1

4        $T0 \Vdash \neg\neg\varphi(c)$ by 2

5        $T00 \Vdash \neg(\forall x)\varphi(x)$ by 3

6        $T00 \Vdash \neg\neg\varphi(c)$ by 2

7        $F0 \Vdash \neg\varphi(c)$ by 4

8        $F00 \Vdash (\forall x)\varphi(x)$ by 5

9        $F00 \Vdash \neg\varphi(c)$ by 6

10       $T01 \Vdash \varphi(c)$ by 7

11       $F000 \Vdash \varphi(c_1)$ by 8

FIGURE 64

It is not easy to see how to construct a frame counterexample from the initial stages of the CSIT. A direct analysis of the semantics shows that we should keep introducing new constants $c_1, c_2, \ldots$ and, while not forcing $\varphi(c_n)$ immediately, guarantee that each $\varphi(c_n)$ is forced in some extension. We can see the beginnings of this phenomena in the cycle generated by line 4 producing lines 7 and 10 on the one hand and in the cycle generated by line 5 producing lines 8 and 11 on the other.

Figure 65 is a simplified frame which gives a counterexample.

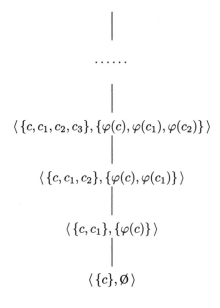

$\langle \{c, c_1, c_2, c_3\}, \{\varphi(c), \varphi(c_1), \varphi(c_2)\} \rangle$

$\langle \{c, c_1, c_2\}, \{\varphi(c), \varphi(c_1)\} \rangle$

$\langle \{c, c_1\}, \{\varphi(c)\} \rangle$

$\langle \{c\}, \emptyset \rangle$

FIGURE 65

We leave the verification that $\emptyset$ does not force $\forall x \neg\neg\varphi(x) \rightarrow \neg\neg\forall x\varphi(x)$ in the indicated frame as Exercise 15. We will, however, show that no finite frame can be a counterexample.

Proposition 5.8: $\forall x \neg\neg\varphi(x) \rightarrow \neg\neg\forall x\varphi(x)$ *is forced by every node p in every frame C with a finite partial ordering R.*

Proof: Let p, C and R be as in the proposition. To verify that $p \Vdash \forall x\neg\neg\varphi(x) \rightarrow \neg\neg\forall x\varphi(x)$ consider any $q \geq p$ such that $q \Vdash \forall x\neg\neg\varphi(x)$. We must show that $q \Vdash \neg\neg\forall x\varphi(x)$. By Lemma 2.13, this is equivalent to the assertion that, for every $r \geq q$, there is an $s \geq r$ such that $s \Vdash \forall x\varphi(x)$. Fix any $r \geq q$. As R is finite, there is a maximal extension s of r in R. Now by monotonicity, $s \Vdash \forall x\neg\neg\varphi(x)$. Thus, for any $c \in C(s)$, $s \Vdash \neg\neg\varphi(c)$. Applying Lemma 2.13 again, as well as the maximality of s, gives us that $s \Vdash \varphi(c)$. Thus (again by the maximality of s), $s \Vdash \forall x\varphi(x)$ as required. $\quad\square$

It is no accident that the sentence in Example 5.7 which has no finite counterexamples contains quantifiers. It is only for sentences with quantifiers that infinite frames are necessary to get counterexamples. Any sentence without quantifiers is either intuitionistically valid or has a finite frame counterexample. This fact supplies us with a decision procedure (albeit a crude one) for the intuitionistic validity of quantifier-free formulas.

Theorem 5.9 (Finite Model Property): *A quantifier-free sentence is forced in all frames if and only if it is forced in all finite frames.*

Proof: Consider any quantifier–free formula φ. We must show that if it is not forced by some $p \in R$ in a frame $\mathcal{C}$, then there is some finite frame $\mathcal{C}'$ in which it is not forced. Let X be the set of all subformulas of φ. (Recall Definition II.2.6 or Proposition II.3.8 which determine the subformulas of φ.) For p in R, define a class $[p]$ of elements of R which force the same elements of X as p:

$$[p] = \{q \in R \mid (\forall \psi \in X)(p \Vdash \psi \leftrightarrow q \Vdash \psi)\}.$$

Let R' be the set of all such $[p]$ for p in R. Now different classes $[p] \in R'$ correspond to different subsets of X. As X, the set of subformulas of φ, is finite, so is R'. Partially order R' by $[q] \leq [p]$ if every formula in X forced by q is forced by p. (Due to the definition of $[p]$ and $[q]$, this is the same as the requirement that every formula in X forced by some r in $[q]$ is also forced by some s in $[p]$.) Define a finite frame $\mathcal{C}'$ with R' as its partially ordered set by setting $A([p]) = A(p) \cap X$ and $C'([p])$ to be the set of constants appearing in $A([p])$. We claim that for all $p \in R$ and all ψ in X, $[p] \Vdash_{\mathcal{C}'} \psi$ if and only if $p \Vdash_{\mathcal{C}} \psi$. This claim clearly suffices to prove the theorem. We proceed to prove the claim by induction on formulas:

Atomic ψ: $A([p]) = A(p) \cap X$ says that if ψ is an atomic formula in X, then $[p] \Vdash_{\mathcal{C}'} \psi$ if and only if ψ is in $A(p) \cap X$, or equivalently, if and only if $p \Vdash \psi$.

Induction Step: Suppose θ and ψ are in X. Suppose, by induction, that for all $q \in R$, $q \Vdash_{\mathcal{C}} \theta$ if and only if $[q] \Vdash_{\mathcal{C}'} \theta$ and $q \Vdash_{\mathcal{C}} \psi$ if and only if $[q] \Vdash_{\mathcal{C}'} \psi$

(1) Disjunction: $p \Vdash_{\mathcal{C}} \theta \vee \psi \Leftrightarrow p \Vdash_{\mathcal{C}} \theta$ or $p \Vdash_{\mathcal{C}} \psi \Leftrightarrow [p] \Vdash_{\mathcal{C}'} \theta$ or $[p] \Vdash_{\mathcal{C}'} \psi$ (by induction) $\Leftrightarrow [p] \Vdash_{\mathcal{C}'} \theta \vee \psi$.

(2) Conjunction: $p \Vdash_{\mathcal{C}} \theta \wedge \psi \Leftrightarrow p \Vdash_{\mathcal{C}} \theta$ and $p \Vdash_{\mathcal{C}} \psi \Leftrightarrow [p] \Vdash_{\mathcal{C}'} \theta$ and $[p] \Vdash_{\mathcal{C}'} \psi$ (by induction) $\Leftrightarrow [p] \Vdash_{\mathcal{C}'} \theta \wedge \psi$.

(3) Implication: Suppose $[p] \Vdash_{\mathcal{C}'} \theta \to \psi$. We must show that $p \Vdash_{\mathcal{C}} \theta \to \psi$. If $q \geq p$ and $q \Vdash_{\mathcal{C}} \theta$, then by induction $[q] \Vdash_{\mathcal{C}'} \theta$, so by our assumption and the fact that $[q] \geq [p]$ follows from $q \geq p$, $[q] \Vdash_{\mathcal{C}'} \psi$. The induction hypothesis then says that $q \Vdash_{\mathcal{C}} \psi$ as required. Conversely, suppose $p \Vdash_{\mathcal{C}} \theta \to \psi$ and $\theta \to \psi$ is in X. We must prove that $[p] \Vdash_{\mathcal{C}'} \theta \to \psi$, that is, if $[q] \geq [p]$ and $[q] \Vdash_{\mathcal{C}'} \theta$, then $[q] \Vdash_{\mathcal{C}'} \psi$. Now as $\theta \to \psi$ is in X and $p \Vdash_{\mathcal{C}} \theta \to \psi$ by assumption, $[q] \geq [p]$ implies that $q \Vdash_{\mathcal{C}} \theta \to \psi$. By our assumption that $[q] \Vdash_{\mathcal{C}'} \theta$ and the induction hypothesis, $q \Vdash_{\mathcal{C}} \theta$. Thus $q \Vdash_{\mathcal{C}} \psi$ and again by induction, $[q] \Vdash_{\mathcal{C}'} \psi$, as required.

(4) Negation is similar to implication and the verification is left as Exercise 16. $\square$

Theorem 5.10: *We can effectively decide the intuitionistic validity of any quantifier–free sentence.*

Proof: We know by the properties of the CSIT expressed in the completeness theorem (Theorems 4.9 and 4.10) that if a given sentence φ is intuitionistically valid then the CSIT will give a (necessarily) finite tableau proof of φ. On the other hand, if φ is not valid then there is, by the finite model property (5.9), a finite frame counterexample. We can thus simultaneously search for a finite frame counterexample to φ and develop the CSIT for φ. We must eventually find either a finite counterexample to φ or an intuitionistic tableau proof that φ is intuitionistically valid. $\square$

The decision procedure embodied in the proof of Theorem 5.10 is not very satisfactory. It give us little information on how large the proof or counterexample must be nor on how long we must search before the required one shows up. All one can say is that, given a quantifier–free sentence φ, it suffices to consider all frames for the atomic formulas appearing in the given sentence which are of size at most that of the set of all subformulas of φ. With considerably more work it is possible to give a more explicit algorithm for generating a possible tableau proof of a quantifier–free φ with a better bound on the number of steps needed to produce either a proof or finite counterexample (see Nerode [1990, 4.2]). We only remark that the decision procedure is considerably more complicated than for classical logic. As we have noted (Theorem I.4.8), quantifier–free predicate logic is equivalent to propositional logic. The decision problem for satisfiability in classical propositional logic is the archetypal NP complete problem. For propositional intuitionistic logic, however, the decision problem is complete for polynomial space (Statman [1979, 5.3]).

Decidability in intuitionistic logic can be pushed a bit farther. In contrast to classical logic, intuitionistic validity for the class of prenex sentences is decidable. The above proof (or any other) for quantifier–free sentences can be extended (Exercise 17) to prenex sentences by applying the existence property (Theorem 2.21) and an intuitionistic version of the theorem on constants (Exercise 3.32). As one should expect, however, the validity problem for all of intuitionistic logic, like that for classical logic, is undecidable. Given the undecidability of the validity problem for classical logic (Corollary III.7.10), we can deduce it for intuitionistic logic by a validity preserving translation due to Gödel.

Definition 5.11: If A is an atomic formula, then $\neg\neg A$ is a *Gödel formula*. If φ and ψ are Gödel formulas then so are $\neg\varphi$, $\varphi \wedge \psi$ and $\forall x\varphi$.

Recall that, in classical logic, A and $\neg\neg A$ are equivalent and $\{\neg, \wedge, \forall\}$ is adequate. So for every formula φ, there is a Gödel formula φ° which is classically equivalent to φ. The decision problem for classical validity is thus reducible to deciding the validity of just the Gödel formulas. We now wish to show that a Gödel formula ψ is classically valid if and only if it is intuitionistically valid. The "if" direction is simply a special case of Theorem 2.6. We need to prove the converse for Gödel formulas.

Lemma 5.12: *If φ is a Gödel sentence and p is a forcing condition in a frame C, then either $p \Vdash \varphi$ or $(\exists q \geq p)(q \Vdash \neg\varphi)$. In particular, if p does not force φ then one of the following cases holds:*

(1) *If $\varphi = \neg\psi$, then $\exists q \geq p(q \Vdash \psi)$.*

(2) *If $\varphi = \psi \wedge \theta$, then $\exists q \geq p(q \Vdash \neg\psi$ or $q \Vdash \neg\theta)$.*

(3) *If $\varphi = \forall x\psi$, then $(\exists q \geq p)(\exists c \in C(q))(q \Vdash \neg\psi(c))$.*

Proof: We proceed by induction on φ. The base case is that φ is $\neg\neg A$ for some atomic sentence A. In this case, if p does not force φ, there is, by the definition of forcing a negation (Definition 2.2 (iii)), a $q \geq p$ which forces $\neg A$ as required in (1). Note that, in general, if $\varphi = \neg\psi$ and $q \Vdash \psi$ then $q \Vdash \neg\neg\psi$ (i.e., $q \Vdash \neg\varphi$) by the intuitionistic validity of $\psi \to \neg\neg\psi$ (Example 2.15).

If φ is $\neg\psi$ and p does not force $\neg\psi$, then, as in the base case, there is a $q \geq p$ which forces ψ and so $\neg\neg\psi$.

If φ is $\psi \wedge \theta$ and p does not force φ, then either p does not force ψ or p does not force θ. Thus by induction there is a $q \geq p$ which forces $\neg\psi$ or $\neg\theta$. (Again, note that by the basic facts about forcing this implies that $q \Vdash \neg(\psi \wedge \theta)$.)

If φ is $\forall x\psi(x)$ and p does not force φ, then, by the definition of forcing, there is an $r \geq p$ and a $c \in C(r)$ such that r does not force $\psi(c)$. The induction hypothesis then tells us that there is a $q \geq r$ such that $q \Vdash \neg\psi(c)$, as required. Of course any such q forces $\neg\varphi$ as well. $\square$

Definition 5.13: A sequence $\langle p_i \rangle$ of forcing conditions in a frame C is a *generic sequence extending p* if $p_0 = p$ and the following conditions hold:

(i) For every i, $p_i \leq p_{i+1}$.

(ii) For every atomic sentence ψ there is an i such that p_i forces ψ or p_i forces $\neg\psi$.

(iii) For every Gödel sentence φ, there is an i such that $p_i \Vdash \varphi$ or p_{i+1} is a condition $q \geq p_i$ as required for φ in the appropriate clause of Lemma 5.12.

Lemma 5.14: *For every forcing condition p in a frame C, there is a generic sequence extending p.*

Proof: Let $\{\varphi_i \mid i \in N\}$ be an enumeration of all the Gödel sentences. We define a sequence $\langle p_i \mid i \in \mathbb{N} \rangle$ by induction. Set $p_0 = p$. If $p_i \Vdash \varphi_i$ and φ_i is $\neg\neg\psi$ for some atomic sentence ψ, then, by the definition of forcing, there is a $q \geq p_i$ which forces ψ. Let p_{i+1} be such a q. If $p_i \Vdash \varphi_i$ but φ_i is not of this form, let $p_{i+1} = p_i$. If p_i does not force φ_i, let p_{i+1} be a condition extending p_i as guaranteed in the clause of Lemma 5.12 corresponding to φ_i. (So, in particular, if φ_i is $\neg\neg\psi$ for an atomic ψ and p_i does not force φ_i, then $p_{i+1} \Vdash \neg\psi$.) It is clear that the sequence p_i satisfies the definition of a generic sequence extending p. □

Theorem 5.15: *For every Gödel sentence φ, φ is classically valid if and only if φ is intuitionistically valid.*

Proof: As we remarked, if φ is intuitionistically valid it is classically valid (Theorem 2.6). To prove the converse suppose that φ is not intuitionistically valid, i.e., there is a frame $\mathcal{C}$ and a forcing condition p such that p does not force φ. We must build a classical model $\mathcal{A}$ in which φ is false. By Lemma 5.14 we can choose an enumeration of Gödel sentences in which $\varphi_0 = \varphi$ and a generic sequence $\langle p_i | i \in \mathbb{N} \rangle$ in $\mathcal{C}$ extending p. Note that, by our assumption that p does not force φ and the definition of a generic sequence, $p_1 \Vdash \neg\varphi$. We let the universe A of our required classical model $\mathcal{A}$ be $\cup\{C(p_i) | i \in \mathbb{N}\}$. We define the relations of $\mathcal{A}$ by $\mathcal{A} \vDash R(\vec{c})$ iff $\exists i (p_i \Vdash R(\vec{c}))$.

We claim that, for every Gödel sentence φ, $\mathcal{A} \vDash \varphi \Leftrightarrow \exists i (p_i \Vdash \varphi)$. As $p_1 \Vdash \neg\varphi$ (and $\neg\varphi$ is a Gödel sentence), this gives us the desired classical model of $\neg\varphi$. The proof is by induction on the formation of the sentence φ. (Note that we specify the levels of formation of formulas in the order given in Definition 5.11 so that $\forall x \psi(x)$ follows $\neg\psi(c)$ for each constant c.)

The base case is that φ is $\neg\neg\psi$ for some atomic sentence ψ. As p_i is a generic sequence, there is an i such that p_i forces ψ or p forces $\neg\psi$. In the former case, $\mathcal{A}$ satisfies ψ (and so $\neg\neg\psi$) by definition. In the latter case, no p_j can force ψ. So by the definition of $\mathcal{A}$, ψ is false in $\mathcal{A}$.

If φ is $\psi \wedge \theta$, then $\mathcal{A} \vDash \varphi \Leftrightarrow \mathcal{A} \vDash \psi$ and $\mathcal{A} \vDash \theta$. By induction this condition holds iff there are j and k such that $p_j \Vdash \psi$ and $p_k \Vdash \theta$. As the p_i form an increasing sequence of forcing conditions, this is equivalent to the existence of an i such that $p_i \Vdash \psi \wedge \theta$, i.e., one such that $p_i \Vdash \varphi$.

If φ is $\neg\psi$, then $\mathcal{A} \vDash \varphi \Leftrightarrow \mathcal{A} \nvDash \psi$. By induction this is true if and only if there is no j such that $p_j \Vdash \psi$. By the definition of generic sequence, this last condition is equivalent to the existence of an i such that $p_i \Vdash \neg\psi$, i.e., $p_i \Vdash \varphi$.

If φ is $\forall x \psi(x)$ suppose first that $\mathcal{A} \vDash \varphi$. If there is no p_i forcing φ, then by the definition of a generic sequence, there is an i and a c such that $p_i \Vdash \neg\psi(c)$. Then, by induction, $\mathcal{A} \vDash \neg\psi(c)$ for the desired contradiction. For the converse, suppose that there is an i such that $p_i \Vdash \forall x \psi(x)$. Then, for every $c \in A$, there is a $j \geq i$ such that $c \in C(p_j)$ and $p_j \Vdash \psi(c)$. By induction, we then know that $\mathcal{A} \vDash \psi(c)$ for every $c \in A$, i.e., $\mathcal{A} \vDash \varphi$ as required. □

Theorem 5.16: *The validity problem for intuitionistic logic is undecidable.*

Proof: If we could effectively decide if any given sentence ψ is intuitionistically valid then we could decide if any sentence φ is classically valid by checking if φ° (as defined in 5.11) is intuitionistically valid. This would contradict the undecidability of validity for classical predicate logic (Corollary III.7.10). □

Corollary 5.17: *Not every sentence is intuitionistically equivalent to a sentence in prenex form.*

Proof: If every sentence had an intuitionistically equivalent prenex form, a systematic search for a tableau proof of such an equivalence would find one. The decision procedure for the validity of prenex sentences (Exercise 17) would then supply one for all sentences. □

Exercises

Below is a list (1–12) of classically valid sentences θ which are not intuitionistically valid. For each one, start a tableau with $F\varnothing \Vdash \theta$ and develop it enough to produce a frame in which θ is not forced. In each example assume that φ and ψ are atomic with either no free variables (1–8) or only x free (9–14).

1. $(\varphi \vee \neg\varphi)$

2. $(\neg\neg\varphi \rightarrow \varphi)$

3. $\neg(\varphi \wedge \psi) \rightarrow (\neg\varphi \vee \neg\psi)$

4. $\neg\varphi \vee \neg\neg\varphi$

5. $(\neg\varphi \rightarrow \neg\psi) \rightarrow (\psi \rightarrow \varphi)$

6. $(\varphi \rightarrow \psi) \rightarrow (\neg\varphi \vee \psi)$

7. $\neg(\forall x)\varphi(x) \rightarrow (\exists x)\neg\varphi(x)$

8. $(\forall x)\neg\neg\varphi(x) \rightarrow \neg\neg(\forall x)\varphi(x)$

9. $(\forall x)(\varphi \vee \psi(x)) \rightarrow (\varphi \vee (\forall x)\psi(x))$

10. $((\varphi \rightarrow (\exists x)\psi(x)) \rightarrow (\exists x)(\varphi \rightarrow \psi(x))$

11. $(\forall x)\varphi(x) \rightarrow \psi) \rightarrow (\exists x)(\varphi(x) \rightarrow \psi(x))$

12. $((\forall x)(\varphi(x) \vee \neg\varphi(x)) \wedge \neg\neg(\exists x)\varphi(x)) \rightarrow (\exists x)\varphi(x)$

13. Show that $\varnothing$ does not force $(\neg\varphi \rightarrow \neg\psi) \rightarrow (\psi \rightarrow \varphi)$ in the frame produced in Example 5.5.

14. Show that $(\varphi \rightarrow \psi) \rightarrow (\psi \rightarrow \varphi)$ is forced by every node in every frame $\mathcal{C}$ in which the ordering on R is a linear ordering.

15. Show that $\emptyset$ does not force $\forall x \neg\neg\varphi(x) \rightarrow \neg\neg\forall x\varphi(x)$ in the frame produced in Example 5.7.

16. Complete the proof of Theorem 5.9 by verifying the negation case of the induction step.

17. Prove that intuitionistic validity is decidable for the class of prenex sentences. Hint: Successively apply Exercises 2.9 and 3.32 to reduce deciding the validity of a sentence in prenex form to deciding the validity of many quantifier–free sentences.

6. A Comparative Guide

In this section we supply a comparative guide to the similarities and differences between modal and intuitionistic logic. We use the presentation of classical predicate logic in Chapter II as a common starting point.

6.1 Syntax

The syntax for classical logic is presented in II.2.1 – II.2.6. For technical reasons we assume in both modal and intuitionistic logic that our language $\mathcal{L}$ has at least one constant symbol but no function symbols other than constants. We also view $\leftrightarrow$ as a defined symbol

$$\varphi \leftrightarrow \psi \quad \text{means} \quad \varphi \rightarrow \psi \wedge \psi \rightarrow \varphi.$$

Of course, modal logic adds two new operators $\Box$ and $\Diamond$ which can be viewed syntactically as unary propositional connectives. Their semantics, however, is really second order.

6.2 Semantics

The semantics for classical logic is presented in II.4 by interpreting the language $\mathcal{L}$ in a structure $\mathcal{A}$ for $\mathcal{L}$. Both modal and intuitionistic logic use systems of structures called *frames* and a new relation, *forcing* ($\Vdash$), to define their semantics. In both cases, a frame consists of a set (W or R) of *possible worlds*, a binary relation S on this set and a function assigning a classical structure $\mathcal{C}(p)$, with domain $C(p)$, to each world p. We let $\mathcal{L}(q)$ be the expansion of $\mathcal{L}$ gotten by adding a constant for each $c \in C(q)$. In modal logic (IV.2.2), the binary relation S can be arbitrary while in intuitionistic logic it is always assumed to be a partial ordering $\leq$. In both cases we assume that the domains of the structures are monotonic: If pSq ($p \leq q$), then $C(p) \subseteq C(q)$. In intuitionistic logic we also require that the sets of true atomic facts be monotonic: If $p \leq q$, φ is an atomic sentence and $C(p) \vDash \varphi$ then $C(q) \vDash \varphi$.

The crucial definition (IV.2.2 and V.2.2) is now that of the *forcing relation* between possible worlds p and sentences φ : $p \Vdash \varphi$. For atomic formulas and for the inductive cases corresponding to $\vee$, $\wedge$ and $\exists$, the definitions for both logics are the same "natural" extension of the classical definition of truth (II.4.3):

> if φ is atomic $p \Vdash \varphi \Leftrightarrow C(p) \vDash \varphi$; $p \Vdash \varphi \vee \psi \Leftrightarrow p \Vdash \varphi$ or $p \Vdash \psi$; $p \Vdash \varphi \wedge \psi \Leftrightarrow p \Vdash \varphi$ and $p \Vdash \psi$; $p \Vdash \exists x \varphi(x) \Leftrightarrow$ there is a c in $\mathcal{L}(p)$ such that $p \Vdash \varphi(c)$. Of course, modal logic also has extra clauses giving the semantics of $\square$ and $\Diamond$.

The crucial differences between modal and intuitionistic logic, however, are in the treatment of $\neg$, $\rightarrow$ and $\forall$. In modal logic, the interpretations continue to follow the "natural" classical style, e.g., $p \Vdash \neg \varphi \Leftrightarrow p$ does not force φ. The situation is quite different in intuitionistic logic. Here $p \Vdash \neg \varphi$ means that no $q \geq p$ forces φ;

> $p \Vdash \varphi \rightarrow \psi \quad \Leftrightarrow \quad$ every $q \geq p$ which forces φ also forces ψ;
>
> $p \Vdash \forall x \varphi(x) \quad \Leftrightarrow \quad$ for every $q \geq p$ and every $c \in \mathcal{L}(q)$, $q \Vdash \varphi(c)$.

Once the forcing relation has been defined, the notions corresponding to classical truth (II.4.3) and validity (II.4.4) are then the same for both modal and intuitionistic logic: φ is *forced in a frame* C iff $p \Vdash \varphi$ for every world p of C; φ is *valid* if it is forced in every frame.

It is worth pointing out that the "unusual" intuitionistic interpretations for $\neg$, $\rightarrow$ and $\forall$ all have a modal flavor. For example, the definitions of $p \Vdash \neg \varphi$ and $p \Vdash \forall x \varphi(x)$ in intuitionistic logic seems much like those of $p \Vdash \square \neg \varphi$ and $p \Vdash \square \forall x \varphi(x)$, respectively, in modal logic. Such ideas form the basis of Gödel's validity–preserving translation of intuitionistic logic into the modal logic S4. (See Gödel [1933, 2.3] and the introductory notes in Gödel [1986, 2.3] vol. 1, 269–299.)

6.3 Tableaux

The *atomic tableaux* are designed to mirror the semantics of the various connectives and quantifiers. Thus it is no surprise that the modal tableaux (IV.3.1) for the atomic sentences and the classical connectives are essentially the same as the classical ones of II.6. For example, the classical tableau beginning with $T(\varphi \wedge \psi)$ adjoins both $T\varphi$ and $T\psi$; the modal one beginning $Tp \Vdash \varphi \wedge \psi$ adjoins both $Tp \Vdash \varphi$ and $Tp \Vdash \psi$.

In addition to the classical concern of using only a new constant as a witness for a true existential sentence (or counterexample for a false universal one), the analysis of the quantifiers in modal logic has to reflect the correct relation among the domains. Thus, for example, given an entry $Tp \Vdash \exists x \varphi(x)$ on a path in a tableau, we can introduce a new c and add the assertion that $Tp \Vdash \varphi(c)$ to the path. On the other hand, given an entry $Tp \Vdash \forall x \varphi(x)$, we can expand it by adjoining $Tp \Vdash \varphi(c)$ for any appropriate c, i.e., any c appearing in any forcing assertion about a world q such that p is accessible from q (and so any one in the intended domain $C(p)$). The modal operators introduce the possibility of creating new worlds. For example, given $Tp \Vdash \Diamond \varphi$ we introduce a new world q such that pSq and $q \Vdash \varphi$. We must also interpret $\Box$ to conform to the semantics and the accessibility relation: given $Tp \Vdash \Box \varphi$, we can adjoin $Tq \Vdash \varphi$ for any appropriate q, i.e., any q such that pSq.

In intuitionistic logic, however, we must make changes that correspond to the new semantics for atomic sentences and the connectives $\neg$ and $\rightarrow$ as well as the quantifiers. The monotonicity assumption for atomic facts tells us to adjoin $Tq \Vdash \varphi$ when given $Tp \Vdash \varphi$ and pSq for any atomic φ. The analysis of the "unusual" connectives involves either the creation of new worlds or looking ahead to future worlds that have already been defined, as is required in the modal analysis of $\Box$. Given $Tp \Vdash \neg \varphi$, for example, we can adjoin $Fq \Vdash \varphi$ for any appropriate q, i.e., any q such that $p \leq q$. On the other hand, given $Fp \Vdash \neg \varphi$ we can introduce a new world q such that $p \leq q$ and adjoin the assertion $Tq \Vdash \varphi$. The analysis for intuitionistic implication is similar: If $Tp \Vdash \varphi \rightarrow \psi$, $p \leq q$ and $Tq \Vdash \varphi$ all appear on a path P, we can adjoin $Tq \Vdash \psi$ to P; if $Fp \Vdash \varphi \rightarrow \psi$ appears, we can introduce a new q and adjoin pSq, $Tq \Vdash \varphi$ and $Fq \Vdash \psi$. The tableaux for the quantifiers are constructed as you would expect: Given $Tp \Vdash \exists x \varphi(x)$, we can introduce a new c and adjoin the assertion that $Tp \Vdash \varphi(c)$; given $Tp \Vdash \forall x \varphi(x)$ we can adjoin $Tq \Vdash \varphi(c)$ for any appropriate q and c, i.e., any $q \geq p$ and any c in the world q.

Once the distinct semantics have been built into the atomic tableaux, the definitions of *tableaux* in modal logic (IV.3.2) and intuitionistic logic (V.3.2) are both essentially the same as in classical logic (II.6.1). The only changes are to the notions of "new" and "appropriate" so they fit the intended semantics and notation. We should point out that it is quite possible to put the ordering relations $p \leq q$ directly on the tableaux in the intuitionistic case as we did in the modal case. We did not do that only because the construction of the ordering is so restricted in the intuitionistic case that it can easily be read off from the rest of the tableau. Thus if one is working solely within intuitionistic logic, it is simpler to stick closer to the classical format and not clutter the tableaux with the ordering facts. The generality of the binary relations constructed in the modal tableaux makes it simpler to record them directly.

In any case, the notions of a *tableau proof* (II.6.2, IV.3.3, V.3.3) are essentially the same in all three logics: A tableau beginning with an assertion of the falsity of φ (or of φ's being forced) in which every path contains a contradiction (the assertion of both the truth and falsity of some sentence) is a proof of φ.

6.4 Soundness and Completeness

The soundness (II.7.2, IV.4.3, V.4.3) and completeness (II.7.7, IV.4.13, V.4.10) theorems are formally the same in all three logics: If φ is provable, it is valid; if φ is valid it is provable. Moreover, at least in outline, the proofs of soundness and completeness are the same as well. For the proof of soundness, the crucial lemma is that if a structure or frame agrees with the root of a tableau, then there is a path through the tableau such that the structure or frame agrees with every entry on the path (II.7.1, IV.4.2, V.4.2). Of course the straightforward notion of agreement used in classical logic ($\mathcal{A}$ agrees with $T\varphi$ iff $\mathcal{A} \vDash \varphi$) must be generalized to deal with frames and forcing but the notions are formally identical in modal (IV.4.1) and intuitionistic logics (V.4.1). The proof of the basic lemma in each case is an induction on the construction of the tableau. The modal and intuitionistic arguments again differ only where the atomic tableaux are distinct. Each then follows the appropriate semantics. Given this basic lemma the proof of soundness is straightforward and identical in all three settings: If one has a proof of φ, it begins with an assertion that φ is false and every path on the tableau includes a contradiction. As no structure or frame can agree with a contradiction, none can agree with the root, i.e., φ is valid.

The completeness theorem is proved by defining a systematic way of producing a tableau with a given root that develops every entry: the *Complete Systematic (Modal or Intuitionistic) Tableau* (CST, II.6.9: CSMT, IV.4.8; CSIT, V.4.6). The modal construction also defines the possible worlds and the accessibility relation among them in the construction of the CSMT as these are built into the atomic tableau. In the intuitionistic case, the restriction of the accessibility relation to a partial ordering allows us to specify in advance both the set of possible worlds and the ordering by choosing any sufficiently complex ordering. We choose the set of finite sequences of natural numbers ordered by extension. The idea that every entry has been developed is expressed by the notions of a *reduced entry* and a *finished tableau* (II.6.7, IV.4.6) in the classical and modal developments. Our proof for intuitionistic logic avoids an explicit definition by building the required properties into the construction of the CSIT and the proof of Lemma V.4.8. (The notion of a *properly developed entry* in Definition V.4.6 replaces that of a reduced entry in Definition IV.4.6 and the notion of a finished tableau is replaced by the properties listed in Lemma V.4.8.) It would be just as reasonable, although somewhat longer, to extract the appropriate definitions for intuitionistic logic and present them as for modal logic in IV.4.6. If, as suggested above, the atomic intuitionistic tableaux are also modified to put the ordering relations directly on the tableaux, the definition of the CSIT could be given as for the CSMT with the corresponding adjustments for the quantifiers and the "unusual" connectives.

The completeness theorem is now proved in all three logics by considering the complete systematic tableau beginning with the assertion of the falsity of φ or of φ's being forced at p. If this tableau is not a proof of φ, it has a noncontradictory path P. We now use the entries on P to build a structure or frame $\mathcal{C}$ which agrees with every entry on P (II.7.3, IV.4.11, V.4.9). In the classical case, φ is not true in $\mathcal{C}$ while in the modal and intuitionistic cases, p does not force φ in $\mathcal{C}$. Thus in each case φ is not valid, as required.

For classical logic, we define a single structure $\mathcal{C}$. Its domain C consists of all terms appearing in assertions on P. The structure itself is defined by letting $\mathcal{C} \vDash \varphi$ for each atomic sentence φ iff $T\varphi$ appears on P. In both the modal and intuitionistic constructions, we must build an entire frame $\mathcal{C}$. The set of possible worlds for $\mathcal{C}$ is the set of p appearing in assertions on P. In the modal proof, pSq is true in $\mathcal{C}$ iff it appears on P. The accessibility relation in the intuitionistic case is determined in advance as extension for the sequences p, q on P. However, had we adjusted the intuitionistic atomic tableaux to directly record the ordering facts, we would define the same ordering by taking the facts appearing on P.

The domains $C(p)$ of the structures $\mathcal{C}(p)$ needed to define the frame $\mathcal{C}$ are the same in both cases because our monotonicity assumptions on them are the same: $C(p)$ consists of the constants of $\mathcal{L}$ as well as all those appearing in any forcing assertion involving a q such that p is accessible from (greater than) q. The definitions of the structures $\mathcal{C}(p)$ on these domains $C(p)$ differ because of the monotonicity assumption on atomic facts in intuitionistic logic. In the modal case, in analogy with classical logic, we define an atomic sentence φ to be true in $\mathcal{C}(p)$ iff $Tp \Vdash \varphi$ appears on P. In the intuitionistic construction, $\mathcal{C}(p) \vDash \varphi$ iff $Tq \Vdash \varphi$ appears on P for any $q \leq p$.

For all three logics, the argument that the frame we have defined agrees with every entry on P is a straightforward induction on the complexity of sentences φ appearing on P. This induction concludes the proof of the completeness theorem.

6.5 Logical Consequences

In both classical and modal logic we defined the notion of a sentence φ being a logical consequence of a set Σ of sentences. Classically, $\Sigma \vDash \varphi$ iff φ is true in every structure $\mathcal{C}$ in which every $\psi \in \Sigma$ is true (II.4.4). In modal logic, we said that φ is a logical consequence of Σ iff φ is forced in every frame $\mathcal{C}$ which forces every $\psi \in \Sigma$ (IV.2.8). For each logic, we then introduced a notion of a tableau proof from Σ. The only modification needed to standard tableau proofs was that we could now add on $T\psi$ ($Tp \Vdash \psi$) to any path P on a tableau for any $\psi \in \Sigma$ (and any p occurring on P). (See II.6.1 and IV.3.11 for the classical and modal cases, respectively.) We then defined the complete systematic tableau from premises (II.6.9, IV.4.14) and proved the appropriate soundness and completeness theorems for deductions from premises (II.7.2, IV.4.13; II.7.7, IV.4.15).

Although we have not explicitly made the corresponding generalizations for intuitionistic logic, they can be modeled routinely on the ones for modal logic. We leave this development to the exercises.

6.6 Decidability and Hilbert–Style Systems

In V.5 we proved the decidability of propositional intuitionistic logic (V.5.10) and the undecidability of full predicate intuitionistic logic. A tableau–based proof for the decidability of propositional modal logic can be found in §7 of Chapter 8 of Fitting [1983, 4.4]. As modal predicate logic includes classical logic, i.e., a sentence φ without modal operators is classically valid iff it is modally valid (Exercise IV.1.10), modal logic is *a foritori* undecidable by Church's theorem for predicate logic (III.8.10).

In IV.6 we give a Hilbert–style system of axioms and rules for modal logic. Describing a corresponding system for intuitionistic logic requires some care. As $\neg$ and $\rightarrow$ no longer form an adequate set of connectives, one must explicitly deal with each of the propositional connectives. Similarly, one must explicitly give axioms and rules for $\exists$. Kleene [1952, 2.3] in §19 supplies such a system for intuitionistic logic which has the advantage of being extendable to a proof system for classical logic by simply adding on the axiom scheme $\neg\neg\varphi \rightarrow \varphi$ or $\varphi \vee \neg\varphi$.

Exercises

We outline a treatment of intuitionistic logic more closely modeled on our treatment of modal logic, as suggested above.

1. Reformulate the intuitionistic atomic tableaux so that the ordering relations appear explicitly. As a sample, the atomic tableau $(F\rightarrow)$ becomes the following:

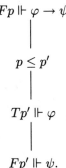

$$Fp \Vdash \varphi \rightarrow \psi$$
$$|$$
$$p \leq p'$$
$$|$$
$$Tp' \Vdash \varphi$$
$$|$$
$$Fp' \Vdash \psi.$$

2. Describe the corresponding notions of "new" and "appropriate" for this system of intuitionistic tableaux and prove the soundness theorem.

3. Define the appropriate notions of a reduced entry and a finished tableau for this system.

4. Define a corresponding notion of a CSIT and prove the completeness theorem.

5. Define the notion of logical consequence for intuitionistic logic as was done for modal logic.

6. Describe the modifications needed in Exercises 2–4 to develop general intuitionistic tableaux from a set of premises and the corresponding notion of a CSIT from premises.

7. Describe the changes needed in Exercises 2–4 to prove the soundness and completeness theorems for deductions from premises in intuitionistic logic.

Suggestions for Further Reading

The description of a Hilbert–style system of axioms and rules in the style of I.7 and II.8 for intuitionistic logic requires some care. As $\neg$ and $\rightarrow$ no longer form an adequate set of connectives, one must explicitly deal with each of the propositional connectives. Similarly, one must explicitly give axioms and rules for $\exists$. Kleene [1952, 2.3] in §19 supplies such a system for intuitionistic logic which has the advantage of being extendible to a proof system for classical logic by simplying adding on the axiom scheme $\neg\neg\varphi \rightarrow \varphi$. Kleene then gives a careful development of logic and recursion theory which tells which theorems have been intuitionistically proved and which not.

In addition to his validity–preserving translation of classical into intuitionistic logic, Gödel [1933, 2.3] also supplied one from intuitionistic propositional logic into an equivalent of the propositional part of the modal logic S4, as described in IV.6. See the introductory note of Gödel [1933, 2.3] in Gödel [1986, 2.3] vol. 1, 296–299, for an explanation of the translation and references for proofs of both the propositional and predicate versions of the translation.

Fitting [1983, 4.1] supplies many variants of the tableau method. For an elementary exposition of intuitionistic logic using natural deduction and algebraic methods, see van Dalen [1983, 3.2]. For a philosophical introduction to intuitionism, see Dummett [1977, 4.1]. For constructive mathematics, see Bishop and Bridges [1985, 4.1], Richman and Bridges [1987, 4.1] and Troelstra and van Dalen [1988, 4.1]. For more advanced topics in the metamathematics of constructive mathematics, see Beeson [1985, 4.1].

For intuitionistic type theory, see Martin–Löf [1984, 4.1]; for its application to a computer system constructive theorem prover, see Constable [1986, 5.6]. For a combination of modal and intuitionistic logics relevant to computer science concerns, see Nerode and Wijesekera [1992, 5.6].

Finally, the "classic" basic text on intuitionism is Heyting [1971, 4.2].

Appendix A
An Historical Overview

We begin with an analogy between the history of calculus and the history of mathematical logic.

1. Calculus

In Athens in the Golden Age of Classical Greece, Plato (c. 428–348 B.C.E.) made geometry a prerequisite for entrance to his philosophical academy, for a master of geometry was a master of correct and exact reasoning (see Thomas [1939, 1.1]). Euclid (c. 300 B.C.E.) emphasized the importance of the axiomatic method, which proceeds by deduction from axioms. (From this point of view, logic is the study of deduction.) Euclid and Archimedes (287–212 B.C.E.) and their predecessors showed how to use synthetic geometry to calculate areas and volumes of many simple figures and solids. They also showed how to solve, using geometry, many simple mechanics, hydrostatics and geometrical optics problems.

In the twenty centuries separating Euclid and Archimedes from Leibniz (1640–1710) and Newton (1640–1722), increasingly difficult problems of calculating areas and volumes and of mechanics and hydrostatics were solved one by one by special methods from Euclidean and Archimedian geometry. Each physical or mathematical advance made by the use of this geometric method required the extraordinary mathematical talent of a Galileo (1564–1642) or a Huygens (1629–1695). Things changed radically after Descartes's discovery, published as the appendix to his *Discours de la Methode* [1637, 2.3], that geometric problems could be translated into equivalent algebraic problems. Geometric methods were replaced by algebraic computations.

There were already strong hints of symbolic-algebraic methods of integration and differentiation in the work of Fermat (1601-1665) and in the works of Newton's teacher Barrow (1630–1677) and Leibniz's predecessor Cavalieri (1598–1647). The symbolic methods of differentiation and integration discovered by Newton and Leibniz made it possible for later generations to use the ordinary calculus to develop science and engineering without being mathematical geniuses. These methods are still the basis for understanding, modeling, simulating, designing, and developing physical and engineering systems. Both Leibniz and Newton were aware of the breadth and importance of these discoveries for our understanding of the physical world. Calculus was well-named in that it reduced many problems of mathematics and physics to largely algebraic and symbolic calculation.

2. Logic

Aristotle's (384–322 B.C.E.) theory of syllogistic also dates from the Golden Age of ancient Greece and the disputations of the Platonic Academy (see Plato's *Euthydemus*). It is found in the collection of his works, called by ancient editors the *Organon*. It consists of the *Catagoriae, De Interpretatione, Analytica Priora, Analytica Posteriora, Topica*, and *De Sophisticis Elenchis*. We discuss only the elements of syllogistic from the *Analytica Priora*.

This was the first successful calculus of reasoning with "all" and "some". In modern terminology, we translate "all" and "some" to the quantifiers "for all" and "there exists". To the modern eye, syllogistic looks quaint with its language of noun expressions, terms universal and particular. But it has solid motivation. For Aristotle, the world consisted of objects c which may or may not possess a given property P. In our modern notation the letter P is called a *predicate symbol*. A particular interpretation of P is given by specifying a nonempty domain C of objects and a set of these objects to be denoted by P. Then, with x a variable ranging over C, $P(x)$ is a logical formula read "x has the property P". Also, if c is a name for a particular object, then $P(c)$ is a logical formula read "c possesses property P".

Now an object may simultaneously have many different properties. An object c may be simultaneously hard, round, red, lighter than water, in this room, on the floor, in the southeast corner. In the late seventeenth century, Leibniz thought that objects should be uniquely characterized by knowing all their properties. Leibniz called the idea the principle of identity of indiscernibles.

Deducing that an object c has one property from the fact that c has some other properties is the kind of question that Aristotle's syllogistic addressed. This use of logic is especially characteristic of the classificatory biology of Linneus (1707-1788) with its genus, species, and varieties. His system is a direct intellectual descendent of Aristotle's biology. Aristotle is often, for this reason, called the "father of biology". His conception of biology and his conception of syllogistic are intimately related. Syllogistic was taught in the standard college curriculum as part of the Trivium of Logic, Rhetoric and Grammar from the middle ages to 1900, and still persists in many Catholic colleges undiminished and unchanged as the main training in logical reasoning, even though outdated by modern mathematical logic.

Syllogistic's chief function was as a check that the quantifiers "for all x" and "there exists an x" were being used correctly in arguments. The aim was to eliminate incorrect arguments which use principles that look like

logically true principles but are not. We follow Aristotle's follower, Chryssipus (d. 207 B.C.E.), in writing syllogistic entirely as rules of inference. An
example of a valid mode of syllogism in this style is the rule of inference
called "mode Barbara".

> From   "All P are Q"
>
> and   "All Q are R"
>
> infer   "All P are R".

In contemporary logical notation we write $P(x)$ for "x is a P", $Q(x)$ for
"x is a Q", $R(x)$ for "x is an R", $(\forall x)$ for "for all x", $(\exists x)$ for "there exists
an x" and "$\rightarrow$" for "implies". Translated to a modern rule of inference,
mode Barbara becomes

> From $(\forall x)(P(x) \rightarrow Q(x))$
>
> and $(\forall x)(Q(x) \rightarrow R(x))$
>
> infer $(\forall x)(P(x) \rightarrow R(x))$.

In this notation P, Q, R are called unary predicate (or relation) symbols.

An invalid Aristotelian mode is

> From   "Some P are Q"
>
> and   "Some Q are R"
>
> infer   "Some P are R".

In modern notation, using $\wedge$ for "and" this "rule" would be translated as
follows:

> From $(\exists x)(P(x) \wedge Q(x))$
>
> and $(\exists x)(Q(x) \wedge R(x))$
>
> infer $(\exists x)(P(x) \wedge R(x))$.

(Give a counterexample to this mode!)

Syllogistic treated four forms of propositions, called categorical propositions, whose medieval names were A, E, I and O:

> A)   "Every P is a Q"
>
> E)   "No P is a Q"
>
> I)   "Some P is a Q"
>
> O)   "Some P is not a Q".

The valid modes were given mnemonic names based on the sequence of
propositions. Thus the valid mode listed above which has the sequence
AAA as the two hypotheses and the conclusion was called "Barbara".

Consider the sequence EAE which had the mnemonic name "Celarent":

> From   "No Q is R"
>
> and   "Every P is Q"
>
> infer   "No P is R".

The modern notation for "not" is $\neg$, so this mode could be translated to modern notation as

> From $\neg(\exists x)(Q(x) \wedge R(x))$
>
> and $(\forall x)(P(x) \rightarrow Q(x))$
>
> infer $\neg(\exists x)(P(x) \wedge R(x))$.

Exercise

Reconstruct the syllogisms from the vowels of the medieval mnemonics, which represent the two premises and the conclusion of the syllogism and then translate them into modern notation. 1. Darii 2. Ferio 3. Cesare 4. Camestres 5. Festino 6. Baroco 7. Darapti 8. Disamis 9. Datisi 10. Felapton 11. Bocardo 12. Ferison 13. Bramantip 14.Camenes 15. Dimaris 16. Fesapo 17. Fresison. (Warning: Aristotle assumes that predicates are nonvacuous. This means that, with modern conventions, the validity of 7, 10, 13 and 16 require that such assumptions be made explicitly.)

Aristotle gave systematic derivations of some of these modes from others. His work was the first axiomatic system for deriving some logical truths from others. In addition, he constructed counterexamples for false modes and rules for negations (contradictories). Aristotle also gave the first systematic discussion of modal logics (discussed in IV) based on the connectives $\Diamond p$, "it is possible that p", and $\Box p$, "it is necessary that p". These connectives, unlike those mentioned above, are not "truth functional". That is, the truth or falsity of p does not determine the truth or falsity of $\Box p$ or $\Diamond p$: p may be possible and false or p may be possible and true. (For a more detailed analysis of the work of the ancient Greek logicians, see Lukasiewicz [1957, 2.2], Bochenski [1951, 2.2] and Mates [1961, 2.2].)

Even though syllogistic was useful in clarifying philosophical discussions, it had no substantial influence on mathematicians. Mathematicians reasoned very tightly even before the time of Aristotle. Indeed, their work was traditionally the model of exact reasoning. However, their reasoning was not fully described by syllogistic. What was missing? With the benefit of hindsight, a short answer is: the rest of propositional logic and the notion of a relation with many arguments.

Developing the work of Philo of Megara (c. 300 B.C.E.), the Stoic Chryssipus of Soli introduced implication (now written $\rightarrow$), conjunction (now written $\wedge$), and exclusive disjunction ("P or Q but not both"). Nowadays, instead of the last mentioned connective we use inclusive disjunction, "P or Q or both", written $P \vee Q$. Chryssipus understood the characteristic property of propositional logic: the truth or falsity of compound propositions built from these connectives is determined by knowing the truth or falsity of the parts.

As for relations, Euclidean geometry is based on the relation of incidence $R(x, y)$, meaning that x is incident with y, where x, y are points, lines, or planes. Thus a point may be incident with (lie on) a line; a line may be incident with (lie on) a plane. What Aristotle missed was the basic building-block character of binary relations $R(x, y)$ such as "x is less than y" and of ternary relations $S(x, y, z)$ such as "z is the sum of x and y", etc. He used only unary relations or predicates $P(x)$ such as "x is red". He generally coded relations $S(x, y)$ such as "x is the grandfather of y" as the property $S_y(x)$, x has the property of being the grandfather of y.

There was no real defect in Aristotle's theory of quantifiers. He rather lacked explicit propositional connectives and relations of multiple arguments in his logical formulas. This lacuna was really only remedied by authors of the late nineteenth century such as C. S. Peirce (1839–1914), E. Schröder (1841–1902) and G. Frege (1848–1925).

3. Leibniz's Dream

Leibniz was the first to assert that a complete formal logic describing reasoning might exist (see Parkinson [1965, 2.2]). He was convinced that he could develop a language for, and calculus of, reasoning which would be as important as the Newton-Leibniz calculus of derivatives and integrals. He called his new subjects the "lingua characteristica" (universal language) and the "calculus ratiocinator" (calculus of reasoning). The mind "will be freed from having to think directly of things themselves, and yet everything will turn out successfully" (Parkinson [1965, 2.2] p. 105). He hoped that these new subjects would expand the capacity of the mind to reason by reducing to symbolic calculation much of the labor required in finding out how to draw a desired conclusion from given premises and how to check the correctness of proposed deductions. To repeat, he thought there should be a calculus of reasoning for dealing with deductions from propositions about the world analogous to the Leibniz-Newton calculus for dealing with solving numerical equations governing the world.

Leibniz knew something of the calculus of classes and the logic of propositions but his work in this area was basically unknown till its publication in Couturat [1903, 2.3]. So his ideas were prescient but not directly influential. Here is Leibniz's dream as expressed by the greatest logician of the twentieth century, Kurt Gödel (1906–1978), in "Russell's mathematical logic" (Gödel [1944, 2.3]).

" ... if we are to believe his words he had developed this calculus of reasoning to a large extent but was waiting with its publication till the seed could fall on fertile ground. He even went so far as to estimate the time which would be necessary for his calculus to be developed by a few select scientists to such an extent 'that humanity would have a new kind of an instrument increasing powers of reason far more than any optical instrument has ever aided the power of vision'. The time he names is five years, and he claims that his method is not any more difficult to learn than the mathematical philosophy of his time. Furthermore, he has said repeatedly that, even in the rudimentary state to which he had developed the theory himself, it was responsible for all his mathematical discoveries, which, one should expect, even Poincaré would acknowledge as a sufficient proof of its fecundity."

(Poincaré (1854–1912) was the most famous French mathematician in 1900. He did not think formal logic was a useful basis for mathematics, but rather, like Cantor (1845–1918), thought mathematics was grounded directly in intuition.)

The algebra of classes and the logic of propositions were rediscovered and then developed much more completely in the mid-nineteenth century by De Morgan (1806–1871) [1847, 2.3] and Boole (1815–1864) [1859, 2.3].

4. Nineteenth Century Logic

Augustus De Morgan [1847, 2.3] extended Syllogistic, introduced propositional connectives and their laws and presented the rudiments of the theory of relations. His friend Boole was an expert in the area of symbolic algebraic methods for solving mathematical problems. Boole's texts on differential and difference equations (reprinted as Boole [1959, 2.3] and [1970, 2.3]) are highly algebraic and algorithmic. They are based on formal algorithms using polynomials in the differential operator D and difference operator $\Delta(f) = f(x+1) - f(x)$ and their formal inverses to solve differential and difference equations, respectively.

Now let us see, in modern notation, some of what Boole did in logic. Suppose that p, q are propositions and consider the following propositional connectives:

Disjunction, written $(p \vee q)$ and read "p or q"

Conjunction, written $(p \wedge q)$ and read "p and q"

Negation, written $(\neg p)$ and read "not p".

The interpretations of these connectives were supposed to be

$(p \vee q)$ is true if and only if at least one of p, q is true

$(p \wedge q)$ is true if and only if p is true and q is true too

$\neg p$ is true if and only if p is not true

To analyze these notions with greater precision, we use the definitions for propositional logic emerging from the work of Wittgenstein (1889-1951) (see [1974, 2.3]) and Post (1897–1954) (see Post [1921, 2.3]) as given in Definition I.2.1: If we are given a stock of primitive (atomic) propositional letters p, q, r ... , then we have the following (inductive) definition of *proposition*:

(i)   Atomic letters are propositions.

(ii) If α, β are propositions, then $(\alpha \vee \beta)$, $(\alpha \wedge \beta)$, $(\neg \alpha)$ are propositions.

(iii) A string of symbols is a proposition if and only if it can be obtained by starting with propositional letters and repeatedly applying instances of (ii).

We next define a *truth assignment* $\mathcal{A}$ to be any mapping of atomic propositions p to a value $\mathcal{A}(p)$ which is either 1 (for true) or 0 (for false) (Definition I.3.1). (Such an assignment $\mathcal{A}$ corresponds to the assignment of values $\mathcal{A}(p)$ to propositional letters p when beginning to fill out one line of a truth table.) Each assignment $\mathcal{A}$ has a unique extension to a *truth valuation* $\mathcal{V}$ which is a map from the set of all propositions to $\{0, 1\}$. The valuation is determined by following the inductive clauses of the above definition and replacing the connectives by the corresponding *Boolean operations* on $\{0,1\}$. These operations are given by the usual tables:

$$0 \vee 0 = 0 \qquad\qquad 0 \vee 1 = 1 \vee 0 = 1 \vee 1 = 1$$

$$1 \wedge 1 = 1 \qquad\qquad 0 \wedge 1 = 1 \wedge 0 = 0 \wedge 0 = 0$$

$$\neg 1 = 0 \qquad\qquad \neg 1 = 0.$$

The inductive definition of the valuation $\mathcal{V}$ corresponding to a given assignment $\mathcal{A}$ is then given as in Definition I.3.2:

(i) $\mathcal{V}(p) = \mathcal{A}(p)$ if p is a propositional letter

(ii) For all propositions α, β,

$$\mathcal{V}(\alpha \vee \beta) = \mathcal{V}(\alpha) \vee \mathcal{V}(\beta), \quad \mathcal{V}(\alpha \wedge \beta) = \mathcal{V}(\alpha) \wedge \mathcal{V}(\beta), \quad \mathcal{V}(\neg \alpha) = \neg \mathcal{V}(\alpha).$$

($\mathcal{V}$ gives the values obtained by filling out the line of the truth table determined by assignment $\mathcal{A}$ as described in I.2.) Thus a proposition can be seen as a two–valued function of the values of its propositional letters. This is what is meant by saying the connectives are truth functional modes of sentence composition. It is Chryssipus's idea in contemporary form. With this view, a proposition is called a *tautology* (or *valid*) if it has truth value 1 under all truth valuations, that is, as a propositional function it is the constant function with value 1. These are the logical truths of propositional logic.

In ordinary algebra over the real or complex numbers, the algebra of formal polynomials and the algebra of polynomial functions are virtually indistinguishable (isomorphic, in modern language) and they were identified with one another in Boole's time. Following the lead from ordinary polynomials, it is natural that Boole should then identify the meaning of a proposition with the induced two–valued propositional function. Under this identification, the logical operations "and", "or", "not" correspond to operations on the propositional functions. This makes the set of propositional functions into an algebraic structure where two propositions are equal if they denote the same propositional function. That is, declare two propositions α and β equal, $\alpha = \beta$, if $\mathcal{V}(\alpha) = \mathcal{V}(\beta)$ for all truth valuations $\mathcal{V}$. (This means that α and β have the same truth table.) For example, $\neg(\alpha \wedge \beta) = (\neg\alpha \vee \neg\beta)$. This equality is one of the laws of Boolean algebra.

Boole also discovered that the algebra of classes and the algebra of propositional functions satisfy the same laws. To explain his insight about the relation between propositional and class calculus, we temporarily adopt a naive nineteenth century point of view due to Frege (which we treat more extensively below).

For every property $P(x)$ we introduce a new abstract object A called a *class*. We define $x \in A$, read x is a member of A, to mean $P(x)$ is true. The *Axiom of Comprehension* states that every property P determines a class A. The *Axiom of Extensionality* says that it determines exactly one class: if A and B are classes, then $A = B$ if, for all x, $x \in A$ if and only if $x \in B$. Thus for any property P, we designate the unique class determined by P by writing $A = \{x \mid P(x)\}$.

Boole's algebra of classes is based on the operations

> *Union*: $A \cup B = \{x \mid x \in A \vee x \in B\}$
>
> *Intersection*: $A \cap B = \{x \in A \wedge x \in B\}$
>
> *Complement*: $-A = \{x \mid x \notin A\}$

Each of these exist by the Comprehension Axiom and are uniquely determined by Extensionality. The laws of the algebra of classes then follow from the laws for propositional functions. For instance, since for each x, the propositional functions determined by $\neg(P(x) \wedge Q(x))$ and $\neg P(x) \vee \neg Q(x)$ coincide, the Axiom of Extensionality implies that $-(A \cap B) = (-A) \cup (-B)$.

It was Boole who discovered truth tables for propositions (§I.2) and the disjunctive normal form (Example I.2.9 and Exercise I.4.9) in the guise of "Boole's law of expansion". It was he who carried out systematic propositional logical reasoning by pure algebra and whose work led to the algebra of logic (Bibliography 3.9). It was Boole who figured out that universal and existential quantifiers were instances of greatest lower and least upper bounds respectively and introduced algebraic notation for them. These concepts were formalized by Schröder (1841–1902) [1877, 2.3] and developed extensively in Schröder [1890–1905, 2.3]. But Boole did not have a good theory of quantifiers as such. He did not improve on Aristotle's treatment of quantifiers except to note that quantifiers were also operations on propositional functions. Schröder also developed the concept of a model of a set of sentences. His work was later taken up by Löwenheim (1887–1940) [1915, 2.3].

5. Nineteenth Century Foundations of Mathematics

The nineteenth century also saw concerted efforts to put a firm foundation under mathematics with precise definitions, axioms and constructions. This effort was motivated by difficulties within the body of mathematics. There was confusion and controversy when definitions were not precise. There were difficulties in distinguishing functions from their symbolic representations. There were difficulties in distinguishing continuity from uniform continuity, convergence from uniform convergence, convergence from forms of summability, differentiability from continuity, etc. What is an integer? a rational? a real? a function? a continuous function? Even Cauchy, one of the great early proponents of the rigorization of analysis, fell prey to such problems giving a "proof" in the early 1820's that the sum of an infinite series of continuous functions is continuous. In 1826, Abel pointed out a counterexample. (See Kitcher [1983, 1.2] p. 254 for a precise description of the "proof" and its inherent error.) What then were to be the foundations of mathematics?

In Euclid's *Elements*, synthetic geometry was taken as the logical foundation for mathematics. Every bit of mathematics was to be reduced to geometry. In the seventeenth century, Descartes reduced synthetic geometry to analytic geometry, and therefore to algebra and numbers, by introducing coordinates. This led, in the nineteenth century, to a great effort to define complex mathematical structures in terms of simpler ones. In this period we find definitions of:

  integers in terms of pairs of nonnegative integers;

  rationals in terms of pairs of integers;

  reals in terms of sets or sequences of rationals;

  complex numbers as pairs of reals.

(Some of the important contributors to this work include Weierstrass (1815–1897) in 1858 (see DuGac [1973, 1.2]), Dedekind (1831–1916) in his calculus course in 1862–63 (see DuGac [1976, 1.2] and the 1872 paper in [1963, 2.3]), Heine (1821–1881) [1872, 1.2] and Cantor [1872, 1.2]. To learn more about this trend see Birkhoff [1973, 1.1] and Struik [1969, 1.1].)

This process of reduction was referred to as the "Weierstrassian arithmetization of analysis". Finally, the nonnegative integers were axiomatized as a set with an element 0 (or 1), and a successor function $S(x)$ (adding 1) by Dedekind (1872 paper in [1963, 2.3]) and Peano (1858–1932) [1894–1908, 2.3] and [1990, 2.3].

To formally and precisely carry out this reduction, two gaps needed to be filled.

Gap I. Logic. All properties of all systems are deduced by logical inferences. What are the axioms and rules of inference of logic?

Gap II. Set Theory. Each system is defined in terms of a simpler system using set constructions such as forming the unordered pair consisting of two sets, the set of all subsets of a given set, the union of a set of sets or the set of all elements of a given set which possess a given property. Also, one has to postulate that some sets exist at the beginning to get going. What sets need to be postulated? What set constructions are needed? What are the needed axioms of set theory?

The situation is perhaps epitomized by the work of Peano. Combining these nineteenth century developments which build more complicated systems from simpler ones, Peano (see [1973, 2.3]) gave the first systematic development of then contemporary mathematics along the lines sketched above. He introduced a systematic notation for both the set theory constructions and the logical connectives and quantifiers, little different from that used today. Nowhere in his work, however, is there a list of either the set theory construction axioms needed or the rules of inference for the logic used. They are simply assumed as already known to the working mathematician. It is worth remarking that Peano's motivation was not to formalize everything completely, dotting i's and crossing t's. Rather, he intended to create a notation which makes thinking about and communicating mathematics entirely independent of the mathematician's native language, be it English, Greek, French, or German. All mathematics would all be written exactly the same way by all speakers of all languages. In this he was quite successful. He was even more ambitious. He also developed a universal scientific language and was involved with the development of what was intended to become a universal everyday language. This was not very popular. It is easier to change the habits of a few mathematicians than the habits of everyman.

Gap I was filled by Frege [1879, 2.3] when he gave the first formal treatment of predicate logic including both quantifiers and relations and propositional connectives. Combining the Aristotelian treatment of quantifiers and the Boolean treatment of propositional connectives and relation symbols R of any number of arguments, he formulated the notion of a logical formula built up from atomic formulas of the form $R(x_1, \ldots, x_n)$ by the propositional connectives such as "and" ($\wedge$), "or" ($\vee$), "not" ($\neg$) and the quantifiers such as "for all x_i" ($\forall x_i$) and "there exists an x_i" ($\exists x_i$).

The precise definition of the syntax of predicate logic in modern notation is given in §II.2. A simplified version can be based on that of the logical connectives of propositional logic given above augmented by a stock of *variables* x, y, z, x_1, y_1 $\ldots$, the *quantifiers* $\forall$ and $\exists$ and, for each n, a stock of relation symbols R, S, $\ldots$ (which are referred to as *n-ary relation symbols*):

(i) If R is an n-ary relation symbol and $x_1, \ldots, x_n$ are variables then $R(x_1, \ldots, x_n)$ is a *formula*. These are called the *atomic formulas*.

(ii) If φ and ψ are formulas and x is a variable, then $(\varphi \vee \psi)$, $(\varphi \wedge \psi)$, $(\neg\varphi)$, $(\forall x)\varphi$ and $(\exists x)\varphi$ are also formulas.

Formulas in algebra represent ways of expressing complicated relations in terms of the basic or atomic relations of the particular algebra considered. So too, formulas of predicate logic intuitively define "relations" between the variables occurring in the formula. (Actually, between the *free variables* of the formula: An occurrence of variable x in a formula φ is called *free* if that occurrence is not within any subformula of φ of the form $(\forall x)\psi$, or $(\exists x)\psi$. A *sentence* is a formula with no occurrences of any free variable.)

Frege [1879, 2.3] gave, also for the first time, a set of axioms and rules of inference, and the definition of a proof as a finite sequence of sentences, each of which is either an axiom or follows from previous sentences in the proof by a direct application of a rule of inference. In [1879, 2.3] he thought of quantifiers as ranging over all objects. He did not have the concept of a model in which a set or domain is given and variables range over that given set. The introduction of the current basis for the semantics of predicate logic was left to Boole's successor in the algebra of logic, Schröder.

It should be mentioned that C. S. Peirce [1870] also independently developed the deductive structure of predicate logic, but this was not well-known at the time. Finally, let us mention that Aristotle's syllogistic is already encompassed in what is called the two-quantifier fragment of predicate logic (without function symbols), for which there is a decision method for logical validity which we give in the text as Exercise II.7.10.

Frege addressed gap II as well. He presented the first fully formal foundation for logic and mathematics, defining the positive integers directly, in Frege [1903, 2.3] (see also [1953, 2.3] and [1977, 2.3]). His treatment of logic was impeccable. We may think of the treatment of classes as based on the intuitively appealing pair of nonlogical axioms given earlier, taking *membership*, $\in$, and *identity*, $=$, as primitive notions:

Axiom of Extensionality: For all classes A, B, if for all x, $x \in A$ if and only if $x \in B$, then $A = B$.

Axiom of Comprehension: For any property $P(x)$, there is a class A such that for all x, $x \in A$ if and only if $P(x)$.

The class A asserted to exist in the axiom of comprehension is unique by the axiom of extensionality and we write $A = \{x \mid P(x)\}$.

Frege's intention was that any property which can be formulated in the formal language is acceptable as P. The class A is regarded as an object too, eligible to be a member of any class. With these axioms, one can immediately deduce the existence of all the usual mathematical objects and operations. As an example, we write out the definitions to which the comprehension axiom can be applied to produce the set constructions which the experienced reader will recognize as the basis of modern axiomatic set theory. They are not needed as separate axioms in Frege's system.

Null class: There is a class $\emptyset = \{x \mid \neg(x = x)\}$

Unordered Pairs: Given classes A, B, there is a class
$$\{A, B\} = \{x \mid x = A \text{ or } x = B\}.$$

Union Axiom: Given a class A, there is a class

$$\cup A = \{x \mid (\exists y)(y \in A \;\wedge\; x \in y\}.$$

Subset Construction (Aussonderung) Axiom: Given a class A and any property $P(x)$, there is a class $B = \{x \mid x \in A \wedge P(x)\}$.

Replacement Axiom: Given any single-valued property $Q(x,y)$, i.e. for every x there is exactly one y such that $Q(x,y)$, and any class A, there is a class $B = \{y \mid (\exists x)(x \in A \wedge Q(x,y)\}$.

Infinity Axiom: There is a least inductive class ω. (A class A is *inductive* if $\emptyset \in A$ and, for every x, $x \in A \rightarrow x \cup \{x\} \in A$.) Note that there is at least one inductive class, the class $\{x \mid x = x\}$ of all classes and that the intersection of a class of inductive classes is again inductive. The least inductive class is then given by comprehension as

$$\{x \mid (\forall y)(y \text{ is inductive } \rightarrow x \in y)\}.$$

(This class ω is the one von Neumann (1903–1957) introduced in [1923, 2.3] as an axiom asserting the existence of the set of integers. It is not, however, the specific definition of the integers that Frege used. Von Neumann redesigned Frege's original definition so that it would extend naturally to the transfinite ordinals. His definition would probably have been equally acceptable to Frege had he wanted to cover transfinite ordinals as well as cardinals.)

So Frege's system was seductively simple. Simply write down a description of your favorite set. The axiom of comprehension immediately guarantees its existence and the axiom of extensionality makes it unique. One can see why Frege was pleased. But, alas, as volume II of his *Grundgesetze* [1903, 2.3] was in preparation, Russell's (1872–1970) paradox appeared:

Let $P(x)$ be the property $\neg(x \in x)$. Let $A = \{x \mid P(x)\}$. Apply this definition of A to A itself to get $A \in A$ if and only if $\neg(A \in A)$, an immediate contradiction.

Frege's structure for foundations of mathematics collapsed into contradiction just as his masterwork was finished. The unrestricted naive Comprehension Axiom had to be abandoned. However, the instances of comprehension listed above, together with the Axiom of Extensionality, form the basis of modern set theory (see list 3.3 in the bibliography).

The 1890's saw the magnificent achievement of Cantor's theory of cardinal and ordinal numbers (Cantor [1957, 2.3]). Russell's paradox cast a temporary shadow on this achievement as it appeared to be based on constructing classes by using instances of the axiom of comprehension. Was Cantor's theory inherently inconsistent? Already in [1885, 2.3], in his review of Frege's [1884, 2.3], Cantor himself described Frege's unlimited comprehension as being based on an inconsistent property. He suggested that his theory used only consistent properties to construct classes. But Cantor gave no hint how we were to tell consistent from inconsistent properties. This did not bother him, since he considered his theory of classes to be based on the same kind of mathematical intuition as that for the natural numbers and thus securely grounded. He was not concerned with axiomatic theories based on formal logic but rather on mathematics based on direct intuition and construction.

6. Twentieth Century Foundations of Mathematics

According to the traditional account of the foundational developments at the beginning of the twentieth century the paradoxes of Russell and others gave rise to three distinct lines of thought. One was called logicism. This was Whitehead (1861–1947) and Russell's [1910–13, 2.3] attempt to rescue both Frege and Cantor by a comprehensive reduction of mathematics to logic by restricting Frege's methods to the theory of types. It was a mathematically awkward theory.

The second line of thought was called formalism. It was the great German mathematician Hilbert's (1862–1943) attempt to restore the set-theoretic paradise that Cantor had created by giving "finitary proofs" of the consistency of formal systems sufficient to encompass branches of contemporary mathematics such as number theory, analysis or set theory. This is mathematical syntax, quite divorced from any intended meaning of the terms. The sentences of mathematics are regarded simply as strings of letters. The axioms are strings, rules of inference are rules for deriving strings from strings and it becomes a combinatorial question whether these chess-like rules lead to a contradiction such as $0 = 1$.

The third line, intuitionism, is that of the great Dutch founder of modern topology, L. E. J. Brouwer (1881–1966) (see Brouwer [1975, 2.3]). (We discuss intuitionism in Chapter V.) He thought that the source of mathematical certitude was in the intuition. In this Cantor and Poincaré would have agreed but Brouwer also concluded that the only meaningful proofs are those for which we have an explicit construction of what the proved theorem asserts to exist. For him, proofs are simply such constructions and theorems simply express their success. So steps in proofs are construction rules. He emphasized constructions as the basic building blocks of mathematics and, in this respect, his views are a precursor of those of computer science, though this was not his intent. He disapproved of creating fixed formal systems of the type Hilbert introduced. He thought that new rules of construction may turn up at any time and that a fixed system limits the mathematician to a fixed set of constructions. He relied, in general, like Cantor did for transfinite ordinals, on an immediate capacity of the educated human intuition to recognize correctness of mathematical principles.

This quick sketch of the influence of the paradoxes on logic and foundations does not do justice to the subject as a continuation of nineteenth century mathematical thought. In his [1899 and 1902, 2.3] *Foundations of Geometry*, Hilbert was the first to give a complete set of axioms for synthetic Euclidean geometry. He examined their consistency and independence quite thoroughly. The framework for finding enough axioms on which to base a subject, and then proving their consistency, is already present there. His later proposals for proving the consistency of number theory, analysis, and set theory are a natural extension of this work. Hilbert himself talked mostly in terms of direct finitistic proofs of the consistency of more and more complicated systems. Many of his followers tried to reduce the consistency of complicated systems, like analysis, to that of apparently simpler systems, like number theory. In this, they were following the model of the construction of the real numbers from rationals, and they, in turn, from the integers. This plan was doomed by Gödel's incompleteness theorem [1931, 2.3].

At that time, the archetypal model for proving consistency was the reduction of the consistency of non-Euclidean geometry to the consistency of Euclidean geometry by interpreting the axioms of non-Euclidean geometry within Euclidean geometry. Hilbert himself gave a consistency proof for Euclidean geometry by interpreting it into analysis. He then hoped to prove the consistency of analysis by interpreting it in a finitary system of arithmetic in such a way that its consistency would be provable in the finitary system. The finitary system itself was to be seen to be consistent by clear and direct intuition.

As for Brouwer, he indicates that his penchant for constructive methods was a propensity from youth, not a consequence of doubt raised by paradoxes. He had the splendid example before him of the nineteenth century algebraist Kronecker (1823–1891), who insisted on explicit algorithms for everything in algebraic geometry and number theory. Kronecker's favorite aphorism was "God created the integers; man the rest". Kronecker meant that every mathematical object can be constructed from the integers and the integers are given directly by intuition. Kronecker gave a constructive treatment of extant algebra and Brouwer extended the constructive method to the analysis and topology of his time. In 1967 E. Bishop (1928–1983) (see Bishop and Bridges [1985, 4.2]) extended the constructive treatment to modern analysis as we know it.

There were other powerful currents coming in with the tide of set-theoretic mathematics initiated by Cantor. Zermelo (1871–1953) [1904, 2.3] published a famous proof that every set can be well-ordered; that is, every nonempty set can be ordered so that every nonempty subset has a least member. The latter was a principle used, without proof from other principles, by Cantor. The proof of Zermelo was attacked on two grounds. First, Zermelo had used (quite consciously) an essentially new axiom of set theory that is now called the axiom of choice:

Axiom of Choice: Given any set of nonempty disjoint sets, there is a set which has exactly one element in common with each.

Second, he used the Cantorian ordinals, which had no rigorous definition at the time. He later gave a second proof without assuming the Cantorian ordinals. Then he revisited set theory in order to lay out its axioms, one of which had clearly been missed earlier. This was the set theory of Zermelo [1908, 2.3]. Zermelo set theory is a collection of informal set construction axioms with no formalization of the underlying logic. These axioms were inadequate to construct large ordinals and cardinals. The axiom of replacement, which we have already discussed informally, filled this gap, and was supplied by Fraenkel (1989–1965) [1922, 2.3] and Skolem (1887–1963) [1922, 2.3]. A satisfactory treatment of ordinals and cardinals and transfinite induction was finally supplied within Zermelo-Fraenkel by von Neumann (1903–1957) [1923, 2.3] and [1925, 2.3] (see van Heijenoort [1967, 2.1]).

Finally, Zermelo–Fraenkel–Skolem set theory emerged the clear winner in the contest for the foundations of twentieth century mathematics. We remark that in the last mathematical axiom to fall into place, the axiom of replacement, the formal use of logic and the formal presentation of set theory come together, a clear indication that both elements are necessary to attain precision in the foundations of mathematics. What this axiom says is that if $\varphi(x, y)$ is a formula of set theory (with parameters) such that for any x there is at most one y such that $\varphi(x, y)$, then for any set A, there is a set B consisting of all those y for which there is an x in A such that $\varphi(x, y)$. Rephrased, the axiom says that the image of a set, under a single–valued relation defined by a formula, is a set. Here the notion of logical formula, $\varphi(x, y)$, is essential.

7. Early Twentieth Century Logic

Now back to pure logic. Post [1921, 2.3] following Whitehead and Russell's *Principia Mathematica* [1910-13, 2.3] gave a definition of formal provability for propositional logic and proved the basic theorems justifying his proof procedure:

Soundness (Theorem I.5.1): Every proposition with a proof is true in all truth valuations.

Completeness (Theorem I.5.3): Every proposition true in all truth valuations has a proof.

The development of predicate calculus to an equivalent point took somewhat longer.

In the 1890's, Schröder had already cleared up the idea of an interpretation or structure for predicate logic. A *structure* consisted of a nonempty set, the domain, together with a relation on the set corresponding to each relation symbol in the language, and a function on the set corresponding to each function symbol in the language. Quantifiers range over the specified domain. (See §II.4.) In a structure it was taken for granted that it makes sense to ask which sentences are true. A logically valid sentence is one true in all domains for all interpretations of all relation symbols, i.e. in all structures for the language.

Löwenheim [1915, 2.3] proved, using Schröder's ideas and notations, that for any sentence S of predicate logic true in some structure with domain D, there exists a countable subset D' of D such that when a structure is formed by restricting relations in D to D', S is true in D'. This result shows that the real numbers, which are uncountable, cannot be characterized by a single sentence of predicate logic. Skolem [1922, 2.3] simplified the proof and extended the theorem from one to a countable number of sentences (see Theorem II.7.7). He observed that, since set theory expressed in predicate logic is a countable set of sentences, there is a model of set theory (i.e., a structure for the language in which all the axioms are true) with a countable domain even though set theory proves that uncountable sets exist. This is called Skolem's paradox although it is not actually a paradox (see Skolem [1922, 2.3], Kleene [1952, 3.1] and, for a particularly good discussion of the "paradox", Fraenkel and Bar-Hillel [1958, 3.3]).

Skolem observed that every sentence is equisatisfiable with a so-called prenex sentence, i.e., one with all the quantifiers in front followed by a quantifier-free formula (see §II.9). (*Equisatisfiable* means one sentence has a model if and only if the other does. Neither he nor Löwenheim gave proof rules.) To see what they did, let us look at the case of one prenex sentence S of the form $(\forall x)(\exists y)\varphi(x, y)$. Suppose S is true in the domain D. Since S is true in D, for every $x \in D$ we can choose a y such that $\varphi(x, y)$. We call this element $y(x)$ and so define a function y from D to D. Let x_0 be any element of D. The desired subset D' can now be taken to be $\{x_0,\ y(x_0),\ y(y(x_0)),\ \ldots\}$. This procedure emphasizes that function symbols and names for individual elements of a domain are useful. So we include in our language for predicate logic a stock of primitive *n–ary function symbols*, $n = 1, 2, 3, \ldots$, and a set of *individual constant symbols*, prospective names for elements of D. We then define the set of *terms* as in §II.2 as follows:

    (i)   All variables and constant symbols are terms.

    (ii) If f is an n–ary function symbol and $t_1, \ldots, t_n$ are terms, then $f(t_1, \ldots, t_n)$ is also a term.

We then extend the class of predicate logic formulas by allowing $R(t_1, \ldots, t_n)$ as an atomic formula for any n–ary relation symbol R and any terms $t_1, \ldots, t_n$. In effect, constructions in the Löwenheim-Skolem style (as above) make sets of terms into structures.

Gödel [1930, 2.3] is usually given credit for the first proof of the completeness theorem for predicate logic (Theorem II.7.8): Every predicate logic sentence true in all structures has a predicate logic proof. Henkin's [1949, 3.4] proof of this theorem (see also Chang and Keisler [1973, 3.4]), which gives a direct construction of a model of a consistent theory, is now one of the basic facts of model theory. This subject has its origins in the early work of Skolem and Löwenheim but its real development begins later with the work of Tarski and his school (see list 3.4 in the bibliography).

Herbrand (1908–1931) [1930, 2.3] had all the ingredients of a proof of the completeness theorem. He associated with each predicate logic sentence $\neg\varphi$ an infinite sequence ψ_n of propositional logic sentences and showed that $\neg\varphi$ is provable if and only if there is an n such that $\psi_1 \vee \ldots \vee \psi_n$ is a tautology. Thus, if $\neg\varphi$ is not provable, there is, for each n, a propositional logic valuation making $\neg\psi_1 \wedge \ldots \wedge \neg\psi_n$ true. His work also shows how to get, from what we would call a model of all of these conjunctions, a model of $\neg\varphi$ and so prove the completeness theorem. What Herbrand refused to do was to use a nonconstructive argument (such as the compactness theorem) to produce, from the individual truth valuations for each finite conjunction, a single structure and valuation that would satisfy them all and so make φ false. Herbrand was aware of how "easily" this could be done. However, he regarded the notions and procedures as being inadmissible metamathematics.

Let us briefly describe, from our point of view, how Herbrand's constructions proceed in one special case: the nonprovability of $\neg\forall x \exists y \varphi(x, y)$ (and so the satisfiability of $\forall x \exists y \varphi(x, y)$). (See II.10 for more details and somewhat greater generality.) Herbrand used the set of ground terms (terms without variables) to create the needed sequence of propositions. We also use them as the domain of the desired model. These sets of terms are now called *Herbrand universes*.

We continue with the notation introduced above in the discussion of the Skolem-Löwenheim theorem. Introduce a constant c to denote the element x_0 of D and a function symbol f to denote $y(x)$ in an extended language. Then the model described above could alternately be described as the Herbrand universe consisting of the set of ground terms $\{c, f(c), f(f(c)), \ldots\}$. The n–ary relation symbols R occurring in φ would then denote the set of all n–tuples of ground terms $(t_1, \ldots, t_n)$ such that $R(t_1, \ldots, t_n)$ is true in the structure D described above. Thus, regarding each atomic sentence $R(t_1, \ldots, t_n)$ as a propositional letter, we have a truth valuation of propositional logic which assigns truth when $R(t_1, \ldots, t_n)$ is true in the original structure and false otherwise.

This hints that the predicate logic problem we started with (of building a model of $\forall x \exists y \varphi(x, y)$) can be replaced by a propositional logic problem about truth valuations of atomic propositions in the Herbrand universes. Namely, there is a structure in which $(\forall x)(\exists y)\varphi(x, y)$ is true if and only if there is a propositional truth valuation of the (infinite) set of quantifier–free sentences:

$$\psi_1 : \varphi(c, f(c))$$
$$\psi_2 : \varphi(f(c), f(f(c)))$$
$$\psi_3 : \varphi(f(f(c)), f(f(f(c))))$$

$$\cdots\cdots$$

making all of these propositional logic sentences true at once. The compactness theorem of propositional logic (Theorem I.6.13) says that there is a truth valuation $\mathcal{V}$ making an infinite sequence $\{\psi_n\}$ of propositional logic sentences all true at once if and only if there is, for each n, a truth valuation $\mathcal{V}_n$ making $\psi_1, \ldots, \psi_n$ all true at once. By this theorem, there is a structure with $(\forall x)(\exists y)\varphi(x, y)$, or equivalently $(\forall x)\varphi(x, f(x))$, true if and only if, for all n, there is a propositional logic valuation making $\psi_1 \wedge \ldots \wedge \psi_n$ true. This is the semantic version of Herbrand's theorem.

Herbrand refused to use nonconstructive methods and so did not prove the completeness theorem: As the nonprovability of $\neg\varphi$ implies the existence of a model of φ, there is a proof procedure which generates all sentences valid in all structures. It was his very insistence on constructivity, however, which has made his work so important. It was Herbrand's method rather than Gödel's, particularly his reduction of provability in predicate logic to propositional logic, which was the inspiration for, and the original basis of, the automation of classical logical inference; this automation has led to such advances as PROLOG, expert systems and intelligent databases.

8. Deduction and Computation

Hilbert was an exponent of the formal axiomatic method. He gave the first complete set of axioms for Euclidean geometry and promoted an abstract point view of many branches of mathematics. In the 1920's, he took such a view of the logic of mathematics itself. He began the study of formal systems, each defined by a set of axioms and a set of rules of inference, as a branch of mathematics called metamathematics (see Kleene (1909–) [1952, 3.2]). In particular, he proposed the project of finding a mathematical proof that formal systems such as that of Whitehead and Russell or Zermelo-Fraenkel set theory are consistent, that is, $0 = 1$ is not derivable.

Hilbert wanted to analyze proofs in such systems in such a way as to be able to give a finitary (i.e., sufficiently elementary so as to be universally acceptable) proof that no contradiction could arise. One approach typical of later followers of his school is to try to find, for each such formal system, a property P such that

(i) P holds of every axiom.

(ii) Whenever P holds of the premises of a rule of inference, it also holds of the conclusion.

(iii) P does not hold of $0 = 1$.

Their expectation was that such a proof would proceed by induction on the lengths of proofs in the formal system. Moreover, the proofs of (i)–(iii) must be "finitary".

Hilbert's textbook on logic, written with Ackermann (Hilbert and Ackermann [1928, 2.3]), singled out predicate logic for study and clearly emphasized this point of view on consistency proofs. His students and followers did give some consistency proofs for simple formal systems. This enterprise gave rise to proof theory as a modern discipline (see list 3.5 in the bibliography).

The purpose of Hilbert's program was to give a convincing proof that formal mathematics as we know it is consistent and so save us permanently from paradoxes like Russell's. This purpose was largely abandoned after Gödel's discovery of his incompleteness theorems [1931, 2.3]. After the proof of the incompleteness theorem, Hilbert still thought a sharpening of his notion of finitary proof might get around the problem it presented (see Hilbert and Bernays [1934 and 1939, 2.3]). However, one of the forms of Gödel's theorem is that mathematical theories which are "sufficiently rich", such as set theory or number theory, do not contain the means to prove their own consistency unless they are themselves inconsistent. Since these systems generally allow us to formalize all known convincing elementary arguments, one cannot expect to find a consistency proof for such rich systems except by using systems which are stronger in some appreciable way. This has been the trend in proof theory for the last sixty years.

The hypothesis that a theory is "sufficiently rich" is nowadays conventionally taken to mean that the deductive power of the theory has to be sufficiently powerful to simulate the steps of the computation of any algorithm. It was the formalization of a mathematical definition of "computable by an algorithm" that marked the beginning of the branch of logic now known as recursion theory or computability theory. We should mention the names of Gödel, Herbrand, Church (1903–), Turing (1912–1954), Kleene, Post (1897-1954) and Markov (1903–1979) as the founders of the subject. The important early papers are collected in Davis [1965, 2.1]. The formulation of a generally accepted definition of the recursive functions, i.e., those effectively computable by an algorithm, presented for the first time the possibility of negative solutions to classical problems asking for algorithms. The first such problem was one from the theory of computability theory itself, the *halting problem*: There is no algorithm which decides if a given computing machine halts on a given input (Theorem III.8.8). Since that first example, many problems from all areas of mathematics and computer science have been shown to have no algorithmic solution. Perhaps the oldest is that of solving Diophantine equations, made famous as Hilbert's tenth problem on his 1900 list of fundamental problems: Find an algorithm for determining if a polynomial equation (in several variables) with integer coefficients has integer solutions (see Browder [1976, 1.2] pp. 1–34). Building on the fundamental work of Putnam (1931–), Davis (1928–) and Julia Robinson (1919–1985), Matijacevič (1949–) finally finished the last step of the proof is that the problem unsolvable: there is no such algorithm (see Davis, Matijacevič and Robinson [1976, 3.6]). Proofs of this sort typically reduce the problem under consideration (such as the solution of Diophantine equations) to the unsolvability of the halting problem. Indeed, from our current perspective, having deduction simulate an algorithm is the heart of the proof of the incompleteness and undecidability (Corollary III.8.10) theorems for predicate logic.

Consider, for instance, the simulation of algorithms by deductions in what is called first order arithmetic inherent in Gödel's idea of the representability of primitive recursive functions [1931, 2.3] and Kleene's [1936, 3.6] extension to all recursive functions. This version of arithmetic is a predicate logic theory starting out with constant symbol 0, successor function s, binary functions $+$ and $\cdot$ for addition and multiplication, respectively, and a binary relation, $=$, for equality. It contains the usual inductive definitions of $+$ and $\cdot$:

$$0 + x = x \qquad x + s(y) = s(x + y)$$

$$x \cdot 0 = 0 \qquad x \cdot s(y) = x \cdot y + x \,,$$

It also has the axiom that $s(x) = s(y)$ implies $x = y$, the usual axioms for equality (see §III.5) and the induction axiom that, for each formula $\varphi(x) = \varphi(x, y_1, ..., y_n)$, asserts that

$$((\varphi(0) \wedge ((\forall x)\varphi(x) \rightarrow \varphi(s(x)))) \rightarrow (\forall x)\varphi(x)).$$

Let n be the term (numeral) corresponding to the integer n. That is, 1 is $s(0)$, 2 is $s(s(0))$, etc. What Gödel and Kleene proved was that for any recursive function f, there is a formula $\varphi(x, y)$ of this language such that $f(m) = n$ if and only if there is a proof of $\varphi(m, n)$ from the axioms of this theory. This theorem says that the deduction apparatus for first order arithmetic, implemented as a deductive engine in software, can compute f by deducing $\varphi(m, n)$. A similar approach to undecidability is presented in §III.8. This is not an efficient way to compute, but it does indicate that deduction as computation is an old theme in twentieth century logic. A great deal of contemporary logic in computer science deals with the various senses in which a deduction is a program and a program is a deduction, especially in intuitionistic logics, where a principle of this kind is the Curry-Howard isomorphism [see Girard [1989, 3.5]).

Over the past few decades recursion theory has moved beyond simple questions of direct algorithmic decidability to develop general theories of computation, effective definability and a whole theory of relative complexity of computation. We refer the reader to list 3.6 of the bibliography for some basic texts.

9. Recent Automation of Logic and PROLOG

After digital computers became available in the late 1950's, Davis and Putnam [1960, 5.7] and a number of other investigators tried to automate theorem proving in predicate logic. (The relevant papers, all from 1960, are in Siekmann and Wrightson [1983, 2.1].) Their success was limited by both their proof procedures and the capacity of the machines used, less powerful than the smallest personal computers today. Inspired by their work, J. A. Robinson (1930–) in 1963 presented a different implementation of Herbrand's theorem (again see Siekmann and Wrightson [1983, 2.1]). In [1965, 5.7], Robinson introduced his resolution method as the sole logical proof procedure for the propositional calculus (§I.8). He included an algorithm, now called the unification algorithm (II.12.3), that originally appeared in Herbrand [1930, 2.3]. Robinson's method considerably cuts down the number of cases to consider in mechanized proofs in predicate logic and, in the words of Martin Davis, "may fairly be said to have revolutionized the subject" (Davis [1983, 5.7], p. 19).

These early works of the 1960's produced interesting machine implementable methods of deduction (§II.13) but they were too slow for anything but research. In the early 1970's, Kowalski [1974, 5.4], building on work of Colmerauer and others [1972, 5.4] on planning systems, introduced the idea of mechanizing deduction for only a certain class of formulas called "Horn clauses". *Horn clauses* (§I.10 and §II.5) are of the form $R_1 \wedge \ldots \wedge R_n \rightarrow T$ where $R_1, \ldots, R_n$ and T are atomic sentences. It was known that Horn clause deduction computes all recursive functions. This was the basis of Kreisel and Tait [1961, 3.6] and Smullyan [1961, 3.6]. However, even this small fragment of predicate logic was still too slow in practice. What has now evolved is PROLOG, a computer language which restricts the proof procedure for Horn clauses to a very special type of deduction, the SLD–trees (§III.1–2). The standard implementations of this deduction procedure are logically incomplete (see §II.2), but even they suffice to compute all recursive functions (Corollary III.8.7).

10. The Future

Calculus became a widespread tool after its algebraic and symbolic algorithms had been developed. With the advent of high performance computing, it is now used for problems of a size and difficulty unimaginable a hundred years ago. We see similar prospects for automated inference in the future, as implementations and applications also make increasing use of high performance computing. There are already "mathematician's assistants" such as Constable's NUPRL [1986, 5.6] or Huet and Coquand's CONSTRUCTIONS (see Huet and Plotkin [1991, 5.7], which keep track of lemmas and proofs and tactics and strategies. We expect that eventually automated inference will be as useful as calculus, with just as many diverse applications. This is simply a modern extension of Leibniz's dream.

Suggestions for Further Reading

For the history of mathematics, Stillwell [1989, 1.2], Boyer [1989, 1.2] and Edwards [1979, 1.2] are good introductions. Kitcher [1983, 1.2] is a very interesting philosophical treatise on the nature of mathematics but it also contains (Chapter 10) a brief study of the development of analysis as an illustrative example of the philosophical forces at work. A good collection of articles dealing with a variety of topics in both the history and philosophy of modern mathematics is Aspray and Kitcher [1988, 1.2].

For early logic, Kneale and Kneale [1962, 2.1] is a good reference. For twentieth century logic, Van Heijenoort [1967, 2.1] should be consulted first. Pre-nineteen hundred references such as Boole or Aristotle or Leibniz, or Russell can be read with profit without further background.

Here are some of the basic modern papers in logic. They were translated and have introductions by leading experts in van Heijenoort [1967, 2.1] These papers will be accessible to the student after reading the first two chapters, or after skimming this chapter:

Fraenkel, A. A., "The notion 'definite' and the independence of the axiom of choice" [1922].

Frege, G., "A formula language, modeled upon that of arithmetic, for pure thought" [1879].

Gödel, K., "The completeness of the axioms of the functional calculus of logic" [1930].

Gödel, K., "On formally undecidable propositions of Principia Mathematica" [1931].

Herbrand, J., *Investigations in Proof Theory*, University of Paris [1930].

Löwenheim, L., "On possibilities in the calculus of relatives" [1915].

Peano, G., "The principles of arithmetic, presented by a new method" [1889].

Skolem, Th., "Logico-Combinatorial investigations in the satisfiability or provability of mathematical propositions" [1920].

von Neumann, J., "An axiomatization of set theory" [1925].

Post, E., L., "Introduction to a general theory of elementary propositions" [1921].

Zermelo, E. "Proof, that every set can be well-ordered" [1904].

Zermelo, E., "Investigations in the foundations of set theory 1" [1908].

Here are some basic papers on the automation of logic which are collected in Siekmann and Wrightson [1983, 2.1]. They should also be accessible after the first two chapters or after skimming this chapter.

Davis, M., "The prehistory and early history of automated deduction" [1983].

Davis, M., "A computer program for Pressburger's algorithm" [1957].

Davis, M., and Putnam, H., "A computing procedure for quantification theory" [1960].

Davis, M., "Eliminating the irrelevant from mechanical proofs" [1963].

Gelernter, H., "Realization of a geometry-theorem proving machine" [1959].

Gilmore, P. C., "A proof method for quantification theory: its justification and realization" [1960].

Robinson, J. A., "Theorem-proving on the computer" [1963].

Robinson, J. A., "A machine-oriented logic based on the resolution principle" [1965]

Wang, H., "Proving theorems by pattern recognition I" [1960].

Wos, L., Robinson, G. A. and Carson, D. F., "Efficiency and completeness of the set of support strategy in theorem proving" [1965].

Another good source of relevant papers is Bledsoe and Loveland [1984, 5.1].

Appendix B
A Genealogical Database

The list of facts of the form "fatherof(a,b)" given below is a transcription of the genealogical information contained in the first few chapters of Chronicles (the last book of the Hebrew Bible). We used it for various programming problems and projects including Exercises II.5.7-8 and III.2.12-14. Warning: When semantically correct programs are run using the database, many unexpected results occur. Several sources of possible difficulties are outlined in Exercise III.2.14. The types of problems they can engender are endemic in real life situations. Grappling with such problems is an interesting and worthwhile exercise.

fatherof(adam,seth).
fatherof(seth,enosh).
fatherof(enosh,kenan).
fatherof(kenan,mahalalel).
fatherof(mahalalel,jared).
fatherof(jared,enoch).
fatherof(enoch,methuselah).
fatherof(methuselah,lamech).
fatherof(lamech,noah).
fatherof(noah,shem).
fatherof(noah,ham).
fatherof(noah,japheth).
fatherof(japheth,gomer).
fatherof(japheth,magog).
fatherof(japheth,madai).
fatherof(japheth,javan).
fatherof(japheth,tubal).
fatherof(japheth,meshech).
fatherof(japheth,tiras).
fatherof(gomer,ashkenaz).
fatherof(gomer,diphath).
fatherof(gomer,togarmah).
fatherof(javan,elishah).
fatherof(javan,tarshish).
fatherof(javan,kittim).
fatherof(javan,rodanim).
fatherof(ham,cush).
fatherof(ham,mizraim).

fatherof(ham,put).
fatherof(ham,canaan).
fatherof(cush,seba).
fatherof(cush,havilah).
fatherof(cush,sabta).
fatherof(cush,raama).
fatherof(cush,sabteca).
fatherof(raamah,sheba).
fatherof(raamah,dedan).
fatherof(cush,nimrod).
fatherof(canaan,sidon).
fatherof(canaan,heth).
fatherof(shem,elam).
fatherof(shem,asshur).
fatherof(shem,arpachshad).
fatherof(shem,lud).
fatherof(shem,aram).
fatherof(shem,uz).
fatherof(shem,hul).
fatherof(shem,gether).
fatherof(shem,meshech).
fatherof(arpachshad,shelah).
fatherof(shelah,eber).
fatherof(eber,peleg).
fatherof(eber,joktan).
fatherof(joktan,almodad).
fatherof(joktan,shelelph).
fatherof(joktan,hazarmaveth).

fatherof(joktan,jerah).
fatherof(joktan,hadoram).
fatherof(joktan,uzal).
fatherof(joktan,diklah).
fatherof(joktan,ebal).
fatherof(joktan,abimael).
fatherof(joktan,sheba).
fatherof(joktan,ophir).
fatherof(joktan,havilah).
fatherof(joktan,jobab).
fatherof(shem,arpachshad).
fatherof(arpachshad,shelah).
fatherof(shelah,eber).
fatherof(eber,peleg).
fatherof(peleg,reu).
fatherof(reu,serug).
fatherof(serug,nahor).
fatherof(nahor,terah).
fatherof(terah,abraham).
fatherof(abraham,isaac).
fatherof(abraham,ishmael).
fatherof(ishmael,nebaioth).
fatherof(ishmael,kedar).
fatherof(ishmael,abdeel).
fatherof(ishmael,mibsam).
fatherof(ishmael,mishma).
fatherof(ishmael,dumah).
fatherof(ishmael,massa).
fatherof(ishmael,hadad).
fatherof(ishmael,tema).
fatherof(ishmael,jetur).
fatherof(ishmael,naphish).
fatherof(ishmael,kedmah).
fatherof(abraham,zimran).
fatherof(abraham,jokshan).
fatherof(abraham,medan).
fatherof(abraham,midian).
fatherof(abraham,ishbak).
fatherof(abraham,shuah).
fatherof(jokshan,sheba).
fatherof(jokshan,dedan).
fatherof(midian,ephah).
fatherof(midian,epher).
fatherof(midian,enoch).
fatherof(midian,abida).
fatherof(midian,eldaah).
fatherof(abraham,isaac).
fatherof(isaac,esau).
fatherof(isaac,israel).

fatherof(esau,eliphaz).
fatherof(esau,reuel).
fatherof(esau,jeush).
fatherof(esau,jalam).
fatherof(esau,korah).
fatherof(eliphaz,teman).
fatherof(eliphaz,omar).
fatherof(eliphaz,zephi).
fatherof(eliphaz,gatam).
fatherof(eliphaz,kenaz).
fatherof(eliphaz,timna).
fatherof(eliphaz,amalek).
fatherof(reuel,nahath).
fatherof(reuel,zerah).
fatherof(reuel,shammah).
fatherof(reuel,mizzah).
fatherof(seir,lotan).
fatherof(seir,shobal).
fatherof(seir,zibeon).
fatherof(seir,anah).
fatherof(seir,dishon).
fatherof(sier,ezer).
fatherof(seir,dishan).
fatherof(lotan,hori).
fatherof(lotan,homam).
fatherof(shobal,alian).
fatherof(shobal,manahath).
fatherof(shobal,ebal).
fatherof(shobal,shephi).
fatherof(shobal,onam).
fatherof(zibeon,aiah).
fatherof(zibeon,anah).
fatherof(anah,dishon).
fatherof(dishon,hamran).
fatherof(dishon,eshban).
fatherof(dishon,ithran).
fatherof(dishon,chran).
fatherof(ezer,bilhan).
fatherof(ezer,zaavan).
fatherof(ezer,jaakan).
fatherof(dishan,uz).
fatherof(dishan,aran).
fatherof(israel,reuben).
fatherof(israel,simeon).
fatherof(israel,levi).
fatherof(israel,judah).
fatherof(israel,isachar).
fatherof(israel,zebulun).
fatherof(israel,dan).

fatherof(israel,joseph).
fatherof(israel,benjamin).
fatherof(israel,naphtali).
fatherof(israel,gad).
fatherof(israel,asher).
fatherof(judah,er).
fatherof(judah,onan).
fatherof(judah,shelah).
fatherof(judah,perez).
fatherof(judah,zerah).
fatherof(perez,hezron).
fatherof(perez,hamul).
fatherof(zerah,nri).
fatherof(zerah,ethan).
fatherof(zerah,heman).
fatherof(zerah,calcol).
fatherof(zerah,dara).
fatherof(nni,achar).
fatherof(ethan,azariah).
fatherof(hezron,jerahmeel).
fatherof(hezron,ram).
fatherof(hezron,chelubai).
fatherof(ram,amminadab).
fatherof(anninadab,nahshon).
fatherof(nahshon,salma).
fatherof(salma,boaz).
fatherof(boaz,obed).
fatherof(obed,jesse).
fatherof(jesse,eliab).
fatherof(jesse,abinadab).
fatherof(jesse,shimea).
fatherof(jesse,nethanel).
fatherof(jesse,raddai).
fatherof(jesse,ozem).
fatherof(jesse,david).
fatherof(jether,amasa).
fatherof(hezon,caleb).
fatherof(caleb,jesher).
fatherof(caleb,shobab).
fatherof(caleb,ardon).
fatherof(caleb,hur).
fatherof(hur,uri).
fatherof(uri,bezalel).
fatherof(hezon,segub).
fatherof(segub,jair).
fatherof(machir,gilead).
fatherof(hezron,ashhur).
fatherof(ashhur,tekoa).
fatherof(jerahmeel,ram).

fatherof(jerahmeel,bunah).
fatherof(jerahmeel,oren).
fatherof(jerahmeel,ozem).
fatherof(jerahmeel,ahijah).
fatherof(jerahmeel,onam).
fatherof(ram,maaz).
fatherof(ram,jamin).
fatherof(ram,eker).
fatherof(onam,shammai).
fatherof(onam,jada).
fatherof(shammai,nadab).
fatherof(shammai,abishur).
fatherof(abishur,ahban).
fatherof(abishur,molid).
fatherof(nadab,seled).
fatherof(nadab,appaim).
fatherof(appaim,ishi).
fatherof(ishi,sheshan).
fatherof(sheshani,ahlai).
fatherof(jada,jether).
fatherof(jada,jonathan).
fatherof(jonathan,peleth).
fatherof(jonathan,zaza).
fatherof(jarha,attai).
fatherof(attai,nathan).
fatherof(nathan,zabad).
fatherof(zabad,ephlal).
fatherof(ephlal,obed).
fatherof(obed,jehu).
fatherof(jehu,azariah).
fatherof(azariah,helez).
fatherof(helez,eleasah).
fatherof(eleasah,sisamai).
fatherof(sisamai,shallum).
fatherof(shallum,jekamiah).
fatherof(jekamiah,elishama).
fatherof(caleb,meshah).
fatherof(mareshah,hebron).
fatherof(meshah,ziph).
fatherof(hebron,korah).
fatherof(hebron,tappuah).
fatherof(hebron,rekem).
fatherof(hebron,shema).
fatherof(shema,raham).
fatherof(raham,jorkeam).
fatherof(rekem,shammai).
fatherof(shammai,maon).
fatherof(maon,bethzur).
fatherof(caleb,haran).

fatherof(caleb,moza).
fatherof(caleb,gazez).
fatherof(haran,gazez).
fatherof(jahdai,regem).
fatherof(jahdai,geshan).
fatherof(jahdai,pelet).
fatherof(jahdai,ephah).
fatherof(jahdai,shaaph).
fatherof(caleb,sheber).
fatherof(caleb,tirhanah).
fatherof(caleb,shaaph).
fatherof(shaaph,madmannah).
fatherof(sheva,machbenah).
fatherof(ephrathah,hur).
fatherof(hur,shobal).
fatherof(hur,salma).
fatherof(hur,hareph).
fatherof(shobal,kiriath-jearim).
fatherof(salma,bethlehem).
fatherof(salma,atroth-beth-joab).
fatherof(hareph,beth-gader).
fatherof(shobal,haroeh).
fatherof(david,amnon).
fatherof(david,daniel).
fatherof(david,absalom).
fatherof(david,adonijah).
fatherof(david,shephatiah).
fatherof(david,ithream).
fatherof(david,shimea).
fatherof(david,shobab).
fatherof(david,nathan).
fatherof(david,solomon).
fatherof(david,ibhar).
fatherof(david,elishama).
fatherof(david,eliphelet).
fatherof(david,nogah).
fatherof(david,nepheg).
fatherof(david,japhia).
fatherof(david,elishama).
fatherof(david,eliada).
fatherof(david,eliphelet).
fatherof(solomon,rehoboam).
fatherof(rehoboam,abijah).
fatherof(abijah,asa).
fatherof(asa,jehoshaphat).
fatherof(jehoshaphat,joram).
fatherof(joram,ahaziah).
fatherof(ahaziah,joash).
fatherof(joash,amaziah).

fatherof(amaziah,azariah).
fatherof(arariah,jotham).
fatherof(jotham,ahaz).
fatherof(ahaz,hezekiah).
fatherof(hezekiah,manasseh).
fatherof(manasseh,amon).
fatherof(amon,josiah).
fatherof(josiah,johanan).
fatherof(josiah,jehoiakim).
fatherof(josiah,zedekiah).
fatherof(josiah,shallum).
fatherof(jehoiakim,jeconiah).
fatherof(jeconiah,zedekiah).
fatherof(jeconiah,shealtiel).
fatherof(jeconiah,malchiram).
fatherof(jeconiah,pedaiah).
fatherof(jeconiah,shenazzar).
fatherof(jeconiah,jekamiah).
fatherof(jeconiah,hoshana).
fatherof(jeconiah,nedabiah).
fatherof(pedaiah,zerubbabel).
fatherof(pedaiah,shimei).
fatherof(zerubbabel,meshullam).
fatherof(zerubbabel,hananiah).
fatherof(zerubbabel,hashubab).
fatherof(zerubbabel,ohel).
fatherof(zerubbabel,berechiah).
fatherof(zerubbabel,hasadiah).
fatherof(zerubbabel,jushab-hesed).
fatherof(hananiah,pelatiah).
fatherof(hananiah,jeshaiah).
fatherof(jeshaiah,rephaiah).
fatherof(rephaiah,arnan).
fatherof(arnan,obadiah).
fatherof(obadiah,shecaniah).
fatherof(shecaniah,shemaiah).
fatherof(shemaiah,hattush).
fatherof(shemaiah,igal).
fatherof(shemaiah,bariah).
fatherof(shemaiah,neariah).
fatherof(shemaiah,shaphat).
fatherof(neariah,elioenaI).
fatherof(neariah,hizkiah).
fatherof(neariah,azriham).
fatherof(elioenai,hodaviah).
fatherof(elioenai,eliashib).
fatherof(elioenai,pelaiah).
fatherof(elioenai,akkub).
fatherof(elioenai,johahan).

fatherof(elioenai,delaiah).

fatherof(elioenai,anani).

fatherof(judah,perez).

fatherof(judah,hezron).

fatherof(judah,carmi).

fatherof(judah,hur).

fatherof(judah,shobal).

fatherof(shobal,reaiah).

fatherof(reaiah,jahath).

fatherof(jahath,ahumai).

fatherof(jahath,lahad).

fatherof(etam,jezreel).

fatherof(etam,ishma).

fatherof(etam,idbash).

fatherof(penuel,gedor).

fatherof(ezer,hushah).

fatherof(ashhur,tekoa).

fatherof(ashhur,ahuzam).

fatherof(ashhur,hepher).

fatherof(ashhur,temeni).

fatherof(ashhur,ahashtari).

fatherof(ashhur,zereth).

fatherof(ashhur,zohar).

fatherof(ashhur,ethnan).

fatherof(koz,anub).

fatherof(koz,zobebah).

fatherof(chelub,mehir).

fatherof(mehir,eshton).

fatherof(eshton,bethrapha).

fatherof(eshton,paseah).

fatherof(eshton,tehinnah).

fatherof(tehinnah,ir-nahash).

fatherof(kenaz,othniel).

fatherof(kenaz,seraiah).

fatherof(othniel,hathath).

fatherof(othniel,meonothai).

fatherof(othniel,ophrah).

fatherof(seraiah,joab).

fatherof(joab,ge-harashim).

fatherof(jephunneh,caleb).

fatherof(caleb,iru).

fatherof(caleb,elah).

fatherof(caleb,naam).

fatherof(elah,kenaz).

fatherof(jehallelel,ziph).

fatherof(jehallelel,ziphah).

fatherof(jehallelel,tiria).

fatherof(jehallelel,asarel).

fatherof(ezrah,jether).

fatherof(ezrah,mered).

fatherof(ezrah,epher).

fatherof(ezrah,jalon).

fatherof(ezrah,ishbah).

fatherof(ishbah,eshtemoa).

fatherof(mered,shamai).

fatherof(mered,ishbah).

fatherof(mered,jered).

fatherof(mered,heber).

fatherof(mered,jekuthiel).

fatherof(jered,gedor).

fatherof(heber,soco).

fatherof(jekuthiel,zanoah).

fatherof(shimon,amnon).

fatherof(shimon,rinnah).

fatherof(shimon,ben-hanan).

fatherof(shimon,tilon).

fatherof(ishi,zoheth).

fatherof(ishi,ben-zoheth).

fatherof(judah,shelah).

fatherof(shelah,er).

fatherof(shelah,laadah).

fatherof(shelah,jokim).

fatherof(shelah,joash).

fatherof(shelah,saraph).

fatherof(shelah,jahubilehem).

fatherof(er,lecah).

fatherof(laadah,mareshah).

fatherof(simeon,nemuel).

fatherof(simeon,jamin).

fatherof(simeon,jarib).

fatherof(simeon,zerah).

fatherof(simeon,shaul).

fatherof(simeon,shallum).

fatherof(simeon,mibsam).

fatherof(simeon,mishma).

fatherof(mishma,hammuel).

fatherof(mishma,shimei).

fatherof(mishma,zaccur).

fatherof(amaziah,joshash).

fatherof(amaziah,jamlech).

fatherof(amaziah,meshoabab).

fatherof(joshibiah,jehu).

fatherof(joshibiah,joel).

fatherof(seraiah,joshibiah).

fatherof(asiel,seraiah).

fatherof(shiphi,eiloenai).

fatherof(shiphi,jaakobah).

fatherof(shiphi,jeshohaiah).

fatherof(shiphi,asaiah).
fatherof(shiphi,adiel).
fatherof(shiphi,jesimiel).
fatherof(shiphi,benaiahi).
fatherof(shiphi,ziza).
fatherof(allon,shiphi).
fatherof(reuben,enoch).
fatherof(jedaiah,allon).
fatherof(shimri,jedaiah).
fatherof(shimri,shemaiah).
fatherof(reuben,pallu).
fatherof(reuben,hezron).
fatherof(reuben,carmi).
fatherof(joel,shemaiah).
fatherof(shemaiah,gog).
fatherof(gog,shimei).
fatherof(shimei,micah).
fatherof(micah,reaiah).
fatherof(reaiah,baal).
fatherof(baal,beerah).
fatherof(azaz,bela).
fatherof(huri,abihail).
fatherof(jaroah,huri).
fatherof(gilead,jaroah).
fatherof(michael,gilead).
fatherof(jeshishai,michael).
fatherof(jahdo,jeshishai).
fatherof(buz,jahdo).
fatherof(abihail,michael).
fatherof(abihail,meshullam).
fatherof(abihail,sheba).
fatherof(abihail,jorai).
fatherof(abihail,jacan).
fatherof(abihail,zia).
fatherof(abihail,eber).
fatherof(abdiel,ahi).
fatherof(guni,abdiel).
fatherof(levi,gershom).
fatherof(levi,kohath).
fatherof(levi,merari).
fatherof(gershom,libni).
fatherof(gershom,shimei).
fatherof(kohath,amram).
fatherof(kohath,izhar).
fatherof(kohath,hebron).
fatherof(kohath,uzziel).
fatherof(amram,aaron).
fatherof(amram,moses).
fatherof(amram,miriam).

fatherof(merari,mahli).
fatherof(merari,mushi).
fatherof(aaron,nadab).
fatherof(aaron,abihu).
fatherof(aaron,eleazar).
fatherof(aaron,ithamar).
fatherof(eleazar,phinehas).
fatherof(phinehas,abishua).
fatherof(abishua,bukki).
fatherof(bukki,uzzi).
fatherof(uzzi,zerahiah).
fatherof(zerahiah,meraioth).
fatherof(meraioth,amariah).
fatherof(amariah,ahitub).
fatherof(ahitub,zadok).
fatherof(zadok,ahimaaz).
fatherof(ahimaaz,azariah).
fatherof(azariah,johanan).
fatherof(johanan,azariah).
fatherof(azariah,amariah).
fatherof(amariah,ahitub).
fatherof(ahitub,zadok).
fatherof(zadok,shallum).
fatherof(shallum,hilkiah).
fatherof(hilkiah,azariah).
fatherof(azariah,seraiah).
fatherof(seraiah,jehozadak).
fatherof(levi,gershom).
fatherof(levi,kohath).
fatherof(levi,merari).
fatherof(gershom,libni).
fatherof(gershom,shimei).
fatherof(kohath,amram).
fatherof(kohath,izhar).
fatherof(kohath,hebron).
fatherof(kohath,uzziel).
fatherof(merari,mahli).
fatherof(merari,mushi).
fatherof(libni,jahath).
fatherof(jahath,zimmah).
fatherof(zimmah,joah).
fatherof(joah,iddo).
fatherof(iddo,zerah).
fatherof(zerah,jeatherai).
fatherof(kohath,amminadab).
fatherof(kohath,korah).
fatherof(kohath,korah).
fatherof(kohath,assir).
fatherof(kohath,elkanah).

fatherof(kohath,ebiasaph).
fatherof(kohath,assir).
fatherof(kohath,tahath).
fatherof(kohath,uriel).
fatherof(kohath,uzziah).
fatherof(kohath,shaul).
fatherof(elkanah,amasai).
fatherof(elkanah,ahimoth).
fatherof(samuel,vashni).
fatherof(samuel,abijah).
fatherof(merari,mahli).
fatherof(mahli,libni).
fatherof(libni,shimei).
fatherof(shimei,uzzah).
fatherof(uzzah,shimea).
fatherof(shimea,haggiah).
fatherof(haggiah,asaiah).
fatherof(samuel,joel).
fatherof(elkanah,samuel).
fatherof(jeroham,elkanah).
fatherof(eliel,jeroham).
fatherof(toah,eliel).
fatherof(aaron,eleazar).
fatherof(eleazar,phinehas).
fatherof(phinehas,abishua).
fatherof(abishua,bukki).
fatherof(bukki,uzzi).
fatherof(uzzi,zerahiah).
fatherof(zerahiah,meraioth).
fatherof(meraioth,amariah).
fatherof(amariah,ahitub).
fatherof(ahitub,zadok).
fatherof(zadok,ahimaaz).
fatherof(issachar,tola).
fatherof(issachar,puah).
fatherof(issachar,jashub).
fatherof(issachar,shimron).
fatherof(tola,uzzi).
fatherof(tola,rephaiah).
fatherof(tola,jeriel).
fatherof(tola,jahmai).
fatherof(tola,ibsam).
fatherof(tola,shemuel).
fatherof(uzzi,izrahiah).
fatherof(izrahiah,michael).
fatherof(izrahiah,obadiah).
fatherof(izrahiah,joel).
fatherof(izrahiah,isshiah).
fatherof(benjamin,bela).

fatherof(benjamin,becher).
fatherof(benjamin,jediael).
fatherof(bela,ezbon).
fatherof(bela,uzzi).
fatherof(bela,uzziel).
fatherof(bela,jerimoth).
fatherof(bela,iri).
fatherof(becher,zemirah).
fatherof(becher,joash).
fatherof(becher,eliezer).
fatherof(becher,elioenai).
fatherof(becher,omri).
fatherof(becher,jeremoth).
fatherof(becher,abijah).
fatherof(becher,anathoth).
fatherof(becher,alemeth).
fatherof(jediael,bilhan).
fatherof(bilhan,jeush).
fatherof(bilhan,benjamin).
fatherof(bilhan,ehud).
fatherof(bilhan,chenaanah).
fatherof(bilhan,zethan).
fatherof(bilhan,tarshish).
fatherof(bilhan,ahishahar).
fatherof(ir,shuppim).
fatherof(ir,huppim).
fatherof(aher,hushim).
fatherof(naphtali,jahziel).
fatherof(naphtali,guni).
fatherof(naphtali,jezer).
fatherof(naphtali,shallum).
fatherof(manasseh,asriel).
fatherof(machir,gilead).
fatherof(machir,peresh).
fatherof(machir,sheresh).
fatherof(sheresh,ulam).
fatherof(sheresh,rekem).
fatherof(ulam,bedan).
fatherof(shemida,ahian).
fatherof(shemida,shechem).
fatherof(shemida,likhi).
fatherof(shemida,aniam).
fatherof(ephraim,shuthelah).
fatherof(shuthelah,bered).
fatherof(bered,tahath).
fatherof(tahath,eleadah).
fatherof(eleadah,tahath).
fatherof(tahath,zabad).
fatherof(zabad,shuthelah).

fatherof(zabad,ezer).
fatherof(zabad,elead).
fatherof(ephraim,beriah).
fatherof(rephah,resheph).
fatherof(resheph,telah).
fatherof(telah,tahan).
fatherof(tahan,ladan).
fatherof(ladan,ammihud).
fatherof(ammihud,elishama).
fatherof(elishama,non).
fatherof(non,joshua).
fatherof(asher,imnah).
fatherof(asher,ishvah).
fatherof(asher,ishvi).
fatherof(asher,beriah).
fatherof(asher,serah).
fatherof(beriah,heber).
fatherof(beriah,malchiel).
fatherof(malchiel,birzaith).
fatherof(heber,japhlet).
fatherof(heber,shomer).
fatherof(heber,hotham).
fatherof(heber,shua).
fatherof(japhlet,pasach).
fatherof(japhlet,bimhal).
fatherof(japhlet,ashvath).
fatherof(shemer,ahi).
fatherof(shemer,rohgah).
fatherof(shemer,hubbah).
fatherof(shemer,aram).
fatherof(helem,zophah).
fatherof(helem,imna).
fatherof(helem,shelesh).
fatherof(helem,amal).
fatherof(zophah,suah).
fatherof(zophah,harnepher).
fatherof(zophah,beri).
fatherof(zophah,shual).
fatherof(zophah,imrah).
fatherof(zophah,bezer).
fatherof(zophah,hod).
fatherof(zophah,shamma).
fatherof(zophah,shilshah).
fatherof(zophah,ithran).
fatherof(zophah,beera).
fatherof(jether,jephunneh).
fatherof(jether,pispa).
fatherof(jether,ara).
fatherof(ulla,arah).

fatherof(ulla,hanniel).
fatherof(ulla,rizia).
fatherof(benjamin,bela).
fatherof(benjamin,ashbel).
fatherof(benjamin,aharah).
fatherof(benjamin,nohah).
fatherof(benjamin,rapha).
fatherof(bela,addar).
fatherof(bela,gera).
fatherof(bela,abihud).
fatherof(bela,naaman).
fatherof(bela,abishua).
fatherof(bela,ahoah).
fatherof(bela,gera).
fatherof(bela,shephuphaN).
fatherof(bela,huram).
fatherof(shaharaim,jobab).
fatherof(shaharaim,zibia).
fatherof(shaharaim,mesha).
fatherof(shaharaim,malcam).
fatherof(shaharaim,jeuz).
fatherof(shaharaim,sachiah).
fatherof(shaharaim,mirmah).
fatherof(shaharaim,abitub).
fatherof(shaharaim,elpaal).
fatherof(elpaal,eber).
fatherof(elpaal,misham).
fatherof(elpaal,shemed).
fatherof(elpaal,beria).
fatherof(elpaal,shema).
fatherof(beriah,zebadiah).
fatherof(beriah,arad).
fatherof(beriah,eder).
fatherof(beriah,michael).
fatherof(beriah,ishpah).
fatherof(beriah,joha).
fatherof(elpaal,zebadiah).
fatherof(elpaal,meshullam).
fatherof(elpaal,hizki).
fatherof(elpaal,heber).
fatherof(elpaal,ishmeraj).
fatherof(elpaal,izliah).
fatherof(elpaal,jobab).
fatherof(shimei,jakim).
fatherof(shimei,zichri).
fatherof(shimei,zabdi).
fatherof(shimei,elienai).
fatherof(shimei,zillethai).
fatherof(shimei,eliel).

fatherof(shimei,adaiah).
fatherof(shimei,beraiah).
fatherof(shimei,shimrath).
fatherof(shashak,ishpan).
fatherof(shashak,eber).
fatherof(shashak,eliel).
fatherof(shashak,abdon).
fatherof(shashak,zichri).
fatherof(shashak,hanan).
fatherof(shashak,hananiah).
fatherof(shashak,elam).
fatherof(shashak,anthothiah).
fatherof(shashak,iphdeiah).
fatherof(shashak,penuel).
fatherof(jeroham,shamsherai).
fatherof(jeroham,shehariah).
fatherof(jeroham,athaliah).
fatherof(jeroham,jaareshiah).
fatherof(jeroham,elijah).
fatherof(jeroham,zichri).
fatherof(mikloth,shimeah).
fatherof(ner,kish).
fatherof(kish,saul).
fatherof(saul,jonathan).
fatherof(saul,malchi-shua).
fatherof(saul,abinadab).
fatherof(saul,eshbaal).
fatherof(jonathan,merib-baal).
fatherof(merib-baal,micah).
fatherof(micah,pithoh).
fatherof(micah,melech).
fatherof(micah,taarea).
fatherof(micah,ahaz).
fatherof(ahaz,jehoaddah).
fatherof(jehoaddah,alemeth).
fatherof(jehoaddah,azmaveth).
fatherof(jehoaddah,zimri).

fatherof(zimri,moza).
fatherof(moza,binea).
fatherof(binea,eleasah).
fatherof(eleasah,azel).
fatherof(azel,azrikam).
fatherof(azel,bocheru).
fatherof(azel,ishmael).
fatherof(azel,sheariah).
fatherof(azel,obadiah).
fatherof(azel,hanan).
fatherof(eshek,ulam).
fatherof(eshek,jeush).
fatherof(eshek,eliphelet).
fatherof(ammihud,uthai).
fatherof(omri,ammihud).
fatherof(zerah,jeuel).
fatherof(meshullam,sallu).
fatherof(hodaviah,meshullam).
fatherof(hassenuah,hodaviah).
fatherof(jeroham,ibneiah).
fatherof(uzzi,elah).
fatherof(michri,uzzi).
fatherof(shephatiah,meshullam).
fatherof(reuel,shephatiah).
fatherof(ibneiah,reuel).
fatherof(hilkiah,azariah).
fatherof(meshullam,hilkiah).
fatherof(zadok,meshullam).
fatherof(meraioth,zadok).
fatherof(ahitub,meraioth).
fatherof(jeroham,adaiah).
fatherof(pashhur,jeroham).
fatherof(malchijah,pashhur).
fatherof(adiel,maasai).
fatherof(jahzerah,adiel).
fatherof(meshullam,jahzerah).
fatherof(meshillemith,meshullam).

Bibliography

1. History of Mathematics

1.1 Sourcebooks for the History of Mathematics

Birkhoff, G., ed., *A Source Book in Classical Analysis*, Harvard University Press, Cambridge, Mass., 1973.
The history of the introduction of rigor in analysis is well represented here.

Midonick, D., *The Treasury of Mathematics*, Philosophical Library, New York, 1965.

Smith, D. E., *A Source Book in Mathematics*, 2 vols., Dover, New York, 1959.

Struik, D., *A Source Book in Mathematics 1200–1800*, Harvard University Press, Cambridge, Mass., 1969.
Characteristic papers by many mathematicians of the period.

Thomas, I., *Selections Illustrating the History of Greek Mathematics with an English Translation*, 2 vols., Loeb Classical Library, Harvard University Press, Cambridge, Mass., 1939.
A Greek–English edition of selections referred to in Heath's History of Greek Mathematics with very informative quotes.

1.2 Histories of Mathematics

Asprey, W. and Kitcher, P., *History and Philosophy of Modern Mathematics*, Minnesota Studies in the Philosophy of Science, vol. XI, University of Minnesota Press, Minneapolis, 1988.
An eclectic collection of articles attempting to present the state of the interdisciplinary endeavor at the time.

Boyer, C., *A History of Mathematics*, 2nd ed., Revised by U. C. Merzbach, Wiley, New York, 1989.

Browder, F. E., ed., *Mathematical developments arising from Hilbert's problems*, *Proc. Symp. Pure Math.*, **27**, American Mathematical Society, Providence, 1976.

Cantor, G., "Über die Ausdennung eines Satzes aus der Theorie der trigono-merischen Reihen", *Mathematische Annalen*, **5**, 123–132, 1872.

Dieudonné, J., *Abrégé d'Histoire des Mathématiques*, 2 vols., Hermann, Paris, 1978.

DuGac, P., "Éléments d'analyse de Karl Weierstrass", *Archive for the History of the Exact Sciences*, **10**, 42–176, 1973.

DuGac, P., *Richard Dedekind et les fondements de l'analyse*, Paris, 1976.

Edwards, C. H., *The Historical Development of the Calculus*, Springer-Verlag, Berlin, 1979.

Eves, H., *An Introduction to the History of Mathematics*, 4th ed., Holt Rinehart Winston, New York, 1975; 6th ed., Saunders College Pub., Phila-delphia, 1990.

Grattan–Guinness, I., *The Development of the Foundations of Mathemati-cal Analysis from Euler to Riemann*, MIT Press, Cambridge, Mass., 1970. *Explains the intellectual difficulties of Euler, Gauss and Riemann in making their mathematics stand on a firm foundation.*

Grattan–Guinness, I., ed., *From the Calculus to Set Theory 1630–1910: An Introductory History*, Duckworth, London, 1980.

Heath, T. L., *Mathematics in Aristotle*, Clarendon Press, Oxford, 1949.

Heath, T. L., *A History of Greek Mathematics I, II*, Dover, New York, 1981.
The two texts above are the standard texts in the area.

Heine, E., "Die Elemente der Functionenlehre", *J. fur die reine und ange-wandte Mathematik*, **74**, 172–188, 1872.

Kitcher, P., *The Nature of Mathematical Knowledge*, Oxford University Press, Oxford, 1983.
In addition to an extensive treatment of the philosophical issues, this book supplies a good history of modern analysis as a case study illuminating the author's views.

Klein, F., *Development of Mathematics in the 19th Century* (M. Acker-mann, tr.), Math. Sci. Press, Brookline, Mass, 1979.
To this day, the best exposition of the evolution of core mathematics in the nineteenth century. It makes clear what the mathematical and foundational difficulties were.

Philips, E., ed., *Studies in the History of Mathematics*, MAA Studies in Mathematics, **26**, Mathematical Association of America, 1987.

Smith, D. E., *A History of Mathematics*, 2 vols., Dover, New York, 1958.

Stillwell, J., *Mathematics and its History*, Springer-Verlag, 1989.

Struik, D. J., *A Concise History of Mathematics*, Dover, New York, 1987.

2. History of Logic

The history of logic itself is intertwined with the history of philosophy as much as the history of mathematics. The references reflect this fact.

2.1 Sourcebooks in Logic

Here are five collections of fundamental papers in modern mathematical logic and its applications which may be consulted to clarify unexplained points. Students will be equipped to read most of these papers after reading the first two chapters of the text. They are also an appropriate basis for the instructor's supplementary reading and essay assignments.

Benacerraf, P. and Putnam, H., eds., *Philosophy of Mathematics: Selected Readings*, 2nd ed., Cambridge University Press, Cambridge, 1983.
For those who would like to understand philosophical issues.

Davis, M., ed., *The Undecidable. Basic papers on undecidable propositions, unsolvable problems, and computable functions*, Raven Press, Hewlett, N.Y., 1965.
This volume contains the 1930–40's papers of Gödel, Church, Kleene, Post and Turing on recursive function theory, incompleteness and undecidability.

van Heijenoort, J., ed., *From Frege to Gödel*, Harvard University Press, Cambridge, Mass., 1967.
Most important papers in mathematical logic from 1879 to 1931 are available in English here, including most of those referred to in the historical appendix. The introductions to the papers, by leading logicians, are extremely informative, especially when the texts are obscure.

Hintikka, J., ed., *The Philosophy of Mathmatics* (Oxford Readings in Philosophy), Oxford University Press, London, 1969.

Siekmann, J. and Wrightson, G. , eds., *Automation of Reasoning*, 1957–70, 2 vols., Springer-Verlag, Berlin, 1983.
This volume contains most early papers in automation of reasoning, many of which make good reading assignments.

2.2 Histories of Logic

Bochenski, J., *Ancient Formal Logic*, North-Holland, Amsterdam, 1951.

Bochenski, J., *A History of Formal Logic*, University of Notre Dame Press, Notre Dame, Ind., 1961.

Boehner, P., *Medieval Logic*, Manchester University Press, Manchester, England, 1952.

Drucker, T., ed., *Perspectives on the History of Mathematical Logic*, Birkhäuser, Boston, 1991.

Hailperin, T., *Boole's Logic and Probability*, North-Holland, Amsterdam, 1976.

Hallet, Michael, *Cantorian Set Theory and Limitation of Size* (Oxford Logic Guides, **10**), Clarendon Press, Oxford, 1984.

Heinzmann, G., ed., *Poincaré, Russell, Zermelo et Peano: textes de la discussion (1906–1912) sur les fondements des mathématiques: des antinomies a la predicativite*, Albert Blanchard, Paris, 1986.

Kneale, W. and Kneale, M., *The Development of Logic*, Clarendon Press, Oxford, 1975.
The standard exposition.

Lukasiewicz, J., *Aristotle's Syllogistic from the Standpoint of Modern Formal Logic*, 2nd ed., Clarendon Press, Oxford, 1957.
A different view of what Aristotle did.

Mates, B., *Stoic Logic*, 2nd ed., University of California Press, Berkeley, 1961.

Mueller, I., *Philosophy of Mathematics and Deductive Structure in Euclid's Elements*, MIT Press, Cambridge, Mass., 1981.

Nidditch, P., *The Development of Mathematical Logic*, Routledge and Kegan Paul, London, 1962.

Parkinson, G., *Logic and Reality in Leibniz's Metaphysics*, Clarendon Press, Oxford, 1965.
Probably the best place to learn Leibniz's logic.

Rescher, N., *The Development of Arabic Logic*, 1964.

Schilpp, P., *The Philosophy of Bertrand Russell*, Northwestern University, Evanston, Ill., 1944 (3rd ed., Tudor Publishers, New York, 1951).

Scholz, H., *Concise History of Logic* (K. Leidecker, tr.), Philosophical Library, New York, 1961.

Styazhkin, N. I., *History of Mathematical Logic, from Leibniz to Peano*, MIT Press, Cambridge, Mass., 1969.

2.3 Primary Sources for the History of Logic

Aristotle, *Selections* (W. D. Ross, ed.), Oxford University Press, Oxford, 1942.

Aristotle, *Categories and De Interpretatione* (J. Ackrill, tr.), Clarendon Press, Oxford, 1966.

Aristotle, *Aristotle's Posterior Analytics* (J. Barnes, tr.), Clarendon Press, Oxford, 1975.

Aristotle, *Aristotle's Categories and Propositions* (H. Apostle, tr.), Peripatetic Press, Grinnell, Iowa, 1980.

Boole, G., *The Mathematical Analysis of Logic*, Macmillan, Barclay and Macmillan, Cambridge, England, 1847 (reprinted B. Blackwell, Oxford, 1948).
This is very enjoyable reading.

Boole, G., *An investigation of the laws of thought, on which are founded the mathematical theories of logic and probability*, Macmillan, London, 1854.

Boole, G., *Collected Logical Works*, Open Court, La Salle, Ill., 1952.

Boole, G., *Studies in Logic and Probability*, Watts, London, 1952.

Boole, G., *A Treatise on Differential Equations*, 5th ed. Chelsea, New York, 1959.

Boole, G., *A Treatise on the Calculus of Finite Differences*, J. F. Moulton, ed., 5th ed., Chelsea, New York, 1970.

Boole, G., *The Boole–De Morgan Correspondence 1842–1864* (G. C. Smith, ed.), Clarendon Press, Oxford, 1982.

Brouwer, L. E. J., *Collected Works*, 2 vols. (A. Heyting, ed.), American Elsevier, New York, 1975.

Cantor, G., "Rezension der Schrift von G. Frege, *Die Grundlagen der Arithmetik*", *Deutsche Littertur Zeitung*, 728–729, 1885 (reprinted in Cantor [1932, 2.3], 440–441).

Cantor, G., *Gesammelte Abhandlungen mathematischen und philosophischen Inhalts* (E. Zermelo, ed.), Springer, Berlin, 1932 (reprinted 1962, Olms, Hildesheim).

Cantor, G., *Briefwechsel Cantor–Dedekind* (E. Noether and J. Cavaillès eds.), Actualitates scientifiques et industrielles, **518**, Hermann, Paris, 1937.

Cantor, *Contributions to the Founding of the Theory of Transfinite Numbers* (P. E. B. Jourdain, tr.), Dover, New York, 1952.
Good to read to see how informal and intuitive Cantor's foundations were.

Cavaillès, J., *Philosophie mathématique,* includes "Correspondence Cantor–Dedekind", Hermann, Paris, 1962.

Couturat, L., *Opuscules et Fragments inédits de Leibniz, extracts des manuscripts de la Bibliothéque royale de Hanovre*, Paris, 1903.

Couturat, L., *L'Algebre de la Logique*, 2nd ed., A. Blanchard, Paris, 1980 (translation of original edition by L. G. Robinson as *The Algebra of Logic*, Open Court, London, 1914).

De Morgan, A., *Formal Logic, or, the calculus of inference, necessary and probable*, Taylor and Walton, London, 1847.

Dedekind, R., *Gesammelte mathematische Werke*, 3 vols. (R. Fricke, E. Noether and O. Ore, eds.), F. Vieweg & Sohn, Brunswick, 1932 (reprinted Chelsea, New York, 1969).

Dedekind, R., *Essays on the Theory of Numbers* (W. Beman, tr.), Dover, New York, 1963.
Dedekind was a master stylist. These papers, on the construction of the reals by Dedekind cuts and on the justification of definitions of functions by inductive definitions, are masterpieces of clarity and very accessible.

Descartes, R., *Discours de la Methode*, Ian Marie, Leyde, 1637 (reprinted Union generale d'editions, Paris, 1963; translated as *Discourse on Method* by J. Veitch, Open Court, La Salle, Ind. 1945).

Euclid, *The thirteen books of Euclid's Elements* (Sir Thomas Heath, tr. and ed.), Dover, New York, 1956.

Fraenkel, A., "Der Begriff 'definit' und die Unabhängigkeit des Auswahlsaxioms", *Sitzungsberichte der Preussischen Akademie der Wissenchaften, Physikalisch–mathematische Klasse*, 253–257, 1922 (translated in van Heijenoort [1967, 2.1] as "The notion of 'definite' and the independence of the axiom of choice").

Frege, G., *Begriffsschrift*, Halle, 1879 (translated in van Heijenoort [1967, 2.1] as "*Begriffsschrift*, a formula language, modeled upon that of arithmetic, for pure thought").

Frege, G., *Die Grundlagen der Arithmetik*, Breslau, 1884 (reprinted and translated as *The Foundations of Arithmetic* by J. L. Austin, Philosophical Library, New York, 1953).

Frege, G., *Grundgesetze der Arithmetik, begriffsschriftlich abgeleitet*, 2 vols., Jena, Pohl, 1903 (partially translated by M. Furth as *The basic laws of arithmetic. Exposition of the System*, University of California Press, Berkeley, 1964).

Frege, G., *Conceptual notation and Related articles* (T. W. Bynum, tr. and ed.), Clarendon, Oxford, 1972.

Frege, G., *Logical Investigations* (P. T. Geach, ed., P. T. Geach and R. H. Stoothoff, tr.), R. Blackwell, Oxford, 1977.
There is much to be learned today by reading these masterworks.

Gentzen, G. (M. E. Szabo, ed.), *The Collected Papers of Gerhard Gentzen*, Studies in Logic, North-Holland, Amsterdam, 1969.
Gentzen explained what he was doing more clearly than most of his successors.

Gödel, K., "Die Vollständigkeit der Axiome des logischen Funktionen-kalküls", *Mon. für Math. und Physik*, **37**, 349–360, 1930 (translated as "The completeness of the axioms of the functional calculus of logic", in van Heijenoort [1967, 2.1] and Gödel [1986, 2.3]).

Gödel, K., "Über formal unentscheidbare ... ", *Mon. für Math. und Physik*, **37**, 349–360, 1931 (translated as "On formally undecidable propositions of Principia Mathematica and related systems I", in van Heijenoort [1967, 2.1], Davis [1965, 2.1] and Gödel ([1986, 2.3]).

Gödel, K., "Eine Interpretation des intuitionistischen Aussagenkalküls", Ergebnisse eines mathematischen Kolloquiums, 4, 1933 (reprinted and translated as "An interpretation of the intuitionistic propositional calculus", in Gödel [1986, 2.3] vol. 1, 300–302.

Gödel, K., "Russell's mathematical logic", in Schilpp [1944, 2.2], 123–153 (reprinted in Gödel [1986, 2.3] vol. 2, 119–141).

Gödel, K., *Collected Works*, vol. 1– (S. Feferman et al., eds.), Oxford University Press, Oxford, 1986– .
These papers have introductions and explanations by experts not equaled elsewhere.

Herbrand, J., *Recherches sur la théorie de la démostration*, Thesis, University of Paris, 1930 (excerpts translated as "Investigations in proof theory: The properties of true propositions" in van Heijenoort [1967, 2.1]).

Herbrand, J., *Logical Writings*, Reidel, Hingham, Mass., 1971.

Heyting, A., *Intuitionism: An Introduction*, North Holland, Amsterdam, 1956.

Hilbert, D., *Grundlagen der Geometrie*, Teubner, Leipzig, 1899 (translated by E. J. Townsend as *Foundations of Geometry*, Open Court, La Salle Ill., 1950).
The first complete treatment of Euclidean geometry. The English version contains some important additions.

Hilbert, D. and Ackermann, W., *Grundzüge der theoretischen Logik*, Springer, Berlin, 1928 (English translation of 1938 edition, Chelsea, New York, 1950).

Hilbert, D. and Bernays, P., *Grundlagen der Mathematik I (1934) II (1939)*, 2nd ed., I (1968) II (1970), Springer, Berlin.
Never translated, yet the most influential book on foundations.

Löwenheim, L., "Über Möglichkeiten im Relativkalkül", *Math. Annalen*, **76**, 447–470, 1915 (translated as "On possibilities in the calculus of relatives" in van Heijenoort [1967, 2.1].

Peano, G., *Formulario mathematico*, Bocca Freres, Turin, 1894–1908 (reprinted Edizioni Cremonese, Rome, 1960).

Peano, G., *Opere Scelte*, 3 vols., Edizioni Cremonese, Rome, 1957–9.

Peano, G., *Selected Works of Giuseppe Peano* (H. C. Kennedy, tr.), University of Toronto Press, Toronto, 1973.

Peano, G., *Arbeiten zur analysis und zur mathematischen Logik* (edited by G. Asser), B. G. Teubner, Leipzig, 1990.
Peano is very readable today, because we have largely adopted his notation (except for his system of dots instead of parentheses).

Peirce, C. S., "Description of a notation for the logic of relatives, resulting from an amplification of the conceptions of Boole's calculus of logic", *Memoirs of the American Academy of Arts and Sciences*, **9**, 317–368, 1870 (reprinted in Peirce [1933, 2.3], 27–98).

Peirce, C. S., *Collected Papers of Charles Sanders Peirce*, C. Hartshorne and P. Weiss eds., vol. 3, *Exact Logic*, The Belknap Press of Harvard University Press, Cambridge, Mass., 1933 (reprinted in 1960).
Peirce independently invented predicate logic and the calculus of relations.

Poincaré, H., *Science and Hypothesis* (W. J. Greenstreet, tr.), Dover, New York, 1952.

Poincaré, H., *Science and Method* (F. Maitland, tr.), Dover, New York, 1952.

Post, E., "Introduction to a general theory of propositions", *American Journal of Mathematics*, **43**, 163–185, 1921 (reprinted in van Heijenoort [1967, 2.1]).

Russell, B., *The Principles of Mathematics*, Cambridge University Press, Cambridge, England, 1903.
An informal very well written book which gives the flavor of the times.

Russell, B., On some difficulties in the theory of transfinite numbers and order types, *Proc. London Math. Soc.* (2), **4**, 29–53, 1907.

Russell, B., *Introduction to Mathematical Philosophy*, Allen and Unwin, London, 1917 (reprinted 1960).
An excellent exposition of the Logistic point of view.

Russell, B., *Logic and Knowledge: Essays 1901–1950* (R. C. Marsh, ed.), Allen and Unwin, London, 1956.

Russell, B., *The Autobiography of Bertrand Russell*, 3 vols., Allen and Unwin, London, 1967.
There is little logic here, but the social context is revealing.

Schröder, E., *Der Operationskreis des Logikkalkulus*, Leipzig, 1877 (reprinted Darmsdat, 1966).

Schröder, E., *Vorlesungen über die Algebra der Logik*, 3 vols., B. G. Teubner, Leipzig, 1890–1905.

Skolem, T., "Einge Bemerkungen zur axiomatischen Begründung der Mengenlehre" in *Matematikerkongressen i Helsingfors*, Akademiska Bokhandeln, Helsinki, 1922 (translated in van Heijenoort [1967, 2.1] as "Some remarks on axiomatized set theory").

Whitehead, A. N. and Russell, B., *Principia Mathematica*, 3 vols., Cambridge University Press, Cambridge, England, 1910–13; 2nd ed., 1925–1927. *This is more quoted than read.*

Wittgenstein, L., *Tractatus Logico–Philosophicus* (D. Pears and B. McGuiness, tr.), Routledge and Kegan Paul, London, 1974. *In his youth Wittgenstein took truth tables more seriously than we do.*

von Neumann, J., "Zur Einführung der transfiniten Zahlen", *Acta literarum ac scientiarum Regiae Universitatis Hungaricae Francisco-Josephinae, Sectio scientarum mathematicarum*, **1**, 199–208, 1923 (translated as "On the introduction of transfinite numbers" in van Heijenoort [1967, 2.1].

von Neumann, J., Eine Axiomatisierung der Mengenlehre, *J. für die reine und angewandte Mathematik*, **154**, 219–240, 1925 (translated as "An axiomatization of set theory" in van Heijenoort [1967, 2.1]).

von Neumann, J., *Collected Works*, vol. 1 (A. H. Taub, ed.), Pergamon Press, Oxford, 1961.

Zermelo, E., "Beweis, dass jede Menge wohlgeordnet werden kann", *Math. Annalen*, **59**, 514–516, 1904 (translated as "Proof that every set can be well-ordered" in van Heijenoort [1967, 2.1]).

Zermelo, E., "Untersuchungen über die Grundlagen der Mengenlehre I", *Math. Annalen*, **65**, 261–281, 1908 (translated as "Investigations into the foundations of set theory I" in van Heijenoort [1967, 2.1]).

3. Mathematical Logic

3.1 Handbooks

(See also list 5.1.)

Barwise, J. ed., *Handbook of Mathematical Logic*, North Holland, Amsterdam, 1977.
A group effort, summarizing in a fairly self-contained way many of the areas of modern mathematical logic. It is the first place to look for an exposition of an unfamiliar branch of logic.

Gabbay, D. and Guenthner, F., *Handbook of Philosophical Logic*, 4 vols., D. Reidel, Dordrecht, 1983–85.
This book has very useful summaries of many branches of nonclassical logics.

3.2 Logic Textbooks

(See also list 5.2.)

Beth, E., *Formal Methods; An Introduction to Symbolic Logic and to the Study of Effective Operations in Arithmetic and Logic*, D. Reidel, Dordrecht, 1962.

Beth, E., *The Foundations of Mathematics: A Study in the Philosophy of Science*, 2nd ed., North-Holland, Amsterdam, 1965.
This book has very extensive discussions of foundations and history.

Boolos, G. and Jeffrey, R., *Computability and Logic*, 3rd ed., Cambridge University Press, Cambridge, England, 1989.

Church, A. *Introduction to Mathematical Logic*, rev. ed., Princeton University Press, Princeton, 1956.
This book has extensive discussions of alternate axiomatics for classical propositional and predicate logic.

Crossley, J. N. et al., *What is Mathematical Logic?*, Oxford University Press, Oxford, 1972 (reprinted Dover, New York, 1990).
This book has been translated into many languages as a brief introduction to incompleteness.

Curry, H. B., *Foundations of Mathematical Logic*, Dover, New York, 1977.
Fun for formalists.

Ebbinghaus, H., Flum, J., and Thomas, W., *Mathematical Logic*, Springer-Verlag, Berlin, 1984.

Enderton, H., *A Mathematical Introduction to Logic*, Academic Press, New York, 1972.

Hamilton, A. G., *Logic for Mathematicians*, Cambridge University Press, Cambridge, England, rev. ed., 1988.

Hilbert, D. and Ackermann, W., *Principles of Mathematical Logic* (L. Hammond et al. tr. of [1928, 2.3].), Chelsea, New York, 1950.
This was the first modern book on first order logic. It is noted for the brevity and clarity of its exposition.

Hodges, W., *Logic*, Penguin, Harmondsworth, England, 1977.

Kalish, D., Montague, R. and Mar, G., *Techniques of Formal Deduction*, Harcourt Brace Jovanovich, New York, 1980.

Kleene, S. C., *Introduction to Metamathematics*, D. Van Nostrand, New York, 1952 (reprinted North–Holland, Amsterdam, 1971).
This book, by a principal architect of recursion theory, develops logic so that the intuitionistic and classical steps can be separated out and has unexcelled explanations of Gödel's theorems and related topics.

Lukasiewicz, J., *Elements of Mathematical Logic* (O. Wojtasiewicz, tr.), MacMillan, New York, 1963.

Manaster, A., *Completeness, Compactness, Undecidability: An Introduction to Mathematical Logic*, Prentice-Hall, Englewood Cliffs, N. J., 1975.
This text is a short exposition of the sequent calculus.

Mendelson, E., *Introduction to Mathematical Logic*, 2nd ed., D. Van Nostrand, New York, 1979.
For thirty years this was the text most used by professional logicians teaching undergraduates.

Monk, J. D., *Mathematical Logic*, GTM **37**, Springer-Verlag, Berlin, 1976.

Ponasse, D., *Mathematical Logic*, Gordon Breach, New York, 1973.

Quine, W. V., *Mathematical Logic*, rev. ed., Harvard University Press, Cambridge, Mass., 1951.
This text introduces Quine's system NF (New Foundations), which is quite different from Zermelo-Fraenkel set theory.

Rosenbloom, P. C., *The Elements of Mathematical Logic*, Dover, New York, 1950.
This text explains Post canonical systems well and uses them for incompleteness proofs following Post.

Rosser, J. B., *Logic for Mathematicians*, 2nd ed., Chelsea, New York, 1978.
This text was written using Quine's system NF as a base.

Shoenfield, J. R., *Mathematical Logic*, Addison-Wesley, Reading, Mass., 1967.
This text is a balanced summary of mathematical logic as of about 1967. It is still a basic reference for graduate logic courses with excellent problems but it is very terse.

Smullyan, R., *First Order Logic*, Springer-Verlag, Berlin, 1968.
This presents many versions of the method of tableaux and uses them with consistency properties to derive a great many results not included in the present book.

Smullyan, R., *What is the Name of this Book?*, Prentice-Hall, Englewood Cliffs, New Jersey, 1978.

Smullyan, R., *Forever Undecided: a Puzzle Guide to Gödel*, A. Knopf, New York, 1987.
The last two are among Smullyan's popular puzzle books, with a quite rigorous treatment of Gödel's theorems in unusual terms.

van Dalen, D., *Logic and Structure*, 2nd ed., Springer-Verlag, Berlin, 1983.
This elegant text covers both intuitionistic and classical logic.

3.3 Set Theory

Cohen, P., *Set Theory and the Continuum Hypothesis*, W. A. Benjamin, Inc., New York, 1966.
This book has a short elegant introduction to logic followed by an outline of the author's famous proofs of the independence of the axiom of choice and the continuum hypothesis.

Fraenkel, A. A. and Bar-Hillel, Y., *Foundations of Set Theory*, North-Holland, Amsterdam, 1958 (2nd ed., with D. van Dalen, 1973).
This book explains the nature and origin of the axioms of set theory with great completeness.

Fraenkel, A. A., *Abstract Set Theory*, 4th ed., revised by A. Levy, North-Holland, Amsterdam, 1976.

Halmos, P., *Naive Set Theory*, D. Van Nostrand, Princeton, 1960.

Hausdorff, F., *Set Theory* (tr. from German 3rd edition, 1937), Chelsea, New York, 1962.
Although first published in 1914, this is still a vibrant text on the use of set theoretic methods in topology by a famous contributor.

Hrbaček, K. and Jech, T., *Introduction to Set Theory*, 2nd rev. ed., M. Dekker, New York, 1984.

Jech, T., *The Axiom of Choice*, North Holland, Amsterdam, 1973.
Collects many independence proofs of forms of the axiom of choice.

Jech, T., *Set Theory*, Academic Press, New York, 1978.
A standard reference at the graduate level for the basic material.

Kunen, K., *Set Theory: An Introduction to Independence Proofs*, North-Holland, Amsterdam, 1980.
A classroom favorite as a basic graduate text.

Kuratowski, K. and Mostowski, A., *Set Theory*, North-Holland, Amsterdam, 1976.

Levy, A., *Basic Set Theory*, Springer-Verlag, Berlin, 1979.

Rubin, H. and Rubin, E., *Equivalents of the Axiom of Choice, I, II*, North-Holland, Amsterdam, 1963, 1985.

Rubin, J., *Set Theory for the Mathematician*, Holden-Day, San Francisco, 1967.

Suppes, P., *Axiomatic Set Theory*, Dover, New York, 1972.
Still a readable exposition of axiomatic set theory.

3.4 Model Theory

Bell, J. L. and Slomson, A. B., *Models and Ultraproducts*, North-Holland, Amsterdam, 1974.
Found by many students to be the most understandable beginning text.

Chang, C. C. and Keisler, J., *Model Theory*, 3rd ed., North-Holland, Amsterdam, 1990.
Still the standard treatise on basic model theory. The authors were two major contributors to the subject.

Henkin, L., "The completeness of the first order functional calculus", *J. Symbolic Logic*, **14**, 159–166, 1949.

Maltsev, A., *The Metamathematics of Algebraic Systems* (B. F. Wells III, tr., ed.) North-Holland, Amsterdam, 1971.
Represents the Russian school's work in the area.

Robinson, A., *Introduction to Model Theory and to the Metamathematics of Algebra*, North-Holland, Amsterdam, 1963.
Standard Western view of logic applied to algebra.

Robinson, A., *Nonstandard Analysis*, rev. ed., North-Holland, Amsterdam, 1974.
The standard exposition of calculus and other subjects with infinitely small elements, by the originator of the subject.

Sacks, G., *Saturated Model Theory*, W. A. Benjamin, Reading, Mass., 1972.
A short clear treatment of model theory in the Morley–Vaught tradition.

3.5 Proof Theory

Girard, J.-Y., *Proof Theory and Logical Complexity*, vol. I, Bibliopolis, Naples, 1987.
A quite readable view of proof theory for the mathematician.

Girard, J.-Y., *Proofs and Types* (with appendices and tr. by Lafont, Y.,

and Taylor, P.) Cambridge University Press, Cambridge, England, 1989.
Contains Girard's famous normalization theorem for second order intuitionistic logic, the basis of polymorphic programming languages.

Pohlers, W., *Proof Theory, An Introduction*, LNMS **1407**, Springer-Verlag, Berlin, 1989.

Prawitz, D., *Natural Deduction*, Almqvist and Wiskell, Stockholm, 1965.
Brought out clearly the view that deductions are the basic mathematical objects of proof theory.

Schutte, K., *Proof Theory* (J. N. Crossley, tr.), Springer–Verlag, Berlin, 1977.

Takeuti, G. *Proof Theory*, 2nd ed., North-Holland, Amsterdam, 1987.

3.6 Recursion Theory

(See also list 5.3.)

Cutland, N., *Computability: An Introduction to Recursive Function Theory*, Cambridge University Press, Cambridge, England, 1980.
Includes an approach to computability via register machines.

Davis, M., *Computability and Unsolvability*, McGraw Hill, 1958 (reprinted Dover, New York, 1982).
An exposition from the Post canonical systems point of view.

Davis, M., Matijasevič, Ju. and Robinson, J., "Hilbert's tenth problem, Diophantine equations: positive aspects of a negative solution" in Browder [1976, 1.2], 323–378.

Kleene, S., "General recursive functions of natural numbers", *Math. Annalen*, **112**, 727–742, 1936 (reprinted in Davis [1965, 2.1]).

Kreisel, G. and Tait, W., "Finite definability of number–theoretical functions and parametric completeness of equation calculi", *Zeit. Math. Log. Grund. Math.*, **7**, 28–38, 1961.

Lerman, M., *Degrees of Unsolvability*, Springer-Verlag, Berlin, 1983.
The standard text on Turing degrees as a whole.

Minsky, M. L., "Recursive unsolvability of Post's problem of tag and other topics in the theory of Turing machines", *Annals of Mathematics*, **74**, 437–454, 1961.

Odifreddi, G., *Classical Recursion Theory*, I, North-Holland, Amsterdam, 1989, vol. II, 1994.
Recursion theory on the integers, with many simplified proofs and expanded explanations.

Rogers, H., *Theory of Recursive Functions and Effective Computability*, McGraw-Hill, New York, 1967 (Reprinted by MIT Press, Cambridge, Mass., 1988).
For many years the best book on recursion theory and still an excellent starting point.

Shepherdson, J. and Sturgis, H., "Computability of Recursive Functions", *J. ACM*, **10**, 217–255, 1963.

Smullyan, R., *Theory of Formal Systems*, rev. ed., Princeton University Press, Princeton, 1961.
Development of recursively enumerable sets of strings based on Horn clause axioms. Not sufficiently known to computer scientists, who have often duplicated the results in PROLOG *language.*

Soare, R. I., *Recursively Enumerable Sets and Degrees*, Springer-Verlag, Berlin, 1987.
The standard current textbook on its subject.

Tourlakis, G., *Computability*, Reston Publishing Co., Reston, Va., 1984.
Also includes a development of register machines.

Weihrauch, K., *Computability*, Springer-Verlag, Berlin, 1987.

3.7 Categorical Logic

Fourman, M. P. and Scott, D. S., "Sheaves and Logic", in *Applications of Sheaves* (Fourman, Mulvey, and Scott, eds.), LNMS **753**, Springer-Verlag, Berlin, 1979, 302–401.
Clear explanation of logical versus sheaf methods.

Goldblatt, R. I., *Topoi, the Categorical Analysis of Logic*, North-Holland, Amsterdam, 1979; rev. ed., 1984.

Lambek, J. and Scott, P. J., *Introduction to Higher Order Categorical Logic*, Cambridge University Press, Cambridge, England, 1986.
The standard text on the relation between category theory (topoi) and higher order intuitionistic logic.

3.8 Algebra of Logic

Birkhoff, G., *Lattice Theory*, 3rd ed., American Mathematical Society Colloquium Pub. **25**, American Mathematical Society, Providence, 1967.

Dwinger, P. and Balbes, R., *Distributive Lattices*, University of Missouri Press, Columbus, Mo., 1974.

Halmos, P., *Lectures on Boolean Algebras*, D. Van Nostrand, Princeton, 1963 (reprinted, Springer-Verlag, Berlin, 1974).

Henkin, L., Monk, J. and Tarski, A., *Cylindric Algebras*, 2nd ed., North-Holland, Amsterdam, 1985.

Rasiowa, H. and Sikorski, R., *The Mathematics of Metamathematics*, Monographie Matematycze, **41**, Pa. Wydawn. Nauk., Warsaw, 1963.

Sikorski, R., *Boolean Algebras*, 3rd ed., Springer-Verlag, Berlin, 1969.

4. Intuitionistic, Modal, and Temporal Logics

(See also list 5.6.)

4.1 Handbooks

Gabbay, D. and Guenthner, F., *Handbook of Philosophical Logic*, 4 vols., D. Reidel, Dordrecht, 1983–85.
This book has very useful summaries of many branches of nonclassical logics.

4.2 Intuitionistic Logic and Constructivism

Beeson, M. J., *Foundations of Constructive Mathematics*, Springer-Verlag, Berlin, 1985.
An encyclopedic treatment.

Bishop, E. and Bridges, D., *Constructive Analysis*, Springer-Verlag, Berlin, 1985.
An update of Bishop's 1967 book, which showed how to give a natural constructive treatment of modern functional analysis.

Bridges, D. and Richman, F., *Varieties of Constructive Mathematics*, Cambridge University Press, Cambridge, England, 1987.
An introduction to constructive methods.

van Dalen, D., Intuitionistic logic, in *The Handbook of Philosophical Logic*, vol. III, 225–339, D. Reidel, Dordrecht, 1986.
The best succinct introduction to the mathematics of intuitionistic logics yet written.

Dragalin, A. G., *Mathematical Intuitionism: Introduction to Proof Theory*, Translations of Mathematical Monographs **67**, American Mathematical Society, Providence, 1988.

Assumes no background and gives some unity to Kripke frames and Kleene's realizability semantics.

Dummett, M., *Elements of Intuitionism*, Clarendon Press, Oxford, 1977
A thorough statement of the philosophical principles behind intuitionism, as well as an expository account of Beth and Kripke semantics.

Fitting, M., *Proof Methods for Modal and Intuitionistic Logics*, D. Reidel, Dordrecht, 1983.
Many variant tableaux methods.

Gabbay, D. G., *Semantical Investigations in Heyting's Intuitionistic Logic*, D. Reidel, Dordrecht, 1981.
An in-depth study of Kripke frame semantics, including decidability and undecidability of various theories and a discussion of recursive and r.e. presentations of frames.

Heyting, A., *Intuitionism, An Introduction*, 3rd ed., North-Holland, Amsterdam, 1971.
Later edition of the standard exposition on early intuitionism.

Martin-Löf, P., *Intuitionistic Type Theories*, Bibliopolis, Naples, 1984.
A predicative intuitionistic type theory. The basis of Constable's NUPRL system.

Nerode, A., "Some lectures on intuitionistic logic", in *Logic and Computer Science* (Lectures given at the 1st session of the C.I.M.E., Montecatini Terme, Italy, 1988), G. Odifreddi, ed., LNMS **1492**, Springer-Verlag, Berlin, 1990.

Nerode, A. and Remmel, J. B., A survey of r.e. substructures, in *Recursion Theory* (A. Nerode and R. Shore, eds.), Proc. Symposia in Pure Math., **42**, American Mathematical Society, Providence, 1985, 323–373.
This article gives an introduction to the methods of recursive algebra, a more completely developed classical analog of intuitionistic algebra. Recursive algebra can be linked to intuitionistic algebra through recursive realizability.

Troelstra, A. and van Dalen, D., *Constructivism in Mathematics*, 2 vols., North-Holland, Amsterdam, 1988.
The standard encyclopedic treatment of material hard to find elsewhere.

4.3 The Lambda Calculus and Combinatory Logic

Barendregt, H., *The Lambda Calculus: Its Syntax and Semantics*, rev. ed., North-Holland, Amsterdam, 1984.
The standard encyclopedic treatment.

Gunter, C., *Semantics of Programming Languages*, MIT Press, Cambridge, 1992.

Hindley, J. R. and Seldin, J. P., *Introduction to Combinators and Lambda Calculus*, Cambridge University Press, Cambridge, England, 1986.
Short and readable.

Revesz, G., *Lambda Calculus, Combinators, and Functional Programming*, Cambridge University Press, Cambridge, England, 1988.

Smullyan, R., *To Mock a Mockingbird and Other Logic Puzzles*, Knopf, NY, 1985.
One of Smullyan's puzzle books. A rigorous, but unconventionally expressed, treatment of self-reference in combinatory logic.

4.4 Modal Logic

van Benthem, J., *Modal Logic and Classical Logic*, Bibliopolis, Naples, 1983.
An advanced text.

van Benthem, J., *A Manual of Intensional Logic*, 2nd ed., CSLI, Stanford, 1988.

Chellas, B. F., *Modal Logic: An Introduction*, Cambridge University Press, 1980.
This seems to be the text most referred to in the computer science literature.

Fitting, M., *Proof Methods for Modal and Intuitionistic Logics*, D. Reidel, Dordrecht, 1983.
An encyclopedic treatment of tableau methods.

Hughes, G. E. and Cresswell, M. J., *An Introduction to Modal Logic*, Methuen, London, 1968.
A good basic text.

Hughes, G. E. and Cresswell, M. J., *A Companion to Modal Logic*, Methuen, London, 1984.

Lemmon, E. J., *An Introduction to Modal Logic: The "Lemmon Notes"* (K. Segerberg, ed.), American Philosophical Quarterly Monograph Series, **11**, Basil Blackwell, Oxford, 1977.

Linsky, L., ed., *Reference and Modality*, Oxford University Press, Oxford, 1971.
A collection of important early articles on modal logic including Kripke's basic work and various articles with a philosophical point of view.

Nerode, A., "Lectures on modal logic", in *Logic, algebra, and computation* (International summer school directed by F. L. Bauer at Marktoberdorf, Germany, 1989) (F. L. Bauer, ed.), Springer–Verlag, Berlin, 1991.

4.5 Temporal Logic

van Benthem, J., *The Logic of Time*, Reidel, Dordrecht, 1983.

van Benthem, J., *A Manual of Intensional Logic*, 2nd ed., CSLI, Stanford, 1988.

Gabbay, D. M., *Investigations in Modal and Tense Logics with Applications to Problems in Philosophy and Linguistics*, D. Reidel, Dordrecht, 1977.

Goldblatt, R., *Logics of Time and Computation*, 2nd ed., CSLI Lecture Notes, **7**, Center for the Study of Language and Information, Stanford, 1992.

Prior, A., *Past, Present, and Future*, Clarendon Press, Oxford, 1967.

Shoham, Y., *Reasoning about Change*, MIT Press, Cambridge, Mass., 1988.

5. Logic and Computation

5.1 Handbooks, Sourcebooks and Surveys

Barr, A., and Feigenbaum, E., eds., *The Handbook of Artificial Intelligence*, 3 vols., Heuristic Press, Stanford, 1981.
The many articles provide a good overview of the field and volume 3 has a number of items directly relevant to the topics covered here.

Bledsoe, W., and Loveland, D., *Automatic Theorem Proving after 25 years*, American Mathematical Society, Providence, 1984.

Boyer, R. S. and Moore, J. S., eds., *A Computational Logic Handbook*, Academic Press, Boston, 1988.
Primarily directed at automatic theorem proving.

Lassez, J.-L. and Plotkin, G., eds., *Computational Logic: Essays in Honor of Alan Robinson*, MIT Press, Cambridge, Mass., 1991.
This book contains a number of surveys of major areas of computational logic as well as current research papers.

van Leeuwen J., ed., *Handbook of Theoretical Computer Science*, 2 vols., North-Holland, Amsterdam and MIT Press, Cambridge, Mass., 1990.
This was a large group effort, and summarizes the state of theoretical computer science at the time, and in particular of many applications of logic, such as logic of programs.

Nerode, A., "Applied logic", in *The Merging of Disciplines: New Directions in Pure, Applied, and Computational Mathematics* (R. E. Ewing, K. I. Gross and C. F. Martin, eds.), Springer–Verlag, Berlin, 127–163.
A brief guide to some applications of logic to computer science as of 1986.

Siekmann, J., and Wrightson, G. , eds., *Automation of Reasoning*, 1957–70, 2 vols., Springer-Verlag, Berlin, 1983.
This volume contains most early papers in automation of reasoning, many of which make good reading assignments.

5.2 General Textbooks

Börger, E. *Computability, Complexity, Logic*, North-Holland, Amsterdam, 1989.

Davis, M., and Weyuker, E., *Computability, Complexity, and Languages*, Academic Press, New York, 1983.

Davis, R. E., *Truth, Deduction and Computation*, Computer Science Press, N.Y., 1989.

Fitting, M., *Computability Theory, Semantics, and Logic Programming*, Oxford University Press, Oxford, 1987.

Gallier, J., *Logic for Computer Science, Foundations of Automatic Theorem Proving*, Harper and Row, New York, 1986.
Sequent and resolution based, with cut elimination, the Hauptsatz, SLD–resolution, and many sorted logic.

Harel, David, *Algorithmics: The Spirit of Computing*, Addison-Wesley, Reading, Mass., 1987.

Lewis, H., and Papadimitriou, C., *Elements of the Theory of Computation*, Prentice Hall, Englewood Cliffs, NJ, 1981.

Manna, Z., *Mathematical Theory of Computation*, McGraw-Hill, New York, 1974.

Manna, Z., and Waldinger, R., *The Logical Basis for Computer Programming*, Addison-Wesley, Reading, Mass., 1985.

Robinson, J. A., *Logic: Form and Function*, North-Holland, Amsterdam, 1979.

Schöning, U., *Logic for Computer Scientists*, Birkhauser, Boston, 1989.

Sperschneider, V., and Antoniou, G., *Logic: A Foundation for Computer Science*, Addison-Wesley, Reading, Mass., 1991.

5.3 Complexity Theory

Balcazar, J. L., Diaz, J. and Gabarro, J., *Structural Complexity*, 2 vols., Springer-Verlag, Berlin, 1988, 1990.
A good current book for an introduction to the realms of complexity theory.

Garey, M. R. and Johnson, D. S., *Computers and Intractability: A Guide to the Theory of NP–Completeness*, W. H. Freeman, New York, 1979.

Still the best place to learn about P *and* NP.

Hartmanis, J., ed., *Computational Complexity Theory*, Proc. Symp. App. Math., **38**, American Mathematical Society, Providence, 1989.
Lecture notes from an AMS short course.

Hopcroft, J. E., and Ullman, J. D., *Introduction to Automata Theory, Languages and Computation*, Addison-Wesley, Reading, Mass., 1979.
The standard text since its publication for computer science students on Turing Machines, automata, and basic complexity.

Machtey, M. and Young, P., *An Introduction to the General Theory of Algorithms*, North-Holland, Amsterdam, 1978.

Odifreddi, G., *Classical Recursion Theory, II*, North-Holland, Amsterdam, 1993.

Statman, R., "Intuitionistic propositional logic is polynomial space complete", *Theoretical Computer Science*, **9**, 67–72, 1979.

5.4 Logic Programing and PROLOG

Apt, K. R., "Ten Years of Hoare's Logic: A Survey — Part I", *ACM TOPLAS* **3**, 431–483, 1981.

Apt, K. R., "Introduction to logic programming", in van Leeuwen [1990, 5.1] vol. B, 493–574, 1990.

Apt, K. R., Blair, H. A. and Walker, A., "Towards a theory of declarative knowledge", in *Foundations of Deductive databases and Logic Programming* (J. Minker, ed.), Morgan Kaufmann, Los Altos, Ca., 1988.

Apt, K. R., and Pedreschi, D., "Studies in Pure Prolog", in *Computational Logic* (J. Lloyd, ed.), Springer–Verlag, Berlin, 1991.

Bezem, M., "Characterizing termination of logic programs with level mappings", *Proc. North American Logic Programming Conference* (E. L. Lusk and R. A. Overbeek eds.), vol. 1, 69–80, MIT Press, Cambridge, Mass., 1989.

Bratko, I., *Prolog Programming for Artificial Intelligence*, Addison-Wesley, Reading, Mass., 2nd ed., 1990.

Clark, K. L., "Negation as failure", in *Logic and Databases* (H. Gallaire and J. Minker, eds.), 293–322, Plenum Press, New York, 1978.

Clocksin, W. F. and Mellish, C. S., *Programming in PROLOG*, 3rd revised and extended edition, Springer–Verlag, Berlin, 1987.

Colmerauer, A., "Metamorphosis Grammars", in *Natural Language Communication with Computers*, 133–189 (L. Bolc, ed.), LNCS 63, Springer-Verlag, Berlin, 1974.

Dodd, T., PROLOG, *A Logical Approach*, Oxford University Press, Oxford, 1989.

Furukawa, K., "Logic Programming as the integrator of the Fifth Generation Computer Systems Project", *Communications of the ACM*, **35**, 82–92, 1992.

Gelfond, M., and Lifschitz, V., "Stable semantics for logic programming", in *Logic Programming, Proc. 5th International Conference and Symposium on Logic Programming* (Seattle, 1985) (R. Kowalski and K. Bowen eds.), MIT Press, Cambridge, Mass., 1988.

Grant, J. and Minker, J., "The impact of Logic Programming on databases", *Communications of the ACM*, **35**, 66–81, 1992.

Kowalski, R., "Predicate Logic as a Programming Language" in *Proc. IFIP-74*, 569–574, North-Holland, Amsterdam, 1974.

Kowalski, R., *Logic for Problem Solving*, North-Holland, Amsterdam, 1979.

Lloyd, J. W., *Foundations of Logic Programming*, 2nd extended edition, Springer-Verlag, Berlin, 1987.
This is the standard exposition of the subject and contains an extensive bibliography.

Maier, D. and Warren, D., *Computing with Logic: Logic Programming with Prolog*, Benjamin/Cummings, Menlo Park, Ca., 1988.
Logic via resolution combined with PROLOG; very strong on the relation with databases.

Martelli, A. and Montannari, U., "An efficient unification algorithm", *ACM Transactions on Programming Languages and Systems*, **4**, 258–282, 1982.

Robinson, J. A., "Logic and Logic Programming", *Communications of the ACM*, **35**, 40–65, 1992.
A recent brief history of the subject by one of its forefathers.

Shepherdson, J. C., "Negation as failure: A Comparison of Clark's completed data base and Reiter's closed world assumption", *Journal of Logic Programming*, **1**, 51–79, 1984.

Shepherdson, J. C., "Negation as failure II", *Journal of Logic Programming*, **2**, 185–202, 1985.

Shepherdson, J. C., "Negation in Logic Programming", in *Foundations of Deductive Databases and Logic Programming* (J. Minker, ed.), Morgan and Kaufmann, Los Altos, Ca., 1987.

Shepherdson, J. C., "Logics for negation as failure", in *Logic from Computer Science* (Y. N. Moschovakis, ed.), 521–583, MSRI Publications **21**, Springer-Verlag, Berlin, 1992.

Sterling, L. and Shapiro, E., *The Art of Prolog: Advanced Programming Techniques*, MIT Press, Cambridge, Mass., 1986.

Thayse, A., ed., *From Standard Logic to Logic Programming*, Wiley, Chichester, 1988.
Motivated by the concerns of AI. *See also Thayse [1989, 5.6].*

5.5 Nonmonotonic Logic

Doyle, J., "A truth maintenance system", *Artificial Intelligence Journal,* **12**, 231–272, 1979.

Ginsberg, M., ed., *Readings in Nonmonotonic Reasoning*, Morgan and Kaufmann, Los Altos, Ca., 1987.

Halpern, J. Y. and Moses, Y. O., "Knowledge and common knowledge in a distributed environment", in 3rd *ACM Conference on the Principles of Distributed Computing*, 50–61, 1984 (revised as IBM RJ 4421, 1984).

Hintikka, J., *Knowledge and Belief*, Cornell University Press, Ithaca, N.Y., 1962.

McCarthy, J., "Circumspection — a form of nonmonotonic reasoning", *Artificial Intelligence*, **13**, 27–39, 1980.

Marek, W., Nerode, A. and Remmel, J. B., "Non–Monotonic Rule Systems" I, II, *Mathematics and Artificial Intelligence*, **1**, 241–273, 1990, to appear 1992.

Minsky, M., "A framework for representing knowledge", in *The Psychology of Computer Vision* (P. Winston, ed.), 211–272, McGraw–Hill, New York, 1975.

Moore, R. C., "Possible world semantics for autoepistemic logic", in *Proceedings 1984 Nonmonotonic Reasoning Workshop* (AAAI), New Paltz, N.Y., 1984.

Moore, R. C., "Semantical considerations on nonmonotonic logic", *Artificial Intelligence*, **25** (1), 75–94, 1985.

Parikh, R., ed., *Theoretical Aspects of Reasoning about Knowledge (TARK 90)*, Morgan Kaufmann, Los Altos, Ca., 1990.

Reiter, R., "A logic for default reasoning", *Artificial Intelligence*, **13**, 81–132, 1980.

Reiter, R., "Nonmonotonic reasoning", *Ann. Rev. Comp. Sci.*, **2**, 147–186, 1980.

Vardi, M., ed., *Theoretical Aspects of Reasoning about Knowledge (TARK 88)*, Morgan and Kaufmann, Los Altos, Ca., 1988.

5.6 Intuitionistic, Modal and Temporal Logics

(See also lists 4.1–4.5.)

Constable, R., *Implementing Mathematics with the* NUPRL *Proof Development System*, Prentice-Hall, Englewood Cliffs, NJ, 1986.
NUPRL *implements Martin-Löf's predicative intuitionistic type theory as a mathematician's assistant.*

Galton, A., *Temporal Logics and their Applications*, Academic Press, London, 1987.

Goldblatt, R. I., *Axiomatizing the Logic of Computer Programming*, LNCS **130**, Springer-Verlag, Berlin, 1982.

Goldblatt, R. I., *Logics of Time and Computation*, 2nd ed., CSLI Lecture Notes, **7**, Center for the Study of Language and Information, Stanford, 1992.

Halpern, J. Y. and Moses, Y. O., "A guide to modal logics of knowledge and belief", *Proc. 9th Int. Joint Conf. on Artificial Intelligence* (IJACI).

Manna, Z. and Waldinger, R., *The Logical Basis of Computer Programming*, Addison-Wesley, Reading, Mass., 1985.

Nerode, A. and Wijesekera, D., Constructive Concurrent Dynamic Logic, *Mathematics and Artificial Intelligence*, to appear, 1992.

Smets, P., Mamandi, E. H., Dubois, D. and Padre, H., *Nonstandard Logics for Automated Reasoning*, Academic Press, London, 1988.

Thayse, A., ed., *From Modal Logic to Deductive Databases*, Wiley, Chichester, 1989.
An impressive presentation of many types of modal logic as a basis for work in artificial intelligence. See also Thayse [1958, 5.4].

Thayse, A., ed., *From Natural Language Processing to Logic for Expert Systems*, Wiley, Chichester, 1991.
An extensive treatment of applications of logical methods to many areas of AI.

Thistlewhite, P. B., McRobbie, M. A. and Meyer, R. A., *Automated Theorem-proving in Nonclassical Logics*, Pitman, London, 1988.

Turner, R., *Logics for Artificial Intelligence*, Halsted Press, Chichester, 1984

Wallen, L., *Automated Proof Search in Nonclassical Logics*, MIT Press, Cambridge, Mass, 1990.
This book and Thistlewhite [1988, 5.6] explore how to automate nonclassical logics of every description.

5.7 Automated Deduction and Program Correctness

(See also list 5.6.)

de Bakker, J., *Mathematical Theory of Program Correctness*, Prentice-Hall, Englewood Cliffs, N. J., 1980.

Bibel, W., *Automated Theorem Proving*, Vieweg, Braunschweig, 2nd rev. ed., 1987.

Bledsoe, W. and Loveland, D., *Automatic Theorem Proving after 25 years*, American Mathematical Society, Providence, 1984.

Boyer, R. S. and Moore, J. S., *A Computational Logic*, Academic Press, New York, 1979.
This represents an automated logic which incorporates many heuristics for finding correct proofs by induction in elementary number theory. It is the basis of a school of program development and verification.

Boyer, R. S. and Moore, J. S., eds., *The Correctness Problem in Computer Science*, Academic Press, New York, 1981.

Burstall, R., "Some techniques for proving correctness of programs which alter data structures", *Machine Intelligence*, **7**, 23–50, 1972.

Chang, C.-L. and Lee, C.-T., *Symbolic Logic and Mechanical Theorem Proving*, Academic Press, New York, 1973.
Takes the Herbrand universe point of view in developing elementary logic.

Davis, M., "The prehistory and early history of automated deduction", in Siekmann and Wrightson [1983, 5.1], 1–28.
A good look at the early history.

Davis, M. and Putnam, H., "A computing procedure for quantification theory", *J. ACM*, **7**, 201–216, 1960 (reprinted in Siekmann and Wrightson [1983, 5.1], vol. 1, 125–139).

Floyd, R., "Assigning meaning to programs", *Proceedings of Symposia in Applied Mathematics*, **19**, 19–32, American Mathematical Society, Providence, 1967.

Gries, D., *The Science of Programming*, Springer-Verlag, New York, 1981.

Harel, D., *First Order Dynamic Logic*, Springer-Verlag, Berlin, 1979.

Hoare, C., "An axiomatic basis for computer programming", *Communications of the ACM*, **12**, 576–583, 1969.

Hoare, C. and Shepherdson, J., eds., *Mathematical Logic and Programming Languages*, Prentice-Hall, Englewood Cliffs, N. J., 1985.

Huet, G. and Plotkin, G., eds., *Logical Frameworks*, Cambridge University Press, Cambridge, England, 1991.

Loeckx, J. and Sieber, K., *The Foundations of Program Verification*, 2nd ed., Wiley, New York, 1987.

Loveland, D., *Automated Theorem Proving: A Logical Basis*, North-Holland, Amsterdam, 1978.
A very complete exposition of variations on resolution.

Robinson, J. A., "A Machine oriented logic based on the resolution principle", *J. ACM*, **12**, 23–41, 1965 (reprinted in Siekmann and Wrightson [1983, 2.1]).

Turing, A. M., "Checking a large routine", in *Report of a Conference on High Speed Automatic Calculating Machines*, University Mathematical Library, Cambridge, England, 1949.

Wos, L., Overbeek, R., Lusk, E. and Boyle, J., *Automated Reasoning*, Prentice-Hall, Englewood Cliffs, N. J., 1984.

Index of Symbols

355

Index of Terms

Texts and Monographs in Computer Science

(continued from page ii)

Edsger W. Dijkstra and Carel S. Scholten
Predicate Calculus and Program Semantics
1990. XII, 220 pages

W.H.J. Feijen, A.J.M. van Gasteren, D. Gries, and J. Misra, Eds.
Beauty Is Our Business: A Birthday Salute to Edsger W. Dijkstra
1990. XX, 453 pages, 21 illus.

P.A. Fejer and D.A. Simovici
Mathematical Foundations of Computer Science, Volume I:
Sets, Relations, and Induction
1990. X, 425 pages, 36 illus.

Melvin Fitting
First-Order Logic and Automated Theorem Proving
1990. XIV, 242 pages, 26 illus.

Nissim Francez
Fairness
1986. XIII, 295 pages, 147 illus.

R.T. Gregory and E.V. Krishnamurthy
Methods and Applications of Error-Free Computation
1984. XII, 194 pages, 1 illus.

David Gries, Ed.
Programming Methodology: A Collection of Articles by Members of IFIP WG2.3
1978. XIV, 437 pages, 68 illus.

David Gries
The Science of Programming
1981. XV, 366 pages

David Gries and Fred B. Schneider
A Logical Approach to Discrete Math
1993. XVII, 497 pages, 25 illus.

John V. Guttag and James J. Horning
Larch: Languages and Tools for Formal Specification
1993. XIII, 250 pages, 76 illus.

Eric C.R. Hehner
A Practical Theory of Programming
1993. IV, 248 pages, 10 illus.

Texts and Monographs in Computer Science

Texts and Monographs in Computer Science

(continued)

Franco P. Preparata and Michael Ian Shamos
Computational Geometry: An Introduction
1985. XII, 390 pages, 231 illus.

Brian Randell, Ed.
The Origins of Digital Computers: Selected Papers, 3rd Edition
1982. XVI, 580 pages, 126 illus.

Thomas W. Reps and Tim Teitelbaum
The Synthesizer Generator: A System for Constructing Language-Based Editors
1989. XIII, 317 pages, 75 illus.

Thomas W. Reps and Tim Teitelbaum
The Synthesizer Generator Reference Manual, 3rd Edition
1989. XI, 171 pages, 79 illus.

Arto Salomaa and Matti Soittola
Automata-Theoretic Aspects of Formal Power Series
1978. X, 171 pages

J.T. Schwartz, R.B.K. Dewar, E. Dubinsky, and E. Schonberg
Programming with Sets: An Introduction to SETL
1986. XV, 493 pages, 31 illus.

Alan T. Sherman
VLSI Placement and Routing: The PI Project
1989. XII, 189 pages, 47 illus.

Santosh K. Shrivastava, Ed.
Reliable Computer Systems
1985. XII, 580 pages, 215 illus.

Jan L.A. van de Snepscheut
What Computing Is All About
1993. XII, 478 pages, 78 illus.

William M. Waite and Gerhard Goos
Compiler Construction
1984. XIV, 446 pages, 196 illus.

Niklaus Wirth
Programming in Modula-2, 4th Edition
1988. II, 182 pages

Texts and Monographs in Computer Science

(continued)

Study Edition

Edward Cohen
Programming in the 1990s: An Introduction to the Calculation of Programs
1990. XV, 265 pages